SMALL BUSINESS MANAGEMENT

FIFTH EDITION

WILEY SERIES IN MANAGEMENT

WILEY

FIFTH EDITION

SMALL BUSINESS MANAGEMENT

Hal B. Pickle
St. Edwards University

Royce L. Abrahamson
Southwest Texas State University

JOHN WILEY & SONS
New York ▪ Chichester ▪ Brisbane ▪ Toronto ▪ Singapore

Library of Congress Cataloging in Publication Data:

Pickle, Hal B.
    Small business management / Hal B. Pickle, Royce L. Abrahamson. —
5th ed.

      p.   cm. — (Wiley series in management)
    Includes bibliographical references.

    ISBN 0-471-50071-2
    1. Small business—Management.   I. Abrahamson, Royce L.
II. Title.   III. Series.
HD62.7.P52   1990
658.02′2—dc20
                            89-36239
                            CIP

Printed in the United States of America

10 9 8 7 6 5 4

Printed and bound by R.R. Donnelley & Sons, Inc.

PREFACE

Although we have written this book for students in the classroom, we have also written it for prospective small business entrepreneurs and for those persons already operating small business firms who desire to improve the overall efficiency and effectiveness of their operations. The format of this book enables the classroom instructor to use one of several teaching methods: lecture, lecture with case assignment before class, case discussion in class, or a combined case–lecture method in class.

As in previous editions, the approach is practice-oriented and the writing style is informal. We have continued to expand our presentation of the techniques and methods used in day-to-day management of the small business enterprise with this edition.

The chapter arrangement for the fifth edition has been rearranged to present discussion of microcomputers earlier in the text. We took this step because microcomputers have an increasing influence in modern small businesses. In addition, risk management is presented in the section dealing with management strategy.

A major addition to the fifth edition is the expanded coverage of the "Business Plan." Chapter 1 contains discussion of this timely topic while Chapter 4 is refocused entirely on the "Business Plan." Furthermore, there is a "Business Plan" section at the end of each chapter that focuses the readers' attention on guidelines and questions centered on the "Business Plan." The last section of the text, an "Entrepreneurial Business Planning Guide," provides the reader with a sequential guide through the activities that are necessary to launch a new small business. In addition, we have included in this section a list of trade associations, of addresses of the Small Business Administration field offices, and of available publications that may be purchased from the Small Business Administration.

Chapter 10, "Microcomputers in Small Business," has been reorganized. The focus of the chapter now is on the microcomputer and software applications in the small business. Attention is directed toward detailing major factors that should be evaluated when the small business owner is in the process of selecting a microcomputer for the firm.

The subject of international marketing has been moved to Chapter 22 to highlight the role that the government can have in assisting small business owners who desire to enter the international business arena.

Many popular features appear in each chapter of the fifth edition to assist the students' comprehension of small business management.

"Learning Goals" are stated at the beginning of each chapter alerting the reader to major points in the ensuing discussion.

"Key Words" are listed at the introduction of each chapter. Each key word is highlighted in boldface type the first time it is defined in the text.

"Entrepreneurial Profiles" focus on successful entrepreneurs. All profiles are new to this edition.

"Small Business Briefs" highlight a specific facet of small business management.

"Summary of Key Points" focus on the major concepts presented in the chapter. These summaries assist the students as they review chapter material.

"Discussion Questions" have been revised to emphasize the major concepts presented in each chapter.

"The Business Plan" guides present a series of questions that the prospective entrepreneur should ask regarding each chapter topic.

"Entrepreneurial Projects" at the conclusion of each chapter involve students in experiential activities pertaining to various aspects of small business management.

"Cases" are presented for each chapter. These cases are based on "real-world" small business situations and illustrate points made in the text discussion. Approximately 40 percent of the cases are new to the fifth edition.

Moreover, new or expanded topics, illustrations, and applications have been incorporated throughout the text. Some of these are listed here:

Women entrepreneurs • Minority entrepreneurs • Master franchising • International franchising • Estimating purchasing power • Theory X • Theory Y • Theory Z • Two-factor theory • Employee morale • Communication process • Communication barriers • Immigration Reform and Control Act of 1986 • Fair Labor Standards Act of 1938 • Microcomputers • Application software • Purchasing agent • Economic order quantity • Market segmentation • Product life cycle • Telemarketing

Finally, we would like to acknowledge the many thoughtful and detailed reviews we received from the following educators around the country. Their suggestions provided us with valuable input as we revised the text. Our special thanks to:

Kathy J. Daruty, *Los Angeles Pierce College*
Larry G. Bailey, *San Antonio College*
Richard L. Hilliard, *Nichols College*
Paul J. Londrigan, *Mott Community College*
Nick Sarantakes, *Austin Community College*
Louis D. Ponthieu, *University of North Texas*
Richard Cuba, *University of Baltimore*
Jerry E. Boles, *Western Kentucky University*
R. B. Keusch, *East Carolina University*

CONTENTS *IN BRIEF*

vii

CONTENTS

SECTION FIVE   MARKETING THE PRODUCT OR SERVICE   463

SECTION SIX   THE GOVERNMENT AND SMALL BUSINESS   585

APPENDIX   ENTREPRENEUR'S BUSINESS PLANNING GUIDE   655

ENTREPRENEURSHIP, SMALL BUSINESS OWNERSHIP, AND FRANCHISING

KEY WORDS

CHAPTER 1

ENTREPRENEURSHIP

LEARNING GOALS

After reading this chapter, you will understand:

1 What an "entrepreneur" is.

2 That there are a variety of personality characteristics that contribute to entrepreneurial success in small business.

3 The importance of a business plan for entrepreneurs.

4 That there are various ways of defining a "small business."

5 The substantial contribution that small business makes to the economy of the United States.

6 That small business provides many opportunities for women and minority-group members to excel.

7 That entrepreneurs derive many rewards from small business ownership.

8 What some of the limitations and problems of small business ownership are.

9 That many small businesses are family operations.

ENTREPRENEURIAL PROFILE

Bill and Julie Brice

I CAN'T BELIEVE IT'S YOGURT

When Bill and Julie Brice were college students at Southern Methodist University, the brother and sister team managed a frozen yogurt store in Dallas. After less than a year, they took $10,000 of their own money and purchased two struggling frozen yogurt stores. As customers began to come into the store, a frequent comment overheard was, "I can't believe it's yogurt." The corporate identity was created. Ten years later, I Can't Believe It's Yogurt is a nationwide franchise network of over 170 stores and sales exceeding $25 million.

Julie Brice recalls that initially they just "winged it" without benefit of a business plan. In fact, their only business plan was to try to figure out how not to lose $100 a day. For the Brices, a typical workweek was 80 hours. To attract business to their stores, they flagged down cars and gave frozen yogurt samples to customers. However, as they increased the number of stores from two to four during the first year of operation, they realized that they needed direction and goals for the company. At that stage, Julie enrolled in an entrepreneurship course at Southern Methodist University. At the end of the semester, she had developed a business plan. Since that time, a business plan has been an integral part of I Can't Believe It's Yogurt.

In retrospect, the Brices understand the value of a business plan. With a business plan, they would have been able to avoid some of the early mistakes and capitalize on additional opportunities.

Source: Developed from Steven Friedlander, "Cold Cash," _Continental Profiles,_ October 1988, pp. 27 and 29, and Roger Thompson, "Business Plans: Myth or Reality," _Nation's Business,_ August 1988, p. 20.

"The business of America is business," said Calvin Coolidge. To this statement we should add that _the key to american business is the entrepreneur_.

The foundation of the United States' free enterprise economic system is "small business." In our nation's formative years, nearly all businesses were small, cottage-type, handcraft firms. The advent of the Industrial Revolution saw the emergence of large-scale businesses and a corresponding decline in the production of goods and services by small businesses. Today, there is a resurgence of the "entrepreneurial spirit" across America, and "small business'' is once again the driving force in our nation's economy, making major contributions in terms of employment opportunities and technological innovations.

Small business owners are confronted by numerous problems beyond their control, such as inflation, taxes, government regulations, high interest rates, and competition from big business. Clearly, these conditions do not seem to provide a healthy environment for new small business ventures. However, the Office of Advocacy reports that between 1,050,000 and 1,250,000 new businesses are started each year and most start-ups require less than $5000 of initial capital. And Dun & Bradstreet reports that new business incorporations number over 700,000 annually and many of these new corporations are small businesses. These data strongly suggest that more and more Americans believe they can achieve the quality of life they desire through small business ownership.

The men and women who initiate these businesses are entrepreneurs. An **entrepreneur** is ''one who organizes and manages a business undertaking, assuming the risk, for the sake of profit.''[1] Entrepreneurs are the cornerstone of the American private enterprise system. They play a leading role in creating and developing new products and services, which results in new business opportunities. Furthermore, enterpreneurs bring together the funds needed to initiate the business, organize and direct it toward goal accomplishment, and often play the leading role in managing the business operation to provide economic goods and services to consumers. Without a doubt, the success of the United States has resulted, in large measure, from the energy and the creativity of its entrepreneurs operating in an environment of private enterprise.

Clearly, small business owners are entrepreneurs. They assume risk and organize and manage all facets of their business. Perhaps the only difference between small business owners and entrepreneurs, in view of our definition, is in terms of their perception of the importance of profit. For example, the psychological satisfaction owners derive from their business is often as significant to them as the economic (profit) satisfaction, as shown in Figure 1-1.

PERSONALITY CHARACTERISTICS AND ABILITIES OF ENTREPRENEURS THAT CONTRIBUTE TO BUSINESS SUCCESS

Extensive research has been conducted in an attempt to identify the personality characteristics of entrepreneurs that contribute to their business success. One research study of 97 small business managers did produce a correlation of .63 between success and five general personality characteristics: drive, mental ability, human relations ability, communications ability, and technical knowledge.[2] Though not identified in the study, two additional abilities—decision making and conceptual—are deemed important for business success.

FIGURE 1-1
ENTREPRENEURS DERIVE ECONOMIC AND PSYCHOLOGICAL REWARDS FROM ORGANIZING, MANAGING, AND OPERATING THEIR SMALL BUSINESSES.

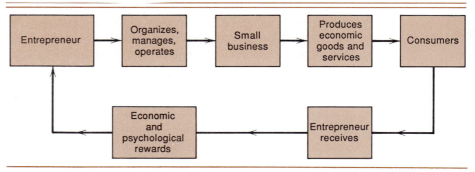

Figure 1-2 shows the relationship between these abilities and small business success.

Drive

In general terms, **drive is a person's motivation or work effort.** It is comprised of such personality traits as responsibility, vigor, initiative, persistence, and ambition. Entrepreneurs must exert considerable effort and energy in establishing and managing their business, and those owners who conscientiously plan, organize, staff, lead, and control the activities of their small business are more likely to have a successful business than are entrepreneurs who manage intuitively.

However, working long hours is no guarantee of success. Much depends

FIGURE 1-2
PERSONALITY CHARACTERISTICS AND ABILITIES OF ENTREPRENEURS THAT CONTRIBUTE TO SMALL BUSINESS SUCCESS.

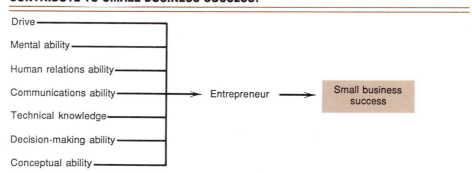

instead on what an entrepreneur does when he or she is at work. Many entrepreneurs are highly motivated and work long hours, and their businesses still do not succeed. In these circumstances, the business often fails because entrepreneurs spend too much time performing nonmanagement tasks and neglecting the essential, more difficult, and challenging management tasks of planning, organizing, staffing, leading, and controlling which shape the future of the firm. In fact, some entrepreneurs seem to feel more comfortable spending most of their time on the nonmanagement tasks because they may feel inadequate to perform the managerial functions or lack the knowledge which is necessary to be an effective manager. By staying busy on nonmanagement tasks, they convince themselves that they don't have time to devote to the management functions. It is not uncommon to hear such comments as ''I know I should be doing more planning, but I am just too busy dealing with the situations and problems that arise each day!''

Mental Ability

Mental ability that contributes to the success of entrepreneurs consists of overall intelligence (IQ), creative thinking ability, and analytical thinking ability. Entrepreneurs must be reasonably intelligent, use **creative thinking** to adapt their actions to the needs of the business in various situations, and engage in **analytical thinking** to analyze systematically problems arising in the business.

For example, the owner of a small drive-through restaurant that sells sandwiches and barbeque wanted to expand her business. The restaurant was located near the downtown business district. After analyzing the situation, she realized that many working people do not have time or take time to eat breakfast. Thus, she created the idea of free delivery of breakfast to offices of businesspeople in the downtown area. Telephone orders are taken, and deliveries go out in 20 minutes. This plan demonstrates how the entrepreneur can use creative and analytical thinking to develop unique opportunities and capitalize on them to increase customer patronage and generate sales.

Human Relations Ability

Human relations ability is demonstrated through such personality factors as emotional stability, skill in interpersonal relations, sociability, consideration of others, tactfulness, and empathy. For example, consider empathy. **Empathy** is the owner's ability to ''put oneself in someone else's place'' and know how the other person feels and perceives the situation. Thus, it is one of the most important facets of human relations ability in dealing with both customers and employees. Entrepreneurs must create and maintain good customer relations to encourage repeat patronage. They must develop and sustain good relations with employees so that they will be motivated to achieve higher levels of performance. In addition, entrepreneurs must be aware of the needs and motives of customers to train employees properly to respond to their needs. Hence, it is clear that human relations ability is a requisite of all entrepreneurs and is an important contributor to entrepreneurial success.

Communications Ability

The skill in conveying written and oral information to others (employees, customers) so that understanding is created between the sender and receiver is the entrepreneur's **communication ability.** Entrepreneurs who effectively communicate with customers, employees, suppliers, and creditors will more likely be successful in their business operation than will entrepreneurs who are deficient in communications skills. For example, an entrepreneur may send a form letter to good customers who have missed a payment deadline. The form letter states, ''We have not received your monthly payment; please remit at once.'' The letter is intended only as a reminder to customers; however, they may interpret it as a dun and an implication that they are irresponsible in meeting their obligations. Some individuals may be offended enough to cease trading with the business, and the entrepreneur would never know the reason. This important topic is covered more extensively in Chapter 8.

Technical Knowledge

If the small business is to succeed, the entrepreneur must offer an acceptable product or service. For example, in an eating establishment, the entrepreneur may be highly motivated, practice good human relations, be an effective communicator, and possess high mental ability. However, if customers are not provided good food and service, they will not return. And the business will undoubtedly fail because repeat patronage is essential for all businesses.

Technical knowledge refers to the entrepreneurial skill of working with ''things.'' Technical knowledge includes expertise in such areas as personal selling techniques, operating a complex piece of equipment (computer), or analyzing and interpreting financial records. Technical knowledge is the one ability that entrepreneurs can learn if they put forth the effort. For example, an entrepreneur who plans to open a restaurant should obtain ''hands-on'' experience by working in that type of business environment for a period of time. This allows the entrepreneur to learn specific technical knowledge needed for this type of business, such as food preparation, equipment usage, supply sources, and recordkeeping.

Decision-Making Ability

Decision-making ability is the skill of selecting a satisfactory course of action from among alternatives to guide the company. The entrepreneur evaluates perceived opportunities and strives to make the decisions that will enable the firm to realize sustained growth.

Conceptual Ability

Conceptual ability refers to the entrepreneur's skill to understand the overall organization of the small business and how each unit (accounting, sales, production) fits together as a unified whole and contributes to the success of the firm. Conceptual ability is important for the entrepreneur as he or she charts the overall direction of the firm. Conceptual ability enables the entrepreneur to recognize opportunities that no one else has been aware of and lead the company as it capitalizes on them.

As the foregoing discussion of personality characteristics and abilities suggests, entrepreneurs who have high levels of drive, mental ability, human relations ability, communications ability, technical knowledge, decision-making ability, and conceptual ability are not guaranteed success. However, they do stand a greater likelihood of success than do those entrepreneurs who possess low levels of these same characteristics.

THE BUSINESS PLAN

Entrepreneurs should have a plan of action to guide them as they chart the direction of the company and strive to make the best possible decisions to increase the likelihood of success for the proposed new business venture or the contribution and growth of the ongoing firm. This plan of action is called the **business plan,** a comprehensive, well-thought-out, written document which establishes the necessary guidelines for entrepreneurs. An often heard complaint of entrepreneurs is that they don't have time to sit down and write out a detailed business plan. However, as the chairman of First Business Bank in Los Angeles says, "The business plan is a necessity. If the person who wants to start a small business can't put a business plan together, he or she is in trouble."[3]

By putting the business plan in writing, entrepreneurs can focus objectively on "where they are now and where they want to be at some specified time." The plan does not guarantee success. But Leo Lauzen, chairman of Comprehensive Accounting Corporation, which has more than 330 independent franchisees nationwide, states: "We have a study of what it is that causes business failure and it's not because the owner couldn't make pizzas or clean carpets or whatever. The problem is he didn't know how to run a business."[4] He adds that 80 percent of the failures his firm handles could have been avoided by proper planning.

The written plan also serves as a vehicle by which entrepreneurs can communicate what the business is all about to others, such as financial sources and employees.

In preparing a strong foundation for the proposed business or examining the status of the ongoing firm, the business plan requires entrepreneurs to ask and answer critical questions about themselves and the business. Specific questions to be answered include

What business will I be in or am I in?

What are my personal strengths and weaknesses?

Where will I be able to obtain financing?

What are the products and services I will offer?

What is the market for my product or service?

How will I market the product or service?

What operational controls are needed to measure performance?

Who will manage the company?

By answering questions such as these, entrepreneurs are forced to consider all areas of the business operation and develop specific objectives to be achieved. For example, when an idea for a new business has been developed and the entrepreneur begins to evaluate the proposal, the business plan may reveal a significant opportunity. Perhaps an even more important contribution may be that the business plan identifies some critical weaknesses or potential hazards and that risks are greater than potential rewards. Thus, the business plan provides the entrepreneur with the foresight to avoid making an expensive mistake. In this instance, the plan has served as a preventative rather than remedial measure.

Eric Siegel, a business consultant, emphasizes the importance of the business plan. He says, "If you do a really good job of writing a business plan, it's more than just putting words on paper. You do a lot of research, and you expose a lot of flaws. Each one that you expose and treat, you enhance the chances of your success."[5]

To assist the reader in relating the various parts of the business plan to the development of a new business or the evaluation of an ongoing concern, we have included questions and guidelines pertaining to specific parts of the business plan at the end of each chapter. In addition, a comprehensive business plan is included in the Appendix. The comprehensive business plan guides the prospective entrepreneur through the stages of small business development, from creation of the idea for the business to implementation of the plan.

A detailed discussion of each element of the business plan is presented throughout the text. To guide the reader, the major components of the business plan are presented here together with the chapter in which each component of the business plan is discussed.

The Business Plan

1. Self-assessment of the entrepreneur: strengths and weaknesses, a description of the business I am in (Chapter 1).
2. Form of ownership: sole proprietorship, partnership, corporation (Chapter 2); franchising (Chapter 3).
3. Business plan: the business plan, buy an existing business or start a new one (Chapter 4).
4. Sources of funds: equity and debt capital (Chapter 5).
5. Facilities plan: location analysis (Chapter 6); physical facility requirements (Chapter 7).
6. Management plan: strategy, objectives, structure, employee relations, motivation, communication (Chapter 8); personnel needs, key personnel, recruitment, training, and development (Chapter 9); microcomputers (Chapter 10); risk management (Chapter 11).
7. Financial plan: financial recordkeeping, cash control (Chapter 12); accounting statements, budgets (Chapter 13).
8. Operational control plan: purchasing (Chapter 14); inventory control (Chapter 15).
9. Marketing plan: strategy, market segmentation, products and services, market research (Chapter 16); pricing (Chapter 17); consumer behavior, personal selling (Chapter 18); promotional strategy (Chapter 19).
10. Legal and governmental relations plan: consumer credit (Chapter 20); legal considerations (Chapter 21); governmental control (Chapter 22).

WHAT IS A SMALL BUSINESS?

From shopping malls to roadside stands, from towering office complexes to basements, small businesses are everywhere. They line this country's Main Streets and side streets . . . even its sidewalks.[6]

What is a small business? Answers to this question would likely include responses as encompassing as those contained in the preceding statement. No doubt some would consider a business small if it had no more than a specified number of employees (i.e., 5 or 10). Others would likely believe that a small business is one that limits its scope of operations to the local market area. Others frequently classify businesses as small by the nature of the firm, such as the local drugstore, clothing store, service station, or jewelry store.

GET FULL VALUE FROM YOUR PLAN

A business plan doesn't belong on the shelf collecting dust. But that's where a lot of plans end up once they have been used to attract the dollars needed to start or expand a business.

Why spend all that time writing a plan and never get full value from it, says Raymond O. Loen, who has a consulting firm in Lake Oswego, Ore.

Loen has spent 30 years helping owners and managers figure out how to make their companies successful. During that period, he has seen a lot of business plans go to waste. Here is his list of the 10 most common ways that executives go wrong in using their plans, plus his antidote for each.

Single-Purpose Use
Management typically prepares a business plan to secure financing and demonstrates little regard for how to implement the plan. Broad generalities take the place of operational details.

Stress implementaton. Write in specific objectives for key managers and describe how those objectives will be attained. Emphasis on implementation will enhance your chances for financing by showing that your plan is for real.

One-Person Commitment
When one person, such as the company president or the chief financial officer, writes the plan, key managers may not develop a full commitment to it. Although they contribute suggestions, it's not the same as having a section of the plan that they personally must write and implement.

Obtain balanced participation from all members of the management team. Have each prepare a section of the plan. If you want to put some muscle into it, link each manager's compensation or incentive performance pay to the successful implementation of his or her part of the plan.

Benign Neglect
The business plan is left on the shelf, with the assumption that its real value was in the preparation. No matter how much you participated in writing the plan, commitment dissipates over time when the plan isn't reviewed. Out of sight, out of mind.

Beat neglect by making follow-up planning easy, rather than something painful you feel compelled to postpone. Schedule regular meetings to discuss only the plan, nothing else. Divide planning into two phases. First, set corporate and individual department goals without regard to financial considerations. Write one-sentence strategies for each. Then go back and fill in the figures and write a finished product. The updated plan can be completed in less than three days of meetings.

Unworkable Document
Executives find they have a bulky, hard-to-use document that discourages its use.

Make the plan workable by distilling its goals to one-page action summaries for each department. Display the information in bar charts for easy presentation at planning meetings. Each month, managers should exchange copies of their bar charts to show progress made on their parts of the business plan.

Unbalanced Application

Sometimes a disproportionate amount of attention is given to one part of the plan, such as marketing or the balance sheet. Or too much attention is devoted to long-range events to the detriment of the short-range goals.

To combat this, be sure to get balanced participation from all key managers. And 90 percent of all management action should be concerned with the next 12 months.

Disillusionment

Executives tend to get disillusioned when they find that reality doesn't match business-plan projections. One reason for this is that they don't plan for the unexpected.

Plan for contingencies, both positive and negative. For example, consider the impact of inflation on sales volume or profit margins. What opportunities will arise if a major competitor drops out? This type of planning will help produce a thoughtful response rather than a seat-of-the-pants reaction.

Too Action-Oriented

Action-oriented managers may contribute to a plan, but after it is finished they tend to forget about it. They want to get back to the "real world" of business.

Take advantage of this action orientation by having managers plan for their individual areas of responsibility, not for the corporation. Force them to confront real problems that they must solve.

No Performance Standard

Most executives can't tell you precisely how well they have implemented their business plan. But if a plan is to have any meaning, there ought to be a way to measure its progress.

Give each manager an objective measurable in dollars. In areas where it is difficult to measure productivity gains, this approach can be used by assigning a dollar value to a particular project. For a typical executive, seek a productivity gain equal to two to five times base salary.

Poor Progress Control

Implementation is difficult to track because progress reports get lost in the jumble of other meeting agenda items.

The key to charting your plan's progress is to hold a monthly meeting solely to evaluate the plan. Don't mix review of the plan with other matters.

Early Consumption

The business plan gets used up because no one is updating it as time passes.

Update the plan every six months. This means that every six months you extend the plan another year. That way, you never run out of plans.

Source: Nation's Business, August 1988, p. 21. Reprinted by permission, *Nation's Business,* August 1988. Copyright 1988, U.S. Chamber of Commerce.

Committee on Economic Development

To provide a framework of understanding of what a small business is, two of the more common definitions are presented. The **Committee on Economic Development (CED)** offers a definition that states that a business will be classed as a **small business** if it meets two or more of the following criteria.

1. Management is independent. (Usually the managers are also owners.)
2. Capital is supplied and ownership is held by an individual or a small group.
3. The area of operations is mainly local. Workers and owners are in one home community. Markets need not be local.
4. Relative size within the industry—the business is small when compared to the biggest units in its field. The size of the top bracket varies greatly so that what might seem large in one field would be definitely small in another.[7]

Small Business Administration

The **Small Business Administration (SBA)** was created by the Small Business Act of 1953 and is an independent agency of the federal government. The purpose of the SBA is to assist and counsel small business owner–managers. The SBA attempts to help people get into business and stay in business. As defined by the SBA, a small business is one that is independently owned and operated, not dominant in its field of operation, and operated for a profit.

The CED and the SBA definitions are similar. Both use qualitative guidelines for size classification. Each emphasizes independent ownership and management and relative lack of dominance in the field of operation as guidelines for defining a business as small. These guidelines are appropriate for our definition of a ''small business,'' as used in our text.

In addition, the SBA uses a quantitative size classification to determine if a business firm is small and thus eligible for loans and other assistance through the SBA. These size classifications are based on either dollar sales or number of employees. These are the quantitative size classifications for a ''small business'' as used by the SBA:

1. *Retail firm* Annual sales of not over $3.5 to $13.5 million, depending on the industry in which the firm is engaged. For example, the sales limit for a hardware store is $3.5 million annually, while for a department store it is $13.5 million.
2. *Service firm* Annual receipts not exceeding $3.5 million to $14.5 million, depending upon the industry in which the firm is engaged. To illustrate, the sales limit for an automotive repair shop is $3.5 million, while for computer-related services it is $12.5 million.
3. *Wholesale firm* Numbers of employees does not exceed 100.
4. *General contractors* Annual receipts do not exceed $17 million. The

ceiling on receipts for special trade contractors, such as roofing, is $7 million.

5. *Manufacturers*   Number of employees does not exceed 500 and large if number of employees exceeds 1500. For employment between 500 and 1500, a size that is standard for the industry is used. For example, the size standard for household furniture manufacturers is 500; construction machinery manufacturers, 750; and aircraft manufacturers, 1500. About 98 percent of all manufacturers have 500 employees or fewer.

The Small Business Owner–Manager

Throughout the text, we make reference to the following terms: manager, management, owner, owner–manager, entrepreneur, entrepreneur–manager, and small business manager. Whenever such references are made, they are descriptive of the **small business owner–manager,** the person in charge of a small business in either of the following situations: (1) where the owner is also the manager or (2) where the manager is a salaried employee.

IMPACT OF SMALL BUSINESS IN THE ECONOMY OF THE UNITED STATES

Small business contributes significantly to our economy. The SBA classifies approximately 98 percent of all businesses in the United States—sole proprietorships, partnerships, corporations, part-time businesses, and unincorporated professional activities—as small businesses.

Small enterprise runs the gamut from corner news-vending to developing optical fibers. Small business people sell gasoline, flowers, and coffee-to-go. They publish magazines, haul freight, teach languages, and program computers. They make wines, motion pictures, and high-fashion clothes. They build new homes and restore old ones. They repair plumbing, fix appliances, recycle metals, and sell used cars. They drive taxicabs, run cranes, and fly helicopters. They wildcat for oil, quarry sand and gravel, and mine exotic ores. They forge, cast, weld, photoengrave, electroplate, and anodize. They also invent anti-pollution devices, quality control mechanisms, energy saving techniques, microelectronic systems—a list would go on for volumes.[8]

The following facts give us evidence of the dramatic influence of small business on our economy.

1.   Small business provides about 67 percent of initial job opportunities and are responsible for most of the initial on-the-job training in basic skills provided young people.

FIGURE 1-3
SMALL BUSINESS EMPLOYERS BY INDUSTRY.

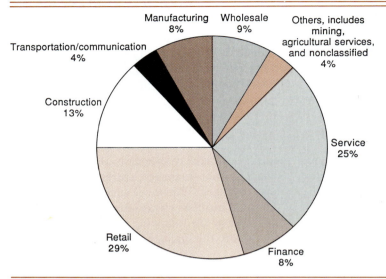

(*Small Business Primer,* The NFIB Foundation, Washington, D.C., 1988, p. 6.)

2. As a source of employment, small businesses provide jobs for about 56 percent of the U.S. work force, excluding farm employment.
3. In terms of output, small businesses account for approximately 38 percent of the gross national product.
4. Small firms account for nearly 42 percent of all sales in the United States.
5. Retailing (29 percent) and service firms (25 percent) make up over half the number of small businesses in the United States. (See Figure 1-3.)
6. Small firms account for nearly $7 out of every $10 made by retailers and wholesalers.
7. The livelihood of more than 100 million Americans is provided directly or indirectly by small business.
8. Almost 70 percent of all U.S. business are sole proprietorships.
9. About 60 percent of small businesses with employees have fewer than 5 employees and 90 percent have fewer than 20.

Small businesses create more jobs than do medium- and large-scale businesses. For example, in the period 1980 to 1986, firms with more than 500 employees provided only about 37 percent of all new jobs created in the private sector. However, small businesses accounted for nearly 63 percent of all new jobs created in the private sector, and the majority of the new jobs was generated by the very small companies! For example, firms with less than 20 employees generated about 39 percent of all new jobs for this period.[9]

FIGURE 1-4
SIXTY-FIVE IMPORTANT INNOVATIONS BY U.S. SMALL FIRMS IN THE TWENTIETH CENTURY[1]

Acoustic suspension speakers
Aerosol can
Air conditioning
Airplane
Articulated tractor chassis
Artificial skin
Assembly line
Automatic fabric cutting
Automatic transfer equipment
Bakelite
Biosynthetic insulin
Catalytic petroleum cracking
Computerized blood pressure controller
Continuous casting
Cotton picker
Defibrillator
Double-knit fabric
Dry chemical fire extinguisher
Electrical wire nuts
Fiber optic examination equipment
Fluid flow meter
Foam fire extinguisher
Front-end loader
Gas chromatograph
Geodesic dome
Gyrocompass
Hand-held fluoroscope
Heart valve
Heat sensor
Helicopter
Hetrodyne ratio
Hydraulic brake
Large-capacity computer

Link trainer
Nuclear magnetic resonance scanner
Nuclear magnetic resonance spectrometer
Optical scanner
Oral contraceptives
Outboard engine
Overnight national delivery
Pacemaker
Personal computer
Photo typesetting
Piezo electrical devices
Polaroid camera
Precast concrete
Prefabricated housing
Pressure-sensitive cellophane tape
Programmable computer
Quick-frozenfood
Reading machine
Rotary oil drilling bit
Safety razor
Six-axis robot arm
Soft contact lenses
Sonar fish monitoring
Spectrographic grid
Stereoscopic map scanner
Strain gauge
Strobe lights
Vacuum tube
Variable output transformer
Winchester disk drive
Xerography
Zipper

[1] An innovation is here defined as the first sale using a discovery. A small firm has fewer than 500 employees.
Source: Small Business Administration.

A significant contribution has been made by workers in small business. The incidence of innovation among small business workers is substantially higher than among workers in large corporations. Small firms produce two and a half times as many innovations as large firms relative to the number of persons employed. Since World War II, small businesses have been responsible for developing more than half of the new products and service innovations. Some of the inventions that have resulted in major new industries and growth companies are shown in Figure 1-4.

WOMEN ENTREPRENEURS

Women are playing an increasingly important role in the labor force. A significant aspect of this emerging role of women in the work force is their growing interest in entrepreneurship. Through previous work experience and increasing educational attainment, women are acquiring the skills and knowledge that can be translated into entrepreneurship. The following facts highlight some of the characteristics of the entrepreneurial woman.

1. Women-owned businesses are the fastest growth segment of the small business community. In one five-year period, from 1980 to 1985, the number of self-employed women increased 47.4 percent, nearly twice the percentage increase in the number of self-employed men.

2. Women-operated sole proprietorships' share of firms is 28.1 percent, up from 26.1 percent five years ago. Most women-owned firms are sole proprietorships.

3. Women are starting businesses in record numbers. There are 3.7 million women-operated nonfarm corporations, partnerships, and sole proprietorships in the United States, according to SBA estimates. This is an increase of 1.9 million since 1977.

4. Share of business receipts of women-operated nonfarm sole proprietorships increased from 8.8 percent to 12 percent in the last five years. Most recent data show annual receipts of women-owned businesses are approximately $65 billion. Receipts of women-owned sole proprietorships increased by almost 79 percent over the last five years, far outdistancing the 31 percent increase in total sole proprietorship receipts. Not only are more women going into business for themselves, but they are consistently enlarging their share of the sole proprietorship market.

5. Women are entering nontraditional businesses for women. For example, ownership by women has normally been concentrated in the retail and service industries. However, women are branching out into other fields. In fact, expansion of women-owned businesses in other industries has greatly outdistanced their growth in the retail industry. To illustrate, ownership of mining, construction, and manufacturing businesses by women increased by 116 percent, and ownership of transportation, communications, and electrical utilities increased by 124 percent in the five-year period 1980–1985. While women entrepreneurs are still a distinct minority in these industrial classes, it is clear that they are greatly increasing their opportunities across a wide range of industries. They also continue to increase their relative presence in the more traditional service industries (personal, business, health, professional) as well as in retail trade.[10]

Lynn Gordon, proprietor of French Meadow Bakery of Minneapolis, started baking a special "health-food" bread in her kitchen and selling 40 loaves a week to a local co-op. News of her bread spread by word of mouth. When gourmet shops and grocery stores began distributing her bread, Gordon had to move from her kitchen to a storefront-bakery to meet increased demand. Her success as an entrepreneur was featured on "60 Minutes," and Neiman-Marcus included her bread in a special gift certificate.

Jean Riffel graduated from college with a bachelor's degree in business administration and after graduation took some computer training. She went to work for Sperry Univac for a while but quit to get software experience in a smaller company. When she was passed over for promotion, she left to become vice president of a still smaller firm. However, she quit this position because she wanted to develop her own business ideas. With an idea and $10,000 of her savings, she opened her firm in her home in 1980, Computer Systems Service Bureau, an automated data processing services and training company. Since then, she has built the firm to 104 employees and annual revenues of nearly $3 million.[11]

MINORITY-OWNED BUSINESSES

Many minority-owned businesses are small and profitable operations. An SBA study on small, family-owned minority businesses suggests these firms often choose to remain small because they are profitable at small sizes. The study found the use of paid family members, who likely are motivated and productive, was a strong indicator of high productivity and profitability.[12]

The principal area of business of minority-owned firms are concentrated in services, retail trade, construction, and finance. Minorities are beginning to enter other fields, particularly wholesale trade, manufacturing, and transportation. Most minority businesses are sole proprietorships. Younger and better educated minority persons are attracted to self-employment today and these businesses have greater prospects for earnings than in previous decades. The likelihood of choosing entrepreneurship varied by ethnic/racial groups as seen in the following ranking: (1) Asians, (2) Hispanics, and (3) blacks.

Blacks and Hispanics have traditionally faced difficulties in entering business, ranging from low family income to inadequate occupational training and differences in educational attainment.[13]

Comer Cottrell's story is an example of the success of minority entrepreneurs. He started his beauty products company, Pro-Line Corporation, 17 years ago with only $600 and a borrowed typewriter. Now, his firm has expanded in a $26 million company with 175 employees. The firm is now the fourth largest ethnic beauty concern and the largest black-owned firm in the Southwest. Cottrell has succeeded, as he puts it, "in selling hope—that's all the beauty business is."[14]

The SBA program designed to provide assistance to small businesses owned and operated by economically and socially disadvantaged persons is the Section 8(a) program of the Small Business Act. The purpose of this program is to award noncompetitive contracts to economically and socially disadvantaged small business operators to assist them in becoming self-sufficient. Small business owners who participate in the Section 8(a) program receive management, technical, marketing, and financial assistance.

REWARDS AND ADVANTAGES OF SMALL BUSINESS OWNERSHIP

The entrepreneur realizes distinct rewards and advantages that are directly related to the size and the form of ownership of the business. The following discussion explores some of these benefits.

Profit Expectation

Profit is an essential product of the small business because it is a measure of the success of the firm, it affords owners with the funds that they need to

FIGURE 1-5
ENTREPRENEUR CONTRIBUTIONS AND REWARDS.

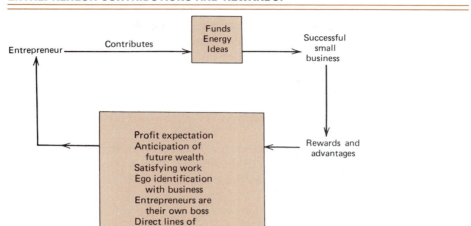

provide for the standard of living they desire for their families, it serves as the salary of the owner–manager, and it provides at least a part of the resources necessary for the stability and growth of the company. To a great extent, entrepreneurs control the amount of their income by their managerial expertise. Thus, earning a profit is one of the strongest motivators for initiating a small business. As shown in Figure 1-5, however, profit is only one reward entrepreneurs may receive from a successful small business.

Anticipation of Future Wealth

Many entrepreneurs work more for the future of their business than for their present well-being. Their dreams of building their business to achieve future wealth and status motivate them and contribute considerable personal satisfaction. Many never realize their dreams, but some do. J. C. Penney, Henry Ford, and King C. Gillette are just a few of the entrepreneurs who saw their small businesses grow into modern corporate giants.

A classic example of the small business owner who turned his company into a corporate giant is H. Ross Perot. Perot started his company, Electronic

Data Systems, Inc., in 1962, when he was 32 years old, with $1000 and an idea. Just 22 years later, EDS was purchased by General Motors for $2.55 billion. Mr. Perot's share of the purchase price was $1.2 billion.

Many small business firms are operated as part-time activities by people who support themselves and often their business by working at other, full-time employment. They create and operate these part-time businesses in expectation of creating a full-time business for themselves. Some realize their dreams, and others just go on supporting their part-time businesses for years with income from their full-time employment. The Office of Advocacy notes that many new businesses are part-time businesses with receipts of less than $25,000 annually.

It should be noted that dreams for some people are more satisfying than the actual realization of the dreams. In this sense, small business firms that are not successful may provide considerable satisfaction to their creators for long periods of time.

Satisfying Work

Most people spend a third or more of their waking hours in a work environment. Unfortunately, there are some people who are very dissatisfied with their work. Some dislike their work so much that they continually look forward to the weekend, dread the thought of the next workweek, and even develop physical and psychological illnesses resulting from the dislike of their work. Conversely, people who experience a high level of job satisfaction approach their work more positively, demonstrate better physical and mental health, exhibit a higher level of commitment to the firm, and have a more constructive outlook on life in general.

Many small business owners realize a high level of personal satisfaction derived from working in their own business. The owner of a TV repair shop may derive a sense of accomplishment each time a set is repaired. However, the owner may gain even greater satisfaction from the management of the business. The challenge of creating a business and achieving the various tasks involved in its operation and growth can be exhilarating to many people. As the owner of a small retail apparel shop observed, "The most important thing today is job satisfaction, and each day I find this is a more attainable goal through owning my own business rather than working for someone else. Owning a business provides me with the opportunity for personal achievement and personal fulfillment."

Ego Identification with the Business

Most owners of small businesses started the firms themselves, often as a result of considerable sacrifice and work. As a result, it is understandable that most of them feel a close ego identification with their business. Many entrepreneur–managers feel the firm is, in a sense, an extension of their own being.

The authors realized early in their consulting experience with small business firms that any criticism of the operations of the firm had to be handled very tactfully because it was common for the entrepreneur–manager to take strong personal offense.

Almost all small business entrepreneur–managers who have established a successful small business exhibit a very strong sense of personal pride in their business, which is certainly justified. In fact, it is not at all uncommon for the entrepreneur–managers to want their children to carry on the family business because of personal pride.

Entrepreneurs Are Their Own Bosses

Everyone at one time or another fantasizes about going into business and being his or her own boss. Now a growing number of Americans are making that fantasy a reality.[15] Many entrepreneurs report that they choose to go into business for themselves because it means, "I am my own boss." Making management decisions for the business represents a continuing challenge and provides a source of personal satisfaction for the entrepreneur. Entrepreneurs feel that they control their own destiny and do not have to answer to anyone except themselves for the actions. And the rewards they receive are in direct proportion to their level of management performance.

Some entrepreneurs have continued to operate their business for years even though they could have earned considerably more money in someone else's employment. Thus, the desire to be one's own boss is undoubtedly a primary motivator for these individuals.

Direct Lines of Communication Between Owner and Employees

Because there is usually only one level of management in the small business enterprise, face-to-face contact is the norm between the manager and the employees when instructions are given or specific problems relating to the business are discussed. The one-to-one communication relationship significantly increases the chances of reducing or eliminating many common communications problems encountered in larger firms. In larger firms, for example, messages ordinarily must pass from the sender through several other persons in the chain of command before the person for whom the communications are intended finally sees or hears them. In this relaying process, messages can easily become distorted or misinterpreted.

In the small enterprise, effective use can be made of upward communication from the employees to the owner–manager. The bottom-to-top communication process is an effective method for improving understanding within the organization.

Effective utilization of the short lines of communication will enable the small business owner–manager to reduce many of the human problems caused by faulty communication. On the other hand, poor communication will have a negative influence on the organizational environment and consequently increase human relations problems.

Personal Contact with Employees and Customers

Small business owners have the opportunity to develop and maintain harmonious working relationships with their employees. With only one level of management, direct interaction is possible between managers and employees. Through this personal relationship, owner–managers and employees have an opportunity to understand each other's position, needs, and wants better. Furthermore, the employees and the manager often work side by side on an informal rather than a formal basis. In this way, each participant learns to respect the other's viewpoints. In the small firm, it is especially vital that all members cooperate to form an effective work team.

One of the particular advantages of the small business firm is that it provides the type of environment in which close, personal customer relationships can be cultivated by the owner-manager. The owner–manager may know customers on a first-name basis, and the manager knows what products they are buying. Customers can be given personal, individualized consideration to fit their specific needs. The small business manager recognizes the value of such relationships to the success of the business. Customers appreciate this personal concern, and it is often a major reason why they patronize a particular business. The manager is also in a better position to handle customer complaints directly. By utilizing the opportunities they have for personal contact and by dealing fairly with their customers, small business owners can do much to ensure the success of the firm. In this small business environment, the entrepreneur has the opportunity to acquire detailed information about the specific market.

Centralized Decision Making

The entrepreneur is directly involved in making all decisions affecting the firm. Whereas managers in large firms often must refer matters to higher management for a decision, entrepreneurs can make decisions quickly since there is only one major level of management in the small firm. This advantage is especially important when time is critical. By being able to respond quickly, the entrepreneur can often take advantage of unexpected business opportunities that require quick response and turn them into profitable gain for the small firm.

Entrepreneurial Status

In most communities, the entrepreneur–manager ranks high in the work status hierarchy. There is a wide range of status even within the small business group. For example, the principal stockholder–president of the local bank is usually assigned a higher status in the community than the service station owner–manager. In spite of this range of status, the community usually perceives a higher status for the small business entrepreneur group than most forms of the blue-collar and white-collar employment. In fact, in many small communities, small business owners are often assigned to the top of the status scale.

It should also be pointed out that perceived status is more important to an individual's satisfaction than actual status assigned by other people. Many entrepreneurs feel they have high levels of status in their communities and derive considerable satisfaction from this impression, regardless of whether or not it is actually true.

Ease of Entry

An attractive feature of the small business operation, particularly the sole proprietorship, is the ease with which one can go into business. All that is required is to open the doors for business is a location, any special operating licenses required by the city or state government, and some capital. No other restrictions are normally placed on the entrance into small business. With the business in operation, the entrepreneur has the unique opportunity to cultivate close ties with the community.

COMMON PROBLEMS OF OWNING A SMALL BUSINESS

While there are many rewards and advantages of entrepreneurship, it would be improper to ignore some of the common problems of small business ownership. Some of the problems confronting not only small business but owners of all sizes of business are reported annually by Dun & Bradstreet in its report on the causes of business failures, shown in Figure 1-6.[16] This report indicates wide-ranging problems that must be confronted by the entrepreneur. As shown in Figure 1.6, some of the causes should be considered major as they contribute to a larger percentage of the failures: economic factors, lack of experience, low sales, and high expenses. Causes considered minor because they account for a smaller percentage of failures include neglect, lack of capital, problems with customers, disaster, fraud, and too few assets. Other problems to be considered but not included in the Dun & Bradstreet study are lack of specialization, confining and long hours of operation, risk of funds, government paperwork and regulations, and stress.

Obviously, each entrepreneur does not encounter all these problems. However, awareness of these problems enables entrepreneurs to take necessary precautions to prevent these problems from developing in their firm.

FIGURE 1-6
SOME COMMON CAUSES OF BUSINESS FAILURE

Cause	Percentage of Total Failures
Economic factors	71.7%
Experience	20.3
Sales	11.1
Expense	8.1
Neglect	1.6
Capital	0.5
Customer	0.4
Disaster	0.4
Fraud	0.3
Asset	0.2

Source: The Business Failure Record, Dun & Bradstreet Corporation.

Economic Factors Causes

Profits are the life-sustaining force of the small business. If profits are insufficient to carry the firm, the business cannot succeed. Reduced profits may result if the firm loses a share of its market to a competitor or if consumer spending declines or is shifted to other products or services. Higher interest rates that must be paid for business loans in inflationary periods also negatively impact on profits.

Experience Factors Causes

In today's dynamic business environment, entrepreneurs must be alert to rapidly changing conditions. For example, they must recognize and react to variables that impact on their firm, such as inflation, technological change, and consumer habits.

Failure to identify and respond to changing social, economic, and environmental conditions will lead to serious problems or eventual failure of the firm. A number of problems encountered by entrepreneurs with inadequate experience are discussed in the paragraphs that follow.

Lack of Experience in Product or Service Line

Sometimes owner–managers may lack experience in the line of business they enter. They may have a strong background in one line of business but be unsuccessful in another owing to their unfamiliarity with the specific problems of the new line of business. A case in point is the mortician who sold his mortuary business and purchased a jewelry store. Within a year the jewelry store closed. The primary cause of this unsuccessful business venture was that the owner entered a business he knew nothing about.

Lack of Management Experience

Another form of inexperience is shown by a lack of management experience. There is a vast difference between being the best machinist, mechanic, or salesperson and being able to manage a machine shop, an auto repair shop, or a retail store. Whereas the manager of the firm usually has a specific job skill, the possession of a particular job skill in no way guarantees success in the new role as manager. Without proper management training, the skills and techniques necessary for effective management will not likely be attained.

Overconcentration of Experience

An overconcentration of experience in one function may present a problem to the small firm owner–manager. Owner–managers must have the ability to view the firm conceptually. This means they should be able to perceive the need for, interrelationship of, and contribution of each activity of the firm. If owner–managers concentrate a major portion of their time and energy on the one function that is their interest and specialty—either sales, production, or finance—and neglect the others, this approach will likely have an adverse effect on the total firm. For example, managers may focus their efforts on sales. To complete a sale, they may promise delivery of merchandise by certain dates when they know the firm does not have the productive capacity to meet such deadlines. When the firm is unable to make a delivery on the scheduled date, customers become irritated and may even cease doing business with the firm. Thus, small business managers must be aware that the health and vitality of the firm depend in large measure on giving balanced attention to all functions of the firm. In addition, this example underscores the need for all business managers to be honest with their customers. Ethical dealings with customers help to build repeat sales and enhance the small business owner's image in the business community.

Incompetence of Management

Of all the problems encountered because of experience factors, manager incompetence is the major cause of failure. Managers are incompetent when they lack the necessary skills and knowedge necessary to lead the firm to accomplish its goals. Specific traits, skills, and knowledge which entrepreneurs should possess were identified earlier: drive, mental ability, human relations ability, communications ability, technical knowledge, decision-making ability, and conceptual ability.

Sales Causes

The lack of experience may be evidenced in various ways in the life of a company. If entrepreneurs lack proper management skills and knowledge, they may encounter problems related to the sales effort of the firm: (1) weak competitive position, (2) lack of proper inventory control, (3) low sales volume, and (4) poor location.

Weak Competitive Position

Competition is the bulwark of our economy. Small businesses must compete with other small businesses as well as big businesses. Firms that cannot efficiently compete in such areas as services offered, prices charged, or quality of merchandise sold definitely have difficulty surviving. For example, a small restaurant manager may lower the price of the lunches served to match lower prices charged by competitors. However, as a result of lowering the price, the manager may have to serve smaller portions. If this action is needed to remain competitive, the outlook for the firm is bleak. Because most business firms and especially small businesses must depend on repeat patronage for survival and growth, reducing the size of portions or lowering the quality of the product will surely lessen patronage.

Inadequate Inventory Control

As small business managers must have general management skill to operate the total business, they may not possess some of the specialized and technical skills required for proper management of the firm, such as control of inventory. If too large an inventory is in stock, the result is that too much of the owner's capital is tied up or there is the possibility of inventory loss through spoilage or obsolescence. When insufficient levels of inventory are stocked, merchandise is not available to meet customer demand. For example, a farm equipment dealer in a small town made only a minimum effort to maintain control of his inventory. Consequently, he had no idea of stock availability or which were the high-turnover items. When customers needed parts, they usually required them immediately. However, the equipment dealer was normally out of stock for most items, but would order the parts from the manufacturer, a process requiring several days for delivery. Because customers could not wait for replacement parts, they were forced to go elsewhere to fill their needs. As a result of this policy on inventory, the farm equipment dealer lost many sales, and the firm went out of business.

Expense Causes

Failure to control operating expenses will reduce profit and pose a potential threat to the firm. Likewise, borrowing too heavily may force the business to close if debts cannot be paid.

Neglect Causes

Whereas only a small percentage of firms fail because of personal neglect, it can be a particular problem of the small business owner. Common reasons for personal neglect include poor management of time, poor health, laziness, family or marital problems, or apathy. Sometimes managers become too involved and devote too much time to community or other outside activities. Although these activities have merit, entrepreneurs must be careful not to place their activities ahead of the firm's interest. Entrepreneurs need to establish priorities for themselves relative to their involvement in their firm and their many other activities. They must keep in mind the objectives of the firm and not become easily distracted by too many outside activities or disenchanted by minor business or personal setbacks.

Capital Causes

Whether taking over an existing business or opening a new firm, the amount of capital required to start the business and to continue operations must be carefully considered. If projected capital needs are too low, the business may open successfully but fail if funds are insufficient to sustain the firm after the "grand opening." For example, too much of the firm's funds may be committed to fixed assets, leaving a shortfall for the funds needed for purchasing inventory or paying current bills, such as rent or utilities.

Customer Causes

A concern of the small business manager is whether to extend credit. Firms that do grant credit must protect against the practice of extending too much credit. One small auto repair garage had at one time $10,000 worth of accounts receivable on the books. Much of the credit had been extended to "friends" of the owner. When bills came due, most were never collected because the friends had disappeared. Even though it was difficult or impossible for the owner to collect on these accounts, he could not postpone payment of his bills. Fortunately, the firm was able to survive. Survival was made possible by a reversal of credit policy. The owner no longer extends any credit. All sales are for cash only. And though the owner was uncertain as to the effect this policy would have on his customers, the results have been positive. Today, the firm is on sound financial ground.

Disaster Causes

There are some circumstances over which the owner may have little or no control. Small business owners may face disasters resulting from fire, employee strikes, burglary, and employee theft. Natural disasters, such as an earthquake, flood, or hurricane, may devastate the small business owner. For example, in 1969, Russel Steiner had just taken over his father's small 15-year-old shipbuilding business in Bayou La Batre, Alabama—the Detroit of trawlers—with plans for expansion. But when Hurricane Camille struck the Gulf Coast, the Steiner shipyard was totally destroyed. The shipyard was able to rebuild with the assistance of a disaster loan from the Small Business Administration. The firm currently builds 36 vessels a year, exporting its ships to Latin America and Western Africa.[17]

Fraud Causes

Fraud is the deliberate misrepresentation of the status of the business by the owner–manager to deceive others. Some means by which fraud is committed include using a misleading name for the company, issuing false and misleading financial statements, and disposing of the assets of the firm in an irregular manner.

Asset Causes

If the entrepreneur expands the business too rapidly, such as enlarging the current facility or opening a second store unit, and sufficient business is not generated from the expansion, serious problems can result. The entrepreneur must take great care not to expand too rapidly or tie up too many funds in fixed assets.

Lack of Specialization

Large firms have the financial resources available to hire individuals who possess the expertise needed to staff the variety of positions in the firm. Accountants maintain company financial records, salespeople make contacts to sell the company's products, and personnel staff members actively recruit the type of qualified persons needed to fill job vacancies.

In the small business, the owner–managers generally perform all or most of the functions because their monetary resources are limited. Hence, they must be generalists rather than specialists. They must be familiar with all phases of the firm's operations—general management, accounting, sales management, production management, personnel management, and any other necessary functions. Because they have many duties to carry out, they frequently do not have enough time to devote to long-range planning of the firm. Instead, most of their time is spent in dealing with the current day's activity or crisis. Thus, a disadvantage to many small firms is lack of resources for hiring and utilizing specialists in the functional area of the business.

Confining, Long Hours of Work

Considerations on the positive side of owning a business include being one's own boss and profit expectations. One disadvantage is that managers of the small business must do most of the work themselves. For example, entrepreneur–managers are usually the first to arrive in the morning and the last to leave at night. If they become ill, they cannot call in sick to their boss. They cannot take off a few days without making special arrangements for someone to operate the business for them.

It is common for most firms to be open six days a week, and many are open seven to remain competitive with other small and big businesses. In addition, owners work long hours, as shown in Figure 1-7. The majority of

FIGURE 1-7
HOURS PER WEEK WORKED BY NEW BUSINESS OWNERS.

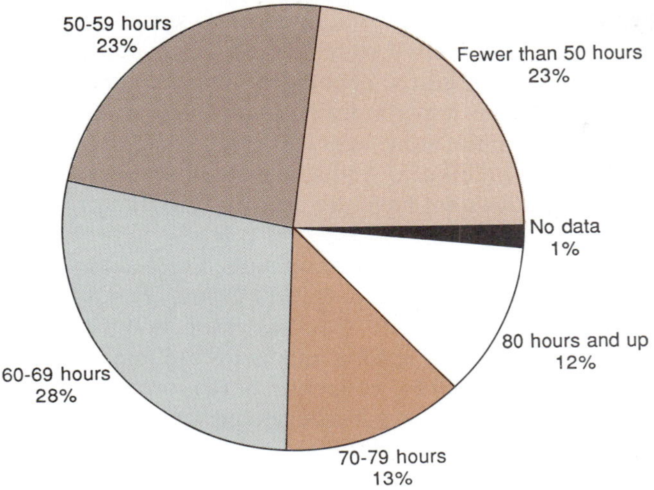

(Small Business Primer, The NFIB Foundation, Washington, D.C., 1988, p. 17.)

business owners in the first year of operation work more than 60 hours per week and 25 percent work more than 70 hours per week.

Risk of Funds

Although profit is one of the major advantages of ownership, entrepreneurship carries with it the risk of loss of funds. Because funds invested in the firm are largely personal funds or borrowed funds, the owner may be personally liable for any and all debts. Hence, it is possible that the small business owner may not only lose a lifetime's personal savings but may also build up liabilities that will take years to repay.

Government Regulations and Paperwork

While not a problem limited to small businesses, the growing number of government regulations and required reports is placing a disproportionately heavier burden on the small business, due in large measure to their limited financial and personnel resources. The report prepared by the White House Commission on Small Business emphasized this point: ''The most maddening obstacles to operating a small business are the inappropriate federal regulations and the overwhelming, often incomprehensible reporting requirements that go with them.''[18]

Small business owners realize that some government regulation is necessary to maintain an orderly society. However, we have seen a dramatic upsurge in the number of regulations, particularly in the areas of affirmative action, hiring, energy conservation, and protection for consumers, workers, and the environment.[19] Currently, some 90 agencies issue thousands of new regulations annually, all of which have a major impact on the small business.

The increase in required paperwork that accompanies the increased number of regulations is a major drain on the small business owner's time and energy. For example, some agencies require separate reports for local, regional, and federal offices. And as we noted at the opening of this section, the small business does not have the personnel to interpret and complete the necessary forms.

Some of the most frequent complaints directed toward the many reports are (1) there are too many reports and forms, (2) reports and forms are overly time consuming to complete, (3) costs associated with the reports and forms are excessive, (4) many reports and forms are unnecessary or useless, (5) not enough time is allowed for collection of the forms or reports, and (6) forms are confusing. As one entrepreneur noted, ''I spent an entire day trying to figure out why I owe an additional $30.00 in taxes. I called my accountant and his calculations showed that I had overpaid by $45.00. The explanation on the form was so confusing that my accountant could not figure it out. Finally, I paid the $30.00 and asked the IRS to explain the form to me!''

A report on the White House Commission on Small Business recognized the magnitude of the twin problems of regulations and paperwork. One major recommendation of this comission was to require all federal agencies to analyze the cost and relevance of regulations to small businesses. This action could then lead to the development of a specific regulatory policy for small business and could result in some businesses being exempt from some regulations and reporting requirements. Furthermore, when new regulations are proposed, small business representatives should have the opportunity to provide input before final regulations are adopted.

Some relief from the burden of rules and regulations has been gained by the small businesses with the passage of the **Regulatory Flexibility Act** or ''Regflex'' in the fall of 1980. The act went into effect in 1981, and its purpose is to require federal agencies to revise or drop excessive rules. The act requires government agencies to give public notice of impending major rules so that small business can comment, to weigh the effect of proposed rules on small business, to explain the need and objective of each proposed rule, and to review all existing rules within 10 years and to eliminate those that are not needed.

Stress

All small business owner–managers face stressful situations not only in the day-to-day management of the firms but in their personal lives as well. **Stress** refers to how people respond to events in the environment that pose a threat.

For example, the small business owner encounters stressful situations when sales are declining, when customers are not paying their bills, when employee productivity is declining, or when employee absenteeism and tardiness are increasing. Stressful situations in the personal life include a change in the goals of the small business owner, aging, children leaving home, or the death of parents.

A moderate level of stress is desirable because it keeps us alert as well as serves to motivate us. However, too much stress or stress handled improperly can lead to adverse physiological and behavioral consequences for the owner, such as heart disease, mental illness, or ulcers. Thus, if stress is not handled properly by the entrepreneur, it can result in serious health problems and cause serious problems that threaten the survival of the small business.

A FAMILY-OWNED BUSINESS

Many small businesses are family owned, and the business plays a central role in the daily lives of the family. Often all family members participate in some aspect of the business, and business matters are the focus of family discussions.

As discussed earlier, more and more women are becoming full-time entrepreneurs. In these situations, the husband often works in the full-time employ of another firm. His role in this case involves support activities, such as maintenance and repair of facilities and equipment.

Children in these family-owned businesses often perform some duties as soon as they are old enough, such as making deliveries, cleaning up, waiting on customers and operating a cash register. In skilled trades, children of the owner often learn trade skills as apprentices to their father. It has been common practice, in all nations throughout history, for many skilled trades to be passed down from father to son. In addition, small business firms are often passed down from parents to their children, and some have operated in the same family for generations.

There are many small businesses in operation that could not exist except as family operations. The profit of the firm is in reality a salary for the family. If the owners of these family operations had to pay salaries to employees outside the family, it would be financially impossible for them to continue to exist.

Problems of managing a family-owned business are both similar to and somewhat different from the management problems in a nonfamily business. In some ways, the management problems faced by the entrepreneur of a family business are identical to those that confront the owner of any small company. In other ways, however, they are different because emotions generated by family relationships often interfere with sound business decisions.

In some family-owned businesses, the firm is owned by two groups. One group consists of silent partners, stockholders, or directors. The other group is represented by those who are involved in the ongoing management of the firm. It is not unusual for these two groups to have conflicting views relating to the operation and management of the firm.

Another problem is that in some family businesses, there is no clear specification of who is in charge of daily operations, and the result is the potential for conflict. At other times, relatives may be hired, but they may not have the necessary job skills. Then there is also the matter of equity in paying family members. A potential difficulty may arise if some family members perceive they are doing more than others but are not paid accordingly.

A survey of 200 owners of family businesses revealed two other problems. One problem centered on who will succeed the family business owner. A second problem is the lack of formal, professional evaluation procedures or written job descriptions.[20]

SUMMARY OF KEY POINTS

1. Millions of Americans have fulfilled their dream of owning their own business, and this entrepreneurial spirit has been the cornerstone for making America the most economically powerful nation in the world. Small business continues to provide avenue for individual creativity and self-expression.

2. Personality characteristics and abilities of entrepreneurs that contribute to business success include (a) drive, (b) mental ability, (c) human relations ability, (d) communications ability, (e) technical knowledge, (f) decision-making ability, and (g) conceptual ability.

3. The business plan is a complete, well-thought-out, written document that establishes the plan of action for the entrepreneur's small business.

4. The Committee on Economic Development defines a business as small when (a) management is independent, (b) capital is supplied and ownership is held by an individual or a small group, (c) the area of operations is mainly local, and (d) the business is small when compared to the biggest units in its field.

5. The SBA defines a small business as one that is independently owned and operated, not dominant in its field of operation, and operated for profit.

6. Small business firms make a substantial contribution to the economy of the United States in terms of providing employment, accounting for a large share of our gross national product, and generating new products and services through research and development.

7. Women and minority entrepreneurs play an increasingly strategic role in the small business economy.

8. Rewards and advantages of small business ownership include profit expectation, anticipation of future wealth, satisfying work, ego identification with the business, being one's own boss, direct line of communication between owner and employees, personal contact with employees and customers, centralized decision making, entrepreneurial status, and ease of entry.

9. Some of the common problems of small business ownership are caused by economic, experience, sales, expense, neglect, disaster, fraud, customers, assets, and capital factors; lack of specialization; confining and long hours of operation; government regulations and paperwork; and stress.

10. Many small businesses involve the entire family in the operation of the firm.

DISCUSSION QUESTIONS

1. How would you explain the term "entrepreneur"?
2. Identify some of the personality traits that contribute to the success of the small business manager.
3. What is a business plan?
4. How does the SBA define a "small business"?
5. Explain the rewards and advantages of small business ownership.
6. Identify the common problems of business failure.
7. What effect can stress have on the small business owner?

THE BUSINESS PLAN: THE ENTREPRENEURIAL SELF-ASSESSMENT

Entrepreneurship can be rewarding and challenging, but it also involves risk. Before you decide to start an entrepreneurial business venture, you should analyze your personal strengths and weaknesses. The following list of personal characteristics is designed to help you determine if you have what it takes to be a successful entrepreneur. Analyze yourself carefully as you answer each question.

	Yes	No
Do I really have the desire to be my own boss rather than work for someone else?		
Do I have the need to do things on my own?		
Am I a self-starter?		
Do I have sufficient management skills?		

	Yes	No
Do I have experience in the type of business I am interested in owning and operating?	✓	
Can I accept the responsibility of seeing things through to the end?	✓	✓
Am I well-organized person?		✓
Can I accept the risk of possible loss of investment if the venture fails?	✓	
Do I have the desire to lead and direct others?	✓	
Do I have the need to be in control of the business?	✓	
Can I make decisions quickly if I have to?	✓	
Do I have good health and the high energy level necessary to be an entrepreneur?		✓
Do I have the financial resources I need to begin as well as future credit resources?	✓	
Can I sustain my business through the early, formative years?	✓	
Can people (customers and employees) trust what I say?		
Do I have the need to set and achieve difficult goals and move on to other challenges?		
Do I have the desire to be innovative and creative?		
Do I prefer having a plan of action (business plan) before I begin an activity?		
Is my spouse supportive of my plan?		
Do I manage my time efficiently?		
Am I willing to work the long hours it takes to be an entrepreneur?		
Do I have the desire to stick with the business even in troubled times?		
Am I willing to do *all* the tasks (glamorous and not so glamorous) which are necessary for the successful operation of the business?		
Am I a hard worker?		

There is no "passing score." However, if most of your answers are "yes," you probably have what it takes to become an entrepreneur. If you answer "no" to about half of the questions, you may need a partner to reinforce the areas where you are weak. If most of your answers are "no," then entrepreneurship is likely not for you.

ENTREPRENEURIAL PROJECTS

1. Write a short paragraph about yourself; indicate your entrepreneurial strengths and weaknesses.
2. Discuss the reasons why you would like to go into business for yourself.
3. List three to five types of businesses you believe you would be interested in starting and the reasons for your interest in these types of business.
4. Give the reasons why you would not want to go into business for yourself.
5. Interview the owner of a small business. Obtain all or any part of the following information.
   a. What were your reasons for going into business for yourself?
   b. Why did you choose this specific type of business?
   c. What personality characteristics do you feel are your strong points and what are those that need strengthening?
      (1) Drive
      (2) Mental ability
      (3) Human relations ability
      (4) Communications ability
      (5) Technical knowledge
      (6) Decision-making ability
      (7) Conceptual ability
   d. Which of the following rewards do you receive from your small business? Is any one more important than the others?
      (1) Profit expectation
      (2) Anticipation of future wealth
      (3) Satisfying work
      (4) Ego identification with the business
      (5) Being one's own boss
      (6) Direct lines of communication with employees
      (7) Personal contact with employees and customers
      (8) Centralized decision making
      (9) Entrepreneurial status
      (10) Ease of entry
   e. Do any members of the owners family work in the business? If so, what are their duties

CASE A
The New Entrepreneurs

John Young and Fred Webster attended college and played football on the same team. After graduation, they went their separate ways in their respective careers. Both worked for companies in the energy business (oil and gas). During their careers, they kept in contact with each other.

With the downturn in the energy industry in the 1980s, both left the field and agreed to form a partnership. They returned to the college town where they had enjoyed good times and surveyed the business opportunities that were available. Both agreed that they wanted to do something completely different from their previous experience in the energy business.

After surveying the business opportunities, they agreed to purchase a restaurant-bar business. The owner of the restaurant, Johnny Adams, was retiring after 25 years of successful operation of the business.

When asked what experience they had in the restaurant-bar business, John and Fred commented: "We've never been in the restaurant-bar business except to frequent them. We hope to take the business Mr. Adams has built up over the years and expand it."

Questions

1. Do John and Fred have the right kind of "experience" needed to succeed in small business?
2. Do you believe John and Fred have the personality characteristics that contribute to small business success?
3. What are some of the negative factors about small business ownership that John and Fred should consider before purchasing the business? How could they overcome these negative factors?
4. What are some positive factors that seem to indicate that they could be successful entrepreneurs?
5. What are some questions that John and Fred should ask themselves before entering into this business partnership?
6. Would you advise John and Fred to go into business as partners in the restaurant and bar?

C A S E B
The Big Chill

Darryl Smith feels like he's being cheated on. His wife, Diane, doesn't get home until late, she has taken several long business trips, and she has been keeping to herself a lot.

So just what's going on? Diane has become an entrepreneur. Three years ago, against her husband's advice, she turned in her full-time job as a housewife and mother of two for 70-hour weeks at Sweet Stuff, her retail cake decorating shop and custom cake bakery in Newark, Calif. "I knew if I didn't do it I'd regret the decision for the rest of my life," she says.

Business at Sweet Stuff is doing just great, says Diane, 38, who started decorating cakes seven years ago as a hobby. Soaring demand for her wedding cakes and unique decorating techniques convinced Diane to turn the hobby into a business. Twice since then she has moved into larger quarters, and the shop now brings in revenues of roughly $20,000 a month with a small profit.

But the way Darryl sees it, he had the sweet life before Sweet Stuff came along, and the business is just robbing him of a wife and their sons, 10 and 8, of a mother. Darryl often finds himself preparing the kids for school and cooking dinner. "It's a relief to know she has a livelihood and that it's fulfilling to her, but I'm jealous," says Darryl, 41, who met and married Diane when they worked togeter in an optometrist's office. "[The business] is a complete emotional involvement separate from the family."

The strain has not been emotional, but financial, too. Diane took a second mortgage on the house to start her business. When she is at home, she spends much of her time alone working on the company books and a newsletter. "Darryl has no say in the business. He has no idea what it even grosses," says Diane, who takes a small salary for herself and plows almost all profits back into the company.

Darryl's anger had remained pent up until the couple recently realized how close their marriage was to blowing up and began seeing a counselor. The Smith's are trying to work through their miscommunications.

Why don't the two try working together in the business? Impossible, they both insist. For one thing, Darryl is a self-admitted pessimist. Diane is just the opposite. And he's simply not cut out for the entrepreneurial life-style, he says. "I like job security, benefits, and paid vacations," says Darryl, who manages an optical store and sticks to strict operating procedures spelled out through union contracts. Diane likes the frenetic life of an entrepreneur. "At Sweet Stuff we're informal, we're more like a family. If someone needs time off, we'll work around it," she says.

And there's the issue of business strategy. Darryl thinks Sweet Stuff should give up the retail business of selling decorating supplies and concentrate on making one-of-a-kind cakes, which can sell for as much as $500 apiece. Diane thinks both businesses will thrive, since hers is one of the few retail outlets for decorating supplies. Traditionally, hobbyists have had to order supplies directly from manufacturers.

Despite his ideas on how to run the business, Darryl has no interest in taking it over if something were to happen to his wife. And Diane worries about having to give half of her company to her husband under California community property laws if they divorce. "But I don't know what would happen if we started talking about a postnuptial agreement," says Diane warily.

The Smiths still have a long way to go in working out their differences. "We're learning to talk to each other," says Diane. But she has no intention of giving up her baby, although she has agreed to cut back her work schedule by 10 hours a week, and the two plan a vacation in the Caribbean. "Eight years ago I was a very different person. I married Darryl because I needed someone to lean on. Now for the first time, I'm doing something for myself, by myself."

Source: Marie-Jeanne Juilland, "The Good, the Bad, and the Ugly," _Venture,_ January 1988, pp. 43–44. Reprinted from the January 1988 issue of VENTURE, for Entrepreneurial & Business Leaders, by special permission. © 1988, Venture Magazine, Inc. 521 Fifth Ave., New York, N.Y. 10175-0028.

Question

1. Discuss the special problems encountered in this small business.

Notes

[1] _Webster's New World Dictionary of the American Language._

[2] Hal B. Pickle, _Personality and Success: An Evaluation of Personal Characteristics of Successful Small Business Managers_ (Washington, D.C.: Small Business Administration, 1964).

[3] "Winning Ideas for Small Business Success," _Small Business Success,_ 1988 edition (Pacific Bell Directory), p. 6.

[4] Roger Thompson, "Business Plans: Myth or Reality," _Nation's Business,_ August 1988, pp. 17–18.

[5] Ibid., p. 23.

[6] "What Is a Small Business," _Time,_ May 6, 1985, Special Advertising Section, "Small Business USA." No page number.

[7] CED, Committee for Economic Development, _Meeting the Special Problems of Small Business_ (New York: 1947), p. 14.

[8] Report to the President, *America's Small Business Economy* (Washington, D.C.: Agenda for Action, White House Commission on Small Business, April 1980), p. 16.

[9] *The State of Small Business* (Washington, D.C.: U.S. Government Printing Office, 1988), p. xvi.

[10] Ibid., pp. 41 and 43.

[11] "Starting Their Own," *Nation's Business,* May 1987, p. 23.

[12] Bruce A. Kirchhoff and Judith J. Kirchhoff, "Productivity and Profitability Among Small Family Businesses," September 1984, reported in *The State of Small Business* (Washington, D.C.: U.S. Government Printing Office, 1985), p. 340.

[13] *The State of Small Business* (Washington, D.C.: U.S. Government Printing Office, 1984), p. 371.

[14] Michael Whittaker, "Making a Mark Beautifully," *Nation's Business,* January 1988, p. 24R.

[15] "Winning Ideas for Small Business Success," p. 5.

[16] *Business Failure Record* (New York: Dun & Bradstreet, 1987), p. 19.

[17] Small Business Administration, *Network* (Washington, D.C.: SBA, September–October 1987).

[18] Report to the President, *America's Small Business Economy,* p. 29.

[19] Kenneth W. Chilton and Murry L, Weidenbaum, "Small Business Performance in the Regulated Economy," Working paper 52 (St. Louis: Center for the Study of Small Business, Washington University, February 1980), p. 1.

[20] "Keeping It in the Family," *Nation's Business,* March 1988, pp. 14, 16.

KEY WORDS

CHAPTER 2

OWNERSHIP

After reading this chapter, you will understand:

1 The needs and characteristics of the business determine which form of ownership best fits the business.

2 The advantages and disadvantages of the sole proprietorship, the partnership, and the corporation.

3 The difference between general and limited partners.

4 What stocks and bonds are and the difference between preferred and common stock.

5 How a joint venture functions and where it is used.

6 The different ways forms of ownership are taxed and how Subchapter S may save you money if you are a small business owner.

7 The difference between dissolution and bankruptcy and the three forms of bankruptcy.

Carl C. Hall

ATKINS PICKLE COMPANY

Like relish on your hot dog? Have a yen for sweet (or dill) pickles? Chances are sometime in the past 30 years, most Americans have enjoyed a product of Atkins Pickle Company of Atkins, Arkansas. Think of the Ozarks the next time you taste a good, long, green pickle. And think of SBA—without it Atkins would have been a modest pickle packer indeed.

In 1959, the pickle company received a $350,000 SBA loan when it had less than $1 million in annual sales and 100 employees. Today Atkins Pickle has $20 million in yearly sales and 400 employees.

Carl C. Hall gained control of the company—which had been started in the 1940s—in 1956 and secured in 1964 what was then the largest SBA loan in Arkansas history—$700,000. The major expansion caused Atkins Pickle to become one of the largest cucumber purchasers from growers in Arkansas, Texas, and Mississippi. More than tens of millions of pickles are produced annually, of a gourmet quality dubbed "the Cadillac of the pickle industry." In 1971, Carl Hall was named Arkansas Small Business Person of the Year.

In 1983, Hall, 83, sold the company to Dean Foods of Franklin Park, Illinois. Atkins Pickle, however, remains the largest employer in

rural Atkins, Arkansas, and one of the top three pickle packers in America. And that relish? In the old days, Hall used to make it with a concrete mixer.

Source: Small Business Administration, Network (Washington, D.C.: SBA, November–December 1987).

FORMS OF BUSINESS OWNERSHIP

There are three forms of business ownership: (1) the sole proprietorship, (2) the partnership, and (3) the corporation. In addition, the joint venture, technically an adaptation of the partnership form of ownership, is increasing in usage.

Small business owners often ask which is the best form of ownership. There is no one answer to this question because it depends entirely on the individual business. The corporation form of ownership is usually not suited to a "mom and pop" operation, and the sole proprietorship form of ownership would be completely impossible for a giant firm like General Motors.

The needs and characteristics of each business dictate which form of ownership is most suited to that business. (See Fig. 2-1). Some of the factors that should be considered when selecting a form of ownership are these.

1. The problems of creating the form of ownership
2. The amount of capital needed in the business
3. The amount of profit available for distribution
4. The authority relationship in operating the business
5. The length of life of the business and need for continuity of the business
6. The extent of liability to the owners
7. Legal restrictions of the form of ownership
8. Taxation

FIGURE 2-1
CHARACTERISTICS OF EACH SMALL BUSINESS DETERMINE BEST FORM OF OWNERSHIP.

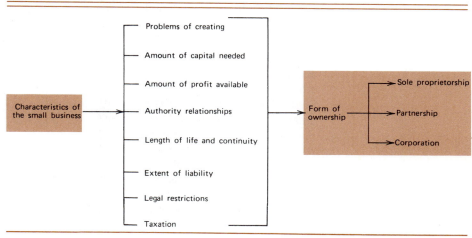

FIGURE 2-2
NUMBER OF SOLE PROPRIETORSHIPS, PARTNERSHIPS, AND CORPORATIONS IN THE UNITED STATES.

Sole proprietorship	70%	11,262,000
Partnership	10%	1,644,000
Corporation	20%	3,171,000

(Statistical Abstract of the United States, 1988.)

THE SOLE PROPRIETORSHIP

The **sole proprietorship,** is the most common form of business ownership in the United States today, as shown in Figure 2-2. The sole proprietorship is owned by one person and has distinct advantages and disadvantages relative to other forms of ownership.

Advantages of the Sole Proprietorship

The advantages of the sole proprietorship are as follows.

1. It is the easiest form of ownership to establish. All the owner must do to create this form of ownership is to acquire the assets (permits are sometimes required, such as a liquor license for a tavern) to begin the business, and it is automatically a sole proprietorship.
2. All profits earned by the business belong to the owner and do not have to be shared with anyone else.
3. The owner of the business has total authority over the business.
4. There are no special legal restrictions on the sole proprietorship form of ownership. Only those general areas of civil and criminal law that apply to all forms of business ownership apply to the sole proprietorship.
5. Because the business is taxed as an individual for federal income tax, there is no double taxation (discussed later in this chapter).

Disadvantages of the Sole Proprietorship

1. The amount of capital available to the business is limited to the assets and credit of the one owner. The degree of the problem rests with the amount of capital needed in the business. Many people in the United

States could finance a small hot dog stand in a rented building. However, no one could amass the wealth necessary to sustain General Motors, which has assets valued at over $45 billion.

2. Length of life of the business is dependent on the owner. In general terms, the owner may close his or her doors and go out of business at any time he or she chooses. In addition, technically, if the owner dies, the business ceases to exist. Of course, the assets are still in existence. The business may be sold, or a relative may take over the firm, at which time it then becomes a new sole proprietorship.

3. The owner has unlimited liability. The owner is liable not only for the amount invested in the business but also for all other assets owned. In cases of bankruptcy or legal judgments, all assets (except those exempted by state law, such as the owner's homestead) may be taken from the owner to satisfy legal claims.

THE PARTNERSHIP

A **partnership** consists of two or more people. The partnership may be established almost on any basis the partners wish.

Although this is not required legally, it is best for partners to have legal counsel draw up an instrument called "articles of copartnership." (See Fig. 2-3.) This agreement should state what each partner is to contribute to the partnership, what authority each partner has, and how the profit or loss is to be shared. If an articles of copartnership agreement is not created, the laws of the state in which the partnership exists determine distribution of authority, profit, and loss in cases of dispute.

Articles of copartnership should contain the following general information.

1. Effective date of the partnership
2. Name of the firm
3. Names and addresses of the partners
4. Nature and scope of business activity of the partnership
5. Location of all business activity
6. Period of time the partnership is to exist
7. Contributions of each partner
8. Distribution of profit and loss
9. Withdrawals and salaries of the partners
10. Contribution of time by the partners to the business
11. Authority relationship of the partners
12. Partners' access to books and records of the partnership
13. Terms and method of withdrawal of any partners
14. Distribution of assets and name of business if dissolved
15. A provision for arbitration of disputes

FIGURE 2-3
ARTICLES OF COPARTNERSHIP.

PARTNERSHIP AGREEMENT

THIS PARTNERSHIP AGREEMENT is entered into this __First__ day of __December__ , 19__85__ , between the following persons whose names and addresses are set forth below:

Eric B. Preston   Harold E. Sims
3326 Main Street   626 North 39th Street
Austin, Texas   78799 Austin, Texas   78711

The above partners hereby agree that upon the commencement date of this partnership they shall be deemed to have become partners in business. The purposes, terms and conditions of this partnership are as follows:

1. **NAME**—The firm name of the partnership shall be
    Custom B.B.Q.

2. **PRINCIPAL PLACE OF BUSINESS**—The principal place of business of the partnership shall be
    221 Main Street
    Austin, Texas   78788

3. **PURPOSE**—The business of the partnership is set forth below and includes any other business related thereto.
    Cook and sell barbecue meats

4. **TERM**—The partnership shall commence on __December 1__ , 19__85__ , and shall continue until __indefinite term__ .

5. **CAPITAL CONTRIBUTION: DISTRIBUTION OF PROFITS AND LOSSES**—Eric B. Preston's contribution to the partnership will be managing and operating the business.

    The principal capital is to be contributed by Harold E. Sims who agrees to provide any capital contribution required after startup to cover losses of partnership. As a consequence of such an agreement, Harold E. Sims will be allocated any net losses sustained by the partnership.

    In as much as Eric B. Preston's contribution will be service, the partnership agrees to allocate 2/3 (two-thirds) of any profits to Eric B. Preston.

    A division of profits and losses shall be made at such time as may be agreed upon by the partners and at the close of each fiscal year. The profits and losses of the partnership shall be divided between the partners according to the above Schedule of "Distribution of Profits and Losses."

6. **CONTROL**—The partners shall have the exclusive control over the business of the partnership and each partner shall have equal rights in the management and conduct of the partnership business. Any differences arising as to the ordinary matters connected with the partnership business shall be decided by a numerical majority of the partners. Any act beyond the scope of this partnership agreement or any contract which may subject this partnership in liability in excess of __5,000.00__ DOLLARS shall be subject to the prior written consent of all the partners.

7. **DISSOLUTION**—In the event of retirement, bankruptcy, death or insanity of a general partner, the remaining partners have the right to continue the business of the partnership under the same name by themselves, or in conjunction with any other persons they select.

IN WITNESS WHEREOF, the parties hereto have signed this partnership agreement on the day and year first written above.

_____
PARTNER

_____
PARTNER

Types of Partners

There are two basic categories of partners in a partnership: the general partner (sometimes called ordinary) and the limited partner (sometimes called special).

General Partner

There is no legal limit to the number of **general partners** a partnership may have, but there is usually a requirement that it have at least one. The general partner has unlimited liability. He or she may be held liable not only to the extent of his or her investment in the business but also any other assets he or

Visual Concepts International, Inc., owned by Jeffrey Burns and Craig Schlagbaum, is a rapidly expanding new publishing company, conceived during a late-night study session back in the fall of 1985 at the University of Colorado. The product responsible for the fledgling company's rapid growth was a full-color poster entitled, "Justification For Higher Education." Projected against a majestic Rocky Mountain background, the poster features a hilltop mansion and a five-car garage, filled with over a quarter-of-a-million dollars worth of exotic automobiles.

she may own (excluding certain homestead items specified by state law). The general partner must also take an active part in the operations of the business.

Limited Partner

There is no legal requirement that a partnership must have any **limited partners,** and there is no limit to the number it may have. The primary difference between the general partner and the limited partner is that the limited partner has limited liability. The limited partner can lose only his or her investment in the partnership. Other assets the limited partner may own cannot be seized to satisfy debts of the partnership. The three basic types of limited partners are these.

Secret partner   The public does not know the individual is a partner in the business.

Silent partner   The partner does not take part in the management of the business.

Dormant partner   The public does not know the person is a partner, and the person does not take part in the management of the business.

Advantages of the Partnership Form of Ownership

1. Creation of the partnership form of ownership requires little effort and involves little cost. Usually, the only cost in creating the partnership form of ownership is a legal fee for drawing up and recording the articles of copartnership. There also may be fees to obtain permits and/or licenses, such as a health permit.
2. Profit may be divided in any manner prescribed by the partners. Sometimes, formulas are created to divide profit on the basis of funds invested in the business or time spent in the business.
3. Usually, more capital can be raised by the partnership than by the sole proprietorship. The amount of capital that can be raised by the partnership is limited to the assets and credit of all the partners.
4. The partnership allows for limited partners who have limited liability. This is important not ony to the limited partners but also to the capital-accumulating ability of the partnership. The protection of limited liability makes it easier to obtain investment funds from people who would not become general partners because of the risk involved.
5. Any type of authority relationship may be established in the partnership. Often, it allows people of widely diverse talents and skills to enter into a business. For example, one person may be a highly skilled technician in the production of a product but not have sales or management skills. Another person may have sales ability and management skills but not have sufficient technical skills to produce the product.

Together in a partnership, they may be very successful, where alone they may have failed.

6. Usually, no special legal restrictions exist for partnerships that do not exist for the sole proprietorship.

7. The partners are taxed as individuals for federal income tax; there is no double taxation (discussed later in this chapter).

Advantages offered by the partnership not offered by the sole proprietorship are (1) its ability to combine capital or skills or both of more than one person and (2) the limited liability of being a limited partner.

Disadvantages of the Partnership Form of Ownership

1. Although the partnership usually has greater capital-accumulating ability than the sole proprietorship, it usually has far less potential than the corporation.

2. There is a great potential for authority disputes in partnership. Although the articles of copartnership generally spell out the authority of each partner, it is impossible to allow for all contingencies. There are usually areas of overlap of authority where conflict may arise. In addition, it is usually difficult for even two people to function in the operations of a business without some friction. The addition of each person to the partnership geometrically increases the potential of friction. It is not at all unusual for a highly successful partnership to break up because of personality clashes in the operations of the business.

3. General partners contribute a limited life to the partnership. The withdrawal or death of any general partner terminates the partnership. The remaining partners may settle claims of the withdrawn partner and start a new partnership. However, it can often be a real problem to obtain enough funds to buy the ownership of a partner. Limited partners aid continuity of the business because they may withdraw, die, or sell their ownership in the partnership without terminating the partnership.

4. The unlimited liability of the general partners can be a serious disadvantage to the general partners. For example, suppose a person with extensive property holdings goes into business with another person to produce canned specialty food items. Also, imagine a negligent employee allowing canned fish to go out of the plant without sufficient cooking, causing several deaths (accidentally uncooked food products causing death has actually occurred). Court judgments against the partnership could cause the individual to lose all of his or her wealth and put the person into debt for the rest of his or her life. Of course, insurance and other methods of dealing with risk (Chapter 11) can help reduce losses.

5. There is more than one person to share the profits of the business.

Primarily, the partnership has disadvantages the sole proprietorship does not have in that it must generate sufficient profit for more than one person, and there is considerable potential for dispute.

JOINT VENTURES

A **joint venture** is a specialized type of partnership. In the regular partnership, persons join together in a *continuous operation* of a business. In a joint venture, individuals join together in co-ownership for a *given limited purpose*.

For example, three men who purchase a tract of land for the sole purpose of developing it with apartments and then selling it for a profit would be engaging in a joint venture. On the other hand, if the three men contributed funds to the purchase and operation of a store on a continuous basis, it would be the creation of the usual partnership.

Although not nearly as common as other forms of ownership, joint ventures are increasing in frequency, particularly in real estate developments. The joint venture is taxed as a partnership. In addition, a formal, signed agreement should be drawn up by legal counsel to avoid future problems and disputes.

THE CORPORATION

The **corporation** form of ownership consists of three or more owners (in most states) who are known as stockholders. The corporation is in a legal sense an artificial being in that it may own property, enter into contracts, be liable for debts, sue and be sued, and conduct day-to-day business.

The corporation form of ownership comprises only 20 percent of all businesses; however, it accounts for 90 percent of all business receipts. (See Fig. 2-4.)

Corporations are created by obtaining a charter from 1 of the 50 states. State laws vary in their requirements and taxation of corporations. Among other things, states usually require that a corporation have three or more stockholders, that the stockholders elect a board of directors, and that records are maintained at a designated location. The board of directors has overall responsibility for operating the corporation. The board of directors also appoints the officers of the corporation and establishes overall policy for the corporation.

The articles of incorporation usually contain such information as

1. Name of the corporation.
2. Period of time the corporation will exist (usually perpetual).
3. Purpose of the corporation.

FIGURE 2-4
RECEIPTS OF BUSINESS BY FORM OF OWNERSHIP.

Sole proprietorships	6%	$516 billion
Partnerships	4%	$375 billion
Corporations	90%	$7,816 billion

(*Statistical Abstract of the United States, 1988.*)

4. Number of shares of stock the corporation can issue and their par value.
5. Initial address of the corporation.
6. Names and addresses of the initial board of directors.
7. Names and addresses of incorporators.

The corporation must also have its own bylaws, which give such information as

1. Stockholders' meetings.
   a. Place and time.
   b. Means of calling special meetings.
   c. Means of establishing a voting list.
   d. What constitutes a quorum.
   e. Voting of shares.
2. Board of directors.
   a. Number and means of election.
   b. Term of office.
   c. Means of removal.
   d. Method of filling vacancies.
   e. Quorum at meetings.
   f. Regular and special meetings—time, place, notification.
3. Officers of the corporation.
   a. Titles and duties of principal officers.
   b. Means of removal and filling vacancies.
   c. Method of fixing salaries.
4. Contracts, loans, checks, and deposits.
   a. Who may enter into contracts for the corporation.
   b. Who may borrow money for the corporation.
   c. Who may write checks and drafts.
   d. Place of deposit of corporation money.

5. Certificates for shares and their transfer (stock).

   a. Form of stock certificates.
   b. Methods of transfer of stock.

6. Fiscal year of the corporation (when it starts and ends).
7. Dividends (how they are declared and paid).
8. Description of the corporation seal.
9. Amendment of bylaws.

Corporations accumulate funds by selling stock (certificates of ownership) or bonds (certificates of debt) or both.

Stock

Ownership in a corporation may exist in two basic forms: preferred stock and common stock. Both preferred stock and common stock may be issued by the corporation with an almost unlimited combination of features available to them. However, most stocks issued do have certain features in common.

Stockholders receive payment from the corporation in the form of **dividends.** The board of directors of the corporation determine if a dividend will be paid and the amount of the dividend if it is paid. There is no legal requirement under normal circumstances that a corporation must pay dividends. One exception to this general rule occurred when stockholders forced Henry Ford to pay dividends after they proved in court that he was unreasonably holding back large profits to the detriment of the stockholders.

Some corporations have never paid a dividend. In fact, some stockholders do not want their corporation to pay dividends. They prefer to have earnings plowed back into the corporation to increase the value and growth of the corporation. This, in turn, almost always increases the value of the stock. Individuals must pay income taxes on all dividends received, and the dividends are treated as current income.

Preferred Stock

Preferred stock has several distinct characteristics, some of which, as its name implies, provide benefits that common stock does not receive. However, preferred stock usually has to give up some desirable features to obtain these benefits.

Par or No-Par Feature

Preferred stock may be either par or no-par stock. **Par value** of a stock is an arbitrary amount of value that is printed on the face of the stock certificate. Preferred stock with a par value usually exists in units of $100. The par value of the stock has no relationship to either the market value (the price it can be sold for on the open market) or book value (all assets minus all liabilities equals book value of all stock). For all practical purposes, it is simply a recordkeeping device. Preferred stock may also exist as no-par; that is, it does not have a stated value printed on the certificate.

Preferred Payment of a Stated Amount of Dividend   Preferred stock usually has a stated amount of dividend that must be paid to the stockholder before any dividends can be paid to common stockholders. Usually, this stated dividend exists in the form of a stated percentage of par value. For instance, it is relatively common for the dividend rate of preferred stock to be 6 percent of par. If the stock is 6 percent, $100 par, then the preferred stockholder must be paid $6 before common stock may receive any dividends. If the preferred stock is no-par, then the certificate will contain a statement as to a standard dividend that must be paid first. For instance, it may state on the face of the certificate that the preferred stockholder must receive $6 before any payment can be made to common stockholders.

Cumulative or Noncumulative   Preferred stock may be cumulative or noncumulative in terms of dividends. A cumulative feature is the most common. Because there is no requirement that dividends be paid to stockholders each year, it would be possible for a corporation dominated by common stockholders to hold back all dividends for several years and then pay preferred stockholders for only one year and distribute the rest to the common stockholders. The cumulative feature prevents this in that it requires the corporation to pay not only the current year's dividend but also all past years' unpaid dividends to preferred stockholders before common stock can receive any dividends. Of course, noncumulative means that previous years' dividends that were not paid do not have to be paid before common stock receives dividends.

Voting or Nonvoting   Preferred stock usually does not have voting rights. It is a feature that is usually reserved for common stock. However, there is no legal requirement that prevents preferred stock from having voting rights, and it does have this privilege in some corporations. Stockholders in a corporation often sign proxies that give another person the right to cast their vote in the corporation. Proxies are usually solicited by the existing board of directors.

Common Stock

There is more **common stock** than any other type of stock in most corporations, and in most small businesses it is the only type of stock.

Common stock usually has full voting rights. In addition, it usually is paid only after preferred has been paid. As a result, it is a higher-risk stock than preferred. However, in a corporation with large profits, it often receives much larger dividends or increases in price per share or both than preferred.

Common stock, as with preferred stock, may also be par or no-par. Also, it is an arbitrary figure that exists only for recordkeeping purposes. More common stock has a par value of $1 per share than any other denomination. In fact, it is not unusual for a common stock to have a par value of $1 per share and have a market value of several hundred dollars per share. Some common stocks do not have an arbitrary value assigned to them and, as a result, are no-par common stock.

A common-stock certificate.

Bonds

Bonds are certificates of long-term debt owned by a corporation. They are usually issued in amounts of $1000 each. Bonds have a maturity date, at which time the corporation must pay the face amount of the bond to the owner of the bond. The corporation must pay the amount of the interest to the bondholder at the prescribed periods of time, usually once a year. For example, a bond with $1000 value and carrying a 10 percent interest rate must pay the bondholder $100 each year and $1000 at maturity. In addition, just because the bond has a face value of $1000 does not mean it is sold for that amount. Depending on the current interest rate, most bonds are sold at either above or below this face value. However, the face value is the amount that must be paid at maturity regardless of how much it brought when first sold.

The bondholders do not have voting rights unless the corporation fails to pay its yearly interest or its face value at maturity. In cases of forfeiture, bondholders usually assume full voting rights, and all forms of stock lose their voting rights until the debt is satisfied.

Advantages of the Corporation Form of Ownership

1. The primary advantage of the corporation is its ability to accumulate capital. Many corporations have accumulated vast amounts of money for investment into assets through the sale of stocks and bonds.
2. The length of life of the corporation is established in its charter. Most charters specify the life of the corporation to be to perpetuity (i.e., its life is without end). Ownership of corporations in the form of stock

An example of a registered bond.

INTERNATIONAL MINERALS & CHEMICAL CORPORATION
11.875% SINKING FUND DEBENTURE DUE MAY 1, 2005
INTERNATIONAL MINERALS & CHEMICAL CORPORATION, a New York corporation (herein referred to as the "Company"), for value received, hereby promises to pay to

CUSIP 459884 AC 6

SEE REVERSE FOR CERTAIN DEFINITIONS

11.875%
DUE 2005

SPECIMEN

11.875%
DUE 2005

FIVE THOUSAND DOLLARS

REGISTERED

makes it easy to transfer ownership without disturbing the corporation. Parents who own businesses may find it very hard to divide their businesses among their children under the sole proprietorship and partnership forms of ownership. In the corporation form of ownership, all they must do is divide the shares of stock.

3. In general, the corporation has limited liability, that is, all a stockholder can lose is the money paid for the stock. There are some exceptions to this general rule. If a very small corporation borrows money, lenders often require the owners to sign personal liability notes in order to obtain the loan. This means that the owners must repay the note with their own assets if the corporation is unable to repay the note. Another somewhat rare exception occurs when a stockholder is also an officer of the corporation and is guilty of fraud or neglect.

Disadvantages of the Corporation Form of Ownership

1. Creating the form of ownership of the corporation requires greater time and money than any other form of ownership. However, it is not an unreasonable amount in most cases. A charter must be obtained from the state. This requires time, legal fees, and state fees. It usually takes several weeks to process the charter application. The cost for attorney and state fees usually is from $500 up, depending on the state.
2. Taxation is sometimes a serious disadvantage, which is discussed later in this chapter.
3. There is a wide range of legal restrictions on corporations. States have

FIGURE 2-5
FEATURES OF THE SOLE PROPRIETORSHIP, PARTNERSHIP, AND CORPORATION FORM OF OWNERSHIP

	Sole Proprietorship	Partnership	Corporation
Creation of form of ownership	One person starts a business	Two or more people sign articles of copartnership	Three or more people obtain state charter
Ability to accumulate capital	Assets and credit of one person	Assets and credit of all partners	Sale or stocks and bonds
Profit sharing	All to owner	To partners based on agreement	Stockholders
Authority	All to owner	Based on articles of copartnership	Board of directors
Life and continuity	Depends on owner	Depends on general partners	Usually perpetual life and transfer of stock provides continuity
Liability	Unlimited liability	Unlimited liability to general partners	Limited to amount of stockholder investment
Legal restrictions	No special ones	No special ones	Several state and federal restrictions

various legal requirements of corporations such as charter limitations, right to do business in other states, and some government supervision, which usually requires reporting to various agencies of the state. The federal government also has various legal restrictions on corporations that engage in interstate commerce. The corporation is also subject to all usual civil and criminal aspects of law to which the sole proprietorship and partnership are subject. Individuals operating the corporation are subject to the law in terms of their conduct in operating the corporation. For example, several years ago some officers of electrical manufacturers were sentenced to terms in prison for price fixing in violation of the Sherman Antitrust law.

Figure 2-5 presents the different features of the three forms of ownership.

TAXATION OF THE FORMS OF OWNERSHIP

There are some areas of government taxation that are common to all types of business ownership. Some of these common forms of taxation are local busi-

FIGURE 2-6
FEDERAL INCOME TAXATION BY FORM OF OWNERSHIP.

	Taxed
Sole proprietorship	As individual
Partnership	As individuals
Corporation	Corporation tax
	Dividends taxed to individuals
Subchapter S corporations	Under conditions small corporations taxed as partnership

ness licenses, licenses for sale of alcoholic beverages, property taxes (real estate and personal property), and payroll taxes.

In addition to these common areas of taxation, there are some taxes that vary according to the form of ownership. (See Fig. 2-6.)

Taxation of Sole Proprietorships

Usually, the only type of tax the sole proprietorship is subject to, other than those listed earlier as common taxes, is the federal income tax. All profit of the sole proprietorship is considered current income to the individual owner. All profit from the business is listed as ''business income'' in the owner's personal income tax return. All profit of the business is taxed in this manner, even if the owner has not withdrawn it from the business. It is never considered as a salary and, therefore, is not an expense of the business.

Taxation of Partnerships

Partnerships are usually taxed differently from other forms of business ownership only in the area of federal income taxes. All profit earned by the partnership is considered personal income to the partners in the proportion of share of profits specified by the articles of copartnership. It does not matter whether the profits are withdrawn from the business. Even when the articles of copartnership specify a salary to one or more partners, it is still considered a distribution of profit rather than wages in the computation of federal income taxes. This treatment of federal income taxes is the same for both general and limited partners.

Taxation of Corporations

The corporation is subject to taxes that are not common with partnerships or sole proprietorships. One of these is the state corporation tax. State laws vary widely in their method and amount of taxation of corporations. However, most states tax corporations on profit and/or on the basis of assets.

Corporations are also subject to a federal **corporation income tax.** The corporation tax rates are

Taxable Income	Rate
$ 0– 50,000	15%
50,000– 75,000	25
75,000–100,000	34
100,000–335,000	39
Over 335,000	34

The 39 percent rate on all income between $100,000 and $335,000 results in all corporations with an income over $335,000 being taxed at an effective rate of 34 percent on all income.

If a corporation had taxable income of $400,000, the tax rate would computed as follows:

$$
\begin{aligned}
15\% \text{ of first } \$50,000 &= \$\ \ 7,500 \\
24\% \text{ of next } \$25,000 &= \ \ \ 6,250 \\
34\% \text{ of next } \$25,000 &= \ \ \ 8,500 \\
39\% \text{ of next } \$235,000 &= \ \ 91,650 \\
34\% \text{ of } \$65,000 &= \underline{\ \ 22,100} \\
\text{Total tax} &=. \$136,000
\end{aligned}
$$

A flat tax rate of 34 percent on all $400,000 would also result in a tax of $136,000. The corporation tax rate is intended to help small corporations with income under $335,000, with most of the help going to corporations with income of less than $100,000.

Salaries of all employees and officers, regardless of whether they are stockholders, are considered an expense to the corporation. However, the salaries of the officers or employees are considered wages in their personal income tax computation. In addition, all dividends distributed by corporations are considered personal income to the individual. In a sense, this amounts to double taxation in that profit of the corporation is subject to a corporate income tax, and the dividends distributed from the remaining profit are also taxed as current income to the stockholder.

Collection of Taxes

Businesses perform as collectors of taxes for some government agencies. They must withhold income taxes and social security taxes from the salaries of their employees. Such taxes are then remitted to the government agencies at regular intervals. In addition, retail and service firms must collect sales tax from customers and remit to a government agency. It is both a burden and a cost to small business to act as a collection agent for these government agencies.

CORPORATE TAXATION CAN BE AN ADVANTAGE

The double taxation of the profits of the corporation would seem to be a serious disadvantage of the corporation form of ownership. Sometimes it can be an advantage. For example, suppose you were earning a good salary and wanted to invest some of your savings in a new business venture with someone else. The business would start small, but you would want it to grow by reinvesting profit into the business. You would not want profits from the business until it had reached its full potential growth. If the business were a partnership, you would have to report the profit as personal income and pay federal income tax on it. Suppose the business made $100,000 profit the first year. As one of the partners, you would report $50,000 as personal income tax. If both of you were at the 28 percent tax bracket plus the 5 percent surcharge as a result of your salaries, together you would pay $33,000 ($16,500 each) in taxes on the business income and only have $67,000 left to invest in the business.

However, as a corporation, the corporation would pay federal income taxes on the profit, and the rest could remain in the business, and you would not have to pay income tax on the profit as an individual. As a corporation, the first-year profit would be taxed as follows:

$$15\% \text{ of } \$50,000 = \$\ 7,500$$
$$25\% \text{ of } \$25,000 = 6,250$$
$$34\% \text{ of } \$25,000 = \underline{8,500}$$
$$\$22,250$$

By being taxed as a corporation, you and your partner would leave $77,750 in the business for growth—a gain of $10,750 more than as a partnership. When the business reached its full potential and you began to take out profit from the business, you could elect Subchapter S (discussed next) and be taxed as a partnership.

SUBCHAPTER S CORPORATIONS

In an attempt to assist small businesses, Congress added Subchapter S to the Internal Revenue Code. Subchapter S permits corporations under certain conditions to be taxed as a proprietorship or partnership. These conditions are as follows:

1. It must be a domestic corporation that is not an ineligible corporation (some corporations are ineligible under Subchapter S, such as some insurance companies).
2. It must not have more than 35 shareholders.
3. It must have only individuals, bankruptcy or decedent's estates, or certain trusts as shareholders.
4. It must have only one class of stock.

5. It must not have a nonresident alien as a shareholder.
6. All shareholders must consent.

People are often confused by the title **Subchapter S corporation.** They mistakenly think it is a special form of corporation. It is a regular corporation chartered by 1 of the 50 states. It is eligible for and does elect to be taxed under Subchapter S of the Internal Revenue Code. In a year in which the corporation elects to be taxed under Subchapter S, all profits of the corporation (whether distributed or not) are *not* subject to the regular corporation tax. The shareholders (stockholders) have their share of the profit added to all their other income and are then taxed as individuals. The election to be taxed as a Subchapter S corporation is effective for all subsequent years, unless it is terminated by an election of the stockholders. A majority of the stockholders must consent to terminate. If a corporation terminates its tax option status and elects to be taxed as a corporation, the stockholders must then wait five years (unless IRS consents) before electing to be taxed as a partnership again. Subchapter S can be of considerable value to a small business. The business gets to keep all the desirable features of the corporation form of ownership without the double taxation disadvantage. For example, if you had considerable wealth but still wanted to enter into a high-risk business, you could possibly lose everything as a sole proprietorship or general partner. However, if the corporation is a Subchapter S corporation, you would only risk your investment and still be taxed as an individual.

Some of the other potential benefits are these:

1. *Income splitting.* In a high-profit year, a father may give stock to his children to take advantage of their lower income tax bracket without giving up control of the corporation.
2. *Availability of fringe benefits for the stockholders.* Employee benefit plans are often not available to sole proprietors and partners simply because they are employers, not employees. Fringe benefits to stockholders as employees (life and health insurance, pension plans, etc.) are a deductible expense to the corporation. Also, some executives may be uninsurable as individuals but insurable under group plans because all employees must be accepted in the plan.
3. *A tax-free death benefit can be provided to selected stockholders.* The company can provide up to $5000 to an employee's family at the time of the employee's death. The company can restrict the benefit to one or as many employees as the company chooses.

Subchapter S is rather complex and technical and the potential for tax savings so diverse that no one should become a Subchapter S corporation without the advice and guidance of an accountant or attorney. On the other hand, the potential benefits are so great to many businesses that almost everyone operating a small business should investigate its potential for his or her business.

DISSOLUTION AND BANKRUPTCY

The form of ownership of a business may be terminated by either dissolution or bankruptcy. Although in a technical sense the business is dissolved in bankruptcy, dissolution is usually considered to be the termination of the business when it is solvent. On the other hand, bankruptcy is an act of terminating the business because of insolvency (except Chapter 11).

Dissolution

Dissolution of the sole proprietorship may result because of the death of the owner or as an act of the owner. The partnership form of ownership may cease owing to withdrawal of a general partner (such as by death), some condition stated in the articles of copartnership (such as a time limit for the partnership to exist), or by consent of the partners. A corporation may be dissolved because of a charter limitation (i.e., time limit) or vote of the stockholders (the charter usually specifies the number of votes necessary for dissolution, such as majority or two-thirds).

Bankruptcy

The Bankruptcy Act was passed by Congress in 1898 and substantially revised in 1938 and 1978. Three chapters in the act established methods of **bankruptcy**—Chapters 7, 11, and 13.

Chapter 7

The purpose of this chapter in the act is to sell the debtor's assets, pay the money to creditors, and legally discharge the debtor from further responsibility. The bankruptcy may be either voluntary or involuntary. The debtor may ask the courts to initiate bankruptcy proceedings. Creditors may also petition the courts to initiate bankruptcy proceedings if the debtor is not paying debts as they become due.

When the debtor's assets are sold, creditors are paid in the following order as long as there is money to satisfy their claims.

1. All cost and expenses involved in the bankruptcy proceedings.
2. All claims for wages, salaries, and commissions earned by individuals in the past 90 days before filing of the petition. A limit of $2000 per individual is imposed.
3. All claims for contributions to an employee benefit plan within 180 days before filing the petition with a maximum of $2000 per individual.
4. All claims of individuals for deposits made of goods or services that were not received with maximum of $900 per individual.
5. Claims of governmental units for taxes.
6. All other creditors in proportion to the amounts of their claims.

Chapter 11

Chapter 11 of the Bankruptcy Act is used when it is felt that reorganization and the continued operation of a business is feasible and preferable to Chapter 7 liquidation. This chapter is intended for use by businesses, but they can be sole proprietorships, partners, or corporations. It can also be voluntary or involuntary. The bankruptcy court will appoint a committee of creditors (and a committee of stockholders if the business is a corporation). The committee(s) will prepare a reorganization plan and submit it to the court. The court will approve the plan if more than two-thirds the amount of claims (and two-thirds the number of stockholders if a corporation) approve and if the court considers the plan fair and equitable. If the plan is approved, the business is discharged from claims not provided for in the plan.

Chapter 13

Chapter 13 of the Bankruptcy Act can only be used by individuals, not by partnerships or corporations. It is a voluntary action only. It is also intended for persons with a "regular" income. The debtor prepares and files an adjustment plan that designates the part of the debtor's future income that will be turned over to creditors. Usually it does not extend past a three-year period. If accepted, the courts will appoint a trustee who will receive and distribute the income as specified in the plan.

SUMMARY OF KEY POINTS

1. The needs and characteristics of each business determine which form of ownership is most suited to that business.
2. The advantages of the sole proprietorship are that (a) it is easiest to form, (b) profits belong to the owner, (c) there is total authority over the business, and (d) there are no special legal restrictions.
3. The disadvantages of the sole proprietorship are (a) limited capital, (b) limited life, and (c) unlimited liability.
4. The partnership agreement is called "articles of copartnership."
5. There must be one general partner, but there can be any number of limited partners or none.
6. The advantages of the partnership are that (a) it is easy to form, (b) profits are divided as desired, (c) there is more capital, (d) it allows for limited partners, (e) there is any authority relationship wanted, and (f) there are no special legal restrictions.

7. The advantages of the partnership form are (a) less capital potential than corporations, (b) potential for authority disputes, (c) limited life of general partners, and (d) unlimited liability of general partners.

8. Corporations are chartered by the states and may issue preferred or common stock or both. They may also issue bonds.

9. Advantages of the corporation form of ownership are (a) ability to accumulate capital, (b) perpetual life, and (c) limited liability.

10. Disadvantages of the corporation form of ownership are (a) time and cost of acquiring charters from the state, (b) taxation, and (c) legal restrictions.

11. Partnerships and sole proprietorships are taxed as individual income. Corporations pay a corporation income tax, and dividends to stockholders are taxed as income to the individual.

12. Under certain conditions, corporations can elect to be taxed as partnerships under Subchapter S.

13. Dissolution and bankruptcy are methods of terminating a business. Dissolution occurs when it is solvent, and bankruptcy usually occurs when it is not solvent.

DISCUSSION QUESTIONS

1. Because more businesses are sole proprietorships than any other form of ownership, the sole proprietorship must be the best form of ownership for small businesses. Evaluate this statement.

2. When would you use the sole proprietorship form of ownership?

3. Would you have articles of copartnership if you formed a partnership? Explain.

4. Explain the two different types of partners.

5. When would you use the partnership form of ownership?

6. If you started a corporation, what instruments might you use to raise capital?

7. Would you issue preferred or common stock?

8. When would you use the corporation as a form of ownership?

9. When would you use a joint venture?

10. What type of taxes must the various forms of ownership pay?

11. What is a Subchapter S corporation, and why is it important to some small businesses?

12. Considering the forms of dissolution and bankruptcy, under which can the firm continue to operate?

THE BUSINESS PLAN: FORM OF OWNERSHIP

How many people will be needed to start and operate the business?
How much time will be required to run the business?
How much money will be required to establish the business?
Do I have all the knowledge necessary to establish and operate the business?
Do any of the owners need to be shielded from unlimited liability?

____ I will be able to establish and operate the business by myself.

____ There is no special reason to shield myself from unlimited liability.

____ The business profit being taxed to me on my personal income tax is no special problem.

____ Continuity of the business is no special problem to me or my family.

If you checked all of the above, there is a strong possibility that the sole proprietorship form of ownership is suited to your needs.

____ Two or more people (but not more than five) will be required to establish and operate the business.

____ The partners are able to get along with each other and operate efficiently.

____ Unlimited liability is no special problem for the general partners. If there is a problem with any other partners, they can meet the requirements to be limited partners.

____ Each partner being taxed on partnership profits on their individual income tax does not create any special problems.

If you checked all of the above, there is a good possibility that the partnership form of ownership will fit your needs. If you decide on the partnership, you should consult an attorney to draw up the Articles of Copartnership. See page 47 for information that will be needed.

If the partnership is not for the continuous operation of a business, but is a joint ownership for a given limited purpose, a joint venture must be considered.

____ A large number of people will be required to provide the capital to start and operate the business.

____ There is a need for limited liability.

____ There is a need for continuity of the business.

If you checked all of the above, the corporation form of ownership is a strong possibility for your needs. If you use the corporation form of ownership, you need to contact an attorney who will obtain a charter from your state. Pages 52–54 list information you will need to provide.

If you wish to retain all the profits in the corporation for growth, you may want to be taxed as a corporation. If you meet the requirements of a Subchapter S corporation, you may want to be taxed as a partnership. Consult a tax expert before you elect to become a Subchapter S corporation.

ENTREPRENEURIAL PROJECTS

Find three businesses in your community—a sole proprietorship, a partnership, and a corporation.

1. Ask each business why it has its form of business ownership.
2. Ask the partnership what type of partners it has in the business.
3. Ask the corporation from what state it obtained its charter.
4. Find out if the corporation uses Subchapter S.
5. Find out what types of securities the corporation has outstanding.
6. Find out if the partnership has articles of copartnership.

CASE A

Joan and Don, Entrepreneurs

Joan Kirby and Don Harris are partners in a successful clothing store and are currently investigating the possibility of buying another business.

Joan and Don live in a city with a population of 400,000. The business they are considering is a local plant that manufactures prefabricated homes. The business has been in operation for 23 years, but the owner recently died. The owner's heirs are not interested in keeping the business and must sell it because they need cash to pay estate inheritance taxes. Joan and Don consider the $1 million asking price to be a bargain.

In addition to the $1 million, they estimated they will need about $300,000 for working capital. They have over $500,000 in cash and other liquid assets, and a local bank is willing to lend them the balance. Don's wife is a real estate agent. For 10 years, she has invested her real estate commissions in local pieces of property. Her investments have been very astute, and as a result, she now owns several pieces of valuable real estate.

Joan and Don's clothing store was formed as a general partnership, and they both work in the business. However, they are not sure what form of ownership they should select for the new venture. In fact, they are not sure if the general partnership is the best form of ownership for their clothing store.

Questions

1. Would you recommend a sole proprietorship? Explain.
2. Would you recommend a partnership? If so, what kind would you recommend? Explain.
3. Would you recommend a joint venture? Explain.
4. Would you recommend a corporation? If so, what kind of securities would you issue? Explain.
5. Would the corporation form of ownership protect their clothing store and Don's wife's property in case of bankruptcy?
6. Is a general partnership the best form of ownership for the clothing store?

CASE B

A Cosmetic and Toiletry Business

Jean and Murray Kenedy are both 37 years old and have been married for 14 years. They have two adopted children, ages 10 and 12. Jean obtained her college degree in chemistry and has worked as a sales representative for a large chemical firm since leaving college. She is one of the company's best salespersons and has consistently earned above average in sales commissions. Murray obtained his college degree in business administration and is now the assistant plant manager in a medium-sized manufacturing plant that produces retail store shelves and counters.

Jean and Murray began talking about starting their own business even before they were married. The challenge of creating a business and making it grow appeals very much to them. Since the second year of their marriage, they have lived on Murray's salary and invested Jean's salary (after paying taxes on it) with the idea of obtaining enough money to start the business. They now have $215,000 and are ready to make their move into their own business.

They have investigated several ventures over the years and have changed their minds several times about what kind of business they wanted to create. About three years ago, Jean began to investigate the possibility of producing a limited line of cosmetics and toiletries. The couple is now convinced it offers them a good potential. Jean has formulated the following items to be their products.

Women's Products	*Men's products*
Face cream	Hair tonic
Hair rinse	Shaving cream
Two perfumes	After-shave lotion
Hand cream	Men's cologne
Hair spray	
Shampoo	

Jean has attempted to make these products as allergy-safe as possible. These products appealed to both Jean and Murray because the manufacturing process is basically mixing and filling containers. The same general purpose machinery needed to produce any one of these products will also produce the rest. As a result, it is possible to produce all of them with a limited investment. Murray has leased a building that will fit their needs. He has also placed orders with manufacturers of the machinery they will need. His estimates show they will have $20,000 left to use as working capital after they have paid for everything required to produce the product.

Murray has turned in his resignation notice effective next week. Jean will keep her job as a safety factor until the business can get off the ground and produce a profit. The last month has been hectic for both of them, owing to their efforts to get the business going. It has just occurred to them that they have not decided on the form of ownership they want for the business.

Questions

1. Would you select the sole proprietorship form of ownership? Explain your answer.
2. Would you select the partnership form of ownership? Explain your answer. If you did select this form of ownership, what type of partners would you use?
3. Would you select the corporation form of ownership? Explain your answer. If you did select the corporation form, would you issue bonds, preferred stock, or common stock or all three? Why?
4. Could things happen in the future that would cause a need for a change in the form of ownership? Explain your answer.
5. Could they be a Subchapter S corporation under IRA regulations? Could it be to their benefit to choose to do so?

KEY WORDS

CHAPTER 3

FRANCHISING

After reading this chapter, you will understand:

1 What franchising is.

2 That franchising is a major force in the distribution of goods and services.

3 The advantages and disadvantages of owning a franchise.

4 The various kinds of assistance franchisors provide franchisees.

5 That franchising is growing in importance in international markets.

6 Why franchising offers an excellent opportunity for minority-group members to become entrepreneurs.

7 The laws and regulations designed to protect the franchisee.

8 Some of the trends predicted for franchising in the 1990s.

DOMINO'S PIZZA

Tom and James Monaghan opened a pizza store in Ypsilanti, Michigan, in 1960, called DomiNicks. In 1961, James left his half of the business to Tom, receiving a Volkswagen delivery car as compensation for his half of the business. Later that year, Tom formed a partnership and additional pizza stores were opened. When the partnership dissolved in 1965, Tom Monaghan owned three stores.

An employee suggested a new name for the corporation, "Domino's." Monaghan adopted the name and created a new logo: a red domino with three dots—one for each store. Sales doubled in 1965. In 1967, the first Domino's franchise was sold, and the first out-of-state store was opened in Vermont in 1968.

The initial progress was followed by a series of setbacks. In 1968, a fire destroyed the corporate office and commissary. A financial crisis caused Tom Monaghan to lose controlling interest in Domino's temporarily in 1970. And Domino's had to contend with a lawsuit from Domino's sugar which sued Domino's Pizza in 1975 for trademark infringement. The suit was finally decided in favor of Domino's Pizza in 1980.

Domino's success is attributed to its original business concept of the free delivery of a fresh-made, quality pizza to the customer's home in 30 minutes or less. Another reason for success is simplicity. Domino's sells only pizza and a cola beverage and stores function in a pickup and delivery capacity only.

Domino's is the world's largest pizza delivery company. Domino's accounts for over half of the pizza delivered in the United States.

Domino's has crossed international boundaries and now has nearly 200 franchises in Australia, Canada, Hong Kong, Japan, the United Kingdom, West Germany, and Puerto Rico. Continuation of international franchising is an integral part of Domino's strategy.

Domino's expansion continues at a rapid rate, with four new stores opening each day. With over 4300 stores in operation, 10,000 stores are expected to be opened by the 1990s.

Source: Developed from information supplied by Domino's Corporation.

Franchising continues its growth in employment, number of units, and sales both in national and international markets. Franchising offers one of the best opportunities for the entrepreneur to compete with large companies. Franchising provides individuals with the opportunity to own their own business and realize the satisfaction that comes from being a part of the free enterprise system.

HISTORY OF FRANCHISING

Franchising has long been an effective form of distribution that is used primarily by manufacturers whose product lines are especially suited to exclusive or highly selective distribution. Historically, the concept of franchising in our country dates back to 1898, begining in the automobile industry when an independent dealer was licensed to sell and service electric and steam automobiles. Until as late as the 1940s, franchise operations were primarily confined to automobile manufacturers, oil refineries, and soft drink companies. However, the early history of franchising is almost completely overshadowed by the dramatic upsurge of franchising in the United States in the relatively recent past. For example, about 90 percent of current franchisors have started their business since 1954. During the 1960s and 1970s, franchising had its greatest impact in the United States. Franchising remains healthy and is a significant force in our economy, accounting for about 34 percent of all retail sales. (See Fig. 3-1.)

Many success stories are prominent in franchising. Certainly, one of the

FIGURE 3-1
FRANCHISING'S SHARE OF THE RETAIL SALES DOLLAR (IN PERCENTAGES).

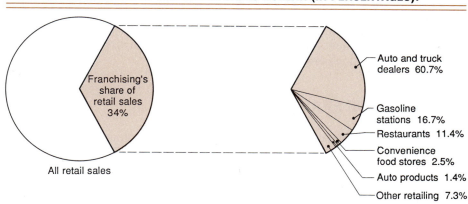

(*Franchising in the Economy, 1986–1988,* U.S. Government Printing Office, Washington, D.C., 1988, p. 15.)

best known franchises is Kentucky Fried Chicken, started by the late Harland Sanders.

Harland Sanders opened a small service station in Corbin, Kentucky, and also served meals to tourists at his family's dinner table in order to make ends meet during the depression of the 1930s. His reputation for food (especially his fried chicken) soon spread, and food preparation became the dominant business. Incidentally, he was made a Kentucky colonel in the 1930s in recognition of his contribution to the state's cuisine.

While catering for a banquet, he added an unusual combination of 11 herbs and spices to his special cooking process, which sealed in the natural juices and flavor. To single out his fried chicken from "southern fried chicken," he designated his product "Kentucky Fried Chicken."

Kentucky fried chicken became his restaurant's specialty item. His restaurant grew to a capacity of 150 seats and prospered until the mid-1950s. Then a new interstate highway was planned that rerouted tourist traffic away from his restaurant. With this turn of events, he auctioned off his business at a loss, paid his debts, and began living on social security benefits.

Dissatisfied with retirement and having confidence in the quality of his fried chicken, the Colonel went into the chicken-franchising business. In 1955, at the age of 65, he took his first social security check, $105, and began traveling cross-country by car from restaurant to restaurant. He cooked his fried chicken, using his special recipe and utensils, for the restaurant owner and employees. If their reaction was favorable, they entered into a handshake agreement that gave the Colonel a profit of a nickel for each chicken sold. The first franchise was opened in Salt Lake City, and by 1963 there were more than 600 Kentucky Fried Chicken franchised outlets. In 1964, Colonel Sanders sold his business to John Y. Brown and two associates. Colonel Sanders was retained as goodwill ambassador and media spokesperson, promoting Kentucky Fried Chicken through national advertising and personal appearances. He resigned his directorship in the company in 1970. He died in December 1980. In 1986, Kentucky Fried Chicken was acquired by PepsiCo.

In 1988, Kentucky Fried Chicken had 7522 food outlets worldwide.[1] This phenomenal growth has occurred from an investment of $105 and the vision of one person.

DEFINITION OF FRANCHISING

The International Franchise Association defines **franchising** as "a continuing relationship in which the franchisor provides a licensed privilege to do business, plus assistance in organizing, training, merchandising, and management in return for a consideration from the franchisee." Thus franchising is a method for the owner (**franchisor**) of a product, service, or method to obtain retail or wholesale distribution through licensed, affiliated dealers (**franchisees**). Frequently, the franchisor grants the franchisee the exclusive right to distribute the product, service, or method in a specific geographical area, usually for a specific term and an option for renewal if the terms of the agreement have been met. In many ways, the franchising system of distribution is similar to a large chain-store operation in that all franchised outlets have an identifying trademark, standard symbols, equipment, and storefronts; standardized services or products; and uniform business practices that are outlined in the franchise agreement.

A former president of the International Franchise Association (IFA) described franchising as "a convenient and economic means for the filling of a drive or desire (for independence) with a minimum risk and investment and maximum opportunities for success through the utilization of a proven product or service and marketing method."[2]

TYPES OF FRANCHISE ARRANGEMENTS

There are two basic types of franchise arrangements—the product and trade name franchise and the business format franchise. The **product and trade name franchise** is the traditional type of arrangement in the United States. It started as an independent sales relationship between supplier and dealer in which the dealer acquired some of the identity of the supplier. Franchise dealers concentrate on one company's product line and to some extent identify their business with that company.[3]

Thus, in the product and trade name franchise, the manufacturer may franchise a number of retailers. Automobile and truck dealers, gasoline service stations, and earth-moving equipment dealers are the most common product and trade name franchises. Another type of product and trade name franchise is that of the producer who franchises wholesalers to sell to retailers. This arrangement is most common in the soft drink industry. A national manufacturer of a syrup (Coca-Cola, Dr Pepper, or Pepsi-Cola) franchises wholesalers (independent bottlers) to serve retail markets.

Business format franchising[4] is a newer form of franchising and has been responsible for much of franchising's growth since the 1950s. Under this method, the franchisor establishes a fully integrated relationship with the franchisee. This is a continuous business relationship between franchisor and franchisee and covers the total operations of the franchise including the product or service, trademark, marketing strategy, quality control, operating manuals, and ongoing two-way communication. Common types of business format franchises include the fast-food restaurant, such as McDonald's and Burger King, rental services, real estate services, personal and business services, and nonfood retailing.

Product and trade name franchises dominate the franchising field, accounting for an estimated 70 percent of all franchise sales. However, since 1972, the number of establishments of product and trade name franchisors has declined rapidly. For example, between 1972 and 1988 there was a net loss of

FIGURE 3-2
BUSINESS FORMAT FRANCHISING

Kinds of Establishments	Percentage of Total
Restaurants	28.5%
Business aids, services, all kinds	19.8
Retailing, nonfood	16.5
Construction, home improvement, maintenance, and cleaning services	8.0
Retailing, food (other than convenience stores)	7.4
Convenience stores	5.4
Educational products and services	3.3
Rental services, auto and truck	3.3
Hotels, motels, campgrounds	3.2
Recreation, entertainment, and travel	2.8
Rental services, equipment	1.0
Laundry and drycleaning services	0.8

Source: Franchising in the Economy, 1986–1988 (Washington, D.C.: Department of Commerce, 1988), p. 28.

almost 110,000 gasoline service stations. Automobile dealers and soft drink bottlers are also experiencing a decline, but the attrition rate is expected to slow in the next few years. The volume of sales and number of units owned or franchised by business format franchisors has risen steadily since 1972.

Figure 3-2 shows the types of business format franchises, with restaurants being the most popular.

ADVANTAGES OF FRANCHISING

A franchise offers distinct advantages to the franchisee. In the following discussion, we will consider the services that a franchisor makes available to the franchisee.

Management Training

In Chapter 1, we discussed some common problems of entrepreneurship and observed that one major cause of small business failure is the entrepreneur's lack of experience. Franchisors provide an extensive amount of management training to franchisees to assist them in overcoming this weakness. Franchisees are given training prior to opening the franchise as well as continued management training and counseling once the franchise is in operation. Management training given prior to the opening covers all phases of franchise operation. Usually training seminars are held at the franchisor's headquarters. Preopening training is designed to instruct the franchisee in the professional and profitable operation of the business. New franchisees receive thorough instruction in all prescribed methods of franchise operation, such as store management, accounting, sales promotions and techniques, advertising, inventory control, and purchasing. Franchisors may also provide training for a limited number of employees of the franchisee prior to the opening. Some types of preopening management training afforded franchisees are presented here.

1. Dunkin' Donuts requires franchise owners to attend a six-week course at Dunkin' Donuts University at Braintree, Massachusetts. Franchisees receive instruction in how to recruit, train, and motivate employees; how to use equipment; inventory control; accounting and budget control; financial statement analysis; and recordkeeping. Owners receive intensive classroom work as well as "hands-on" instruction and a complete set of operational manuals. Refresher courses in advanced management are available to franchisees for the life of the franchise agreement.

2. Burger King operates regional training centers that provide detailed instruction in restaurant operation, equipment, and administration for franchisees or management or both. Burger King University in Miami, Florida, also offers ongoing and advanced training for franchisees in restaurant operations and administration.

3. Postal Instant Press (PIP), the world's largest while-you-wait printing operation, provides two weeks of intensive training at the PIP headquarters national training center. Training covers the use of all machines and equipment, advertising, promotional aids, marketing, estimating, and recordkeeping, inventory and cost control, counter procedures, sales, all phases of business management and procedures, employee relations, and communication skills.

Furthermore, training continues after the franchisee opens for business. Kentucky Fried Chicken, for example, provides assistance and training in operational activities of customer service, general restaurant management, quality control, and accounting methods. At PIP, following the initial training, a field coordinator spends one week assisting with the opening of the location. This is followed by a 3-day visit after 30 days of operation and another 3-day visit after 60 days of operation. After 90 days, a marketing specialist visits the owner. Quarterly visits are made thereafter.

The postopening training may be conducted at the franchise location, or selected franchise personnel may attend a training session at a model store near the franchise location. Some franchisors bring franchisees together periodically at regional meetings, where they may exchange views and opinions and receive additional management assistance.

Franchisors recognize that the continuing management training and consultation that they provide franchise owners is a primary reason for a franchisee's success. Individuals with a minimum of business experience are given the opportunity to learn the management skills needed to operate their own business successfully. And the success of the franchisor is reflected in the success of the franchisees.

Established Brand Name Products or Service

When franchisees are licensed, they acquire the right to use the brand name or trademark of the franchisor. The identification with an established name provides the franchisee with the distinct advantage of the drawing power of well-known products or services. Customers recognize a certain characteristic—the "Golden Arches" of McDonald's—and quickly identify that attribute as a symbol of courteous service, quality food, and cleanliness. These associations are important factors when consumers are selecting which firm to patronize.

Standardized Goods and Services

Because the franchisee uses the franchisor's brand name or trademark, the franchisor's reputation depends to a large extent on the quality of the product or service provided by the franchisee. To assure that goods and services are consistent through all franchised outlets, the franchisor makes available to the franchisee various types of assistance that extend to all phases of activity in the franchise. For example, Shakey's provides an operations manual to its pizza parlor owners that details the following:

Food preparation and recipes

Product specifications

Personnel procedures

Customer service

Management control

Maintenance and sanitation

Safety and security

By adhering to standard operating procedures of the franchisor, the goal of uniform products and services can be achieved and the image of the franchisor enhanced.

National Advertising

Association with a nationally known franchisor permits the franchise owner to benefit from the broader promotion of the product or service than would be possible for the independent businessperson. National advertising campaigns are financed by each franchisee's contribution of a stated percentage of monthly sales or a flat monthly sales or a flat monthly rate to the franchisor. For example, Wendy's franchisees contribute 2 percent of their sales to be spent on national advertising campaigns. Wendy's National Advertising Program (WNAP) is headed by a committee made up of corporate executives and franchise owners which provides input and feedback on national advertising of the franchisor. Another advantage is that the advertising is prepared by professionals, either advertising agencies or personnel on the staff of the franchisor.[5]

To supplement national advertising, franchisors require local franchisees to spend a minimum amount or percentage of sales on local advertising. For example, Wendy's requires each franchisee to spend at least 2 percent of gross sales on local advertising efforts. Company offices around the country offer franchisees support and suggestions in preparing the local advertising.[6]

Financial Assistance

Franchisors offer a wide range of financial assistance to franchisees. The following methods are illustrative of the financing arrangements available as reported by franchisors in *Franchising Opportunities Handbook*.

1. McDonald's has no financial assistance plan for franchisees.
2. Dunkin' Donuts provides financing assistance for real estate acquisition and development. Equipment and sign assistance is available to qualified franchisees.
3. Sir Speedy (print centers) makes financing available for the entire package to qualified individuals, excluding working capital.

Other financial assistance may be provided in the form of short-term credit for the purchase of certain food and paper products if the franchisee elects to purchase these items from the franchising company. One major franchisor offers both short- and long-term financing arrangements to franchisees whose credit rating qualifies them. The advantages of this financing method include a lower down payment than required by outside lending agencies, competitive interest rates, flexible repayment terms, and preparation of all necessary paperwork by the franchisor at no cost to the franchisee.

One form of nonfinancial assistance provided by the franchisor is to counsel franchisees on how to establish a good working relationship with lending agencies and on how to seek long-term financing for the site and building through conventional loan sources. Some franchisors assist with the presentation to the financial institution. For example, Kampgrounds of America, Inc. (KOA), does not provide direct financing to franchisees for campground construction. However, it does provide assistance in obtaining financing such as assisting the franchisee in preparing the prospectus, developing operating

ESTIMATED STORE COST OF A FREESTANDING LOCATION FAST-FOOD FRANCHISE

The estimated costs for a freestanding location for an international fast-food franchise are detailed below. These costs are based on estimates provided by the franchiser to prospective franchisees.

		Range of Costs
Land		$ 85,000–140,000
Building		110,000–170,000
Site improvements		30,000–40,000
Equipment		90,000–150,000
Working capital and non-recurring expenses		
Preconstruction Expenses (land surveys, topographical surveys)	$2,000	
Construction coordination	3,000	
Equipment installation coordination	2,200	
Interest expense for construction	6,000	
Utility deposits	1,000	
Legal fees	1,000	
Training program, living, and travel expenses	3,000	
Salaries	3,000	
Uniforms	1,500	
Opening equipment and supplies	2,000	
Opening inventory	8,000	
Cash on hand	7,300	
Total		$40,000–40,000
Franchise fee		40,000–40,000
Total		$395,000–580,000

projections, and meeting with potential lenders. Because franchisees have access to the franchisor's business expertise, they are often able to obtain more favorable credit terms from lending agencies.

Established Business Methods

A benefit of franchising is that the franchisee does not have to build the operation from the ground up. Instead, the franchisee is buying into a business firm that has established a record for success. The franchisee is able to capitalize on the accumulated knowledge and skills of the franchisor that are based on

Blockbuster Entertainment Corporation is the nation's largest video-cassette rental chain with company stores and franchise operations in 39 states and in Canada and the United Kingdom. Blockbuster provides franchisees with an integrated and comprehensive operating package.

sound business management principles and practices. Thus, the franchisee can avoid many of the common pitfalls encountered by the independent small business owner mentioned in Chapter 1.

Furthermore, the franchisee profits by capitalizing on the franchisor's developmental work in creating goodwill, building a consumer-accepted image, designing the physical facility and equipment, and providing proven products and services. The assistance received by franchisees in organizing and promoting the product, service, or business method enables them to concentrate their energy on managing the business. Reliance on the tested and proven methods of operation of the franchisor increases the chance of franchisee success.

Volume Purchasing Power

Franchisors require franchisees to use standardized products and services. This policy enables the franchisor to negotiate systemwide purchasing contracts with suppliers whereby volume purchases can be made, similar to the advantages enjoyed by chain stores. The systemwide purchasing arrangement may be on a national or regional basis (depending on the scope of franchise operation) and enables the franchisees to obtain the highest-quality products and supplies at lowest prices. Another alternative is the formation of a purchasing cooperative that is operated jointly by the franchisor and franchisees. Franchisees contribute an initial membership fee and quarterly fees for each franchise location. Through the cooperative, mass purchasing and distribution are available to individual franchisees. These quality purchases mean lower costs for products and supplies to each franchisee.

One franchisor has established a nationwide commissary system that provides food, equipment, and supplies through approved independent companies. Everything needed for the operation of the franchise can be purchased at lower cost through the commissary system.

Higher Success Rate

Owning a franchise does not guarantee success, but historically the success ratio is much higher for franchisees than for independently owned businesses. According to one source, nearly 38 percent of individual start-ups go out of business in the first year; by contrast, less than 4 percent of franchises are discontinued after one year. And as reported by the Department of Commerce, this success rate has been consistent since 1971. After five years, 92 percent of the franchisees are still in operation versus only 23 percent of independent businesses.[7] The variety of support services that the franchisor is able to offer the franchisee largely accounts for the higher rate of success.

The fast-food franchiser profiled in the chapter opening, Domino's Pizza has designed a policy to strengthen the position of the franchisee and discourage transience among operators. Domino's does not sell franchises to outside investors, only to Domino's employees who are former store managers or supervisors. A minimum of 12 months of management experience in a Domino's Pizza store is required before an application can be made for a franchise. And most of these managers have worked for a year as delivery persons or pizza makers.

This policy has enabled Domino's to keep rapid growth under control. Although the company is opening hundreds of new restaurants each year, it boasts a stable work force and has an annual failure rate among outlets of less than 1 percent. An advantage of this policy is that since Domino's management knows the potential franchisee before the sale is completed, it can assure lending agencies that the employees are reliable. This often results in more favorable treatment on loan applications.

Uniform Control Systems

An important component of the franchisor's program of support services is assistance provided in the control over franchise operations. For example, the franchisor furnishes the franchisee with a standardized system of financial and inventory controls, such as standardized reporting procedures and forms. These financial controls are a valuable aid for the franchisee in the preparation of financial statements and tax returns. An inventory control system enables franchisees to maintain a more accurate count of merchandise available and merchandise needed. By using these operational controls, the franchisee is in a more favorable position to improve overall efficiency and effectiveness of the franchise.

Income Potential

Because of the association with a franchisor with a proven business system as well as the franchisee's initiative, the franchise has a more favorable income potential than does the independent business operation. For example, the Department of Commerce reports that average yearly sales for all franchised outlets in 1988 was $1.25 million. While the numbers obviously vary among the different types of franchises, the figures do reflect the sales potential possible in the franchise operation.

Territorial Protection

Territorial protection policies vary among franchisors. Some have a policy of assigning an exclusive territory or area to the franchised outlet. This method protects both franchisor and franchisee interests. Other franchisors do not assign exclusive territories but rather an area of primary responsibility. This policy stipulates that the area of primary responsibility will be assigned at the time that the franchise agreement is signed and during the term of the agreement the franchisor will not operate or grant a franchise whose area of primary responsibility significantly overlaps another franchisee's area of primary responsibility.

LIMITATIONS OF FRANCHISING

As with any business undertaking, there are limitations to the franchise method of distribution that must be taken into account. Some of these limitations are discussed in the following section.

Franchise Fees and Royalties

Initial financial requirements vary. Some franchisors have a range of financial requirements depending on such factors as size of the franchise operation and its location. For example, Swensen's Ice Cream requires a franchisee to have a minimum net worth of $250,000, of which $150,000 is in cash or assets convertible to cash.[8] H & R Block requires equity capital of from $2000 to $3000.[9] For another franchisor, total investment depends on the size of the franchised operation. For a smaller unit the investment is $120,000; for a full-sized outlet, the investment is $400,000.

Franchise costs include a license fee, which is a fee charged for the initial processing of the franchise application. This fee is payable when the franchise agreement is signed, and it is not refundable under any circumstances. For one franchisor, this fee is $6500. Other costs include a down payment on equipment and building decor, sign package for the business, office furniture, and nonrecurring expenses, such as architectural costs, labor expenses prior to opening, and initial accounting fees. Operating capital expenditures cover supplies and inventory, wages and expenses while training key people, promotion and advertising of the grand opening, cash reserves for operating the franchise, licenses and fees (health permits, business licenses), and other deposits, such as insurance and utilities. Franchisees are ordinarily required to pay their travel and living expenses while attending training classes prior to the opening at the franchise headquarters and also for any follow-up training as well as any compensation of the franchisee and employees while attending these classes.

In addition, royalty payments to the franchisor represent a continuing cost. Royalties are paid to franchisors based on a predetermined percentage of sales. The royalties must be paid for the continuing use of the franchisor's trademark, service mark, trade name, and other related items. The royalty fee is stated in the franchise agreement as a stated percentage of gross sales (to be paid weekly, monthly, or annually) or a flat annual fee. For example, one franchise agreement calls for the franchisee to pay a weekly royalty of 5 percent of total receipts while another franchise agreement calls for a 5.5 percent royalty payment monthly for the life of the agreement.

Other fees must be recognized. As discussed earlier, franchisees must remit a specific percentage of sales for both national and local advertising. The franchisee may have other fees which cover the cost of continuing operational advisory services, such as financial management services.

Conformity to Standardized Operations

Although franchisees own the business, they do not have the autonomy to run the firm as do independent business owners. The franchisor ordinarily exercises varying degrees of continuing control over the franchisee's operation to assure the quality and uniformity of standards of products and services at all outlets. Franchisors representatives have the right to visit a store at any time during regular business hours without prior notice to conduct a reasonable inspection of the store. Failure of the franchisee to comply with the terms of the franchise agreement can result in termination of the franchise agreement.

Restricted Freedom in Purchasing

While the franchisee is not required to purchase food and nonfood items directly from the franchisor, the franchisor does maintain control over the purchases made by the franchisee. The franchisor establishes the specifications and quality standards for all items used in the franchise. Control is accomplished by providing the franchisee with a list of approved products and specifications. The franchisee has the option of buying directly from the franchisor, on the open market, or from distributors licensed by the franchisor. However, in all cases, purchasing is limited to suppliers who meet the franchisor's standards for quality.

Limited Product Line

The franchisor controls the products or services that may be sold through the franchise outlet. The franchisee cannot introduce other products or services except as they are introduced by the franchisor or approved by the company.

Restriction on Sale of Franchise

If a franchisee desires to sell, transfer, or assign his or her ownership interest, such action must be approved by the franchisor. The franchise agreement which details the specific reasons for approval of a transfer of ownership interest thus limits the freedom of the franchisee. In all instances, the franchisor has the right of first refusal in the proposed sale by the franchisee. When approval is given for a transfer of ownership, the new owner must meet all requirements of the franchisor.

Termination or Expiration of the Agreement

When a franchise agreement is executed, it is binding on both parties. Specific language in the agreement details the reasons by which the agreement may be terminated by either party. For example, the franchisee can terminate the agreement if the franchisor breaks any part of the contract and fails to take

FIGURE 3-3
LENGTH OF FRANCHISE AGREEMENTS

Number of years	Percentage
1	1.1
3	1.5
5	14.8
10	33.1
15	14.6
20	19.6
25	0.9
Perpetual	12.5
Other	1.9

Source: Franchising in the Economy, 1986–1988 (Washington, D.C.: U.S. Department of Commerce, 1988), p. 13.

corrective action within a stated time. The franchisor can terminate the agreement for specific actions of the franchisee, such as misrepresentation, bankruptcy, or failure to comply with the terms of the agreement.

The length of the franchise agreement varies from one year to a perpetual agreement. In a Department of Commerce survey, the most common term was for 10 years, but 33 percent were for 20 years or longer. If the agreement has been fulfilled by the franchisee, then the franchisee has the opportunity to enter into a new agreement at the end of the original term. Figure 3-3 shows the length of time for which franchise agreements are valid.

A summary of the advantages and disadvantages of franchising is presented in Figure 3-4.

FIGURE 3-4
ADVANTAGES AND LIMITATIONS OF FRANCHISING

Advantages	Limitations
Management training	Franchise fees and royalties
Established brand-name product or service	Conformity to standardized operations
Standardized product or service	Restricted freedom in purchasing
	Limited product line
National advertising	Restrictions on sale of franchise
Financial assistance	Termination of agreement
Established business methods	
Volume purchasing power	
Higher success rate	
Uniform control system	
Income potential	
Territorial protection	

CODE OF ETHICS OF THE INTERNATIONAL FRANCHISE ASSOCIATION

The **International Franchise Association (IFA),** founded in 1960, is a nonprofit trade association that represents franchising companies in the United States and around the world. The purpose of the IFA are to serve as a spokesperson for franchising, provide services to member companies and those interested in franchising, set standards of business practice, serve as a medium for exchanging experience and expertise, and offer educational programs for top executives and managers.

The IFA has developed a Code of Ethics that is designed to enhance mutual trust and confidence between franchisor and franchisee and to set high standards of business ethics and conduct. Specifically, the Code of Ethics includes the following.

Code of Ethics—International Franchise Association
Each member company pledges:

1. In the advertisement and grant of franchises or dealerships a member shall comply with all applicable laws and regulations and the member's offering circulars shall be complete, accurate, and not misleading with respect to the franchisee's or dealer's investment, the obligations of the member and the franchise or dealer under the franchise or dealership and all material facts relating to the franchise or dealership.
2. All matters material to the membership's franchise or dealership shall be contained in one or more written agreements, which shall clearly set forth the terms of the relationship and the respective rights and obligations of the parties.
3. A member shall select and accept only those franchisees or dealers who, upon reasonable investigation, appear to possess the basic skills, education, experience, personal characteristics and financial resources requisite to conduct the franchised business or dealership and meet the obligations of the franchise or dealer under the franchise and other agreements. There shall be no discrimination in the granting of franchises based solely on race, color, religion, national origin, or sex. However, this in no way prohibits a franchisor from granting franchises to prospective franchisees as part of a program to make franchises available to persons lacking the capital, training, business experience, or other qualifications ordinarily required of franchisees or any other affirmative action program adopted by the franchisor.
4. A member shall provide reasonable guidance to its franchisees or dealers in a manner consistent with its franchise agreement.
5. Fairness shall characterize all dealings between a member and its franchisees or dealers. A member shall make every good faith effort to resolve complaints by and disputes with its franchisees or dealers

through direct communication and negotiation. To the extent reasonably appropriate in the circumstances, a member shall give its franchisee or dealer notice of, and a reasonable opportunity to cure, a breach of their contractual relationship.

6. No member shall engage in the pyramid system of distribution. A pyramid is a system wherein a buyer's future compensation is expected to be based primarily upon recruitment of new participants, rather than upon the sale of products or services.[10]

FRANCHISE INFORMATION

An excellent source for information on hundreds of franchises is the *Franchise Opportunities Handbook,* published by the U.S. Department of Commerce. This guidebook provides a description of the operation, the number of franchises and the length of time the franchise has been in operation, how much equity capital is needed, the financial and managerial assistance available, and the training provided by the franchisor. Here is an example of the kind of information available on a particular franchise.[11]

COMPUTERLAND CORPORATION
2901 Peralta Oaks Court
Oakland, California 94606

Description of Operation: ComputerLand offers franchises for retail stores dealing in microcomputers, computer systems and related items, in a protected location, supported by marketing and purchasing services, under the name ComputerLand.

Number of Franchisees: 800 in 50 states and 24 foreign countries.

In Business Since: 1976

Equity Capital Needed: $200,000 to $600,000, depending on market size and location.

Financial Assistance Available: Financing of franchise fee available to qualified applicants. Franchisor will assist franchisee in preparing a loan proposal package to present to a bank or other loaning institution.

Training Provided: There is an initial training program for franchisees. Subjects covered are product knowledge, sales training and management, accounting, merchandising, and general franchise operation management. Updated and refresher courses are offered. Specific retail sales trainings are offered on an ongoing basis.

Managerial Assistance Available. Upon opening of the store, franchisor offers in-store aid and also supplies and keeps an updated operations manual which includes bookkeeping direction. Franchisor develops advertising aids for the franchisee, makes available inventory for purchase by franchisee at cost and protects the ComputerLand name.

INTERNATIONAL FRANCHISING

The Department of Commerce reports that U.S. franchisors are currently operating in most major markets or are engaged in negotiations for entering foreign markets. Opportunities in foreign markets are dramatically expanding the potential for franchise expansion. For example, in 1971, there were 156 U.S. companies with 3365 franchise outlets in foreign countries. By 1986, the number of franchisors had climbed to 354 and the number of franchising outlets increased to 31,626. An additional 228 franchisors have indicated they are strongly considering expanding their operations across international borders.[12]

McDonald's and Kentucky Fried Chicken are prime examples of success in international franchising. Kentucky Fried Chicken has over 2700 international units and McDonald's nearly 2500.[13]

Franchising operations in foreign markets involve many of the same problems that confront other business ventures: language barriers, cultural differences, and sometimes unpredictable government decision making. When compared to other service sectors, however, the problems of franchise companies in international transactions are relatively less formidable. Franchisors must comply with the same local requirements as domestic businesses, and franchise agreements must comply with local and national laws. There are no specific trade barriers that discriminate against U.S. franchises.[14]

There are a number of ways to enter a foreign market: franchising directly to individuals in the local market, establishing a company-owned franchise, or master franchising. **Master franchising,** sometimes referred to as subfranchising, is the major method of entry into a foreign market. Among U.S. franchisors that operate internationally, master franchising is the preferred form of entry. Under this arrangement, the franchisor divides a market into large areas (major sections of a country, a single country, a few contiguous countries, or a region), and each area is assigned to a master franchisee. The franchisor provides the master franchisee with the management and technical training and trademark licenses. The master franchisee has authority to subfranchise to individuals in the area and is responsible for providing the support to the local franchisees. Local franchisees pay a franchise fee and royalties to the master franchisor who in turn pays an agreed-upon percentage to the franchisor, such as 10 or 15 percent. The franchisor also makes money from license fee payments by the master franchisee to the franchisor, franchise opening fees, sales of supplies and products and equipment, or equity ownership in the master franchise. A major advantage of master franchising is that the franchisee is familiar with the local customs and territory.

Some specific areas that should be evaluated by the franchisor prior to entering an international market are the following:

1. Official limitations on royalty payments or licensing and trademark contracts. In some cases royalties on trademarks and brand names are taxable and payable by the franchisor whether he or she is domiciled in or out of that particular country.

2. Problems may exist in the protection of trademarks, as no facility exists for their registration.

3. In some cases, franchising agreements remain solely the concern of contracting parties, and there are no regulations to safeguard franchising agreements. Tie-in arrangements are discouraged and sometimes forbidden.

4. In some countries, a significant percentage of ownership share of the business activity is required by local nationals; in others, aliens cannot own real estate property; and in others, they cannot own retail businesses.

5. There are also important restrictions on equipment. This may impose a significant problem with respect to equipment or systems considered essential to the distinctiveness of the end product or the end service.

6. Wide economic variation as a result of inflation and currency valuation, exchange controls, and price ceilings on products pose problems affecting various types of franchising business categories.[15]

Franchisors must give serious consideration to the cultural differences throughout the world. For example, consider what happened to Hardee's in Saudi Arabia. There, the government regulations require businesses to close down several times a day to allow employees and customers to pray to Allah. Hardee's had to adjust its franchise policies to accommodate the local custom.[16]

Long John Silver's Seafood could not sell fish in Japan for a variety of business and cultural reasons. In 1977, a group of Japanese businesspeople offered to help Long John Silver's gain entry into the Japanese market. The company sold master franchising rights, but the Japanese market presented challenges that could not be overcome. One problem was the high cost of real estate. Another barrier was the shortage of real estate. In some instances, one had to know the right people or make payments to the right people just to have the privilege of getting some land. Sometimes up-front money, called "key money," was required just to obtain a lease. Distribution problems were encountered because of Japan's road and street system. Many times a store could not be reached by a regular delivery truck because the truck was too large for the street or road and supplies had to be hauled by handcart. While the franchisor tried to adapt its menu items to the local taste, the Japanese did not accept them and Long John Silver's pulled out of the Japanese market.[17]

Markets in many foreign, developed countries are exhibiting the same characteristics as those that contributed to the growth of franchising in the United States. These characteristics are a rising level of disposable income; rising demand for consumer goods and services; more working women; increasing urbanization, which makes critical masses of the population more reachable; and greater consumer mobility. There are more young people who like to try new products and services, and there is a growing middle class that has potential investors.[18]

In world markets, U.S. franchisors have the most units in Canada, followed by Japan, Australia, the United Kingdom, and continental Europe, especially France, West Germany, the Netherlands, and Belgium. The reasons for the heavy influx of U.S. franchisors into these markets are the relative sophistication of their economies, fewer governmental controls on investment in these developed countries than those in developing countries, and the generally high level of prosperity of their citizens.[19]

The predominant type of franchisees in international markets are in the food categories: restaurants, donut shops, ice cream shops, and convenience stores. However, other forms of franchising such as nonfood retailing and business aids and services are demonstrating growth.[20]

The United States is also the focus of franchising interests from abroad. There are no precise figures on the number of foreign franchisors in America, but the number is increasing. Some examples of inroads in the United States include Molly Maids (Toronto), Uniglobe Travel International (Vancouver), Dosanko Foods (Japan), and Copy 2000 printing centers (France).

MINORITY-OWNED FRANCHISES

Two common problems for small investors, especially minority entrepreneurs, are the lack of business and management experience and inadequate financing. The franchising distribution system has made it possible to overcome these obstacles in many situations because of the various services and assistance that franchisors make available to franchisees. Thus, franchising is an avenue for minority-group members to become entrepreneurs and to enhance the likelihood of success.

The greatest number of minority-owned franchises are owned by Orientals followed by blacks, persons with Spanish surnames, and American Indians. According to the Department of Commerce, franchises most popular among minority entrepreneurs are restaurants, automotive products and services, food retailing other than convenience stores, convenience stores, and business aids and services.[21] There are 365 black-owned McDonald's (6.6 percent of the total) and 195 black-owned Popeye's (30 percent of the chain), the two top companies with the most black-owned franchises, according to the Small Business Administration.

FRANCHISING AND THE LAW

The enthusiasm for franchising must be tempered with the reality of some of the risks and problems associated with this fast-growing distribution system. A regulation enacted in 1979 by the Federal Trade Commission (FTC) seeks to put an end to some of the abuses and unjustified claims by franchisors, such as arbitrary terminations of franchises or unsubstantiated profit claims. Franchising has also become a focal point of regulation in many states.

Franchise Disclosure Statements

The Federal Trade Regulation Rule issued by the FTC requires franchisors in all states to provide a **franchise disclosure statement** to prospective franchisees at the first meeting with a representative of the franchisor or at least 10 days before signing a franchise agreement or paying any money toward a franchise purchase. In addition, 15 states require franchisors to register their franchise offer with a state agency or provide disclosure statements similar to the FTC regulation to prospective franchisees in order to sell franchises in that state.

The disclosure statement has proven to be useful in evaluating franchises. In a recent survey sponsored by the FTC, 69 percent of those surveyed who eventually purchased a franchise indicated the disclosure statement assisted them in making their decision.

The FTC disclosure statement makes available detailed information on 20 separate areas that may influence the decision to invest or not invest in the franchise. These areas are now described.

1. Information identifying the franchisor and its affiliates and describing their business experience.
2. Information identifying and describing the business experience of each of the franchisor's officers, directors, and management personnel responsible for franchise services, training, and other aspects of the franchise program.
3. A description of the lawsuits in which the franchisor and its officers, directors, and management personnel have been involved.
4. Information about any previous bankruptcies in which the franchisor and its officers, directors, and management personnel have been involved.
5. Information about the initial franchise fee and other initial payments that are required to obtain the franchise.
6. A description of the continuing payments franchisees are required to make after the franchise opens.
7. Information about any restrictions on the quality of goods and services used in the franchise and where they may be purchased, including restrictions requiring purchases from the franchisor or its affiliates.

8. A description of any assistance available from the franchisor or its affiliates in financing the purchase of the franchise.
9. A description of restrictions on the goods or services franchisees are permitted to sell.
10. A description of any restrictions on the customers with whom franchisees may deal.
11. A description of any territorial protection that will be granted to the franchisee.
12. A description of the conditions under which the franchise may be repurchased or refused renewal by the franchisor, transferred to a third party by the franchisee, and terminated or modified by either party.
13. A description of the training programs provided to franchisees.
14. A description of the involvement of any celebrities or public figures in the franchise.
15. A description of any assistance in selecting a site for the franchise that will be provided by the franchisor.
16. Statistical information about the present number of franchises; the number of franchises projected for the future; and the number of franchises terminated, the number the franchisor has decided not to renew, and the number repurchased in the past.
17. The financial statements of the franchisors.
18. A description of the extent to which the franchisees must personally participate in the operation of the franchise.
19. A complete statement of the basis of any earnings claims made to the franchisee, including the percentage of existing franchises that have actually achieved the results that are claimed.
20. A list of names and addresses of other franchisees.[22]

Legal Rights of Prospective Franchisee

The FTC regulation prescribes a number of legal rights to the prospective franchisee. They are

1. The right to receive a disclosure statement at your first personal meeting with a representative of the franchisor to discuss the purchase of a franchise; but in no event less than 10 business days before you sign a franchise or related agreement or pay any money in connection with the purchase of a franchise.
2. The right to receive documentation stating the basis and assumptions for any earnings claims that are made at the time the claims are made, but in no event less than 10 business days before you sign a franchise or related agreement or pay any money in connection with the purchase of a franchise. If an earnings claim is made in advertising, you have the right to receive the required documentation at your first personal meeting with a representative of the franchisor.

3. The right to receive sample copies of the franchisor's standard franchise and related agreements at the same time as you receive the disclosure statement and the right to receive the final agreements you are to sign at least 5 business days before you sign them.
4. The right to receive any refunds promised by the franchisor, subject to any conditions or limitations on that right that have been disclosed by the franchisor.
5. The right not to be misled by oral or written representations made by the franchisor or its representatives that are inconsistent with the disclosures made in the disclosure statement.[23]

A violation of the federal law could result in a civil penalty against the franchisor of up to $10,000 for each violation. If a prospective franchisee has been injured by a violation, the FTC may be able to provide a remedy for the injury suffered, such as compensation for any money lost or the setting aside of future contractual obligations.

However, your best protection as a prospective franchisee is to investigate the franchisor thoroughly, evaluate your own abilities, and be aware of your legal rights.

EXCLUSIVE DISTRIBUTORSHIP

A somewhat different method of distribution from franchising is the **exclusive distributorship.** This method of distribution may be used for products that are purchased rather infrequently, such as autos. In an exclusive distributorship, a manufacturer signs an **exclusive agency contract** with a distributor (wholesaler, retailer, agent). The agreement specifies that the manufacturer gives the distributor exclusive rights to sell the goods or sevices within a designated geographical area. In addition to restricting the sales territory, a manufacturer may provide the dealer with marketing services, such as sales training and cooperative advertising. In return, the distributor agrees to certain requirements of the manufacturer, such as stocking adequate levels of inventory, charging the prices established by the manufacturer, or not stocking competitive products. This arrangement gives manufacturers greater control over the distribution of their products.

However, there are legal limits to this distribution arrangement. These restrictions are discussed in Chapter 22.

WHAT'S AHEAD IN FRANCHISING?

The Department of Commerce projects franchising to continue to expand at both the national and international level. Franchising's growth will create opportunities for current franchises and pave the way for the development of a new generation of franchises of products, services, and methods. Franchising's growth will set the stage for the entrance of new entrepreneurs and the creation of new jobs in the economy.

The continued growth of business format franchising in both sales and number of units is forecast. Fast-food restaurants will remain the most popular of this kind of franchising.

Franchising will continue its expansion into various types of service firms. Quick lube and oil change centers, diet services, beauty salons, maid services, temporary help services, and carry-out restaurant services are targeted growth areas. International markets are predicted to be strong growth areas for franchising in the 1990s.

Another move is toward conversion franchising for selected types of businesses. **Conversion franchising** permits an independent business owner who is already established to affiliate with a franchisor and realize the benefits of the franchising relationship. Century 21, a real estate sales firm, and Jiffy Lube International, quick lube franchisor, are among the franchisors using this strategy.

In an attempt to reduce real estate and management costs and to increase food traffic, combination franchising has been test marketed, particularly by fast-food chains, convenience stores, hotels, and automotive aftermarket chains. **Combination franchising** is a plan whereby two franchises share a location and management. For example, Popeye's Famous Fried Chicken and Biscuits franchisees in California have implemented combination franchising with Carl Jr's., a franchised hamburger chain. Results thus far are mixed on the combination franchising concept.[24]

Thus, it appears that major changes are in store for the entire economy. In the 1990s creativity and imagination will be rewarded as new products, services, and business methods are introduced. Education, computer usage, and the ability to work with and manage people will be profitability utilized by these new businesses. These developments suggest that franchising will play a strategic role in the business developments of the 1990s.[25]

SUMMARY OF KEY POINTS

1. Franchising, as defined by the International Franchise Association, is "a continuing relationship in which the franchisor provides a licensed privilege to do business, plus assistance in organizing, training, merchandising, and management in return for a consideration from the franchisee."

2. Two basic types of franchise arrangements are product and trade name franchising and business formal franchising.

3. Specific advantages of franchising include (a) management training, (b) established brand name or service, (c) standardized product or service, (d) national advertising, (e) financial assistance, (f) established business methods, (g) volume purchasing power, (h) higher success rate, (i) favorable income potential, (j) uniform control systems, and (k) territorial protection.

4. Limitations of franchising include (a) franchisee fees and royalties, (b) conformity to standardized operations, (c) restricted freedom in purchasing, (d) limited product line, (e) restriction on sale of franchise, and (f) termination of franchise agreement.

5. The IFA has adopted a Code of Ethics that is designed to strengthen the relationship that exists between franchisor and franchisee.

6. Franchising has expanded to an increasingly important role in international markets.

7. Minority entrepreneurs may receive management and financial support through franchise ownership that increases their chances of successful business ownership and operation.

8. The Federal Trade Commission has established regulations that require franchisors in all states to provide disclosure statements to prospective franchisees. The FTC has also outlined the legal rights of prospective franchisees.

9. In an exclusive distributorship, a manufacturer makes an agreement with a dealer (wholesaler, agent, or retailer) specifying that the manufacturer will sell goods or services in a particular area only through a single dealer.

10. Franchising should continue to be a significant force in the U.S. economy through the 1980s and 1990s.

DISCUSSION QUESTIONS

1. Explain the difference between a product and trade name franchise and a business format franchise.

2. Explain some of the advantages of owning a franchise.

3. What are some of the limitations of franchising?

4. What is the purpose of the Code of Ethics for franchisors developed by the IFA?

5. Why should a prospective franchisee make a thorough analysis of the franchisor before signing a franchise agreement?

6. What are some of the legal issues involved in franchising?

7. What is an exclusive distributorship?

THE BUSINESS PLAN: FRANCHISE ANALYSIS

The 25 questions that follow should be answered when evaluating the potential of a franchise.

Checklist for Evaluating a Franchise

The Franchise

1. Did your lawyer approve the franchise contract you are considering after he studied it paragraph by paragraph?

2. Does the franchise call upon you to take any steps that are, according to your lawyer, unwise or illegal in your state, county, or city?

3. Does the franchise give you an exclusive territory for the length of the franchise, or can the franchisor sell a second or third franchise in your territory?

4. Is the franchisor connected in any way with any other franchise company handling similar merchandise or services?

5. If the answer to the last question is yes, what is your protection against this second franchisor organization?

6. Under what circumstances can you terminate the franchise contract and at what cost to you, if you decide for any reason at all that you wish to cancel it?

7. If you sell your franchise, will you be compensated for your goodwill, or will the goodwill you have built into the business be lost by you?

The Franchisor

8. How many years has the firm offering you a franchise been in operation?

9. Has it a reputation for honesty and fair dealing among the local firms holding its franchise?

10. Has the franchisor shown you any certified figures indicating exact net profits of one or more going firms that you personally checked yourself with the franchisee?

11. Will the firm assist you with
    a. A management training program?
    b. An employee training program?
    c. A public relations program?
    d. Capital?
    e. Credit?
    f. Merchandising ideas?

12. Will the firm help you find a good location for your new business?

13. Is the franchising firm adequately financed so that it can carry out its stated plan of financial assistance and expansion?

14. Is the franchisor a one-person company or a corporation with an experienced management trained in depth (so that there would always be an experienced individual at its head)?

15. Exactly what can the franchisor do for you that you cannot do for yourself?

16. Has the franchisor investigated you carefully enough to assure itself that you can successfully operate one of their franchises at a profit both to them and to you?

17. Does your state have a law regulating the sale of franchises and has the franchisor complied with that law?

You—the Franchisee

18. How much equity capital will you have to purchase the franchise and operate it until your income equals your expenses? Where are you going to get it?

19. Are you prepared to give up some independence of action to secure the advantages offered by the franchise?

20. Do you really believe you have the innate ability, training, and experience to work smoothly and profitably with the franchisor, your employees, and your customers?

21. Are you ready to spend much or all of the remainder of your business life with this franchisor, offering his or her product or service to your public?

Your Market

22. Have you made any study to determine whether the product or service that you propose to sell under franchise has a market in your territory at the prices you will have to charge?

23. Will the population in the territory given you increase, remain static, or decrease over the next five years?

24. Will the product or service you are considering be in great demand, about the same, or less demand five years from now than today?

25. What competition exists in your territory already for the product or service you contemplate selling?
    a. Nonfranchise firms?
    b. Franchise firms?[26]

ENTREPRENEURIAL PROJECTS

1. Write a short essay in answer to the following question: Why should I choose to become a franchisee instead of opening my own independent business operation?
2. What are my strengths that would make me a successful franchisee?
3. Review the classified ads of your local newspaper or some other paper such as *The Wall Street Journal*. From the business opportunities section, compile a list of the types of franchise opportunities available in your community.
4. Select a specific franchisor. Request the franchisor to send you information about what it takes to start the franchise and the types of services the franchisor provides franchisees.
5. Interview a franchisee in your community. Have him or her explain the assistance provided by the franchisor.

CASE A
Promises, Promises

It was hard not to be seduced, Gail Casano remembers, when she and her husband were considering buying a Movieland U.S.A. franchise in early 1986. The video rental shops, all slick and colorful, came replete with giant movie screens and popcorn machines. ''Well, look at my car,'' said Mark Baron, Movieland's president, pointing to his late-model Mercedes-Benz when she and her husuband asked how much they could make with a franchise. One store, Casano was told, was making $40,000 a month in sales. It was, Baron said, a business that ran itself. Just sit back and reap the rewards.

Now, two years later, Casano and her husband are $50,000 in debt. They sold two houses they had bought as investments and mortgaged their own to pay the $125,000 start-up costs, which included a $55,000 franchisee fee. Casano had been told by Baron the start-up would be $95,000 tops. The franchisor is no longer in existence; Baron has disappeared; and several civil suits have been filed against Movieland—filled with charges of fraud, deceit, incompetence, drug abuse, and intimidation. ''Buying the franchise was the worst thing I ever, ever did,'' laments Casano, 35, from Setauket, N.Y.

The business of franchising is surrounded by a grand myth, myth given life by the legitimate successes of franchising. Buy a franchise—buy someone else's idea, his or her expertise and support—and you buy success. The reality is much starker. Especially when you buy into a new franchise. By investing in a franchise less than five years old, you can often get a huge break on the price, but you assume a much greater risk. "Any fast-growing company could be a rocket to the sky or a fast-burner," says Patrick J. Boroian, president of Francorp, Inc., Olympia Fields, Ill., a franchising development and consulting firm. "It's all too easy for a franchisor to take a check and not service the franchisee."

Movieland, Jericho, N.Y., which offered its first franchise in April 1985 claimed to have added 20 units by the beginning of 1987, giving it a spot at No. 25 on last year's Venture Franchisor 50 list based on unit growth. Although the majority of companies on our list have grown and prospered, others have suffered fates similar to Movieland's, underscoring the unpredictability of young franchise systems.

In February, 1986, Casano, a real estate agent, and her husband, chief of respiratory therapy at a nearby hospital, met with Baron, 50% owner of Movieland. He handed them a disclosure document. "He said that none of the other franchisees had used an attorney. He made us feel we weren't going to get the spot we wanted if we used a lawyer," says Casano. (Other franchisees also claim in court papers that Baron told them they did not need lawyers.) Casano admits she did not read the entire document because she didn't understand the legalities, and that she signed the franchising agreement a week after receiving it. All this despite a warning from the Federal Trade Commission on the front of every disclosure document that advises a potential franchisee to study it and show it to a lawyer or an accountant. In addition, the Movieland disclosure document carried a warning from the state of New York that 10 business days must pass before the principals can sign a binding agreement. "I don't remember getting that page," says Casano.

Casano claims—other franchisees have made similar claims in their suits— that once she handed her check over to Baron, all support ended. "Neither Movieland nor Baron ever bothered to even visit our store once it opened [in August 1986]. We never received promotional material. We never saw any advertising, though we, and other franchisees, were responsible for paying 3% of our monthly gross to Movieland for this service," Casano charges in an affidavit filed in Nassau County (N.Y.) Supreme Court.

What the franchisees didn't know at the time was that the two owners of Movieland were engaged in a brutal struggle over the company, according to court papers. After months of battling Baron, Barry Geister, who owned the other 50% of the company, finally agreed to let Baron buy him out. He resigned from the company in August 1986. But Baron never paid Geister for his shares of the company, and in October 1986, Geister filed suit, asking for his share of the company back and that a receiver be appointed for Movieland. The court ordered Baron to pay, but Geister, now an independent consultant with FranchiseIt, Inc., Bohemia, N.Y. claims he has received only $15,000 of the $300,000 he's owed. Geister also says Movieland only had "13 or 14 franchises at the most," not the 20 Baron claimed to Venture.

At the same time in August 1986, many franchisees, citing lack of support, stopped paying their 5% royalties and advertising fees. Baron threatened to terminate their agreements. According to court documents, he broke into one store that was waiting to open in an attempt to take back the lease. Baron's assistant called Casano and threatened to break into her store as well. Then Baron slapped a number of franchisees with lawsuits—including Casano, six weeks after she opened. Casano had paid her monthly fees but was charged with failure to pay for $15,102 worth of goods sold and delivered.

At least six franchisees countersued Movieland for failure to honor their franchise agreement, requesting the termination of the agreement and the return of their franchise fees. Threats continued, with one franchisee, Ray Van Capella of Commack, N.Y., stating in an affidavit that on "January 2, 1987 . . . Baron entered my store with two shady looking characters, his 'goons.' Only my wife was present. They were very physical looking and Baron was very high-strung and nervous. . . . Baron stated to my wife that . . . the thugs he was with 'want their money and they don't care how or where they get it.'"

At least three formal police complaints have been filed against Baron. In June 1987, a judge issued preliminary injunctions prohibiting Baron from interfering in the operations of three franchisees and ordering the franchisees to continue paying royalties. "The problem is there is no Movieland to pay a royalty to," says Jay L.T. Breakstone, the attorney for six Movieland franchisees. According to several of the litigants, as well as the attorney general, Baron has disappeared. Venture's many attempts to track him down turned up only one cue. A lawyer from Minolta Corp. which had successfully sued Baron's previous company over nonpayment for equipment, claims Baron called him in December, 1987, asking him for a job refererence.

With the drawn-out legal headaches, the tight, competitive video rental market, and no support from a franchisor, many franchisees have had trouble making a go of their stores. Casano, who had to quit her $45,000-a-year real estate job to run the store, says she is barely existing. But she swears that she will make it work. "It's my whole life savings. I will not kiss off that money." Meanwhile the New York attorney general is conducting an investigation of Movieland.

Source: Jeannie Ralston, "Promises, Promises," *Venture,* March 1988, pp. 55–56. Reprinted from the March, 1988 issue of VENTURE, For Entrepreneurs & Business Leaders, by special permission. © 1988 Venture Magazine, Inc., 521 Fifth Ave., New York, N.Y. 10175-0028

Questions

1. Analyze this situation and identify the problems that the franchisee experienced.

2. How could these problems have been prevented?

CASE B
Michael Davis

Since graduating from college in 1965, Michael Davis has been employed as a personnel manager in the Department of Education in a large Southwestern state. Michael majored in business management in college, and his personnel management position enabled him to put his educational experience to good use.

However, Michael has been experiencing a common problem encountered by highly motivated individuals—job burnout. His job provides a comfortable and secure living for Michael, his wife, and their two children. However, Michael feels that working in the strict confines of a state bureaucracy is stifling his growth. He has assessed his situation and feels that he wants out. He wants to be in control, and the way to do this is by owning his own business. He has had this desire since his college days but never felt he was in a position to take such a step. Now, he realizes that unless he makes the move, he may never be able to take this career step. Michael is 41 years old.

He lives in a city with a population of 250,000, and the city and the surrounding area are experiencing rapid economic growth. During the last two years, he has been reading extensively about new business opportunities that have good potential. One of the opportunities he has examined is a quick lubrication system (10-minute service) for motor vehicles and recreational vehicles. The size of these service centers is approximately 2000 square feet and they are open 10 hours daily, six days a week. The potential for such a center is very good because the general public has less time to wait for this type of auto service and prefers the convenience of a drive-in lubrication service.

Michael is concerned about his lack of experience but feels that one method of reducing risk in starting a new business is through franchising. He has been assured by the franchisor that the company training program will equip him with the knowledge he needs to manage the business. The company provides an intensive 14-day training course for new franchisees at the franchisor's headquarters. Employees of the franchise receive a five-day training session at the franchise site, which is conducted by a representative of the franchisor.

In addition, the franchisor offers continuing management support for the life of the franchise in the area of accounting, advertising, policies and procedures, and operations. Complete operational manuals are provided. Regional managers of the franchise work closely with franchisees, and the company sponsors annual seminars for franchisees.

The amount of equity capital needed is $40,000. The franchisor will provide financing to qualified franchisees and will assist franchisees in locating additional sources of financing.

Michael has visited two other franchise owners in other parts of the city, and both are very satisfied with the business. One had average sales of $385,000, and the other had sales of $415,000. The average salary for one owner was $49,000, and for the other it was $58,335.

The area of the city in which the franchise is available is experiencing the fastest growth of the entire city. It is on a major thoroughfare, and 50,000 automobiles are registered within a 25-minute drive of the proposed site.

In addition to the previously discussed requirements, the franchisor's expectations of the franchisee are set forth as follows.

1. You must have long-range business goals and commitment. This is not a get-rich-quick scheme but a method to enjoy what you are doing while building financial security.
2. You must be willing to become actively involved in the business.
3. You must have a strong desire to succeed in this business and not be trying to escape from your present situation.
4. You must be able to interact well with employees, customers, and the community as a whole.

Questions

1. List the advantages you can see in the franchisor's offer.
2. Are there any disadvantages in the franchisor's offer? If the answer is yes, what are they?
3. What additional information should Michael obtain to assist him in making his decision?
4. What should Michael do, based on the information given?

Notes

[1] "The Franchise 100," *Venture*, December 1988, p. 41.

[2] *Franchise Opportunities Handbook* (Washington, D.C.: U.S. Department of Commerce, 1988), p. xxix.

[3] *Franchising in the Economy, 1986–1988* (Washington, D.C.: U.S. Department of Commerce, 1988), p. 1.

[4] Ibid., p. 4.

[5] Annual Report, Wendy's International, Inc., 1986, p. 8.

[6] Ibid.

[7] E. Jan Hartmann, "As Franchising Grows, So Can You," *Venture*, July 1988, p. 60.

[8] "Opportunity Now," brochure of Swensen's, Inc., undated.

[9] *Franchise Opportunities Handbook*, p. 32.

[10] Ibid., p. xxxiii.

[11] Ibid., p. 224.

[12] *Franchising in the Economy, 1986–1988*, Pp. 7 and 9.

[13] "The Franchise 100," *Venture*, December 1988, pp. 37 and 41.

[14] *Franchising in the Economy*, p. 9.

[15] *Franchising in the Economy, 1976–1978* (Washington, D.C.: U.S. Department of Commerce, 1978), p. 7.

[16] John F. Persinos, "New Worlds to Franchise," *Venture,* November 1987, p. 50.

[17] Ibid., p. 52.

[18] Carol Steinberg, "Economic Lifestyle Changes Fuel Explosive Expansion, *Venture,* July 1988, p. 62.

[19] *Franchising in the Economy, 1986–1988,* p. 9.

[20] Ibid., p. 10.

[21] Ibid., p. 11.

[22] *Franchise Opportunities Handbook,* pp. xxx and xxxi.

[23] Ibid., p. xxxii.

[24] Echo M. Garret, "Combination Franchising," *Venture,* December 1988, p. 36.

[25] *Franchising in the Economy, 1986–1988,* p. 6.

[26] *Franchise Opportunities Handbook,* pp. xxxiii and xxxiv.

ESTABLISHING THE FIRM

KEY WORDS

THE BUSINESS PLAN

LEARNING GOALS

After reading this chapter, you will understand:

1 The advantages and disadvantages of buying an existing business.

2 The advantages and disadvantages to starting a new business.

3 If you plan to buy an existing business you must analyze (a) why the owner wants to sell, (b) the physical condition of the business, (c) the market in which the business exists, (d) the financial condition of the business, and (e) legal aspects of the purchase in order to arrive at a true value of the business.

4 You are buying future profit of the business and how you can capitalize this yearly profit to arrive at a guideline for a fair price.

5 If you ever plan to start a new business, the feasibility study should include investigation of (a) the need for the business, (b) location, (c) market, (d) physical facilities, (e) operations and personnel, and (f) projected financial information.

6 Why you must spend time, effort, and money in investigating business opportunities to lessen the risk of business failure.

ENTREPRENEURIAL PROFILE

Mel Farr

MEL FARR FORD, INC.

For every sports star who makes it big, there are many others who lose out when the limelight fades. Bad management skills, drugs, naive investments—these are only a few of the pitfalls. But Mel Farr, Former All-American halfback for UCLA and star runner for the Detroit Lions, stutter-stepped away from those things.

Mel Farr Ford, Inc., in Oak Park, Michigan, is one of the largest car dealers in America, ranked 37 of the nation's top 100 black-owned businesses by *Black Enterprise.* But Farr does not forget a helping hand.

"When SBA granted my loan, it was the very key to what I needed at that time," Farr recalled. "Without it, I more than likely would have had to postpone or even forget about my dream of becoming an automobile dealer."

Retail car sales were bleak in the late 1970s. Mel Farr Ford, Inc., was born at that time (1978), and in two years the company had sustained severe losses and employees were halved in number, to 45.

But in 1980, the SBA made an auto dealer loan of $200,000 to Farr, when sales were $6 million. Today there are two more Mel Farr dealerships (Lincoln-Mercurys) in Detroit and Aurora, Colorado, and aggregate sales are $52 million. There are 140 employees.

Farr out!

Source: Small Business Administration, *Network* (Washington, D.C.: SBA, January–February, 1988).

The entrepreneur has many decisions to make once he or she decides to become engaged in a small business venture. One of the first—and one of the most important—decisions is whether to start a new business or buy an existing business. The answer to this question may vary in each case, and there are many factors to consider.

This chapter investigates the advantages and disadvantages of both buying an existing firm and starting a new one. In addition, the chapter provides an overview of the information needed to arrive at a realistic decision when buying an existing firm or starting a new one.

In some respects, information required for buying or starting a business and the methods of obtaining this information pertain to the entire field of small business management. Consequently, specific knowledge and methods of obtaining information are contained throughout the entire book. Therefore, this chapter serves as an overview and introduction to the knowledge necessary to perform adequate investigation for purchasing an existing business or starting a new one.

BUY AN EXISTING BUSINESS

There are both advantages and disadvantages to buying an existing business. If the small business entrepreneur decides to buy an existing business, there are many things he or she must investigate and analyze about the business if he or she is to make a good purchase decision.

Advantages of Buying an Existing Business

There are several factors that may make an existing business an attractive purchase.

1. It is a proven business, which reduces the risk and often makes it easier to finance.
2. The business often has well-established customer goodwill.
3. Lines of supply and credit have already been established.
4. Employees have already been hired and trained.
5. The physical facilities are sometimes available for rent rather than purchase, which reduces the amount of capital necessary to buy the business.
6. Sometimes it is difficult to find potential buyers for business firms because of lack of skills, lack of interest, or lack of capital. Consequently, one may find an existing business that is being sold at a very low price relative to the value of the business. This is often true of manufacturing firms, which are sometimes sold far below the replacement value of the building, machinery, and equipment.
7. Equipment and inventory are already on hand. There is no need to find vendors and purchase.
8. Usually, the methods and systems of operation have already been created, the "bugs" are worked out, and they are running.

Disadvantages of Buying an Existing Business

There are also factors that may make an existing business unattractive as a purchase.

1. The business may be offered for sale because it is losing money. The buyer of an existing business must be very careful to determine the

true reason why the business is being sold. The reason the seller gives may not be the real reason.

2. Customer, supplier, and creditor ill will, rather than goodwill, may have been established and may carry over to the new owner.

3. The employees working in the firm may not be desirable employees, and it may be difficult to get rid of them because of unionization or other reasons. Also, firing undesirable employees often has an adverse effect on the morale of good employees in situations where they don't know what to expect when a new owner takes over the business.

4. It may not be the best location for the business.

5. The facilities may not be completely suited to the needs of the business. If remodeling is required, the cost may be excessive.

6. Innovations in the business may be difficult owing to present facilities. For example, the size of the building may prevent the addition of new lines of products that would help sales.

7. There may not be a business for sale of the type you are looking for in a given market, or it may cost an excessive amount of money to purchase.

8. The equipment and inventory may be old, outdated, or in need of repair.

FACTORS TO INVESTIGATE AND ANALYZE

To arrive at a wise purchase decision, the small business entrepreneur must investigate various aspects of the existing business. The entrepreneur must analyze and evaluate (1) why the owner wants to sell, (2) the physical conditions of the business, (3) the market in which the business exists, (4) the financial condition of the business, and (5) legal aspects of the purchase, in order to arrive at (6) a true value of the business. (See Fig. 4-1.)

Why Does The Owner Want to Sell?

There can exist an almost endless list of reasons why a business is up for sale. Sometimes the reason the seller gives for selling the business is the real reason, and sometimes it is not. The owner may wish to sell because of such reasons as retirement, other business opportunity, or reduction of his business activities. On the other hand, the owner may wish to sell because the business is losing money; there is a continued trend of decreasing sales, new competition, and legal problems; or excessive effort is required for the level of profit being produced.

When the reasons for selling are factors that will ultimately mean the failure of the firm, the reason given for selling is usually not the real motivation. Few people would volunteer information that would automatically preclude anyone buying the business. For example, one individual looking for a small

FIGURE 4-1
FACTORS TO INVESTIGATE WHEN BUYING AN EXISTING FIRM.

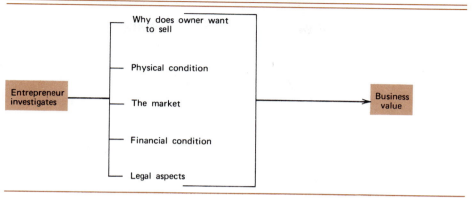

business to buy was offered a small grocery–gasoline store at a price that seemed very reasonable. An income statement provided by the owner indicated a very profitable business. However, a careful examination of sales and purchase records showed the firm to be making much less profit than claimed. In addition, talking to people in the nearby town revealed a new highway was being planned that would eliminate a large part of the store's business.

Rather than end up with a failing business and lost savings, any prospective buyer should expend considerable energy in evaluating the business.

Physical Condition of the Business

The **physical facilities** condition of the business is an important part of the total value of the business and the amount of capital that will be needed in the business.

The age and condition of such items as the building, equipment, and even inventory determine how much money must be spent in addition to the purchase price to get the business in proper operating condition. A buyer who must spend considerable money in remodeling a business should make sure that he or she can obtain the necessary funds when the business is purchased. The buyer must consider the cost of remodeling a part of the total cost of the business.

Old machinery and equipment may have to be replaced soon after the purchase, and the buyer must consider total cost and availability of funds for this before making the purchase. Inadequacy or obsolescence of inventory is also an expense and should be considered. In addition, if the buyer decides to purchase the business, a complete list of all inventory and equipment should be included in the purchase/sale agreement. There have been instances when a person agrees to buy a business at a specific price and then finds, on taking over the business, that the former owner has sold a large part of the inventory without replacing it. This reduction in inventory may represent a loss of thousands of dollars.

The prospective buyer must also evaluate the appearance of the business to determine if it provides an adequate image to customers. For example, a restaurant that is badly in need of paint does not produce an image of cleanliness to customers, and the cost of painting should be considered before purchasing the business.

Another consideration is that of adequacy of equipment. The manufacturing firm that has machinery and equipment that are not efficient and cause high labor costs may not be a good buy. In retail and service firms, the location of the business is an important factor to sales and should be evaluated during the purchasing decision.

The Market

To evaluate the market in which the business exists, the entrepreneur must determine (1) the composition of the population, (2) competition, and (3) attitudes of customers.

Composition of the Population

The first step in analysis of the **composition of the population** is to define the market in terms of where it exists. It may exist as the entire town, a large section of the town, or as a neighborhood. Studying maps, lists of customers, traffic patterns, and **travel times** (this is achieved by traveling major traffic arteries from the store at legal speed limits and marking the time it takes to reach various points on a map) help define the normal market area of the business.

Often looking for natural or psychological **barriers** helps define the **market** for a small business. Expressways, highways, and rivers with few crossings are examples of natural and psychological barriers. Figure 4-2 shows how highway and expressway locations in one town define the market for many small businesses in the area.

Once the market area has been defined, the composition of the population should be determined to help identify the number of potential customers in the market. The following information about the population of the market area should be collected and analyzed.

1. Characteristics of the population—such as income, education, unemployment, ethnic composition, average family size, and size of age groups.
2. The trend of size of the population over the past years.
3. Any significant changes in characteristics of the market area over the past 10 years.

FIGURE 4-2
MARKET BARRIERS IN A CITY AREA.

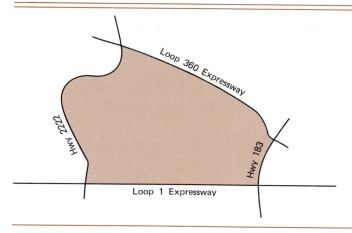

4. Predictions of any future changes in size or characteristics of the market area.
5. Estimation of the number of potential customers for the business from the population data collected.

Some of this information can be found from census tracts in U.S. Bureau of Census publications (found in many public libraries). However, it may be out of date (the census is only taken every 10 years) in areas that are growing or changing.

Sometimes, much of these data are available from local groups, such as city governments, local chambers of commerce, or other civic organizations. In other cases, little or none of the information is available and must be collected by statistical sample techniques (discussed in Chapter 16). Often, this information may be collected at the same time that customer attitude surveys are conducted.

Competition

The prospective buyer should measure competition of the business in the market area by obtaining the following information.

1. How many direct competitors are there in the area (stores of the same type)?
2. How many indirect competitors are there in the area (stores that are different types, but handle some of the same merchandise)?
3. How many competitors have gone out of business in the past five years?

4. How many new competitors have entered the area in the past five years?
5. What is the volume of business of competition in the market area as compared to the store being investigated?
6. What are the pricing policies of the competition?
7. What customer services do competitors offer?
8. What is the extent and effectiveness of the sales effort (including advertising and promotion) of the competition?
9. What is the appearance of the competition? Are their establishments attractive?
10. Identify and rank all competition as either strong or weak.
11. Is there any information concerning the possibility of future competition?

Most of this information concerning competition can be obtained by either direct observation or by talking to merchants and people in the marketing area. Many competitors will answer some questions themselves.

Customer Attitudes

The **attitude** of previous and current **customers** of the business is important to the prospective buyer. Goodwill of customers has value and definitely affects the purchase price of the business. A negative attitude, on the other hand, decreases the value of the business and should be studied to determine if the new owner can reverse these opinions.

The prospective buyer should perform a sample survey of people in the market area to obtain information about their attitudes toward the business. Often, this can be one of the most important types of information the buyer can obtain because it identifies actions that should be taken if the business is purchased. A discussion of the method of taking statistical **customer attitude surveys** is found in Chapter 16. A sample customer attitude survey device is presented in Chapter 18.

Financial Condition of the Business

There are several financial areas of the business that should be investigated. Some of the questions that should be answered are

1. What has been the trend of profit and cash flow over the past 10 years?
2. Has profit been consistent each year or are there wide fluctuations in profit?
3. What has been the trend of sales for past years?
4. Are assets valued realistically in the balance sheet? Significant amounts of intangible assets (goodwill, organization costs, etc.) and unrealistic depreciation may distort the true value of the assets.

5. Will there be sufficient funds after the purchase to meet current expenses and debt?
6. Are the expenses listed in the income statement realistic, or are there some that could be eliminated without harming the business?
7. Do you feel the profit record of the business is in line with the purchase price?

The prospective purchaser of the business should insist on at least the previous five years' (1) balance sheets, (2) income statements, (3) income tax returns, and (4) cash flow statements (accounting statement analysis is discussed in Chapter 13). Unfortunately, many small business firms do not maintain cash flow statements (Chapter 13) in spite of the fact that it is so important to a prospective buyer. However, cash flow statements can be almost always created from the records of the firm by an accountant if adequate records have been kept. The wise buyer will have this function performed by an accountant.

The wise buyer should also remember that the accounting statements provided by the seller may not be correct because of error or dishonesty. In addition, the income tax return is only a copy of the original and may not be accurate. The buyer (or preferably his or her accountant) should verify at the least the latest year of each different statement by examining sales, expenditures, and inventory records. The buyer should rely heavily on his or her accountant for the anaysis of the **financial condition** of the business.

Legal Aspects

There can be many **legal aspects** to consider when a business is being investigated for possible purchase. Some of these are

1. The prospective buyer should investigate evidence of ownership of the business. It is wise to purchase title insurance because the title insurance company will conduct a complete search of legal records to make sure the buyer receives a clear title.
2. Is the business location zoned properly? Sometimes, businesses are in existence when zoning is created by the community, and they are allowed to continue in a nonconforming status. The nonconforming status prohibits additions to the business and can be a serious block to growth of the business.
3. Are there any liens or liabilities outstanding against the business that will be assumed by the new owner?
4. Does the business have the required licenses and permits and will these be available in the future?
5. Are patents, trademarks, copyrights, and trade names protected under the law? Can an adequate defense of these be made if contested? (Defense of these must be made in court by the holder if contested.)

6. Does the firm have any exclusive dealerships, and do they pass on to the new owner? When do these agreements expire, and what are the terms of the agreements?
7. Does the firm have a union contract, and what does it specify?
8. Does the business have employment agreements with any other person or persons?
9. Obtain copies of all leases on buildings, equipment, and so forth, and study the terms of the leases.
10. Does the firm have any pending litigation against it?
11. Does the firm have any existing commitments?
12. Require the seller to sign an agreement that prohibits the seller from future competition with the buyer for a reasonable number of years.

The prospective buyer must obtain complete information about all legal aspects concerning the business because failure to do so can result in loss of thousands of dollars or even failure of the business.

VALUE OF THE BUSINESS

All previously discussed areas of investigation make a definite contribution to the value of a business. However, they contribute to the value of the business by helping determine the future profitability of the business. A prospective buyer, in reality, is buying the future profit of the firm. In a very real sense, future profit is the **return on investment** in money, time, and effort.

A fair return on investment is also dependent to some degree on the amount of risk sustained. For example, a person might receive 10 percent interest on a money market account in a savings and loan association. The risk is relatively low because the account is insured by a federal government agency. Investment in most small business firms is usually much more risky than a money market account.

The **capitalization** (determining the value of a business firm from the amount of yearly profit) of the yearly profit of a firm usually varies between four and eight times the yearly profit figure (this would be from 12.5 percent to 25 percent return on investment). Consequently, a firm that was expected to produce a profit of $20,000 per year should reasonably expect to bring a price of between $80,000 and $160,000, depending on the degree of risk involved. Of course, price is established by the buyer and the seller, and what is paid often has no relationship to this capitalization guideline. However, a wise buyer will generally follow this guideline on future profit expectations in determining what price the buyer is willing to pay.

Probably the most common method of determining the price of an existing business is value of its assets. This is usually done by (1) estimating the current market value, (2) taking the book value of the assets in the balance sheet, or (3) estimating what it would cost to replace the assets. The capitalization of profit is a more realistic method of determining price for the buyer, but the buyer or seller may want to use value of assets in price negotiations in an attempt to get the best price possible.

Many prospective buyers do not expend the time, effort, and money necessary to evaluate the purchase of a business adequately. This is definitely a mistake. It is far better to expend some time, effort, and money to make sure that the buyer is getting a fair deal than to take a chance that the purchase will turn out all right. If the prospective buyer does not perform an adequate analysis, the individual stands a strong chance of losing savings and being in debt for some period of time in the future. An analysis also helps the buyer operate the business more effectively once it is purchased because there is a considerable amount of information on which to base operating decisions. The buyer should be conservative and realistic in the analysis. In addition, the buyer should avoid being unrealistic about what can be done to improve the business.

Many people who buy or start a business want to do so very badly and as a result take a "best case scenario" toward the business. Buying or starting a business is certainly no time for self-deception. A conservative and "eyes open" approach is always a must for the entrepreneur. The authors never cease to be amazed at the businesses some people start or buy. Ones that have no chance of being a success. Businesses that even the most inexperienced novice should recognize as being immediate failures. These entrepreneurs want to start the business so much that they talk themselves into believing other than what is obvious.

START A NEW BUSINESS

Starting a new business also has advantages and disadvantages. Starting a new business also requires extensive investigation and analysis if the business is to have the best chance of success.

Advantages of Starting a New Business

Factors that may make it attractive to start a new business rather than purchase an existing business are these.

1. Location is many times one of the most critical decisions for a business firm. It can be the difference between success and failure in many businesses. Often the only way to obtain the best location is to start a new business.
2. Physical facilities can be constructed to conform to the most efficient use for the business planned. Existing buildings seldom can be arranged to provide the most efficient work flow possible, particularly in manufacturing firms, without having wasted space.

After three years of hard work in their kitchens, in food labs, and with people from all across the country, Richard and Randye Worth, creators of R. W. Frookies, have created a cookie that is not only healthy but tastes great. To capitalize on the health consciousness trend, these cookies are naturally sweetened with fruit juices and contain no cholesterol or sugar. They are high in dietary fiber, low in sodium, and contain only 45 calories per cookie.

3. Innovating in a new business is much easier than in an existing one because of physical limitations of the existing business.
4. All phases of the new business can be established by the owner without having to change something as when buying an existing business.
5. Existing businesses sometimes have ill will of some customers, suppliers, creditors, and employees. The existing business may also have an image (such as a price image) that the new owner does not want. Starting a new business allows the entrepreneur to establish whatever image is desired.
6. In many cases, there just are not any businesses of the type that fit the capabilities of an entrepreneur. Consequently, the only alternative left is to start one.
7. When purchasing an existing business, the buyer usually pays for the profitability of the firm. Sometimes a new firm can be established for less money and still realize the same profit.

Disadvantages of Starting a New Business

Factors that make it undesirable to start a new business rather than buy an existing business are

1. There is a higher risk factor in starting a new business.
2. It often takes considerable time and expenditures of funds for a new business to build its customer patronage.
3. Funds are usually harder to obtain to start a new business than to buy an existing, successful firm.
4. It usually takes time to work out the "bugs" in a new business, both in facilities and procedures.
5. Lines of credit and supply must be established.
6. An existing business has sales, expenditures, and profit records to help project future profit. These must be estimated when starting a new business. This makes them much less accurate and dependable.

THE FEASIBILITY STUDY—THE BUSINESS PLAN

Investigation and analysis of a new business is much more difficult and much less accurate than studying the purchase of an existing firm. Past records of the business operations with which to make evaluations of the business are not available. The **feasibility study** or business plan should include investigation of (1) the need for the business, (2) location, (3) market, (4) physical facilities, (5) operations and personnel, and (6) projected financial information. (See Fig. 4-3).

FIGURE 4-3
FACTORS TO INVESTIGATE WHEN STARTING A NEW BUSINESS.

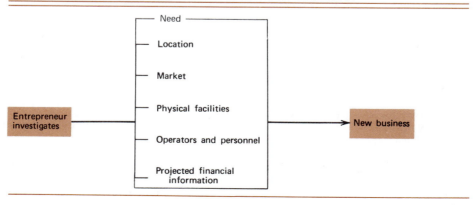

CHECKLIST FOR STARTING A NEW BUSINESS

Check if answer is yes

Check if answer is yes

Are You the Type?

Have you rated your personal qualifications? _____

Have you carefully considered your weak points and taken steps to improve them or to find an associate whose strong points will compensate for them? _____

What Business Should You Choose?

Have you written a summary of your background and experience to help you in making this decision? _____

Have you considered your hobbies and what you would like to do? _____

Does anyone want the services you can perform? _____

Have you studied surveys and/or sought advice and counsel to find out what fields of business may be expected to expand? _____

Have you considered working for someone else to gain more experience? _____

What Are Your Chances for Success?

Are general business conditions good? _____

Are business conditions good in the city and neighborhood where you plan to locate? _____

Are current conditions good in the line of business you plan to start? _____

What Will Be Your Return on Investment?

Do you know the typical return on investment in the line of business you plan to start? _____

Have you determined how much you will have to invest in your business? _____

Are you satisfied that the rate of return on the money you invest in the business will be greater than the rate you would probably receive if you invested the money elsewhere? _____

How Much Money Will You Need?

Have you filled out worksheets similar to those shown in Chapter 5 of this book? _____

In filling out the worksheets have you taken care not to overestimate income? _____

Have you obtained quoted prices for equipment and supplies you will need? _____

Do you know the costs of goods which must be in your inventory? _____

Have you estimated expenses only after checking rents, wage scales, utility, and other pertinent costs in the areas where you plan to locate? _____

Have you found what percentage of your estimated sales your projected inventory and each expense item is and compared each percentage with the typical percentage for your line of business? _____

Have you added an additional amount of money to your estimates to allow for unexpected contingencies? _____

Where Can You Get the Money?

Have you counted up how much money of your own you can put into the business? _____

Do you know how much credit you can get from your suppliers—the people you will buy from _____

Do you know where you can borrow the rest of the money you need to start your business? _____

Have you selected a progressive bank with the credit services you may need? _____

Have you talked to a banker about your plans? _____

Does the banker have an interested, helpful attitude toward your problems? _____

Should You Share Ownership with Others?

If you need a partner with money or know-how that you don't have, do you know someone who will fit—someone you can get along with? _____

Check if answer is yes

Do you know the good and bad points about going it alone, having a partner, and incorporating your business? _____

Have you talked to a lawyer about it? _____

Where Should You Locate?

Have you studied the makeup of the population in the city or town where you plan to locate? _____

Do you know what kind of people will want to buy what you plan to sell? _____

Do people like that live in the area where you want to locate? _____

Have you checked the number, type, and size of competitors in the area? _____

Does the area need another business like the one you plan to open? _____

Are employees available? _____

Have you checked and found adequate: utilities, parking facilities, police and fire protection, available housing, schools, and other cultural and community activities? _____

Do you consider costs of the location reasonable in terms of taxes and average rents? _____

Is there sufficient opportunity for growth and expansion? _____

Have you checked the relative merits of the various shopping areas within the city, including shopping centers? _____

In selecting the actual site, have you compared it with others by using a score sheet similar to the one shown in Chapter 7? _____

Have you had a lawyer check the lease and zoning? _____

Should You Buy a Going Business?

Have you considered the advantages and disadvantages of buying a going business? _____

Have you compared what it would cost to equip and stock a new business with the price asked for the business you are considering buying? _____

How Much Should You Pay for It?

Have you estimated future sales and profits of the going business for the next few years? _____

Are your estimated future profits satisfactory? _____

Check if answer is yes

Have you looked at past financial statements of the business to find the return on investment, sales, and profit trends? _____

Have you verified the owner's claims about the business with reports from an independent account's analysis of the figures? _____

Is the inventory you will purchase a good buy? _____

Are equipment and fixtures fairly valued? _____

If you plan to buy the accounts receivable, are they worth the asking price? _____

Have you been careful in your appraisal of the company's goodwill? _____

Are you prepared to assume the company's liabilities, and are the creditors agreeable? _____

Have you learned why the present owner wants to sell? _____

Have you found out about the present owner's reputation with his or her employees and suppliers? _____

Have you consulted a lawyer to be sure that the title is good? _____

Has your lawyer checked to find out if there is any lien against the assets you are buying? _____

Has your lawyer drawn up an agreement covering all essential points including a seller's warranty for your protection against false statements? _____

Should You Invest in a Franchise?

Have you considered how the advantages and disadvantages of franchising apply to you? _____

Have you made a thorough search to find the right franchise opportunity? _____

Have you evaluated the franchise? _____

Have You Worked Out Plans for Buying?

Have you estimated what share of the market you think you can get? _____

Do you know how much or how many of each item of merchandise you will buy to open your business? _____

Have you found suppliers who will sell what you need at a good price? _____

Do you have a plan for finding out what your customers want? _____

Have you worked out a model stock assortment to follow in your buying? _____ *Check if answer is yes*

Have you set up stock control plans to avoid overstocks, understocks, and out-of-stocks? _____

Do you plan to buy most of your stock from a few suppliers rather than a little from many, so that those you buy from will want to help you succeed? _____

How Will You Price Your Products and Services?

Have you decided upon your price ranges? _____

Do you know how to figure what you should charge to cover your costs? _____

Do you know what your competitors charge? _____

What Selling Methods Will You Use?

Have you studied the selling and sales promotion methods of competitors? _____

Have you studied why customers buy your type of product or service? _____

Have you thought about why you like to buy from some salespeople whereas others turn you off? _____

Have you decided what your methods of selling will be? _____

Have you outlined your sales promotion policy? _____

How Will You Select and Train Personnel?

If you need to hire someone to help you, do you know where to look? _____

Do you know what kind of person you need? _____

Have you written a job description for each person you will need? _____

Do you know the prevailing wage scales? _____

Do you have a plan for training new employees? _____

Will you continue training through good supervision? _____

What Other Managmeent Problems Will You Face?

Do you plan to sell for credit? _____

If you do, do you have the extra capital necessary to carry accounts receivable? _____

Have you made a policy for returned goods? _____

Have you planned how you will make deliveries? _____

Have you considered other policies that must be made in your particular business? _____ *Check if answer is yes*

Have you made a plan to guide yourself in making the best use of your time and effort? _____

What Records Will You Keep?

Have you planned a system of records that will keep track of your income and expenses, what you owe other people, and what other people owe you? _____

Have you worked out a way to keep track of your inventory so that you will always have enough on hand for your customers but not more than you can sell? _____

Have you planned on how to keep your payroll records and take care of tax reports and payments? _____

Do you know what financial statements you should prepare? _____

Do you know how to use these financial statements? _____

Have you obtained standard operating ratios for your type of business that you plan to use as guidelines? _____

Do you know an accountant who will help you with your records and financial statements? _____

What Laws Will Affect You?

Have you checked with the proper authorities to find out what, if any, licenses to do business are necessary? _____

Do you know what police and health regulations apply to your business? _____

Will your operations be subject to interstate commerce regulations? If so, do you know to which ones? _____

Have you received advice from your lawyer regarding your responsibilities under federal and state laws and local ordinances? _____

How Will You Handle Taxes and Insurance?

Have you worked out a system for handling the withholding tax for your employees? _____

Have you worked out a system for handling sales taxes? excise taxes? _____

	Check if answer is yes		Check if answer is yes
Have you planned an adequate record system for the efficient preparation of income tax forms?	——	Are the goals specific so that you can measure performance?	——
Have you prepared a work sheet for meeting tax obligations?	——	Have you developed a business plan, using one of the SBA aids to record your ideas, facts, and figures?	——
Have you talked with an insurance agent about what kinds of insurance you will need and how much it will cost?	——	Have you allowed for obstacles?	——

Will You Set Measurable Goals for Yourself?

Will You Keep Up to Date?

	Check if answer is yes		Check if answer is yes
Have you set goals and subgoals for yourself?	——	Have you made plans to keep up with improvements in your trade or industry?	——
Have you specified dates when each goal is to be achieved?	——	Have you prepared a business plan that will be amended as circumstances demand?	——
Are these realistic goals; that is, will they challenge you but at the same time not call for unreasonable accomplishments?	——		

Source: Small Business Administration, *Starting and Managing a Small Business of your Own* (Washington, D.C.: SBA).

As mentioned earlier, methods and sources of collecting information concerning areas of the feasibility study are discussed in detail in many chapters of this book. The following discussion of the information needed in a feasibility study is intended to give an overview of some of the information an entrepreneur must analyze to arrive at a realistic evaluation of the proposed firm's chances of success. This information is also necessary for good planning and successful establishment of the business. It should also be noted that much of the information needed for a feasibility study of a new business is related to the information needed to evaluate the purchase of an existing firm.

Need for the Business

The entrepreneur should determine if there is a need for the business in the market area. If there is not sufficient demand, there will not be enough income for the firm to be profitable.

Usually, the most efficient way to estimate how much income the business will receive is to perform a marketing research survey in the market area (Chapter 16). A survey device that asks people where they trade, why they trade there, how much they spend on the product or service, and other related questions will allow the entrepreneur to estimate potential sales for the new firm. The entrepreneur can evaluate each survey response to estimate if the firm can "take away" the business from the source potential customers are currently using. By projecting the total dollar volume of business from the sample survey to the total number of customers in the area, the entrepreneur

FIGURE 4-4
NATIONAL AVERAGE OF NUMBER OF INHABITANTS PER STORE BY TYPE OF BUSINESS, RETAIL AND SERVICE.

Kind of Business	Number of Inhabitants per Store
RETAIL	
Building Materials, Hardware, Garden Supply, and Mobile Home Dealers	
Building materials and supply stores	5,339
Hardware stores	8,008
Retail nurseries, lawn and garden supply stores	26,028
Mobile home dealer	20,823
General Merchandise Group Stores	
Department stores	26,029
Variety stores	9,465
Food Stores	
Grocery stores	1,073
Meat, fish stores	12,248
Fruit stores and vegetable markets	26,028
Candy, nut, and confectionery stores	16,018
Retail bakeries	10,959
Automotive Dealers	
Motor vehicle dealers, new and used cars	6,407
Motor vehicle dealers, used cars only	6,548
Auto and home supply stores	5,480
Gasoline Service Stores	921
Apparel and Accesory Stores	
Women's clothing	5,368
Men's and boy's clothing and furnishing stores	9,053
Family clothing stores	11,568
Shoe stores	7,712
Furniture, Home Furnishings, and Equipment Stores	
Furniture and home furnishings stores	3,107
Household appliance stores	10,411
Radio, television, and music stores	6,941
Eating and Drinking places	
Eating places	823
Drinking places (alcoholic beverages)	1,964
Drugstores and Proprietary Stores	4,004
Miscellaneous Retail Stores	
Liquor stores	4,957
Used merchandise stores	6,310
Automatic merchandising machine operators	16,017
Fuel and ice dealers	10,412

FIGURE 4-4
(CONTINUED)

Kind of Business	Number of Inhabitants per Store
Florists	8,676
Cigar stores and stands	52,058
Sporting goods stores and bicycle shops	9,053
Bookstores	26,028
Stationery stores	34,705
Jewelry stores	8,329
Hobby, toy, and game shops	20,823
Camera and photographic supply stores	41,646
Gift, novelty, and souvenir stores	8,465
Luggage and leather goods stores	115,683
Sewing, needlework, and piece goods stores	11,568

SERVICE

Hotels, Motels, Trailer Parks, Camps

Hotels	14,873
Motels	4,658
Sporting and recreational camps	28,920
Trailering parks and campsites for transients	15,199

Personal Services

Coin-operated laundries and dry cleaning	6,589
Photographic studios, portrait	6,948
Beauty shops	1,101
Barber shops	2,263
Shoe repair, shoeshine, and hat cleaning	16,141
Funeral service and crematories	9,963

Automotive Repair, Services, and Garages

General automotive repair shops	2,896
Top and body repairs shops	6,548
Automotive rental and leasing	19,869
Automotive parking	19,812

Miscellaneous Repair Services

Radio and television repair shops	5,983
Reupholstery and furniture repair	8,499

Amusement and Recreation Services

Motion picture production, distribution, services	24,326
Motion picture theaters	16,396
Billiard and pool establishments	35,594
Bowling alleys	24,643

Dental Laboratories — 24,383

Legal Services — 1,442

Source: Computed from Bureau of Census publications.

can obtain an estimated sales volume for the proposed business. However, the entrepreneur should remember that the answer obtained is no better than the survey device, the sampling technique, the size of the sample, and the accuracy of the judgment used to estimate the amount of "take away" on each sample.

Also the entrepreneur can obtain the total number of inhabitants in the market area from census tract information or city government information and compare it to the national average of number of inhabitants per store shown in Figure 4-4. Using the total number of inhabitants in the market area, the national average number of inhabitants per store, and the number and quality of competitors in the area will provide an estimate of the need for the new business.

Location

Selection of the site for the business will usually require information that will include

1. Determining who your customers are and what causes them to buy the products of services, or both, you plan to offer. For example, if you were going to sell imprinted tee shirts, you would know that most of your customers would be below 35 years of age and generally buy this product on impulse. Consequently, the best location for your store would be in a high customer traffic area. A mall that was visited by a high percentage of young people would be an ideal site. Also, comparing the characteristics of your customers (age, education, income, etc.) with the distribution of these characteristics in city areas would show which areas would provide the most customers. Generally, retail, service, and wholesale businesses and manufacturers like to locate as near as is practical to their customers.

2. Determining who your potential competitors are, how effective they are, and where they are located. A comparison of the areas that have the most customers with areas that have the most competition will provide insight into which is the best area for your new business.

3. Deciding to build, buy an existing building, or rent based on the needs of the business, the amount of capital available, and the availability of adequate sites and structures.

4. Listing all available sites and their cost. Local realtors are a good source of this information. Location site is often a trade-off between desirability of site, cost, and available capital.

5. Identifying the major traffic arteries.

6. Making a traffic survey of automobiles and pedestrians (depending on the type of business) at the best sites.

7. Getting zoning information from the city on the various possible sites.

The Market

In many types of business, selection of a good location also depends to a large degree on the market. Some of the information that should be collected and analyzed includes the following.

1. Population size and characteristics (income, education, age groups, etc.).
2. Projections of population size and characteristic changes in future years.
3. Number, effectiveness, and characteristics of competition in the market.
4. A statistical customer survey. As discussed earlier, such a survey should be conducted in the selected market area to determine where and why people currently buy products or services the new business will offer.

Physical Facilities

If the decision is to build, rather than to rent or to purchase an existing building, the following information must be acquired.

1. Determine work flow and layout of equipment.
2. Determine building specifications and type of construction.
3. Establish amount of parking space needed based on number of employees and customers. Cities usually require a minimum number of parking spaces based on the type of business and size of the building.
4. Identify the type of and access to loading and unloading facilities needed by the business.
5. Based on the type of business, arrive at the type and cost of equipment needed.
6. Obtain city building requirements.
7. Design a floor plan for the business.

Operations and Personnel

Information needed to arrive at operations and personnel planning includes the following.

1. Create job descriptions for all personnel needed in the business.
2. Draw up an organization chart showing lines of authority and responsibility.

3. Set a salary schedule for each job position based on current wage rates in the community.
4. Establish a work schedule showing hours and days worked for each position.
5. Establish a list of products to be carried with the amount of each that will be carried in initial inventory.
6. Determine sources of supply from all inventory items.
7. Determine if there will be any seasonal patterns of sales or if there will be seasonal items carried in inventory.
8. Establish price policies for all merchandise. Determine markups and obtain prices of competitors.
9. Create a plan for opening promotion and advertising.
10. Establish policies for amount and type of advertising to be conducted regularly after opening.

Projected Financial Information

Using the information gathered in the previous investigations creates the following financial information.

1. Create a projected budget for the first year of operation. Try to estimate all income and expense items as accurately as possible.
2. Create a projected balance sheet based on all assets you have determined the business will need plus all debts you plan to incur as a result of financing.
3. Create a projected cash flow statement for the first year's operation using income, expense, asset, and financing data.
4. If possible, draw a breakeven chart. (See Fig. 4-5.)
5. Determine your source of funds by contacting banks and other financial sources listed in Chapter 5.

The financial statements in Chapter 11 can be used as guides for the projected budget, projected balance sheet, and projected cash flow statement.

The breakeven chart is drawn by calculating sales revenue and costs at various levels. In the example, the number of units sold is multiplied by the selling price to determine the total dollars of revenue. Fixed costs are those costs that are sustained no matter how many units are sold. This figure would include such items as depreciation and insurance on plant and equipment. Variable costs increase as the number of units sold increases. They include such items as direct labor and raw material costs. The amount of these costs is computed at various levels of number of units sold. The breakeven point is the point at which the cost and sales lines cross.

For example, suppose a manufacturer had the following costs.

Fixed Costs (yearly)		Variable Costs (per unit)	
Plant and equipment depreciation	$30,000	Direct labor	$.4000
Utilities, taxes, and insurance	5,000	Raw materials and supplies	.2667
Office expenses	5,000	Variable cost per unit	$.6667
Total yearly fixed costs	$40,000		

Selling price for each unit of production is $2 per unit.

Figure 4-5 illustrates what this firm's breakeven analysis would look like. Sales at 30,000 units would cost $40,000 in fixed costs and $20,000 in variable costs, for a total of $60,000. Sales of 30,000 units at $2 each would produce revenue of $60,000. Therefore, if the firm produces and sells 30,000 units, it will not incur a loss or a profit.

As with the investigation of buying an existing business, the feasibility study for establishing a new business requires the expenditure of time, effort, and money. However, this expenditure of time, effort, and money greatly

FIGURE 4-5
A BREAKEVEN CHART.

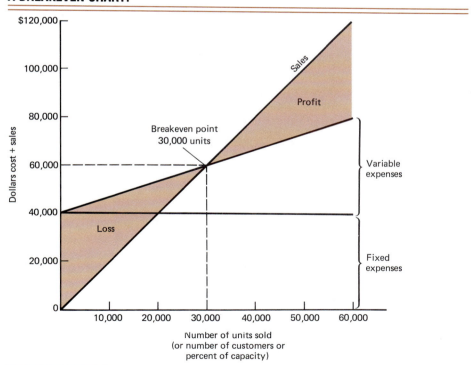

enhances the chances of success for the new firm. If a feasibility study is not made, the entrepreneur stands a very real risk that much more time, effort, and money will be lost as a result of failure of the business. Very few entrepreneurs perform adequate feasibility studies. If they did, the high failure rate of new business firms during the first year of operation would be reduced drastically. Most of the waste of business failure could be avoided.

SUMMARY OF KEY POINTS

1. The advantages of buying an existing business are (a) proven business, (b) established customer goodwill, (c) lines of supply and credit established, (d) employees hired and trained, (e) possibility of renting facilities, (f) possibility of being sold at low price because of lack of buyers, and (g) methods of operation and system in place.

2. The disadvantages of buying an existing business are (a) the prospective business may be losing money; (b) business may be curtailed by customer, supplier, and creditor ill will; (c) employees may not be good employees and may have a union; location may not be good; (e) facilities may not be adequate; (f) innovations may be difficult; and (g) a suitable business may not be for sale.

3. The factors to investigate in buying a new business are (a) why does the owner want to sell, (b) physical conditions, (c) the market, (d) financial condition, and (e) legal aspects.

4. The market analysis should include an analysis of the composition of the population, competition, and customer attitudes.

5. The value of the business usually should be computed by capitalizing the profit of the business. A general guideline is from four to eight times the yearly profit.

6. The advantages of starting a new business are (a) one can select best location, (b) facilities are constructed to needs of business, (c) innovating is easier, (d) all phases of the business can be established by the owner, (e) there is no existing ill will, (f) it fits the capabilities of the owner, and (g) a new business may cost less for the same amount of profit.

7. The disadvantages of starting a new business are (a) higher risk factor, (b) time and funds needed to build customer patronage, (c) funds usually harder to obtain, (d) time to work out "bugs" in business, (e) lines of credit and supply must be established, and (f) lack of sales, expenditure, and profit records.

8. The feasibility study should include (a) need for business, (b) location, (c) market, (d) physical facilities, (e) operations and personnel, and (f) projected financial information.

9. A breakeven chart shows sales, fixed expenses, variable expenses, loss, and profit at various levels of units sold (can be number of customers or percentage capacity). The location where the sales and cost lines cross is the breakeven point.

DISCUSSION QUESTIONS

1. Give three advantages and disadvantages of buying an existing business firm.

2. Why would an owner want to sell his or her small business?

3. What would be some factors of population in the market area you would want to investigate when deciding whether or not to buy an existing business firm?

4. What are some legal aspects to look for when buying an existing business?

5. How does a small business entrepreneur determine the value of an existing firm he or she plans to buy?

6. Give three advantages and disadvantages of starting a new business.

7. How should a person go about deciding whether or not to start a new business?

8. Why should a person spend time, money, and effort investigating the purchase of an existing business or the feasibility of starting a new business?

THE BUSINESS PLAN: BUY AN EXISTING FIRM

The business plan listed at the end of each chapter in this book is the feasibility study for starting a new business. In addition, the special interest feature ''Checklist for Starting a New Business'' is a type of business plan. In reality, this entire chapter is a type of business plan. Therefore, the business plan for this chapter will feature buying an existing firm.

_____ Why does the owner want to sell? If the business is really making an adequate profit, does the reason given sound reasonable?

Physical Facilities

____ Are the physical facilities adequate for the business you are planning?

____ Will you have to spend money to improve the building, equipment, machinery, inventory, and so on?

____ Do you have sufficient funds to achieve these improvements?

The Market

Composition

____ Have you studied maps, lists of customers, traffic patterns, and travel times to determine the actual market area of the firm?

____ Have you defined the natural and psychological barriers in defining the market area? Do you expect them to change?

____ What are the characteristics of the population in the market area—income, education, unemployment, ethnic composition, average family size, and size of age groups.

____ What has been the trend in population for the past 10 years and what trend do you expect in the future? Watch for factors that would indicate a decrease in population for your business.

____ Estimate the number of potential customers in the market area.

Competition

____ How many direct and indirect competitors are there in the area? Plot them on a map.

____ How many competitors have gone out of business or entered the market area in the past 5 years? Try to find out the reasons for those that went out of business.

____ Compare the volume of business of the competition with the business you are investigating. Try to find out reasons for any differences. Can you change them?

____ What are the pricing policies and customer services of the competition? Do you plan to meet or exceed them?

____ How much effort does the competition put into advertising, promotion, and sales effort? What do you plan to do in each of these areas relative to your competition?

____ How attractive to customers are competitors?

____ Is there any information about possible future competition in the market area?

Customer Attitudes

_____ Do the customers have a positive attitude toward the business? If not, can these attitudes be reversed with reasonable effort? A customer attitude survey will answer these questions.

Financial Condition

_____ What has been the trend of profit and cash flow over the past 10 years?

_____ Have profit and cash flow been consistent?

_____ What has been the trend in sales for the past 10 years?

_____ Are assets valued realistically in the balance sheet? Watch out for large amounts of intangible assets and/or unrealistic depreciation.

_____ Will you have sufficient funds to operate the business after the initial purchase? Consider purchases, current debt, salaries, living expenses, and so on.

_____ Are expenses listed in the income statement realistic? Can you reduce some?

_____ Can you obtain (at least 5 years) balance sheets, income statements, income tax returns, and cash flow statements? If the owner is not willing to provide any of these, you should ask yourself why. You probably will need an accountant.

Legal Aspects

_____ Investigate the evidence of ownership.

_____ Is the business properly zoned?

_____ Are there any liens or debts that will be assumed by you?

_____ Does the business have the required licenses and permits and will they be available to you in the future?

_____ Are any patents, trademarks, copyrights, and trade names defensible in court? Make sure they are transferred to you.

_____ Are any exclusive dealerships or franchises transferrable to you? When do they expire and what are the terms of the agreement?

_____ Is there a union contract and what is in the agreement?

_____ Obtain copies of all leases.

_____ Is there any litigation pending?

_____ Are there any existing commitments of any kind?

_____ Is the seller willing to sign an agreement that prohibits future competition from the seller for a reasonable number of years?

Value

____ Compare the book, market, and replacement value of the assets of the business with the asking price. Use any favorable to you in the price negotiations.

____ Determine the degree of risk of the venture.

____ Multiply the expected yearly profit of the business times a factor that is representative of the risk involved to determine a fair price for you to pay. This factor is normally between four and eight times with a normal range of risk.

ENTREPRENEURIAL PROJECTS

Select a small business in your community, and do the following.

1. Ask the owner if he or she were to sell the business, what price he or she would ask for it.
2. Ask questions to determine, in general, physical conditions of the business, the market, financial condition of the business, and legal aspects of the business.
3. Decide if you would purchase the business, and, if so, set a price that you believe is a fair one. Compare this price with the owner's price.

CASE A
The Hobby Shop

When David Barnes graduated from college, he went to work for a large oil corporation. After 15 years, David has received several promotions and makes a good salary. David has never really liked working for a large corporation and has recently begun to dislike it even more. He has been able to build up a money market account to $80,000 through savings and investments in the stock market. He has been looking at small business opportunities for the last year.

David has been a model builder since his high school days, and one of the businesses he has investigated and liked best is a hobby shop. It is located in a small shopping center, the rent is $1,600 per month, and there are still eight years to go on the long-term lease. The owner claims he has made between $40,000 and $50,000 per year all seven years the store has been open. The hobby shop offers a wide range of models, radio-controlled cars and airplanes, games, and other hobby items. The store has two full-time and three part-time employees. The owner has agreed to turn over all records and train David in the operation of the store.

The owner is 60 years old and has told David he wants to sell the store so he and his wife can move back to a town in another state where they grew up and where all their relatives live.

The owner says he is willing to sell the store for the value of the inventory, fixtures, and furniture. He claims their value to be $100,000. He is willing to accept $70,000 down and a 10-year note for the remaining $30,000 at no interest. David is concerned about the asking price because he estimates the inventory, fixtures, and furniture to worth about $20,000 less. He estimates he could open a new hobby store for $80,000.

Questions

1. What do you think of the reasons the owner gave for selling the business?
2. What are some of the things David should investigate before deciding whether or not to buy the business?
3. If the owner has been making the profit he claims, do you consider his asking price to be fair?
4. If everything checks out as presented by the owner, would you recommend that David purchase the hobby shop, or should he start a new hobby shop?

CASE B
Susie Q

Susan Quintas has been interested in music for many years. She is 26 years old and unmarried and has $150,000 in municipal bonds inherited from an aunt. Susan tried a musical career as a pop singer (Susie Q) for three years after she graduated from the local college. Her singing career never amounted to much, so she decided to try some other career. She would now like to start a stereo store selling medium- and high-quality stereo equipment.

Susan divided the town into five sections based on the location of physical and psychological barriers. She then created a customer questionnaire and hired several college students to conduct a survey. Her survey revealed that customers who bought the most stereo equipment were between the ages of 18 and 35, had incomes of between $15,000 and $35,000, and had a high school or higher education. When medium- and high-quality stereo owners revealed where they had bought their stereo equipment, three stores (we call them X, Y, and Z) accounted for about 72 percent of the sales. Customers listed equipment specifications as the first reason for their selection, with price a close second.

Susan has obtained information from census tracts, the city government, and the local chamber of commerce. She has broken this information down into the five areas of her survey.

Section	Median Income	Average Age	Average Years of Education	Competition	Characteristics of Section
1	$18,000	30	12	Firm X—Discount image	Fastest growing
2	24,000	24	13	Firm Y—High price line	Old, established
3	40,000	38	14	Two minor stores	Old, established
4	12,000	30	13	Firm Z—Discount image	Old, becoming industrial
5	25,000	25	13	Three minor stores	New, growing

Firm Y is located in a shopping mall whereas X and Z are located in stores on major streets. A new shopping mall is being built in Section 5.

Questions

1. Which section of town would you pick in which to locate? Why?
2. Outline the steps Susan must go through to start her store.

KEY WORDS

CHAPTER 5

SOURCES OF FUNDS

LEARNING GOALS

After reading this chapter, you will understand:

1   The difference between short-term capital needs and long-term capital needs.

2   That equity capital comes from personal savings, partners, or sale of stock or from all three.

3   That commercial banks make several different types of loans—traditional bank loans, installment loans, discount accounts receivable, and discount installment contracts—and that they also have lines of credit for business firms.

4   That vendors and equipment manufacturers and distributors finance purchases for small business firms.

5   How factors and sales finance companies finance customer credit for small business firms.

6   That insurance companies and private investors make limited loans to small business.

7   How Small Business Investment Corporations (SBICs) provide funds to small businesses.

8   The many different types of financial assistance the Small Business Administration (SBA) provides small business firms.

9   Who is eligible for an SBA loan and how one goes about applying for such a loan.

10   What sources provide funds for different types of needs.

ENTREPRENEURIAL PROFILE

Stephen Wozniak and Steven Jobs

APPLE COMPUTER

An Apple a day? More like two Apples a minute. By 1987 Apple Computer—in its first decade—had averaged selling 1370 computers a day.

The legend began in 1976 when Stephen Wozniak, 26, a Berkeley college dropout with a passion for computers, collaborated with Steven Jobs, 21, on the *Breakout* video game for Atari, where Jobs worked. When Jobs saw Wozniak's crude, home-built computer kit—Apple I—he was sure they could market it to other hobbyists. He wasn't thinking, then, of the *whole world.*

Wozniak feverishly worked on a superior second computer which, with its keyboard, power supply, ability to generate color graphics, and BASIC programming language in an attractive case, would revolutionize the computer industry. Apple II—which took the computer into the average home—was born.

Apple Computer incorporated in 1977 and moved out of Steve Jobs's parents' garage. The first seed capital came from the proceeds of the sale of Jobs' Volkswagen van and Wozniak's programmable calculator.

Two things happened in a hurry which gave the new company's crazy product invention credibility and explosive profit potential. First, Mike Markkula, an alumnus of Intel who had retired at the ripe old age of 35, joined the firm as chairman, threw in $225,000 of his own money, as well as a business plan. Second, the infusion of approximately $3 million in venture capital gave the green Apple a sizable advantage over struggling competitors. The effect was that of giving one of many miners at the Klondike a sharper pick.

People remember the investors in round

one in early 1977—the legendary venture capitalist Arthur Rock, as well as Capital Management Services. But few corporate heads at Apple today can remember who joined Venrock Associates to spearhead a crucial second round of financing in September 1977.

That was Continental Illinois Venture Corp.—an SBA-backed Small Business Investment Company (SBIC)—which provided $504,000 in equity financing. Apple had just finished its first fiscal year with $774,000 in sales and a modest $42,000 in profit. The company had 63 employees in Cupertino, California.

Only 10 years later, Apple Computer has annual sales of $2.6 billion and employs 6500 people.

In 1980, Apple's initial public stock offering was one of the largest in Wall Street's history, raising $100 million. In 1982, the company donated personal computers and training to 10,000 public and private schools in California in its "Kids Can't Wait" program. The Macintosh and Apple's LaserWriter printer catalyzed desktop publishing in the mid-eighties. Apples are sold in 80 countries.

Today Wozniak and Jobs are gone, with Pepsi-Cola magnate John Sculley wresting the Apple reins in 1985. One thing is for certain—Apple's annual taxes bypassed the SBIC investment figure long ago, and probably left the $4 million SBA needs to run the 307 SBICs annually in the dust!

It's nice to know SBA—and the U.S. taxpayer—helped to grow that giant Apple tree.

Source: Network (Washington, D.C.: Small Business Administration, SBA, March–April, 1988.

The small business failure rate discussed in Chapter 1 indicates that many small business entrepreneurs make fatal mistakes when they start their business. It also indicates that one of the major causes of business failure is lack of sufficient capital when the business is first started. The high failure rate of small businesses also makes it difficult to borrow funds to start a new firm. Knowing the correct amount of capital needed and the possible sources where these funds may be borrowed is extremely important to the small business entrepreneur.

AMOUNT OF CAPITAL, TIME, AND INTEREST RATE

Many small business entrepreneurs mistakenly feel that if they are able to rent a store, purchase equipment, and purchase the initial inventory, they have sufficient funds to start the business. These are major items requiring capital, but they are certainly not all that is required. There are many other costs that require a considerable amount of money. For example, most businesses are not immediately profitable, and the owners must sustain themselves and their families until the business can provide them a living. Also, they may have to finance customer credit until it begins to turn over and produce funds for the business. Figures 5-1 and 5-2 show worksheets that indicate the amount and type of capital that are usually needed by a new business. Please note that the entrepreneur must have funds to cover several months' worth of expenses that recur each month. Most firms sustain greater cash payments than cash receipts during the first several months of operations.

In addition to the list in Figures 5-1 and 5-2, if the owner borrows money to start the business, the owner must also pay back the principal and interest of all loans. The amount of the payments of these loans is very important to the small business owner. It is not uncommon for a small business entrepreneur to establish a business that produces good profit but have it fail because of large monthly payments on loans. What normally would be sufficient profits are drained into repaying the loan.

The amount of the monthly payments is subject to three factors: (1) the total amount of money borrowed, (2) the time in which the loan must be repaid, and (3) the interest rate charged by the lender.

FIGURE 5-1
CAPITAL NEEDS WORKSHEET.

ESTIMATED MONTHLY EXPENSES

Item	Your estimate of monthly expenses based on sales of $_____ per year	Your estimate of how much cash you need to start your business (See Column 3.)	What to put in Column 2 (These figures are typical for one kind of business; you will have to decide how many months to allow for in your business.)
	Column 1	Column 2	Column 3
Salary of owner—manager	$	$	2 times column 1
All other salaries and wages			3 times column 1
Rent			3 times column 1
Advertising			3 times column 1
Delivery expense			3 times column 1
Supplies			3 times column 1
Telephone and telegraph			3 times column 1
Other utilities			3 times column 1
Insurance			Payment required by insurance company
Taxes, including social security			4 times column 1
Interest			3 times column 1
Maintenance			3 times column 1
Legal and other professional fees			3 times column 1
Miscellaneous			3 times column 1

FIGURE 5-1
(CONTINUED)

STARTING COSTS YOU ONLY HAVE TO PAY ONCE

Fixtures and equipment	Column 2	Fill in Figure 5-2 and put the total here
Decorating and remodeling		Talk it over with a contractor
Installation of fixtures and equipment		Talk to suppliers from whom you buy these
Starting inventory		Suppliers will probably help you estimate this
Deposits with public utilities		Find out from utilities companies
Legal and other professional fees		Lawyer, accountant, and so on
Licenses and permits		Find out from city offices what you have to have
Advertising and promotion for opening		Estimate what you'll use
Accounts receivable		What you need to buy more stock until credit customers pay
Cash		For unexpected expenses or losses, special purchases, etc.
Other		Make a separate list and enter total
Total estimated cash you need to start with	$	Add up all the numbers in column 2

Source: *Checklist for Going into Business* Washington, D.C.: Small Business Administration, 1973), p. 7.

FIGURE 5-2
FIXTURES AND EQUIPMENT WORKSHEET.

LIST OF FURNITURE, FIXTURES, AND EQUIPMENT

Leave out or add items to suit your business. Use separate sheets to list exactly what you need for each of the items below.	If you plan to pay cash in full, enter the full amount below and in the last column.	If you are going to pay by installments, fill out the columns below. Enter in the last column your down payment plus at least one installment.			Estimate of the cash you need for furniture, fixtures, and equipment.
		Price	Down Payment	Amount of Each Installment	
Counters	$	$	$	$	$
Storage shelves, cabinets					
Display stands, shelves, tables					
Cash register					
Safe					
Window display fixtures					
Special lighting					
Outside sign					
Delivery equipment if needed					
Total furniture, fixtures, and equipment (Enter this figure also in Fig. 5-1 under "Starting Costs You Only Have to Pay Once.")					$

Source: Checklist for Going into Business (Washington, D.C.: Small Business Administration, 1973), p. 12.

Amount

The more the small business entrepreneur must borrow, the greater the burden it becomes to repay. For example, if the following amounts are borrowed at 12 percent interest for 10 years, the payments will be

Amount	Monthly Payment	Total Interest Paid
$ 10,000	$ 143.47	$ 7,216.40
25,000	358.68	18,041.60
50,000	717.35	36,082.00
100,000	1434.71	72,165.20

Time

The length of time in which the loan must be repaid can be critical to the success of the business. For example, if a small business entrepreneur borrows $50,000 at 12 percent interest to start a business, the following amounts would have to be repaid depending on the length of repayment time:

Time to Repay	Monthly Payment	Total Interest Paid
5 years	$1112.22	$16,733.20
10 years	717.36	36,083.20
15 years	600.08	58,014.40
20 years	550.54	82,129.60

Of course, this does not mean that the small business owner should always take as long to repay a loan as possible. The longer it takes to repay a loan, the more the borrower will pay in interest.

Interest Rate

Interest rates may fluctuate widely over a period of time and have a definite effect on how much an entrepreneur must pay for borrowed money. For example, if an entrepreneur borrows $50,000 to be repaid in 10 years at the following interest rates, the monthly payments and total amount of interest paid on the loan will be these:

Interest Rate	Monthly Payment	Total Interest Paid
10%	$660.75	$29,290.00
12%	717.35	36,082.00
14%	776.33	43,159.60
16%	837.57	50,508.40

Variable interest rates are a method of calculating interest payments. A method of determining interest rates for a specific period of time, such as the prime interest rate at a six-month or year period, is used. For example, the mortgage might specify two points above the prime interest rate on a specific date each year. If the interest rate is 14 percent because the prime interest rate on January 1 was 12 percent, it would drop to 12 percent the next year if the prime rate drops to 10 percent.

FIGURE 5-3
FACTORS THAT INCREASE LOAN PAYMENTS.

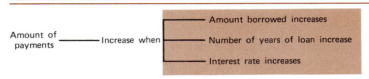

Amount of payments —— Increase when
- Amount borrowed increases
- Number of years of loan increase
- Interest rate increases

Refinancing is another popular device to lower interest rates in years of lower interest rates. Suppose a firm signs a mortgage note with a 14 percent interest rate. If the interest rates drop to 10 percent, the firm would find it less expensive to sign a new mortgage note at 10 percent and use the money to pay off the old mortgage note.

Of course, all three factors together determine the payment amount. For example, borrowing a smaller sum of money for a longer period of time than planned could still result in the same payment amount. (See Fig. 5-3.)

SOURCES OF EQUITY CAPITAL

Equity capital (ownership) may come from personal savings, from partners, or by selling stock in a corporation. The best and most common source of funds to start a business is from a person's own savings. As a general rule, most small business authorities suggest that the small business entrepreneur provide at least 50 percent of the starting funds in the form of equity capital. Usually, any amount under 50 percent requires a level of borrowing that creates payments that are extremely difficult, if not impossible, to meet.

If small business entrepreneurs do not have sufficient equity capital themselves, they may consider taking in partners or selling stock in a corporation. They may take in general or limited partners, but they must remember that they may have to give up some control over the businesses. If they incorporate and sell stock, they obtain the features of the corporation form of ownership (which may or may not be good for them), and they may have to give up some control of their businesses. In addition, if they decide to add partners or sell stock, they must be sure that there will be sufficient profits in the business to sustain themselves while providing funds for the equity investors.

Venture capital has become an increasing source of equity funds for new business ventures. Venture capital individuals or firms supply funds for new firms in exchange for a percentage ownership of the new business. This source of equity capital has been popular in business start-ups involving new technology.

SOURCES OF DEBT CAPITAL

Possible sources of **debt capital** (borrowed funds) for the small business entrepreneur are commercial banks, vendors, equipment manufacturers and distributors, factors, sales finance companies, insurance companies, private investors, Small Business Investment Corporations, and the Small Business Administration.

Commercial Banks

Commercial banks are primarily a source of **short-term loans.** In fact, they lend more short-term funds than any other type of financial institution.

The bank receives both demand (checking accounts) and savings deposits from its customers and lends out a percentage of these deposits to businesses and individuals. Generally, five years is the maximum length of time of any loan made by a commercial bank and usually the loan doesn't exceed three years. However, banks do participate in loans with the Small Business Administration that are for longer periods of time (discussed later in this chapter).

As a rule, commercial banks usually do not lend funds for long-term fixed assets, such as building and land. Often, they do lend money for the purchase of equipment and inventories and for financing customer credit.

The commercial bank may lend money in several ways—by traditional bank loans, installment loans, line of credit, discounting accounts receivables, and discounting installments sales contracts. (See Fig. 5-4.)

FIGURE 5-4
COMMERCIAL BANKS' FINANCIAL ASSISTANCE TO SMALL BUSINESS.

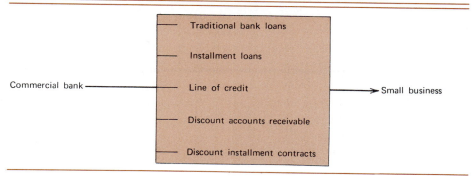

Commercial bank — Traditional bank loans / Installment loans / Line of credit / Discount accounts receivable / Discount installment contracts — Small business

SMALL BUSINESS BRIEF

HIGH INTEREST RATES CAUSE PROBLEMS

Small businesses often must borrow money for various reasons. As demonstrated earlier, the interest rate determines to a large degree the amount of their payments. Relatively stable interest rates at reasonable levels are very important to most small businesses. If interest rates climb to very high rates, many of these businesses find it impossible to borrow funds and repay them.

In years of high interest rates these rates have been a particularly troublesome problem for many small businesses. In fact, they probably have been a primary cause of many small business failures. Figure 5-5 shows how much the prime interest rate has fluctuated in recent years.

FIGURE 5-5
PRIME INTEREST RATE FROM 1977 to 1989.

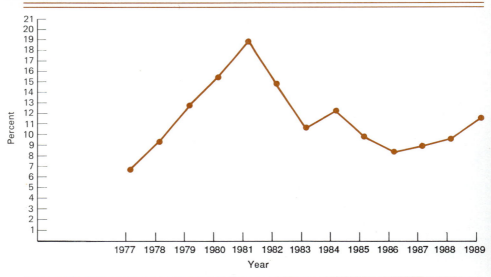

Traditional Bank Loan

The **traditional bank loan** may extend for a few days to finance such things as taking advantage of a cash discount. Also, it may extend for several months or years to finance various purchases or to provide working capital. Traditional bank loans are repaid when due and are not installment-type loans.

Installment Loans

Installment loans are made to businesses by commercial banks usually to finance purchases of equipment and other fixed assets. Generally, they are for a year or more. For example, a business might borrow $9000 for three years from a commercial bank to purchase a panel delivery truck. At 12 percent interest, the business would be required to pay the bank $298.93 per month for three years. The actual or true interest rate on this type of loan is almost always higher than the interest rate on the traditional bank loan for the same borrower.

Line of Credit

The **line of credit** is not a true type of business loan but rather an established limit of credit a business may automatically borrow. All loans above an amount established by a bank must be approved by a committee made up of officers of the bank. To avoid delay and save effort, a commercial bank's loan committee will usually establish a line of credit for a business firm. The business may then simply notify the bank that it is borrowing the money, and the money is automatically made available.

Discount Accounts Receivable

Another method by which commercial banks help businesses finance customer credit is called discount accounts receivable. The bank loans a business a percentage of the amount of its accounts receivable, and the business pledges its accounts receivable as collateral. For example, a business, to provide working capital, might take $10,000 worth of customers' 30-day accounts to the bank for discounting. The bank would make an estimate of the collectability of the accounts and lend a percentage of the total amount, for instance, $8000. The business would receive cash immediately to use as working capital. As the business receives cash from customers on these accounts receivable, it turns them over to the bank until the entire loan plus interest is repaid. After the bank is repaid, the business retains any additional funds it collects. If it does not collect enough accounts to repay the bank, it must make up the difference.

Discount Installment Contracts

Commercial banks also assist businesses in their customer credit by discounting **installment sales contracts.** To illustrate, a customer makes a purchase of merchandise and signs an installment contract with a business. The business then takes the contract to a bank, where it receives money for the contract.

Most customer installment sales contracts contain an effective or true interest rate of between 21 and 24 percent. Banks usually will loan the business the full face value of the contract. The interest charged in the installment sales contract is then their fee for making the loan. The bank or business then collects the payments from the customer, which go to the bank to repay the loan. If the customer fails to repay the contract, the business must reimburse the commercial bank.

Prime Interest Rate and Interest Rates to Small Business

The **prime interest rate** is the rate of interest the commercial bank currently charges its best customers. In other words, it is the lowest interest rate at which it will loan money. It varies considerably from small business customer to small business customer, but the average interest rate charged small businesses probably is about 2 to 3 percent above the prime rate. This interest rate applies to small businesses that have been in business a sufficient period of time to prove their profitability (ability to repay the loan). Because of the high failure rate of new small businesses, commercial banks usually will not lend money for a new venture unless the entrepreneur has "good" collateral that is about twice the amount of the loan to pledge against the loan.

Applying for a Loan

Bankers generally look for three things when considering a loan application: (1) ability to repay the loan, (2) collateral, and (3) credit record. The small business entrepreneur should take along three recent financial statements when applying for a loan or a line of credit: (1) a balance sheet, (2) an income statement (a copy of the business's federal income tax statement may be substituted or added), and (3) a cash flow statement (see Chapter 11 for samples and a discussion of these statements). The entrepreneur should also take along a personal financial statement when applying for venture capital. Figure 5-6 is a financial statement used by one entrepreneur to obtain a $10,000 unsecured loan and a line of credit of $50,000.

Vendors

Vendors can be an important source of short-term credit for small business firms. Firms that sell inventories to a business usually will finance the purchase of these goods for short periods of time, usually from 30 to 90 days. For example, a drug wholesaler might sell merchandise to a drugstore on credit, with the store having 30 days to pay. For 30 days, the drugstore would then be selling merchandise for which it had not paid. At the end of the 30-day period, the drugstore would then take money that it had received from the sale of the merchandise and pay the amount owed the drug wholesaler.

Vendors also have needs for working capital, so it is a common practice for them to offer their business customers a cash discount. When they offer a cash discount, the terms of the purchase, such as "3/10, n/30," mean that the

FIGURE 5-6
SAMPLE FINANCIAL STATEMENT PRESENTED TO A COMMERCIAL BANK.

BALANCE SHEET

Assets

Cash	$ 8,192	
Note receivable from sale of land	136,266	
Rent houses (two, current market value)	124,000	
Home	78,000	
Mineral rights (two, both leased)	50,000	
Personal property	40,000	
Total Assets		$436,458

Liabilities

Mortgages on rent houses	$101,800	
Mortgage on home	39,000	
Personal credit (automobile and personal)	2,500	
Total liabilities		$143,300

Net Worth | | $293,158

INCOME

Salary	$ 53,460	
Interest income	17,831	
Cash from note receivable (principal)	6,500	
Income		$ 77,791

MONTHLY PAYMENTS

Rent		
Payments to mortgage company	$1,268	
Rental income	875	
Balance paid		$393
Home mortgage		418
Automobile and credit cards		400
Monthly payments		$1,211

total amount of the purchase is due in 30 days; however, if the customer will pay the total amount of the purchase within 10 days, he or she is allowed to subtract 3 percent from the total amount. Business firms often find that they can borrow money from a commercial bank for 20 days to take advantage of this discount and the cost of the loan is less than the cash discount.

Equipment Manufacturers and Distributors

To encourage businesses to purchase their **equipment, manufacturers and distributors** often will finance the purchase. Usually, such loans take the form of an installment sales contract. The manufacturers or distributors may actually carry the note themselves or discount the installment sales contract with a financial institution. Machinery, equipment, display shelves, cash registers, and office equipment are some of the more common items financed by manufacturers and distributors.

Factors

Factors are financial firms that finance accounts receivable for business firms. They may either purchase or discount accounts receivable.

If they discount accounts receivable, they function exactly as the commercial bank example discussed previously. They will lend a certain amount of money based on their analysis of the collectability of the accounts, and the business turns them over to the factor until the original amount borrowed plus interest is repaid. All remaining collections are kept by the business firm. If the small business fails to collect the amount owed the factor (including interest), it must make up the difference.

When factors purchase accounts receivable, they make an analysis of the collectability of the accounts and pay the business firm a percentage of the total amount. The business firm (sometimes the factor) then collects the accounts and turns all collections over to the factor. It is very important to the factors that they judge the collectability of the accounts with considerable accuracy because the total they collect must cover what they loan and their expected profit. If they collect less, then they must suffer the loss.

Sales Finance Companies

Sales finance companies purchase installment sales contracts from business firms. The customer will sign an installment sales contract, after which the business firm sells the contract to the sales finance company. Usually, the business firm will receive the full face value of the contract, and the profit of the sales finance company is derived from the interest of the contract.

Sales finance companies also engage in what is known as "floor planning." Floor planning is common in the retail automobile trade and in retail sales of large appliances. To illustrate, the sales finance company finances the purchase of the dealer's stock of automobiles. In return for this financing, the dealer then pays the sales finance company interest on the loan until the car is sold. When the car is sold, the dealer then turns the contract over to the sales finance company and receives the full amount of the purchase. The sales finance company then collects principal and interest in monthly installment payments from the automobile purchaser. The automobile serves as collateral to the sales finance company until the loan is repaid.

Insurance Companies

Insurance companies make some **long-term loans** to small businesses for the purchase of fixed assets. Insurance companies collect premiums on their policies and then invest them in stocks, bonds, and business loans. Moreover, insurance companies are regulated by both state and federal agencies, and the type of loans they are able to make is controlled to some degree by government agencies to protect the policyholders. Insurance companies usually loan funds to small businesses that have high-value collateral to pledge to ensure the repayment of the loan. Loans for shopping malls and apartments are common business loans made by insurance companies. Other than these types of loans, insurance companies provide a limited source of small business loans.

In 1975 William Ackerman and Anne Robinson collected $300—from friends who donated $5 apiece—and produced 300 copies of *In Search of the Turtle's Navel,* a recording of acoustic instrumentals performed by Ackerman. They stuffed and labeled the blank, white album covers by hand. Today, this company, named Windham Hill Productions, Inc., is a $30-million-a-year enterprise employing 45 people—and still headed by Ackerman and Robinson. The company has expanded to include several labels and a video and film division. It has no debt and no interest in going public.

Private Investors

Private citizens who lend their savings are often a source of capital for small business. They usually lend their funds for a time period of one to five years. The **private investor** is generally an individual who is willing to risk his or her funds for a higher interest rate than he or she would be able to obtain from savings and loan associations or bonds. The interest rate that private investors charge is usually above that of most financial institutions. It often is in the range charged by small loan companies for consumer loans.

Small business owners should investigate private sources to make sure they are not dealing with someone who is associated with crime or usury or both.

Small Business Investment Corporations

Small Business Investment Corporations are privately owned financial corporations that are licensed, regulated, and promoted by the Small Business Administration, an agency of the federal government. SBICs may only loan or invest money in small businesses according to the SBA definition of a small business. They themselves may obtain loans or guarantees of loans from the SBA to lend and invest in small businesses. An SBIC must have a minimum initial investment of at least $150,000. Often the investment exceeds more than $1 million. The SBIC may obtain loans or guarantees (the SBA guarantees the financial institution making the loan that the loan will be repaid) of loans that amount to twice the SBIC's paid-in capital and surplus, with a $7.5 million maximum.

The SBIC then takes the funds it has invested and funds obtained through the SBA and either (1) makes loans that must exceed five years to small businesses or (2) invests in small businesses. SBIC's often invest in small businesses but are prohibited from obtaining a controlling interest in the businesses. Many SBICs provide management consulting to the business firms to protect their investment.

In 1969, the SBA established a program of SBICs to aid minority enterprises. These are called MESBICs (Minority Enterprise Small Business Investment Corporations).

Small Business Administration

The **Small Business Administration SBA** was established as an agency in the Department of Commerce in 1953 to help promote small business. The SBA engages in various types of activities that assist small businesses, including financial assistance (other types of assistance will be discussed in Chapter 22).

Loans

The SBA is authorized to make loans directly to small businesses or to participate in loans with private financial institutions. When it is a participating loan, the SBA and the private financial institution each put up part of the loan. There is seldom any money provided the SBA to make such loans, and they comprise an extremely small percentage of the total loan financing made possible by the SBA.

Loan guarantees are the primary type of loan the SBA provides small businesses. The SBA is allowed by law to guarantee up to 90 percent of a loan to a financial institution, with a maximum of $350,000 ($500,000 in special situations). The lending institution lends all the money, but the SBA guarantees a specific percentage repayment. If the borrower defaults on the loan, the SBA reimburses the lending institution the amount of the loan guarantee.

Guaranteed loans comprise a large percentage of the total financing by the SBA. The bank can charge any interest rate up to a rate maximum set by the SBA. The SBA usually sets the interest rate between 2 and 3 percent above the prime interest rate charged by large New York banks. For instance, in the past it has been 2.75 percent above prime if the loan was for less than seven years, and 2.25 percent above prime if the loan was for more than seven years. The SBA prefers guaranteed loans rather than direct or participation loans because this allows the SBA to make many times more money available to small businesses.

Eligibility Requirements

The SBA makes loans only to small businesses. The SBA does not compete with financial institutions in making loans. If the applicant can obtain sufficient money at a private financial institution, federal law does not allow the SBA to make that person a loan. Before applying to the SBA, the applicant must seek private financing at a local bank or other lending institution. If the applicant lives in a city of more than 200,000 people, he or she must apply to two lending institutions before going to the SBA.

The SBA also specifies six general credit requirements.

1. The applicant must be of good character.
2. The applicant must show ability to operate the business successfully.
3. The applicant must have enough capital so that, with an SBA loan, he or she can operate on a sound financial basis.
4. The applicant must show the proposed loan to be of sound value or secured so as to assure repayment reasonably.
5. The applicant must show that the past earnings or future prospects indicate ability to repay the loan out of profit.
6. If the venture is a new business, the applicant must invest a reasonable amount of money to provide for any losses that might occur during the early stages of business operations.

Ineligible Applicants

The SBA cannot make loans under certain circumstances.

1. When funds are otherwise available at reasonable rates.
2. When the loan is to "(a) pay off a loan to a creditor or creditors of the applicant who are inadequately secured and in a position to sustain loss, (b) provide funds for distribution of payment to the principals of the applicant, or (c) replenish funds previously used for such purposes."
3. When the loan is for speculation in any kind of property.
4. When the applicant is a nonprofit organization.
5. When the applicant is a newspaper, magazine, or book publishing company.
6. When any of the gross income of the applicant is derived from gambling.
7. When the loan provides funds to lending institutions.
8. When the loan is used to purchase real property to be held for investment.

Loan Application

Businesses that are in existence follow different steps from an entrepreneur trying to start a new business.

1. Prepare a balance sheet (see Chapter 13) listing all assets and liabilities of the business (not personal items).
2. Prepare an income statement (see Chapter 13) for the previous full year and the current year to the date of the balance sheet.
3. Prepare a current personal financial statement of all owners (excluding stockholders who hold less than 20 percent of the stock).
4. Prepare a list of all collateral to be offered as security for the loan with present market value of each.
5. State the amount of the loan desired and the purpose for which it will be used.
6. Take all this material to a bank and apply for a loan. If the loan is refused, ask about a guaranteed loan. If the bank is interested, have it contract the SBA. Remember, you must go to two banks before applying to the SBA if the city has more than 200,000 population.
7. If a guaranteed loan is not available, write or visit the nearest SBA office.

Entrepreneurs Starting a New Business

1. Describe in detail the type of business you wish to start.
2. Describe your experience and management capabilities.
3. Prepare a statement of how much you or others have to invest in the business and how much you need to borrow.

FIGURE 5-7
SOURCES OF CAPITAL FOR SMALL BUSINESS.

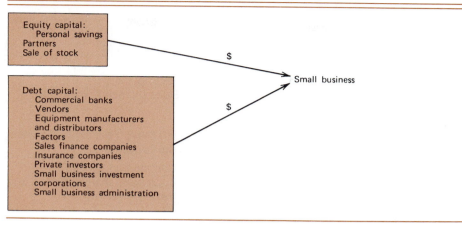

4. Prepare a current financial statement listing all personal assets and liabilities.
5. Prepare a detailed projection of earnings for the first year of operation.
6. Prepare a list of all collateral to be offered as security and your estimate of the current market value of each.
7. Take all this material to a bank and apply for a loan. If the loan is declined, ask about a guaranteed loan. If the bank is interested, have it contact the SBA. You must go to two banks before going to the SBA if the city has more than 200,000 population.
8. If a guaranteed loan is not available, write or visit your nearest SBA office.

SOURCES OF FUNDS BY TYPE OF CAPITAL NEED

A general picture of sources of capital for small business is shown in Figure 5-7. However, small business firms have various types of short-term and long-term needs. Short-term needs may include such items as working capital, customer credit, and inventories. Long-term needs include such items as land, buildings, machinery, fixtures, furniture, and equipment. Very few sources extend loans for all these needs. Most financial institutions specialize in lending money for only one or two areas of these needs. Figure 5-8 presents various sources of capital for small business listed by the general areas of needs for which they specialize in providing funds.

FIGURE 5-8
SOURCES OF FUNDS BY TYPE OF CAPITAL NEEDED.

SHORT-TERM CAPITAL

Working Capital (salaries and other expenses)	Customer Credit	Inventories
Commercial banks	Commercial banks Factors Sales finance companies	Commercial banks Vendors

LONG-TERM CAPITAL

Land and Buildings	Machinery, Fixtures, and Furniture, and Equipment
Insurance companies Private investors	Commercial banks Equipment manufacturers and distributors Private investors

ALL TYPES OF CAPITAL NEEDS

Private Sources	Government Sources
Small Business Investment Corporations	Small Business Administration

SUMMARY OF KEY POINTS

1. The total paid on loans increases when (a) the amount borrowed increases, (b) the number of years of the loan increases, and (c) the interest rate increases.

2. Equity capital may come from personal savings, from partners, or by selling stock in a corporation.

3. Possible sources of debt capital are commercial banks, vendors, equipment manufacturers and distributors, factors, sales finance companies, insurance companies, private investors, SBICs, and the SBA.

4. Commercial banks lend money by traditional bank loans, installment loans, line of credit, discounting accounts receivables, and discounting installment sales contracts.

5. The prime interest rate is the rate the commercial bank is currently charging its best customers. Loans to small business average about 2 to 3 percent above the prime rate.

6. A small business should provide (a) a balance sheet, (b) an income statement or a federal income tax return or both, and (c) a cash flow statement when applying for a loan.

7. Vendors that sell inventories usually will finance the purchase for 30 to 90 days.

8. Equipment manufacturers and distributors will often finance purchase of their equipment to small business.
9. Factors purchase or discount accounts receivable.
10. Sales finance companies purchase installment sales contracts and provide "floor planning" for many businesses.
11. Insurance companies are a source of funds for large buildings, shopping malls, and apartments.
12. Private investors sometimes lend money to small businesses, but their rate is usually higher than those of many other sources.
13. Small Business Investment Corporations borrow money from the SBA and either lend money to small businesses or invest in them.
14. The SBA guarantees loans made by private financial institutions. They guarantee up to 90 percent of the loan.

DISCUSSION QUESTIONS

1. What are some of the items for which a small business needs money?
2. Where may a small business obtain equity capital?
3. If you wanted to finance customer credit using a commercial bank, what types of loans might you ask for at the bank?
4. How do vendors help finance small businesses?
5. How do equipment manufacturers and distributors help finance small businesses?
6. How does a factor operate?
7. How does a sales finance company operate?
8. Where do insurance companies get money to lend, and what type of loans do they usually make to small businesses?
9. Why do private investors lend money to small businesses?
10. What is a Small Business Investment Corporation?
11. What type of loan does the SBA make?
12. If you were a small business owner, where would you look for funds to purchase machinery and equipment?

THE BUSINESS PLAN: SOURCE OF FUNDS

The funds to buy or start a business come from money you have, money for which you can sell part ownership of the business, or money you can borrow.

_____ Fill in Figures 5-1 or 5-2 to help you determine how much money you need to start or buy the business. Try to think of other costs you will have that may not be on these two figures (such as purchase of land).

_____ How much money do you have to contribute to the business? Do you plan on taking in a partner or selling stock in a corporation? How much money will this contribute to the business? Have you considered a Small Business Investment Corporation or venture capitalists?

_____ Will you have to borrow additional funds? Take into consideration the amount, time, and interest rate to determine if you will have the ability to repay the borrowed funds.

_____ Will you use a commercial bank for some of your funds? Talk to several banks about working capital loans and a line of credit. Try to obtain the best interest rate possible. Could you use a commercial bank to discount accounts receivable or installment contracts?

_____ If you are buying an existing business, do you have balance sheets, income statements, and cash flow statements to take with you when you talk about a loan? If you are starting a business, do you have a projected balance sheet, income statement, and cash flow statement?

_____ Create a personal financial statement like the one presented in Figure 5–6. Take this with you when you talk to any financial institution.

_____ Determine who your vendors will be and find out their credit terms.

_____ Can you finance your accounts receivable by using factors? Will you use sales finance companies to purchase your installment sales contracts?

_____ Have you considered insurance companies if you are financing shopping malls, apartments, or other large real estate ventures?

_____ Are private investors a possible source of funds? Take into consideration that their interest rates may be higher than other sources of funds. Make sure you are not dealing with someone associated with crime or usury.

_____ If you are turned down by commercial banks (one in small towns and two in large cities), you may be eligible for a Small Business Administration guaranteed loan. Check the eligibility requirements and ineligible applicants section in this chapter to see if you are eligible for a loan.

_____ If you plan on obtaining a SBA-guaranteed loan, read carefully the loan application information in this chapter.

_____ From the amount of money you decided you needed, subtract the amount of money you have and the amount of money you can obtain from selling part ownership in the business, to determine how much you will have to borrow. Can you obtain this amount from the financial sources listed in the chapter?

ENTREPRENEURIAL PROJECTS

Interview a small business owner and find out the following.

1. What were the sources of his or her starting capital? What percentage was equity capital and what percentage was debt capital?

2. Does he or she use any of the following financial sources? Are they used for short-term or long-term funds? What does he or she use them to finance?

   a. Commercial banks
   b. Vendors
   c. Equipment manufacturers and distributors
   d. Factors

   e. Sales finance companies
   f. Insurance companies
   g. Private investors
   h. SBIC
   i. SBA

CASE A

The Hole-in-One Golf Shop

Kevin Hogan plans on opening a golf supply shop in a city of 300,000 population when he graduates from college in about six months. He has $22,000 in savings. Kevin has located a store for rent at $800 per month that he feels is suited to his needs and has made a list of various things he will need to open and their price.

Merchandise	$18,000
Shelves, racks, and displays—free installation	4,000
Remodeling	2,000
Cash register (used)	400
Checkout counter	200
Used desk	100
Adding machine	200
Office supplies (3 months' supply)	90
Telephone	
Deposit	75
Rate per month	16
Utilities	
Deposit	200
Estimated monthly bill	40

Kevin has made some other estimates and plans as follows:

1. He can completely turn over his inventory every four months.
2. He plans a 100 percent markup on cost of all merchandise.
3. He plans to hire a part-time clerk at $90 per week.
4. He feels he can get by on $900 per month for himself.
5. He plans to spend $1000 on opening promotion and advertising.
6. He feels he can get by with $100 a month advertising thereafter.
7. Kevin estimates that 75 percent of his sales will be on credit in the form of 30-day accounts.

Questions

1. Estimate how much money Kevin will have to obtain by filling in a worksheet similar to Figure 5-1 (provided in *Study Guide*).
2. Should Kevin try to obtain equity or debt capital? Explain.
3. Which of the following sources could Kevin use and for which items?

Source	Money for
Commercial bank	
Vendors	
Equipment manufacturers and distributors	
Factors	
Sales finance companies	
Insurance companies	
Private investors	
Small Business Investment Corporations	
Small Business Administration	

4. Which sources of financing would you advise Kevin to use and for what uses?

CASE B
Marvin Matlock

Marvin Matlock has operated a restaurant in a town of 18,000 for the past 10 years. His restaurant is located at one of the off-ramps of a major highway, and his sign and building are visible for several hundred yards. He features "down home cooking" at reasonable prices with fast service. During the 10 years he has been in business, Marvin has gone to considerable effort to make sure that the quality of his food stays constant and that the appearance of his establishment is always clean and neat. As a reward for his efforts, profits have always been good. The past two years the business has cleared about $40,000 per year.

Two weeks ago someone left a burner on under a skillet filled with grease. This resulted in a fire that completely destroyed the restaurant. Marvin had taken out fire insurance when he first started 10 years ago. The agent had asked Marvin on several occasions if he wanted to increase his insurance owing to increased costs, but Marvin had never done anything about the value of the policy.

The fire insurance policy paid Marvin $150,000. After checking with contractors and equipment dealers, Marvin finds that a new building will cost him $175,000, and equipment and furniture will cost another $60,000. Even with his savings and the insurance money, Marvin only has $180,000. It will take five months to get back into business. Marvin feels he must have at least $1500 a month to meet his personal needs. He has estimated that he needs about $65,000 more to get him back into business and provide enough money for working capital to get him going again.

Marvin lists his needs as follows:

Building	$175,000
Equipment	40,000
Furniture	20,000
Personal draw	7,500
Working capital and miscellaneous expenses	2,500
Total funds needed	$245,000
Funds on hand	−180,000
Additional funds needed	$ 65,000

Marvin wants you to help him find the money.

Questions

1. Examine the following sources of small business financing and determine which might give Marvin a loan and for what purpose.

   a. Commercial bank
   b. Vendors
   c. Equipment manufacturers and distributors
   d. Factors
   e. Sales finance company
   f. Insurance company
   g. Private investor
   h. SBIC
   i. SBA

2. Which sources would you suggest Marvin borrow from, and how much should he borrow?

KEY WORDS

CHAPTER 6

LOCATION ANALYSIS

After reading this chapter, you will understand:

1   That many factors must be evaluated to establish the potential of the proposed trade area.

2   That accessibility of the site is important to the success of the firm.

3   The difference between consumer, shopping, specialty, and impulse goods.

4   Why adequate parking space is an important criterion in site selection.

5   The differences between various locations: central business district, neighborhood locations, shopping centers and malls, string street locations, and isolated locations.

6   The importance of site economics.

7   The impact of zoning laws on the small business.

8   Why a traffic study of the proposed location should be conducted.

ENTREPRENEURIAL PROFILE

Harvey and Zena Hafetz

Z & H UNIFORMS

"I was fired into greatness," jokes Harvey Hafetz of his dismissal from a job as a sales representative for a cosmetics distributor in 1971. Of course, that's today—then it was a painful experience.

Harvey's wife, Zena, had decided just that year to leave her job as an elementary school teacher and try another challenge. The couple purchased a small uniform shop in Reading, Pennsylvania, as an investment and to give Zena part-time on-the-job training for a new career. But when Harvey lost his job, he joined his wife at the little store. Z & H Uniforms was born.

In the first year, their manager quit and the redevelopment authority condemned their building. Things looked grim. But they moved the little store to the Park City Mall in Lancaster, decorated it fashionably, and the business prospered. Opportunity in hardship.

Today, the company has 20 retail stores, mostly in shopping malls and 11 leased departments catering primarily to health care professionals. A contract sales department furnishes executive-type apparel, hospitality, food service, and industrial-type clothing to industry.

In 1985, Z & H added 10 stores after acquiring a Philadelphia-based competitor's stores with the help of a $600,000 SBA-guaranteed

loan from Meridian Bank. The firm had 75 employees then; only three years later, it has 170. Annual sales have doubled in that time, from $3.5 million to $7 million.

Zena directs the buying and merchandising for the stores, adopting some of the current fashion into uniforms unique in the industry. Harvey handles sales. Their son, Andrew, may be next in line for Z & H; he's a student at the Philadelphia College of Textiles and Science.

Source: Network (Washington, D.C.: Small Business Administration, March–April 1988).

IMPORTANCE OF LOCATION ANALYSIS

The entrepreneur who is planning to launch a new business venture and the owner of the ongoing business both understand the importance of the firm's location to its economic vitality. Two of the most critical factors that contribute to the success of the firm are (1) analysis of the potential site and (2) choice of the specific location. These two factors are especially important for retailing firms where competition is usually intense. In fact, location may be the deciding factor when customers shop in one store in preference to another.

Location analysis is a dynamic rather than a static process. It does not end when the firm opens for business but continues for the life of the firm. The owner must choose the management strategy that best meets the firm's location requirements and reflects changing environmental and business conditions. For example, when a lease expires, should the owner renew the lease at the present location or relocate? If business conditions are good and the entrepreneur plans to expand by adding a second outlet, the choice of the location is as critical for the new store as it was for the original outlet.

It is not unusual for an entrepreneur to select a location based primarily on convenience or cost. For example, a location may be chosen because of the availability of a vacant building, proximity to the owner's residence, or low rent. Merely because a location is convenient or the rent is low should not be the dominant reasons for selecting a specific site without first making a thorough analysis of the overall location's potential for the firm's survival and growth.

In the ensuing discussion, our attention is focused on the two most common types of small business, retailing and service firms. Separate discussions are devoted to wholesaling and manufacturing firms. Although the material emphasizes starting a new business, it can easily be adapted to the needs of the owner of an ongoing business who is considering relocation or expansion.

The principal variables that should be analyzed include (1) trade area analysis, (2) strategic factors in location analysis, (3) accessibility of the location, (4) parking availability, (5) types of goods sold or services provided, (6) site choices, (7) site economics, (8) zoning regulations, and (9) traffic analysis.

TRADE AREA ANALYSIS

The **trade area** is the geographic area that provides a major portion of the continuing patronage necessary to support the individual business or a larger shopping district, such as a shopping center. The trade area can usually be divided into three zones of influence.

1. The "primary trading area" is ordinarily viewed as the zone where a given establishment can serve consumers better than, or as well as, major competitors from the standpoint of convenience and accessibility. It is normally expected to contribute about two-thirds of total sales volume.
2. The "secondary trading area" is the zone beyond the primary area where a given establishment can still exert a reasonably strong pull but is at some disadvantage with respect to convenience and accessibility. This zone may generate from 15 to 20 percent of all sales.
3. The "tertiary area" is often not definable in geographic terms and con-

sists of customers who patronize the shopping center or store for reasons not related to proximity to their residence. These may be consumers with a strong attachment to a store, workers in nearby business establishments, or people responding to a well-publicized promotional event. This zone often contributes 5 to 20 percent of the total business of a shopping center.[1]

The search for the preferred location begins by answering the question, "Which location affords the greatest potential for the business in three target areas: the town or city, the area within the town or city, and the specific location in the trade area?"

STRATEGIC FACTORS IN LOCATION ANALYSIS

Analysis of the trade area begins when the entrepreneur conducts an economic feasibility study to aid in determining the potential of the trade area for the proposed business venture. The same factors should be evaluated for each of the three target areas (town or city, area within the city, and the specific location) to ensure consistency of the study in attempting to determine market potential. The factors to be evaluated include population characteristics, income level, occupational analysis and educational level, nature of competition, site history and future, and community attitudes.

Population Characteristics

A population study enables the small business owner to create a profile of the general population in the area as well as of the firm's potential customers. The profile should reveal significant characteristics of the population, such as the following:

1. What is the age distribution of the general population? Of my potential customers?
2. How many one-person households and family households are there in the area? How has this changed in the last 10 years?
3. How many families (or single persons) own their homes? How many live in apartments?
4. What is the value of the homes? Are home values increasing or decreasing?
5. How much is monthly rent for apartments?
6. Are families chiefly younger families with children or older, retired couples?
7. Are young people able to find employment in the area after graduation, or do most have to relocate to find employment?

To illustrate, a population study of an area that is growing rapidly was undertaken to establish the area's potential for a family fitness center. The study revealed that dual-career, young married professionals with children were the predominant group buying homes in the area. A large majority of these new residents were employed in professional and managerial occupations. With the interest of Americans in a healthy life-style, this area appears to offer the potential level of support necessary for a family fitness center.

Income Level

Another important indicator of a site's potential is the income level of residents in the trade area. Income level measures disposable personal income, the amount of money that consumers have available to spend, and is a measure of purchasing power. For retailers, **disposable personal income** indicates the amount of income available for expenditures in the various categories of food, beverages, and tobacco; clothing; accessories and jewelry; personal care; housing and household operations; medical care; personal business; transportation; and recreation. As income levels rise, discretionary buying power increases. **Discretionary buying power** is that portion of one's income that is not required for purchasing the basic necessities of life but can be spent on ''luxury'' items, such as VCRs or designer clothing.

Estimating Purchasing Power

Purchasing power for a trade area can be estimated from several sources. One popular source is the Census Bureau, which publishes extensive data on characteristics of the population, such as income, education, housing, and occupation. Census Bureau data are available for various geographical designations, called Metropolitan Statistical Areas, or MSAs. The MSA is either a (1) city of at least 50,000 population or (2) an urbanized area of at least 50,000 population with a total metropolitan population of at least 100,000 that have a high degree of social and economic integration.

In areas of more than 1 million population, Primary Metropolitan Statistical Areas (PMSAs) are identified that have a large urbanized county or cluster of counties with very strong internal economic and social links. The Consolidated Metropolitan Statistical Areas (CMSAs) are large metropolitan complexes within which PMSAs have been defined.

Census tracts are subdivisions of MSAs. Each tract is divided into areas of 4000 to 9000 residents. Statistical information and a map of each tract are published. In urban areas, block statistics are available that contain housing and population characteristics of city blocks.

A second resource is the *Survey of Buying Power,* published by *Sales and Marketing Management* magazine. This annual survey reports data on individual and family purchasing power. A third source of data is information available from local sources, such as the chamber of commerce or trade asso-

FIGURE 6-1
ESTIMATION OF PURCHASING POWER AND SALES POTENTIAL FOR A GROCERY STORE.

1. Determine number of household (family) units in trade area from census data or utility company	1,500
2. Multiply number of household (family) units by average household income in census tract	$20,000
3. Equals total purchasing power (total disposable income)	$30,000,000
4. Multiply total purchasing power by percentage of disposable income spent for grocery items	12%
5. Equals total potential purchasing power for grocery items in the trade area	$3,600,000
6. Multiply by percentage of money that will be spent in this particular store (from survey of consumers or management estimate)	10%
7. Equals total projected sales for this store in this trade area	$360,000

ciations. Finally, a market survey can be made to collect buying power data for the specific trade area. Many of these sources and a market survey technique are discussed in Chapter 16.

We can illustrate the estimation of purchasing power with an example of a retailer who is studying the possibility of opening a neighborhood grocery store. A method for the retailer to obtain a general forecast of the trade area's purchasing power and ability to support his or her business is presented in Figure 6-1. The retailer needs five sets of data. First, the number of households (family units) in the trade area can be determined from such sources as census data or utility companies. Second, the average household income in the store's trade area can be obtained from census data. Third, the percentage of disposable income that families spend for grocery items can be determined from the retail trade association or from census data. Fourth, the total potential purchasing power for grocery items in the area is obtained by multiplying the number of households by the average household income. Fifth, the percentage of household income that will be spent in the particular store (obtained from a local market survey or management estimate) multiplied by total potential purchasing power for grocery items equals total projected sales for the particular store.

Occupational Analysis and Educational Level

Income, occupation, and level of education are closely related. The occupational and educational survey should disclose the types of employment in the area as well as the percentage in each employment category. (See Fig. 6-2.) These data will reflect the stability of employment in the area. To illustrate, a

FIGURE 6-2
PERCENTAGE OF EMPLOYED PERSONS IN ORLANDO, FLORIDA, ON
NONAGRICULTURAL PAYROLLS CLASSIFIED BY INDUSTRY DIVISION.

Industry Division	Percentage of Employed Persons
Government	11.4%
Services	32.0
Finance, insurance, real estate	7.0
Wholesale and retail trade	26.1
Transportation and public utilities	5.5
Manufacturing	11.0
Construction	7.0
Mining	N/A

(*Employment and Earnings*, U.S. Department of Labor, Washington, D.C., June 1988, pp. 78–79.)

high percentage of the work force employed in seasonal jobs would indicate a fluctuating employment picture for the area and thus involve a higher risk factor for a new or expanding firm.

The educational analysis will also reveal significant data about the area. Generally, a population with a higher educational level will have higher-level jobs and greater income. With more income, consumers have greater discretionary buying power to spend for nonstaple merchandise.

Analysis of the Competition

Analysis of competitors in the trade area is one means of forecasting business potential. Evaluation of competitors should provide a conceptual view of the nature, location, size, quantity, and quality of competition in the trade area. The analysis will likely reveal trends in the local business environment. For example, the analysis will enable the small business owner to determine if other competitors are moving into the local area. The survey should also provide a perspective of the actions of established competitors; for example, are they expanding or maintaining the status quo or closing? If there are only a limited number of competitors, it does not necessarily suggest that an additional firm has a strong potential for success in the community. Instead, it may be an indicator that the local area cannot or will not support an additional firm of the proposed type.

Site History and Future

The history of the proposed site should be studied. If a site has an unfavorable history, one marked by a succession of failures, the owner should seek to ascertain the reason for the failures. Did other firms fail because the site was a poor location, it was the wrong type of business for the site, management was incompetent, products or services were unacceptable, or was it some combination of these factors? While failures at a site do not automatically condemn the site for future occupants, it does suggest that the prospective occupant needs to use the knowledge of causes of earlier failures to prevent similar mistakes.

The future of the site also bears investigation. What, if any, changes are planned in the area of the proposed site? Are street improvements planned that could make access to the site difficult if not impossible? Is public transportation service to the area going to be increased, decreased, or rerouted? Are new shopping malls planned for the trade area, bringing in more competition? Will land use in the area be rezoned that will have a direct impact on the firm's clientele? The answer to these types of questions will provide the entrepreneur with a wealth of information with which to gauge the potential of the proposed location.

Community Attitudes

Prevailing community attitudes have a substantial influence on shaping the character of the town or city and, consequently, the small business. Positive attitudes encourage growth through aggressive programs and plans designed to stimulate the local area's economy. The development and implementation of plans to attract new businesses and to stimulate growth of existing firms reveal a healthy environment for businesses in the area. Specific plans may include giving special tax breaks or making low-interest loans available for new businesses locating in the area or renovating established businesses. Another program is the formation of community action groups for the purpose of encouraging consumers to patronize businesses in the area.

To illustrate one such cooperative venture, a group of business owners and citizens in an area of a large city joined together to promote the local community as a quality, convenient place to live, work, and shop. Meeting together, business owners and citizens determined that the plan should consist of several parts. First, they established the length of time the promotion should cover (one year) with the expectation that the plan would be successful and carried forward. Second, goals were established that outlined the purpose of the venture: promote the community, boost morale by developing a general positive attitude throughout the community, and benefit the entire community through worthwhile projects and events. Third, a committee was formed to detail how the plan was to be implemented. Special events were planned throughout the year to correspond to seasonal themes centered on fall, winter, spring, and summer. Events include coordinated sales events by area merchants, discount coupon booklets distributed by local merchants at area stores, parades, distance runs, communitywide garage sales, carnivals at local schools (Halloween), Christmas lighting contests, and street dances. To date the program has been very successful, and it is being continued by the citizens in the community beyond the one-year initial plan.

ACCESSIBILITY OF THE LOCATION

Accessibility is an integral part of site analysis. Accessibility refers to the ease and safety consumers experience when entering and leaving a site. For retailers, such as apparel shops, and service firms, such as drive-in businesses (dry cleaners), accessibility is one of the most important factors in site selection.

In site selection, careful analysis must be made to identify any factors that could impede pedestrian and vehicle movement to and from the site. These limitations must be weighed in relation to the specific area chosen: central

H & R Block has nearly 7500 company owned and franchised tax offices in the United States. These tax offices are located in accessible and visible shopping areas and are open weekdays, evenings, and weekends, to reach its target market.

business district, shopping centers, or locations along heavily traveled streets and highways.

Traffic congestion often discourages shoppers from patronizing a particular store, especially in downtown business districts. Another major consideration is how easily and safely autos can enter and exit from a particular site. If the entrance or exit poses a hazard to the driver, getting onto or off the parking lot may keep customers away from a shopping center or a drive-in type of business. Furthermore, a site with only limited access or located at an intersection may discourage shoppers.

Likewise, owners should study pedestrian accessibility to identify potential obstacles that discourage shoppers. For example, a location that generates much vehicular traffic as well as large crowds of nonshoppers creates congestion and limits accessibility. Or a noisy, cluttered, hazardous, or run down area also inhibits pedestrian traffic. Other obstacles to pedestrian traffic include driveways or other interruptions in the sidewalks, the necessity of climbing stairs or walking down dark hallways to enter a business, or pedestrian or vehicular cross traffic.

Another matter is the accessibility of the site by public transportation (bus, streetcar, subway). Convenient public transportation to and from residential areas is an inducement to customers to patronize a business.

Studying the traffic pattern and traffic arteries allows small business owners to determine the accessibility of their specific location. They can develop a time travel map detailing peak periods of traffic that assist them in deciding on their hours of operation.

Inaccessibility is frequently a prime reason for business failure. To illustrate, a restaurant opened in a small shopping center located near a larger shopping mall. Luncheon business was good, but the lack of traffic for the evening meal spelled the failure of the restaurant. The restaurant was located down a dark street between a park and a lower-middle-class neighborhood. To reach the restaurant, customers had to pass many other restaurants. Nine months after its opening, the restaurant closed its doors. And a second food establishment was also unsuccessful at the same site for the same reason—inaccessibility.

PARKING AVAILABILITY

In our highly mobile society, consumers rely on the automobile as the primary form of transportation to complete their shopping trips. In addition to availability, the ease with which customers can park is a key contributor to the success of the business. Some store owners have been known to park their own vehicles in the prime spaces in front of their business, a practice that clearly frustrates shoppers, and they respond by patronizing competitor stores.

For shops in downtown locations in large metropolitan areas, lack of available parking has long been a major problem. To combat the problem, merchants have taken steps to ease parking congestion. Old buildings have been razed and replaced by parking lots and garages. A common action is for merchants to make arrangements with parking lots or parking garages whereby customers are given free or reduced price parking while shopping. To encourage downtown shopping, some cities allow free on-street parking on Saturdays. A recognized advantage of shopping centers is the capacity to provide adequate customer parking.

There are no uniform standards for determining parking adequacy for retail and service establishments. The Urban Land Institute surveyed parking space needs and found that a supermarket requires five times more parking space than a furniture store of equal size. Their studies of parking space requirements in shopping centers indicated that a general standard of 5.5 spaces per 1000 square feet of gross leasable area (GLA) is satisfactory for meeting the demand for most shopping periods during a year. Shopping center parking needs vary by size of center, as the following parking standards developed for shopping centers by the Urban Land Institute suggest.[2]

4.0 spaces per 1000 square feet of GLA for centers with 25,000–400,000 square feet.

4.5 spaces per 1000 square feet of GLA for centers with 400,000 to 600,000 square feet.

5.0 spaces per 1000 square feet of GLA for centers with 600,000 square feet and over.

A list of the basic considerations for use in determining parking requirements should include the following:

1. Type of neighborhood in which the business is located
2. Frequency of store visits by shoppers
3. Length of time of store visits by shoppers
4. Accessibility of store by public transportation and number of customers who use public transportation to visit the store.
5. Volume of walk-in traffic
6. Variation or fluctuation in business on daily, weekly, and seasonal pattern
7. Extent of competition

SELECTING A RETAILING LOCATION

The location guidelines provided by one seafood franchisor to franchisees include the following.

For a 74-seat location, we suggest you select a lot that is a minimum of 115′ by 200′. Smaller lots such as 100′ by 150′ will not be adequate.

Parking spaces for customers should number one space for each two seats plus parking for employees.

Level and clear lots are less expensive in the final cost figure than lots that require a great deal of site preparation, that is, removing or hauling in dirt, blasting rock, removing existing buildings.

Electricity, sewer, water, and gas must be available at the site or furnished to the site by the owner.

Access to the highway or màin road must be available for highway access permits.

Sign permits must be available for the company sign that has a total of 112 square feet per side.

Select a Location that is . . .
In a neighborhood or trade area with 40,000 people
On a main traffic artery
On a straight road—no locations on curves or hills
Visible from all approaches
Not on a high-speed artery
Not bottled up by traffic at stop signs or traffic lights

TYPES OF GOODS SOLD OR SERVICES PROVIDED

In choosing a location, the types of goods sold or services provided must be taken into account. Some of these issues are discussed here.

Retailers

A retailer's location decision is greatly influenced by the type of goods sold. Retailers sell consumer goods that are goods purchased by the ultimate consumer for personal use. Consumer goods can be classified into four categories: convenience, shopping, specialty, and impulse.

Convenience Goods
Convenience goods are those items that the customer needs immediately and are usually purchased from a source that is most convenient to the shopper.

These goods are sold through many outlets, and generally the price per unit is low. These goods are advertised nationwide, the frequency of purchase is high, little selling effort is required by the retailer, and consumers give little thought either to the purchase of these items or where they are purchased. Types of convenience goods include gum, candy bars, and soft drinks. For stores handling convenience goods, a high volume of customer traffic is of utmost importance.

Shopping Goods

Consumers ordinarily spend a considerable amount of time and effort in comparing products when purchasing a shopping good. **Shopping goods** are sold through a selected number of outlets. The per unit cost is usually substantial, so customers normally compare quality features and cost of the merchandise. These items are purchased infrequently and have a relatively long life expectancy. It takes a concerted effort by retailers to sell shopping goods that include such items as automobiles, refrigerators, TVs, and furniture. For retailers of shopping goods, the quality of customer traffic is more important than the volume of customer traffic.

Specialty Goods

Specialty goods refer to items that have a special quality or characteristic and the customer will not accept a substitute. They are distributed through a small number of outlets. Price is not a consideration in the purchase of specialty goods, since prices may range from very inexpensive to very expensive. Instead, a specialty good is an item that customers will go out of their way to purchase. Some examples of specialty goods are exclusive brands of clothing, exotic perfumes, precious jewelry, and special types of foods. Since customers seek out the specialty retailer, they may locate in isolated areas because they generate their own consumer traffic.

Impulse Goods

Impulse goods are ''spur-of-the-moment'' purchases. Impulse items usually have a low or moderate price per unit and appeal to personal taste; they are distinguished from staple or necessity goods. Impulse goods are placed in store locations that have heavy customer traffic and afford high visibility, such as drive-in stores along major traffic arteries or in stores at the checkout stations.

Services

For service firms, the choice of location is heavily influenced by the type of service provided and the reputation of the firm. For example, personal-service firms where clients visit the place of business, such as a bookkeeping service, should be as accessible as possible. If the service firm makes calls to the clients, as do plumbers or electricians, the choice of location can be determined by such factors as owner's convenience, space, and rent. In fact, many of these small service firms operate out of their own home. When the firm has built an excellent record for service, location becomes less of an issue because customers will go out of their way to patronize the firm.

Some of the pertinent questions for the service firm owner to evaluate are

1. If you choose a remote location, will savings in rent offset the inconvenience?
2. If a remote location is selected, will you have to pay as much as you save in rent for advertising to make your service known?
3. If a remote location is chosen, will the customer be able readily to locate your business?
4. Will travel time to customers be excessive?
5. Will you pick up and deliver?

SITE CHOICES

In the smaller town, the choice of a site may be limited to the availability of a structure or a site. In larger areas, multiple sites are usually available, and the selection of the site is made more complex. There are several kinds of locations available, each having its own advantages and disadvantages. The site choices include (1) central business districts, (2) neighborhood locations, (3) shopping centers and malls, (4) string street locations, and (5) isolated locations.

Central Business Districts

The central business district has been the traditional center of a town's or city's shopping area because of the early development of this section of town and the convergence of the transportation systems in the central area. A business locating in a central business area has the advantage of being able to draw customers from the entire trading area. Another advantage is that small businesses capitalize on the drawing power of the larger downtown stores, such as major department stores. In addition, the large number of employees of companies and financial institutions located in the central city represent a huge potential market. Stores that sell convenience, shopping, specialty, and impulse goods find the central business district a suitable location.

However, certain drawbacks are associated with the central business district. One disadvantage is that this location usually has higher operating costs and higher rental rates. Furthermore, competition is usually very keen in the downtown area. With increased traffic congestion, downtown locations have had increasing difficulty in attracting customers. To counteract these problems, some cities have initiated programs to revitalize the downtown business areas to make them more appealing. Building renovations and the creation of pedestrian walkways are part of the plan to breathe new life into central cities.

Neighborhood Shopping Areas

Within most cities are found clusters of several stores scattered throughout the residential areas. Ordinarily, these stores are convenience-type stores. Stores located in neighborhood shopping areas include drugstores, hardware stores, grocery stores, and small variety stores. Service establishments (barber, beauty shops, dry cleaners) also find neighborhood locations attractive.

Neighborhood shopping area stores depend largely on the patronage of people who live in the area immediately surrounding the location. Compared to downtown locations, neighborhood stores have lower operating costs and lower rental rates. A distinct advantage of neighborhood locations is the opportunity afforded the owner–manager to enjoy direct, personal contact with customers. Through personalized attention, such as knowing customers by name, the small business manager is able to promote repeat patronage for the store.

Shopping Centers and Malls

The period following World War II ushered in major changes in the United States. A major change was the movement away from the inner city to the suburbs as the population became more mobile. The relocation of large segments of the population was instrumental in the rise of the planned, suburban shopping centers. A **shopping center** is a "group of commercial establishments planned, developed, and owned, and managed as a unit related in location, size, and type of shops to the trade area the unit serves; it provides on-site parking in definite relationship to the types and sizes of stores." [3] Planned shopping centers include convenience, neighborhood, community, and regional. According to the Urban Land Institute, a center's type is determined by tenants or major tenants, not by site area or square feet of the structure. [4]

Convenience Shopping Centers

Convenience shopping centers are usually located along a heavily traveled street. They may consist of from 5 to 10 outlets for convenience goods and personal services. The major tenant is normally a convenience store, such as 7-Eleven. Other tenants may include various types of service establishments, such as a washateria, a hair styling salon, and a dry cleaning establishment. This is the smallest of the planned centers.

Neighborhood Shopping Centers

Neighborhood shopping centers usually serve a population of from 2500 to 40,000 living within a driving time of 6 to 10 minutes. The firms in the center offer convenience goods (food, drugs, sundries) and personal services (barber and beauty shops, dry cleaning). A supermarket or drugstore or both comprise the chief tenants in the center and are responsible for pulling most of the traffic into the center. These centers may have from 10 to 25 tenants and from 30,000 to 100,000 square feet of leasable space.

Community Shopping Centers

The trading area of the **community shopping center** usually overlaps with other trading areas, and the population served ranges from 40,000 to 150,000. In addition to convenience goods and personal service shops, these centers have many shops that offer shopping goods. Thus, community centers offer shoppers a greater assortment of merchandise—with a greater range of prices, clothing sizes, styles—than the neighborhood centers. This enables shoppers to make price and quality comparisons. The major store in this center may be a junior department store, a variety store, a supermarket, or a discount department store. The number of tenants may range from 25 to 50, and gross leasing area ranges from 100,000 to 300,000 square feet.

Regional Shopping Centers

Regional shopping centers cater to a trade area that has 150,000 or more people, and the area may extend from 10 to 15 miles or more in all directions. The trading area of the center depends on the location of competitors as well as on travel time needed to reach the center (usually 20 to 40 minutes of driving time). Regional centers have 50 or more stores and one or more full-line department stores as the anchor tenant serving as the prime customer attraction. These stores are usually not smaller than 100,000 square feet. This type of center offers a wide range and depth of shopping goods: apparel, furniture, general merchandise, and home furnishings. Other features of the center that attract customers are community rooms, theaters, medical clinics, banks, and postal services. In addition to major department stores, regional centers may have as many as 200 small specialty shops. Gross leasable area ranges from 300,000 to 750,000 square feet.

Many modern centers have enclosed, weather-controlled malls. These centers provide the added advantages of making it convenient and pleasant for customers to shop at all times because a consumer can complete all shopping under one common roof. These centers have other features such as fountains and landscaped interiors that add to their attractiveness.

When a regional center exceeds 750,000 square feet, it is then classified as a superregional center. This center may include three to six department stores of not less than 100,000 square feet as anchor tenants and a unique location within the largest trade area of the city. Gross leasable area ranges from 750,000 to more than 1,000,000 square feet.

A number of variations have occurred in conventional shopping centers that are discussed in the paragraphs that follow.

Minimall

Minimalls are designed for customer convenience. The major tenants are a junior department store; a food, drug, or variety store; and a number of specialty and service outlets. In addition to offering convenience of location for goods and services, the center is designed to reduce energy consumption and lessen the distance traveled to reach the center.

Small Regional Mall

Small regional malls are scaled-down versions of the regional center. The tenants are similar to tenants of the larger mall and can serve the needs of smaller markets. This mall may be desirable for the small business owner who desires having an outlet in a smaller center.

Specialty or Theme Centers

Specialty centers cater to unusual market segments. The theme center can be adapted to historical buildings. An example is Ghiradelli Square in San Francisco. This complex consists of eight buildings originally used for manufacturing chocolate and spices. The buildings have been renovated and converted into many small specialty shops and restaurants.

Fashion Centers

Fashion centers more suited for high-income areas, consist of apparel shops, boutiques, and handcraft shops that sell high-quality and high-priced specialty goods. These centers usually draw customers from a wide trade area because of their offering of specialty merchandise.

Advantages and Disadvantages of Shopping Centers

Locating in a shopping center has several advantages. Store owners can coordinate their advertising effort and direct them toward centerwide sales promotions. Centers also provide adequate parking near stores so parking problems are minimized. Store hours for the center are generally standardized, and hours of operation are longer than for independent stores. There is also a common theme for the center. With its modern, attractive interior and exterior, the shopping center can provide a pleasant and inviting place to shop.

Centers also have some disadvantages. Store owners in a center have certain restrictions on their operations, such as store hours, higher rent than in independent locations, and products or services that can be sold.

String Street Locations

When a group of retail outlets develops in an unplanned manner along a street or highway which is served by mass transportation and also has a high automobile traffic count, the result is referred to as a **string street location.** Each outlet must be able to stand on its own and attract its own customers. Drive-in grocery stores, furniture stores, auto parts houses, and fast-food restaurants are common types of retailers who choose a string street location. Small service firms that cater to the immediate needs of passing traffic also find this type of location adequate.

Isolated Locations

When a single retailer or service firm chooses to locate in urban areas or along heavily traveled streets or highways, the choice is referred to as an isolated location. As no other retailers or service firms are in the area, the business must be able to attract its own customers. A fruit and vegetable stand or a pottery store is an example of a type of retailer who may choose an isolated location. Merchandise is usually lower priced, there is usually ample parking, and rent and other operating costs are lower in these locations. The reputation of the retailer or service firm will be a significant factor in attracting customers to this type of location.

RETAIL AFFINITY

Stores selling some types of consumer goods, such as shopping goods, have a strong **retail affinity** to one another because they sell similar or complementary merchandise. Retailers of shopping goods choose to locate near competitors because customers need travel only a short distance to compare the products of the various stores. Locating near the competition gives shop owners greater customer drawing power than they would have individually. For example, automobile dealers tend to locate in close proximity to facilitate comparison shopping. Further groupings of retail affinity are used by furniture stores, antique shops, and theaters. In deciding whether to locate near establishments that sell similar or complementary merchandise, retailers should consider several factors, such as how many competitors there are in the trade area, the buying power of prospective customers, and the size and financial strength of competitors. Some examples of retail affinity follow.

In shopping centers, the grouping of certain kinds of stores has been found to be desirable. The retail affinity of stores in fashion centers or convenience centers illustrate this grouping.

Dual-level shopping malls typically have one level, with fashion stores located close to upscale department stores; the other level contains nonfashion stores.

Almost all kinds of shopping goods stores have a strong affinity for department stores. For example, men's or women's clothing stores can benefit from a location near a department store.

Other stores in certain groupings have a strong affinity for one another, either because they sell similar merchandise or because the merchandise offerings are complementary or related as the following examples demonstrate.[5]

Men's clothing, men's shoes, men's furnishings

Women's apparel, accessories, shoes, and millinery, and children's clothes and toys

Paint, furniture, curtain and drapery; upholstery, hardware

Stores that sell personal services and conveniences naturally go together. In shopping centers, they should be located as close to the parking area as possible.[6]

Some kinds of stores do not appear to benefit from proximity to other related businesses. As discussed earlier, jewelry stores selling specialty goods have no strong affinity for other kinds of retail establishments. Convenience stores that depend more on the volume of traffic than its character are to be found in all types of locations.

SITE ECONOMICS

For each type of business, there is an optimum location. For example, studies of specific sites show that one side of the street is preferable for retail stores, and this is especially true for those sections of the country that have long, hot summers. The optimum location is referred to as the **100 percent location.** Location analysis may reveal an optimum site, such as accessibility or population income level, but the occupancy cost may be prohibitive. In this instance, a site with lower occupancy costs may be the only satisfactory alternative. Occupancy costs include taxes, purchase or lease or rental rate, utilities, maintenance, and remodeling if necessary.

The unique requirements of each firm must be studied when evaluating the economic feasibility of the site relative to occupancy cost. For example, the optimum location for a store selling convenience goods is a corner site that has two traffic flows and a large window display.

When renting, small business owners must evaluate the rent-paying capacity of the site. Certain businesses, such as convenience stores, drugstores, and apparel shops, can sustain high-rent areas. Other stores, such as furniture and furnishings, locate in a low-rent site. Some characteristics of stores appropriate for high- and low-rent areas are shown in Figure 6-3.

ZONING REGULATIONS

In the search for a site for the business, the owner–manager must be aware of the zoning regulations in the area under consideration. Zoning refers to the

FIGURE 6-3
CHARACTERISTICS OF STORES SUITABLE TO HIGH- AND LOW-RENT LOCATIONS.

Locations	Type of Firm
High-Rent Location	
High value of merchandise in proportion to bulk	Jewelry store
Window display important	Department store
High rate of merchandise turnover	Fashion apparel store
Low gross margin of profit per item	Drugstore
Impulse or convenience items sold	Convenience stores (7-Eleven)
Appeal to transient trade	Hair styling salon
Relatively little advertising	Specialty food shop
Low-Rent Location	
Low value of merchandise in proportion to bulk	Agricultural and garden supply store
Large amount of floor space needed for floor display	Office furniture store
Low rate of merchandise turnover	Hardware store
High gross margin of profit per item	Furniture store
Shopping goods sold	TV store
Established clientele	Small, neighborhood drugstore
Much advertising	Variety store

division of a city or county into districts to control the location and the use of buildings, land, and construction. The three broad categories of zoning include residential, business or commercial, and industrial, although there may be subcategories within the major classification. In cities or counties, a governing body, either a zoning commission or a city or county planning commission, establishes zoning regulations that define the purpose for which land or buildings are to be used. This commission can also bring action to prevent or restrain the construction or remodeling of a building or the use of a building or land that violates the city or county zoning regulations.

A basic aim of zoning laws is to ensure a degree of consistency in the types and uses of buildings in a given area. The owner–manager must be aware that zoning laws affect not only the type of business that may be permitted to be established in an area but may also determine the kind of building that may be constructed as well as its height and size.

For example, an individual purchased a home in an area zoned residential with the expectation of starting a small hair styling salon in the home. She applied to the zoning commission for a change in zoning category that would have permitted the overlapping of commercial and residential zone areas. Her application was denied on the basis of objections from the neighbors as well as on the basis of traffic and parking problems that would have been caused.

This case directs a word of caution to small business owners about the prospective site. They must ascertain that the intended business will not violate the zoning laws of an area. Hence, a site may be a good location, but city or county zoning regulations may prohibit locating there. Thorough investigation into zoning laws is an essential part of the site selection process. A zoning map of the city and surrounding territory can be useful in determining location and boundaries of zoning categories in a city or county.

Although it may be possible to get a site rezoned, the small business owner should not purchase a site until the site's classification has been changed. Too often, a site is purchased with no assurance, only hope, that it can be rezoned. Purchasing on the expectation that it may be rezoned is at best a risky business venture and fatal to the business if a reclassification cannot be obtained.

Sometimes, the small business owner may follow the required procedures and still encounter an insurmountable zoning hurdle as seen in the following case. The owner of a residential real estate firm purchased some property for the purpose of constructing an office building for his firm. The property was located in an environmentally sensitive area and was zoned for residential use but not commercial or industrial. However, the planning commission and the city council both approved a preliminary zoning change that would allow him to construct the office building on the site. When he came back to the city council for final zoning approval a year later, a new city council had been elected. The new council voted not to approve the zoning change.

TRAFFIC ANALYSIS

Traffic flow is a basic factor in location analysis for many types of businesses. A traffic study is a valuable tool in location analysis for at least two reasons. First, the **traffic count** measures the amount of pedestrian and vehicle traffic passing a site that represents potential customers. Second the study serves as one measure for comparing the relative desirability of sites under consideration.

Pedestrian Traffic Count

To make a pedestrian traffic study, the owners must decide (1) who is to be counted, (2) when the count will take place, and (3) where the count should be made. The purpose of this study is to establish the number of potential customers passing by the proposed site during the store's hours of operation.

Prior to taking the count, small business owners should decide who is to be counted in order to give the count more reliability. A heavy volume of traffic is of little or no value if it does not represent potential customers. For example, a ladies' apparel shop owner would be more interested in the number of women passing the site whereas the drugstore owner would be interested in total traffic volume.

Another criterion for counting should possibly be the age categories of pedestrians. Pedestrians should also be classified according to their purpose in passing the site. Employees rushing to work or rushing home are not potential customers for shopping goods. The in-between hours are the best hours to study traffic for some store owners. For example, the best time for an owner of a downtown store to make a study is between the hours of 10 and 5. However, shopping center traffic is heavier during the afternoon, evening and weekend hours.

Other considerations in determining traffic flow are the season as well as the month, week, and day. Traffic normally is much heavier before holidays and during the latter part of the week.

When a day with normal traffic flow has been selected, it is a good policy to divide the day into half-hour and hour intervals. This enables traffic to be counted and recorded for each half-hour interval that the store is open for business.

Another factor in pedestrian traffic counting is to establish where the count will be made. Will all traffic passing near the site or just the traffic passing in front of the site be counted? Care must also be taken not to count people twice, as when customers enter and leave a store.

Thus, the pedestrian traffic study can provide data as to the sales potential for the site. If the following information is known, based on either past experience of the retailer or from a trade association, a reasonable estimate of sales volume can be forecast.

1. Characteristics of individuals who are most likely to be store customers (from pedestrian interviews)
2. Number of such individuals passing the site during store hours (from traffic counts)
3. Proportion of passersby who will enter the store (from pedestrian interviews)
4. Proportion of those entering who will become purchasers (from pedestrian interviews)
5. Amount of average transaction (from past experience, trade association, and trade publications)[7]

Automobile Traffic Count

The sales potential of many convenience-type firms and service firms depends on the quantity and composition of automobile traffic past a site. The technique used to ascertain the who, when, and where of pedestrian traffic analysis may be used also to establish auto traffic flow and potential. Data on traffic flow along major streets are available from city and state government agencies or outdoor advertising companies. However, the traffic analysis should be conducted with emphasis on any unique requirements of the company.

Auto traffic may be classified on the basis of the kind of trip taken: work trip, planned shopping trip, or pleasure trip. For example, along heavily traveled arteries, a dry cleaning establishment finds the location on the work-bound side of the street favorable whereas the drive-in grocery store effectively utilizes the homeward-bound side. Location analysis shows that a good retail location for the planned shopping trip is the right-hand side of the main street going into a shopping district and next to the streets carrying traffic into, out of, or across town. Motels, restaurants, and service stations attract pleasure-trip traffic by locating along heavily traveled highways with easy exit and access.

Analysis of pedestrian and auto traffic makes it possible for small business owners to develop a time-travel map. This map allows a picture of the quality and quantity of traffic flow during normal shopping hours to be developed and is one major element in evaluating whether a site will generate a sufficient sales volume for profitable operation.

Traffic analysis is more significant for some types of outlets than for others when considered on the basis of the type of consumer goods sold. As earlier discussed, outlets distributing convenience goods must rely on the quantity of pedestrian and auto traffic as the most important measure. Drive-in stores that sell convenience goods are more attractive to consumers if they are located close to their residence. Shopping goods outlets depend more on quality than quantity because people who visit these stores usually make a deliberate effort to shop there. Specialty goods outlets are usually able to locate in a more out-of-the-way site because customers seek them out. Hence, traffic analysis is not as essential for specialty outlets as it is for convenience and shopping goods stores.

A bakery located in a small town was able to expand its market by putting two small portable enclosed trailers along two of the heaviest traveled highways leading into a major metropolitan area. At these sites, motorists easily and safely exit and enter on their way to work and buy pastries and coffee that they take to their place of work. The owners operate the sites from 6 A.M. to 11 A.M. daily, five days a week. These additional outlets have proven very beneficial in enlarging the market for the bakery's products.

LOCATION ANALYSIS FOR SMALL WHOLESALERS

Wholesalers are intermediaries. Their sales are usually made to retailers or to other wholesalers. Small wholesalers usually serve a local market, such as the wholesale grocer who supplies merchandise to grocers in a relatively small geographical territory.

Small wholesalers must consider many of the same location factors we have outlined earlier for the retailer and service firm owner. However, they must be evaluated in light of any special needs of the wholesaler. For example, the wholesaler must consider the trade area's potential. In most towns or cities, there is a wholesaling district that must be studied to determine its suitability and accessibility. Some wholesalers have begun to locate on the edge of towns or cities that provide more flexibility and relief from some of the inner-city traffic congestion.

LOCATION ANALYSIS FOR SMALL MANUFACTURERS

As with other establishments, the choice of locating a new small manufacturing firm or relocating an established firm is one of the ingredients of the successful firm. A major cause of the manufacturer's ability to move from a position of marginal profit to a healthy profit position is often attributed to choice of site. In the serarch for the most desirable location, many factors must be analyzed: general area and the specific site, markets and raw materials, labor supply, transportation systems, community attitudes, and community services and facilities.

General Area and Specific Site

In selecting an area for locating the manufacturing operation, the small owner should identify specific needs, such as immediate land requirements as well as planned expansion, type of plant, and labor supply. With these data, the search to find the general area that meets the specific needs can progress. Once a general area has been selected, the next phase consists of determining the availability and suitability of a site to meet the firm's needs, such as the proper terrain required for the plant's foundation.

Markets and Raw Materials

Another option facing a manufacturer is the choice of locating the plant close to the source of raw materials and near customers. If a firm manufactures products whose raw materials are more costly to ship than the finished goods, the owner will usually locate near the source of raw materials. If the firm depends primarily on the local customers or manufactures a product that is perishable, however, it may be more advantageous to locate near customers so that they can have convenient access to the finished goods.

Transportation

The importance of rail, water, highway, or air transportation is usually determined by the weight, size, and price of the product. When the firm produces goods that sell for a relatively low price and the cost of shipping is high relative to the cost, such as concrete, transportation costs are significant, and the firm will usually compete only in the local market. Conversely, if the shipping cost is low relative to selling price, as for electronic parts, transportation costs are not as significant, and the manufacturer will distribute goods in a broad market. Another factor to be considered in choosing the transportation system is the speed with which customers demand delivery. Thus, the relative importance of the various transportation systems depends on the kind of business to be served. Furthermore, the manufacturer must try to evaluate not only current transportation needs but future needs as well.

Labor Supply and Wages

One of the more important considerations in plant location is the availability of an adequate labor supply. A small electronics manufacturer that requires highly technical personnel pays much greater attention to availability of that type of labor than does the plant that requires unskilled labor almost exclusively. If the firm employs chiefly unskilled labor, the prevailing wage rates and the extent of unionization of employees in an area may be critical. Should other factors outweigh the availability of labor in an area, the owner should determine if the site will offer enough amenities to attract employees.

Community Attitudes

In site selection, the manufacturer should determine if the people in the community favor the firm's locating in the area. Some cities permit only "clean" manufacturing operations in the community, that is, those firms that do not pollute the environment, such as electronics firms. A community that is anxious to attract the new facility often makes special tax concessions, such as exempting the firm from taxes for a specific period of time. However, there is no assurance that this advantage will endure, because it can be changed by local governments.

Community Services and Facilities

The types of community facilities that are available or will be supplied by the city may become a strategic factor in site selection. Frequently cited service and facility requirements are housing, education, recreation, hospitals, police and fire protection, adequacy of power supply, and ability to provide utilities to the firm.

The factors just mentioned plus a number of other considerations are presented in Figure 6-4. By assigning a point value to each item to be considered, the small manufacturer can be in a stronger position to evaluate location alternatives.

FIGURE 6-4
FACTORS TO BE EVALUATED IN SELECTING A LOCATION FOR A SMALL MANUFACTURING FIRM.

Factors	Quality of each factor in meeting firm's specific requirements: 1 (lowest) to 10 (highest)	×	Importance of each factor to the success of company: 1 (least important) to 5 (most important)	=	Points
1. Accessibility to market and customers served	_____		_____		_____
2. Quantity and quality of labor supply	_____		_____		_____
3. Wage and salary rate in community	_____		_____		_____
4. Adequate supply of raw materials	_____		_____		_____
5. Tax burden of business in the community	_____		_____		_____
6. Community attitudes toward business	_____		_____		_____
7. Adequacy of transportation systems	_____		_____		_____
8. Suitable climate	_____		_____		_____
9. Community services and facilities (housing, schools, police and fire protection, hospitals)	_____		_____		_____
10. Adequacy of utilities	_____		_____		_____
11. Potential of site for expansion	_____		_____		_____
12. Evaluation of site chosen in relation to site chosen by competitors	_____		_____		_____
			Total Score[1] =		_____

[1] Reflects potential of proposed location.

SUMMARY OF KEY POINTS

1. Major factors to study in location analysis are the size and potential of the trade area, accessibility, parking availability, site choices, site economics, zoning regulations, and traffic analysis.

2. Small business owners should evaluate three categories of the trade area

and its potential: the town or city, the specific area of the town or city, and the specific site.

3. A retail location is dependent in part on the type of goods sold: convenience, shopping, specialty, and impulse.

4. The location of a service firm is influenced partly by the type of services provided.

5. The small business owner must include as a part of location analysis the accessibility to the site by auto and pedestrian traffic.

6. Adequate parking facilities are a key factor in determining a site's potential.

7. The small business owners may choose a location from among many alternatives: central business district, neighborhood location, shopping centers and malls, string street locations, and isolated locations.

8. An economic study of the proposed location should be conducted to determine its feasibility for the business.

9. Zoning regulations govern the location and use of buildings, land, and construction.

DISCUSSION QUESTIONS

1. Explain why accessibility of a site is one of the major factors to be evaluated when choosing the location for the small business.

2. Identify the four types of consumer goods.

3. What are some of the chief factors to consider when evaluating the parking facilities of a proposed site?

4. Explain the advantages and disadvantages of the central business district.

5. Explain why site economics is important in the choice of location.

6. How do zoning regulations influence site selection?

7. Discuss the factors to be evaluated when making a pedestrian and automobile traffic count.

8. Identify and briefly discuss the factors that should be evaluated by a small manufacturer in choosing a location for a factory.

THE BUSINESS PLAN: LOCATION ANALYSIS

The questions that follow have proven useful in evaluating location alternatives. This analysis can assist the entrepreneur in developing a profile of the potential trade area, accessibility, competition, the potential for attracting new business, and cost.

Potential of the Trading Area

1. How big is the trading area? _____ sq mi

2. What is the customer potential within 5 mis? _____ customers. Within 30 min travel time? _____ customers.

3. What is the density of population? _____ people per sq mi

4. Is there adequate transportation? _____ Yes. _____ No.

5. What is the income level of the trading area? $ _____ per capita.

6. Is the local employment pattern good? _____ percent people unemployed.

7. What is the general makeup of the community? _____ Residential. _____ Old. _____ Growing.

8. What are the trends in population and income? _____ Up. _____ Down.

9. Is new construction on the increase? _____ Yes. _____ No.

10. Are school enrollments up? _____ Yes. _____ No.

11. Are retail sales on the increase? _____ Yes. _____ No.

12. Have average business improvements been made recently? _____ Yes. _____ No.

13. Is there a high vacancy rate for business property? _____ Yes. _____ No.

14. Have shopping patterns changed drastically in recent years? _____ Yes. _____ No.

15. Are customers moving to or away from the potential location? _____ To. _____ From.

16. What are the present zoning restrictions? _____ _____

Can Customers Get to the Location?

1. Is the area served by adequate public transportation? _____ Yes. _____ No.

2. How broad an area does the transportation service encompass? _____ sq mi

3. Is the area generally attractive to shoppers? _____ Yes. _____ No.

4. Can it be easily reached by automobile? _____ Yes. _____ No.

5. Is public parking adequate and relatively inexpensive? _____ Yes. _____ No.

6. How many spaces in the available, nearby parking space are taken up by all-day parkers? _____ Many. _____ Few.

7. If located on a highway, is the location easily accessible from the main traffic flow? —————— Yes. —————— No.

8. What are restrictions on signs and store identification? —————— ————————————————————————————

9. If on a limited-access road, how close is the nearest interchange? —————— miles.

10. Is the location accessible to delivery trucks? —————— Yes. —————— No.

11. Is the traffic speed too fast to encourage entrance by automobile? —————— Yes. —————— No.

12. Are the customers who drive past the location on their way to work or on shopping trips? —————— On way to work. —————— On shopping trip.

13. Will nearby stores help you? Are the other stores in the shopping center, neighborhood, or highway location of a nature that will attract customers who will also become patrons of your store? —————— Yes. —————— No.

14. What are the prospects for changes in traffic flow in the near future? —————— Slight. —————— Likely.

15. Will anticipated changes improve or damage the location? —————— Improve. —————— Damage.

16. Are zoning changes planned which would affect accessibility of the location? —————— Yes. —————— No.

Judging the Competition

1. Are there other businesses of the same kind, and, if so, how many, between the prospective location and the most highly populated area? —————— stores.

2. Is this spot the most convenient store location in the area? —————— Yes. —————— No.

3. How many other stores of the same kind are in this trading area? —————— stores.

4. How many of them will compete with you for customers? —————— stores.

5. Do they have better parking facilities? —————— Yes. —————— No.

6. Do they offer the same type of merchandise? —————— Yes. —————— No.

7. Do you consider them more aggressive or less aggressive than your own operation will be? —————— More. —————— Less.

8. What other competing stores are planned in the near future? —————— ————————————————————————————

9. Are other potential sites that are closer to the majority of customers likely to be developed in the near future? _____ Yes. _____ No.

10. Are your major competitors well-known, well-advertised stores? _____ Yes. _____ No.

11. Is there actually a need for another store of this kind in the area? _____ Yes. _____ No.

12. How well are the demands for this product being met? _____ Good. _____ Fair. _____ Poor.

13. If there are empty stores or vacant lots near the location, what is planned for them? A competitor store? _____ Yes. _____ No.

Can the Location Attract New Business?

1. Is the location in an attractive business district? _____ Yes. _____ No.

2. Are there numerous stores which will draw potential customers for you into the area? _____ Yes. _____ No.

3. Is the location near well-known and well-advertised stores? _____ Yes. _____ No.

4. Is this location the most attractive one in the area? _____ Yes. _____ No.

5. Is the location on the side of the street with the biggest customer traffic? _____ Yes. _____ No.

6. Is the potential location nearer to the general parking area than locations of competing firms? _____ Yes. _____ No.

7. Is the location in the center of or in the fringe of the shopping district? _____ Center. _____ Fringe.

8. Is it near the common meeting places for people, such as public offices? _____ Yes. _____ No.

9. Are most of the people passing the store prospective customers? _____ Yes. _____ No.

10. Are the people who pass usually in a hurry or are they taking time to shop? _____ In a hurry. _____ Out shopping.

Cost of the Location

1. What will your rent be? $ _____ per month.

2. Who will pay the utility costs? _____ You. _____ Others.

3. Who pays additional costs such as taxes, public services, and costs of improvements? _____ You. _____ Others.

4. What are the possibilities for eventual expansion? _____ Good.
   _____ Poor.

5. Are good employees available? _____ Yes. _____ No.

6. Will potential income justify your costs? _____ Yes. _____ No.

Source: *Starting and Managing a Small Retail Hardware Store,* Starting and Managing Series, Vol. 10 (Washington, D.C.: Small Business Administration), pp. 17–20.

ENTREPRENEURIAL PROJECTS

1. Select a line of merchandise as reported in *Sales and Marketing Management* magazine. Lines of merchandise reported are groceries and other foods, health and beauty aids, women's and girl's clothing, footwear, major household appliances, and furniture and sleep equipment. Choose these data for a specific city (or the city in which you live if it is reported in the magazine). Then find the population for the city selected and the effective buying income for that city. Use this information to make an estimate of the area's purchasing power for the potential of the line of merchandise selected.

2. Visit the local chamber of commerce to inquire about the types of assistance they offer firms considering moving into the local trade area.

3. Contact a trade association and determine the types of assistance they provide members regarding location analysis.

4. Consult Census Bureau data and determine the percentage of people employed in each industry for your city, county, state, or all three areas.

5. Assume you have been asked to serve as a consultant to a group of individuals planning to open a restaurant. What factors would you identify as most important to this type of business?

6. Assume you have been asked to serve as a consultant to a group of individuals who want to build a small manufacturing plant in your area. They plan to manufacture wooden desks and student chairs for elementary schools. What facors should be identified as important for this business?

7. Use the profile of the characteristics of stores in high-rent and low-rent areas. Select a store in your community in the high-rent and low-rent area and determine how each matches the profile. If differences are noted, what are they?

C A S E A
Big Scoop

Ray Langston has contacted Big Scoop, a national franchisor of ice cream shops, about the possibility of obtaining a franchise for his area of the city. The franchisor provides Ray with the following demographic information for the specific area of the city in which Ray is interested.

A map included in the franchisor's information packet shown here details the location selected for the next franchise in the city of 300,000.

THE PARKWAY SHOPPING CENTER.

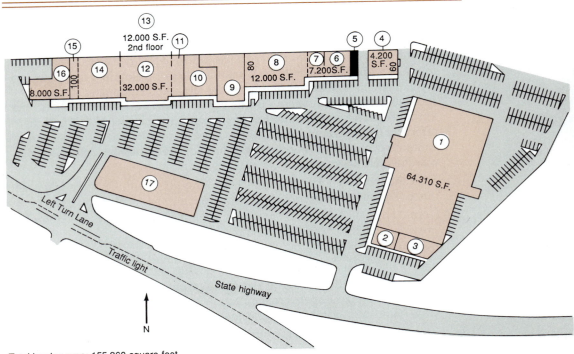

Total leasing area: 155,360 square feet

Parking: 809 cars

1. Supermarket
2. Western wear apparel
3. Pizza restaurant
4. Savings and loan branch office
5. Big Scoop proposed site
6. Children's clothing store
7. Medical doctor's office
8. Vacant
9. Drugstore (Nat'l chain)
10. Vacant
11. Bar BQ Restaurant
12. Department store
13. Health and fitness center
14. Vacant
15. Dry cleaning establishment
16. Auto tire store
17. Fast-food restaurant
    (Hamburger)

Demographics	Primary Trade Area 1.0-Mile Radius	Secondary Trade Area 2.0-Mile Radius
Population		
Current	9,779	36,328
5-year projection	12,175	45,648
% change	+24.5%	+22.5%
Households		
Current	4,028	14,259
5-year projection	5,105	18,063
% change	+26.7%	+26.7%
Estimated Households by Income Level		
$50,000 or more	10.58%	10.40%
$35,000 to $49,999	17.61%	17.35%
$25,000 to $34,999	20.46%	21.20%
$15,000 to $24,999	24.79%	25.05%
$7,500 to $14,999	14.52%	14.66%
Under $7,500	12.05%	11.35%
Occupied Units		
Owner occupied	46.11%	51.34%
Renter occupied	53.89%	48.66%
Average Number of Persons per Household	2.45	2.59
Year Round Units at Address		
Single dwelling unit (home)	60.67%	67.68%
2–9 units (apartments)	23.29%	17.65%
10+ units (apartments)	14.10%	13.13%
Mobile home or trailer	1.94%	1.55%
Estimated average household income	$27,623	$27,631
Estimated median household income	$25,307	$25,172
Per capita income	$11,367	$10,706

A traffic study conducted by the city transportation department has shown a daily traffic count past the potential site of 20,390 vehicles.

The only ice cream competition in the area is from an independent shop located ½ mile north of the proposed Big Scoop site. This competitor shares its location with a hamburger restaurant.

The estimated store cost is $97,446. This cost includes the capital investment (equipment, franchise fee, leasehold improvements) and the cash allocations (opening inventory, advertising, insurance deposit, security deposit, first month's rent and first month's rental extras).

Based on average sales of Big Scoop franchisees, the gross sales projection is $135,400 and a net income of $12,200. The average salary of Big Scoop franchisees last year was $13,000.

Questions

1. How would you estimate the total potential purchasing power for ice cream sales in this trade area?
2. What is the total purchasing power for households within 1.0 miles of the center?
3. What other factors should Ray consider in his evaluation of the potential for a Big Scoop franchise in this area?

CASE B

Kristy's Pizza Palace

Kristy has been associated with the food business in some capacity all her working life. While in high school and college, she worked part-time for various fast-food restaurants. Since graduation from college, she has been employed as a salesperson for a large wholesale grocer. She has been extremely successful as a salesperson but has been seriously considering opening her own fast-food restaurant, Kristy's Pizza Palace.

She knows that the eating habits of millions of Americans have undergone significant change in recent years. Dining out and carryout food are growing in popularity. Kristy has read a National Restaurant Association report that indicates about 40 percent of all food dollars are spent on meals eaten away from the home. The association's report also emphasized that per capita sales of fast-food restaurants increased by almost 86 percent between 1972 and 1984. Furthermore, there is expected to be a major increase in the dollars spent for carryout food items.

These data support her view that potential is good in the fast-food industry, but she also realizes that competition is intense. Fast food has become a staple of a majority of American's diets, and pizza is one of the most popular of the many types of fast foods. National Restaurant Association figures indicate that pizza is more popular than other foods, such as Chinese and Mexican, and pizza's share of the fast-food market continues to grow.

Kristy knows that location is one key to the success of her proposed restaurant, and she is currently evaluating an available site. This site has a suitable building that would require some remodeling and is located on one of the most heavily traveled arteries in the city—a six-lane, east–west divided street that intersects a four-lane, north–south artery. However, the six-lane thoroughfare becomes four lanes beyond the intersection with the north–south street. There is adequate parking, but the parking lot has only a single entrance and exit ramp. Traffic flows one way, east, in front of the restaurant. Traffic must enter the restaurant's parking lot from a "right-turn-only" lane that feeds traffic from the six-lane street onto the four-lane street. Traffic must exit and travel west.

Traffic is steady all day but is particularly congested at the peak travel time during the afternoon and early evening from approximately 4 to 7 P.M. Entering and exiting is difficult during these times as well as somewhat difficult for the remainder of the day.

The other businesses on the block include a combination self-service gas station and drive-in grocery, a barbecue restaurant, and a drive-through bank. Competition in a small convenience shopping center across the six-lane street consists of a Mexican food restaurant, a fast-food hamburger restaurant, a fast-food chicken restaurant, and a national pizza franchise, which has been in this location for three years.

Kristy knows that the number of automobiles passing the site is very high,

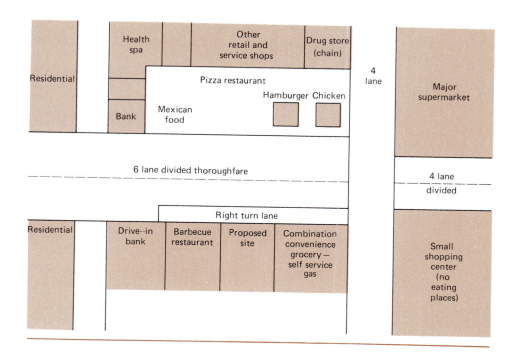

but there is practically no potential for pedestrian drop-in customers. Kristy has studied the site's history and knows the following.

1. The site was originally a Mexican fast-food restaurant, a franchise similar in type to Taco Bell. The land was developed and a building erected. Eight months after opening, the restaurant closed.
2. About six months after that closing, a national pizza franchise leased the site. The original Mexican restaurant facility was razed, and a building to house the pizza restaurant was constructed. In one year, the pizza restaurant closed.
3. Three months later, a Western-type steak house replaced the pizza restaurant. Extensive remodeling was done to emphasize the Western atmosphere. Within 11 months, the steak house closed its doors for good.

Questions

1. What does the history of the site suggest as far as the likelihood of success for the proposed pizza restaurant?
2. How do you explain the failure of three businesses at this site?
3. Would you recommend Kristy lease this site?

Notes

[1] William R. Davidson, Daniel J. Sweeney, and Ronald W. Stampfl, *Retailing Management,* 5th ed. (New York: John Wiley, 1984), pp. 188–189.
[2] *Shopping Center Development Handbook* (Washington, D.C.: Urban Land Institute, 1985).
[3] *Dollars and Cents of Shopping Centers: 1987* (Washington, D.C.: Urban Land Institute, 1987), p. 3.
[4] *Shopping Center Development Handbook.*
[5] William R. Davidson, Daniel J. Sweeney, and Ronald W. Stampfl, *Retailing Management,* 6th ed. (New York: John Wiley, 1988), p. 252.
[6] Ibid.
[7] James R. Lowry, *Using a Traffic Study to Select a Retail Site,* Management Aid No. 2.021 (Washington, D.C.: U.S. Government Printing Office, 1980).

KEY WORDS

CHAPTER 7

PHYSICAL FACILITIES

LEARNING GOALS

After reading this chapter, you will understand:

1 The value of physical facility planning to the entrepreneur.

2 The variety of issues involved in choosing between occupying a new facility or an existing structure.

3 Why each business must define its unique space and construction requirements.

4 How the architectural style and interior features of the facility help to shape the image of the firm.

5 The importance of layout for retailers, service firms, and manufacturers.

6 The difference between process layout and product layout in a manufacturing facility.

7 How merchandising service establishments and processing-type service establishments differ.

Anthony and Thomas Zanitos

ANTHONY THOMAS CANDY COMPANY

In 1914, a small candy kitchen—Anthony's Confectionary—was started by a Greek immigrant in Columbus, Ohio. The store was basically run by five family members until 1969, when Anthony Zanitos's son, Thomas, got the itch to expand.

It's that kind of itch for which the SBA was created.

BancOhio awarded Zanitos a $50,000 loan guaranteed by SBA. He immediately began opening new stores in other neighborhoods of Columbus. The company's gross annual sales grew from $800,000 at the time of SBA's loan, to $5.8 million today. At loan time there were 16 employees; today there are 150 employees in 14 Anthony Thomas Candy stores in the Ohio capital.

In 1982 and 1983, the candy kitchen plant expanded into a depressed area of Columbus targeted as a "revitalization" zone. It did so in care of two SBA 503 loans issued by a local development company specifically for community improvement projects. This facility now produces over 1 million pounds of candy annually.

Zanitos has been a leader in the candy industry, serving as a past board member of the Retail Confectioners Institute. Along the way he has invented two candy manufacturing machines and a unique process for melting chocolate. To increase profitability,

Zanitos's manufacturing plant now prints and makes its own boxes.

In a very competitive industry, the Anthony Thomas Candy Company has surged ahead, thanks to a boost from SBA.

Source: Network (Washington, D.C.: Small Business Administration, September–October 1987).

THE PHYSICAL FACILITY

Physical facility planning refers to the exterior and the interior design of the physical facility, including the layout of the store's interior. The exterior design of the physical facility can be considered an asset in attracting customers. Franchisors realize the prominent role of exterior design in customer recognition. By requiring uniformity of facility design for their franchised outlets, franchisors believe consumers will associate quality goods and services with the franchise whenever they see the familiar facility.

Total store planning must be a high-priority item for small business owners. The building's exterior and interior features should be carefully studied from the standpoint of establishing its suitability for serving the needs of customers as well as the store owner. **Physical facility design** represents the type of image that the business seeks to project to consumers by means of both exterior and interior features. In this chapter, we examine some of the factors that should be evaluated regarding physical facility design.

PHYSICAL FACILITY PLANNING

The small business owner must answer some basic yet crucial questions in selecting the appropriate physical facility. One question centers on whether to construct a new facility or occupy an existing facility. Another centers around whether to lease (rent) or purchase the facility.

Construct a New Facility

The ideal situation for small business owners is to determine the building requirements and design the facility from the ground up. The advantage of this approach is that modern, energy-efficient features can be incorporated into the building plan. The exterior design as well as the interior features can be arranged to match the special requirements of the business. In addition, the physical location can be chosen that best meets the needs of the business. Regarding location, a critical dimension of constructing a new facility is determining the suitability of the terrain to support the foundation of the business. A small business owner purchased a piece of property and constructed a brick structure on the site. Three years later, the site had to be demolished because the structure was built on clay soil that contracted and expanded with changing moisture conditions in the soil. The result was a cracked foundation and walls in the building's structure. The owner is currently suing the building architect and engineer who did soil tests.

Occupy an Existing Facility

Most small business owners occupy facilities that are already constructed. In evaluating an available freestanding building or a vacancy in a shopping center, small business owners must not only determine if the location is suitable but also if it will match their requirements or can be modified to satisfy the firm's specifications.

As seen in Chapter 3, thousands of gasoline service stations have closed since the early 1970s, due primarily to problems in the energy industry. Many of the buildings that housed these stations have been sold to franchises and small business owners who have converted them into facilities for various businesses. Fast-food operations have been especially successful in converting service stations into satisfactory facilities. Service stations have also been converted into dry cleaning plants, printshops, used-car lots, muffler shops, bookstores, doughnut bakeries, pawn shops, and various types of service repair shops. The net result is that the cost of remodeling is considerably less than constructing a new facility, and the remodeling process is faster than constructing a new facility.

Buy or Lease

Following the decision of whether to locate the business in an existing structure or build a new one, the next step is the decision of whether to buy or lease the facility. Several issues must be considered.

In smaller towns or in areas where real estate values may not be excessive, small business owners may choose to buy their building. Another alternative is to lease the facility. Leases may be negotiated in a number of different ways. Leases may be stated as a flat amount per year, and the owner pays a fixed amount each month. A straight percentage lease requires the small business owner to pay a percentage of annual sales or profits. A percentage with a guaranteed minimum requires the tenant to pay on the same basis as the straight percentage lease, but the landlord is guaranteed a minimum amount regardless of profit or sales. Most small firms lease their facility.

Advantages of Buying

When owner–managers buy their building, they have the option to maintain it in the way they desire. They do not have to obtain permission from the landlord if they wish to modernize the structure. Furthermore, by owning the building, small business owners do not have to be concerned about being evicted as long as the business is solvent. Another advantage of ownership is that if the property appreciates in value, the small business owner reaps the benefit. Still another advantage is that building depreciation is an expense of business operations for income tax purposes, as are taxes and mortgage interest payments.

Disadvantages of Buying

On the other side of the coin are the negative factors of ownership. Property may decline in value if a business district declines. A large initial capital outlay is required if the building is purchased plus the cost of regular interest and mortgage payments. Additionally, ownership limits the mobility of the owner. If owners wish to relocate, they must dispose of their owned building in some manner. In addition, there are substantial costs involved in taxes and maintenance and repairs that may limit the amount of working capital available for ongoing business operations or expansion.

Advantages of Leasing

Leasing offers several advantages to small business owners. By leasing, the owners do not have to make a large initial cash outlay as they would if they purchased a building. Hence, more funds are available for current operations. Leasing also increases the mobility of owners if they decide to move when the lease expires. By leasing, they do not suffer the financial loss if the building declines in value. For income tax purposes, rent is also an expense of doing business. Moreover, the lease agreement may stipulate that the building owner pay for all or part of any renovation desired by the building occupant.

Disadvantages of Leasing

One disadvantage of leasing is that the building owner may elect not to renew the lease, forcing the small business owner to relocate when the lease expires. If the tenant wishes to make any modifications to the building, he or she must have the owner's permission, which may or may not be granted. In some instances, only the landlord can make the modifications, and he or she may not be willing to undertake the time and expense of this activity. Economic conditions may decline and the lease payments may put a severe financial strain on the business. Some leases contain restrictions or provisions as to what actions the small business manager can take with regard to the facility. For example, one small business owner leased a building. After signing the lease, the owner read the fine print in the lease agreement and discovered that the lease prohibited the display of any type of store sign on the property. To advertise the store's location, the owner had to rent a portable sign trailer and park it off the property to display the store's name. Another restriction may be on the lines of merchandise that may be sold at the location.

SPACE REQUIREMENTS ANALYSIS

A principal goal of the entrepreneur is to assess accurately the space requirements of the firm. However, this is one of the more difficult needs to gauge because the firm's needs must be projected into an uncertain future, and each firm has varying space needs, depending on the nature of the business and the products or services sold.

If projected space needs are underestimated, a move to a new facility or modification of the existing structure becomes necessary, resulting in additional cost to the owner and inconvenience to both customer and owner. Overestimating space needs results in underutilized space and corresponding increased costs until the volume of business matches available space.

Not only should the entrepreneur define initial space needs, but he or she should also determine if the facility's construction is of the type that will make remodeling relatively easy and can be accomplished economically. To illustrate, if an entrepreneur plans to open a specialty apparel shop, initial spatial requirements must be set for the selling and nonselling areas. The existing structure should also be evaluated in terms of its flexibility and adaptability for modification. For example, are there existing walls that can be easily removed if future growth dictates the need for more space in the selling area?

ANALYSIS OF TYPE OF CONSTRUCTION

The building should be both functional and attractive for the specific type of business. Whether constructing a facility or occupying an existing structure, the small business owner must be certain that it complies with all zoning regulations and local building codes. Some specific concerns to be addressed pertaining to construction requirements follow.

1. Exterior walls: masonry, precast concrete
2. Interior walls: permanent, freestanding, partitions, materials, such as sheetrock
3. Flooring: carpeting, wood, tile
4. Ceiling: material (such as acoustical tile), high ceilings, suspended ceilings
5. Roofing: wood, tile, composition shingles, built-up roof
6. Design of structure: appropriate for area

Before making a final decision, the entrepreneur would be well advised to use the services of professional building contractors or architects when analyzing space and construction requirements.

ARCHITECTURAL STYLE

For retailers and many types of personal service firms, the architectural style establishes the image that the entrepreneur wishes to convey to consumers. As suggested earlier, a unique exterior can have a strong influence in a con-

After learning the restaurant business in his father's delicatessen, Richard Melman went into business for himself, founding Lettuce Entertain You Enterprises, Inc. Melman's approach to physical facility planning is unique. Each of his restaurants has one-of-a-kind designs rather than the standardized appearance that is common for a multiunit firm.

sumer's decision to shop in a particular store, and this may afford the owner a significant competitive advantage. The factors discussed in the following sections are representative of physical facility design considerations that should be analyzed.

Storefront

Small business owners should choose building materials and a storefront design that are consistent with the store image the store owner is trying to create. The type of building materials used for the storefront may be dictated

FIGURE 7-1
A CHECKLIST FOR WINDOW DISPLAYS.

Merchandise Selected
1. Is the merchandise timely?
2. Is it representative of the stock assortment?
3. Are the articles harmonious—in type, color, texture, use?
4. Are the price lines of the merchandise suited to the interests of passersby?
5. Is the quantity of display suitable (that is, neither overcrowded nor sparse)?

Setting
1. Are glass, floor, props, and merchandise clean?
2. Is the lighting adequate (so that reflection from the street is avoided)?
3. Are spotlights used to highlight certain parts of the display?
4. Is every piece of merchandise carefully draped, pinned, or arranged?
5. Is the background suitable, enhancing the merchandise?
6. Are the props well suited to the merchandise?
6. Are the window cards used, and are they neat and well placed?
8. Is the entire composition balanced?
9. Does the composition suggest rhythm and movement?

Selling Power
1. Does the window present a readily recognized central theme?
2. Does the window exhibit power to stop passersby through the dramatic use of light, color, size, motion, composition, and/or item selection?
3. Does the window arouse a desire to buy (as measured by shoppers entering the store)?

(John Wingate and Seymour Helfant, *Small Store Planning for Growth,* Small Business Management Series no. 33, Small Business Administration, Washington, D.C., 1977, p. 77.)

by the funds available. More expensive materials, such as brick or fieldstone, or less expensive materials, such as aluminum, wood, or special types of structural glass, may be used. Remodeling the storefront of the older building can project a modern refreshing appearance or an historical look.

Display Windows

Consumers enjoy window shopping. Small business owners should use this knowledge of shopping habits to their advantage as they plan their window displays. Some vital questions to be studied and answered in relation to the display windows are shown in Figure 7-1. Attractive display windows not only are used as one form of promotional strategy to display merchandise but also to project the store's image to the community and to introduce new seasonal merchandise. Attractively designed display windows may catch the eye of the casual shopper, causing them to stop, look, enter, and purchase merchandise.

Thoughtful planning should go into deciding how display windows can be used most effectively. For example, they should be designed so that they are appropriate for the merchandise lines handled by the store. Displays of small items, such as jewelry, should be set at between waist and eye level, whereas larger items, such as shoes or luggage, can be displayed much lower (below waist level).

Some retail outlets have a recessed storefront. This arrangement permits people to window shop in a more relaxed atmosphere out of the mainstream of pedestrian traffic.

Entrances and Exits

Store entrances and exits establish how smoothly customer traffic flows in and out of the business. Obstacles that impede the smooth flow of traffic may drive customers to competitors. Obstacles that may discourage customers are doors that are difficult to open, poor location of doors, doors that are too narrow, no provision for entry for the handicapped or elderly (such as steps leading up to the entrance), or poor condition of the walkway leading to the store entrance.

To facilitate customer traffic, the small business facility should have an adequate number of properly located entrances and exits. Actions that may be taken to accomplish this objective are the installation of doors that open automatically, removal of obstacles to permit ease of entry by all (including the handicapped or elderly), and clearly marking and lighting entrances and exits. Awnings placed over the store entrance may provide an added measure of shopper comfort and convenience.

Store Signs

A properly placed store sign guides customers to the store. If shoppers are looking for a store location with which they are not familiar and the store location is not clearly marked, they become frustrated, may give up the search, and shop at a competitor's store.

There are some problems that small business owners may encounter with regard to the store sign. Some signage problems are

Improperly designed signs.

Signs placed in the wrong position, such as behind a structural barrier, so that they are not readily visible to the potential shopper.

Signs that are of the wrong size (too small to assist in identifying the store's location, too large and thus too costly).

Signs that are no longer readable because of faded lettering.

Signs that are the wrong color (not enough contrast so they can easily be read).

Signs that convey the wrong image of the store.

BUILDING INTERIOR FEATURES

Shoppers tend to have favorable attitudes toward shopping in stores where the interior is both appealing and inviting. The small business owner should pay special attention to those features that help to create a favorable shopping environment: floors, walls and ceilings, lighting and fixtures, color scheme, and year-round climate control.

Flooring

Flooring should be sturdy enough to handle traffic as well as the weight of materials that will move over it. In a factory, a painted concrete floor may be satisfactory. For a retailing firm, flooring should have a type of covering that matches the decor of the store and also be safe and comfortable for the customer. This may include various kinds of tile, hardwood, carpet, linoleum, or terrazzo. The condition of the flooring should be considered also. Some questons need to be answered regarding flooring. How difficult is it to maintain the floor? Is the floor covering unsuitable or dangerous (e.g., does it become slick if it gets damp)? Is the floor covering an unsuitable color or of poor material? Does the flooring add to the noise or reduce the noise in the store? Is the flooring durable? What is its cost?

Walls and Ceilings

Like flooring, the walls and ceilings are an essential part of the store's overall image. Walls should be of sufficient strength to support the requirements of the building, such as holding up shelving as well as matching the color scheme of the store. Partitions are useful in that these movable walls allow for a variety in the arrangement of the store. Likewise, the ceiling requirements must be analyzed. Will it be plaster or acoustical tile? By the use of a suspended acoustical tile ceiling, some flexibility in ceiling height can be obtained. Lowering the ceiling can also reduce the cost of operation, as with lower heating and cooling costs. Inclusion of fireproof partitions can also help to reduce insurance costs. Use of the proper type of paint on the interior walls and partitions helps to reduce maintenance costs. Structural columns and posts should not interfere with store operations.

Lighting and Fixtures

Proper lighting aids the shopper. Lighting requirements must be studied for each type of store. A proper lighting system enhances the environment of the store. Equally important, proper lighting enables the customer to see merchandise clearly and makes selection of desired items easier. Insufficient lighting can cause customers to shy away from a store. Glaring or obscure lights are examples of this problem. In the factory, lighting must be adequate for workers to perform their job efficiently. Lights should be bright but not glaring.

With higher energy costs, a lighting system must be designed that is energy-efficient. It must also be a flexible system so that it can be increased at some future time if the need arises. Moreover, it must have the proper appearance, be maintained easily and inexpensively, and be sturdy in construction.

Color Scheme

The choice of colors can give the store a specific appearance. Paint manufacturers suggest that colors can be used to create certain visual effects, such as making a building appear larger. Painting a rear wall a darker color makes a long, narrow building seem wider.

When choosing colors, the owner should select those that are appropriate for the merchandise being sold and for the store image that the owner is trying to create. For example, warm colors (yellow, orange, and red), though they attract attention, may tend to overpower merchandise. They should be used in the proper setting, such as in youth-oriented shops (children's clothes, toy store) or sportswear stores.

Soft, neutral colors (beige, off-white) lend themselves to overall store decor. Black and pastels (mauve, peach) and cool colors (blue, green, gray, blue-green, blue-gray) can best be used with displays of more expensive merchandise, such as jewelry.

Colors can also be used to brighten a store and make it more appealing and more conducive to promoting employee efficiency. Certain colors are also cost effective since they reflect light and aid in lowering lighting needs and reducing energy consumption.

Climate Control

Year-round temperature control is a necessary feature for the comfort of customers and employees. Care must be taken to see that the climate-control equipment selected or in place in the building is energy efficient, especially in light of rising energy costs.

Other Facility Requirements

In surveying the additional requirements of the facility, the small business owner needs to ascertain if the following factors are adequate for the business.

1. Electrical wiring, gas pipes, and plumbing
2. Restroom facilities and rest area equipment

3. Water fountains
4. Shelving and display cases
5. Transportation for personnel, freight, and merchandise (elevator, escalator, conveyor)
6. Security system
7. Fire prevention equipment (sprinkler system, fire extinguishers)
8. Loading docks (location, size, type, protective covering)
9. Waste disposal facilities

STORE LAYOUT

The layout design of the retail store, service firm, and manufacturing facility is a critical factor in the efficient operation of the firm. Manufacturing and service firms will be discussed later in the chapter. In the retail establishment, **layout** means "the spatial arrangement of selling and nonselling departments, aisles, fixtures, display facilities, and equipment in the proper relationship to each other and to the fixed elements of the structure."[1]

Considerable attention should be given to planning the store layout. The goals of retail store layout are to attract customers, to serve them efficiently, and to provide for the efficient operation of the business. The attainment of these goals is facilitated by such features as lighting, colors, and the ease with which the premises can be maintained and made secure (store security is discussed in Chapter 11). In selecting the appropriate store layout, owners should evaluate a number of factors that will now be discussed.

Type of Merchandise

Each store layout must be designed with the type of merchandise and customer in mind. For retailers, the store's success depends almost entirely on sales. Properly designed store layout makes products easily accessible. The layout of the sales floor should be planned with customer convenience uppermost in importance. Related merchandise should be displayed in close proximity to ensure ease of shopping. For example, shirts, slacks, ties, shoes, and belts should be located in adjacent areas.

CHECKLIST FOR INTERIOR ARRANGEMENT AND DISPLAY

Layout   Yes   No

1. Are your fixtures low enough and signs so placed that the customer can get a bird's eye view of the store and tell in what direction to go for wanted goods? ____ ____

2. Do your aisle and counter arrangements tend to stimulate a circular traffic flow through the store? ____ ____

3. Do your fixtures (and their arrangement), signs, lettering, and colors all create a coordinated and unified effect? ____ ____

4. Before any supplier's fixtures are accepted, do you make sure they conform in color and design to what you already have? ____ ____

5. Do you limit the use of hanging signs to special sale events? ____ ____

6. Are your counters and aisle tables not overcrowded with merchandise? ____ ____

7. Are your ledges and cashier-wrapping stations kept free of boxes, unneeded wrapping materials, personal effects, and odds and ends? ____ ____

8. Do you keep trash bins out of sight? ____ ____

Merchandise Emphasis   Yes   No

1. Do your signs referring to specific goods tell the customer something significant about them rather than simply naming the products and their prices? ____ ____

2. For your advertised goods, do you have prominent signs, including tear sheets at entrances, to inform and guide customers to their exact location in the store? ____ ____

3. Do you prominently display both advertised and nonadvertised specials at the ends of counters as well as at the point of sale? ____ ____

4. Are both your national and private brands highlighted in your arrangement and window display? ____ ____

5. Wherever feasible, do you give the more colorful merchandise in your stock preference in display? ____ ____

Layout	Yes	No		Yes	No

6. In the case of apparel and home furnishings, do the items that reflect your store's fashion sense or fashion leadership get special display attention at all times? ___ ___

7. In locating merchandise in your store, do you always consider the productivity of space—vertical as well as horizontal ___ ___

8. Is your self-service merchandise arranged so as to attract customers and assist them in selection by the following means:

  a. Is each category grouped under a separate sign? ___ ___

  b. Is the merchandise in each category arranged according to its most significant characteristic—weather, color, style, size, or price? ___ ___

c. In apparel categories, is the merchandise arranged by price lines or zones to assist the customer in making a selection quickly. ___ ___

d. Is horizontal space usually devoted to different items and styles within a category (vertical space being used for different sizes—smallest at the top, largest at the bottom)? ___ ___

e. Are impulse items interspersed with demand items and not placed across the aisle from them, where many customers will not see them? ___ ___

Source: John W. Wingate and Seymour Helfant, _Small Store Planning for Growth_ (Washington, D.C.: Small Business Administration, 1977), pp. 100–101.

If feasible, merchandise should be displayed openly so customers can examine the products. For some types of merchandise, such as jewelry and cameras, open displays are not practical. Impulse or convenience goods should be placed near the front of the store so that as many people as possible will see them. Shopping goods should be placed in areas that are reached only after passing impulse and convenience goods. Specialty goods should be located some distance from the front of the store because customers make an extra effort to purchase them.

FIGURE 7-2
PREFERRED LOCATION FOR HIGH-DEMAND MERCHANDISE.

N	A	N
A	P	S
P	S	S

N = Nonproductive A = Average P = Prime S = Superior

(Packard/Carron, START YOUR OWN STORE: Managing, Merchandising, and Evaluating;
© 1982, p. 56. Reprinted by permission of Prentice-Hall, Inc., Englewood Cliffs, N.J.)

Size of Store

The well-designed layout allows the owner to utilize the total square footage of the store in the most efficient way. Obviously, selling is the most important activity in the retail outlet and must receive the major space allocation. Packard and Carron report that a small store will allocate about 75 to 80 percent of available space to sales activities.[2] The nonselling areas (stockroom, office, storage, fitting rooms, washroom) should be provided enough space so that all nonselling activities support the selling activities efficiently.

Certain areas of the store produce more customer traffic and sales than others. High-demand merchandise should be placed in optimum locations. Figure 7-2 identifies the important traffic and selling areas and the preferred location for merchandise that is in high demand.

Customer Traffic Flow

In planning the store arrangement, the owner should give thought to how many customers will be in the store at the peak hours and how readily these customers can be served. Fast, efficient service is especially important in retail and service establishments. Locating cash registers convenient to the selling area reduces the time a salesclerk must spend walking to and from the sales floor; hence, customer service is improved. More customer traffic can be accommodated if self-service fixtures (display cases, counters) are situated for customer convenience. By using a counter with several tiers, one can use vertical space efficiently. Stock areas should be located as near the selling area as practical to reduce the amount of time a salesclerk must be away from the selling area getting additional stock. In a shoe store, for example, the shoe stock is ordinarily located on shelves immediately behind the displayed stock. Because only a limited stock can be displayed, the salesclerk ordinarily must go to the stockroom to obtain the size and style of shoe desired. The salesperson merely steps through a curtained opening, selects the shoes requested, and is back on the sales floor in a very short time. By considering these factors, the small business owner will be able to serve his or her customers more efficiently at peak hours of business and, in turn, increase store sales.

Display Fixtures

Fixtures are an integral part of effective layout design. A useful guide to the small business entrepreneur for deciding on the kind of display fixtures needed is a realization that the most practical and economical fixtures permit merchandise to be displayed in proper arrangement for each line of merchandise with maximum exposure and minimum amount of distractions.

Other factors that should be considered in determining store layout are building construction, fire and security protection measures, the number of employees and facilities, and service to customers (restrooms and fitting rooms). A checklist for evaluating the interior arrangement and display of a retail store is the subject of the special interest feature in this chapter.

LAYOUT PLANS

The store layout should make merchandise accessible to customers. In considering which type of layout plan to employ, the retailer should be guided by selecting the plan that best facilitates consumer shopping. As noted, certain areas of the store generate most of the sales and customer traffic. For example, as much as two-thirds of the store's annual sales may be made in the front quarter of the store near the entrance and checkout station. In small retail firms, the grid layout and the free-flow layout are the two plans most commonly used.

Grid Layout

The **grid layout** is a rectangular store arrangement pattern that features a main aisle and secondary aisles that are located at right angles to the main aisle, as shown in Figure 7-3. The main aisles carry a large share of the traffic and provide the best location for convenience goods, impulse, and seasonal merchandise. Shopping goods may be displayed on the secondary aisles, and specialty goods may be placed in less traveled areas of the store, such as the rear

FIGURE 7-3
THE GRID LAYOUT PLAN.

Nonselling Area

of the store. Thus, the grid layout forces customers to follow the planned traffic flow.

An advantage of the grid layout is that it is conducive to low building costs and is easily adapted to situations where structural columns are numerous and close together. Other advantages of this layout plan are that total floor space requirements are minimized because aisles are of consistent width, and a greater amount of merchandise can be displayed in a given amount of space because of the regularity of the arrangement; it is easier to use a standardized type of display fixture throughout, resulting in fixture economies; and it is easier for customers to become familiar with the regularity of the features of the grid layout.[3] This layout plan makes it easier to control store security also.

Free-Flow Layout

Store owners using the free-flow layout recognize that customers normally move to their right when they enter a store. Under this plan, the store layout may be circular, octagonal, or U-shaped. Figure 7-4 shows the free-flow layout plan. Unlike the grid, the **free-flow layout** has no uniform pattern of arrangement. This plan has considerable flexibility because display counters can be added, removed, or rearranged without disrupting the overall layout pattern. Another advantage of this plan is that it allows customers to move easily in any direction from one display area to another. As a result, customers have access to a variety of merchandise assortments that may result in increased sales.

The grid layout is the most commonly used retail layout plan. It is less expensive to design and better suited to the needs of the small business. However, some owners use a free-flow layout to create a distinct store personality even though floor space is used less efficiently under this layout pattern.

MANUFACTURING FACILITY LAYOUT

Layout in the plant refers to the efficient arrangement of the manufacturing facilities and employees. In the plant layout, attention is centered on how the equipment is to be set up as well as the location and space requirements of support services, such as maintenance, receiving and shipping, and storage. Some of the benefits of good factory layout are listed as follows.

1. Lower cost of manufacturing
2. More efficient use of floor space
3. Reduced manufacturing bottlenecks
4. More effective control
5. Better quality of products
6. Better service to customer
7. Minimized material handling
8. Less time needed to manufacture goods

FIGURE 7-4
THE FREE-FLOW LAYOUT PLAN.

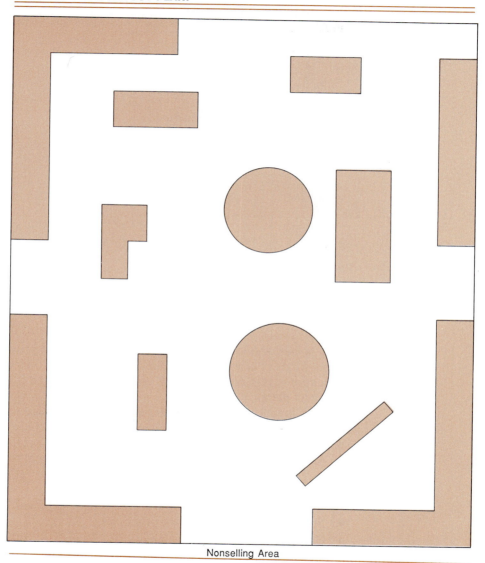

Nonselling Area

FIGURE 7-5
PROCESS LAYOUT OF A SMALL MANUFACTURER PRODUCING WOODEN PRODUCTS (CHAIRS AND DESKS).

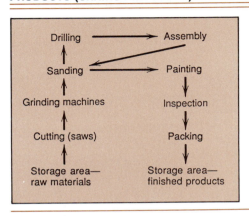

Types of Manufacturing Layout Plans

There are two basic patterns of layout used in manufacturing operations: the process layout and the product layout.

Process Layout

Process layout, shown in Figure 7-5, is usually found in plants where many different kinds of products are produced or are produced for customer specifications. It is often called job order production and is characteristic of many small plants.

Process layout means that similar equipment is located in one area or department of the plant. Hence, all lathes or drills would be in one area. In this arrangement, all work of a specific kind is sent to the specific department or area. All lathe work required in the factory would be sent to the lathe machine area.

The advantages of the process layout are these.

- Superior control of intricate processes.
- Greater utilization of machinery.
- Lower capital investment in equipment.
- Increased flexibility; readily adaptable to frequent rearrangement of operational sequence.
- Steadier operation; production can be maintained better during absenteeism. Machine breakdown are not serious because work may be routed to other machines.
- Improved service; maintenance requirements of equipment can be grouped for specialized service.

FIGURE 7-6
FLOOR DIAGRAM OF PRODUCT LAYOUT IN SMALL FACTORY.

	Product A					
Storage raw materials	Saws	Drills	Sanding machines	Assembly	Painting	Storage finished product
	Product B					
Storage raw materials	Lathes	Milling	Sanding machines	Assembly	Varnishing	Storage finished product
	Product C						
Storage raw materials	Saws	Lathe	Heat treating	Plating	Assembly	Painting	Storage finished product

- Lower unit cost; more economical where volume of work is too small to justify a production line.
- Best suited for items requiring a flexible sequence of operations.
- Reduced equipment; fewer dupicate machines necessary to meet production requirements.
- Production stimulated; more incentive to workers to increase production through incentive plans.[4]

Product Layout

Manufacturing facilities that use a **product layout** ordinarily mass-produce goods. (See Fig. 7-6.) Product layout has all equipment needed to produce a specific product arranged in sequence as on an assembly line. This equipment is used only for producing the one product. Raw materials enter the manufacturing sequence, and as each stage of the operation is completed, the material moves to the next stage until all stages have been completed and the product "rolls off the assembly line." Thus, there may be a considerable amount of duplication of kinds of machinery in the manufacturing operation.

Product layout is usually too sophisticated and expensive a system for the small business, but it is adaptable to the requirements of the larger, mass-production industries. This system is especially suitable for automated manufacturing processes.

The product layout

- Simplifies controls and reduces cost accounting.
- Reduces materials-handling costs.
- Provides smoother flow of materials.

- Reduces floor space required for goods in process.
- Cuts production time.
- Reduces investment in work in process.
- Develops efficient labor through job specialization.
- Provides better overall supervision and reduces paperwork.
- Reduces floor space required per unit produced.[5]

LAYOUT OF THE SERVICE FIRM

Layout for service establishments is determined primarily by whether they are a merchandising or processing-type service establishment. **Merchandising service establishments** include motels and most personal service firms, such as hair styling salons and travel agencies. It is important for these firms to cater to customer needs and project an attractive physical appearance. The exterior should appear inviting to customers, and the layout should be designed to serve the customer in the most efficient manner. For example, the layout of the hair styling salon must have sufficient stations to serve customers in a timely manner and project an inviting image. The waiting area for customers should be uncluttered, and if the shop is large enough, there needs to be a receptionist station as well.

Processing-type service establishments include alteration shops, dry cleaners, and printshops. These service businesses are similar to a manufacturing firm. The processing operations are separated from where customer orders are taken. For example, the receptionist in the printshop takes customer orders in the small front area, and the printing equipment is located in the back. The layout in the work area depends on the type of equipment used and the size of the building. It is important that the front area present an air of professionalism and cleanliness, not cluttered, and free of obstacles. Chairs may be available for customers while they wait. The separation of the work area and customer service area makes for greater efficiency as well as safety.

ASSISTANCE IN LAYOUT PLANNING

The small business owner should seek as much assistance as possible in determining the most efficient layout of the business. Many sources are available to provide this assistance. Retail trade associations provide planning services to their members. Manufacturers of store equipment and fixtures will also provide assistance. Other valuable resources are contractors, financial advisors, architects, interior designers, business suppliers, and government agencies, especially the Small Business Administration. Many of these services are offered free or at a minimal cost. Careful thought-out plans can avoid unnecessary waste and expense later in relation to store or plant layout.

SUMMARY OF KEY POINTS

1. Physical facility planning refers to the exterior and interior design of the facility, while physical facility design represents the type of image the firm expects·to convey to the public.
2. The small business owner must choose between constructing a new facility or occupying an existing facility and whether to buy or lease (rent) the facility.
3. The size and type of building must be analyzed for both current and future needs.
4. Exterior building features to be evaluated are architectural style, storefront, display windows, entrances and exits, and outside signs.
5. Building interior analysis should include flooring, walls and ceiling, lights and fixtures, color scheme, climate control, and any special features required by the firm.
6. To design the proper store layout, the store owner should consider the type of merchandise, size of store, customer traffic, and display fixtures.
7. Two types of store layout for retail firms are grid and free-flow.
8. Manufacturing facilities may be organized on a process layout or product layout basis.
9. Service firm layout depends on whether it is a merchandising service establishment or a processing-type service establishment.
10. A variety of sources are available from which the small business owner can receive assistance in planning store layout.

DISCUSSION QUESTIONS

1. What are some decisions the small business owner has to make when choosing a physical facility?
2. List several factors that should be evaluated when deciding whether to buy or lease a facility.
3. Identify some of the issues that need to be studied when determining the size and type of facility desired.
4. Briefly discuss the interior building features that should be evaluated by the small business owner.
5. What is the meaning of layout for the retailer?
6. What should be the basis for determining the appropriate retail store layout?
7. What is the difference between a grid layout and a free-flow layout?
8. Explain the difference between process and product layout in a factory.
9. Discuss the difference between a merchandising service firm and a processing-type service firm.

THE BUSINESS PLAN: PHYSICAL FACILITY PLANNING

In developing the plans for the physical facility for a retail firm, the entrepreneur should consider the following points as an aid in developing this section of his or her business plan.

Facility Plans

1. Shall a new facility be constructed or shall the firm be housed in an existing structure?
2. Shall the facility be leased or purchased?

Store Exterior

1. Does the store's exterior design project the image the entrepreneur wishes?
2. Does the store's exterior blend with the other shops in the surrounding area?
3. Does the facility have an appropriate store sign (proper size, easy to read, clearly identifying the business, correct placement and positioning)?
4. Is there a display window that allows merchandise to be displayed effectively?
5. Are store entrances adequate (located correctly, clearly marked, easy to open and close, nonthreatening—no obstacles or barriers to shoppers entering or leaving the store)?

Store Interior

1. Does the store's internal environment encourage shopping and project the desired image (flooring, walls and ceiling, lighting and fixtures, climate control, color scheme)?
2. Is maximum space allocated to selling activities, making sure that nonselling activities do not infringe on valuable selling space?
3. Does the layout plan demonstrate a true concern for the convenience of the customer?
4. Does the layout encourage self-selection of merchandise whenever possible so that customers have "hands-on" opportunities to examine the merchandise?
5. Is the layout plan appropriate for the type and size of store?

ENTREPRENEURIAL PROJECTS

1. Select a small retail store, and evaluate the store's interior and exterior features.
   a. Building exterior
      (1) Type of building architecture
      (2) Storefront
      (3) Display windows
      (4) Entrances
      (5) Store signs
   b. Building interior
      (1) Flooring
      (2) Walls
      (3) Ceiling
      (4) Lights and fixtures
      (5) Color schemes
      (6) Climate control
2. Draw the floor plan of the layout of the store. Describe the layout plan. What recommendations do you suggest for improving the layout plan?
3. Assume you are asked to serve as a consultant to a group of individuals who are interested in starting a retail card shop. Would you advise them to buy or lease the physical facility? Why?

CASE A

Burk's Jewelers, Inc.

Alex Burk, age 72, has been a jeweler all his working life. He has built a successful jewelry store in a town with a population of 24,000. A family operation, his son and daughter with their spouses are now actively involved in the operation of the store (sales, watch and jewelry repair).

Mr. Burk has retired from the business, and his son Larry has become the president of the corporation. Larry has a goal of expanding the business into another town or city. One possible choice is a small town of about 1000 population located about 30 miles from the existing business. The second possible site is a major metropolitan area located about 60 miles away from the existing business. After studying the potential of both sites, Larry has decided that the metropolitan area offers the best potential for expansion. Larry has decided to go ahead with these plans and locate the new store in a shopping center.

Larry's sister, Tammy and her husband, Allen, will manage the new store. Allen has been in the construction business in the metropolitan area, but the economy of the area has been depressed for the past two years and the construction business has been very sluggish. Thus, he and Tammy welcomed the opportunity to manage the new store.

When the economy of the metropolitan area was booming, excessive retail space was developed. With the business downturn, there is now an oversupply of retail space. Many buildings and shopping centers have "For Lease" signs adorning building fronts.

With the economic downturn, it is a buyer's market, and retail space is available at reasonable rates. Shopping center owners are willing to make "good deals." For example, space that rented for $1.50 per square foot (psf) 18 months ago is now available for $1.00 psf. The toughest choice is selecting the best site from the many that are vacant. Furthermore, Larry has defined the Southwest portion of the city as the area where the new store will be located because this area is easily accessible by major highway from the smaller town where the company's main store is located. Tammy and Allen will operate the store, and Larry will be in the new store on Tuesday's to handle all jewelry repair since Allen is not qualified to repair jewelry.

Larry has narrowed his choice of location to two sites, both within 1 mile of each other. Site 1 is an older center with a drugstore (national chain), office supply store, video rental, two restaurants, a small furniture store, bookstore, liquor store, tanning salon, and the vacated space of a jeweler whose business closed late last year. The owner of the closed shop was retired from the military and had no expertise in jewelry repair except to replace batteries in watches.

Site 2 is a recently opened center with a major grocery-drug store, junior department store, variety store, three restaurants, travel agency, card shop, dentist, full-service bank, and a retail supplier of beauty products.

Within 6 miles of this section of town is a regional shopping center with six jewelry stores, both independents and chains.

Both sites are equally accessible by car and have the approximate square footage in each. Both will require signing an 18 month lease. A comparison of the sites reveals the following:

	Site 1	Site 2
Monthly rent (psf)	$1.00	$1.50
Center	Older	Newer

Questions

1. What factors should Mr. Burk consider in choosing between sites 1 and 2?
2. Comment on the suitability of the proposed layout for the jeweler. Would you recommend a different store layout plan?

PROPOSED LAYOUT OF BURK'S JEWELERS.

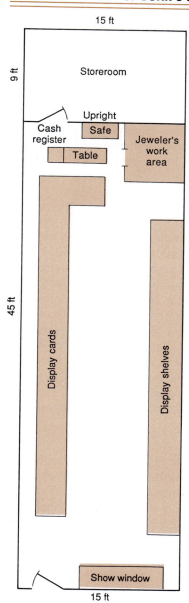

CASE B
House's Jewelry Store

House's Jewelry Store is a small, single-unit retail jewelry store located in the downtown shopping area of a city of 10,000 population. The business opened in 1959 in a small store but moved to its present location in 1969. The location has been good, and rental payments are relatively low. There is one other competitor in the downtown area.

Floor space is 3000 square feet. One-fourth of the floor space is allocated to repair facilities, clerical space, and storage areas. The remaining floor space is divided into four areas. Diamonds, expensive gemstones, and wedding sets comprise one-fourth of the selling area. Watches, gold necklaces and bracelets, gold-filled jewelry, and other assorted pieces occupy about one-fourth of the selling floor. Gift items, pottery and china, silver and pewter serving pieces, and stemware utilize another one-fourth of this space. The remaining floor space is aisle space.

In addition to the owner and his wife, three full-time employees and one part-time employee work in the store. Each person performs a wide range of duties in the store. The watch repair department is a leased-out service department designed to increase sales by attracting additional customers to the store. The store's downtown competitor has no in-store watch repair service. All watches brought in for repair are sent out of town.

During the past two years, the Houses have been evaluating whether to move the business to a new shopping center located at the edge of the city. Population shifts, the movement of other retailers, the deterioration of the downtown area, and the favorable atmosphere at the shopping center area have been the factors that have made them decide to move.

There is a suitable location in the new center. The Houses want their new store to have an efficient, well-planned layout.

Specifically, they want the following to be incorporated into their design layout.

1. A workshop area located in the store rather than behind the store as is the case with the present location. This would allow the owner to have closer contact with actual store operations.
2. Pieces of jewelry that have a similar function, such as watches, bracelets, and chains, should be placed in close proximity to each other. This arrangement will facilitate customer shopping.
3. Use track lighting to enable displays to be mobile and to add to the flexibility of the layout.

4. All display cases should be lined with materials of a related color scheme to allow jewelry to be accentuated by reflection of light on its surface.

The proposed store layout is now shown.

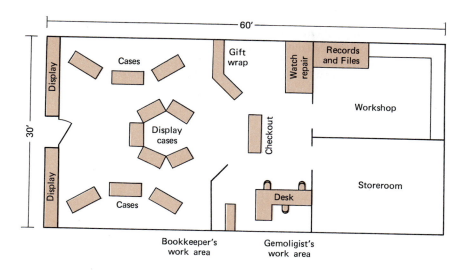

Proposed Layout

Area (30 feet by 60 feet)

Space allocation

> Space should be divided into departments.
> Dropped ceilings over certain areas will enhance different items.
> Wall space should be used for display.

Layout spaces

Record room (6 feet by 8 feet) for security files

Workshop (10 feet by 20 feet) for jewelry repair and casting

Watch repair room (6 feet by 8 feet)

Checkout stand placed at back of store

Gift-wrapping area

Desk and working area for bookkeeper

Desk and diamond salon for owner (L-shaped desk with three chairs)

Question

1. Evaluate the store layout as to its suitability for the new jewelry store.

Notes

[1] William R. Davidson, Daniel J. Sweeney, and Ronald W. Stampfl, *Retailing Management,* 6th ed. (New York: John Wiley, 1988), p. 278.

[2] Sidney Packard and Alan J. Carron, *Start Your Own Business* (Englewood Cliffs, N.J.: Prentice Hall, 1982), p. 55.

[3] Davidson, Sweeney, and Stampfl, *Retailing Management,* p. 279.

[4] Raymond Newton, *Principles of Plant Layout for Small Plants,* Technical Aids for Small Manufacturers (Washington, D.C.: Small Business Administration, 1971), p. 3.

[5] Ibid.

MANAGING THE
SMALL BUSINESS

KEY WORDS

MANAGEMENT STRATEGY AND EMPLOYEE RELATIONS

LEARNING GOALS

After reading this chapter, you will understand:

1. What a manager of a small business does.
2. The management functions that all small business managers perform.
3. Why a small business manager must set objectives.
4. That managers have different assumptions about people.
5. That there are different styles of leadership.
6. The benefits of efficient time management.
7. The importance of good management–employee relationships.
8. The different types of needs and wants that individuals have.
9. What employee morale is as well as the indicators of low employee morale.
10. Some of the problems encountered in disciplining employees.
11. The need for effective communcation.

ENTREPRENEURIAL PROFILE

Ben Cohen and Jerry Greenfield

BEN AND JERRY'S HOMEMADE, INC.

Ben Cohen and Jerry Greenfield, friends from a junior high school on Long Island, New York, opened Ben and Jerry's Homemade, Inc., an ice cream manufacturer, in 1978 with $8000 in personal savings and help from their parents. The firm has grown to be the third largest ice cream manufacturer in the United States, with 200 employees and annual sales of $32 million. Their ice cream is sold in 35 states.

Before starting their business, Ben was a craft teacher at a school for disturbed children but was suffering from job burnout. Jerry was a lab technician who tried to get into medical school but was turned down.

Ben and Jerry wanted to go into the food business. Initially, they considered making bagels, but the bagel-making equipment, costing $40,000, was too expensive.

As an alternative, they decided to open an ice cream parlor. But at that stage neither had any thought of manufacturing ice cream. The location they chose was a rundown gas station with holes in the roof and the walls were falling apart. They selected this building because of its excellent location—across from city hall.

Their personal and business goals were to go into the ice cream business and have fun, create a product that made people happy, and operate a business in a way that would benefit the community.

The firm is committed to doing well for its stockholders, employees, and the community. It has a compressed salary ratio of 5 to 1, which means the highest-paid employee cannot earn more than five times the low-

est-paid employee. They have created a profit-sharing plan for employees. They distribute 5 percent of pretax profits to employees based on length of employment rather than salary.

The firm has established a foundation that awarded in a one-year period over 100 grants that totaled $250,000. They have a policy of donating free products to any Vermont nonprofit organization that makes a request.

In 1988, Ben and Jerry were chosen as National Small Business Persons of the Year.

Source: Network (Washington, D.C.: Small Business Administration, May–June 1988).

The ability of small businesses to retain their strategic position in our economy and to compete effectively with large business firms depends in large measure on the skill of the owner–managers. Small firms that have survived the early, formative years and demonstrated a capacity for growth have been led by owner–managers who not only perceived and capitalized on the opportunities available to them, but in countless situations created the opportunities that made them successful. Thus, the leadership provided by the firm's managers is paramount for solidifying the firm's position in the business community.

A **manager** supervises the work activities of employees to see that they accomplish their specific tasks. In a large company, "managing" activities are distinct from "doing" activities of employees. However, this separation is not so clear in the small firm, where owner–managers commonly work side by side with employees, performing many of the same tasks. Nevertheless, owner–managers must give a high priority to managing and not devote their major energies to nonmanagement activities.

THE MANAGEMENT FUNCTIONS

Owner–managers' responsibilities involve coordinating and leading all the human, physical, and financial resources of the firm toward its goals. These responsibilities are fulfilled by managers when they perform the management functions: planning, organizing, staffing, leading, and controlling.

Planning

Planning is defined as the process of setting the objectives of the firm and then choosing the course of action the firm will follow to move from where it is currently to where it wants to be at some future time. The primacy of planning recognizes that planning is the first and most basic of all the management functions. Planning enables the managers to chart the direction of the company and provide the foundation for the other functions by identifying the kind of organization structure that is needed, the type of employees that are required, the most effective leadership style, and the type of controls needed to reach the objectives. Because all businesses operate in a constantly changing environment, planning is a dynamic process.

Managers must concentrate on both long-range and short-range plans. The time span for long-range plans is ordinarily five years or more, and short-range planning usually covers a year or less. Long-range plans focus attention on matters pertaining to the overall direction of the company, whereas short-range plans signal the specific measures needed to reach the long-range goals. Most small business managers spend the bulk of their time and energy on short-range planning, usually the result of daily job pressures. However, the pressure of immediate issues should not preclude managers from devoting a substantial portion of the time and energy to long-range planning.

Objectives

The first phase of the planning process involves developing the objectives of the firm. It is preferred that they be stated in writing. Because the firm operates in a dynamic environment and these changes may present obstacles to the original goals, managers must constantly monitor objectives and modify them when the situation demands, such as when consumer interest shifts from one product or service to another.

Objectives reflect concern and attention for the various parties at interest to the firm: ownership (sole proprietorship, partnership, corporation, stockholders), employees, customers, and the community at large. Representative objectives that recognize the various constituencies of the firm may be as follows.

To ownership   It shall be the goal of the owner and manager of this company to attempt to maximize profits.

To employees   To pay a fair, competitive wage or salary and afford employees with opportunities for training and development that will allow them to utilize and expand their talents.

To customers   To provide products and services of the highest quality at the lowest prices possible.

To community   To use all available safeguards to protect and improve the environment in the area in which the business operates.

Objectives also serve as the foundation for the policies, procedures, and rules of the firm.

Policies

Policies serve as the broad guidelines for making decisions and taking actions necessary to accomplish objectives. Policies provide the guidelines for action in each of the functions areas of the enterprise, such as sales, production, finance, and personnel. For example, the vacation policy of a small retail grocer is stated as follows: "After 12 months of continuous full-time employment, one workweek of paid vacation is earned. After 24 months or more of continuous full-time employment, two workweeks of paid vacation are earned. After 10 years or more of continuous full-time employment, three workweeks paid vacation are earned."

Procedures

Procedures detail the exact actions or steps for accomplishing a certain activity. Procedures usually specify how a policy should be carried out. For example, the following procedure outlines the steps to be followed when a customer presents a credit card for payment for gasoline purchases.

1. Check card to determine that it is honored in this location and has not expired.
2. Set imprinter for amount of sale, insert card, insert invoice, and imprint the invoice.
3. Check hard copy to see that all information has been printed.
4. Fill in all appropriate information such as number of gallons, price per gallon, vehicle license number, and initials of person filling out the card.
5. Get signature of cardholder and give tissue copy to copyholder, ring up sales on gas sale key, and put hard copy into cash register.

Rules

Rules are specific guides. They define the personal conduct required of employees in specific work situations. They specify the actions that should or should not be taken in regard to a situation. A set of company rules for a small, drive-in convenience store, include the following.

"Never sit on the counter."

"Employees only behind the checkout stand."

"Never turn your back on an open cash register."

Decision Making

The owner is constantly called upon to make decisions regarding actions to be taken in the firm. How effective the manager is at making decisions when and where they are needed is crucial in establishing the degree of success enjoyed by the firm. Decision making permeates every activity of the company. Objectives, policies, procedures, and rules provide the manager with the framework needed for making many of the routine, repetitive decisions. The decision-making process has four phases: (1) define the problem, (2) develop alternatives, (3) evaluate alternatives, and (4) implement the plan of action. Each of these steps is discussed in the following sections and is diagrammed in Figure 8-1.

FIGURE 8-1
THE STEPS IN THE DECISION-MAKING PROCESS.

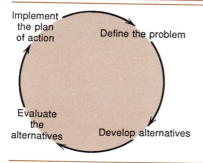

Implement the plan of action

Define the problem

Evaluate the alternatives

Develop alternatives

Define the Problem   The first phase of decision making begins with an examination of the current status of the business. The owner–manager's attention is centered on identifying problems and analyzing if there are problems. If a problem exists, the manager must state specifically what is wrong or what area of the company should be producing better results.

The problems must be correctly defined, because if it is diagnosed incorrectly, the solution will fail, no matter how well thought out and applied it may be. For example, the service firm owner may be experiencing a leveling off of demand for services. However, the owner knows that if the business is to remain competitive, sales must increase by at least 6 percent annually over the next three years. If examination reveals that the cause of the problem is a new competitor, then what alternatives can be developed to increase competitiveness and reverse the leveling off of sales?

Develop Alternatives   After correctly defining the problem(s), the owner must consider satisfactory alternative courses of action that will yield positive results. In most situations, several alternatives can likely be developed that will lead to desired outcomes. For example, possible alternatives to be considered for increasing the business activity of the service business are

1. Increase the amount of advertising done by the firm.
2. Add new types of services to those already offered.
3. Provide service personnel with additional technical training.
4. Offer special performance incentives available to service personnel.
5. Offer a discount on seasonal services, such as a $10 discount on pre-season air conditioning check.
6. Relocate the service center, such as moving to a more accessible site.

Evaluate Alternatives   After preparing a list of satisfactory alternatives, the owner should evaluate each in terms of its advantages and disadvantages. The owner should consider the following points when studying the feasibility of each alternative.

1. Will this alternative provide a satisfactory solution to the problem?
2. If this alternative is adopted, will it likely prevent the problem from redeveloping in the future?

Alternatives that do not appear feasible are set aside for consideration at a later date. In this case, the relocation may not be feasible because financial resources are not available.

Implement the Plan of Action   After analyzing the alternatives, the owner should have an indication of the course of action that offers a satisfactory solution to the problem. In many situations, instead of choosing a single alternative, the manager may incorporate several alternatives into the final plan of action. To increase demand for the services of the firm, the owner may choose several alternatives, such as increasing advertising, offering special discounts on some seasonal services, providing more training for service personnel, and instituting an incentive program for service technicians.

Organizing

The management function of **organizing** is the process of identifying jobs that must be performed, defining authority and responsibility of employees, and establishing authority relationships between employees so that the objectives developed in the planning function can be attained. The organizing function consists of three related steps: (1) identification of jobs, (2) define authority and responsibility, and (3) determining authority–responsibility relationships.

Identification of Jobs

In the first phase of the organizing function, managers are concerned with identifying the essential jobs that must be performed if objectives are to be reached. In a manufacturing firm, these tasks include the essential enterprise functions of sales, production, and finance. In retailing, these functions are sales, buying, and finance. Division of work is desirable because it allows for task specialization that is designed to achieve greater efficiency in task performance. Insofar as it is possible in the small business, it is desirable to divide the jobs to achieve specialization and group them into logical units (departments) or some similar arrangement, usually on the basis of similarity of activities. Grouping makes coordination of enterprise functions possible.

By dividing and grouping tasks, each department is held accountable for its specific part of the business operation. For example, all sales activities are grouped together in the sales department as are all recordkeeping activities in the office administration department.

Define Authority and Responsibility

How much authority and responsibility each employee has should be clearly defined. Even in the small firm, it is preferable that this information be in writing. Authority is the right of persons to take action and make the necessary decisions for completing the tasks assigned to them. Responsibility is the obligation employees have to perform the tasks assigned to them to the best of their ability.

In the small business, the owner–manager has complete and final authority and responsibility. As often happens, however, owner–managers find that they do not have time to devote to every detail in the company. Effective managers realize that one of the most practical methods of running a successful company is to delegate some authority to their employees. Delegation of authority enables employees to make decisions in areas where they are qualified. It also allows the manager to devote extra time to more important matters. Delegation encourages key employees to take initiative. In addition, employees can have authority delegated to them to keep the company running if the owner–manager must be away from the business. When authority is delegated, employees are responsible for performing the tasks satisfactorily.

One small manufacturer recognized the necessity for establishing the formal organization. He divided the firm into three departments: production, sales, and administrative.

He then designated the responsibilities for each department manager. The production manager was given authority and responsibility for manufacturing, packing, and shipping. The sales manager's authority and responsibility included advertising, attracting new customers, and customer service. The administrative department manager's authority and responsibility were for accounting, purchasing, and personnel activities.

After working with department managers, both individually and as a team, the owner–manager was able to establish the job procedures and to avoid the overlapping of authority and responsibility between departments. All these procedures were then written down. Thus, managers had specific information on what decisions they could make and which actions needed approval by the owner. The owner also designated the production manager to be in charge during the owner's absence.

Determining Authority–Responsibility Relationships

Authority and responsibility relationships among personnel must be clearly defined to avoid confusion and overlapping authority. The **organization chart** is useful in this regard for representing graphically the authority and responsibility relationships among people in the various departments as well as for delineating the channels of formal communication. Usually, the organization chart is quite simple in the small business because of the relatively small size of the company. For example, Figure 8-2 depicts the organization structure of a small store with the owner–manager and two salespersons. However, as the firm grows, an assistant manager and additional employees may be added.

Staffing

Once tasks have been identified, the need is to match personnel to jobs. The goal of **staffing** is to see that employees are selected and placed in tasks for which they are qualified. This management function is discussed more completely in Chapter 9.

Leading

Leading is the process of influencing employees toward the accomplishment of company goals. Through their daily interaction with employees in the firm, owner–managers have the unique opportunity to create an atmosphere that encourages a spirit of teamwork. Clearly, the quality and style of leadership is a major factor in shaping the success of the business and managers must ac-

FIGURE 8-2
ORGANIZATION CHART OF A SMALL RETAIL STORE WITH TWO SALESPERSONS.

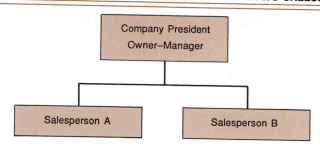

REVISED ORGANIZATION CHART OF AN ASSISTANT MANAGER
AFTER ADDITION OF A SALESPERSON.

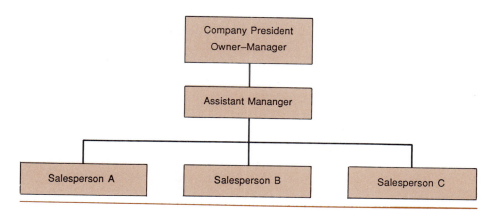

cept this responsibility. What determines a manager's leadership style is likely influenced by their assumptions about people, as shown in Figure 8-3. These assumptions are found in Theories X, Y, and Z.

Theories X, Y, and Z and Styles of Leadership

Douglas McGregor[1] contends that there are two extreme assumptions that managers make about people, Theory X and Theory Y. The assumptions a manager makes determines the leadership style he or she adopts. **Theory X** and **Theory Y** assumptions are beliefs about the nature of people and the nature of work.

Theory X Assumptions

1. The average human being has an inherent dislike of work and will avoid it if he or she can.

FIGURE 8-3
THEORY X AND THEORY Y ASSUMPTIONS RESULT IN LEADERSHIP STYLES.

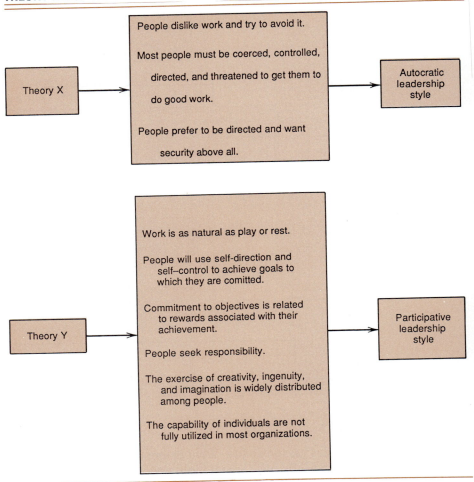

2. Because of the human characteristic of dislike of work, most people must be coerced, controlled, directed, and threatened with punishment to get them to put forth effort toward the achievement of organizational objectives.

3. The average human being prefers to be directed, wishes to avoid responsibility, has relatively little ambition, and wants security above all.

Autocratic Leaders Managers who follow Theory X will likely be autocratic managers. **Autocratic leaders** strive for maximum control. They delegate little or no authority and provide few outlets for employee creativity. Close supervision is the practice, and pressure is applied to obtain greater employee productivity. Because formal communications flow primarily downward from managers to employees, there is little opportunity for the exchange of information and ideas. Employees are usually reprimanded for mistakes. Autocratic leadership usually has a negative impact on employees, especially if they have strong needs for independence and participation.

Theory Y Assumptions

1. The expenditure of physical and mental effort in work is as natural as play or rest.
2. External control and the threat of punishment are not the only means for bringing about effort toward organizational objectives. People will exercise self-direction and self-control in the service of objectives to which they are committed.
3. Commitment to objectives is related to the rewards associated with their achievement.
4. The average human being learns, under proper conditions, not only to accept but also to seek responsibility.
5. The capacity to exercise a relatively high degree of imagination, ingenuity, and creativity in the solution of organizational objectives is widely, not narrowly, distributed in the population.
6. Under the conditions of modern industrial life, the intellectual potentialities of the average human being are only partially utilized.

Participative Leaders   Theory Y managers are likely to practice participative leadership. **Participative leaders** have a positive view of employees and as such they strive to involve them in the ongoing operations of the company. These leaders encourage employees to share in making decisions that affect them. By encouraging participation, the manager desires to have employees become ego-involved in their work and in the company. The leader strives to build an organizational environment that recognizes the value of the individual. Participative leaders trust subordinates to act responsibly.

In the small business, the participative leader not only seeks out ideas and suggestions from subordinates but also tries to make constructive use of time. This method of tapping the creative talents of employees underscores a basic ingredient of the participative leadership philosophy: employees are more likely to support ideas and actions that they have had a part in creating.

Communication flows freely in this type of company—horizontally and vertically. Instead of a company made up of individual performers, such a company emphasizes extensive use of teamwork. Thus, employees are encouraged to take greater responsibility for guilding their own efforts and work in a supportive relationship with their coworkers and the entrepreneur.

The basic principles of the Japanese style of management that is widely publicized today are found in the basic tenets of McGregor's Theory Y.

Rosemary Garbett assumed active control of Los Tios, a Tex-Mex restaurant in Houston, Texas, after her husband's death in 1976. Since then, she has turned a marginal mom-and-pop business into a successful restaurant chain. Garbett practices participative leadership by actively listening to employee suggestions and delegating authority and responsibility. To increase employee motivation, she has instituted a profit-sharing plan.

Theory Z Assumptions

Theory Z is a contingency theory. The basic premise of contingency theory is that no one leadership style is best for all occasions. Instead, employee efficiency may be increased by use of either an autocratic or a participative style, depending on the circumstances involved in each situation. Whereas Theory X and Y rely on the assumption that there are only two variables that interact within the organization, work and the nature of man, Theory Z recognizes that there are many variables that interact within the organization. Contingency factors include the kind of work to be performed, time pressures, characteristics of the subordinates, and the leader's own behavior. Depending on the situation, autocratic or participative leadership may be the appropriate leadership style to use. A third style, **free-rein leadership,** may be suitable for those situations where employees have the ability to take charge and control their own work behavior.

FIGURE 8-4
THE CONTROL CYCLE.

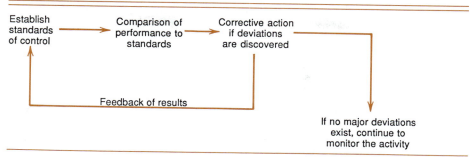

Controlling

Planning and controlling are closely related. Planning involves setting objectives. **Controlling** is the process of measuring current operations to determine if actual performance conforms to objectives and the plans to accomplish them.

The purpose of the control function is to provide managers with continual feedback on the progress of the company toward goal attainment. Without an effective system of controls in place, owners have no way of gauging performance. The basic control process, shown in Figure 8-4, consists of (1) establishing standards of performance, (2) comparison of performance to standards, and (3) corrective action if deviations from standards are indicated.

Establishing Standards of Performance

Objectives indicating desired results must be established before standards can be set. Once objectives have been set, standards, which are the performance levels expected if goals are to be realized, may be established. Thus, planning and controlling are linked together by performance standards. Various types of control standards appropriate for a small business are presented in Figure 8-5. For example, salespersons have a performance standard of the number of

FIGURE 8-5
STANDARDS USED IN FUNCTIONAL AREAS TO GAUGE PERFORMANCE.

Production	Marketing	Personnel Management	Finance and Accounting
Quality	Sales volume	Labor relations	Capital expenditures
Quantity	Sales expense	Labor turnover	Inventories
Cost	Advertising expenditures	Labor absenteeism	Flow of capital
Machine	Individual salesperson's	Safety	Liquidity
Individual job	performance		
performance			

SMALL BUSINESS BRIEF

TIME MANAGEMENT

Managers in all sizes of firms can realize substantial improvement in their own performance and in their company's performance through more efficient use of their time. Small business owners are certainly no exception. The statement "Time is money" is especially appropriate for the entrepreneur. **Time management** is a systematic analysis of how the owner and employees use their time at work. Time-use analysis can reveal to owners the types of activities on which they are spending their time and consequently enable them to devote their time to more critical, high-priority matters. High-priority activities can then be identified for the owner, other managers, and each employee. In this way, activities of less importance can be delegated, and these activities become high-priority items for that level. The goal is to improve the quality of time that owners and employees invest on the job, not the quantity. The following guidelines can aid the owner and employees to gain greater control over their work and to accomplish more.

Observe how your time is spent   Keep a record for at least two weeks of how each hour of your day is spent. You can prepare a chart with 30-minute time slots to fill in during the day. Include all activities, even personal calls, commuting, coffee breaks, and reading the newspaper. At the end of each week, you should have a fair understanding of how much time every activity consumes.

Define hours available for work   Establish a working schedule or calculate how many hours a week you want to commit to your business. This schedule will provide a time frame to fill with business responsibilities.

Outline all tasks   Make a list of all your responsibilities and how much time each one requires. These can be daily, weekly, or monthly activities. Include time for personal responsibilities, and list those tasks for which you don't now have time but feel you should do or want to do.

Set priorities   Make a realistic assessment of all the tasks you have outlined and the number of hours you have available. Eliminate those activities that can be delegated or are not essential. Notice which activities are taking more time than necessary and explore ways to be more efficient. For example, you might consider creating a more practical filing system or investing in office equipment that will facilitate the flow of paper; you can learn to keep phone conversations short.

Delegate responsibility   A lot of your time may be wasted making decisions that can be made by your staff. Realistically, you cannot do everything, and once you have established your priorities, the rest should be delegated.

Organize your day   Each day, list what you need to accomplish in order of priority. Plan how and when you will do the various tasks. List only what is feasible and realistic for the day. Although you may not be a habitual list maker, organization is the key to controlling your time. In addition, planning ahead reduces the amount of time wasted between tasks.

Evaluate your system   Frequently reevaluate your priorities and responsibilities. As your business grows, the demands on your time will change. Always maintain a basic awareness of how your time is spent and of the need to be more efficient.

Source of guidelines listed above: For Women: Managing Your Own Business (Washington, D.C.: Small Business Administration, 1984), pp. 20–21.

customers they are expected to contact in a specified time period and the sales quota they are expected to reach.

Comparison of Performance to Standards

If standards are to be useful, they must be compared with actual performance of employees. This information permits the owner to determine if employees are performing at the desired level. Control standards that are clearly defined can more easily be compared to actual performance. For example, the sales quota and number of client calls expected of the salesperson can readily be monitored. When the salesperson's performance is checked at various intervals—hourly, daily, weekly, monthly—any variations in performance become apparent.

Corrective Action

If the comparison of standards and performance reveals no deviations, the only action required of the owner is to continue to monitor the activity. However, if variations are revealed, steps must be taken to correct the deviation so that future performance is redirected toward the standard. If a salesperson is not reaching the standard performance level, specific actions may be needed that include additional training or a reevaluation of standards and adjusting them to a more realistic level.

EMPLOYEE RELATIONS IN THE SMALL BUSINESS

Of the many issues that confront the owner–manager, one of the most challenging is found in the area of employee relations. As stated in Chapter 1, small business managers often possess technical skills. For a person in the role of owner–manager, however, one of the most valuable skills is human relations, the ability to work effectively with employees to achieve individual and company goals.

In our text, the term **employee relations** refers to the interpersonal relationships that occur daily as small business managers and employees interact. The quality of interpersonal relationships determines the organization environment that is found in the firm. The **organization environment** is shaped by the interaction of three factors in the workplace.

1. Social factors (group interaction, superior–subordinate relationships)
2. Physical factors (working conditions, job layout)
3. Economic factors (wages and salary, fringe benefits)

The perception that employees have of the organization environment influences, either directly or indirectly, their attitudes and resulting behavior toward the owner–manager and the company as well as their expectations from their job and their actual level of performance.

Many small firms have at least a few employees on the payroll. A primary goal of managers is to have employees work together as a team rather than as individuals. Teamwork stresses mutual understanding and cooperation for goal achievement at both the individual and company level.

In this section, we will explore some of the prominent "employee relations" issues. This discussion should provide an owner–manager with the foundation for understanding employee behavior. The need to understand the cause of employee behavior is very real for the small firm owner–manager. With a small number of employees, cooperation and support among all employees are essential for goal accomplishment.

MOTIVATION

People spend a substantial portion of their lives at work. Consequently, the workplace has a profound impact on each individual. Modern managers realize that employees are unique, each with his or her own values, attitudes, interests, physical makeup, and emotional set. Each person's behavior at work is shaped by the combination of such factors as physiological makeup, work experience, goals, and the influence of cultural background (family, peers, race, education).

Since each employee is unique, owners must seek to understand what motivates their behavior. **Motivation** is the inner drive that ignites behavioral actions to satisfy needs.

EMPLOYEE NEEDS

Just as each person has his or her own physiological makeup, values, attitudes, and interests, so does each have a unique set of needs. In our discussion, needs are defined as all the "things" people must have to survive as well as the things they want above the survival level. Thus, all human behavior is directed toward the satisfaction of needs.

The need satisfaction process is shown in Figure 8-6. To illustrate, an employee has a need to be promoted. This desire causes tension within the individual, which in turn causes the individual to be motivated. The individual undertakes the action he or she perceives will result in a promotion, such as raising the level of their performance. When the employee raises his or her performance level to a higher level, and the owner rewards the performance with a promotion, the need is satisfied. As Figure 8-6 indicates, need satisfaction is a continuous process.

Employees may be motivated either positively or negatively. Positive motivation occurs when employees strive toward a goal, such as a salary increase.

FIGURE 8-6
THE NEED-SATISFACTION PROCESS.

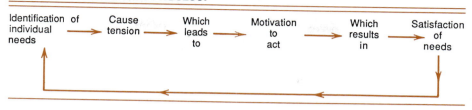

Negative motivation results from such reasons as fear of failure or frustration and causes an employee's motivation to be aimed toward protection. Negative motivation may cause employees to reject new work methods or a promotion, become apathetic, sabotage the system, or leave the company.

Reseachers have theorized various explanations of human needs and individual behavior. We will focus our discussion on three: Abraham Maslow's hierarchy of needs, Frederick Herzberg's two-factor theory, and David McClelland's acquired needs theory.

Hierarchy of Needs

The hierarchy of needs[2] suggests which needs are most important for an individual at a given time in their life. This needs hierarchy suggests a priority in which one level of needs must be reasonably well satisfied before needs at the next higher level become prominent. This theory offers an explanation of why employees behave the way they do on the job, and this aids in understanding human behavior. Knowledge contained in the need hierarchy is beneficial to managers, as they can use this information to build an organization environment that offers opportunities for higher-order needs to be satisfied. In companies where employees are provided with opportunities to fulfill their needs, they tend to have more favorable attitudes toward the organization and their work assignments. The need hierarchy, shown in Figure 8-7, consists of five levels of needs: physiological, safety and security, social, ego, and self-actualization. The need hierarchy is based on the assumption that individual needs affect behavior in accordance with two basic principles.

1. *The deficit principle:*   A satisfied need is not a motivator of behavior. People act to satisfy "deprived needs," that is, needs for which a satisfaction "deficit" exists.
2. *The progression principle:*   The five need categories exist in a strictly ordered hierarchy of prepotency. A need at any one level only becomes activated once the next lower-level need has been generally satisfied. The following discussion highlights each of the needs of the hierarchy.

FIGURE 8-7
THE HIERARCHY OF NEEDS.

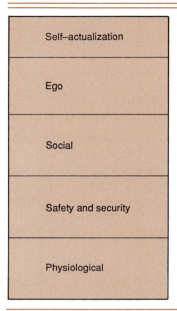

(Abraham Maslow, ''A Theory of Human Motivation,'' *Psychological Review,* Vol. 50, no. 4, July–August 1943, pp. 370–396, and Abraham Maslow, *Motivation and Personality,* Harper & Row, New York, 1954.)

Physiological Needs

Everyone has physiological needs. These are the basic needs everyone must have to survive—food, oxygen, water, shelter. The owner–manager of the firm provides a wage or salary that allows employees to obtain the resources that will satisfy these basic maintenance needs.

Safety and Security Needs

A need to feel safe and secure from anything that might cause harm exists in all persons. Safety and security needs can be satisfied in many ways. Safety needs may be satisfied through such actions as when the owner purchases equipment with special safety features or maintains a physical environment that is free from pollution.

Security needs may be fulfilled when the owner offers employees job security, a health insurance plan, or a pension plan. These actions remove many of the employee's concerns over economic insecurity.

Social Needs

A social need is one's desire to interact with others. Social needs include the need to belong, to be accepted by coworkers, and to give and receive attention. Americans are frequently described as a "nation of joiners." People are members of many groups simultaneously—social, civic, religious, and of course, work groups. Social needs are satisfied through group membership. Belonging and acceptance needs can be satisfied on the job when employees are accepted as members of the work group. Owner–managers offer employees the opportunity to satisfy their social needs through a variety of actions, such as company picnics and the design of jobs so that interaction is possible among employees.

Ego Needs

Ego needs include self-esteem (self-confidence, independence) and personal reputation (recognition, status). As people mature, they develop a need to be independent both on and off the job. On the job, employees express the need for independence by their desire to have some control over how their work is performed and freedom from close supervision. When given this type of independence, employees can demonstrate their maturity.

Employees have a need for recognition. This need can be satisfied when employees are given recognition for their contribution to the company, such as a bonus for the salesperson of the month or a cash award for a suggestion. When an employee is given recognition, his or her status is elevated.

Status is the relative social ranking a person has compared with others in the group. Status may be either formal or informal. Formal status refers to the rank of people as specified by the authority structure of the organization. Sources of formal status include job title, occupation, and organization level. Informal status refers to the social rank given people because of feelings toward them. Informal sources of status include such personal facts as seniority, work schedule, age, education, and expertise.

The visible status symbols that identify one's rank in the social hierarchy include size and location of office, type of office equipment (desk, chair, computer), job title, and number of windows in an office.

Self-actualization Needs

The highest-order need becomes dominant when other needs have been satisfied. This need refers to a person becoming all he or she is capable of becoming. Maslow suggested that only 10 percent of the population ever achieves this level.

Awareness of the need hierarchy equips managers with an understanding of the behavior exhibited by employees. For example, the owner should realize that if a lower-order need is threatened, employees will revert to functioning at the lower need level that is threatened until it is again reasonably well satisfied. If an employee faces the loss of a job, he or she will regress to functioning at the lower physiological and safety and security need level until the threat is removed, such as by getting a job. He or she is then ready to begin functioning at the higher need levels again. Figure 8-8 indicates some of the means by which needs may be satisfied on the job.

FIGURE 8-8
HOW NEEDS ARE SATISFIED ON THE JOB.

Need Level	Satisfied on the Job by
Physiological	Good working conditions
Safety and security	Modern equipment with safety features, job security
Social	Interaction on the job, company-sponsored activities
Ego	Position, title, office, parking space
Self-actualization	Self-expression, growth, achievement, personal development

Two-Factor Theory

Frederick Herzberg has developed a two-factor theory of motivation.[3] Herzberg identifies the two factors as motivator factors and hygiene factors. Motivators are classed as satisfiers and hygiene factors as dissatisfiers. Herzberg viewed these factors as separate dimensions, not as points on a continuum.

Hygiene Factors

Hygiene factors include company policies and administration, pay, working conditions, and supervision. These factors, also called "maintenance factors," can only lead to dissatisfaction because they relate more to the work setting, or "job context," than to the nature of the work itself. To the manager, the message is that if hygiene factors are present in the work environment in high quantity and quality, they will not serve as motivators to increase job satisfaction but will only result in "no dissatisfaction." However, the absence of hygiene factors in the workplace will lead to varying degrees of employee dissatisfaction, which has a negative impact on the company.

Motivation Factors

The second group of factors were labeled "motivators" or "satisfiers." These factors include achievement, recognition, work itself, responsibility, advancement, and personal growth on the job. These factors are part of what employees actually do in their job and are related to the nature of the work. They are classified as "job content factors." The presence of these factors can increase job satisfaction but will not prevent job dissatisfaction.

A list of each of the motivator and hygiene factors is given in Figure 8–9.

Acquired Needs

David McClelland[4] assumes that there are three needs that are acquired over time and are the result of life experiences. All three needs are active simultaneously within an individual, but one need tends to be dominant. Consequently, employees are motivated by their needs, and the challenge for the

FIGURE 8-9
MOTIVATOR AND HYGIENE FACTORS.

Motivators	Hygiene
Meaningful and challenging work	Pay
Recognition for accomplishment	Status
Feeling of achievement	Security
Increased responsibility	Working conditions
Opportunities for growth and development	Fringe benefits
	Policies and administrative practices
The job itself	Interpersonal relations

No job satisfaction   Job satisfaction

←——————————————————————————————————————→

Motivators
(derived from the job itself)

Job dissatisfaction   No job dissatisfaction

←——————————————————————————————————————→

Hygiene Factors
(derived from the environment)

manager is to learn to identify which need is dominant for each employee and develop a work environment that will allow employees to fulfill these needs. The knowledge of which need is dominant also helps in placing a person in the correct job. The three needs in this theory are the need for affiliation, the need for power, and the need for achievement.

Need for Affiliation
The desire to establish and maintain friendly and warm relations with other persons is the affiliation need. This is the same as the social need in the hierarchy of needs theory.

Need for Power
Power is the capacity to influence or control. An individual expresses this power need when he or she seeks to be dominant over, or control the use of, physical objects or the actions of others. In an organization, power may be acquired in a number of ways, as described here.

1. Legitimate power refers to the power a person has because of his or her formal position in the organization. The further ones goes in the company hierarchy, the more legitimate power he or she has.
2. Coercive power is based on the superior's ability to apply sanctions

either in the form of direct punishment, such as a temporary suspension, or discharge.

3. Reward power is based on the superior's ability to grant or withhold rewards, such as promotions or wage increases.

4. Expert power is that which accrues to an individual because of certain special knowledge or skill he or she possesses. People will follow this person's lead because they have confidence that the "expert" knows what he or she is doing or saying.

5. Referent power is based on the follower's admiration of and identification with the leader. The leader has a certain charisma which attracts people and causes them to be willing to follow.[5]

Achievement Need

The achievement need tends to be characteristic of people who have a strong desire to accomplish a task through their own efforts. David McClelland identified the characteristics of the people who have a strong achievement need as follows.

1. They prefer situations in which they take personal responsibility for finding solutions.

2. They tend to set moderate, realistic, attainable achievement goals and to take "calculated risks."

3. They want concrete feedback on how well they are doing.[6]

According to McClelland, an individual who is likely to have a strong achievement need is the entrepreneur. When employees have a high need for achievement, the owner–manager should allow them to work at tasks in which they can assume greater responsibility and can take the initiative to solve their own problems.

ORGANIZATIONAL CHANGE

Managers should consider that all decisions they make and actions they undertake will affect employees. A method of building strong employer–employee relations is to assess the impact that proposed actions and decisions will have on employees prior to taking the action and to ascertain what steps should be taken to lessen an adverse impact.

One common problem deals with changes in the company that affect operations and personnel of the firm. Change may be reflected in methods or procedures of work, such as a change to automated facilities, a change in personnel, or a move by the company to a new location. Change has a definite impact on individuals and should be undertaken so as to encounter as few obstacles as possible.

Change is a fact of an organization's life and is desirable if the firm is to remain abreast or move ahead of the competition. Yet the major barrier to change is resistance. The owner–manager resists change on the grounds that the business has been successful. Therefore, why is there a need to change? Employees resist change because they fear the unknown and desire to maintain the status quo in which they feel secure. Relationships between managers and employees can be adversely affected if employees feel they are being pressured or manipulated into making changes. Employee resistance to change may be evidenced by increased hostility or aggressiveness on the job. They may resort to sabotage in the work area, absenteeism and tardiness may increase, or they may develop apathetic attitudes toward their work.

Although resistance to change can never be totally eliminated, it can be reduced through positive actions taken by the owner–manager. One constructive measure is to communicate complete information of why the change is necessary and what the benefits of the change will be for the owner and employees. Another major action that managers should take is to involve all employees who will be affected by the change early in the discussion about the change. They should be encouraged to contribute their ideas and suggestions on the change and how it should be implemented. Employee participation is the most constructive action that managers can take to reduce resistance to change.

EMPLOYEE MORALE

The organizational environment has a major impact on employee morale. **Morale** is defined as the attitude of individuals toward factors in the work environment, such as their job, pay, or supervision. In this context, employees may be described as having either high or low morale. Since morale is an attitude held by individuals, a feeling that employees have, it is difficult to measure. In fact, morale cannot be measured directly as can the number of dollars of profit earned annually. Instead, indirect techniques are used to measure the attitudes of employees and provide a reading of employee morale.

One technique of measuring employee attitudes is an objective survey. This survey technique asks employees to check how they feel about particular factors in the company. Questions may be true-false, multiple choice, or scaled, ranging from completely satisfied to completely dissatisfied. Figure 8-10 presents one method of collecting data on employee morale.

A descriptive survey is another method of collecting morale data. Employees are requested to supply written answers to questions. Regardless of the method employed, morale surveys can profitably be used regularly to identify the strengths and weaknesses of the company.

Indicators of Employee Morale

There are indicators, or warning signals, that alert owners to the realization that employee morale is low. Some of the indicators that the small business owners should be aware of are shown in Figure 8-11.

FIGURE 8-10
EMPLOYEE MORALE SURVEY

Listed below are 18 statements about your job and the company in which you work. Please check each statement according to how you perceive them: Agree with the statement; Disagree with the statement; or Uncertain (if you do not know or cannot decide).

	Agree	Disagree	Uncertain
1. I have the opportunity to participate in decisions that affect me.	_____	_____	_____
2. Communications within the company keep me informed about company plans.	_____	_____	_____
3. My supervisor does not use unreasonable pressure to get employees to meet work schedules.	_____	_____	_____
4. My job performance is evaluated fairly and constructively.	_____	_____	_____
5. I have considerable freedom to use my initiative and judgment in my job.	_____	_____	_____
6. I have assurance of job security as long as my job performance is satisfactory.	_____	_____	_____
7. Opportunities for promotion are based on ability and job performance.	_____	_____	_____
8. My pay is fair compared to the pay others receive.	_____	_____	_____
9. The company provides safe and satisfactory physical working conditions.	_____	_____	_____
10. My job is interesting and challenging.	_____	_____	_____
11. Grievances and disciplinary matters are handled fairly.	_____	_____	_____
12. My coworkers are friendly and cooperative.	_____	_____	_____
13. I receive recognition for doing good work.	_____	_____	_____
14. Supervisors and subordinates work together as a team.	_____	_____	_____
15. Standards of performance for my job are realistic.	_____	_____	_____

FIGURE 8-10
CONTINUED

	Agree	Disagree	Uncertain
16. Fringe benefits are satisfactory.	_____	_____	_____
17. I derive a feeling of personal satisfaction from doing my job well.	_____	_____	_____
18. I have a feeling of pride in working for this company.	_____	_____	_____

Any of these negative morale indicators will adversely affect the small firm. Considerable amounts of time and money are expended in employee selection and placement. Employees who are properly placed in a job tend to have higher morale. Poor selection and placement procedures lead to frustration and low morale. Eventually, employees will leave the firm or be low producers. Firms that have a high turnover rate of employees experience increased costs of operations as new employees must be selected and placed. While they are being trained, their productivity is below standard, and chances for error or waste of material are greater. When the firm begins to experience a high turnover rate, the manager's efforts should be directed toward discovering the reasons and take corrective action.

If absenteeism increases, the small business will be understaffed. If this happens in the retail or service establishment, it is difficult to provide the kind

FIGURE 8-11
INDICATORS OF LOW EMPLOYEE MORALE.

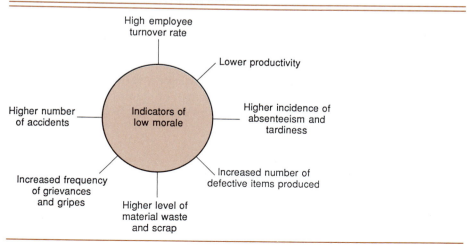

of customer assistance needed, especially during peak business hours. This may result in driving customers to competitors or at least inconveniencing them while shopping. In the small manufacturing firm, the absence of a skilled machine operator means that a machine must be idled, thus reducing the firm's output. Or, if the machine is operated, it will likely have to be operated by a marginally qualified worker. The result will be lower productivity because of an increased number of defective products.

If accidents increase, not only must the personal injury be a matter of real concern but also the effect that the accidents have on the company. A valuable worker is lost for a period of time, productivity suffers, and the cost of employee accident insurance increases.

The negative effect of low morale should be an area of major concern for small business managers. Consequently, they should attempt to maintain up-to-date information relating to the state of employee morale and take appropriate actions to improve employee morale.

If these indicators begin to surface, small business managers should recognize that they are merely "symptoms." The critical task is to establish the "cause." Why is turnover increasing? Why is productivity suffering? Why are accidents increasing? Only by ascertaining the "cause" of these problems will it be possible to take constructive steps to correct them.

EMPLOYEE DISCIPLINE

When employees work together, conflict may develop. If managers fail to cope with the conflict and take appropriate action, the result can be a lowering of employee morale. Employees lose respect for managers who cannot tolerate mistakes, who are too lax and apply discipline only under the most severe circumstances, or who apply discipline inconsistently.

One way to reduce the number of instances where discipline is required is to inform employees of company rules and regulations. For example, many firms specify employee actions that are prohibited and that, if engaged in, will result in disciplinary action being taken. It is essential, however, that employees perceive the rules as being fair and related to their job performance.

Disciplinary problems arise for a variety of reasons: lack of knowledge, poor attitudes, lack of interest, or carelessness. Some of the acts that call for disciplinary action are shown in Figure 8-12.

Progressive Discipline

Progressive discipline is one approach that applies a minimum of discipline to a first offense but increases the degree of discipline for subsequent violations of rules or policies. Progressive discipline actions may include the following sequence:

FIGURE 8-12
EMPLOYEE ACTS PROHIBITED IN THE COMPANY.

Disorderly conduct: reporting to work under the influence of liquor or consuming intoxicants on company premises or while on company business.
Conclusive evidence of dishonesty.
Obtaining employment by using false or misleading information.
Continued violation of safety practices.
Selling or soliciting in the company.
Gambling.
Excessive tardiness or absenteeism without reason.
Refusal to work as directed (insubordination).
Willful destruction of company property.

1: Oral warning

2: Written warning stating the consequences of future violations

3: Disciplinary layoff or demotion

4: Discharge

The "hot stove rule" has been recommended as a series of steps to make discipline more effective. It uses the analogy of touching the hot stove and administering discipline. The sequence should include

1. A forewarning—all are warned by the heat generated not to touch the stove.
2. Immediate action—touching the stove results in being immediately burned.
3. A consistent rule—each time the stove is touched, you are burned.
4. Impersonal administration—all who touch the stove are burned.[7]

Positive Discipline

The most effective type of discipline is positive, that which corrects or strengthens an individual. It is also the most difficult type of discipline to apply. Disciplining should be conducted in a private setting, away from the noise of the job and certainly not in front of fellow employees. When disciplining, managers should concentrate on the mistake rather than on the person. It is essential that managers listen carefully to the employee's view as to what occurred in order to get the complete facts and clarify any misunderstanding. The manager should explain not only that something is being done incorrectly but also explain why employees should be doing it another way.

An equitable solution that is fair to both employer and employee should be the result.

Some guidelines that will enable the owner to establish a climate of positive discipline are suggested as follows.

1. There must be rules and standards that are communicated clearly and administered fairly.
2. Rules and standards must be reasonable.
3. Rules should be communicated so that they are known and understood by all employees.
4. While a rule or a standard is in force, employees are expected to adhere to it.
5. Even though rules exist, people should know that if a personal problem or a unique situation makes the rule exceptionally harsh, the rule may be modified, or an exception may be granted.
6. There should be no favorites, and privileges should be granted only when they can also be granted to other employees in similar situations. This means that it must be possible to explain to other employees who request a similar privilege with less justification why the privilege cannot be extended to them in their particular situation.
7. Employees must be aware that they can and should voice dissatisfaction with any rules or standards they consider unreasonable as well as with working conditions they feel are hazardous.
8. Employees should understand the consequences of breaking a rule without permission.
9. There should be an appeals procedure when an employee feels you have made an unfair decision.
10. Employees should be consulted when rules are set.
11. There should be recognition for good performance, reliability, and loyalty.[8]

COMMUNICATION

A fundamental need in the small business is for information pertaining to business operations to be accurate and to flow freely between the owner–manager and employees. **Communication** is defined as the interpersonal process of transmitting information between two or more people so that understanding is created. As emphasized in Chapter 1, communication skill is one of the abilities that contributes significantly to small business success. A communication network that enables employees to be informed about forthcoming actions in the company is likely to generate a feeling of trust between the owner–manager and employees. A two-way communication system provides employees with opportunities to be involved in company matters and affords managers with insight into employee attitudes toward the company.

FIGURE 8-13
THE COMMUNICATION PROCESS.

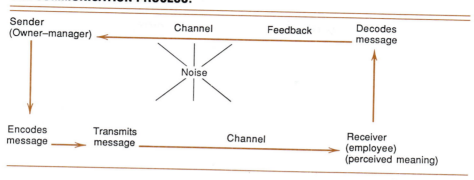

In the small business, most communication is exchanged on a face-to-face basis because the manager has direct, personal contact with employees. The communication process is presented in Figure 8-13. The communication process begins when the sender (the small business manager) needs to send a message to employees. He or she is responsible for encoding an intended meaning into a message. The message may be verbal, written, or nonverbal (gestures) or a combination of all. The message is sent through the proper channel to the receiver who decodes the message into the perceived meaning. To complete the process, the receiver should provide feedback to the sender indicating what he or she understands the message to mean. This completes the loop of the communication process. In this way, any misunderstanding can be corrected.

Barriers to Communication

"Noise" in the communication process refers to anything that interferes with the transmission of the written or oral message or distorts the message. Common types of noise include psychological barriers, semantic barriers, communication overloading, physical distractions, and an absence of feedback.

Psychological Barriers

Psychological barriers refer to the communication breakdown that occurs because of various forms of distortion of information and problems revolving around interpersonal relationships. A common psychological barrier is filtering information. For example, employees may filter out negative information and pass on to the entrepreneur only the positive information they perceive is desired by the owner. Another psychological barrier is selective perception, which means that people hear only what they want to hear, not what is actually being said. A psychological barrier that revolves around interpersonal relationships occurs when the receiver does not trust the sender, the "credibility gap."

Semantic Barriers

Semantic barriers result because words have different meanings for people. In our language, a single word may have multiple meanings. For example, the word "round" has 50 different meanings printed in *Webster's New Collegiate Dictionary*. When an entrepreneur uses a word that has many meanings, he or she must ensure that the word is understood in the way he or she is using the word. Another type of semantic barrier results when terms are used with which the receiver is not familiar. This barrier most likely occurs when technical terms, or the special language of the company, called "jargon," are used to convey information and the receiver has not been told the specific meaning of the term as used in the company.

Communication Overload

Too much information may result in employees receiving so many written reports and verbal instructions that they are unable to separate the important from the unimportant. When this overload occurs, it can short-circuit the communication process and cause a blockage. Managers should realize that too much information can sometimes be just as detrimental as too little.

Physical Distractions

There are many types of physical distractions that can interfere with the effectiveness of an intended message. When two people are talking, any type of movement, such as people walking by or sounds, such as machinery or the ringing of a telephone, are common physical distractions that interfere with the messsage.

Absence of Feedback

If the sender does not get feedback from the receiver, it cannot be assumed that the sender's message was the same as the receiver perceived it to be. Feedback is essential to promote effective communication.

SUMMARY OF KEY POINTS

1. A manager supervises the work activities of employees to see to it that they accomplish their specific tasks. The owner frequently works side by side with employees in the daily operations of the firm.
2. The management functions of the owner–manager include planning, organizing, staffing, leading, and controlling.
3. Planning is the process of defining objectives and then choosing the course of action the firm will follow to reach objectives.

4. The planning process involves developing objectives, policies, procedures, and rules to provide direction for the owner and the employees.

5. Decision making consists of four phases: define the problem, develop alternatives, evaluate alternatives, and implement a plan of action.

6. The organizing function is the process of identifying the jobs to be performed, defining the authority and responsibility of each employee, and determining authority–responsibility relationships.

7. Leading is the process of influencing employees toward attainment of company goals.

8. Theories X, Y, and Z are different assumptions of human nature and work and influence the leadership style of managers. The appropriate leadership style varies, depending on the circumstances of each situation.

9. Control is the function of determining if efforts conform to plans and objectives.

10. Time management is the systematic analysis of how owners and employees use their time in performing their activities.

11. Employee relations refer to the interpersonal relationships that occur between small business owners and employees.

12. Motivation is the inner drive that ignites behavioral actions to satisfy needs.

13. Three theories of human behavior are Maslow's hierarchy of needs, McClelland's acquired needs theory, and Herzberg's two-factor theory.

14. Employees have many needs that must be satisfied on the job.

15. All organizations experience changing conditions. A major problem of change is reducing employee and owner resistance to change.

16. Employee morale is the attitude that employees have toward the owner–manager, the firm, their job, and their fellow employees.

17. Indicators of low morale include higher rates of turnover, absenteeism, and tardiness; lower productivity; more grievances and gripes; higher incidence of accidents; and increased spoilage and waste of materials.

18. Employee discipline is necessary to maintain order in the firm. The owner should specify guidelines that govern employee conduct.

19. Effective communication keeps employees informed and is instrumental in creating higher employee morale.

DISCUSSION QUESTIONS

1. What are the five management functions?
2. What are the four phases of decision making?
3. What is the relationship of planning and controlling?

4. What is Theory X? What leadership style would likely be used if a manager believed Theory X to be true?
5. What is time management?
6. Explain the motivation process.
7. List several indicators of low employee morale.
8. What is the "hot stove" rule of discipline?
9. What are some barriers to effective communication?

THE BUSINESS PLAN: GUIDELINES FOR EFFECTIVE COMMUNICATION, EFFECTIVE LEADERSHIP, AND MANAGEMENT ORGANIZATION

Effective Communication

Small business managers must realize that effective communication does not occur in a vacuum. Instead, it is the result of conscious efforts by the manager to create an effective communication network. Some guides for creating an effective communication network are listed here.

As an Owner–Manager, Do I . . .

1. Encourage employees to express their ideas and opinions?
2. Listen with understanding to ideas, suggestions, and complaints?
3. Keep employees informed on all changes affecting work?
4. Keep informed on how employees are feeling and what they are thinking?
5. Encourage two-way communication?
6. Award recognition for good work and express appreciation for jobs well done?
7. Try to make communication messages accurate, complete, and clear?
8. Explain the "why" of decisions?
9. Strive to create a climate of trust and confidence by reporting facts honestly to employees?

Effective Leadership

Through their leadership role, owner–managers have a unique opportunity to create positive employee relationships. These guidelines offer some specific suggestions for becoming a more effective leader.

As a Leader, Do I . . .

1. Strive to improve my understanding of human behavior?
2. Accept the fact that others do not always see things as I do?

3. Respect differences of opinion and consider the possibility that I may not have the right answer when there are differences of opinion?

4. Show employees that I am interested in them as individuals as well as employees?

5. Treat employees as individuals; never deal with them impersonally?

6. Give explanations insofar as possible for management actions?

7. Provide information and guidance on matters affecting employees' security?

8. Make reasonable efforts to keep jobs interesting?

9. Encourage promotion from within?

10. Express appreciation publicly for jobs well done?

11. Offer criticism privately in the form of constructive suggestions for improvement?

12. Keep my staff up to date on matters that affect them?

Management Organization Guidelines

1. Do you have a written organization chart?

2. Are all important activities adequately supervised?

3. Does each person in the company know to whom he or she reports?

4. Is authority and responsibility delegated to key members in the company?

5. Does each person clearly understand his or her job?

6. Are you giving thought to where the company will be five years from now?

ENTREPRENEURIAL PROJECTS

Interview a small business manager and obtain the following data.

1. What are the objectives of the business? Are the objectives written down?

2. Does the firm have an organization chart? If so, obtain a copy of the chart.

3. Are morale surveys conducted in the firm? If so, how often?

4. Does the firm have written rules and regulations? If it does, what are they?

C A S E A
The Apparel Shop

Harry Wilson, office manager, and Robert Ellison, manager of the men's department, were leaving The Apparel Shop on their way to lunch. As they approached the front door, they observed Daniel Masters, the owner and president of the firm, in conversation with Norma Jackson, manager of the jewelry department. Mr. Masters was trying to end the conversation, and he appeared anxious to leave. Finally, in a voice expressing some impatience, he told her he had to leave, but added, "Drop by my office anytime. The door is always open."

Daniel Masters took control of the store a year ago when his father unexpectedly died of a heart attack. Daniel has had a difficult time adjusting to his role as president. He worked in the store while in high school and college, and his father taught him all the technical operations of the different departments.

As Harry and Robert were eating their lunch, they discussed the situation at The Apparel Shop. Both agreed that Daniel knew all phases of store operations, but one of the main problems was getting Daniel to listen to ideas or suggestions. Harry remarked, "I have been with the store for about two years. During the year that I worked for Daniel's father, he gave me a great deal of freedom in the office operations. He let me make a lot of changes after we had discussed them. He was easy to talk to and encouraged ideas."

Robert agreed and added, "Daniel is just the opposite. We don't have a chance to discuss ideas or problems with him. And we are strongly discouraged from making our own decisions. Everything has to be decided by Daniel. And I have stopped dropping in that 'open door.' Just last week I made an appointment to discuss our new lines of merchandise that we have been handling for the past month."

Robert continued by describing his meeting with Daniel. When Robert walked in, Daniel was on the telephone, and he motioned for Robert to sit down. When he hung up, he rushed out of the office, without a word to Robert, to talk to his secretary. He returned, wrote some notes on his desk pad, and turned to Robert and said, "Well, what's your problem today?"

Robert reminded him that they were to discuss the merchandise lines as well as sales figures, customer relations, and salespersons. When Robert mentioned the salespersons, Daniel interrupted him to comment about the shortage of salespersons in the women's department. Then the conversation was interrupted by another phone call. Finally, the discussion returned to the purpose of the meeting, but as they were looking at the sales figures, Daniel interrupted again, commenting on how he felt one of the salesperson's performance had begun to decline.

Robert was ready to give up on that session when they were interrupted by another phone call. Daniel was clearly angry when he ended the telephone conversation. He said, "Trouble in the jewelry department again. Norma is always asking for assistance. But I believe we have your problems worked out, Robert, haven't we? Norma is coming up now. But when you have a chance, drop back, and let's take a close look at all phases of your department, especially the new merchandise lines we have added."

As Robert got up to leave, Daniel commented, "Thanks for coming, *Harry*. Come back anytime. You know my door is always open."

Questions

1. What leadership style best describes Daniel?
2. What is likely to happen to the general state of employee motivation and morale if Daniel continues to manage in the manner described earlier?

CASE B
Frank Mason

Frank Mason earned the funds necessary to put himself through college by working in a machine shop in a small manufacturing company. He learned his trade well and became a skilled tool and die maker.

After graduating with a BBA degree, he accepted employment as a first-level supervisor in the Dawson Manufacturing plant. He earned less at Dawson than he could have earned at a larger company, but he preferred working in a smaller company. Furthermore, he liked the particular geographical area with the many recreational facilities found there. Frank considered his entry-level position an excellent method for gaining management experience as well as offering advancement opportunities. His employment goal was to advance to a supervisor's position within two years, a goal he felt was achievable and realistic with the smaller company.

After 15 months, Frank's supervisor retired for health reasons. Frank felt that with his technical skill and the management experience he had acquired, he would be the most likely candidate for the vacated position. However, Roger Hartfield, a first-level supervisor in another department with more seniority than Frank and also a long-time personal friend of the owner, was promoted and became Frank's supervisor.

Frank felt that he was more qualified than Roger even though Roger had been with the company for a longer period. Frank felt that the only reason that Roger was promoted was because of the personal friendship with the owner. Frank was disappointed but not discouraged with this turn of events. He felt that if Roger would provide him with the opportunity, he could prove his value to the company and be given the recognition he felt he deserved. And then the next promotion would be his.

It soon became apparent to Frank that Roger was not aggressive but managed in a very relaxed manner. Roger did not encourage employees to participate or come up with creative solutions to manufacturing problems in the department. Instead, Frank discovered that work relationships with Roger were much better if he did only what he was told to do, offered no solutions to problems in the department, and did not volunteer to take on extra responsibilities.

Frank enjoys working with machinery. A year ago, he developed a new process that reduced the number of steps in the production process and saves the company about $15,000 a year. However, Frank never received any recognition for his contribution. He feels that the chief obstacle to his gaining recognition is his immediate supervisor who is intentionally holding Frank back.

Although Frank likes the job and the location, he is beginning to lose enthusiasm for the job and the company. He is giving serious thought to seeking employment with another company, but this would require a move to another town 400 miles away.

Questions

1. Describe the leadership style of Frank's new supervisor, Roger.

2. What are the factors that have contributed to the lowering of Frank's morale?

3. Describe the breakdown in formal communication in this situation.

4. Is Frank correct in considering other employment? Or should he first go directly to the owner of the company and explain the situation as he perceives it? If he does go to the owner, role play what Frank should say to the owner.

5. What problems are encountered when it appears that promotions are based more on friendship than on performance?

6. If you were in Frank's position, what would you do?

Notes

[1] Douglas McGregor, *The Human Side of Enterprise* (New York: McGraw-Hill, 1960).
[2] Abraham Maslow, "A Theory of Human Motivation," *Psychological Review,* Vol. 50, no. 4 (July–August 1943), pp. 370–376.
[3] Frederick Herzberg, Bernard Mausner, and Barbara Block Synderman, *The Motivation to Work,* 2nd ed. (New York: John Wiley, 1967).

[4] David C. McClelland, "Business Drive and National Achievement," *Harvard Business Review,* Vol. 40. no. 4 (July–August 1962), pp. 99–112.

[5] John R. P. French and Bertram Raven, "The Bases of Social Power," in *Group Dynamics,* 2nd ed., eds. Dorwin Cartwright and A. F. Zander (New York: Row, Peterson, 1960), pp. 607–623.

[6] *"Business Drive and National Achievement,"* pp. 104–105.

[7] Burt Scanlon and Bernard J. Keys, *Management and Organization Behavior* (New York: John Wiley, 1979), p. 382.

[8] "Employee Relations and Personnel Policies," *Business Basics,* no. 1023 (Washington, D.C.: Small Business Administration, 1980), pp. 15–17.

KEY WORDS

PERSONNEL MANAGEMENT

LEARNING GOALS

After reading this chapter, you will understand:

1   The purpose of a job analysis, job description, and job specification.
2   That there are many sources from which employees may be recruited.
3   The sequence of steps in the hiring process.
4   The purpose of the orientation process.
5   The types of employee training used in small businesses.
6   The role of employee counseling.
7   The purposes of performance appraisal.
8   The types of compensation plans that small business owners use.
9   Some of the federal laws that affect the employees.
10 What fringe benefits are.

ENTREPRENEURIAL PROFILE

Paul Orfalea

KINKO'S GRAPHICS CORPORATION

Paul Ofalea, founder of Kinko's Corporation, a photocopy chain, recounts that as a member of a study group preparing a paper for a college course, he decided that instead of proofreading the paper as his contribution, which his disability—dyslexia—prevented, he would ensure that the paper would be photocopied. This event led him to marvel at the possibilities of photocopying as a business opportunity. "It was a print shop all in one machine concept," he realized. Orfalea started with one store on the campus of the University of California, Santa Barbara, in 1972. The company today has 400 stores and is growing at the rate of 25 percent a year.

Source: Network (Washington, D.C.: Small Business Administration, March–April 1988).

In the small business, owners must put forth their maximum effort to attract the most talented employees because they are the key asset of the company. Owners who employ competent people know that this is one of the most effective ways of staying competitive because these employees are likely to be more highly motivated and their job performance higher.

In large firms, personnel management specialists are delegated authority and assigned responsibility to administer all personnel activities. However, small business owners usually do not enjoy the luxury of a full-time personnel manager because of the size of the firm and its limited financial resources. Instead, owners personally take care of all personnel activities or delegate the assignment to an employee who performs these activities in conjunction with other job assignments.

The absence of a full-time personnel manager in no way diminishes the value of this function. Rather, it should signal to owners the necessity for intensifying the energy to expend on this vital function so that the objectives of the personnel function may be achieved efficiently and effectively.

The goal of owners is to ensure that competent people are hired and placed in job assignments that match their unique qualifications. To realize this goal, these personnel management activities must be accomplished: define job requirements, engage in employee recruitment, establish selection procedures, and provide employee training and development.

DEFINE JOB REQUIREMENTS

The process of selecting competent personnel for each position can be accomplished more efficiently through a systematic definition of the requirements of each task and the skills, knowledge, and other qualifications that employees must possess to perform each task satisfactorily. Identifying the requirements of tasks and the qualifications of employees encompasses three phases: conducting a job analysis, developing a job description, and preparing a job specification.

Job Analysis

The job analysis forms the foundation for developing the job description and job specification. The **job analysis** is a systematic investigation to collect all pertinent information about each task. From the job analysis, the skills, knowledge, and abilities that employees need to perform a task effectively and efficiently plus the duties, responsibilities, and requirements of each task are identified. The job analysis should provide the following information for each task.

1. Job title
2. Department in which the job is located
3. Line of supervision
4. Description of job, including major and minor duties.
5. Relation to other jobs (promotion opportunities, transfer possibilities, experience required, normal sources of employees)
6. Unique job characteristics (location, physical setting)
7. Supervision (type given and received)
8. Types of material and equipment used
9. Qualifications
   a. Experience requirments
   b. Education requirements
   c. Mental requirements
   d. Manual dexterity requirements
   e. Physical requirements (walking, climbing, standing, kneeling, lifting, talking, etc.)
10. Working conditions (inside, outside, hot, cold, dry, wet, noisy, dirty, etc.)

Job description

The job description is prepared from information revealed in the job analysis. The **job description** is a written record that defines the major and minor duties of each task. It also contains a description of the responsibilities of each task, such as maintenance of equipment, safety and health of others, and contact with the public. The description further defines the various task requirements, such as physical activities, working conditions, and any hazards associated with the performance of a task. It should also indicate the approximate percentage of time that the employee spends on each activity. The job description focuses on the "what, why, where, and how" tasks are to be performed.

Small business owners can collect job-related information from a number of sources that will be beneficial in preparing the job description. The most immediate source of information is the employees themselves. When writing a new job description, a government publication, the *Dictionary of Occupational Titles,* can be extremely useful. It contains 20,000 actual job descriptions. A third source of information is SCORE and ACE consultants of the SBA.

Job Specification

Whereas the job description describes the job, the **job specification** describes the person expected to fill the job. It details the qualities, knowledge, skills, and abilities an individual should possess to perform a task satisfactorily. Included in the job specification is the identification of employee characteristics (planning, leading others, making decisions) and the experience, education, and skills needed to perform the tasks outlined in the job description. The job specification provides a standard against which to measure how well an applicant matches the job opening. For example, a specification for a salesperson should define any special aptitude or technical knowledge needed to sell a product or service. Figure 9-1 contains the job description and specification of a credit manager–bookkeeper in a small business.

RECRUITMENT OF EMPLOYEES

Personnel qualifications for the essential jobs in the small business are defined in the specification. To translate job specifications into action, small business owners must recruit those individuals whose qualifications match the job requirements. Owners should explore many sources of prospective employees. The discussion that follows, though not exhaustive, represents some of the major sources for recruiting employees for the small business.

FIGURE 9-1
THE JOB DESCRIPTION AND JOB SPECIFICATION.

Job Title:	Credit Manager and Bookkeeper
Report to:	Store Manager
Job Summary:	Manages credit and bookkeeping functions of the business, controls the firm's assets and expenditures, acts as assistant to store manager, manages store in store manager's absence.
Job Description:	Processes credit applications: analyzes financial status and payment record of customers, checks references and credit bureau to determine credit responsibility.
	Sends collection notices to customers who accounts are past due.
	Checks the accuracy and completeness of price, stock classifications, and delivery information.
	Prepares bank deposit, listing checks and cash, and takes deposit to bank.
	Does all bookkeeping and prepares balance sheet and profit and loss statements of store.
	Sells merchandise during rush hours of the store.

Job Specification:	Education:	A minimum of a high school education is required.
	Experience:	Some prior bookkeeping and/or credit and collection experience is desirable.
	Skills:	Ability to keep a set of books and prepare balance sheet and profit and loss statements.

Job Duties	Approximate Time Spent On Each Assignment (percent)
Bookkeeping	40%
Credit and collection	20
Selling on retail floor	20
Inventories and stock control	10
Miscellaneous functions	10

Current Employees

Whenever possible, current employees should be given first consideration for any job openings within the company. Furthermore, a policy of advancement from within has a positive impact on employee morale because it signals the owner's support of current employees. In addition, present employees may be able to refer qualified friends or relatives for a job vacancy. ''Word of mouth'' is one of the most commonly used sources of recruitment in the small business.

Media Advertising

Advertising is an often used technique to attract prospective employees. Job vacancies may be publicized in the newspaper classified section or broadcast over a local radio station or television station. Job announcements in newspapers in nearby cities and in trade association magazines may also produce job applicants.

In-Store Advertising

Many owner–managers use in-store advertising to call attention to job openings. "Help wanted" signs are placed in the store window, or the vacancy may be announced on the store's marquee or on a portable sign trailer located in front of the store.

Drop-in Applicants

Occasionally, individuals will stop and inquire if any jobs are open even though no vacancy has been advertised. Even if a job is not open at the time, the owners should take down some information about the interested parties, such as name and phone number and the type of position wanted, or they may be asked to fill out an application blank so they can be contacted if a vacancy occurs.

Vocational–Technical Schools

Area schools provide a large pool of highly trained individuals. Many high school programs offer excellent training in vocational and technical skills, and community colleges have outstanding technical training programs. In addition, private technical training schools, such as business colleges or electronics schools, train many qualified candidates.

Former Military Personnel

Persons retired from military service may possess technical skills and knowledge that can fill the firm's employment needs. These personnel may also have extensive management experience.

Colleges and Universities

Placement offices at colleges and universities maintain an active file of candidates who posses a wide range of qualifications. The owner–manager should consider this source, especially if the firm needs an employee who has received specialized training such as in accounting. In addition, the owner–manager should not overlook contacting teachers for recommendations of possible employees.

Public Employment Agencies

Public employment agencies, such as state and federal government agencies, offer their services in helping to locate and place employees. State employment agencies, for example, maintain employment offices at strategic locations throughout the state, and each office has direct contact with all other offices. They have on file an up-to-date listing of potential employees who possess a wide range of skills. Unskilled, skilled, technical, and professional employees may be recruited through these agencies. An advantage of public employment agencies is that their services are provided at no cost to users.

Private Employment Agencies

Private employment agencies maintain an extensive listing of applicants who possess skills necessary for performing a variety of tasks. Private employment agencies charge a fee for their placement services, which must be paid by either the applicant or the employer.

Labor Unions

Some firms may consider labor unions as possible sources of personnel. Unions can be especially helpful in supplying workers for certain types of occupations, such as carpenters or brickmasons.

Former Employees

Employees who may have voluntarily quit for personal or health reasons may be rehired at a later date. For example, someone who moved to another city and later returned to the local area may be reemployed.

Part-Time Employees

For many types of business, sales fluctuate sharply upward as a particular holiday season approaches, such as Christmas or Easter. This upturn in business activity often puts pressure on the regular work force to provide all customers with personalized service. Hence, the owner–manager can effectively employ part-time employees to fill in during the rush season. Part-time employees can also work odd-hour shifts, such as in the evenings or on Saturdays.

Other firms have need of extra help certain times of the day or week, but business activity is not sufficient to justify hiring a full-time employee. For example, a small retail store in a shopping center found its peak business hours were from 2 P.M. to 9 P.M. and its peak days were Friday and Saturday. The manager was able to hire two part-time employees to help meet the needs of the peak hours and days. A small hardware store owner and his wife operate their store by themselves. When peak busines periods develop or when the owners want to get away for a vacation, they employ their neighbors, a retired military officer and his wife, to manage the store.

A large number of part-time employees is usually available. Possible sources include students of high schools and colleges, retired persons who desire only a few hours of employment a day or week, and people whose health permits only limited hours of work each day or week.

Temporary Personnel Services

Temporary personnel services offer specialized assistance to the small business owner, such as a word processing operator, a secretary, or a bookkeeper. When it is not feasible to hire a full-time employee, a temporary personnel service may be utilized. Temporary personnel services hire their own employees and assign them to firms requiring assistance. When a small business owner uses a temporary's service, he or she is not hiring an employee but is buying the use of their time. The temporary service is responsible for all matters relating to employees, such as payroll, workers' compensation, social security, fringe benefits, and withholding taxes. Most national temporary personnel services offer performance guarantees and fidelity bonding at no additional cost.

THE SELECTION PROCESS

The purpose of the selection process is to obtain as much information about an individual as possible relative to skills, knowledge, and attitudes to determine if that person is suited to and qualified for the type of work available. Small business managers can prevent unpleasant situations from developing if they do not short-circuit the selection process. In most instances, it is equally as poor a decision to hire someone who is overqualified as one who is underqualified for a position.

What can happen when highly qualified persons are hired and their skills are not utilized is shown in the following situation. Jean, an ambitious law school graduate, accepted a position as an assistant to the president of a small public relations firm. After a period of job orientation, she was told she would be assigned to handle clients of the firm.

Instead of handling legal matters, Jean was assigned secretarial–receptionist responsibilities. She scheduled the president's luncheons, arranged his tennis matches, and spent much of her time on the job reading novels. As a result of her job skills being underutilized, she became so bored and frustrated that she quit.

The underqualified person will likely become frustrated because of the lack of skill or knowledge, job performance will likely be substandard, and the person will usually quit or have to be replaced or retrained because he or she

When a small business owner gives employees a complete orientation into the company and thorough job training, they will most likely respond with higher levels of job performance and derive more satisfaction from their job.

is not producing at a satisfactory level. Hiring overqualified or underqualified persons results in undesirable consequences for both the individual and the company. This underscores the need to find the proper match between people and jobs.

The selection process involves a number of activities, all of which are designed to elicit pertinent data about job candidates. These activities include the application blank, personal interviews, and employee testing.

The Application Blank

An **application blank,** as shown in Figure 9-2, presents managers with a written record of an applicant's qualifications and enables them to compare and evaluate applications for a position. Generally requested information on the application form is the name, address, telephone number, kind of work desired, social security number, work experience, education, and job references. By having the applicant complete the application form, managers can evaluate the candidate's skill in organizing and presenting information.

The completed application form is a useful reference for the interviewer when conducting the personal interview. Some restrictions on the information requested on the application form are discussed in a later section, "The Civil Rights Act of 1964 and the Equal Employment Opportunity Act of 1972."

FIGURE 9-2
APPLICATION FOR EMPLOYMENT.

EMPLOYMENT APPLICATION

(An Equal Opportunity Employer)

Date _____

Name _____ Social Security Number _____

Last   First   Middle Initial

Address _____ Telephone Number _____

Street   City   State   Zip Code

Military Service
Branch _____ from _____ to _____   Rank Achieved _____   Position Desired _____

Special Schools or Training in Military _____

Job applying for _____

If Related to an Employee of This Firm, State Name: _____

Person to Notify in Case of Emergency _____

Name   Telephone

List Equipment and Office Machines You are Qualified to Operate: _____

EMPLOYMENT RECORD

(List most recent employment first)

Name and Address of Company	Position and Duties	Dates Employed	Ending Salary	Supervisor's Name	Reason for Leaving

May we contact your present employer?   Yes _____   No _____

EDUCATION

Schools Attended	Number of Years Attended	Major Subject Studied	Degree or Certificate

REFERENCES

Name	Address	Telephone	Relationship or Title

Personal Interviews

An extensively used selection technique is the personal interview. During the interview, the manager has the opportunity to learn more about the applicant through face-to-face contact. A requirement of the interview session is that the prospective employee be made to feel at ease because the applicant is likely to be a bit edgy. Putting the applicant at ease may be accomplished by adopting an informal approach at the interview to help break the tension. After the preliminaries, the interview should be guided but not dominated by the manager. It is especially important to let the candidate speak freely, answering as well as asking questions about areas of concern. By using the application blank as a reference, the manager will be able to guide the discussion and obtain in-depth information about the applicant's background. The personal interview also affords the opportunity for the manager to observe the applicant's personal appearance. The special interest feature addresses the issue of how to improve interview skills.

The manager should check the references listed by the applicant. A telephone call to the former employer (immediate supervisor where possible), teacher, or personal reference provides a quick means of validating the accuracy of the data supplied on the application form and in the interview. Another means of obtaining references is by letter, but it takes much longer to get the desired information this way. Some factors to evaluate in checking references are inflated salary figures, incorrect dates of employment, false claims on the amount of education and experience, and claiming a higher level of job responsibility than actually held.

A note of caution is appropriate with regard to reference checks. Some firms do not give information about former employees because of the risk that former employees may claim an unfavorable reference caused them to not be hired for a better position. Such action may result in a former employee bringing legal action against a former employer.

In the personal interview, the untrained interviewer may commit three major errors according to John Franco, president of Learning International, a training company in Stamford, Connecticut.[1]

1. Not spending enough time analyzing the requirements of the job you are trying to fill.
2. Failing to ask candidates the right questions to find evidence of their suitability, including both their strengths and their weaknesses.
3. Trusting too much to your gut reaction instead of evaluating candidates objectively against the criteria you established for the job.

Though most small business managers are busy with the many day-to-day activities of the firm, they should not neglect the job interviews because this is an integral step in the selection process.

SMALL BUSINESS BRIEF

POLISHING YOUR INTERVIEW SKILLS

The small business owner who wants to fill a job with the best-qualified person should avoid some ''common interview pitfalls,'' says Ed Kiradjieff, former director of personnel for Price Waterhouse and now head of his own Boston-based recruitment firm.

A poor interview not only may result in hiring an unsuitable candidate but may drive a better prospect away, says Kiradjieff, who has interviewed thousands of job hunters during his 25 years of employment experience. He offers 10 ways managers can improve their interviewing ability.

Prepare a written job description. List job duties, professional qualifications, and the kind of work experience needed.

Break the ice. Establish a friendly atmosphere with small talk and questions about personal interests.

Develop an interview time plan. Try to avoid phone calls and other interruptions. Tell the candidate, for example, ''We have 45 minutes. I'd like to spend the first 15 minutes discussing the job, the next 15 minutes on your background, and the remaining time on any questions you may have.''

Keep an open mind. Guard against forming hiring decisions too early.

Give the candidate time to tell his or her story. One of the biggest errors of the untrained interviewer is to talk too much.

Present a truthful picture of the company and the job. Give both the positives and the negatives.

Listen carefully. Pay attention to repetitions, consistency, and convictions. Is the candidate passionate about outside interests? Concentrate, and take notes.

Avoid salary hide 'n' seek. Don't ask ''What will it take to get you on board?'' This is threatening. Better to inquire about salary history and compare it with the job's salary range.

Tell the candidate about the next step. Don't leave the candidate hanging. Stick to the plan, and communicate as promised.

Mind your manners. ''Extend the kind of courtesy you would give your best customer,'' says Kiradjieff. ''Above all, don't just act interested. *Be* interested.''

Source: Harry Bacas, ''Hiring the Best,'' *Nation's Business,* October 1987, p. 70. Reprinted with permission *Nation's Business,* October 1987. Copyright 1987, U.S. Chamber of Commerce.

Employment Tests

Some owners use tests advantageously as part of the selection process. However, the role of the employment test is to serve as an aid to owners in making employee selection more efficient. Tests should not be the sole criteria for selection. Some types of tests that are used are aptitude, achievement, intelligence, and personality tests.

Aptitude Test

Aptitude tests measure mechanical and clerical aptitude, manual dexterity, or other potential talents a person has for learning a new job.

Achievement Test

The achievement test seeks to measure the skill proficiency that a person has for a specific job. Some of the more familiar achievement tests, also referred to as performance tests, measure a person's skill level in typing, shorthand, or operation of office machines.

Intelligence Test

Intelligence tests measure general mental ability, such as verbal ability (ability to learn, associate, and understand words). It may also measure specific abilities, such as reasoning or visualizing.

Personality Test

Personality tests are often used to aid in selecting managers or salespersons. These jobs require skills in interpersonal relations. Hence the manager may find this test useful as a guide in evaluating applicants on this trait.

When employment tests are used, they must be valid and reliable. Test validity is concerned with the relationship of the test score and performance on the job. A test is valid if the score on the test is a predictor of subsequent job performance. Test reliability is consistency. A test has high reliability when test results are approximately the same when a person is retested with the same test or an equivalent test form over time. Validity is more important than reliability because a test must measure what it purports to measure or else it has no value.

Caution must be exercised in the use of employment tests. Provisions of the Civil Rights Act, discussed later in the chapter, will note restrictions on the use of employment tests.

Physical Examination

Some firms require employees to undergo a physical examination as part of the selection process. A physical exam enables the manager to determine if applicants meet all health standards demanded by the job, such as a health certificate required for food handlers. The exam also indicates if candidates can meet the physical demands of the task. For example, can they tolerate working in dusty or damp areas, or do they have the physical strength and stamina to lift and move heavy materials throughout the day?

Requiring a physical exam is a constructive policy for the small business owner for a number of reasons. First, if the company provides health insurance for employees, the cost of premiums escalates if persons in poor health are hired. Second, the exam should reveal any past injury the candidate may have suffered elsewhere.

ORIENTATION

When the decision has been made to employ an individual, the manager should direct his or her energies toward ensuring that the new employee receives a thorough orientation regarding the general company policies and the specific nature of the job. The orientation process markedly reduces the normal apprehension of new employees, especially during the first days of employment. New employees should be introduced to other employees and made to feel welcome, receive an explanation of how the job fits into the overall company operation, and be given information about conditions of employment, methods of pay, deductions, and work schedules.

Employee Handbook

Small business owners should consider the value of an employee handbook as a vehicle for communicating vital information about the company to employees. The handbook covers such topics as company expectations of employees; pay policies, working conditions, and fringe benefits; and company philosophy toward customers.

Handbooks range from a few typewritten pages to professionally printed booklets. In addition to its use for orientation, older employees find it beneficial as a reference. Even though most small businesses do not have an employee handbook, its value should not be overlooked as a means of reinforcing communication and promoting positive employer–employee relations. Figure 9-3, which presents a table of contents of a small manufacturer's handbook, illustrates the wide range of topics of interest to employees.

TRAINING AND DEVELOPMENT

Whether new employees have had prior experience or this is their first formal job, some type of training must be given. Some of the purposes of employee training are (1) to improve employee job performance, (2) to develop employees for new responsibilities, (3) to prepare employees for a promotion, (4) to reduce accidents, and (5) to instruct employees in the operation of new equipment.

Training should not be considered a one-time event but rather a continuous process. Training seeks to upgrade employee knowledge and skills in order to keep them abreast of changes occurring in the competitive business environment and give them the preparation required for advancement to more challenging opportunities. The overall effect of a continuous training program is mutual benefit for both the employees and the company.

In the small business, the owner–manager has the responsibility for developing and conducting the training program. The kind of training given de-

FIGURE 9-3
TOPICS COMMONLY COVERED IN THE EMPLOYEE HANDBOOK.

Welcome message to employees
History of company
Introduction to company's products
  and services
Your future with the company
Hours of work
Holidays
Insurance
  Hospitalization and surgical
    benefits
  Group life insurance
Jury duty
Military leave
Parking facilities
Personal appearance and work
  habits
  Cleanliness
  Dress
  Leaving the plant premises during
    work hours
  Personal debts
  Personal work

Use of telephones
Prohibited acts
Absence from work and reporting
  absences
Pay policies
  Accrued vacation pay for ter-
    minated employees
  Loss of time due to death in im-
    mediate family
  Overtime pay
  Shift pay differential
  Pay period
  Profit-sharing plan
  Bonuses
  Suggestion system and awards
Retirement plan
Training program
Safety and accident prevention
Disciplinary procedures
Termination of employment
Vacations

pends largely on the kind of work to be performed. Some types of training used in small business are discussed here.

On-the-Job Training

On-the-job-training (OJT) is the most practical and most often used training technique in the small business. Depending on the complexity of the task and the experience level of employees, training may vary from a few hours to several full days.

This training is given by the manager or a designated employee and involves three phases. First, the job is demonstrated, and each step of the process is thoroughly explained. The demonstration should be done slowly, instructions should be given clearly, and the trainees should be asked questions to provide feedback on their understanding of the work procedures. Second, the trainees perform the task by applying what they have learned in step 1. In the third step, the work is inspected, and immediate feedback of performance is given. This technique provides immediate reinforcement of correct performance or immediate feedback to correct improper job techniques at the outset.

On-the-job training is used to provide continuous training to employees to keep their job skills as well as prepare them for a promotion.

Most of the training given salespersons in the small store is on-the-job training given by either the store owner–manager or another experienced salesperson. This training can be supplemented by ''role playing,'' a technique that helps salespersons to identify with customers. In this approach, one person assumes the role of the customer and the other, the salesperson. Role playing permits salespersons to view the sale through the eyes of the customer. After one or more role-playing sessions, the roles may be reversed. This type of training can be conducted on the sales floor during slow times of the business day.

Apprenticeship Training

Apprenticeship training is a formal type of training that combines both formal classroom learning and on-the-job experience. This kind of training program is provided mainly in the skilled trades—plumbers, electricians, meat cutters, bakers, etc. The length of time spent in apprenticeship varies from two years to four or five years, depending on the kind of skill being learned.

Job Rotation

Particularly in the small business, it is beneficial if each employee has a thorough understanding of the different functions performed in the firm. In this way, if an employee is absent, another employee can fill in. One way to accomplish this objective is by job rotation. This technique moves employees from job to job for a few hours a day, a few days, or several weeks, depending on the difficulty of the task. Job rotation should best be done during the slack periods of the business day or season. Job rotation helps employees combat the problems of monotony and boredom on the job because of the varied work experiences. Employees often experience higher levels of morale when they are involved in job rotation.

Computer-Assisted Instruction

Computers can be used to facilitate training. Computer-assisted instruction (CAI), a type of programmed instruction, is self-paced, individualized instruction. Problems, questions, or facts are presented to the learner who responds and gets immediate feedback to his or her answer, thus reducing the risk of error. As a form of programmed learning, CAI can easily be modified to reflect up-to-date innovations in technology. Employees can be given simulation training whereby they face real-world, complex problems or tasks to which they must respond. Their responses are then evaluated for their applicability to the simulated problem.

Group Training

The conference method is one means of achieving group training. A particular advantage of this technique is that participants in the training session have the opportunity to express their viewpoints and share experiences while listening and learning from the contributions that others make in discussing common problems or expressing opinions.

Some group training aimed at increasing the salesperson's knowledge of merchandise and services may be accomplished in sales meetings. These meetings may focus on a discussion of new products, additional services, a special sale, or a change in store policies. These group meetings can be conducted before the start of the business day or during slow periods during the day. When group training is used, care should be taken to see that there are specific goals to be accomplished so that valuable employee time is not wasted.

Training Off Company Premises

Sources outside the company may be a valuable training resource. Some of these sources are now given.

University and Community College Courses

Some small businesses pay for all or part of the cost for some of their employees to continue their education at the university and community college level. The employee may attend on-campus classes in the evening, early morning, or late afternoon and still be available for employment either all day or a major portion of the workday. Often this type of training is specialized training such as in engineering, accounting, or computer technology.

Extension Courses and Correspondence Courses

Colleges and universities offer a number of extension courses. Regular faculty members go to a particular locale where there is a demand for a course. They usually teach the course in the evening so that it does not interfere with the employees work schedule.

Correspondence courses enable a person to receive high school or college credit or learn other skills by completing prescribed lessons in his or her own home. A wide range of courses are offered through correspondence, as in accounting or business law.

Business Suppliers

Business suppliers may serve particular training needs. For example, suppliers frequently provide specific training in technical operations of new computer equipment or instruct employees in the procedures of a new accounting or recordkeeping system.

Training Films

Training films are available from private sources, trade associations, and the Small Business Administration (SBA). Films are available to serve a variety of training needs, such as group training, job procedures, communication, and leadership.

Training Guidelines for the Small Business

In setting criteria for training in the small firm, owner–managers will be aided in determining their training needs by evaluating the following questions.

1. What are the objectives of the training?
2. What do employees need to learn?
3. How much will the training program cost?
4. What type of training should be offered?
5. What method or methods of instructions should be used?
6. What kind of physical facilities will be needed?
7. How long will the training period be?
8. Will training be conducted during or after working hours?
9. Who will conduct the training?
10. Will special equipment be required (such as audiovisual)?
11. Which employees should be selected to attend the training sessions?
12. What type of feedback will be given employees?
13. How will the effectiveness of the program be measured?
14. What is the applicability of the training to the specific needs of the firm?
15. How should the program be publicized?

COUNSELING EMPLOYEES

Counseling is a vital link in interpersonal communication between owners and employees. Counseling may be conducted formally, as in the performance appraisal, or on an informal continuous basis. This type of counseling occurs when employees require information and feedback concerning the method to be used in coping with day-to-day situations. Counseling serves at least four purposes.

1. To give instructions (to explain new job procedures).
2. To gain employee cooperation (to explain changes in company policies, work assignments and work schedules to get employees to support these changes).
3. To obtain information (to deal with employee grievances, one must gather information as to the nature of the complaints).

4. To give advice (employees may request advice on personal matters). In this situation, the best posture is for the owner–manager to be a good listener and offer advice sparingly.

Counseling in the Probationary Period

Many companies have a probationary period for new employees. The length of time for the probationary period varies, depending on the time it takes to learn the task. During the probationary period, owners can monitor the performance level of the new employees and their capacity for learning. During the probationary period owners can offer guidance and constructive feedback to assist new employees in greater understanding of the task and how to improve performance. During this time, employees have the opportunity to form their opinion of the company.

At the end of a specified time, preferably at the end of the first week, new employees should be interviewed. This counseling session serves a number of purposes.

1. Employees can raise questions about company rules or policies about which they are not clear.
2. Employees can offer their impressions of the job.
3. Employees can identify types of assistance or instructions they need.

Throughout the probationary period, periodic counseling should be given to evaluate employees' peformance. In addition to the immediate supervisor, fellow employees are valuable resources for counseling. This counseling process enables owners to ascertain if new employees, the job, and the company are compatible at the end of the probationary period. If they are, the firm has potentially good employees. If they are not compatible, separation should be as painless as possible.

Guidelines for Effective Employee Counseling

Some specific guidelines for formal counseling that the owners should find helpful are enumerated here.

1. Have a purpose for the counseling interview.
2. The counseling interview should be conducted in private.
3. Use the "we" viewpoint insted of "I" to gain the cooperation of the counselee.
4. Such questions as who, what, where, why, when, and how can be used effectively.
5. Listen without interrupting.
6. Conclude each interview with a positive emphasis.

PERFORMANCE APPRAISAL

Performance appraisal is a form of counseling and coaching employees. **Performance appraisal** is the process by which owners gather information about each employee's performance effectiveness and communicate this information to them. Evaluating employee performance is essential if managers wish to help their employees raise their level of performance. In the small business, managers do not spend much time on employee appraisal because they are usually occupied with the daily matters of trying to get the product or service to the customer.

The performance appraisal process is a control function. Consequently, performance appraisal includes (1) establishing standards, (2) recording performance, (3) reviewing performance in accordance with standards, and (4) taking corrective action where and when necessary.

In actuality, employee performance in the small firm is evaluated daily by owners on an informal basis while working directly with employees. However, there should be a regular schedule for performance reviews, such as once or twice a year. When the company is small, the owner–manager does the evaluation. However, as the company grows, the employees should be evaluated by their immediate supervisor and the owner. These appraisals enable the owner to chart employees' progress and suggest areas that need improvement. The following guidelines are recommended for anyone conducting performance reviews.

1. Decide in advance on the purpose of your performance reviews: evaluation, criticism, training, coaching, morale building.
2. Don't wait until the review occurs to let your staff know what you expect from them. Tell them early on exactly what the job requires; what specific goals, standards, and deadlines you expect them to meet; and how you plan to evaluate and reward their performance.
3. Keep a written record of your subordinates' performance throughout the year so that you can cite specific examples to back up any criticisms or comments you make during the review.
4. The review should not be a one-way process. Let the employees participate, and listen to what they say.
5. Go over the evaluation with each employee. They don't have to agree completely with your ratings, but if they strongly disagree, they are not likely to try to improve.
6. When critiquing an employee's performance, make sure you also do some "stroking." Reinforce the good habits with praise.
7. Be specific and constructive in your criticism. Don't just tell someone he or she is not productive enough. Tell him or her how he or she has fallen short and what you expect in the future.[2]

FIGURE 9-4
GRAPHIC RATING FORM.

EMPLOYEE'S NAME _____ **DATE** _____

EMPLOYEE'S TITLE _____ **DEPARTMENT** _____

Check the appropriate term for each factor
that describes the employee being rated.

Factor	Excellent 1	Good 2	Satis-factory 3	Fair 4	Unsatis-factory 5
1. Quality of Work. Thorough, neat, and accurate work that meets standards set for job; needs supervision only occasionally.					
2. Quantity of Work. Acceptable volume of work; does work quickly.					
3. Knowledge of Job. Complete understanding of all factors relating to job; able to proceed alone on almost all work.					
4. Attitude. Cooperative, interested in work; ability and willingness to work with supervisor, peers, and clients to achieve goals.					
5. Dependability. Conscientious, thorough, reliable, excellent attendance record; can always be counted on.					
6. Initiative. Seeks increased responsibility; contributes new ideas; willing to proceed alone.					
7. Judgment. Decisions based on sound knowledge.					
8. Personal Qualities. Sociability, leadership, appearance, integrity.					

In the small business, the review should be kept as simple as possible. The sample appraisal form shown in Figure 9-4 is the graphic rating scale. This is the simplest and most popular technique of all the many methods for appraising performance and is well suited to the requirements of the small business. Employees are rated on various factors (such as quality and quantity of work) and on a range of performance (from unsatisfactory to excellent). The evaluator checks the performance level that best describes the employee's performance level for each trait. The assigned values for each rating are added and totaled for each employee. For example, excellent has a value of one while unsatisfactory has a value of 5.

Purposes of Performance Appraisal

The success of performance appraisal and follow-up counseling depends on whether employees comprehend and accept the purposes of the review. By observing the guidelines listed, a number of important functions can be served by the appraisal.

1. Evaluation of performance over a specified time
2. Motivation of employees by providing them with relevant feedback of job performance
3. Evaluation of potential for growth and development of each employee, such as the potential for promotion to a position of more authority and responsibility
4. Accumulation of data for decisions concerning the distribution of rewards for outstanding performance, such as merit increases
5. Accumulation of information for decisions concerning transfers and terminations
6. Evaluation of effectiveness of training programs and training needs
7. Effective method for communicating the goals of management

The results of the appraisal should be communicated to each employee. Because most people are apprehensive about any type of evaluation, the owner should create an atmosphere that will put employees at ease throughout the counseling session. If the evaluation reveals that a worker's performance is below standard, steps are taken to improve performance, such as giving the employee additional training. If standards have been met, the employee should be commended; if standards have been exceeded, employees should be rewarded, such as with a bonus or merit raise.

EMPLOYEE COMPENSATION

The objectives of a compensation plan are to motivate employees to function at higher levels of performance and to attract and keep employees in the company. If the plan is to accomplish these objectives, it must be perceived as equitable by employees. Employees compare their rewards with others who perform essentially the same kind of task, either in the company or in competitor firms. The primary basis of comparison is money (wages or salary). Equity is evaluated in terms of the effort put into a task and the rewards received for that effort. If the rewards are perceived as equitable, employees will likely stay and be productive. However, if they perceive their rewards are less than those of a coworker, they will tend to react negatively, as by lowering their rate of output.

To establish equity of rewards, the small business owners should use a **job evaluation.** This is a systematic and orderly process for determining the correct rate of pay for each job in relation to other jobs.

Employee Compensation Plans

In addition to equity, compensation plans that are easy to understand and to administer are ideally suited to the small business. Some of the compensation plans commonly used by small business owners are now discussed.

Straight Salary

One popular payment method in the small business is straight salary. Employees receive a fixed amount each pay period, and the plan is quite easy to understand and administer. A disadvantage is that this plan does not provide an incentive for performance of employees.

Hourly Wage

Employees may be paid a specific rate for each hour worked. This method of payment can be used to reward employees where it is difficult to measure output or where the employee has no control over the work output. This plan is quite easy to understand and to administer but also does not provide for employee incentives.

Piece Rate

Piece rate is an incentive pay plan that rewards employees for the number of acceptable units produced. This incentive pay plan is especially suited to manufacturing operations. Piece rates may be paid on the basis of individual output or group output.

Straight Commission

A straight commission plan is well suited to sales positions. It provides a built-in incentive because earnings are proportionate to the amount of sales. This plan is often used with big-ticket items, such as appliances or automobiles. A disadvantage of this plan is that salespersons may use high-pressure sales tactics to close a sale.

Combination Plans

The combination plan is another method for rewarding salespersons. It provides a base salary plus a commission on sales. Advantages of the combination plans are that they provide for both economic security and as an incentive for generating higher levels of sales. These plans may be somewhat complicated to deal with, however.

Bonus Plan

A bonus plan is suited for managers. This plan compensates managers above their base salary and is tied to company profits. These payments are made to managers who are in a position to have a significant effect on profits. A disadvantage is that managers may take a short-time perspective to increase sales that do not benefit the company in the long term.

THE IMMIGRATION REFORM AND CONTROL ACT OF 1986

Small business owners must understand the **Immigration Reform and Control Act of 1986.** The purpose of this law is to reduce the number of illegal immigrants seeking jobs in the United States. The law granted amnesty to many illegal aliens living in the United States and imposed tough sanctions on employers who continue to hire undocumented workers.

Under the law, employees hired after November 6, 1986, must show proof of their identity and eligibility to work and they must fill out an I–9 form of the Immigration and Naturalization Service (INS). This form is shown in Figure 9-5. This form must be kept on file for three years from date of employment. Employers must verify the identity and eligibility to work of all employees hired after the November 1986 date. If an employer fails to keep appropriate records, paperwork violations are punishable by fines of up to $1000 per employee. If an illegal alien is hired, sanctions range from fines of $250 to $10,000 per worker and prison sentences of up to six months.

FAIR LABOR STANDARDS ACT OF 1938 AND WAGES

Generally known as the Wage and Hour Law, the **Fair Labor Standards Act of 1938** (FSLA) applies to most private employers and federal, state, and local governmental agencies. The basic provision of the law requires employers to pay a minimum wage to employees. The law also sets regulations governing the maximum number of hours employees can work (40) without receiving overtime pay. Employees must be paid at least time and one-half of their regular rate for all hours of overtime. Special rules apply to state and local government employment involving fire protection and law enforcement activities, volunteer services, and compensatory time off in lieu of cash overtime pay.

FIGURE 9-5
EMPLOYMENT ELIGIBILITY VERIFICATION.

EMPLOYMENT ELIGIBILITY VERIFICATION

1 **EMPLOYEE INFORMATION AND VERIFICATION:** (To be completed and signed by employee.)

Name: (Print or Type) Last	First	Middle	Maiden
Address: Street Name and Number	City	State	ZIP Code
Date of Birth (Month/Day/Year)		Social Security Number	

I attest, under penalty of perjury, that I am (check a box):

☐ A citizen or national of the United States.

☐ An alien lawfully admitted for permanent residence (Alien Number A _____).

☐ An alien authorized by the Immigration and Naturalization Service to work in the United States (Alien Number A _____,
or Admission Number _____, expiration of employment authorization, if any _____).

I attest, under penalty of perjury, the documents that I have presented as evidence of identity and employment eligibility are genuine and relate to me. I am aware that federal law provides for imprisonment and/or fine for any false statements or use of false documents in connection with this certificate.

Signature	Date (Month/Day/Year)

PREPARER/TRANSLATOR CERTIFICATION (If prepared by other than the individual). I attest, under penalty of perjury, that the above was prepared by me at the request of the named individual and is based on all information of which I have any knowledge.

Signature	Name (Print or Type)	
Address (Street Name and Number)	City	State	Zip Code

2 **EMPLOYER REVIEW AND VERIFICATION:** (To be completed and signed by employer.)

Examine one document from those in List A and check the correct box, _or_ examine one document from List B _and_ one from List C and check the correct boxes.
Provide the *Document Identification Number* and *Expiration Date,* for the document checked in that column.

List A Identity and Employment Eligibility	List B Identity	and	List C Employment Eligibility
☐ United States Passport	☐ A State issued driver's license or I.D. card with a photograph, or information, including name, sex, date of birth, height, weight, and color of eyes. (Specify State)_____)		☐ Original Social Security Number Card (other than a card stating it is not valid for employment)
☐ Certificate of United States Citizenship			
☐ Certificate of Naturalization	☐ U.S. Military Card		☐ A birth certificate issued by State, county, or municipal authority bearing a seal or other certification
☐ Unexpired foreign passport with attached Employment Authorization	☐ Other (Specify document and issuing authority)		☐ Unexpired INS Employment Authorization Specify form
☐ Alien Registration Card with photograph	_____		# _____
Document Identification	*Document Identification*		*Document Identification*
# _____	# _____		# _____
Expiration Date (if any)	*Expiration Date (if any)*		*Expiration Date (if any)*
_____	_____		_____

CERTIFICATION: I attest, under penalty of perjury, that I have examined the documents presented by the above individual, that they appear to be genuine, relate to the individual named, and that the individual, to the best of my knowledge, is authorized to work in the United States.

Signature	Name (Print or Type)	Title
Employer Name	Address	Date

U.S. Department of Justice
Immigration and Naturalization Service

(U.S. Department of Justice, Immigration and Naturalization Service, Form I-9, March 20, 1987, OMB No. 115-0136.)

The law also contains an equal pay provision that prohibits wage differentials based on sex, between men and women employed in the same establishment, on jobs that require equal skill, effort, and responsibility and that are performed under similar working conditions.

The child labor provisions stipulate that the minimum legal age for employing minors (outside of agriculture) is 14, but the employment must be outside of regular schools hours and for no more than 3 hours on a school day, 18 hours in a school week, 8 hours on a nonschool day, or 40 hours in a nonschool week and not in a hazardous job. At age 16, a youth may be employed for an unlimited number of hours in any nonhazardous job, and at 18, a youth may be employed in any job for an unlimited number of hours.

What Firms Are Covered by the FLSA?

All employees of a business are subject to the law's provisions if the company

1. Is engaged in interstate commerce.
2. Produces goods for interstate commerce.
3. Handles, sells, or otherwise works on goods or materials that have been moved in or produced for interstate commerce for any person.
4. Is beyond a certain size (measured by dollar volume of business) and have at least two employees covered under the interstate commerce criteria.

A covered enterprise is the related activites performed through unified operation or common control by any person or persons for a common business purpose and is

1. Engaged in laundering or cleaning or repairing of clothing or fabrics.
2. Engaged in the business of construction or reconstruction.
3. Comprised exclusively of one or more retail or service establishments whose annual gross volume of sales made or business done is not less than $362,500.
4. Any other type of enterprise having an annual gross volume of sales made or business done of not less than $250,000.
5. An activity of a public agency.

Tipped employees are those who customarily and regularly receive more than $30 a month in tips. The employer may consider tips as part of wages, but such a wage credit must not exceed 40 percent of the minimum wage. If an employer elects to use the tip credit, he or she must inform the employee in advance and must be able to show that the employee receives at least the minimum wage when direct wages and tip credit are combined. The law has been interpreted liberally, and today there are few small businesses entirely outside the coverage of the law. However, there are exemptions from the minimum wage and overtime provisions. Owners should carefully check the exact terms of the exemptions before applying them to their employees. Where questions exist, the owner should contact the Wage and Hour Division of the Department of Labor. Some examples of exemptions include the following.

Exemptions from Both Minimum Wage and Overtime Pay

1. Executive, administrative, professional employees, and outside salespersons
2. Employees of certain individually owned and operated small retail or service establishments not part of a covered enterprise
3. Employees of certain seasonal amusement or recreational establishments
4. Farm workers employed by anyone who used no more than 500 "person-days" of farm labor in any calendar quarter of the preceding calendar year

Exemptions from Overtime Pay Provisions Only

1. Certain highly paid commissioned employees of retail or service establishments
2. Employees of motion picture theaters

Records That Employers Must Maintain Regarding FSLA Standards

The law requires employers to remain specific records covering the following topics, and the required records must be maintained for a period of three years.

1. Personal information, including the employee's name, home address, sex, occupation, and date of birth if under 19
2. Hour and day when workweek begins
3. Regular hourly pay rate for any week when overtime is worked
4. Total hours worked each workday and each workweek
5. Total daily or weekly straight-time earnings
6. Total overtime pay for the workweek
7. Deductions or additions to wages
8. Total wages paid each pay period
9. Date of payment and pay period covered

EMPLOYEE BENEFITS

Employee benefits, or **fringe benefits,** have increased substantially both in type and cost. For example, the U.S. Chamber of Commerce surveys a cross section of firms concerning type and extent of fringe benefits. The chamber's survey indicates that employee benefits now amount to about 40 percent of payroll costs.

Wages and salaries are classified as "direct compensation," while fringe benefits are identified as "indirect payments." A broad range of fringe benefits are common in large firms (see Fig. 9-6), but small businesses cannot afford such an extensive benefit package. Some are required by law; others are offered as a result of agreement between employer and employee. However, a small business's ability to attract and maintain a quality work force is directly related to the benefits it offers. The profitability of a small employer is the primary determinant of whether pension and health care programs are provided for employees.

Because small businesses have a lower margin of profit than big businesses, small businesses are less able than large businesses to afford the premiums of pension and health benefits. For example, the Department of Labor reports that in large firms (over 500 employees), 72 percent had retirement pensions, 85 percent had health insurance, and 65 percent had both retirement and pension benefits. In firms with 500 or fewer employees, 26 percent had pension benefits, 54 percent had health coverage, and 23 percent had both types of coverage.

Another factor in offering a fringe benefit program is the administrative

FIGURE 9-6
TYPES OF FRINGE BENEFITS.

Legally required payments (old age, survivors, disability and health insurance)
Pension plan
Insurance plan (life insurance, health insurance, accident insurance)
Discounts on goods and services purchased by employees from the company
Employee meals furnished by company
Paid rest periods, lunch periods, wash-up time, travel time, etc.
Paid vacations
Paid holidays
Payment for jury duty, National Guard, or Military Reserve duty
Profit-sharing payment
Bonuses (Christmas, year end)
Employee education
Workers' compenstion
Unemployment compensation

costs. These costs are relatively fixed, requiring about the same amount of time and money to establish a plan for 5 or 50 employees. One study[3] shows that it costs a small firm about $1080 per employee, but a large firm pays only $574 per employee to establish a pension program.

Thus small business owners face difficult challenges when they try to match benefits with big firms. However, the small firm can enjoy the benefits of greater flexibility and innovativeness in offering their employees a wider range of options related to employee performance. For example, small businesses can design profit-sharing and stock option plans that aid in recruiting employees, which in turn can generate a strong incentive for employees to perform well and be rewarded for their efforts.[4]

Employee leasing or contract staffing is a technique used by small business owners to have competent people on the job and be able to compete with larger firms that offer more liberal fringe benefits to employees. Under the employee leasing arrangement, employees are leased to a small business by a leasing firm. The leasing firm assumes all administrative and fiduciary responsibilities, such as providing fringe benefits, paying employment taxes, and meeting payroll. The owner of the small business leasing employees sends a single check to the leasing firm each pay period. Because the leasing firm has a larger number of employees, it can negotiate lower rates for benefits than can the individual small businesses they serve.

The company's policies regarding fringe benefits should be clearly stated and communicated. For example, what is the vacation policy and what are sick leave benefits? The company's policy should indicate the paid holidays. Frequently, holidays allowed are New Year's Day, Memorial Day, Independence Day, Labor Day, Thanksgiving Day, and Christmas Day. Vacation time varies, but usually one or two weeks are given after a year's employment. After five or ten years, vacations may increase to three weeks. Sick leave benefits are also important to employees. A policy of many firms is to allow employees to earn from one-half day to one full day of sick leave per month.

As with wages and salaries, it is an essential policy to observe the pattern of employee benefits in the local community and follow this pattern in setting guidelines for the firm's fringe benefit package (See Fig. 9-6).

EMPLOYEE SAFETY

Employee safety must be a top-priority item for all managers. One key to successful accident prevention in the small business is to motivate employees to observe work rules that make the job as safe as possible. Employee safety is of primary concern because of the costs that both employer and employee incur when a job-related injury keeps the employee off the job. For the employee, there is the waste of a productive human asset, the suffering, the medical expense, and the financial loss that may result in the loss of future earnings potential if the employee is unable to return to the same task. For the employer, lost-time accidents result in higher costs of operation. Productivity is lowered if a less qualified employee must be hired as a replacement while the injured employee recovers or if the business tries to operate without a replacement during the recovery period.

No business is immune from accidents. In the small business, the best managerial strategy in regard to safety is one that emphasizes accident prevention. Employee safety should be continuously emphasized as part of the company's training program and education process. Reminders in the form of posters or notices of the need for safety should be placed in conspicuous places around the company. Employees should be encouraged to wear protective clothing or goggles and should be given the reasons why the protection is necessary. Training films may be beneficial for emphasizing certain aspects of safety. A safety campaign can be used and recognition given to employee or departments that have the longest period without an accident. Periodic checks should be made of employee work habits. When unsafe acts are discovered, they should be explained to the employee so they can be corrected. If unsafe working conditions are discovered, steps should be taken to correct them. The Occupational Safety and Health Act of 1970, discussed in Chapter 22, is a major law enacted to assure that every working person has a safe and healthful working environment.

Worker's Compensation

Many states require employers, regardless of size of the firm, to provide **workers' compensation** benefits in the form of insurance. Employers purchase insurance, and the rates they pay are based on the hazards of the industry. Where accident and injury may be expected more often, rates are higher. Hence, by reducing the accident and injury rate, a single firm can reduce its insurance premium costs. Workers' compensation provides for financial reimbursement or payment for medical expenses or both. Payment is made to employees for any physical loss of disease resulting from working conditions.

THE CIVIL RIGHTS ACT OF 1964 AND THE EQUAL EMPLOYMENT OPPORTUNITY ACT OF 1972

The **Civil Rights Act of 1964** and the **Equal Employment Opportunity Act of 1972** apply to employers engaged in industry affecting interstate commerce who have 15 or more employees for each working day in each of 20 or more calendar weeks in the current or preceding year. These acts stipulate that an employer cannot discriminate in hiring, firing, promotion, or any other terms and conditions of employment, including fringe benefits, on the basis of race, color, religion, sex, or national origin. There are a restricted number of instances where the employer can discriminate on the basis of religion, sex, or national origin. These distinctions are allowed when it can be shown that any of these factors is a **bona fide occupational qualification or BFOQ.** For example, employees of a religious organization are not subject to the ban on religious discrimination. The law also makes an exception regarding occupations for which sex is a FBOQ, such as acting, modeling, and attending washrooms. Under these acts, race and color can never be a BFOQ for any job, Likewise, it is unlawful to advertise jobs separately as for "help wanted—male" and "help wanted—female."

Employers covered by the act must refrain from requesting information on the employment application form that violates either federal or state fair employment practice laws or the right to privacy. For example, the following questions are almost always illegal and should be avoided.

1. What is your height? weight? age?
2. What is your date of birth?
3. What church do you attend? What is the name of your minister, priest, rabbi?
4. What is your marital status? (Note: You may ask Mr., Mrs., Miss, or Ms.)
5. What is your maiden name?
6. What is your father's surname?
7. What is your place of birth?
8. What are the names of your dependent children under 18 years of age?
9. Who resides with you?
10. How many children do you have?
11. Who will care for the children while you are working?
12. Are you available for Saturday and Sunday work?
13. Have you ever been arrested?
14. Have you ever had your wages garnished?
15. Do you own or rent your place of residence?
16. Where does your spouse or parent live or work?
17. What are the organizations, clubs, and societies to which you belong?
18. Will you attach a photograph to the application form?

Some state laws conflict with the federal Civil Rights Act. For example, some states have restrictions on the hours women can work or how much weight they are permitted to lift. The federal law prevails, prohibiting such discrimination in those firms subject to the act. Thus, small business owners must determine if their firm is subject to state or federal law and then abide by the proper regulations.

The laws also place restrictions on the use of tests for hiring and promotion. Employment tests must be shown to be specifically related to the specific job involved and must be designed so as not to discriminate against a specific group on the basis of race, color, religion, sex, or national origin. As a result, many firms no longer use employment tests.

SUMMARY OF KEY POINTS

1. Personnel management activities include defining job requirements, recruitment, establishing selection procedures, and providing training and development.

2. To define job requirements properly, owner–managers must conduct a job analysis and then develop a job description and job specification from the results of the job analysis.

3. Recruitment is the process of locating persons whose skills and knowledges and abilities match the requirements of the job. Employees may be recruited from within and outside the company.

4. In selecting employees, the owner–managers attempt to collect pertinent data about candidates from such sources as the application blank, personal interviews, and employment tests.

5. There are a variety of employment tests that may aid the owner–managers in the employee selection process. Some of these tests are aptitude, achievement, intelligence, and personality tests. Some firms require a physical examination for all new employees.

6. A thorough orientation into the company will assist employees in adjusting to the new work environment. An employee handbook is an effective vehicle for communicating information about company policies, procedures, and rules.

7. Small business managers should offer to employees opportunities for training and development. Types of training programs that are feasible for small business operations include on-the-job training, apprenticeship training, job rotation, computer-assisted instruction, group training, training provided by suppliers of goods and service, training films, and various types of community college and university courses.

8. Counseling provides small business owners with the opportunity to work more closely with employees and to play a supportive role with their employees.

9. Performance appraisal is a control function in which the owner–managers obtain information about each employee's performance, communicate this information to the employee, and provide avenues for improvement in the situations that demand it.

10. A requisite of employee compensation plans is that they be perceived as being equitable by employees. Compensation plans used by small business owners include straight salary, hourly wage, piece rate, straight commission plan, combination salary and commission plan, and bonus plan.

11. The Immigration Reform and Control Act of 1986 makes it illegal to hire

illegal aliens and provides sanctions for those employers who engage in this practice.

12. The Fair Labor Standards Act of 1938 requires employers to pay a minimum wage to employees and establishes the number of hours employees can work without receiving overtime.

13. Fringe benefits offered by small business owners may be a positive factor in attracting and keeping employees in the firm.

14. Many states require all businesses to provide worker compensation as a form of insurance to reimburse employees for job-related illness or injury.

15. Employee safety should be of utmost concern in the small business. The Occupational Safety and Health Act of 1970 was enacted to require employers to provide employees with a workplace free from hazards that are likely to cause injury or death to employees.

16. The Civil Rights Act of 1964 and the Equal Employment Opportunity Act of 1972 governs hiring, firing, promotion, and fringe benefit practices of some small businesses. The acts stipulate that employers shall not discriminate in hiring practices on the basis of sex, national origin, race, color, or religion. The acts also specify limitations on employment tests.

DISCUSSION QUESTIONS

1. Distinguish between the job description and the job specification.
2. Explain the significance of employee orientation.
3. Identify and explain the different types of training programs given in the small business.
4. Make a list of questions a small business owner should ask when planning to implement a training program.
5. What are the purposes of performance appraisal?
6. Explain the different types of compensation plans used by small business owners.
7. What is the significance of the Fair Labor Standards Act of 1938 to the small business owner of the 1980s.
8. What effect does the Civil Rights Act of 1964 have on the hiring practices of the small business owner?
9. What is a bona fide occupational qualification?

THE BUSINESS PLAN: PERSONNEL MANAGEMENT GUIDELINES

The following guides will assist the small business owner in implementing a more effective and efficient personnel management plan for his or her firm.

1. Are job descriptions and job specifications based on job analysis?
2. Are employees recruited from sources both within and outside the company?
3. In the selection process, are the application blank, personal interview, and employment tests used to fullest advantage?
4. Are new employees given a complete orientation to the job and the company?
5. Are training opportunities made available to all employees according to their unique needs?
6. Are a variety of training techniques used to provide for all needs of the company and employees?
7. Are counseling services available both formally and informally?
8. Are performance appraisals used to enhance employee performance and are they provided on a regular basis?
9. Is the compensation plan perceived as equitable by all employees?
10. Are the laws that affect the small business understood and followed?

ENTREPRENEURIAL PROJECTS

1. Assume that you own a small business. You may choose the type (retail, service, manufacturing, wholesaling). Develop the personnel policies for several or all of the topics listed here that will provide the guidelines for employees in your company.

   Hours of work
   Vacations
   Sick leave
   Fringe benefits
   Pay policies, such as pay period, bonuses, overtime pay
   Retirement
   Holidays

Reasons for termination

Training program

Promotion

Performance review

Time off for personal needs

2. Interview a small business manager and request a copy of his or her employment application form.

3. If the owner has a personnel handbook, examine it and make a list of the major topics it contains.

CASE A

Friendly Auto & Truck Company

Friendly Auto & Truck Company is a family-owned dealership that is headed by the owner's son, who is the general sales manager. The service departments are managed by Mr. Paul, the service manager. New and used cars and trucks are sold through the dealership. A service department provides all types of mechanical repair and vehicle body repair and painting.

The service department is divided into two units: the body repair and painting services, supervised by Ralph, and the mechanical service, supervised by Dave. Ralph and Dave report directly to Mr. Paul, who keeps very tight supervisory control over both service areas. In fact, there is an unwritten policy that an employee is never to go directly to the owner or his son with any problems or suggestions. Instead, everything must be cleared with Mr. Paul. In the past, a violation of Mr. Paul's informal, unwritten policy has resulted in the immediate firing of the employee who bypassed Mr. Paul.

The body and paint shop supervisor, Ralph, and the mechanical repair service supervisor, Dave, have been with the company 10 years. Both have always tried to treat their employees fairly and have done all they could to counsel them regarding personal and work problems. Whenever there was a problem with pay or working conditions, these supervisors always listened to the complaints and tried to get the problems solved to the satisfaction of both the employee and the company. John Friendly, the owner's son, has no interest in any aspect of service, only in the sales end of the business. As a result, John has delegated complete authority to Mr. Paul to manage both service departments. With this much power and authority, Mr. Paul often acts in an arbitrary fashion.

A situation developed that resulted in conflict in the body shop and paint department. Specifically, it concerned the auto–truck painters and their rate of pay. In the past, body repairers and painters have always been paid at the same hourly rate. However, Mr. Paul arbitrarily changed this policy. Two weeks ago, he increased the body repairers' pay rate but not the painters' rate. He went through a lengthy discussion of why he took this action, such as the contention that body repairers had to supply their own tools for their work while the painters did not.

Not surprisingly, the painters were very dissatisfied with this decision because they felt their expertise as painters should be as important as the tools required by the body repairers. The painters demanded a return to the policy where both groups were paid at the same rate. Mr. Paul refused their demand.

Ralph and Dave presented the employees' point of view to Mr. Paul. Ralph emphasized the fact that in all the other body shops in the area both repairers and painters were paid at the same rate. Ralph also stated that painters in other shops in the city were paid more than painters at Friendly even though their skill and work performed are the same as for employees of Friendly.

Mr. Paul maintained his position that repairers were worth more. He noted that in his previous job as a service manager in another city painters were paid less than body repairers. He steadfastly refused to reinstate the previous equal-pay policy and to raise the rates of the painters. All the painters are threatening to quit unless their pay rate is adjusted.

Questions

1. What factors affecting compensation are overlooked by Mr. Paul?
2. What effect is this kind of arbitrary action likely to have on all employees in all service departments, not just the painters?
3. What should be done to resolve the problem in the body and paint shop department?

CASE B

The Morale Survey

Gage Manufacturing Company is a relatively young firm, employing 405 unskilled, semiskilled, skilled, and technical personnel. The company manufactures smaller leisure craft boats (under 20 feet in length). The owner, Bill Gage, has seen his firm expand rapidly in terms of numbers of employees on the payroll and physical facilities. Since the firm has experienced rapid growth, Bill wants to keep current on the general state of the environment within the company. If any problems do exist, he wants to be aware of them and take corrective action.

The following morale survey of Gage Manufacturing Company was conducted by the authors using the survey form shown in Figure 8-10.

EMPLOYEE MORALE SURVEY

Listed below are 18 statements about your job and the company in which you work. Please check each statement according to how you perceive them: Agree with the statement; Disagree with the statement; or Uncertain (if you do not know or cannot decide).

	Agree	Disagree	Uncertain
1. I have the opportunity to participate in decisions that affect me.	23	68	9
2. Communications within the company keep me informed about company plans.	39	55	6
3. My supervisor does not use unreasonable pressure to get employees to meet work schedules.	74	19	7
4. My job performance is evaluated fairly and constructively.	27	63	10
5. I have considerable freedom to use my initiative and judgment in my job.	74	18	8
6. I have assurance of job security as long as my job performance is satisfactory.	73	27	0
7. Opportunities for promotion are based on ability and job performance.	53	47	0
8. My pay is fair compared to the pay others receive.	22	78	0
9. The company provides safe and satisfactory physical working conditions.	36	28	38
10. My job is interesting and challenging.	65	29	6
11. Grievances and disciplinary matters are handled fairly.	21	74	5
12. My co-workers are friendly and cooperative.	89	10	1

**EMPLOYEE MORALE SURVEY
(CONTINUED)**

	Agree	Disagree	Uncertain
13. I receive recognition for doing good work.	60	35	5
14. Supervisors and subordinates work together as a team.	45	51	4
15. Standards of performance for my job are realistic.	58	36	6
16. Fringe benefits are satisfactory.	17	9	74
17. I derive a feeling of personal satisfaction from doing my job well.	88	5	7
18. I have a feeling of pride in working for this company.	82	13	5

Questions

1. What are the strengths of the company as perceived by the employees?
2. What are the areas that need attention by Mr. Gage?
3. What is the meaning of the response, "Uncertain"?
4. What should Mr. Gage do to correct the problem areas?

Notes

[1] Harry Bacas, "Hiring the Best," *Nation's Business,* October 1987, p. 68.
[2] Berkley Rice, "Evaluating Employees," *Venture,* September 1985, p. 34.
[3] James Bell and Associates, "Coverage, Characteristics, Administration, and Costs of Pension and Health Care Benefits in Small Business" (Washington, D.C.: Office of Advocacy, Small Business Administration, March 1984).
[4] *The State of Small Business* (Washington, D.C.: U.S. Government Printing Office, 1985), p. 248.

KEY WORDS

MICROCOMPUTERS IN SMALL BUSINESS

LEARNING GOALS

After reading this chapter, you will understand:

1   What microcomputers are and why they are suited to the needs of the small business owner.

2   Some advantages realized by small business owners when they install a computer system.

3   That small business owners must have realistic expectations about what computers can do for the business.

4   The importance of conducting a computer feasibility study.

5   What software applications are available to small business owners.

6   The importance of computer security.

7   What the functions of a computer service center are.

8   The potential impact on employees when a computer system is installed.

ENTREPRENEURIAL PROFILE

John T. C. Yeh

INTEGRATED MICROCOMPUTER SYSTEMS, INC.

John Yeh, who was born deaf, started his company, Integrated Microcomputer Systems, Inc., out of the frustration with the burdens his deafness placed on his career. He was the first person to receive a Master of Science degree from the University of Maryland. However, he could not find a job that utilized his knowledge and skills.

In 1979, he opened his firm and currently employees 350 persons. Annual sales have risen to $20 million.

John Yeh's firm offers a full range of office automation, telecommunications, software systems, and local area networks. He is also involved in new product development.

In 1988, John was chosen as first runner-up to the National Small Business Person of the Year.

Source: Network (Washington, D.C.: Small Business Administration, May–June 1988).

An advertisement for AT&T declares: "The right computer system can give you a competitive edge in business. That's the long and short of it." The ad's theme highlights the significant role that computers play in the modern business world. Unquestionably, computers are playing a prominent role in small businesses.

Without question, computer technology is advancing at a rapid pace. For example, today's computers are small in size yet significantly more powerful and substantially less expensive than models on the market a few years ago. With the widespread availability of relatively low-cost computers, small business owners are in a position to enjoy the advantages of computer technology that just a short time ago could be afforded by only big businesses.

MICROCOMPUTERS IN SMALL BUSINESS

Microcomputers were introduced in the early 1970s. They are the smallest and least expensive class of computer, and they are ideally suited to the needs of the small business operation.

Microcomputers, called personal computers, home computers, desk-top computers, or portable computers, are small enough so that the entire computer fits easily on a desk top. Portable computers are lightweight, and users can hand carry them from one location to another. They are well-suited to the needs of the person who must be away from the office for long periods of time, such as a salesperson who travels extensively.

Microcomputers are either IBM compatible or noncompatible, such as the Apple Macintosh. Microcomputer components consist of a keyboard for inputting data, one or two disk drives for storage, a monitor, and a printer for data output. The **microprocessor,** which is referred to as a ''computer on a chip,'' is the foundation for the microcomputer. The microprocessor is an integrated circuit that contains the central processing unit (CPU). The CPU performs the arithmetic, storage, logic, and control processing functions. The microcomputer performs these processing functions according to a set of instructions, the **computer program.**

As we have noted, microcomputers are relatively inexpensive. A complete unit for a small business can be purchased for approximately $2000. However, the cost can escalate to many thousands of dollars if a more sophisticated microcomputer and peripheral equipment, such as more expensive printers and larger auxiliary storage units are purchased.

When analyzing whether the business needs a microcomputer, the small business owner may conclude that a computer system is not feasible because the firm is too small. In some cases, this may be a correct conclusion. However, small businesses are definitely able to benefit from the major technological advances that have been made in computer technology, and more and more small business owners are discovering that computers can assist them in improving the firm's efficiency and effectiveness. With increasing regularity, new and improved computer applications are introduced, and others are in the developmental stage. Clearly, the microcomputer has an important role to play in the operation of many small businesses.

There are substantial data to support this view. Microcomputer sales amount to about $40 billion annually, or about two-thirds of all computer sales, according to Dataquest. Small businesses are the fastest-growing segment of this market. A survey of small business owners[1] found that 40 percent of small business owners now own or lease computers. However, usage varies with the size and industry of the business, as shown in Figure 10-1. In this survey, 95 percent of the firms with 100 or more employees own or lease computers while 26 percent of small firms (1–4 employees) use microcomputers. The study also reported that computer usage is more widespread in pro-

FIGURE 10-1
COMPUTERS IN SMALL BUSINESS.

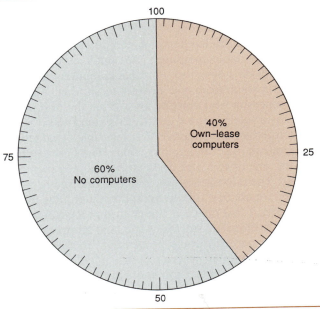

(*Small Business Primer,* The NFIB Foundation, Washington, D.C., 1988, p. 27.)

fessional services (64 percent) and in financial, insurance, and real estate firms (63 percent). Microcomputers are used to perform a variety of office tasks in the small business. Over half the firms with computers use them for word processing and accounting. At least 40 percent of the firms with computers use them to do spreadsheets, payroll, billing, and mailing lists.

In the small business, detailed information is necessary for continuous monitoring of the company's performance. We have observed in Chapter 1 that a common problem contributing to business failure is lack of information, such as inadequate inventory or accounts receivable data. One purpose of a computerized system is to provide owners with detailed, current, and accurate business information that will aid them in managing their operations more efficiently. The following case study illustrates the use of computer technology by a small wholesaler.

A family-owned wholesale glass distributor in New Jersey has 40 employees, 500 to 600 customers, and $5 million in sales annually. When the controller left the company, the owner felt the firm was at a crossroad. Up to this time, accounts receivable had been recorded and processed on a ledger-card machine that used 8½-by-11-inch cards to record accounts receivable information. One card was assigned to each customer, which meant there were between 500 and 600 cards. Accounts payable and general ledger procedures were done manually.

The company management faced the decision of hiring another controller plus a secretary to handle the increased work load. In addition, the service contract on the ledger-card machine was $700 a month. Or should another alternative be considered?

A decision was made to install a microcomputer and an accounting package that combined the general ledger, payroll, accounts receivable, accounts payable, inventory, and customer order entry. The result was an initial savings of $60,000! Since then, the wholesaler has also introduced word processing and a program that combines a spreadsheet, file manager, and word processing.[2]

ADVANTAGES OF COMPUTERS

The preceding illustration points to distinct advantages that can be derived when a computer system is installed. The following representative list of advantages suggests how performance in small businesses may be improved with the introduction of a computer information system.

1. *Timely Information* Information can be made available on a more timely basis because of the rapid speed with which data can be processed. Computerized statements and invoices can be prepared and sent within the specified time. Preparation of many required reports, such as those mandated by governmental agencies, is facilitated.

2. *Cost Reduction* Manual systems replaced with computerized systems result in lower costs of operation. The computerized system enables operations to be streamlined with a corresponding reduction in paper shuffling, thus increasing the overall efficiency and effectiveness of the firm.

3. *Improved Customer Service* Customer relations are improved through more efficient handling of customer accounts, such as more accessible records and ability to complete transactions more quickly.

4. *More Efficient Utilization of Human Resources* Employees are freed from many dull and routine recordkeeping activities and concentrate their attention and effort on more productive and demanding tasks.

5. *Improved Management Decisions* Owners can be supplied with more data and newer kinds of data that provide them with a stronger foundation on which to base their decisions.

6. *Accurate Information* Many of the routine transactions can be performed by the computer, and a reduction in "human errors" is realized.

7. *Better Control over Operations* More comprehensive information is available, and, as a result, internal control over the firm's operations is improved. For example, inventory control is more efficient because

current and complete information concerning shipments and inventory levels is available.

REALISTIC EXPECTATIONS OF A COMPUTER SYSTEM

Despite the advantages that the computer offers, the small business owner should have realistic expectations of what the computer can do for the company. To expect a computer to turn a poorly managed company into a well-managed, profitable company is unrealistic. It is important for the small business owner to be aware of what not to expect from the computer.

1. Don't expect a computer to clean up a mess in the office. The mess will only get worse if you attempt to computerize it.
2. Don't put in a computer because you don't have the right people to do the jobs in your organization. At least initially, the computer will make more demands on your organization, not fewer.
3. Don't install a computer with the idea that any information you want will be instantly available. Computers require structured, formal processing that may not produce some information as fast as an informal system.
4. Don't expect the installation of a computer to help define the jobs that must be done. The computer is a tool to get those jobs done, but the jobs must be well-defined first.
5. Don't expect a computer installation to occur like magic. Computer selection and installation will be successful only through a lot of hard work.
6. Don't expect any computer system to fit exactly your present methods of getting jobs completed. If you are not willing to listen to new ideas on solving problems, you will not be able to install a computer successfully or at a reasonable cost.
7. Don't acquire a computer to generate information you will not use. Growing companies may benefit from structured management information systems, but many owner–managers of small companies already have their fingers on the pulse of their businesses and do not need a formal, electronic system.[3]

FEASIBILITY OF COMPUTER INFORMATION SYSTEMS IN SMALL BUSINESS

Before small businesses conclude whether a computer is practicable, a comprehensive evaluation should be undertaken to include the overall objectives and the information needs of the firm. This analysis should compare the benefits versus the costs of the system.

A feasibility study should be conducted regarding the computer's practicability in the small business. A **feasibility study** is a survey of the current information requirements of the firm, the areas of the company that would benefit the most from a computer information system, an evaluation of the possible computer systems that would meet the firm's requirements, the anticipated cost savings of the system, and a recommendation of the preferred system.

Because the small business owner's knowledge of computers is often limited, specialized advice should be sought before any decision on computer utilization and acquisition is reached. Sales representatives of the various computer systems are available to explain the advantages and uniqueness of their system. However, the small business owners should realize that the sales representatives' views are biased in favor of the system they represent. Although the cost of acquiring the services of outside advice may be considered high in the short term, the expert knowledge and advice of a consultant may offer the small business owner an alternative that is more cost effective in the long run in regard to identifying the needs and selecting a system that will meet those needs.

Some specific concerns to be analyzed in the feasibility study are suggested here.

1. Analysis of the current operations of the company, its goals, and objectives.
2. Determination of the desirability of using a computer to achieve information processing goals. Current operations may be revised that may eliminate the need for the computer.
3. Determine the jobs that should be placed on a computer, such as inventory, payroll, accounting, names of customers and suppliers.
4. Determination of the cost–benefit relationship of the computer. Will the costs be offset by the benefits? Will the computer system increase the firm's ouput capability, as by producing more statements and letters, faster processing of orders, reducing errors in billing?
5. Evaluation of purchasing or leasing.
6. Determination of the effects of the system on the personnel. Will a higher level of motivation result? Will greater employee productivity be achieved?
7. Determination of the costs of training personnel to use the computer.
8. Determination of the specific output needs of the firm.
9. Determination of the weaknesses or inadequacies of the current information processing method.
10. Study of the desired overall information flow in the company.

COMPUTER SOFTWARE

Computer hardware refers to the physical components that make up the computer system, such as the keyboard, monitor, computer itself, and printer. In contrast, **computer software** is the set of instructions or programs that direct the operations of a computer system and tells the computer what operations to perform. There are two classes of software: operating systems software and applications system software.

Operating Systems Software

The programs that control the overall operations of the computer components are called **operating system software,** or **OS**. In the microcomputer, the OS controls the computer's instructions to the printer, monitor, and storage devices as well as receiving and directing inputs from the keyboard. Operating systems software come with the purchase or lease of the computer and must be present before application software systems can be run.

Applications Systems Software

The software that instructs the computer to perform specific tasks, such as processing data or performing computations, and produce desired output, such as payroll or inventory information, is called **application systems software.** A wide array of application programs that are used by small business owners are discussed in the paragraphs that follow. A list of some of the best selling business software packages is presented in Figure 10-2. Most of the best selling software packages are available in versions for both IBM compatibles and noncompatibles. A small business owner can generally use the standard, off-the-shelf packages for most processing needs and attain satisfactory results. Representative software programs for each application system are identified for the reader.

Word Processing

Word processing software enables the small business manager to compose, edit, format, store, and print text electronically by using the keyboard, com-

FIGURE 10-2
BUSINESS SOFTWARE: THE 10 BEST SELLING BUSINESS SOFTWARE PROGRAMS, MARCH 1987–1988.

Rank	Program	Category	Company
1	Lotus 1-2-3	Spreadsheet	Lotus Development
2	WordPerfect 4.2	Word processing	WordPerfect
3	dBASE III Plus v.1.1	Database	Ashton-Tate
4	PFS:First Publisher	Desktop publishing	Software Publishing
5	Microsoft Word v. 4.0	Word processing	Microsoft
6	Lotus Freelance Plus	Graphics	Lotus Development
7	MultiMate Advantage II	Word processing	Ashton-Tate
8	Quattro	Spreadsheet	Borland International
9	PFS:Professional Write	Word processing	Software Publishing
10	Microsoft Word 3.02 (Mac)	Word processing	Microsoft

(Egghead Discount Software, Bothell, Wash. Reported in *Office Guide,* an *INC.* magazine supplement, July 1988, p. 7.)

puter, and printer. If the information is to be saved, it is stored on floppy disks or hard disks.

Word processing has made it possible for office operations to be streamlined, and productivity has been greatly increased. Word processing software enables users to prepare materials, such as mailing lists, labels, reports, form letters, and legal documents. This is the most widely used application program. Special features of word processing software include the ability to enter, edit, delete, format, underline, and store text and create italics and boldface. More advanced features include automatic page numbering and spelling checker, subscript and superscript, and varying types of fonts.

Word Processing Application Programs

WordPerfect: WordPerfect Corporation

Word Star 5.0: MicroPro Corporation

Microsoft Word 4: Microsoft Corporation

PFS Professional Write: Software Publishing Corporation

Spreadsheets

Next in usage to word processing software is the electronic spreadsheet. A **spreadsheet** is a program that is modeled after the spreadsheet used in accounting. Electronic spreadsheets are used to record routine business transactions and as an aid in the planning and budgeting process. It is divided into cells that are formed by intersecting rows and columns. The spreadsheet enables the user to manipulate numerical data that are placed in the cells.

The electronic spreadsheet enables the user to answer "what-if" questions for a proposed business plan or budget. For example, after a preliminary budget is set up, the small business owner can determine the effect on the entire budget by asking a question such as, "What if sales were $200,000 instead of $150,000 next year?" The computer recalculates the entire spreadsheet whenever any number is changed and enables the small business owner to evaluate various proposals. The spreadsheet enables the manager to have more alternatives to evaluate. Thus the spreadsheet usually allows the manager to make a better, more informed decision. Features to evaluate in spreadsheets are built-in mathematical formulas that enable the user to solve problems in budgeting, cash flow management, and rate of return.

Spreadsheet Application Programs

Lotus 1-2-3: Lotus Development

PFS Professional Plan: Software Publishing Company

PlanPerfect: WordPerfect Corporation

Excel: Microsoft

DataBase Management Systems (DBMS)

The third most widely used application program is database. **Database** refers to collecting and storing business information in a central file (floppy disk or hard disk). A file is made up of the records of the business. Each record in a file should contain the same type of information. For example, employee records contain such information as name, social security number, address, telephone number, educational record, job skills, and previous work experience. Each of these categories in a record is called a field, and a record is the set of fields relating to one person. The database file is composed of a number of related records, in this case, all employee records. If the manager needs information about an employee's educational record, the database program enables the manager to access, retrieve, manipulate, and summarize the desired type of information from the file. The small business manager should study the flexibility, capacity limits, and special features of the database software to determine the most appropriate package for the firm.

Database Application Programs

dBase III Plus: Ashton-Tate

pfs:Professional File: Software Publishing Corporation

Data Management: Data Products

Graphics

Business graphics programs enable the manager to use visual presentations of data. A chief advantage of graphics is that they supplement the numerical data, enabling the small business owner to have a picture of any trends that may be developing in the business operation. If any trends or significant changes in business activity are highlighted, the small business owner then analyzes the numerical data more closely to ascertain the cause. Common types of business graphics include line charts, bar charts, pie charts, and scattergrams. Graphics are used to display more types of business information, such as comparing the sales performance of various products, the sales of the firm, or cost of merchandise.

Graphics Application Programs

Lotus Freelanced Plus: Lotus Development

Windows Draw: Micrografix

Harvard Presentation Graphics: Software Publishing Company

Graphwriter: Graphwriter Corporation

Accounting and Inventory Control

Every small business must maintain accurate financial records, such as accounts payable, accounts receivable, inventory, purchase orders, billing, pay-

After gaining experience in several advertising agencies, Tony Caputo decided to test the entrepreneurial waters. He transformed a hobby that began in a walk-in closet in his home into an $11 million a year publishing company that publishes *Now Comics*. In 1986, his company introduced the world's first full-color computer graphics comic book, "Vector."

roll, and job costing. These records provide the foundation for the balance sheet and income statement. These application programs allow the small business manager to record financial entries faster and more accurately. The microcomputer can generate accounting reports that provide the most up-to-date information on the financial status of the small business. Some features of accounting and inventory packages include analyzing flexibility, capacity limitations, and special features, such as sending data to the general ledger from other information sources.

Accounting and Inventory Application Programs

Peachtree: Peachtree Corporation

Dac-Easy Accounting: Dac Software

Quicken: Intuit

Entrepreneurs in all types of businesses realize many benefits from a microcomputer, such as better control over inventory, more timely accounting information, and lower costs of operation due to increased efficiency.

Tax Advantage: Monogram

Business Sense: Monogram

Fiscal Inventory/POS: Fis-Cal

Great Plains Inventory Management: Great Plains.

MAI Purchase Order: MAI

MAI Order Entry: MAI

Real World Job Cost: Real World Corporation

Real World Inventory Control: Real World Corporation

Real World Order Entry/Billing: Real World Corporation

Real World Purchase Order: Real World Corporation

Telecommunications

The process of sending information from one computer to another is **telecommunications.** There are a number of general-purpose communication programs that enable the microcomputer to exchange information with other PCs, retrieve information databases, and send and receive electronic mail. To be able to communicate with another computer, both computers must have a **modem,** an acronym for MOdulator/DEModulator. A modem converts a computer digital signal to analog signals that are carried over telephone lines. The analog signals from the telephone are converted into digital signals that the computer on the receiving end can understand. By means of a modem, computers are able to ''talk'' to each other.

Telecommunications Application Programs

Cross Talk MK.IV: Crosstalk Communications

Smartcom III: Hayes Microcomputer Products

Microsoft Access: Microsoft Corporation

Integrated Software

An integrated software package permits two or more applications in one program. An integrated software package may include word processing, spreadsheet, database management, and telecommunications.

Integrated Systems Application Programs

Symphony: Lotus Development

Framework II: Ashton-Tate

WordPerfect Library: WordPerfect Corporation

PFS:First Choice: Software Publishing Corporation

Open Access: Software Products International

When developing his business plan for a figure skating school, a small business owner included the computer as an integral part of the plan. Because he would have to teach the various skating classes as well as keep the books, the owner did not want to have to spend several hours a day pouring over the accounting records.

For $2300, he purchased an IBM-compatible computer with extra memory, a printer, and two floppy disk drives. He reviewed software manuals and decided on an accounting package from Dac Software, a $70 package.

The computer provides him with up-to-date information on taxes owed and how far ahead or behind the firm is with regard to revenue projections. One positive feature of the system is that the owner spends only about 15 minutes a day at the terminal inputting and processing information.[4]

EVALUATING A MICROCOMPUTER FOR THE SMALL BUSINESS

The decision to incorporate a microcomputer into the firm's operations should be guided by a well-planned strategy. Because there is such an extensive assortment of hardware and software available, the initial step is to specify the firm's current and future information needs. Once information needs have been defined, users should select the software that matches the information needs "before" selecting the computer hardware. A number of the criteria to analyze before making the final choice are presented in the following list.

1. *Software*   Should be "user friendly," flexible, expandable, compatible with the microcomputer system; complete packages should be available (accounting, word processing); packaged software should be available off the shelf, or packaged software can be customized to user requirements.

2. *Hardware*   Should be expandable, compatible; clock speed (the speed of the microprocessor) should be in the range of 8 to 12 megahertz; video display of monitor should be of good quality; unit should fit available space.

3. *User memory*   Random access memory (RAM) is the computer's main memory and stores software applications temporarily. The computer's RAM is measured in kilobytes. A kilobyte equals 1024 characters of information. A RAM of 640K should be adequate for the small business owner's needs.

4. *Hard disk drive and floppy disk drive*   A 20-megabyte hard-disk drive allows storage of up to 20,000K, or about 10,000 pages of material. Both 5¼-inch and 3½-inch hard-disk drives are on the market. The smaller disk should be considered by the first-time user as it is beginning to replace the larger disk drive. Storing programs and information on the hard-disk drive allows faster access to information and more convenience than inserting and removing floppy disks from the disk drive. A 1.2-megabyte floppy disk drive is adequate to load new programs and store backup copies of files.

5. *Vendor's qualifications*   Vendor should have knowledge of industry, type of professional assistance offered small business owner in selecting computer system, financial stability, size of vendor's firm, application experience, installation support, responsiveness to needs of customers, length of time in computer business, extensiveness of line of computer hardware and software in stock.

6. *Training and continuing education*   "Hands-on" experience should be provided, professional seminars offered that are designed to expand computer's applications, on-site training provided for all company personnel, continual technical assistance and support, availability and quality of manuals for computer user.

7. *Service and maintenance support*

There should be provisions for delivery and installation of system, type of service agreement, provision for on-site service and maintenance, cost of service agreement, location of service facilities, response time for service when computer is down, availability of backup system when computer is down, after the sale, vendor has a staff of technically qualified customer service representatives available to support and assist the owner in adapting the system to specific company requirements.

8. *Security*   Security system should prevent unauthorized access and use of system or to make unauthorized program modifications.

9. *Cost of hardware and software*   Lowest price should not be the prime evaluation criterion.

10. *Expandability and compatibility*   Expandability relates to the ability of the user to increase the capability of the computer by the addition of peripheral equipment. Compatibility refers to the software written for one computer to be run on another, even though it is a different model, or the ability of the computer hardware to work together.

COMPUTER SECURITY

As computer use increases in small businesses, a concern of the owner must be computer security. Computer security includes the policies and procedures to protect not only the computer hardware but also the confidentiality and availability of business information.

Without adequate security measures, a small business owner can suffer severe information and hardware losses through either accidental or intentional acts. There are at least four major types of security hazards that the small business owner must guard against.

1. *Environmental and natural hazards*   Natural catastrophes, such as flood or fire, and power fluctuations that can damage or destroy the computer or the data stored in the computer.

2. *Hardware and equipment failure*   Mechanical or electrical failure of the computer or any of the peripheral equipment.

3. *Accidental errors and omissions*   Incorrectly entering data (typographical errors), accidental destruction of business records, and failure to keep backup copies of data and application programs.

4. *Intentional acts*   Sabotage, such as an employee purposely destroying records to get even; alteration of financial records for monetary gain; unauthorized use of computer time for personal gain; and theft of computer equipment, data, or programs.[5]

The following suggested business security checklist will afford a measure of protection against these types of hazards and risks.

1. Is your computer and peripheral equipment in a safe and secure location?
2. Is your computer and peripheral equipment protected against fire, natural disaster, water damage, temperature and humidity changes, electrical power surges, and electrical power losses?
3. Do you have and use backup procedures?
4. Do you have a tested contingency plan?
5. Do you have the exact insurance coverage for your computer equipment?
6. Are your employees bonded?
7. Do you have separation of duties with respect to the data processing function?
8. Are programs fully tested before implementation?
9. Is the computer area restricted to a limited number of employees?
10. Is the computer area locked at night?
11. Is a log of computer job runs maintained and reviewed?
12. Are passwords and/or other security procedures used?
13. Does your computer system provide verification of input?
14. Is the documentation sufficient to maintain and operate the computer system?
15. Are the changes to the software reviewed by someone other than the programmer?[6]

COMPUTER SERVICE CENTERS

If small business owners elect not to install a computer system, the advantages of computerized information processing may be gained by using the services of firms that process information, **computer service centers.**

A computer service center's purpose is to process data of the small business and produce the required reports. In this system, data (checks, sales slips, etc.) are delivered to the service center, where they are processed, and output is generated in the form of the specific report required by the small business owner. The computer service center is able to furnish a single report or many reports, for example, transaction records (sales register, payroll register) and statements (balance sheet, income statement), depending on the needs of the small firm owner. Fees charged by the computer center include the cost of writing a specific program for processing the firm's data and the charge for information processing. If the small business can use a standard or "canned" program, the costs are substantially less than for a custom-designed program package. If a canned program is used, recordkeeping and reporting systems of the small business must be designed to conform to the standardized programming package. The cost for using a standardized package is based on the computer time required to generate the needed reports.

This may be the information system best suited to the needs of many small businesses. For example, a firm experiencing rather stable growth may achieve greater operational efficiency through a service center.

IMPACT OF THE COMPUTER ON EMPLOYEES

Extensive planning should precede any type of change that will be made in a firm's operations. As suggested in Chapter 8, before implementing any type of change in the small business, the impact that the proposed change may have should be thoroughly explored. Employees oppose change for many reasons. Resistance is likely to be encountered even when the change is designed with the best interests of the employees in mind. When proposing to introduce a computer into the firm's operations, it may take time for employees to accept and adapt to the new system even though the system offers many advantages. For example, there will usually be extra work and frustration when the system is being installed and the "bugs" in the system have to be worked out before the system operates smoothly. If employees hold negative attitudes toward the acquisition and installation of a computer system, they must be overcome, or these attitudes will likely lead to behavior that will devastate a system that would otherwise be successful.

To minimize resistance to change, the owner must create a positive environment, following the suggestions presented earlier so that the change can be implemented in an orderly manner. Employers must communicate openly about the proposed change, the purposes, and the advantages. Employees must be encouraged to participate in the planned change from early on and to participate in the implementation of the system. The advantages of the system both to the company and employees must be emphasized. Approaching the change in this manner will lessen the impact on employee morale, reduce resistance to the computer system, and increase the likelihood that the new system will be utilized to its potential in the small business.

The wholesale glass distributor mentioned earlier has these comments about the introduction of a computerized information system. "If you want the benefits of microcomputer software, you don't push it on people. In general, people feel threatened by computerization. It's all so new to many of them, and you just can't force people to use something that they find threatening. My door is open if someone wants to see what a word-processing program can do. I think you have to let them take the initiative. These programs can never really replace people, but they'll make people's jobs easier. They are tools that when properly used are extremely powerful."[7]

SUMMARY OF KEY POINTS

1. Advances in computer technology have resulted in more compact and powerful computers than are relatively inexpensive when compared to early models. Consequently, a computer is now a feasible alternative for information processing in millions of small businesses.

2. Microcomputers are suitable for filling the needs of the small business owner.

3. Firms that utilize computers realize many advantages, such as more timely information, cost reductions, improved customer services, more efficient utilization on human resources, better management decisions, more accurate information, and more effective operational control.

4. Before the owner–manager decides whether a computer is practicable, a feasibility study should be undertaken to analyze thoroughly the needs of the business.

5. An extensive number of application programs are available that facilitate information processing.

6. A number of criteria should be carefully evaluated before a decision is made to purchase or lease a computer.

7. With the increased frequency of use of computers, the owner must be alert to the need for security measures to protect the integrity of the system.

8. A computer service center can process information for the small business that elects not to install a computer system.

9. Before a computer system is installed, the potential impact on people should be thoroughly studied.

DISCUSSION QUESTIONS

1. What is a microcomputer?
2. Explain some of the advantages of computers to a small business owner.
3. Why should the small business owner conduct a feasibility study before deciding to use a computer system?
4. What is meant by an application program?
5. What factors should be evaluated when selecting a computer?
6. Discuss how a computer service center serves the needs of the small business owner.
7. Explain the potential impact on employees when a computer information system is installed in the small business.

THE BUSINESS PLAN: MICROCOMPUTER ANALYSIS

The following questions should be addressed to study all aspects of the microcomputer: applications system software, hardware, and the vendor. This step is necessary to determine the suitability of the microcomputer system to the unique needs of the small business owner.

Software Analysis

1. Does the software package come with effective documentation?
2. Is the operations manual written for the inexperienced computer operator?
3. How easy is the software to use ("user friendly")?
4. How easy is the software to change? (Can data be changed that has already been processed? Can the user change the program instructions, such as payroll withholdings rates, or does the vendor have to make the necessary changes?)
5. Will the user be required to change any business practices? If so, will the changes provide the type of accounting and decision-making information the user needs?
6. Does the software system have security features, such as passwords or user identification codes?
7. Is it easy to increase the size of the files?
8. Does the software have all the features that you must have for your particular business?

Hardware Analysis

1. Does the microcomputer have sufficient storage capacity for the needs of the business now and in the future?
2. Does the printer produce the desired quality of output?
3. Is the speed of the printer satisfactory?
4. Is the monitor adequate in terms of size, color, and so on?
5. Is the processing speed of the microcomputer adequate?
6. Can the microcomputer system be expanded when the need arises?

Vendor Analysis

1. Is the vendor an authorized distributor for the microcomputer system under consideration by the small business owner?

2. Do salespeople listen to customer needs and problems and genuinely try to offer a system that addresses those needs and problems?

3. Does the vendor offer a financing plan?

4. Does the vendor deliver the system, set it up, provide for on-site continuing education and training, and make a complete set of user manuals available to the small business owner?

5. Is the vendor reliable and is the business stable?

6. Does the vendor emphasize business needs first and price only after business needs have been analyzed?

7. Does the vendor offer a complete demonstration of the system's capability?

8. Does the vendor offer a service contract (for a fee) that extends beyond the basic warranty period?

9. Will the vendor provide you with a list of names of customers who are using the system that the vendor installed to verify vendor claims of customer satisfaction?

10. Will the vendor provide on-site service at your place of business?

ENTREPRENEURIAL PROJECTS

1. Report on the content of an article from a magazine or newspaper that describes a computer application in small business.

2. Visit a retail computer store and prepare a report on the kinds of computers that are available for a small business. If possible, collect some literature, and bring it to class.

3. Assume you received a telephone call this morning from Josephine, who owns a ladies' apparel shop. How would you answer her question, "How can a computer help my business?"

4. Have a small business owner who uses a computer in the firm's operation explain why the decision was made to use the computer in the firm.

CASE A

Page Office Supply Company

Page Office Supply Company was founded in September 1945 by Nick Page's father, Gene A. Page. Nick took control of the firm in 1975, when his father retired. Nick has worked in the firm since high school days, so he has a thorough understanding of the firm's operations. Page Office Suppy is a distributor of office supplies to retail office supply stores and larger business firms, educational institutions, and hospitals in the area. Sales volume has increased to $3.5 million annually and is projected to continue at a steady pace in the future.

To maintain an adequate inventory level to meet sales, Page's purchasing system required that approximately 4000 office supply items be evaluated for reordering each week. Sales and accounting records are maintained by two women, both of whom have had long service with the firm. They post sales all day on two rather out-of-date bookkeeping machines.

The sales staff consists of two in-house salespersons and 10 outside sales representatives. Last year, the salespersons generated over 75,000 sales invoices. To maintain their clientele, the company must provide customers with the quick response to their orders that they expect, such as overnight delivery of many items.

One of the long-service women employees will be retiring in two months. Nick is faced with the decision of replacing her. If he follows one plan, he will have to hire two or more employees to replace her to meet the growing sales volume and the corresponding recordkeeping requirements. Or he will have to change the entire recordkeeping system of the firm.

Nick finds the second alternative very appealing, although he realizes that, before making a final decision, he will have to conduct a rather thorough analysis of the firm's needs to justify the implementation of a new system. He wants to see his firm continue to grow, and he ponders whether this goal will be enhanced if a changeover to a computer system is implemented.

Questions

1. What advantages could accrue to Page Office Supply Company with the changeover to a computerized system?
2. What would be some of the possible applications of a computer system in a firm of this type?
3. What possible cost savings could result from the addition of a computerized system instead of maintaining the present system?
4. Should Nick Page install a computer?

CASE B

The Microcomputer

When Roy LeDuff set out three years ago to automate his family business in Phoenix, Arizona, he thought he knew what he was getting into. Phoenix Paint Supply, Inc., has more than 4000 line items in inventory, and "paperwork was getting out of control," he recalls. "We could not afford to hire a new employee. I reckoned a computer would simplify my life—not just the handling of inventory but all my administrative and bookkeeping chores as well."

So LeDuff decided it was time to get computer-literate. He began to canvass popular trade journals and spend his lunch hour in stores comparing the bits and bytes of computer hardware. "That was mistake No. 1," he says, "I should have evaluated my software needs first and then backed into hardware."

Like many first-time buyers, LeDuff found himself frustrated by jargon and at the mercy of salespeople—many of whom, he says in retrospect, did not know the difference between a spreadsheet and a bedsheet. But providing he stayed within his $10,000 budget, LeDuff was ready to take his chances.

That was mistake No. 2. Listening to marketing hype raised his expectations far beyond what was realistically achievable, he says.

LeDuff eventually settled on a microcomputer and a small business software package for under $7000. The purchase, which seemed like a bargain at the time, would cost him months of frustration and disappointment leading to the not uncommon sight of a computer unused, gathering dust on a desk.

The problem, he explains, was a mismatch between hardware and software. The microcomputer's speed was too slow and memory too small to run the software efficiently. Although Phoenix Paint Supply is a small business, the volume of its inventory and daily transactions exceeded what a microcomputer could handle. Moreover, the software had so many bugs in it that "although I had better things to do with my time than sit at a terminal all day, I had to learn programing to try to save my investment," LeDuff says, "That computer became my second wife; I was spending 60 hours a week with it."

As valiant as his efforts were, they met with little success—the software was still bug-ridden. LeDuff, at the end of his rope, called in a computer consultant. Working closely with the software manufacturer, the consultant made numerous design changes in the program to accommodate the computer. But the best he managed was to automate the store's inventory. LeDuff's dream of reaping efficiencies from computerized bookkeeping was no closer to coming true than when he had first started 18 months earlier.

Source: Karen Berney, "Computerizing with Confidence, Part I," *Nation's Business,* November 1986, p. 3.

Question

1. Analyze the situation Mr. LeDuff faced and the mistakes that were made in the computer acquisition.

Notes

[1] Russell W. Rumberger and Henry M. Levin, *Computers in Small Business* as reported in a brochure, "Research in Review" (Washington, D.C.: Institute for Enterprise Advancement, 1987).

[2] "Software in Wholesaling," *Venture,* Vol. 6, no. 5 (May 1984), pp. 126 and 129.

[3] Michael M. Stewart and Alan C. Schulman, *How to Get Started with a Small Business Computer,* Management Aid No. 2.027 (Washington, D.C.: Small Business Administration, 1987) p. 3.

[4] Karen Berney, "Computerizing with Confidence, Part 2," *Nation's Business,* December 1986, p. 26.

[5] *A Small Business Guide to Computer Security* (Washington, D.C.: Small Business Administration, n.d.), p. 5.

[6] Laurence Beitman, "A Practical Guide to Small Business Computer Security," *The Office,* Vol. 96, no. 2 (August 1982), p. 86. Reprinted by permission.

[7] "Software in Wholesaling," p. 129.

KEY WORDS

CHAPTER 11

RISK MANAGEMENT

LEARNING GOALS

After reading this chapter, you will understand:

1   That all small businesses face risks on a daily basis.

2   That small businesses control risk by (a) avoiding/reducing risk, (b) assuming risk, and (c) shifting risk.

3   Small businesses often need fire, theft, liability, loss of earning power, surety, automobile, and life insurance.

4   The difference between the three basic types of life insurance—whole life, endowment, and term.

5   The various benefits a business may derive from life insurance and the relative cost of each type.

6   That there are different types of people who are shoplifters.

7   The different methods you may use to discourage shoplifting.

8   That employee theft is a major problem in business, that there are different methods employees use to steal, and that there are various ways to discourage employee theft.

9   How to discourage burglary.

LaRaine McGuirk

D & L TRUCK LINES

D & L Truck Lines of Kansas City, Kansas, is a woman-owned firm which has experienced remarkable growth and diversification over its 19-year history. President LaRaine McGuirk attributes the growth and success of her company to assistance from the Small Business Administration through its bank-guarantee loan program.

McGuirk worked with Kansas City's Guaranty State Bank and consulted her banker, Mike Johnson, regularly. But when she outgrew the bank's capability to provide additional capital, Johnson suggested an SBA bank-guaranteed loan. In 1983, she secured such a loan for $430,000. Sales increased from $2.2 million to $3 million in 1987, and today the firm has 30 road-tested drivers.

"I saved money because I was able to use the bank that gave me the best interest rate and the bank benefited because they kept what they felt was a good customer and realized the profits from the interest," McGuirk explained.

McGuirk originally started as the firm's bookkeeper in 1968 and was approached by the owner to take over payments on five trucks because he was going out of business. She and her son, Steve, now operate the business from a strategic site near the Missouri and Kansas interstate highways.

At first some suppliers had difficulty accepting McGuirk in the nontraditional role of truck line owner—operator. But her drivers have had little difficulty in accepting her as boss.

As a result of recent trucking deregulation, competition has been keen. But with a sizable portion of her equipment paid for,

McGuirk could afford to let trucks sit idle at times and "hold on" while many newcomers went out of business.

From McGuirk's perspective, perhaps one of the most challenging aspects confronting the trucking industry is driver drug testing. She also projects key changes within the industry will occur due to new legislation which allows a higher maximum gross load of 80,000 pounds. When she started in business, average trailer length was 38 to 40 feet; now 50-foot trailers are common, and require the most skilled drivers.

Escalating equipment costs in the industry have been difficult. But McGuirk's firm generally keeps a truck (average cost: $65,000) four years, because she finances equipment three years only. This cuts interest costs and allows the fourth year to be interest-and-payment free. In this manner, she has no cash flow problems as maintenance costs accelerate.

The liability insurance cost to McGuirk's company in 1986 rose 2 cents per mile, or a $53,619 increase for one year.

As national vice president in charge of membership for the National Association of Women Business Owners (NAWBO), McGuirk has served as a strong supporter and catalyst of women's entrepreneurship. Recalling her experiences as a 1986 delegate to the White House Conference on Small Business, she takes pride in the increased number of women business owners who were elected delegates.

Her personal management philosophy includes honesty first, last, and always; analysis and study of all information pertaining to her business; detailed recordkeeping; and faith in God.

McGuirk's successful ways of doing business have influenced her daughter, Lisa, to obtain SBA business plan information before she started Blooming Pails, a florist shop. "The result was a smooth, intelligent, less costly start than D & L Truck Lines experienced," confides the trucking mother. "I'm teaching my 11-year-old granddaughter to do bank deposits for the flower shop," McGuirk smiled. All in the family!

Source: Lonah Birch, *Network* (Washington, D.C.: Small Business Administration, September–October 1987).

Small business owners face risk on a continuing basis. **Risk** to small business owners exists in many forms. Every time they purchase merchandise, they take a risk that it will not sell. They face a risk every time the delivery driver drives the company truck. This list is almost endless. Many of the risks to which the small business is exposed are major risks that could result in failure of the business.

RISK CONTROL

Small business owners must control risks if their businesses are to survive and prosper. There are three basic methods by which they are able to deal with risks: (1) avoid/reduce the risk, (2) assume the risk, and (3) shift the risk. (See Fig. 11-1.)

Avoid/Reduce the Risk

Sometimes it is possible for a small business owner to avoid or reduce risks, particularly high-level risks. A small business owner may avoid or reduce risks by substitution, screening, elimination, or good management practices.

FIGURE 11-1
RISK CONTROL IN SMALL BUSINESS.

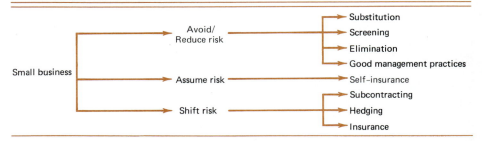

Substitution

A small business may avoid risk by substituting high-risk materials and processing with low-risk materials and processes. For example, a manufacturer using a highly explosive chemical in the manufacturing process may find it is possible to substitute a chemical that is safer and achieves the same results.

Screening

The small business owner may avoid risk by screening out high-risk items. To illustrate, a small business should not extend credit to everyone; rather, it should screen out high-risk individuals to aid in helping reduce bad debt losses.

Elimination

Sometimes the small business is able to avoid risk by elimination of high-level risks. The firm that requires employees to wear eye goggles when operating a grinder is eliminating one chance of injury to the employee.

Good Management Practices

Many risks the small business faces may be greatly reduced with good management practices. To illustrate, periodic inspections and training often contribute greatly to reducing risk of injury to customers and employees. Good hiring procedures help to reduce the risk of employee theft.

Even when risks are shifted to others, as in the case of insurance, good management practices can still reduce the risks and lower the cost of insurance to the business. Insurance premiums can be reduced by installing sprinkler systems, properly placing fire extinguishers, installing burglar alarms, proper care and cleaning of facilities, and so on.

Assume the Risk

Some small businesses assume certain risks because it is either impossible to avoid the risk or too costly to shift the risk to someone else. Often some types of insurance cost too much to justify the protection. For example, shoplifting insurance premiums are often too expensive for the purpose they serve. The small business may elect not to carry this insurance but rather to institute as many deterrents to shoplifting as are practical. There are many risks that the small business must face on a continuing basis. Often the only thing the business can do is practice good management to reduce the risk as much as possible.

To illustrate, a small women's clothing store must purchase clothing several months in advance of its being sold. It is often very difficult to determine what fashions will be so far in advance. If the store purchases the wrong style of clothing, it may lose a considerable amount of money. To reduce the risk it must take, the store needs to evaluate continually its customers' tastes, study the market, and find out what authorities in the fashion field are predicting.

Shift the Risk

The small business owner may shift many risks to other persons by subcontracting, hedging, and insurance.

Subcontracting

A small business may be willing to perform certain functions but may feel other functions are too high a risk for the capabilities of the business. To illustrate, a small contracting firm may feel that it has the ability to perform adequately all construction activities on a new building except the electrical work. To avoid the risk of failure on electrical work and still get the contract, the small business may bid on the contract and **subcontract** the electrical work to another firm for a specified price.

Hedging

Small business firms that deal in goods traded on the commodity market often shift the risk of price fluctuations by **hedging.** For example, a cattle feedlot may buy and sell cattle futures in the commodity market to avoid price fluctuations that could ruin the company.

Insurance

The most common method of shifting risk in small businesses is by purchasing insurance. For premium payments, insurance companies are willing to insure a business agent against a wide range of risks.

The small business may shift the entire risk or a part of the risk. It usually depends on the probability of the risks occurring and the cost of shifting the risk.

TYPES OF INSURANCE FOR SMALL BUSINESS

The principal types of insurance used by small businesses are fire, theft, liability, loss of earning power, surety, automobile, and life. (See Fig. 11-2.)

FIGURE 11-2
TYPES OF RISKS SHIFTED TO INSURANCE COMPANIES.

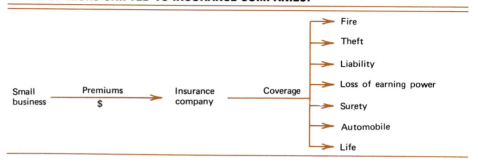

Fire

Fire insurance policies insure the small business from loss due to fire and lightning. Both the building and its contents may be insured in a policy. In addition, a small business may obtain insurance against all the loss or part of the loss. Most small businesses carry fire insurance against part of the loss due to the difference in cost. For example, a small business may have 90 percent coverage, in which case, the insurance company pays for 90 percent of the loss and the small business pays for the other 10 percent of the loss.

Additional riders may be purchased to accompany the fire insurance policy. For an additional premium, the small business firm may purchase insurance against explosion, riot, windstorm, hail, aircraft- and vehicle-caused damage, and smoke damage.

Theft

The small business firm may purchase **theft insurance** for all types of thefts. It may be protected against loss from theft by persons outside (burglary and robbery) and inside (employee theft) the business. Small businesses with employees who handle money often insure against embezzlement of funds by bonding these employees.

Liability

Owners of small business firms may be liable for (1) their own acts, (2) acts of their employees while at work, (3) conditions within the business, (4) products they manufacture or sell, or (5) all of these. If an individual is injured while on the firm's premises, the business is liable for damages if the injury is the result of neglect. For example, if a customer fell and was seriously injured because of a broken step, the business would be liable.

Good management practices are important to keeping down liability claims and premiums. For example, one firm did not check the driving record of employees it hired that were to drive on company business. One employee had a very bad driving record and, while driving himself and another employee, passed in a no-passing zone. A head-on collision killed the passenger, and a very large judgment against the business resulted because it had failed to check the driving record of the driver.

Liability insurance is one of the most important forms of insurance for the small business to carry. Injuries to individuals often result in very large damages being awarded by the courts against the business. Damage awards may amount to several hundred of thousands of dollars and sometimes into millions of dollars. Very few small businesses are able to sustain this type of loss. In addition, unlimited liability for the general partner and the sole proprietor may not only result in business failure but may also put them personally in debt for long periods of time.

There are many types of coverage by liability insurance. Some of the forms of liability coverage are damages resulting from elevator operations, druggists' mistakes, physicians' malpractice, and contractor accidents.

Insurance to protect against **product liability** is very important to most retailers and manufacturers. For example, it was claimed that a fire had been started by a defective television set in a building. Both the manufacturer and the retailer who sold the set were involved in an expensive damage suit. A doctor, hospital, and manufacturer were sued because a patient claimed that failure of a certain piece of equipment caused permanent damages to a patient. This suit is still in litigation 11 years later. Even if litigation is resolved in favor of the retailer or manufacturer or both, each can incur considerable expense in legal fees. Insurance companies usually provide legal representation to clients who carry their liability insurance.

It is also important that the small business purchase sufficient amounts of liability insurance. The small business may have a $50,000 liability policy against losses, but this does not limit the amount of the judgment that may be obtained against the business in court. If the same business were to sustain a $100,000 judgment, then the insurance company would pay only $50,000, and the small business would be required to pay the rest.

Loss of Earning Power

The small business firm may sustain losses not only to physical aspects of the business but also to its ability to earn income. Loss of income may be very damaging and can result in failure of the business in some cases. For example, a fire might cause the business to cease operations for several months, but the need for income to the owner still exists and may not be covered by the fire insurance policy. Also, the owner of a business might sustain an injury that would prevent him or her from working in the business, resulting in the loss of income.

Insurance covering **loss of earning power** may be purchased for many different occurrences. The owner may purchase disability insurance, which provides against loss from disability. He or she may also purchase insurance against loss of income due to the business's not operating as a result of property damages. Loss of income may prevent the owner from meeting debt payments.

Surety Insurance

Some types of small business firms obtain bonding, **surety insurance,** to assure their customers of their ability to complete contracts. To illustrate, a small business contracting company may bond itself against losses to customers arising from its failure to complete contracts. If it fails to complete a contract, the bonding company will hire some other business to complete the terms of the contract. It is common in some industries that a business must bond itself or find it very difficult to obtain business, as in the construction industry.

Automobile Insurance

Automobile insurance is in reality another form of property and liability insurance. There are several types of property insurance available covering the automobile, such as collision, theft, fire, glass breakage, and damages from malicious mischief. Automobile liability insurance covers other peoples' property, other automobiles, persons in other vehicles, and persons in the insured automobile.

Property-type automobile insurance often has a deductible clause. For example, a small business may carry $100 deductible on collision. If the car is damaged in an accident, the owner must pay the first $100, and the insurance company pays anything above $100 of the damages.

Small businesses may feel that it is not economical to carry property type insurance on their automobiles and trucks after they are several years old. However, a small business should carry liability on its vehicles regardless of age. Liability claims may be so expensive that they ruin a business. In fact, many states require businesses and individuals to carry liability insurance to protect other people.

Cost of Protection

Insurance premiums differ by coverage, type of business, and location. However, adequate coverage is a significant expense for most small businesses. One small fast-food hamburger restaurant currently spends $2700 in premiums each year just for property and liability insurance (including $300,000 personal injury liability). A feed and seed ranch store is spending $3500 a year in premiums. To most small businesses, this is a major expense; however, when you consider the protection it provides against loss, it is well worth the cost. Businesses face many losses that could easily bankrupt them.

Life Insurance

Many people feel that **life insurance** is for individuals and is not important to business firms. This is not true, particularly in the case of small business firms. If a general partner or sole proprietor dies, the form of ownership ceases to exist, and the sale or transition usually results in some loss. Even if it is a corporation, the death of a principal officer often creates some problems and losses. In many partnerships, the firm may carry life insurance on the partners as a means of the other partners' having the funds with which to buy out the partner to create a new partnership.

It is not at all unusual for a person to build a very profitable business and then have it sold at less than it is worth at his or her death. When the businessperson dies, the estate must pay estate taxes. Often the businessperson has considerable assets but not large sums of cash. To pay the estate taxes, the heirs often must sell the business to raise the cash. The time that is allowed to raise the cash is often not sufficient to get the best price for the business. Rush sales usually result in a low price.

There are all types of attachments that can be added to life insurance policies, such as a rider that provides for insurance premiums to be waived in case of disability of the person paying the premium. However, there are only three basic categories of life insurance policies: whole life, endowment, and term.

Whole Life

Whole life insurance insures an individual for the remainder of his or her life as long as premium payments are maintained. Usually, premium payments continue until the person dies or reaches 100 years of age. However, there are exceptions in that the person may pay the entire premium at one time or compact the payment into a limited time, such as 20 years. The amount of the premiums is based on the age of the insured when the policy is first taken out. An individual at 25 years of age would expect to pay premiums for many more years than would a person 50 years of age. The younger the individual, the lower the cost of premiums. When the insured dies, the heirs are paid the face value of the policy.

Whole life insurance also has a cash or loan value. The policyholder may obtain cash or a loan on the policy after it has been in effect for a specified length of time, usually 3 years. The longer premiums are paid, the greater the cash or loan value. If the policyholder takes out a loan, the amount of the loan is subtracted from the face value if he or she dies before it is repaid. Often interest rates on policy loans are lower than the market rate. Many owners of small businesses have found insurance policy loans to be a cheap source of debt capital.

Endowment

Endowment insurance policies insure the individual for a specific period of time. If he or she dies during that period of time, the heirs are paid the face value of the policy. However, if the individual does not die, he or she is paid the face value of the policy at the end of the specified period. Premiums are usually paid for the entire period of coverage. Although it is not common, the insured may also elect to pay one lump-sum payment or compact the premiums into a shorter period of time than the coverage.

Endowment insurance premiums are also based on the age of their insured when the policy is purchased and the time period of the policy. Endowment insurance also has a cash or loan value. For most small businesspersons, endowment insurance is not the best type of life insurance to obtain because of the cost of premiums.

Term

Term life insurance insures an individual for a specific period of time and then terminates. The term policy may be for any length of time, but the most common period is five years. The insured pays premiums on a regular basis for five years, and if he or she dies within the five-year period, the insurance company pays the full face amount to the heirs. The cost of premiums is based on life expectancy for the individual's age during the five-year period. Term life insurance does not have a cash or loan value.

Another type of term life insurance is decreasing term. This type of insurance is popular with homeowners. If they borrow a specific amount of money to purchase a home, say, $30,000 for 25 years, then they take out a decreasing term insurance policy on the life of the main provider in the family. The term policy would be valued at $30,000 and decrease in the same proportion as the home loan over the 25-year period. Small business owners sometimes find decreasing term insurance very attractive to protect payment of their loans on land and buildings.

Term insurance is the best type of life insurance for most small businesses because of the lower cost of premiums.

Cost of Life Insurance

The cost of life insurance varies by type of insurance, company, age, and riders added to the policy. As an illustration of the differences between types of insurance, one large insurance company charges the yearly premiums shown in Figure 11-3 for each $1000 of the face value of the policy for a person 25 years of age.

FIGURE 11-3
ANNUAL PREMIUMS FOR VARIOUS TYPES OF INSURANCE.

Type of Insurance (no special riders)	Yearly Premium per $1000 at Age 25
Whole life	$11.44
Endowment with maturity at age 65	20.00
5-year term	3.49
25-year decreasing term	2.51

SHOPLIFTING

Authorities report that business crime in the United States is currently amounting to more than $50 billion each year. This amounts to about $220 for each man, woman, and child in the United States. **Shoplifting** accounts for a large part of this loss. Shoplifting is a major problem for retail stores. Department stores continually try to control shoplifting and still estimate they lose about 2.2 percent of their total sales to shoplifting. Small business retail firms that do not make a continuing effort to control shoplifting undoubtedly lose much more to shoplifters.

Shoplifting is not only a burden to the business firm, but it is also a cost to every consumer. Losses due to shoplifting are a cost of business, and retail stores pass this cost on to their customers in the form of higher prices. In addition, they must pass on to the consumer the more than $14 billion per year they spend trying to control various types of theft. Many small businesses that close their doors each year report they were forced to do so as a result of employee and customer theft.

Types of Shoplifters

There are several different types of shoplifters; in fact, most are amateurs rather than professionals. Some of the types of shoplifters are (1) juveniles, (2) housewives, (3) psychologically sick persons, (4) vagrants, (5) addicts, and (6) professionals.

Juveniles account for more than half of all shoplifting. Almost all juvenile shoplifting occurs, not because of need of the goods, but from dares or for "kicks." The problem has become so bad around large high schools that some merchants will not allow more than a few students in their store at a time.

Women comprise the largest number of adult shoplifters. Most of the women who are caught shoplifting are married women. The reason is probably because women traditionally have done a major part of the shopping for their families. Most of these women shoplift on impulse and, if caught early, will stop before it becomes a regular pattern of behavior.

Some individuals shoplift for psychological reasons. The more common name for this group is *kleptomaniacs*. The value of the goods is seldom any motivation for this group. Their motivation is the act of stealing. These individuals are in dire need of psychological therapy. If being caught results in their receiving psychiatric attention, the merchant has done them a service.

Vagrants and habitual drunkards shoplift because of a real need. They usually steal for food, drink, and clothing. This group is usually the easiest to detect because of appearance and clumsiness.

Narcotic addicts must have large sums of money daily to support their habit. Some of these individuals obtain money by shoplifting items and selling them for money. Of all the shoplifters, this group is usually the most dangerous for the merchant to apprehend.

The professional engages in shoplifting strictly for the money obtained by "fencing" stolen goods. This individual is also the most adept at shoplifting and is usually difficult to detect. The professional shoplifter is also adept at picking the easiest stores from which to steal. As a result, the store owner who does not practice good shoplifting prevention techniques is more likely to be the target of the professional shoplifter than the store owner who does practice good prevention techniques. The professional shoplifter may also be a member of a crime organization. These shoplifters usually have a ready market for their stolen goods and, often, an organization that helps them out with bail and attorneys when they are arrested.

Prevention of Shoplifting

Often merchants may have a serious shoplifting problem and not even know the problem exists. Consequently, one of the most important aspects of shoplifting control is to recognize it as a problem and also know the extent of the problem. This can best be achieved by adequate records and a good inventory control system. The merchant who keeps good records of sales, purchases, and inventory will recognize if merchandise is getting out of the store without anyone's paying for it. By this method, the merchant is able to determine the extent of losses due to shoplifting and employee theft.

There are many things a merchant can do to help prevent shoplifting, but the most effective is a sales force trained in shoplifting detection. Another major weapon for discouraging shoplifting is a consistent policy of prosecuting all shoplifters. Persons caught shoplifting usually have some type of "heart-rending story" and claim it is their first time. Most of the time it is not true, and even if it is, letting them get by with it usually encourages them to do it again. Stores that have a reputation for apprehending and prosecuting shoplifters are usually shunned by professionals, and, to some extent, by many amateurs.

Some other practices that can help to reduce shoplifting losses are these.

1. Post signs around the store saying that shoplifters are prosecuted by the store. One store posted the number of shoplifters it had caught and prosecuted as of that date and found it to be very effective.
2. Keep small expensive items in an enclosed display case and near where a clerk can see it at all times.
3. Have clerks keep a watchful eye on restrooms and fitting rooms.
4. Keep unused checkout lanes closed.
5. If possible, post a guard at the exit door. Keep the number of exits as few as possible.

6. Have an adequate number of salespeople at all times. Part-time help can be valuable in rush periods.
7. Place large convex mirrors and two-way mirrors around the store.
8. Utilize two-way radios, closed-circuit television, and store detectives.

To inhibit the amateur shoplifter, a store owner may find that simple devices and techniques may be of help in reducing shoplifting. To illustrate, one of the authors assisted a small store that had an extremely bad shoplifting and employee theft problem. The store was in such bad shape financially that the author obtained an old home movie camera, installed a small red bulb in front of it, wired the bulb so that it could be plugged into an electrical socket, mounted the camera in a prominent place, and placed a sign below it that said the store was electronically surveyed to prevent shoplifting. This simple device proved to be so effective in frightening amateur shoplifters that the night after the second day it was installed, someone fired a rifle shot through a door window into the camera.

One of the more effective means of preventing shoplifting being used by many clothing stores is a 1- by-3-inch tag embedded with a simple microwave transmitter the size of a pencil point that is attached to the items of clothing. The tag can only be removed by the cashier with special shears. Anyone leaving the store with the tag still on the garment sets off an alarm from a hidden receiver. Cashiers must be very conscientious in removing the tags. One woman sued a clothing store when the clerk forgot to remove a tag and the alarm sounded as she left the store. She was detained by store personnel until the mistake was discovered.

One form of shoplifting is what is called "ticket switching." Some shoplifters change price tags or exchange them with a cheaper item. Some methods of preventing ticket switching are as follows.

1. Hide an extra price tag on the merchandise.
2. Place hard-to-break strings on tags.
3. Use gummed labels that tear apart when removed.
4. Use rubber stamps or machines to mark tags; do not use pencils.
5. Use special type staples when attaching price tags so clerks will know if a tag has been removed and restapled.

Merchants must be very careful in apprehending shoplifters so that they do not leave themselves open to lawsuits for false arrest. In some states they must wait until the shoplifter is out of the store to detain and have him or her arrested. The shoplifter may claim that he or she intended to pay for the merchandise, and it is up to the merchant to prove otherwise. There have been cases where the item was concealed under the person's clothing and the individual maintained successfully in court that he or she was still going to pay for the item before leaving. Also, sometimes a shoplifter will have a confederate and pass the merchandise on to the other person before leaving the store. Fortunately, many states have adopted new legislation aimed at protecting the merchant from so much risk of suits for false arrest. These new laws often have ''willful concealment'' clauses, which permit the merchant to move on the shoplifter before the shoplifter leaves the premises. Every small business person should check the law in his or her state. In addition, local police departments are usually able to provide valuable advice on shoplifting prevention and prosecution.

EMPLOYEE THEFT

Everyone likes to think his or her employees are honest, particularly small business owners, because they are usually close to their employees. Unfortunately, **employee theft** is widespread and accounts for business losses in the billions of dollars each year. Most authorities claim that employee theft accounts for more losses than either shoplifting or burglary.

As is the case with shoplifting, many small business owners do not even know they have a problem with employee theft. For example, one small grocery store recorded an almost unbelievable theft record by having $59,000 cost of goods sold and sales of only $56,000. The owner was convinced employee theft was not a factor. It turned out that two nephews had pocketed several thousand dollars while working the cash registers during the year. In another case, an employer found that a trusted employee had been systematically pocketing $100 a week for several years. One of the most important factors in stopping employee theft is keeping adequate records of sales, purchases, and inventory to determine if a problem exists and, if it does, the extent of the problem.

Employee theft may occur by several different methods. Many times employees will carry merchandise out of the business hidden in pockets, lunch boxes, or somewhere on their person. Employees sometimes leave merchandise in trash boxes carried out of the business. They return at night and recover the merchandise.

One person found 14 watches in a box behind a large discount store when he was collecting boxes to store some of his personal belongings. When he returned them to the store, the owner was completely unaware any watches were missing. A restaurant owner found several top-quality steaks wrapped in a plastic bag when searching the garbage for knives, forks, and spoons. Employee theft may also take the form of salespeople's charging friends or accomplices lower prices or not charging for all the goods they purchase.

Some stores sell damaged goods to employees. Employees have been known to remove a part from a piece of merchandise, buy it at greatly reduced price, and then restore the part when they get it home.

Cash thefts by employees also may occur in different ways. Clerks may not register all sales and pocket the cash. Some shortchange customers and pocket the extra cash. This practice is particularly bad in that the business may also lose customers. Some employees theft occurs in the form of embezzlement through manipulation of accounting books and checks.

Most employee theft is done by people who would never think of committing any other type of crime and do not consider themselves to be dishonest. They rationalize their theft in various ways with the most common excuse being that the business is not paying them what they are really worth and it is a way of supplementing their salary. This is why some small business persons are completely taken by surprise when they discover an employee, who they thought was incapable of stealing, stealing from the business.

Prevention of Employee Theft

The best way to prevent employee theft is to be aware that a problem exists. Good accounting records, good cash control procedures, and a good inventory control system are the keys to controlling theft. Without these a small business can go bankrupt and never even know the primary reason was theft.

The following is a list of things a business should do to help prevent employee theft.

1. Let your employees know you expect honesty and will not tolerate theft.
2. Inspect all employee packages leaving the premises.
3. Keep all doors, except customer exit doors, locked, and make someone responsible for the key.
4. Keep trash from accumulating in the store, and inspect it at *irregular* intervals to make sure no merchandise is going out of the store in this way.
5. Watch the loading–unloading area. Collusion between drivers and employees sometimes occurs. Spot-check incoming merchandise to make sure you receive all of it. Do not let drivers load their own trucks from stock.
6. If at all possible, assign clerks to one register only. Check the register tape against the amount of cash at the end of the employee's time on the register. If trading stamps are given, check these against the tape and cash to spot missing stamps or cash.
7. Have your books audited regularly by a competent accountant.
8. Watch cashiers to make sure they are ringing up all sales and ringing them up at the correct price.
9. Above all, check out each employee hired in an attempt to determine his or her honesty and character.
10. Many of the devices used to detect shoplifting may also be used to identify employee theft, such as two-way mirrors, closed-circuit television, and convex mirrors.

11. Have persons not known to the employees periodically buy an item in the business, and have them watch to make sure the correct amount is rung up on the cash register.

BURGLARY

Burglary is also a problem for small businesses. More than 80 percent of all burglaries are never solved. This is a crime that is committed mostly at night. Apprehension of burglars should be left to the police because the thief often can be a very dangerous person.

Burglary Prevention

Although small business owners should never try to apprehend a burglar, they can perform many functions that will lessen the likelihood of loss due to a burglary. The following are some of the things they may do.

1. Install good locks and sturdy doors.
2. Install a burglar alarm system. Silent alarms direct to the police are very effective.
3. Maintain adequate indoor and outdoor lighting.
4. Use steel gratings over windows when possible.
5. Keep show window advertising in a manner where the inside of the store can still be seen from the outside.
6. Don't leave more cash than is absolutely necessary for starting the next day's business in the store. Take all other funds to bank night depositories.
7. Have a good safe if change must be kept overnight in the store.
8. Change the locks on your doors on a periodic basis. Control the keys with records of what employees have what keys. If keys are lost, have the lock or locks changed immediately.
9. Ask the local police to inspect your store to point out things you might change to protect your store from burglary.
10. Post signs that state no money is kept in the premises overnight.
11. Check the possibility of an armored car service if large amounts of funds are used in the business.
12. Check the feasibility of using a guard dog. Even a pet dog that barks can often scare off a would-be burglar.

BURGLAR ALARM SYSTEMS

There are eight basic systems used in burglar alarm systems. These are

Electromechanical   Electromechanical devices are simple alarm systems that rely on something activating an electrical circuit. For example, windows and doors can be equipped so that a spring and plunger will function to make contact if they are opened, thereby setting off the alarm.

Pressure   Pressure devices are often used under mats and carpeting. Any pressure on them closes the circuit and the alarm sounds.

Taut wire   Taut wire detectors consist of wire strung along a fence or wall so that anyone climbing them will disturb them. They are often used on roofs. Any change in the tension of the wire will set off the alarm.

Photoelectric   Photoelectric devices use a beam of light that is transmitted for a distance to a receiver. If the beam is broken, the alarm is sounded. For best protection, infrared or ultraviolet light is used.

Motion detection   Motion detection alarms may be either radio frequency or ultrasonic wave transmissions. The first method uses a set radio frequency, which is transmitted to a receiver. Any disturbance in the wave patterns sets off the alarm.

Ultrasonic involves transmitting specific ultrasonic waves to a receiver. The alarm sounds when the waves are disturbed.

Capacitance alarms   Capacitance alarms are proximity alarms used to protect metal containers, such as safes. They may also be used on doorknobs. An electromagnetic field is set up on an ungrounded metal object by using two oscillator circuits, which are set in balance. Whenever these circuits are disturbed, the alarm sounds.

Sonic systems   Sonic alarms consist of microphones connected to a receiver, which sets off the alarm when noise is detected in the area. They are usually set above normal noise to avoid false alarms.

Vibration alarms consist of special type microphones attached to an object. If the object is disturbed, the vibrations are picked up by the microphone and sent to the receiver, which sounds the alarm.

Cost

Burglar alarm systems range from simple systems to very sophisticated systems. They may be alarms that are sounded at the business, or the may be silent alarms that are activated only at a police station. Their cost may range from a few hundred dollars to several thousand dollars. Most small businesses should have some form of burglar alarm system. It can save them in insurance premiums and losses from burglary. The firm's resources and individual situation determine which system is best for them.

This chapter has discussed many risks the small business firm faces in its operations; however, these risks should not discourage the prospective small business entrepreneur. Good management practices allow the small business owner to control these risks and operate a profitable business.

SUMMARY OF KEY POINTS

1. Small businesses may avoid and/or reduce risk by substitution, elimination, screening, and good management practices.
2. Small businesses may assume risk by self-insurance.
3. Small business may shift the risk by subcontracting, hedging, and insurance.
4. Fire insurance insures the business from loss due to fire and lightning.
5. Theft insurance provides protection from burglary, robbery, and embezzlement.
6. Liability insurance insures a business against liability due to its own acts, acts of employees while at work, conditions within the business, or products the business manufacturers or sells or all of these.
7. Loss of income may be shifted to insurance companies.
8. Surety insurance bonds small businesses to insure their ability to complete contracts.
9. Automobile insurance provides protection for various losses due to damage or liability.
10. The three basic types of life insurance are whole life, endowment, and term.
11. Types of shoplifters are juveniles, housewives, psychologically sick persons, vagrants, addicts, and professionals.
12. There are many methods of reducing shoplifting.
13. Employee theft is a serious problem, but there are methods of controlling it.
14. Burglar alarm systems and other methods of protecting the facilities can greatly reduce the chances of burglary.

DISCUSSION QUESTIONS

1. Give an example of each of the following methods of controlling risk in a small business.
   a. Avoid/reduce the risk.
   b. Assume the risk.
   c. Shift the risk.
2. Why is liability insurance so important to small businesses, and what types of liability may a small business be protected against?
3. If a small business burns to the ground and the owner has 100 percent

fire insurance coverage, is he or she completely covered against all types of loss? Explain.

4. What is surety insurance?

5. What is the basic difference between coverage of whole life, endowment, and term insurance?

6. What is the difference between cash and loan value of the three basic types of life insurance?

7. Identify the following shoplifters.

   a. The most common.
   b. The most common of adult women.
   c. The one who needs therapy.
   d. The easiest to detect.
   e. The hardest to detect.
   f. Usually, the most dangerous.

8. Give three ways that a drugstore could help prevent shoplifting.

9. What is ticket switching, and how can it be discouraged?

10. Why is employee theft a problem in small businesses?

THE BUSINESS PLAN: RISK MANAGEMENT

Insurance

____ Do you need fire insurance on the building, equipment, fixtures, or furniture?

____ Is burglary, robbery or embezzlement a possibility?

____ Could you be liable for

    ____ Acts of you or your employees?
    ____ Conditions in the business?
    ____ Products you manufacture or sell?

____ Would loss of earning power be serious to you?

____ Will customers require surety insurance?

____ Will the business own or lease any automobiles or trucks?

____ Is there a need for life insurance to assure survival of the business if you or a key member dies? Be sure to consider term insurance.

If you answered yes to any of the above questions, you should contact at least one insurance agent. Consulting two would be better so you can compare prices. Be sure to weigh risk to cost.

Shoplifting

—— Do you carry any merchandise that could be shoplifted?

If your answer is yes, then follow the practices to reduce shoplifting and ticket switching listed in this chapter.

Employee Theft

—— Will you need to employ people in the business?

If the answer is yes, follow the steps listed in this chapter that reduce employee theft.

Burglary

—— Will you keep money or anything of value in the business facilities?

If you answered yes, follow the list for burglary prevention in this chapter. Police in most towns will inspect your business and give advice for burglar protection.

ENTREPRENEURIAL PROJECTS

Visit a small business that is a retail store, and find out the following information:

1. What types of insurance does the business carry? Do you personally feel the insurance coverage is sufficient? Explain.
2. Is shoplifting a problem for the store?
3. What methods of shoplifting prevention does the store use?
4. Are employee theft and burglary a problem for the store?
5. Does the store do anything to prevent employee theft and burglary?
6. Could you make recommendations that would help the business prevent the different types of theft?

CASE A
The Pharmacist

Oscar Mulkey has just graduated from pharmacy school and he plans to open a neighborhood drugstore. His father is giving him a lot about a block from the local high school that he has owned for years. His uncle is loaning Oscar the money to open the business on a 15-year, no-interest loan.

Oscar plans to operate the pharmacy department by himself and hire one full-time and two part-time clerks to wait on customers in the rest of the drugstore. He plans to carry the usual merchandise found in a drugstore, such as gifts, some photography equipment, toiletries for men and women, small appliances, tobacco products, and various drug items. He plans on offering credit and making deliveries to offset discount house competition.

Since you had a course in small business management in college, Oscar has asked you to help him plan certain phases of his business.

Questions

1. Give Oscar one example each of the three ways to control risk in his drugstore.
2. Should Oscar carry life insurance and what types would you recommend?
3. What other types of insurance, if any, should Oscar carry?
4. Do you feel shoplifting could be a problem for the new drugstore? If so, draw up a plan helping Oscar prevent shoplifting.
5. While he is still having his building designed, help Oscar prevent other types of theft.

CASE B
Pretty Pets

Eric Oram is getting ready to open his new pet store, which he has named Pretty Pets. The building is completed, and all shelves, equipment, fish tanks, furniture, and inventory are being installed and stocked. The store should be ready for opening in about 10 days. Eric owns the store building and everything inside it. However, he does have a $75,000 Small Business Administration loan, which has a first lien against his store and everything in it. Eric has hired one full-time employee and one part-time employee. Eric has been so busy he has not thought about insurance or theft until today.

He is stocking a wide range of tropical fish, some birds, hamsters, white mice, fish and pet medicine, pet toys, grooming products, fish and pet foods, and other miscellaneous products normally associated with a pet store. The building has a front and a back door with large windows in the front.

The store will have a panel truck, which will be used to pick up tropical fish at the local airport when they arrive and to pick up and deliver pets that the store grooms. The part-time employee will drive the truck most of the time.

The layout of the store follows.

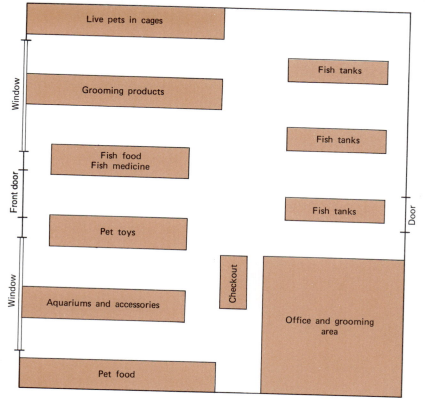

Questions

1. What kinds of insurance does Eric need? Explain.
2. Do you think Eric should expect shoplifting problems? Explain.
3. What can Eric do to minimize shoplifting?
4. What can Eric do to minimize employee theft?
5. What can Eric do to minimize the chances of burglary?

MANAGEMENT INFORMATION AND MERCHANDISE CONTROL

KEY WORDS

CHAPTER 12

FINANCIAL RECORD KEEPING AND CASH CONTROL

LEARNING GOALS

After reading this chapter, you will understand:

1. That financial recordkeeping is vital to the successful small business and that it should be custom-built for the business.

2. The accounting equation and how it is the basis for double-entry bookkeeping.

3. How debits and credits are used to record increases and decreases in assets, liabilities, capital, income, and expenses.

4. The difference between the cash and accrual methods of accounting.

5. How the sales journal is a record of daily income to the business and the disbursement journal is a record of expenditures of funds by the business

6. How a firm keeps a record of credit purchases by individual customers and how it bills them for the amount they owe.

7. That the books in a small business may be kept by use of a computer, a manual system, or a public accountant.

8. How a change fund operates for a business that handles many cash transactions.

9. How a sales and cash receipts form works and why it is important to the small business.

ENTREPRENEURIAL PROFILE

Phil Knight and Bill Bowerman

NIKE

In 1975, SBA loan officer Jack Washburn in the Portland, Oregon, office had a decision to make. A firm manufacturing and importing running shoes wanted a loan. It had been founded 10 years before by Phil Knight, a college running star with an MBA degree, and Bill Bowerman, his former track coach. For the first few years, the office and warehouse were contained in Knight's basement, and most sales were made from the trunks of employees' cars.

Bowerman had created, however, a "revolutionary" shoe sole by pouring rubber into a kitchen waffle iron. The company's brand name was that of a Greek goddess who appeared to a company executive in a dream: Nike.

When the Nike guaranty loan application landed on Jack Washburn's desk, the company had matured a bit. Sales had reached $4.8 million by 1974. The problem was that the growth rate had been around 50 percent for the past five years. Sales were swelling, but working capital was tight. Was Nike a giant in the making or a bubble about to burst?

Washburn, now retired, describes himself as, "a conservative credit professional, with a background in banking." He is also—even now, at age 75–a runner, and so he had a feel for the product. His research showed an excellent product, a promising market, and stellar management. In October 1975, SBA joined the First State Bank of Oregon in a guaranty loan for the maximum amount of $350,000.

Over the next five years, Nike's sales grew

at an annual rate of over 100 percent. The SBA loan was paid in full in 1979. In 1980, the firm went public with an offering of 2 million shares.

Of course, Nike went on to become a household name. The company's complete line of sport and leisure shoes and clothing are sold internationally. Currently, Nike employs 2,290 people and in 1987 had sales of $877 million. Not a bad return on the government dollar!

Source: (Washington, D.C.: Small Business Administration, July–August 1988).

It is not unusual for a small business firm to have adequate sales and still fail because of inadequate financial control. **Financial control** is vital to the success of a small business firm. Good financial records must be constantly maintained in a business if it is to have effective financial control.

Good recordkeeping does not mean that a complex accounting system is required for every business. In fact, recordkeeping should be as simple as possible and still get the accounting job done. To illustrate, a small, one-chair barber shop used an old cash register, a drawer in the cash register stand, a loose-leaf notebook and a checkbook to maintain its financial records. The owner would "ring up" each receipt of cash on the cash register during the day. At the end of each day, he would compare his cash register tape against the amount of cash in the register and record it in a loose-leaf notebook. Every time he purchased supplies or paid a bill in cash, he would put the receipt in the drawer. He also kept check stubs of every bill he paid by check in the drawer. At the end of each week, he would add up daily cash sales records, all expense receipts, and all check stubs for the week. He would then subtract the expense items from the cash sales total to determine the amount of his net cash gain for the week. At the end of the year, he divided his expense receipts and canceled checks into categories of expenses, figured depreciation on his equipment, and totaled his cash sales book. From these records he prepared his income tax return. It was a very simple system, but it fulfilled his accounting needs.

Larger firms, on the other hand, often require rather complex accounting systems with many different types of journals, ledgers, and report forms. In addition, many small business firms and almost all large firms perform their recordkeeping functions on computers (most small firms should be using computers). However, no matter whether it is a simple or complex system, hand- or computer-based, the accounting system depends on the same general concept—recording changes in the basic accounting equation.

THE ACCOUNTING EQUATION

The basic **accounting equation** is **assets = liabilities + capital** (net worth) or **assets − liabilities = capital.** For a simple illustration of the equation, imagine that all your possessions consisted of an automobile valued at $600, personal property (clothing, etc.) worth $800, and $200 in a bank checking account. Your total **assets** would be $1600. Now imagine your only debt was $400 in payments on your automobile. Using the accounting equation, you would find you were worth $1200.

$$\text{Assets} = \text{Liabilities} + \text{Capital (net worth)}$$
$$\$1600 = \$400 + \$1200$$

If you earned $100, the accounting equation would change as follows.

$$
\begin{array}{rcccc}
\text{Assets} & = & \text{Liabilities} & + & \text{Capital} \\
\$1600 & = & \$400 & + & \$1200 \\
+\ 100 & & & & +\ 100 \\
\hline
\$1700 & = & \$400 & + & \$1300
\end{array}
$$

If you made a $75 payment on your automobile, the accounting equation would change as follows:

$$
\begin{array}{rcccc}
\text{Assets} & = & \text{Liabilities} & + & \text{Capital} \\
\$1700 & = & \$400 & + & \$1300 \\
-\ 75 & & -\ 75 & & \\
\hline
\$1625 & = & \$325 & + & \$1300
\end{array}
$$

If you then spent $25 for a night on the town, your equation would be

$$
\begin{array}{rcccc}
\text{Assets} & = & \text{Liabilities} & + & \text{Capital} \\
\$1625 & = & \$325 & + & \$1300 \\
-\ 25 & & & & -\ 25 \\
\hline
\$1600 & = & \$325 & + & \$1275
\end{array}
$$

Recording the effect of every change in the accounting equation is the basis for the foundation of bookkeeping, which is called double-entry bookkeeping.

Every financial transaction should leave the accounting equation in balance. Therefore, each time there is a transaction, there must be (1) equal minuses and pluses on one side of the equation or (2) the same amount of minuses and pluses on both sides of the equal sign. For example, purchasing a shirt for $10 gives the results under assets of adding $10 to personal property and reducing cash by the same amount. Also, receiving an asset, such as cash, means increasing an asset on one side of the equal sign and capital on the other side.

The entire process of bookkeeping and accounting, no matter how simple or complex the system, is based on this concept of keeping the accounting equation in balance by the process of double-entry bookkeeping.

Income and Expenses

To keep records of what is earned by the business and what is paid out by the business, the categories of **income** and **expenses** are used rather than adjusting the capital section for each transaction. For example, suppose you bought fruit for $20 from a farmer and sold it to customers for $100. The difference between all income and all expenses could then be adjusted to the capital account. This difference would also be equal to the difference in cash.

	Income	Expenses	Cash
Sale of fruit	$100		$100
Purchase of fruit		$20	− 20
	$100 −	$20 =	$ 80

The $80 increase in cash would be equal to an $80 increase in capital when adjusted to the capital account. Your basic accounting equation would then appear as follows:

$$
\begin{array}{ccc}
\text{Assets} = & \text{Liabilities} + & \text{Capital} \\
\$1600 = & \$325 & + \$1275 \\
+\ 80 & & +\ 80 \\
\hline
\$1680 = & \$325 & + \$1355
\end{array}
$$

Debits and Credits

Accounting language uses the terms **debit** and **credit** to describe increases or decreases in the categories of the accounting equation (assets, liabilities, and capital) and income and expenses. Assets have a debit balance, while liabilities and capital carry a credit balance. In the example of the accounting equation, the debits and credits would also balance.

$$
\begin{array}{ccc}
\text{Assets} = & \text{Liabilities} + & \text{Capital} \\
\$\ 1680 = & \$\ 325 & \$\ 1355 \\
\text{Debit} & \text{Credit} & \text{Credit}
\end{array}
$$

An increase in an asset would be a debit entry—a decrease would be a credit. Conversely, an increase in liabilities or capital would be a credit entry—a decrease would be a debit. Since income and expenses are adjustments in the capital section, an increase in income is a credit, and an expense is a debit.

$$
\begin{array}{ccc}
\text{Debit} & \text{Credit} & \text{Credit} \\
\text{ASSETS} = & \text{LIABILITIES} + & \text{CAPITAL} \\
+\ \text{Debit} & +\ \text{Credit} & +\quad \text{Credit} \\
-\ \text{Credit} & -\ \text{Debit} & -\quad \text{Debit} \\
& & \text{INCOME} \\
& & +\quad \text{Credit} \\
& & \text{EXPENSE} \\
& & +\quad \text{Debit}
\end{array}
$$

Figure 12-1 shows debits and credits relative to increases and decreases in these categories. Figure 12-1 also shows what type of balance the account

FIGURE 12-1
ACCOUNTING CATEGORIES AND DEBIT AND CREDIT ENTRIES.

Category	A Transaction Increasing the Amount	A Transaction Decreasing the Amount	Usual Balance Carried in the Category
Asset	Debit	Credit	Debit
Liability	Credit	Debit	Credit
Capital	Credit	Debit	Credit
Income	Credit	Debit	Credit
Expense	Debit	Credit	Debit

usually carries at any given time. Notice that increases in income have the same effect as *increases* in the capital category and that increases of expenses have the same effect as *decreases* in the capital category.

In double-entry bookkeeping, for every debit there must be an equal amount of credits, and vice versa.

CASH OR ACCRUAL ACCOUNTING

The Internal Revenue Service (IRS) requires many firms to use the accrual method of accounting. Firms in which inventory is a major part of the business are usually required to use the accrual method. However, the majority of small businesses use the cash method of accounting. Once a method of accounting is selected, the firm must stay with the method unless it receives special permission from the IRS.

Cash Method

Using the **cash accounting method,** a business records all monetary transactions, both income and expenses, as they occur. For example, a small business might pay its property taxes for the previous year in January. If January 1 is the start of the firm's fiscal year, then the deduction cannot be counted until the year it is paid, even though the tax expense was incurred during the previous year. (See Fig. 12-2.)

The cash method is usually the easiest in terms of keeping accounting records. However, it sometimes distorts the financial picture of the business when applied to a specific period of time. Because it is easier to use and understand, the cash method is the better method for most small businesses.

Accrual Method

The business that uses the **accrual accounting method** records income and expenses at the time they are earned or incurred regardless of when the monetary transaction occurs. For example, the small business in the previous ex-

FIGURE 12-2
CASH VERSUS ACCRUAL ACCOUNTING METHOD.

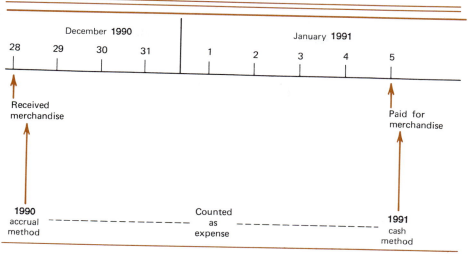

ample would record the property tax expense during the year it was incurred regardless of when it paid the tax. (See Fig. 12-2).

Figure 12-2 illustrates the cash versus the accrual method of accounting, Imagine a firm has December 31 as the closing day of its fiscal year. It has ordered merchandise that arrives December 28, 1990. It sends a check to the vendor on January 5, 1991.

If the firm uses the cash accounting method, it will not record the transaction until January 5, 1991, and it will become a reduction of cash and an expense for the year.

If the firm uses the accrual method of accounting, it will record the transaction December 28, 1990, and it will be an account payable and an expense for the year 1990. When the account is paid in 1991, it will be a reduction of cash and a reduction of a liability.

The IRS requires the accrual method in businesses where inventories play an important part in creating income. This means that many retail stores must adopt this method. The accrual method is more complex in terms of accounting records and statements. However, it is usually a more accurate picture of the financial state of the firm over a specific period of time.

BASIC BOOKS OF RECORD

Although some very small stores can manage to keep adequate accounting records with very few books, such as our barber example, most small stores need at least two basic books of record. These are the sales journal and disbursement journal.

Sales Journal

Basically, the **sales journal** is a record of daily income to the business. Figure 12-3 presents a simple sales journal for a small business that operates on a cash rather than accrual basis. Additional columns may be added to the example when additional information is desired by the small business owner. Many days of income can be shown on very few pages. In the example, the business owner found it desirable to break the sales down by product group. If the owner felt a more extensive breakdown of sales were not needed, all retail sales could have been combined into one column (it is best to have wholesale sales separate for state sales tax information). Having the separate column for sales tax is desirable because all the business owner has to do when it is time to remit sales tax collections to the state is total the column for the period.

Sales information usually comes from sales tickets made out during the day or from cash register tapes.

All income and expenditures should go through the firm's bank account. Consequently, the column entitled "Total Cash Received" is also the amount that is deposited in the bank each day. This column can be of value when reconciling the bank statement.

Firms that have other sources of income than sales may want to add another column called "Other Income." The sales journal can also be called the sales and cash receipts journal, income journal, receipts journal, and so on.

Firms that operate on the accrual basis and finance their own accounts must use different columns. Figure 12-4 illustrates a simple sales journal for these firms. The entry for April 30 in Figure 12-4 shows the business had $890 in total sales. Of this amount, $570 ($890 − $320) was in the form of cash sales, and $320 was in customer credit sales. The business collected $210 from customer credit accounts, the cash register was short $8 owing to change errors, and the business deposited $772 in the bank.

By totaling the separate columns for a specific period of time, the business is able to derive information for its financial statement (financial statements are discussed in Chapter 13). For example, by totaling its sales column, it knows the total amount of sales for the period to be used in the income statement.

Errors are easily detected in the sales journal by adding the total of all credit columns and all debit columns. If the two totals are not the same, then there is an error in the entries. Totaling of debit and credit columns for all daily entries pinpoints the error because daily entries must also balance.

Disbursement Journal

The **disbursement journal** is a record of expenditures of funds by the business. (Some small business owners attempt to keep their personal and business

FIGURE 12-3
SALES JOURNAL.

Date	Description or Account	Total Cash Received Dr.	Sales Tax Cr.	Retail Sales Product Group A Cr.	Product Group B Cr.	Other Products Cr.	Commercial Sales Cr.
Apr. 1	Daily sales	$ 433.50	$13.50	$100.00	$ 90.00	$ 80.00	$150.00
2	Daily sales	455.50	15.50	120.00	100.00	90.00	130.00
3	Daily sales	515.00	15.00	100.00	100.00	100.00	200.00
4	Daily sales	505.50	15.50	120.00	140.00	50.00	180.00
5	Daily sales	547.00	17.00	130.00	150.00	60.00	190.00
	Total for week	$2,456.50	$76.50	$570.00 (A)[1]	$580.00 (B)[1]	$380.00 (C)[1]	$850.00 (D)[1]

[1]Letters under the totals indicate where they belong in the income statement and will be discussed in Chapter 13.

FIGURE 12-4
SALES JOURNAL OF FIRM ON THE ACCRUAL BASIS AND FINANCING ITS OWN CREDIT.

Date 19__	Description and/or Account	Total Sales Cr.	Credit Sales Dr.	Collected on Account Cr.	Misc. Income and Expense Items Income Cr.	Misc. Income and Expense Items Expense Dr.	Cash Deposited in Bank Dr.
4/30	Daily summary	$890.00	$320.00	$210.00			$772.00
	Cash short					$8.00	
5/1	Daily summary	940.00	290.00	180.00			832.00
	Cash over				$2.00		

funds together, but this is a serious error and causes many problems.) With only one exception, all expenditures of the firm should be paid by check. The one exception is the petty cash fund. The petty cash fund is maintained to pay in cash for items of very small value (usually less than one dollar). However, a check should be processed through this journal to establish and replenish the petty cash fund. Records of expenditures from the petty cash fund should also be maintained by the business for tax and control purposes.

Figure 12-5 shows a simple disbursement journal. (Additional columns may also be added to the disbursement journal if needed by the small business.) Daily entries in the disbursement journal must balance in terms of debits and credits. The total of the columns must also balance in terms of debits and credits. Errors are easily recognized by checking debit and credit totals in the columns.

At the end of specific periods of time (the end of every month is recommended), totals of the columns in the disbursement journal may be used to derive various items for accounting statements. Also, combining information from both the sales journal and the disbursement journal provides valuable information for the business. For example, the total of "Total Cash Received from Sales" or "Cash Deposited in Banks" and the total of the "Amount of Check" column is an excellent device for checking bank statements.

Firms should recognize that when they write payroll checks, the amount deducted from the salaries of employees no longer belongs to them. It belongs, at that point, to the federal government. Some small firms get into cash flow binds and use sales tax, deducted FICA taxes, and/or deducted income taxes to meet debt. This is a serious mistake because the government agencies have vast powers to close the business and sell assets to obtain the money that is due.

Accounts Receivable

Most retail small businesses no longer carry 30-day charge accounts (discussed in detail in Chapter 20) because of the money required and the cost and time involved in keeping records and collecting accounts. Instead, they accept bank credit cards for sales that are essentially the same as a cash sale. However, some businesses still carry 30-day charge accounts. Those firms that do must keep records of each customer's charges and payments. Figure 12-6 shows a simple **accounts receivable** card that can be maintained on each customer.

The firms may keep these on cards that are easily reproduced on a copier and put in a window envelope and mailed to the customer on the billing day. They may also be maintained on a computer, and the computer can print out monthly statements to send customers (the computer can also print the mailing labels).

FIGURE 12-5
DISBURSEMENT JOURNAL.

Date	Payee or Account	Check No.	Amount of Check Cr.	Merchandise Purchased Product Group A Dr.	Product Group B Dr.	Other Products Dr.	Commercial Products Dr.	Office Supplies Dr.	Gross Salaries and Wages Dr.	Payroll Deductions FICA Cr.	Income Tax Cr.	Utilities Dr.	Other Expenses Dr.	Nonexpense Payments Dr.
Apr. 1	Smith Wholesale	101	$ 100.00	$100.00										
1	Alford Supply	102	120.00		$120.00									
2	Jones Supply Co.	103	150.00			$150.00								
2	Johnson Products	104	100.00				$100.00							
2	Austin Office Sup.	105	30.00					$30.00						
2	Austin Utilities	106	200.00									$200.00		
3	Trust Insurance Co.	107	50.00										$ 50.00	
3	SBA on note ($20.00 interest)	108	220.00										20.00	$200.00
4	Texas International (airline ticket)	109	140.00										140.00	
4	Petty cash fund	110	25.00										25.00	
5	Weekly payroll	111	420.00						$500.00	$30.00	$50.00			
5	State of Texas	112	76.50											76.50
5	Payroll taxes paid to IRS	113	60.00										60.00	
5	FICA and income tax deduction paid to IRS	114	80.00											80.00
	Total for week		$1771.50	$100.00 (E)[1]	$120.00 (F)[1]	$150.00 (G)[1]	$100.00 (H)[1]	$30.00 (I)[1]	$500.00 (J)[1]	$30.00	$50.00	$200.00 (K)[1]	$295.00 (L)[1]	$356.50 (M)[1]

[1] Letters below the totals indicate where they belong in the income statement, which will be discussed in Chapter 13.

FIGURE 12-6
ACCOUNTS RECEIVABLE CARD.

Mr. & Mrs. Joe Paul Jackson
3232 Blue Herron Road
Santa Monica, Calif. 90401

Date	Item	Charge	Payment	Balance
1/20	Hardware	$28.50		$28.50
2/5			$28.50	0

MAINTAINING THE ACCOUNTING SYSTEM

Small businesses can maintain a bookkeeping system by using a computer or a manual system. Most firms can use computer hardware and software that is relatively inexpensive today to perform their financial recordkeeping and accounting analysis. The software is easy to learn and provides a complete system.

Other firms have such a low volume of recordkeeping requirements that they can easily use a manual system for their financial control. They may use a public accountant to design their accounting system. Also, there are firms that have established general bookkeeping systems and have created copyrighted books and forms for small businesses to use in maintaining their financial records.

Small business owners may use public accountants to maintain their accounting records and analysis. They perform the complete bookkeeping service, auditing, periodic preparation of accounting statements, and preparation of income and other tax returns. Some small business firms perform their own bookkeeping but use public accountants to perform some or all of these other accounting functions.

No matter what system owners use, they must be constantly exposed to their financial records and accounting analysis. This insures that they are aware of their financial status at all times.

FINANCIAL CONTROL AND COMPUTERS

Greatly reduced cost and capabilities of computers, particularly microcomputers, have made them feasible for almost all small businesses. They can greatly increase the efficiency of small businesses in many areas, such as inventory control, theft control, and word processing. Two of the more important functions that may be performed with computers are cash control and accounting.

Cash control can be achieved by tying the cash register to the computer. The inventory control function and cash control function can then be performed by the computer from input into the cash register at the time of sale. As the inventory change is made, the computer records the selling price and totals the sales at the end of the day and reports how much should be in the cash register. Even if a cash register is not tied to the computer, it is possible to run the total inventory sold during the day from records in the computer and compare them to the total amount of cash from the register.

There are many software packages (computer programs) small businesses may use to perform their accounting functions. Examples of some of these software packages for microcomputers and some of the more important things they do for the small business are listed below.

Accounts Receivable System
Maintains on a continuing basis all customer accounts.
Calculates and records interest charged on the accounts.
Calculates and prints statements to be sent to the computers.

Payroll System
Calculates withholding items from each employee's wages.
Calculates payroll taxes to be paid by the business.
Calculates amount of paycheck for each employee and prints checks.
Prints payroll journals.
Calculates and prints W-2 forms at the end of the year.

Accounts Payable
Maintains accounts payable records.
Reports complete vendor listing, cash requirements, and so forth.
Calculates and prints checks.

General Ledger
(This takes the place of the sales and disbursement journals.)

Posts to all accounts (cash, sales, supplies, etc.).
Posts checks to accounts.
Calculates and prints income statements.
Calculates and prints trial balances.
Calculates and prints balance sheets.

Software packages have become very user friendly. You do not have to be a computer programmer to maintain your financial recordkeeping on a computer.

CASH CONTROL

Daily cash control is important to a small business that handles volumes of cash, particularly retail stores. The function of cash control is to compare and balance what is actually received in cash to what should have been received.

Having less cash on hand at the end of the day than should have been received may be the result of (1) recording or ringing up an amount larger than the sale, (2) money taken from the register without being recorded, or (3) giving a customer too much change.

Having more cash on hand at the end of the day than should have been received may result from (1) not recording or ringing up a sale, (2) not ringing up or recording the full amount of a sale, or (3) not giving a customer enough change.

No matter what the cause of the overage or shortage of cash, it should be detected and steps taken to help prevent any future errors. Of course, any firm handling large volumes of cash transactions will have some small amount of human error that cannot be totally eliminated.

In addition, cash control is vital to preventing employee theft. No one likes to think that their employees would steal from the business, but the fact is that billions of dollars are lost each year to employee theft. In fact, many authorities feel employee theft exceeds losses from both shoplifting and burglary.

Change Fund

Most retail stores must have currency and coins on hand at the start of business each day to make change. A small business should determine what amount of change is needed for each cash register based on past history. This should include a specific number of tens, fives, ones, halves, quarters, nickels, and pennies.

This change should be available in each cash register at the start of the day's business. The same amount should be deducted from the total cash in the register at the end of the day and kept for the next day. All other cash should be placed in the night depository of the bank. The **change fund** should be left in a safe overnight if possible and, if not, in the cash register itself. Some businesses that handle excessively large amounts of cash for change and that open later than the bank opens, deposit all their cash in the bank each night. They then obtain cash for the next day's change fund from the bank before the store opens.

Sales and Cash Receipts Balance

A **Sales and cash receipts record,** as shown in Figure 12-7, should be completed at the end of the business each day.

FIGURE 12-7
SALES AND CASH RECEIPTS.

Date 5/1/90
Total Sales

1. Cash sales		$650.00
2. Credit sales		290.00
3. Total sales		$940.00

Cash Receipts

4. Cash sales		$650.00
5. Collections on accounts receivable		180.00
6. Total cash to be accounted for		$830.00

Cash on Hand

7. Cash in register or till:		
Coins	$ 30.00	
Bills	609.00	
Checks	268.00	
Total cash in register or till		$907.00
8. Less change fund		75.00
9. Total cash deposit		$832.00
10. Cash short		$
11. Cash over		$ 2.00

All sales during the day should be recorded on either a cash register, if used, or some other record, such as a sales slip, if a register is not used. There should also be some method of identifying cash and credit sales. Credit tickets, which are posted to customer accounts, are usually used to identify credit sales and then subtracted from total sales on the cash register to arrive at the amount of cash sales.

Cash that is received from customers on their credit accounts should be recorded separately. In addition, any withdrawals from the register should be recorded with full information and placed in the register or cash till.

The small business firm that is able to identify cash sales, credit sales, cash received on customer credit accounts, and cash withdrawals from the business has the information necessary to complete the sales and cash receipt form at the end of the business day. Completion of this form identifies errors and the amount of the error. The sales and cash receipts form may also be combined with inventory control techniques (discussed in Chapter 15) and aid in the control of mistakes, shoplifting, and employee theft.

Financial recordkeeping, as discussed in this chapter, is vital to the day-to-day operations of the small business firm. It must be performed adequately if the small business is to realize the full benefits of accounting analysis, which is presented in the next chapter.

SUMMARY OF KEY POINTS

1. Recordkeeping systems should be custom designed for each business, and they do not have to be complicated for small businesses.
2. The accounting equation is stated thusly: assets = liabilities + capital (net worth).
3. The bookkeeping system is based on the concept of keeping the accounting equation in balance by the process of double-entry bookkeeping.
4. The cash method of accounting means that transactions are recorded when there is a cash transaction. The accrual method records income and expenses at the time they are earned or incurred regardless of when the monetary transaction occurs.
5. The basic books of record are the sales journal and the disbursement journal.
6. The sales journal is a record of daily income to the business.
7. The disbursement journal is a record of all expenditures (except for petty cash items) made by the business.
8. If the small business grants 30-day charge accounts, it must record charges, payments, and balances on accounts receivable cards or in its computer.
9. Most firms can use inexpensive computer hardware and software to perform their financial recordkeeping and accounting analysis. Other firms that have a low volume of recordkeeping requirements may use a manual system designed by public accountants or copyrighted bookkeeping systems.
10. The function of cash control is to compare and balance what is actually received in cash to what should have been received.
11. Cash control is vital to preventing employee theft.
12. Most retail stores must have currency and coins on hand each day to make change for customers.
13. A sales and cash receipts form should be completed at the end of each business day.

DISCUSSION QUESTIONS

1. Does every small business firm need the same type of accounting system?
2. What is the relationship between double-entry bookkeeping and the accounting equation?
3. What is the relationship among income, expenses, and capital?
4. What is a sales journal, and how do you find errors in its entries?
5. What is a disbursement journal, and how do you find errors in its entries?
6. What are the various ways a firm may use to keep its books?
7. Why is cash control important?
8. How does the change fund operate?
9. How does the sales and cash receipts record function?
10. What is the difference between cash and accrual methods of accounting?

THE BUSINESS PLAN: FINANCIAL RECORDKEEPING AND CASH CONTROL

_____ Can you use the cash method of accounting?
Contact the IRS to see if you can use the cash method of accounting. If you are allowed to use it, it is probably the best method for you. If you must use the accrual method, you may need an accountant to help you.

_____ Can you use a manual bookkeeping system?
Unless you have a large number of accounting transactions each day, you should start out using a manual system so you have more intimate knowledge of your financial dealings and status. If you have a large number of transactions, you should obtain a computer of the size you need and inquire about software packages.

_____ What column do you need in your sales journal?

_____ What columns do you need in your disbursement journal?
Construct your sales journal and disbursement journal using the examples in the chapter as guides.

_____ Will you need to offer types of credit that will require you to maintain accounts receivable cards? It is usually better to accept bank credit cards unless competition forces you to carry customer accounts.

_____ Who will keep your accounting books—you, employee, part-time employee, or public accountant? You will probably need an accountant to file your income tax return each year.

_____ Will you need a change fund?

—— Can you avoid keeping currency overnight in the business? If not, how will you keep it safe?

—— Will you need a sales and cash receipts form to be completed each business day?

ENTREPRENEURIAL PROJECTS

Visit a small retail establishment, and find out the following information.

1. What type of bookkeeping system does the business use?
2. Who keeps the books, and are they audited?
3. What method does the business use for cash control? Does it use a daily cash and sales receipt form? If so, compare it to the one in the textbook, and try to obtain a copy to show the class.
4. Does the business use the cash or the accrual accounting method? What is its reason for using this method?

Visit a software store and obtain information on software packages that are available to small businesses for financial recordkeeping.

CASE A

Davis Shoe Store

Sandra Davis owns a shoe store that is located in the central business district in a small town. Davis Shoe Store sells medium-priced shoes for men, women, and children. Sandra carries 30-day charge accounts for some customers who have traded with her for a long time. There is only one cash register, and it starts each day with a $75 change fund. The store has one full-time clerk in addition to Sandra. Sandra keeps her own accounting records, but does have a CPA prepare her federal income tax return each year. Sandra's store uses the accrual method of accounting.

On January 15 the store had the following transactions.

1. The cash register tape recorded $342 in sales for the day.
2. Customer charge tickets showed $80 in credit sales for the day (these are rung up on the cash register along with cash sales).
3. Checks and cash totaling $70 were received from customers on their charge accounts.
4. The following checks were issued by the store:

Check No.	To	For	Amount
524	Acme Shoe Corporation	Shoes	$125
525	City Utilities	Utilities	150
526	Sam Robertson	Weekly payroll	161 (total earned $200, withheld income tax $25, FICA $14)
527	First City Bank	Loan payment	280 (interest $100, principal $180)

5. There was $406 in the cash register in cash and checks at the end of the day.

Questions*

1. Set up a sales journal similar to the one in Figure 12-4 and a disbursement journal similar to the one in Figure 12-5, and record the day's transactions in them.
2. Set up and complete a sales and cash receipt form for the day.
3. Do you think Sandra would have been better off to use the cash method rather than the accrual method of accounting?
4. Do you think Sandra should keep her own books? Should she keep them on a computer?

---

*Forms are provided in the Student Study Guide for this case.

CASE B
Pete's Parts (A)

Peter Wagner worked for a wholesale automobile parts warehouse for 16 years before he decided to open an automobile parts store that would sell retail to individuals and wholesale to service stations, garages, and other businesses that bought automobile parts. Pete found a building for rent on a busy street and remodeled it to fit what he felt was a good layout for a parts store. The store has been open for a week. Business has been good, and Pete feels he is making a profit.

All retail sales are for cash only, but he does carry 30-day accounts for his wholesale customers. Pete employs three people—one full-time and two part-time employees.

Pete's experience with the wholesale automobile parts warehouse did not include an exposure to accounting, and Pete feels he does not have the knowledge to set up his books and keep them.

You have been hired to establish Pete's bookkeeping system and train one of the employees to operate it. A study of Pete's records reveals the following transactions for the first week.

CASH RECEIVED FOR THE FIRST WEEK

Day	Total Cash Received from Retail Sales	Sales Tax	Total Cash Received from Wholesale Sales[1]
May 1	$126	$ 6	$40
2	105	5	20
3	147	7	50
4	126	6	60
5	168	8	80
6	210	10	20

[1] Sales tax is not collected in this state on wholesale sales.

CHECKBOOK ENTRIES FOR THE FIRST WEEK

May 1	U.S. Post Office	(stamps)	$ 15
2	Sam's Office Products	(office supplies)	$ 25
3	World Parts Suppliers, Inc.	(parts)	200
4	Menton Insurance Agency	(insurance payment)	60
5	Jones Supply Co.	(parts)	40
6	Week's payroll (gross salaries, $200; FICA withheld, $13; income tax withheld, $30)		157
7	First State Bank (payment on loan: principal, $50, interest, $2)		52

After talking to Pete, you feel he needs the following columns in his disbursement journal: "Parts," "Utilities," "Office Supplies," "Gross Salaries," FICA Withheld," "Income Tax Withheld," "Miscellaneous Expenses," and Nonexpense Items."

Jim's Service Station started trading with Pete the first day he was open. He bought parts on credit the following days: 5/1, $10; 5/2, $15; 5/4, $10. He came in 5/5 and paid his entire bill for the week.

You feel Pete should operate on the cash accounting basis and have his sales broken down only into retail and wholesale sales.

Questions

1. Set up a sales journal similar to the one in Figure 12-3, and record the week's sales.
2. Set up a Disbursement Journal similar to the one in Figure 12-5, and record the week's transactions.
3. Set up an accounts receivable card for Jim's Service Station, and record the week's charges and payment.
   (Note: Forms are provided in the Student Study Guide.)
   (Save a copy of your journals for use in Chapter 13.)

KEY WORDS

CHAPTER 13

ACCOUNTING STATEMENTS AND ANALYSIS

LEARNING GOALS

After reading this chapter, you will understand:

1 That a balance sheet is a measure of the basic accounting equation: assets = liabilities + capital.

2 That the balance sheet is an estimate of value of the business for one moment in time.

3 The various uses of the balance sheet by small business owners and other groups.

4 That the income statement measures profit or loss over a period of time by subtracting all expenses from all income of the business.

5 The various uses of the income statement by small business owners, investors, creditors, and governmental agencies.

6 That the budget is an estimate of next year's income statement and is a major planning and control device for the small business.

7 Why the cash flow statement is important to the small business owner and the investor.

8 How to create a monthly income and cash flow statement from the information in the sales and disbursement journals.

9 Various accounting ratios and how they act as guidelines to the small business owner.

ENTREPRENEURIAL PROFILE

Joe Pacheco

CERTIFIED PUBLIC ACCOUNTANT

Sound management, especially sound financial management, is critical to the success of a fledgling business: that has been Joe Pacheco's message to new business owners in Utah. Pacheco, a Utah certified public accountant, has also been an articulate spokesman on behalf of small business's contributions to a dynamic economy. Within governmental agencies and business organizations, he has worked to ensure their profitability and growth.

Joe opened his own practice in 1969, performing accounting and tax services for small commercial businesses. While he developed a primary expertise in auditing, he also counseled many small businesses in accounting system design, taxation, management assistance, and other accounting services. In 1980 he established his present business in Murray, Utah.

In his work, Pacheco saw a need for educating the new business owner and took a special interest in those minority and women business owners who may have been less equipped by education or experience for managing a business. Pacheco cooperated in organizing the first Women and Business conference in the state of Utah; now one of the largest in the western states, the annual conference includes many courses in financial management.

Stressing the need for good recordkeeping, Pacheco has often set up accounting systems on a gratis basis for startup companies. In 1975, he took a leave of absence from his firm to volunteer his services as acting director of the Minority Economic Development Coalition of Utah, a nonprofit financial and management assistance organization, until a new director could be hired.

In 1977, under contract with the Small Business Administration, he assisted with the special problems of minority small business owners in the 8(a) procurement program, helping them find ways to make their businesses more profitable—or to make the difficult decision to terminate the venture. In letters and discussions with members of Congress, he advocated improvements in assistance targeted to minority and disadvantaged business owners.

Pacheco has taken a special interest in the education of young entrepreneurs: while

Accounting statements are very important to the small business firm because they provide a basis for planning and control in the business. The principal accounting statements are the balance sheet, the income statement, the budget, and the cash flow statement.

BALANCE SHEET

The **balance sheet** provides a measure of the value of the business at one moment in time. Balance sheets should be prepared periodically for the small business firm. Usually, small businesses have accountants prepare a balance sheet at the end of their fiscal year (January 1 and July 1 are the most common). (See Fig. 13-1.)

Components of the Balance Sheet

The balance sheet is a measure of the basic accounting equation.

$$\text{Assets} = \text{Liabilities} + \text{Capital}$$

Assets

Assets are usually divided into three categories in the balance sheet—current assets, fixed assets, and intangible assets.

Current Assets
Current assets are assets that can be easily and quickly converted into liquid assets (cash). Current assets include such items as cash, accounts receivable, notes receivable that are due in less than a year's time, raw materials inventory, finished goods inventory, supplies, and stocks and bonds of other corporations that are traded regularly on the securities market. Generally, most current assets are used up or change in amounts on hand over relatively short periods of time.

FIGURE 13-1
BALANCE SHEET.

DOVE WHOLESALE PAINT COMPANY
Balance Sheet
January 1, 1990

Assets
Current Assets

Cash		$ 9,000	
Accounts receivable	$ 10,000		
Allowance for bad debts	500	9,500	
Merchandise		24,000	
Supplies		2,000	
General Motors stock		3,500	
Total current assets			$ 48,000

Fixed Assets

Land		12,000	
Building	130,000		
Depreciation allowance	40,000	90,000	
Equipment	60,000		
Depreciation allowance	15,000	45,000	
Delivery truck	4,000		
Depreciation allowance	1,000	3,000	
Note receivable from Acme Products due 1/1/91		2,000	
Total fixed assets			152,000

Intangible Assets

Organizational costs	1,000	
Total intangible assets		1,000
Total Assets		$201,000

Liabilities
Current Liabilities

Accounts payable	$18,000	
Income tax payable	1,500	
FICA tax payable	500	
Total current liabilities		$ 20,000

Long-Term Liabilities

Mortgage payable	25,000	
Note payable to bank 6/1/93	5,000	
Total long-term liabilities		30,000

Capital

Carl Dove, capital	151,000
Total Liabilities and Capital	$201,000

Fixed Assets   Fixed assets are items of property that are not used up over short periods of time. They usually are not easily converted into cash, and they often are depreciated over long periods of time. Fixed assets (sometimes called plant assets) include such items as land, buildings, machinery, equipment, automobiles, trucks, and notes receivable that are due in excess of one year's time.

Intangible Assets   Intangible assets are items that have value to the business but do not exist as tangible property. Some intangible assets that are sometimes listed in the balance sheet are goodwill (the reputation of the business), patents, copyrights, and organizational costs (cost of establishing a form of ownership).

Liabilities

Liabilities Are debt of the business. Liabilities are broken down in the balance sheet into current liabilities and long-term liabilities.

Current Liabilities   Current liabilities consist of debts that are due in less than one year's time. Current liabilities include such items of debt as accounts payable, notes payable within a year, and cash that is paid to governmental agencies on a regular basis (e.g., income taxes withheld from employee salaries and paid to the government every three months).

Long-Term Liabilities   Long-term liabilities are debts that are due in more than a year's time from the date of the balance sheet. Long-term liabilities include such items as notes payable that are due in excess of one year's time, mortgages, and bonds payable.

Capital

Capital is a measure of the value of the business to the owner or owners. It is a measure of all assets minus all liabilities. The result is the net worth of the business.

Characteristics of the Balance Sheet

The balance sheet is both an estimate of the value of the business and an estimate for only one moment in time.

Estimate

Except for cash, almost all other assets listed in the balance sheet are estimates. All accounts receivable cannot be collected, and an estimated amount is subtracted for bad debts. Prices of inventories change from time to time, and their value is not always certain. All fixed assets are estimates. Buildings, machinery, equipment, automobiles, and trucks are listed at cost, and depreciation is estimated and deducted each year. To illustrate, many firms have depreciated buildings and machinery over several years and carry them on their books at scrap value; yet they still have considerable market value. Intangible assets, such as goodwill and patents, are very subjective judgments and are extremely difficult to value because they are intangible.

Liabilities are accurate in the balance sheet because they are specific debts the business owes. By subtracting accurate liabilities from estimated assets, one obtains an estimated capital section of the balance sheet. The only real way to determine the exact value of a business would be to sell it.

Moment in Time

Theoretically, the balance sheet measures the value of the business at one moment in time and represents only that moment in time. Assets, such as machinery, are used up a little each day. Consequently, the estimated value of machinery, on the balance sheet, is an estimate for the day the balance sheet is prepared. In addition, raw materials are constantly being used up and regularly being replaced. Therefore, the value of inventory is an estimate only for the day of the balance sheet date. Liabilities are continually being incurred and paid by the business; consequently, liabilities on the balance sheet represent only that day's amount. Because assets and liabilities change from day to day, capital changes from day to day and is estimated for that day only on the balance sheet.

Uses of the Balance Sheet

Because balance sheets are prepared periodically, they present measures of changes in the business. By looking at balance sheets of several years, one can recognize growth or decline in various phases of the company's financial position. The balance sheet also reveals the company's ability to meet both short-term and long-term debt. By computing ratios from balance sheet data, the firm is able to recognize weaknesses or strengths in its financial position. Balance sheets are also important to creditors who make loans to the business because they reveal the firm's potential for repayment of debts.

INCOME STATEMENT

The **income statement** is a measure of how the business has performed over a specific period of time—usually a month or a year. (See Fig. 13-2.) It measures all income less all expenses to arrive at the profit or loss generated by the business for the period it covers. The income statement is also called the expense and revenue summary, profit and loss statement, income and expense statement, and so on.

Components of the Income Statement

The main components of the income statement are income and expenses.

FIGURE 13-2
INCOME STATEMENT.

DOVE WHOLESALE PAINT COMPANY
Income Statement for 1990

Revenue from Sales			$430,000
Cost of Goods Sold			
Beginning inventory 1/1/90	$ 30,000		
Purchases	264,000		
Merchandise available for sale	294,000		
Less: Ending inventory 12/31/90	24,000		
Total cost of goods sold			270,000
Gross Profit on Sales			$160,000
Operating Expenses			
Advertising	20,000		
Insurance	6,000		
Depreciation expenses			
Building	4,000		
Equipment	6,000		
Truck	1,000		
Sales personnel	35,000		
Entertainment	2,000		
Travel	1,000		
Total operating expenses		$75,000	
General Expenses			
Office expense	12,000		
Postage	800		
Telephone	1,200		
Payroll taxes	3,000		
Utilities	4,000		
Total general expenses		21,000	
Other Expenses			
Interest expense	3,000		
Bad check expense	1,000		
Total other expenses		4,000	
Total Expenses			100,000
Net Income			$ 60,000

Income

All **income** that flows into the firm is listed in this section. There are several items that may come under the heading of income, such as revenue from sales, interest earned, and dividends earned.

Expenses

Expenses in the income statement are usually broken down into cost of goods sold (in retail and wholesale firms), cost of goods manufactured (in manufacturing firms), operating expenses, general expenses, and other expenses.

Cost of Goods Sold **Cost of goods sold** in wholesale and retail firms is comprised of the beginning inventory for the period plus all purchases for the period minus the inventory at the end of the period. (See Fig. 13-3.)

Cost of Goods Manufactured **Cost of goods manufactured** in manufacturing operations is comprised of all direct labor, raw materials, and factory overhead (depreciation on building and machinery, supplies, supervisors' salaries, etc.) that have gone into the manufacturing process during the year. (See Fig. 13-4.)

Operating Expenses Operating expenses are expenses that contribute directly to the sale of goods. Some of the items commonly included under operating expenses are advertising, insurance, truck depreciation, salespersons' salaries and commissions, entertainment, and travel.

General Expenses Items usually presented under general expenses are those that are indirect costs incurred in the administration of the business. Some of the expenses commonly included under this category are office expenses, postage, telephones, payroll taxes, and utilities.

Other Expenses The category other expenses usually contains all other items that do not seem to fit into the other expenses categories, items such as interest expense and bad checks expense.

FIGURE 13-3
COST OF GOODS SOLD SECTION OF THE INCOME STATEMENT FOR A RETAIL FIRM.

Cost of Goods Sold	
Beginning merchandise inventory 1/1/90	$160,000
Purchases for the year	150,000
Merchandise available for sale	$200,000
Less: Ending inventory 12/31/90	40,000
Total cost of merchandise sold	$160,000

FIGURE 13-4

COST OF GOODS MANUFACTURED SECTION OF THE INCOME STATEMENT FOR A MANUFACTURING COMPANY.

Cost of Goods Manufactured	
Direct labor	$120,000
Raw materials	80,000
Factory overhead	90,000
Total cost of goods manufactured	$290,000

Characteristics of the Income Statement

The income statement is an estimate of profit or loss, and it measures profit or loss over a period of time.

Estimate

The income statement, shown in Figure 13-2, presents several items of expenses that exist in the form of depreciation. Building, equipment, and truck depreciations for the year appear as operating expenses. If any expense items are an estimate, then the total expenses figure for the firm is an estimate. Income for the firm is accurate, but when the total of all expenses is an estimate, then the profit or loss figure is an estimate.

Measures Profit over a Period of Time

The income statement deducts all expenses from all income for a specific period of time to arrive at the firm's profit or loss for that period. The income statement usually is prepared once a year at the end of the fiscal period; however, it may be prepared for shorter periods. Some business firms feel they gain better control of their business by preparing their income statements monthly.

Uses of the Income Statement

The small business firm uses its income statement to analyze the success of operations of the business over a specific period of time. Investments, purchases of assets, and distribution of profit are just a few of the decisions that rely on the information provided in the income statement.

The income statement is also used by other groups. Federal income tax returns of the business could not be properly prepared without the income statement. Other government agencies, including various state and local taxing agencies, require income statements from the business for their use. Creditors and investors consider the income statement very valuable, and few would be willing to loan or invest money without its availability for their analysis.

DEPRECIATION AND PROFIT

As a general rule, firms should write off depreciable items as fast as the Internal Revenue Service (IRS) will allow. A simple illustration of the benefits could be illustrated by the following example. Suppose a firm saved $1000 the first year it depreciated the asset and invested it in a money market fund paying 10 percent interest. The business would earn $100 the first year in interest on the amount saved on its taxes. Of course, it will save less in later years by accelerating depreciation, but it will have earned more interest in the early years to reinvest. Inflation would also be a factor in that the firm can realize today's purchasing power.

Firms may manipulate their depreciation in various ways to show different levels of profit. Suppose you bought a light delivery truck to use in your business that cost $25,000. You normally keep delivery trucks for seven years, and you expect to use this one for seven years. The rates currently allowed by the IRS the first year on this class of asset are (1) straight line for five years, (2) any straight line in excess of five years elected by the taxpayer, or (3) modified accelerated cost recovery system (MACRS) of 200 percent declining-balance method. Once a method of depreciation is elected, the firm cannot change it without permission from the IRS. In addition, the IRS has a history of changing the allowable methods every few years. These changes affect newly acquired assets only, the old assets continue to be depreciated as they were started. Under the currently allowable methods of depreciation, your truck could be depreciated the first year as follows.

Depreciation Method	Years Depreciated	First-Year Depreciated
Straight line	7	$ 3,571
Straight line	5	5,000
MACRS	5	10,000

This firm could show a profit that could deviate by as much as $6,429 the first year depending on which of the three methods the firm selects. People investing in or loaning a business money should realize that the income statement is an estimate, and they should check such items as the method of depreciation very carefully.

BUDGET

In reality, the **budget** is the estimate of next year's income statement. It is a major planning and control device for the small business firm. (See Fig. 13-5.)

Components of the Budget

The budget is comprised of (1) income, (2) cost of goods sold or cost of goods manufactured, (3) controllable expenses, and (4) uncontrollable expenses.

FIGURE 13-5
BUDGET.

DOVE WHOLESALE PAINT COMPANY
Budgeted Income Statement for 1991 (All figures are estimates)

Expected Sales Revenue		$450,000
Expected Cost of Goods Sold		275,000
Estimated Gross Margin		$175,000
Controllable Expenses		
Advertising	$25,000	
Sales personnel	37,000	
Entertainment	1,500	
Travel	2,500	
Total controllable expenses		66,000
Margin for Uncontrollable Expenses and Income		$109,000
Uncontrollable Expenses		
Insurance	$ 6,000	
Depreciation expenses		
Building	4,000	
Equipment	1,000	
Truck	1,000	
Office expense	12,000	
Postage	900	
Telephones	1,300	
Payroll taxes	3,600	
Utilities	4,200	
Interest expense	3,000	
Total uncontrollable expenses		42,000
Estimated Net Income Before Federal Income Taxes		$ 67,000

Income

Expected sales revenue is forecast by the business and is the basis for almost all the budget. The number of units forecast to be sold during the next year determines the cost of goods sold or manufactured, controllable expenses, and, to some extent, uncontrollable expenses.

Cost of Goods Sold; Cost of Goods Manufactured

The cost of goods sold section in retail and wholesale firms is estimated usually on the basis of past experiences in markup on the total volume of expected sales. For example, the income statement in Figure 13-2 shows the firm's cost of goods sold is usually about 60 percent of sales. Therefore, with expected sales of $450,000 in its budget, it can expect about 60 percent or $275,000 to be the cost of goods sold figure in the budget.

The cost of goods manufactured section in manufacturing firms is estimated by taking the total number of units estimated to be manufactured for the next year and multiplying by the standard per unit labor and raw material cost. For example, if it requires $1.40 in direct labor and $1.60 of raw materials to produce one unit, it would cost $300,000 of direct labor and raw materials to produce 100,000 units. Factory overhead is usually applied on a past experience basis, usually as a percentage of the total direct labor cost. To illustrate, if factory overhead has usually been about 60 percent of direct labor costs, then 60 percent of the forecasted direct labor expense would be used as the forecasted factory overhead expense.

Controllable and Uncontrollable Expenses

Instead of operating expenses, general expenses, and other expenses shown in the income statement, the budget uses controllable and uncontrollable expense categories.

Controllable expenses are those expenses that the firm has some control over. Advertising, number of sales personnel, entertainment, and travel may be controlled by the firm.

Uncontrollable expenses are expenses that are relatively fixed if the business is operating in a normal business manner. Insurance, all depreciation, office expenses, postage, telephones, payroll taxes, utilities, and interest are expenses that occur as a result of normal business activity. (See Fig. 13-5.)

Characteristics of the Budget

The characteristics of the budget are the same as the income statement because it contains the same items and estimates profit or loss over a future period. Whereas the income statement contains many items that are accurate and some that are estimates, all figures in the budget are estimates because they are amounts forecasted for a future period of time. The budget also covers a period of time, usually the coming year. However, some firms do have budgets for shorter periods of time. They forecast the budget for the next year and then break it down into months or quarters.

Uses of the Budget

The budget is one of the most important accounting tools small business owners have at their disposal. It helps to control the business, and it aids them in making decisions that concern the business.

The budget is a valuable controlling device in that it is a standard against which to measure current performance of the business. The business has expenses on a continuing basis, and the manager can compare these against those projected in the budget. If the current expenditures deviate from the budgeted amount, the manager knows something is wrong and may then investigate to discover the problem and correct it.

The budget also tells the manager what funds are available for different expenditures. The expected profit figure will allow the manager to estimate how much profit can be taken out of the business and how much will be left for purchases of fixed assets, such as machinery.

The budget is also an excellent device for forecasting future financial needs. For example, the manager knows of financial needs months in advance. As a result, he or she is able to arrange for the money in advance rather than waiting until the need arises.

CASH FLOW STATEMENT

The **cash flow statement** is a measure of changes in cash the business has on hand from month to month. It records or projects all cash receipts less all cash disbursements. A business may use the cash flow statement as a record of what has occurred to cash or as a projection into the future to determine future needs for cash or as both. (See Fig. 13-6).

FIGURE 13-6
CASH FLOW STATEMENT.

DOVE WHOLESALE PAINT COMPANY
Projected Cash Flow

	January	February	March
Beginning Cash Balance	$ 9,000	$11,850	$19,825
Cash Receipts			
Cash sales	22,000	23,000	23,000
Cash from accounts receivable	8,000	14,000	16,000
Total cash received for month	$30,000	$37,000	$39,000
Cash Disbursements:			
Cash payments on accounts payable	18,000	20,000	20,000
Advertising	2,500	2,500	2,500
Insurance	500	500	500
Sales salaries and commissions	3,000	3,000	3,000
Entertainment	150	125	125
Travel	200	100	100
Office expenses	1,000	1,000	1,000
Postage	100	100	100
Telephone	100	100	100
Utilities	350	350	350
Interest expense	250	250	250
Payroll taxes	0	0	900
Total cash disbursed for month	$26,150	$28,025	$28,925
Cash Increase or Decrease from Operations	3,850	8,975	10,075
Mortgage Payment	1,000	1,000	1,000
Net Change in Cash Position	2,850	7,975	9,075
Cash Balance Carried into Next Month	$11,850	$19,825	$28,900

Components of the Cash Flow Statement

The cash flow statement takes the amount of cash on hand at the beginning of the month, adds all cash receipts to the balance, and subtracts all cash disbursements to arrive at the amount of cash on hand at the end of the month.

Cash Receipts

Cash receipts include all funds that are received in the form of cash. It usually includes such items as cash sales and cash received in payment of accounts receivable. It does not include sales in the form of credit.

Cash Disbursements

This category contains all expenses, purchases, and payments made in cash. It does not include depreciation or amounts for any items purchased on credit. The cash disbursement category often includes such items as advertising, payments to vendors for purchases, insurance premiums, salaries, travel, utilities, office expenses, and long-term debt payments. Such items as payroll taxes, which are incurred monthly but are only paid quarterly, are not recorded until they are actually paid.

Characteristics of the Cash Flow Statement

The cash flow statement is accurate when it is a record of past receipts and disbursements and an estimate when it is projected for future months. The cash flow statement is usually calculated on a monthly basis for an entire year.

Uses of the Cash Flow Statement

The projected cash flow statement is important to small business owners because it identifies future problems with cash. The cash flow statement will warn them months in advance when there will be a cash shortage and tell them how much so that they are able to plan in advance. By knowing in advance, they can often obtain debt funds at the best interest rate available to them. If it shows surplus funds will be available that are not needed in the business, it allows them to make arrangements for use of the funds in other investments.

For an investor, it is one of the most important accounting statements he or she can use. It is possible for a business to show a loss on the income statement and still be an attractive investment. For instance, it is quite common for entrepreneurs to build apartments, take accelerated depreciation on them, show a loss on the income statement for several years, and still have increases in cash each month even after making the mortgage payment. By doing this, the entrepreneur usually keeps the apartments until they are depreciated to the point where he or she is showing a profit.

COMBINED MONTHLY INCOME AND CASH FLOW STATEMENT

The authors recommend to small businesses that they post their sales and disbursement journals to a combined income and cash flow statement each month. When the columns in their sales and disbursement journals are totaled each month, the business should carry each column total to the statement shown in Figure 13.7. The sales Journal (Fig. 12-3) and the disbursement journal (Fig. 12-5) in Chapter 12 are keyed to the various items that appear in Figure 13-7.

By posting to the income and cash flow statement, the small businesses are able to see how well they are doing each month. They do not have to wait until the end of the year, when it may be too late to correct anything that might be going astray.

RATIOS

Accounting **ratios** are calculated on various items that appear in the accounting statements of a business firm. They are important to the firm in that they provide measures of performance against a guideline to let the business know if it is operating as planned. (All sample calculations shown in the following sections are based on data in the accounting statements shown in Figs. 13-1 and 13-2.)

Current Ratio

The **current ratio** is a measure of the firm's ability to meet current debt. It measures the relationship between current assets and current liabilities.

$$\frac{\text{Current Assets}}{\text{Current Liabilities}} = \text{Current Ratio}$$

$$\frac{\$48,000}{\$20,000} = 2.4$$

Acid Test Ratio

The **acid test ratio** is sometimes called the *quick ratio*. It measures the firm's ability to meet current debt by measuring the relationship between its liquid assets (cash plus other current assets that are quickly converted into cash) and current debt. It is a more specific measure of the firm's ability to meet debt than the current ratio.

$$\frac{\text{Cash} + \text{Accounts Receivable} + \text{Marketable Securities}}{\text{Current Liabilities}} = \text{Acid Test Ratio}$$

$$\frac{\$9000 + \$9500 + \$3500}{\$20,000} = 1.1$$

FIGURE 13-7
MONTHLY INCOME AND CASH FLOW STATEMENT.

CASH FLOW AND INCOME STATEMENT[1]		
Sales		
Retail		
Ⓐ Product group A	$ 570	
Ⓑ Product group B	580	
Ⓒ Other products	380	
Total retail sales	1530	
Ⓓ Commercial	850	
Total sales		$2380
Cost of Goods Purchased		
Retail		
Ⓔ Product group A	100	
Ⓕ Product group B	120	
Ⓖ Other products	150	
Total retail purchases	$ 370	
Ⓗ Commercial	100	
Total cost of goods purchased		470
		$1910
Sales Less Cost of Goods Purchased		
Expenses		
Ⓘ Office supplies	30	
Ⓙ Salaries and wages	500	
Ⓚ Utilities	200	
Ⓛ Insurance	50	
Ⓛ Interest on note	20	
Ⓛ Travel	140	
Ⓛ Payroll taxes	60	
Ⓛ Other expenses	25	
Total expenses		1025
Net Cash Increase		$ 885

Cash Flow		Income	
Net cash increase	$885	Net cash increase	$885
Ⓜ Less: Principal paid		Add any decreases in in-	
on debt	200	ventory level	160
Cash flow for the		Deduct any increases in in-	
period	$685	ventory level	
		Less: Depreciation for	
		period	230
		Net taxable income	$815

[1] Letters indicate column totals from the sales journal (Fig. 12-3) and the disbursement Journal (Fig. 12-5.)

Debt to Net Worth Ratio

The **debt to net worth ratio** measures creditor contributions relative to owner contributions. It is a measure of the firm's ability to meet creditor and owner obligations in case of liquidation of the firm. It is also a measure of whether the firm is overextended in terms of debt.

$$\frac{\text{Total Liabilities}}{\substack{\text{Tangible Net Worth} \\ \text{(Net Worth} - \text{Intangible Assets)}}} = \text{Debt to Net Worth Ratio}$$

$$\frac{\$\ 20{,}000 + \$30{,}000}{\$151{,}000 - \$\ 1000} = 0.33$$

Rate of Return on Assets

The **rate of return on assets** ratio is a measure of profitability of the firm. It indicates the amount of assets necessary to produce the current level of profit.

$$\frac{\text{Profit}}{\substack{\text{Total Tangible Assets} \\ \text{(Total Assets} - \text{Intangible Assets)}}} = \text{Rate of Return on Assets}$$

$$\frac{\$60{,}000}{\$201{,}000 - \$1000} = 0.3$$

Inventory Turnover

The inventory turnover is a ratio that measures how often inventory is sold and replaced. The **inventory turnover** ratio indicates the adequacy of the amount of inventory on hand relative to the amount of sales. Inventory turnover is usually calculated in terms of how many times it completely turns over each year.

$$\frac{\text{Net Sales (Cost of Goods Sold)}}{\substack{\text{Average Amount of Inventory for the Year} \\ \text{[(Beginning Inventory} + \text{Ending Inventory) Divided by 2]}}} = \text{Inventory Turnover}$$

$$\frac{\$270{,}000}{\$30{,}000 + \$24{,}000/2} = 10$$

A small business firm should strive to maintain each of its ratio measures near some optimum point. To illustrate, if the optimum point for a specific business for its acid test ratio was 1.5, then any figure much below this would indicate the business is not maintaining enough liquid assets in relation to its current debt. The firm could expect to have problems in meeting its debts during the year. On the other hand, if the figure is much above 1.5, the business is maintaining too many liquid assets that could be invested elsewhere for additional profit.

An optimum ratio figure differs not only by type of ratio but also by type of business. For example, one would not expect the same inventory turnover figure of a jewelry store as for a supermarket. Small business owners often establish optimum ratio figures based on experience in their business. Also, they should compare their firm's ratio analysis with industry averages that are published in sources such as the Almanac of Business and Industrial Financial Ratios. Many trade organizations also publish financial ratios for their industry.

In conclusion, the authors have found that one of the most common weaknesses of small businesses is their accounting system and analysis. Many activities of the small business firm cannot be fully effective without adequate accounting practices and analysis, for example, inventory control, which is discussed in Chapter 15.

SUMMARY OF KEY POINTS

1. The components of a balance sheet may be shown as assets = liabilities + capital, and this is also the basic accounting equation.
2. The balance sheet is an estimate of the value of the business at one moment in time.
3. The balance sheet measures changes in the business, reveals the company's ability to meet debt, and can be used to compute ratios.
4. The income statement is a measure of income less expense, which equals profitability.
5. The income statement is an estimate and measure of profit over a period of time.
6. The method of depreciation selected can change the profit for the period.
7. The income statement measures the success of the business for the period and is required by the IRS and other groups.
8. The budget is an estimate of next year's income statement, which measures estimated income less controllable and uncontrollable expenses.
9. The budget is important because it is next year's plan and is a controlling and decision-making device.
10. The cash flow statement is a record of all cash receipts and disbursements.
11. The projected cash flow statement is important in that it warns of future

cash problems. Past cash flow statements are extremely important to investors.

12. Ratios are important to businesses because they provide measures of performance against a guideline to let the business know if it is operating as planned.

DISCUSSION QUESTIONS

1. What is the balance sheet, and what are some of its components?
2. Why is a balance sheet an estimate for one moment in time?
3. If you were a small business owner, how would you use the balance sheet?
4. What is an income statement, and what items are contained in the income statement?
5. Why is the income statement an estimate, and why does it measure profit or loss over a period of time?
6. Can the small business owner do without some form of income statement? Explain.
7. Why is the budget like the income statement?
8. Why is the budget important to the small business?
9. What is a cash flow statement?
10. Why is a cash flow statement important to the small business and the investor?
11. Why would a small business owner compute ratios?

THE BUSINESS PLAN: ACCOUNTING STATEMENTS AND ANALYSIS

Set up a balance sheet that will represent the value of the business the first day of operations. Use the one presented in the chapter as a guide.

—— Estimate the budget for the first year's operations using the chapter example as a model.

—— Project the first year's cash flow statement, month by month.

—— Set up a combined monthly income and cash flow statement format. Be sure to key the columns in the sales and disbursement journals to the items in the statement. Duplicate this form and fill in the blanks from the totals in the journals each month.

—— Go to the library and find one or more financial ratio books. Decide which ratios would be important to you. At least once a year, calculate these ratios and compare them to the ratio standards for your type of business. Be sure you know what each ratio measures and how to use it.

ENTREPRENEURIAL PROJECTS

1. Prepare a balance sheet for yourself, listing all assets and liabilities to arrive at your net worth.
2. Keep a record of all income and expenditures for a week's period, and from this record prepare an income statement and a cash flow statement.
3. Prepare a budget for the next week.

CASE A
The West Bookstore

Richard West owns and operates a bookstore in a shopping mall on the west side of a large city. At a recent small business clinic sponored by a local college and the Small Business Administration, Richard learned that financial ratios are valuable tools in evaluating and controlling a small business. Richard knows very little about ratios and has asked your help. The following are copies of his latest income statement and balance sheet.

THE WEST BOOKSTORE
Income Statement for Year Ending 12/31/90

Sales		$230,000
Cost of Goods Sold		
Beginning inventory 1/1/90	$120,000	
Purchases	110,000	
Merchandise available for sale	$230,000	
Less: Ending inventory 12/31/90	130,000	
Total cost of goods sold		100,000
Gross Profit on Sales		$130,000
Operating Expenses		
Advertising	8,000	
Rent	22,000	
Depreciation on furniture and fixtures	6,000	
Salaries and wages	15,000	
Insurance	4,000	
Total operating expenses	$ 55,000	
General Expenses		
Postage	600	
Telephone	1,200	
Payroll taxes	1,500	
Utilities	5,700	
Total general expenses	9,000	
Total Expenses		64,000
Net Income Before Taxes		66,000

THE WEST BOOKSTORE
Balance Sheet

Assets
Current Assets

Cash	$20,000	
Merchandise	130,000	
Supplies	1,000	
ABC Company stock	40,000	
Total current assets		$191,000
Fixed Assets		
Furniture and fixtures	40,000	
Total fixed assets		40,000
Intangible Assets		
Organizational costs	1,000	
Total intangible assets		1,000
Total Assets		$232,000
Liabilities		
Current Liabilities		
Accounts payable	$ 20,000	
Income tax payable	5,000	
FICA tax payable	3,000	
Total current liabilities		$ 28,000
Long-Term Liabilities		
Note payable to bank 6/1/93	60,000	
Total long-term liabilities		60,000
Capital		
Richard West, capital		144,000
Total Liabilities and Capital		$232,000

Questions

1. Compute the following ratios for Richard.
   a. Current ratio
   b. Acid test ratio
   c. Debt to net worth ratio
   d. Rate of return on assets
   e. Inventory turnover
2. Tell Richard how he can use these ratios.

CASE B
Pete's Parts (B)

See Pete's parts (A) (Case B in Chapter 12) for background information. After setting up Peter Wagner's sales and disbursement journal, you decided he should have a monthly income and cash flow statement. To illustrate how it is done, you plan to create a sample statement keyed to his journals.

Pete's inventory system involves reordering all items that he sold from stock each day. He has ordered replacements for everything he sold the first week. However, only $240 worth of parts (at cost) have come in, and he still requires $200 worth of parts (at cost) that have not come in to restock his inventory completely. This means he currently has a decrease of $200 in inventory. Depreciation for the first week amounted to $50.

Questions*

1. Set up a monthly Income and cash flow statement similar to the one in Figure 13-7.
2. Post the sales and disbursement journals to your income and cash flow statement. (It will be a weekly statement in this case.)

---

* Forms are provided in the Student Study Guide.

KEY WORDS

PURCHASING

After reading this chapter, you will understand:

1 The purchasing process in the small business.

2 Why purchasing policies and procedures are needed in the small business.

3 The purpose of economic order quantity.

4 The questions to be answered in make or buy decisions.

5 The factors that should be evaluated in vendor analysis.

6 When title to merchandise passes from seller to buyer.

7 What consignment purchasing is and how it can be advantageous to the small business owner.

8 The importance of purchase discounts to the small business owner as well as the different types of purchase discounts.

ENTREPRENEURIAL PROFILE

Ed and Joyce Bratt

COAST-TO-COAST HARDWARE STORE

The number one hardware store in the 1500-store Coast-to-Coast chain rests in the mountain town of Casper, Wyoming. Says owner Ed Bratt, "If it hadn't been for the SBA loan, I doubt we would have even got off the ground."

In 1974, when Ed and Joyce Bratt tried to find funds to start a retail hardware store, they were shut out by banks. But by year's end SBA came to the rescue with a start-up guaranteed loan of $175,000. "On opening day we sold 12 percent of our inventory," Ed relates. No surprise that the loan was paid off in three years. With 10 employees then, the Bratts now employ 39; their annual sales are $3 million.

Total body paralysis stunned Ed Batt in 1976. He was unable to speak. For nine months he did the store's book work in the hospital. But the husband-wife team overcame that big blow.

Today the store has expanded to 23,000 square feet, almost three times its original size. In 1986 the Bratts opened a new Coast-to-Coast store in Rock Spring, Wyoming. A secret of success? "We always take our discounts on all purchases," Ed affirms.

Source: Network (Washington, D.C.: Small Business Administration, May–June 1988).

Purchasing is a major cost of operation in the small business. According to the Department of Commerce, 57 cents of each sales dollar goes to pay for purchases of materials and services in manufacturing firms; in apparel firms, 52 cents; and in the food business, 71 cents. Efficient performance of the purchasing function is mandatory to attain higher profits.

Small manufacturers plan for purchasing the proper quality and quantity of raw materials that can be processed into finished goods for sale. Small wholesalers base their purchase decisions on projected demand from retailers and service firm operators. Small retailers analyze consumer buying habits, and purchase decisions regarding finished goods are shaped by the expectation of consumer demand. Service firm owners plan the purchases of special parts and standard items in stock with the objective of having all parts and materials they require to perform their specific services.

AUTHORITY AND RESPONSIBILITY FOR PURCHASING

Purchasing activities must be coordinated with all other operations of the firm. In a small business, the owner usually decides whether or not to purchase an item, the number to buy, when to buy, and the specifications and quality needed. As the business grows, the owner should delegate the function of purchasing. This individual becomes the **purchasing agent,** the person who has authority to make purchases for the company. Therefore, it is essential that any limitation on the purchasing agent's authority be clearly defined. For example, the policy may limit the dollar amount the purchasing agent may authorize. Expenditures exceeding this amount must have the approval of a higher authority, say, the owner of the firm.

Centralizing the purchasing function affords greater efficiency, uniformity, and control in performing the purchasing activity. A centralized purchasing authority makes it possible to develop better relations with vendors. If a problem develops, the vendor can negotiate with the purchasing agent.

When we make reference to the purchasing agent or **purchasing manager,** we are referring to the owner or a designated employee who has the authority and responsibility for coordinating purchasing in the small business.

THE PURCHASING PROCESS

When a small business consistently outperforms its competitors, this advantage is not achieved accidentally nor is it solely attributed to luck; rather it results primarily from good management practices. Good management practices are reflected in many ways, and one measure is the quality of purchasing decisions made by the purchasing agent.

For purchasing to be effective, a purchasing manager must coordinate the interdependent activities described in the following statement and shown in Figure 14-1.

Purchasing is the process of buying the right quality of materials, products, and supplies in the correct quantity at the best price and at the proper time from the right vendor. Small business owners realize that they are buying in

**FIGURE 14-1
THE PURCHASING PROCESS.**

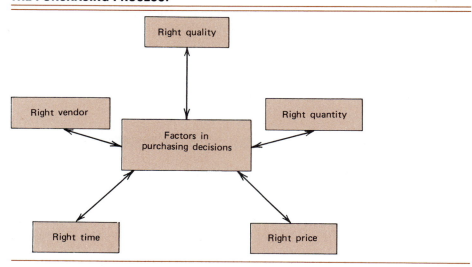

anticipation of customer demand. In essence, they serve as "buying agents" for customers and not as "selling agents" for suppliers.

Quality

Quality is related to the suitability of the raw materials or product for the intended purpose. The raw materials purchased by the manufacturer should be of the best quality needed to meet the manufacturer's specifications at the lowest possible price. Quality requirements can be ascertained through value analysis. **Value analysis** is the systematic study of a component or a product to determine whether any changes in parts or function can be made that will provide the same "value" to users at less cost or greater "value" at the same cost.

Quality specifications can be stated in terms of essential features, such as shape, strength, size, color, flexibility, or appearance. Conducting value analysis may result in eliminating a part, substituting one part for another, or changing the design or material requirement of the part. The list shown in Figure 14-2 indicates some factors to be examined in value analysis.

Quantity

A second objective of purchasing is to buy the proper quantity of materials or products. What is the correct quantity to buy? If the retailer, service firm owner, or wholesaler purchases in large quantities, substantial savings may

FIGURE 14-2
FACTORS TO BE EVALUATED IN VALUE ANALYSIS.

What is the precise function of the item?

Can the item be eliminated?

If the item is not standard, can a standard item be substituted?

Are there any similar items used by the company that can be substituted?

Can the item be redesigned to allow greater tolerances?

Will a design change permit the item to be made from a lower-cost process or a lower-cost material?

Could the item be produced within the firm at less cost?

Are the finishing requirements greater than necessary?

If different sizes of the item are stocked, can some of these be combined to reduce inventory and take advantage of quantity buying?

Is there difficulty in obtaining the part at present?

Are there ways of economizing in packing or shipping techniques?

(Gary J. Zenz, *Purchasing and the Management of Materials*, 6th ed., John Wiley, New York, 1987, p. 240.)

result from the quantity discounts offered by the supplier. However, a large merchandise inventory may tie up an unusually high proportion of funds. There is also the likelihood of spoilage or obsolescence of merchandise as well as the added cost if additional storage space is needed for the large orders. Conversely, buying in small quantities results in frequent reordering and higher per unit costs. There is also the possibility that a product is out of stock when requested by consumers. A technique to aid in deciding the correct quantity to buy is presented later in the chapter.

The small manufacturer must be assured that an adequate stock of raw materials will be available to minimize or eliminate any disruptions in production activity. The manufacturer can use the guidelines in the following list to aid in assessing their quantity of material to be purchased.

1. How much material will be used in production?
2. How much material may be lost through damage or defects?
3. How much material is in inventory when the order is placed?
4. What is the average inventory carried? [1]

Price

The best price is not necessarily the lowest purchase price. The firm offering the lowest price may not be able to meet the quality requirements of the buyer or may not provide the best service. As discussed regarding value analysis, the best price is the lowest price at which merchandise can be purchased that is consistent with the quality specifications. Consequently, the aim of the

Beverly Margolis, founder of Beverly Pac, identified a business opportunity when she sought to buy a color-coordinated kitchenware package for her vacation home but was unable to find one. Margolis assembles a color-coordinated package of kitchen supplies that she sells to resorts and hotels. She has also created packages for other markets, such as recreational vehicle owners. Margolis takes advantage of purchase discounts by buying large quantities of supplies directly from manufacturers.

small business owner is to secure the highest value of merchandise that meets the specific requirements at the lowest purchase price.

Time

The decision of when to purchase materials or services is crucial. In anticipating demand, small business owners must determine the "lead time" for delivery of materials or services so that they will be available when demand occurs. **Lead time** is the elapsed time between the issuance of a purchase requisition and the delivery of the required goods or services. Buyer and supplier actions must be coordinated with regard to the timing of the purchase order and the capacity to deliver materials or services when needed. For example, if the small retailer orders too far in advance of the selling season, operating capital is tied up in inventory. Orders placed with insufficient lead time often result in the delivery of merchandise after the selling season has peaked. Consequently, the small retailer will have a large unsold inventory that must be disposed of at cost or at a loss.

Manufacturers plan their purchase of raw materials so that these materials are available at the time they are needed in the manufacturing process in order to convert raw materials into finished goods. Manufacturers produce goods for stock in anticipation of demand, or they manufacture them to customer specifications. Whichever situation exists, they must be able to deliver according to the date promised. Wholesalers plan their merchandise needs to allow sufficient lead time to ensure delivery of goods when they are needed. By planning purchases with sufficient lead time, the wholesaler will be able to make delivery of merchandise to retailers or operators of service firms as the need arises. In turn, retailers or service establishment operators then have merchandise in stock when consumer demand arises.

The purchasing manager tries to avoid the dual problems of excessive inventory and stockouts. These problems are the result of poor planning and incorrect application of the **safety factor.** The safety factor is the volume decided upon to be kept in inventory to meet contingencies in the company. This inventory level is a judgmental decision based on the knowledge of the firm's operations, suppliers' abilities, industry conditions, and the general economic situation.[2] Procedures for inventory control are discussed in Chapter 15.

Vendor

Selection of the vendor is another of the principal factors that contribute to efficient purchasing. Vendors should be selected who can meet the quality, quantity, price, and time specifications of the small business owner. Follow-up evaluation of vendors is essential to make sure that they continue to provide the type of service that the firm requires. The best purchasing strategy can be defeated if an incompetent vendor is selected. A detailed discussion of vendor analysis is presented later in this chapter.

PURCHASING POLICIES

To facilitate the performance of the purchasing function, purchasing policies must be set to guide employees. Purchasing policies should address issues such as the following.

1. The person who has authority to purchase for the company.
2. Categories of purchases the authorized person may make (specifically state what purchases may not be made by your purchasing agent, if other than owner of the business).
3. A variety of vendors to ensure sufficient competition. A general rule is that three current quotations will constitute evidence of adequate competition.
4. Careful review of prices in a noncompetitive situation.
5. Criteria for selection of vendors.

6. Who, besides you or your purchasing agent, may contact vendors and under what circumstances.
7. Purchases from customers (reciprocal buying).
8. Purchases from employees of your business.
9. Personal purchases for employees and sales to them.
10. Contracts and blanket orders. Specify the basis for pricing and overall dollar limitations.
11. Statement of business principles, such as the standards of the National Association of Purchasing Management.
12. Fairness, honesty, and courtesy. Avoid ''sharp practices,'' for example, kickbacks, gratuities, excessive entertainment, revealing competitor's quotations, and obtaining personal loans from suppliers.
13. Conflict of interest.
14. Gratuities and loans.
15. Confidentiality.
16. Entertainment.
17. Laws and regulations.
18. Procedures required to implement the policies of your business.[3]

The following statement is an example of a policy on authority for purchasing: ''All purchases, with certain exceptions, must be made by the purchasing agent. All exceptions must be approved in writing by the owner or the purchasing agent.''

THE PURCHASING PROCEDURE

The purchasing procedure spells out in detail the actions that are required to complete the purchasing function. The purchasing procedure must correlate with the goals and policies of purchasing stated earlier to achieve the desired results. The purchasing procedure shown in Figure 14-3 outlines a basic format of activities that are necessary for completing the purchasing cycle.

Issuance of Purchase Requisition

When a department requires specific materials or supplies, a purchase requisition is issued. This requisition serves as the basis for action by the purchasing agent. The purchase requisition contains a description of the materials or supplies wanted, the quantity required, the date the materials should be available, the place they are to be delivered, and who is making the request. The purchase requisition should be a standard form used throughout the company. To make sure that the appropriate quality and quantity are ordered, the purchaser must specify on the requisition an accurate and complete description of the materials and supplies needed.

FIGURE 14-3
THE PURCHASING PROCEDURE.

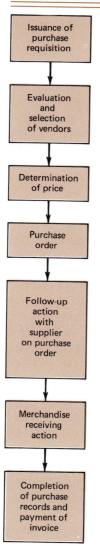

Evaluation and Selection of Vendors

Decisons concerning the source of supply from whom to secure prices is the next phase of the purchasing procedure. For some special materials, there may be only a single supplier. However, in most instances, there will be a number of vendors. In this situation, the vendor selection process consists of narrowing the choices to a relatively few suppliers. The number of vendors from whom prices should be obtained, wherever possible, should be spelled out in the policy statement. The extent of investigation of suppliers will depend on whether the purchase is a routine or nonroutine purchase.

Determination of Price

Prices may be determined from several sources. One method is from current catalogs of manufacturers containing price quotations. A second method is through price negotiation between buyer and seller. A third method is through competitive bidding. This latter method involves considerable time to write product specification and secure price quotations and usually is not used in a small business except for specialized needs.

The Purchase Order

The **purchase order** is the legal order that requests the vendor to supply the materials or services to the firm. The purchase order should be (1) in writing; (2) filled out completely; (3) clearly and precisely cover the purchase quantities, type of product or service, price, delivery, and any other terms of the agreement between supplier and the firm; and (4) signed by the authorized company official. This action will aid in preventing misunderstanding between buyer and supplier. The importance of the purchase order as a legal document must be underscored. It represents the supplier's authorization to ship and charge for the goods or services in the order and the purchaser's obligation to reimburse the supplier for the value of the goods or services ordered. The purchase order should be a preprinted form similar to the one shown in Figure 14-4.

Follow-up Action with Supplier on the Purchase Order

An effective control technique is the follow-up of the purchase order with the vendor. This action will confirm that the order has been received and that the vendor will be able to meet the delivery date. The procedure described as follows is used by a small machine tool manufacturer.

Purchase orders are prepared in quadruplicate. Two copies, the official copy and an acknowledgment copy, are sent to the vendor (both white). A pink copy is placed in a loose-leaf folder in chronological sequence. The fourth copy (blue) is filed alphabetically by vendor in an unfilled order file. The file of pink copies is checked weekly, and if the acknowledgment copy has not been received after the lapse of a short period of time, a reminder is sent to the supplier.

When the acknowledgment copy is received, it is filed in a loose-leaf folder of unfilled orders which are arranged chronologically. At this time the pink

FIGURE 14-4
THE PURCHASE ORDER OF A SMALL BUSINESS.

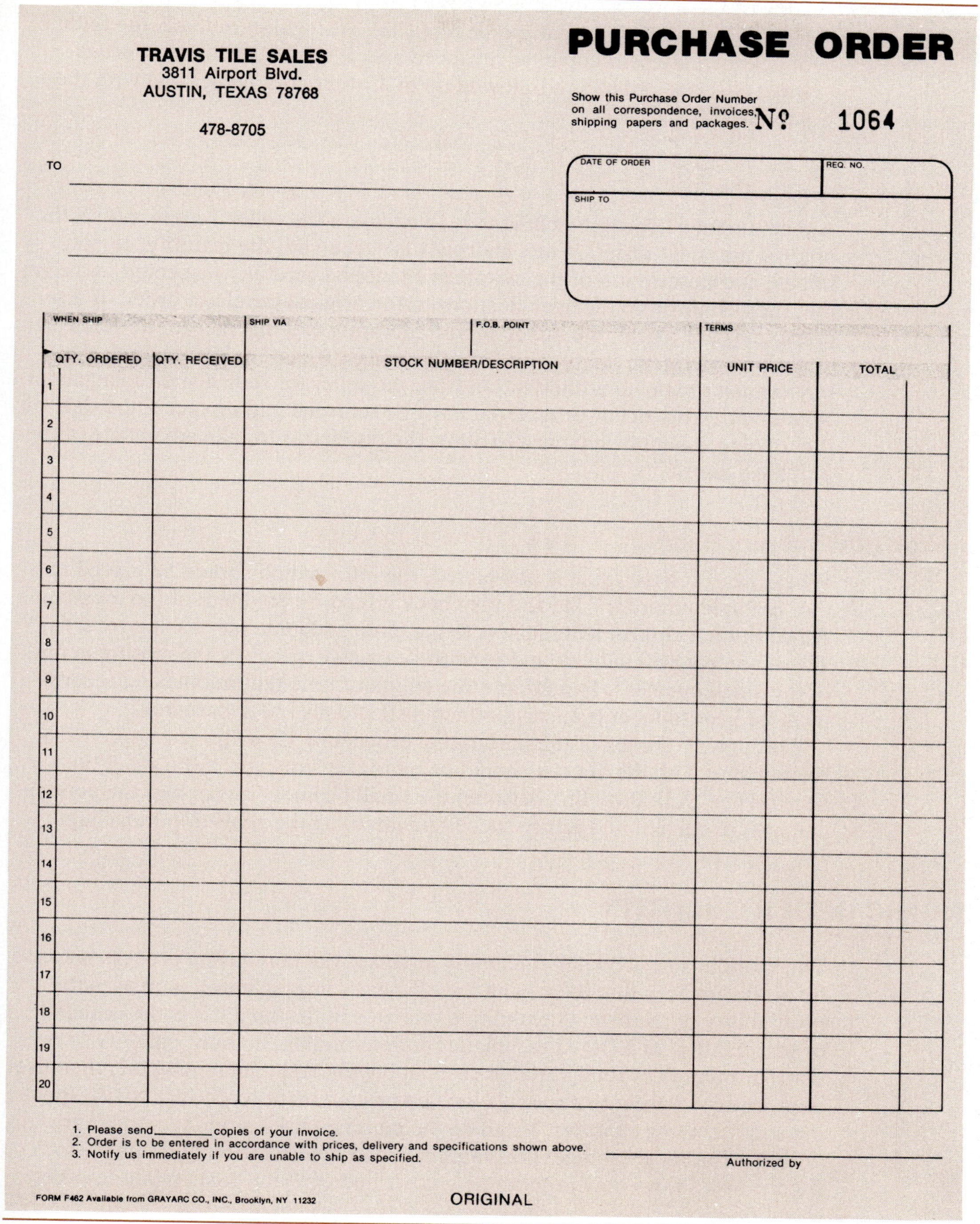

TRAVIS TILE SALES
3811 Airport Blvd.
AUSTIN, TEXAS 78768

478-8705

PURCHASE ORDER

Show this Purchase Order Number on all correspondence, invoices, shipping papers and packages. Nº 1064

TO

DATE OF ORDER | REQ. NO.

SHIP TO

WHEN SHIP | SHIP VIA | F.O.B. POINT | TERMS

	QTY. ORDERED	QTY. RECEIVED	STOCK NUMBER/DESCRIPTION	UNIT PRICE	TOTAL
1					
2					
3					
4					
5					
6					
7					
8					
9					
10					
11					
12					
13					
14					
15					
16					
17					
18					
19					
20					

1. Please send________copies of your invoice.
2. Order is to be entered in accordance with prices, delivery and specifications shown above.
3. Notify us immediately if you are unable to ship as specified.

Authorized by

FORM F462 Available from GRAYARC CO., INC., Brooklyn, NY 11232

ORIGINAL

(Grayarc Co., Inc., Brooklyn, N.Y., Form F462.)

copy of the purchase order is removed from the folder and permanently filed as a record of purchase orders placed. At regular intervals the folder of acknowledgment copies is reviewed and, if the buyer thinks it necessary, past due orders are followed up by further communication with the supplier.[4]

Merchandise Receiving Action

A recommended control technique is to compare the seller's invoice with the original purchase order. When materials are received, the quantity, terms, prices, and description of the materials should be carefully inspected to assure that they conform to the specifications in the original purchase order. If discrepancies are found, the buyer should promptly call this fact to the seller's attention and return the invoice for corrections. If material is rejected, the buyer must obtain an authorization from the seller for return and replacement. Whenever errors occur or material must be returned and replaced, the date on the invoice should be changed to allow the purchaser to take advantage of the purchase discounts.

Completion of Purchase Records and Payment of Invoice

When the purchase cycle is completed, the information should be placed in the "completed order" file and the check issued for payment of the invoice. An additional control technique is to maintain adequate purchasing records. These records will indicate the vendor's capacity to satisfy the requirements of the small business. In addition, the length of time that purchasing records must be kept to meet legal requirements should also be ascertained.

Through all phases of the purchasing procedure, developing a supportive relationship with the vendor should be a primary concern of the small business owner. A healthy link between the small business owner and the vendor can ensure current and future success in attaining the goals of purchasing.

ECONOMIC ORDER QUANTITY

The small business owner constantly analyzes the purchasing process because he or she realizes that increasing the efficiency in purchasing increases the profitability of the firm. A technique that aids in this analysis is the **economic order quantity,** or **EOQ,** a technique for determining the right quantity to order that minimizes total variable costs in buying and maintaining merchandise in inventory. Purchase expenses include procurement (ordering) costs—placing and receiving an order, handling the merchandise—and inventory carrying costs—insurance, storage, obsolescence, and deterioration of items in stock. Figure 14-5 shows how procurement costs and carrying costs relate to order quantity.

HOW TO ESTABLISH SOUND PURCHASING PRIORITIES

A method of analysis called the 80/20 rule can help you establish priorities as to how much effort and how much of your resources you will spend on various purchasing areas. It says you should analyze your operations so you give the highest priorities to matters of greatest importance to your business, and conversely, less time and fewer resources, to items of less significance. Examples of how the rule should be applied appear below. (Percentages should be adjusted to your business operations.)

Value of inventory items   Say in the typical inventory, you determine that 20 percent of the items represent 80 percent of the value of materials in inventory. And conversely, 80 percent are low-cost inventory items that represent 20 percent of the inventory dollar valuation.

Sales volume of inventory items   Assume that 20 percent of the stock items represent 80 percent of the volume.

Customer service   Assume that 20 percent of your customers contribute to 80 percent of your sales volume. Also assume that these will be repeat customers.

Devote the bulk of your time to the 20 percent of the items constituting the top 80 percent of the inventory dollar valuation

Maintain high stock levels on the 20 percent fast-moving items

Concentrate your efforts on pleasing these customers   The 20 percent typically are very loyal to you. Even so, remember that expansion opportunity lies in careful screening of the 80 percent who currently represent only 20 percent of your sales volume.

Source: Purchasing and Cost Control (Washington, D.C.: U.S. Government Printing Office, 1984), p. 39.

As Figure 14-5 indicates, procurement costs decline with larger order sizes as fewer individual orders have to be placed and the average handling cost decreases as individual orders increase in size. Carrying costs increase directly with size of order quantity because they are a function of the size of the average inventory, which is larger with larger quantity orders. Adding procurement and carrying costs results in the U-shaped total cost line. The lowest point on the total cost curve, where procurement costs and carrying costs are lowest, gives the order quantity (EOQ) resulting in lowest annual cost.

A formula can be used to arrive at the EOQ. In firms that use this technique, the EOQ calculations are computerized.

$$EOQ = \sqrt{\frac{2UP}{C}}$$

FIGURE 14-5
ECONOMIC ORDER QUANTITY.

where

U = annual usage of items in units
P = procurement cost per order
C = carrying cost per unit

Therefore, if $U = 1000$, $P = \$4.00$, and $C = \$0.20$, then

$$\text{EOQ} = \sqrt{\frac{2 \times 1000 \times \$4.00}{\$0.20}}$$

$$= \sqrt{40,000}$$

$$= 200 \text{ units per order}$$

MAKE OR BUY DECISION

Small manufacturers are confronted with a make or buy decision. They must decide whether to make product components (or complete products) or buy them from suppliers. In the small firm, owners should seek out the advice of others rather than rely solely on their own judgment or intuition to make this decision. Value analysis is also useful for determining whether it is more economical to make or to buy. The factors of quality, quantity, price, time, and suppliers enter into this decision as well.

FIGURE 14-6
FACTORS TO EVALUATE BEFORE DECIDING TO MAKE OR BUY A COMPONENT.

Prior to Deciding to Buy

1. Is the supplier reliable?
2. Can the supplier meet the quality standards needed for the component?
3. Will the supplier guarantee quality of the product?
4. Can components be delivered on schedule?
5. What are all costs per unit involved in buying the component (such as packaging, freight, shipping, handling, and receiving costs) versus making?
6. What is the likelihood of suppliers being unable or unwilling to supply you because of such occurrences as a strike or fire or demands of a more important customer?
7. How many suppliers are available? If there are few, extra risks are incurred.

Prior to Deciding to Make

1. Can present equipment be used, or will new equipment have to be leased or purchased?
2. Do current employees have the skill and knowledge necessary to produce the component?
3. Can the desired quality standards be produced by the firm?
4. Will the required quantitites be large enough to justify setup costs and personnel training needed to produce the part?
5. What are all costs involved in product (labor, material, overhead)?
6. Is demand for the part stable throughout the year permitting longer production runs or seasonal, requiring only short production runs.
7. Can better suppliers than current ones be found?

The small manufacturer evaluates three alternatives: purchase the complete product or component, purchase some parts and make others, or make all components. As a general guide, growth companies should buy parts because they can use their funds more profitably to expand product lines. Companies in highly competitive industries may find it more efficient to make as many of their components as possible to reduce operating costs. Many of the considerations entering into the make or buy decision are included in Figure 14-6.

VENDOR ANALYSIS

Vendor analysis is one of the most important evaluations performed by the small business managers. Vendors that are selected should be those best able to serve the demands for quantity, quality, service, price, time, and place. The vendor has a strong influence on the firm's competitive position and marketing strategy. There are many factors to consider in vendor analysis. The factors described in the following sections are suggestive of some of the major items that small business owners should incorporate into their evaluation of vendors.

Dependability and Reliability

To determine whether a vendor is dependable and reliable, the small business owner must measure the supplier's performance, such as a change in shipping performance from shipping merchandise on time to missing delivery dates. Consider the following situation. The owner of a dance studio ordered merchandise (T-shirts, leotards, dance shoes) from a catalog description of a new supplier. She wanted the merchandise for a special sales promotion in conjunction with the beginning of the summer dance classes starting the first week in June. The order was placed in March with the assurance by the supplier that it would be delivered by the first week in May. On May 1, the owner of the dance studio received notice from the supplier that the merchandise would be delivered six months late. As a result, the owner canceled the order, and plans for the sales promotion had to be scrapped.

A number of factors concerning dependability and reliability should be examined by the owner. For example, is the quality of the product supplied by the vendor consistent? Does the vendor have the capability of supplying merchandise in the quantity required whether it be in large or small lots? Is the supplier's operation stable so that an uninterrupted flow of goods or services can be maintained? Has the supplier served your firm well in the past? Developing and maintaining good long-term relations between buyer and supplier is vital.

Services of the Vendor

The owner must judge the type of service the vendor is capable of providing. One concern is the manner in which the supplier adjusts shortages in delivery and provides repair and replacement of unsatisfactory or defective materials. A second area of concern is the vendor's capability to provide technical assistance. For example, if technical equipment is purchased by the small manufacturer, what service, such as installation and servicing of equipment, does the vendor provide? Or can the supplier advise the purchaser in technical aspects of the purchase, such as the suitability of a product to the buyer's needs? Other services that the vendor may extend are suggestions on how materials may be more efficiently utilized and assistance in adapting equipment to the owner's special needs.

A supplier may offer special services. To illustrate, suppliers who agree to space deliveries are more desirable than those who will not. They allow the buyer to take advantage of both quantity and quality discounts by purchasing larger quantities yet do not require the buyer to increase storage space or inventory costs by taking delivery of the entire order at once.[5]

FIGURE 14-7
ADVANTAGES OF CONCENTRATING PURCHASES WITH A LIMITED NUMBER OF SUPPLIERS.

The supplier may provide special help in solving merchandising problems.

Credit terms are better.

Competition for the purchasing dollar stimulates suppliers to provide better quality, delivery, and service.

A smaller investment in inventory is needed.

Suppliers may offer special price concessions other than quantity discounts.

Suppliers may offer an opportunity for prior selection of desirable merchandise.

Interrupted service is less likely when there are several suppliers.

Number of Vendors

Another factor in the evaluation process is the determination of whether a single vendor or multiple suppliers can best meet the needs of the small firm. Certain problems may arise if the firm utilizes a single vendor. To illustrate, the vendor may encounter financial difficulties or unanticipated catastrophic events may occur, such as a fire or labor problem, making it impossible to deliver the materials on the date promised. Furthermore, a single supplier may be unable to supply the small firm's needs adequately at peak sales periods or may lack the motivation to provide goods or services promptly when there are no competitors. Ordinarily, most small business owners find it advantageous to split their purchases between two or three vendors and strive to develop a close, harmonious relationship with them. This policy offers the best assurance of maintaining the level of service and supply of merchandise necessary to carry on business activity because each supplier desires to maintain or increase their share of purchases by small business owners and they accomplish this goal only by providing timely delivery and dependable services and quality merchandise. Figure 14-7 lists the advantages of purchasing from several vendors.

Vendor's Location

The geographical location of the vendor is crucial for a variety of reasons. First, transportation costs can substantially increase the cost of the product if the supplier is located some distance from the buyer. Second, correlated with this consideration is the time involved in shipping materials to their destination. Third, the greater distance materials have to be shipped increases the chances for transportation services to be interrupted due to strikes, weather conditions, or other unforeseen events. Fourth, delivery over longer distances may require higher levels of safety stock if delivery is unreliable. If a local vendor can adequately supply the firm, it may be advantageous to buy locally. Because they are more accessible, local vendors should be able to respond more quickly to fill order requests or handle any supply problems that may develop. Purchasing locally demonstrates the small business owner's commitment to the local community as well.

Terms of Sale

The terms of sale should be studied carefully because there may be considerable variation among vendors. For example, does the vendor offer a cash discount for payments made within the regular credit period? Cash discounts have a substantial impact on cost of goods sold. Another criterion to judge is the length of the credit period. One vendor may offer a 30-day credit period, whereas another may extend credit for 60 days.

Vendor's Sales Representatives

Small business managers rely on the vendor's sales representatives to make regular calls to provide them with prompt and accurate price quotations, to follow through on their orders, to expedite delivery, and to handle complaints in a satisfactory manner. Small business managers also expect sales representatives to be knowledgeable about the company and the products they are selling. Furthermore, sales representatives can provide information about possible sources of supply of noncompeting products or services.

Vendor representatives may perform an inventory function for the small retailer. In cases when the vendor's representatives visit regularly and are considered dependable, the owner will have them check inventory items and recommend how much stock should be purchased. Other considerations that should be analyzed are the ethical standards, the financial strength, the labor-management relations, and the management capability of the supplier.

TRANSFER OF TITLE

When the purchase transaction occurs, the time and place where **title** to the merchandise passes must be established to determine legal ownership. Although some transactions may be very simple, the usual transaction is more involved as was indicated in the discussion of purchasing procedures earlier in this chapter. The question of when title passes is ordinarily answered by the designation "free on board" (F.O.B.) seller or buyer.

F.O.B. Seller

The designation **F.O.B. seller** means that title to goods passes as soon as the seller delivers the merchandise to the shipper (airline, truckline, bus, or railway system). Under the terms of this arrangement, the buyer pays for the shipping costs and is responsible for all activities relating to the movement of

FIGURE 14-8
F.O.B. SELLER.

goods, such as providing insurance protection against damage or loss during shipment. Figure 14-8 depicts when title passes under F.O.B. seller.

The responsibility of the seller and the buyer under F.O.B. seller are listed as follows.

F.O.B. (named point of origin)

A. Seller must

1. Place goods on or in cars or vehicles.
2. Secure receipted bill of lading from carrier.
3. Be responsible for loss and damage until goods have been placed in or on cars or vehicles at point of origin and clean bill of lading has been furnished by carrier.

B. Buyer must

1. Provide for the movement of goods after they are on board.
2. Pay all transportation charges to destination.
3. Be responsible for loss or damage or for filing claims with carrier for loss or damage to shipment while in transit.
4. Pay any demurrage and storage charges.

C. Title passes to buyer when shipment is turned over to carrier.[6]

F.O.B. Buyer

Transactions designated as **F.O.B. buyer** indicate that the title of goods does not pass until the merchandise is delivered to the buyer's place of business. Under the terms of this arrangement, the seller pays for shipping charges to the buyer's firm. In addition, the responsibility for insurance protection of goods in transit remains with the seller. Figure 14-9 illustrates when title passes under the F.O.B. buyer agreement.

FIGURE 14-9
F.O.B. BUYER.

By mutual agreement, the buyer and seller may select any other intermediate points for delivery of goods where title would then pass.

The responsibilities of the seller and the buyer under F.O.B. buyer are listed as follows.

F.O.B. (named destination)

A. Seller must

1. Place goods on or in cars or vehicles.
2. Secure receipted bill of lading from carrier.
3. Pay all transportation charges until goods have arrived at destination.
4. Be responsible for loss or damage or for filing claims with carrier for loss or damage to shipment while in transit.

B. Buyer must

1. Provide for any movement of the goods after arrival at named destination.
2. Be responsible for any loss and damage incurred after arrival of goods at named destination.
3. Pay any demurrage and storage charges.

C. Title remains with seller until the shipment is delivered to buyer.[7]

CONSIGNMENT PURCHASING

Consignment purchasing is a stockless purchasing system. Under consignment purchasing, the vendor's merchandise is usually displayed in the small owner's establishment, and the vendor is responsible for maintaining the merchandise display. Ownership of the inventory resides with the vendor until the materials are used or sold. Consignment purchasing has certain advantages to the small business owner. While merchandise is available for sale on the premises, the owner's funds are not tied up in inventory. The problem of obsolescence of merchandise is reduced for the small business owner because unsold or unused merchandise is reclaimed by the vendor. The consigned merchandise may attract customers to the store and may result in additional purchases of regular merchandise as well.

For example, a rack jobber often consigns merchandise to retail firms. The rack jobber places his or her own display rack of merchandise in the store. Rack jobbers regularly check the merchandise rack to see that there is an adequate stock of goods and that they are priced and displayed properly. Title does not pass, and payment for the merchandise is not made until the products are sold or are used by the small business manager.

The small business owner must have a complete understanding with the vendor regarding the status of the consigned goods. The following factors should normally be included, and the consignment agreement should be in writing.

1. Listing of items to be consigned, prices, quantities, and maximum and minimum levels.
2. Duration of consignment agreement, which should not exceed a year's period.
3. Title of consigned inventory remains with the vendor until withdrawn from stock.
4. Designation of insurance responsibility.
5. Policy on rejects—seller responsible for defects; buyer to be responsible for any missing or damaged materials resulting from buyer's negligence.
6. Termination provisions.
7. Provisions for disposition of any unused consigned inventory at the end of the consignment agreement.[8]

PURCHASE DISCOUNTS

Small business owners should continuously search for and take advantage of all opportunities to reduce their costs of operation and consequently improve the firm's operating efficiency. One avenue of profit improvement is achieved by taking purchase discounts that may be available. Discounts represent a reduction in price of the purchased material from the vendor. A high-priority item to be evaluated in deciding whether to take the discount is to weigh the cost of money at prevailing interest rates versus the amount of the discount allowed.

The decision of whether the discount should be taken becomes a financial decision. If interest rates rise and the cash position of the buyer becomes tight, the small business owner should try for longer terms of payment—60 days or more—unless discounts of at least 2 percent are offered.[9]

Principal types of discounts offered to small business owners are the following: cash, trade, quantity, seasonal, and promotional. (See Fig. 14-10.)

Cash Discounts

Vendors offer cash discounts to small business owners as an incentive for prompt payment. **Cash discounts** reduce the purchase price, making these funds available for other uses in the company. The most common cash discount is stated as "2/10, net 30." These discount terms mean that the vendor extends credit to the small business owner for the amount of the purchase for a period of 30 days from the date of the invoice. The total bill is payable at the end of 30 days. However, if the bill is paid within 10 days from the invoice date, the owner is given a 2 percent discount on the net purchase price. Hence, if the purchase order is substantial, sizable cash savings can result.

Many other discount terms are available from suppliers, such as "1/10, net 30"; "2/10, net 60"; and "2/10, EOM." The "2/10, EOM" means that a 2 percent discount can be taken if the owner pays the bill by the tenth of the

FIGURE 14-10
TYPES OF PURCHASE DISCOUNTS.

month following the purchase. For merchandise purchased in September, the owner–manager would be able to take the 2 percent discount if the bill were paid by October 10.

Another way of evaluating the value of the cash discounts is to calculate them on the basis of annual interest rates. To illustrate, the "2/10, net 30" cash discount is equivalent to earning an interest rate of approximately 36 percent on the amount involved in the transaction because there are 18 periods of 20 days each in a year that might be anticipated if the owner receives merchandise shipments regularly throughout the year. Other examples of the range of discounts available on an annual basis are shown here.

1% 10 days, net 30 days = 18% per annum
2% 10 days, net 60 days = 14% per annum
2% 30 days, net 60 days = 24% per annum
3% 10 days, net 30 days = 54% per annum

Quantity Discounts

Quantity discounts are justified on the basis that it is more economical to process and ship fewer large orders than many smaller orders involving the same quantity. However, the small business owner must compare the carrying costs of the larger inventory with the quantity discounts savings as well as the spoilage and obsolescence problems.

Two types of quantity discounts are found in business practice. One plan is the **noncumulative quantity discount.** Under the terms of this plan, quantity discounts are granted if a larger volume of merchandise is purchased in a single order. To illustrate, a supplier may put forward the following schedule.

Size of Order	Percent Discount on Order
Under a dozen	0%
1–2 dozen	2
3–4 dozen	4
5–6 dozen	6

The second plan is a **cumulative quantity discount.** The discount plan calls for the supplier to allow the purchaser a discount if purchases exceed a specified quantity or dollar amount over a predetermined time period. The time span may be a month, but a yearly basis is more common. For example, a manufacturer may permit a 3 percent discount if a small business firm's purchases total $5000 for a year.

Trade Discounts

Manufacturers in some lines of trade may establish a system that allows discounts off the list price or suggested retail price on the basis of their trade classification, that is, wholesaler or industrial buyer. These discounts are called **trade discounts,** and to qualify for them, a firm must perform some of the marketing functions for the manufacturer. These discounts are available to the purchaser regardless of the size of the order.

A manufacturer that sells to both wholesalers and industrial buyers may allow different percentage discounts to each based on the marketing functions performed for the manufacturer. Wholesalers store goods and sell to small users in the area and would be allowed a higher discount than the industrial buyer who purchases directly from the manufacturer. For example, the manufacturer may grant the wholesaler a 40 percent discount off the list price and the industrial buyer a 25 percent discount.

It is helpful to point out that trade discounts are often tied to catalog or price lists. Many suppliers publish comprehensive and costly catalogs at infrequent time periods. The wholesaler or manufacturer can use the same catalog or price list for different types of customers. For example, a manufacturer might publish a list price of a specific item at $10, then allow the wholesaler to take a 30 percent discount, the retailer a 20 percent discount, and the consumer a 10 percent discount. The discounts are often used to allow a business to adjust prices in a catalog or price list without having to reprint the entire catalog or price list. For example, an item might sell to wholesalers for $10 with a 20 percent discount. If the firm wishes to reduce the price for clearance, it may offer a 20 percent, 10 percent chain discount. Or if the firm wishes to increase the price, it may only offer a 10 percent discount on the item.

In other situations, suppliers may provide for a string of chain discounts available to the various classes of firms in the selling chain. In addition, a firm may qualify for more than one discount on a purchase depending on the services performed. Each additional level for which the firm qualifies is applied to the previous net amount. For example, a wholesaler may be offered a chain discount of 30, 20, and 10. Thus, the wholesaler would receive a discount of the manufacturer's list price of 30 percent less an additional 20 percent less an additional 10 percent. The chain discount allowed is calculated in the following manner.

Manufacturer's list price	$100.00
Less 30%	30.00
	$ 70.00
Less 20%	14.00
	$ 56.00
Less 10%	5.60
Net price paid by wholesaler	$ 50.40

If the wholesaler repeatedly offers the same terms on purchases from the same supplier, a shorter method can be used. In the illustration, the $50.40 that is the net figure to be paid is 50.4 percent of the original list price. Each of the discounts in the chain (30, 20, 10 percent) is subtracted from 100 percent and the remainder multiplied together.

$$100\% - 30\% = 70\%$$
$$100\% - 20\% = 80\%$$
$$100\% - 10\% = 90\%$$
$$0.70 \times 0.80 \times 0.90 = 50.4\% \text{ (or a discount of 49.6\%)}$$

Seasonal Discount

Seasonal discounts are offered by suppliers during off-seasons. For example, air conditioners are purchased on a seasonal basis. Manufacturers of air conditioners may wish to grant a seasonal discount of 5, 10, or 15 percent to a customer who places an order during the slow season. The off-season orders enable the manufacturer to use the manufacturing facilities more efficiently year round. Before taking advantage of the seasonal discount, the small business owner should consider all aspects of the purchase, including disadvantages, such as style change, overbuying, high inventory costs, spoilage, theft, and technical obsolescence.

Promotional Discount

A supplier may give buyers a price discount for performing special promotional activities. One form of **promotional discount** is when the supplier pays for the portion of the advertising done by the buyer that features the supplier's product. Other types of promotional discounts include giving a certain quantity of free mechandise to buyers who display the supplier's products and paying for the services of individuals who are employed to demonstrate supplier products in the buyer's place of business.

SUMMARY OF KEY POINTS

1. Purchasing is the process of buying the right quality in the right quantity from a reputable supplier at the best price and at the right time to meet demand.

2. Purchasing policies must be created that will guide company personnel as they make purchasing decisions.

3. Purchasing procedures detail the specific actions necessary to complete the purchasing process.

4. Economic order quantity (EOQ) is a technique for determining the right quantity to order that minimizes total variables costs of purchasing: procurement costs and carrying costs.

5. One decision that must be made by the small business owner is whether to make or buy components or complete products from suppliers.

6. Vendor analysis requires determining the best source of supply. Factors to be evaluated include dependability and reliability, services offered, number of vendors, vendor's location, terms of sale, and vendor's sales representatives.

7. The point at which title to goods passes must be established in the purchase transaction. When title passes may be determined by F.O.B. seller or F.O.B. buyer.

8. Consignment purchasing is a stockless purchasing system.

9. Types of discounts are cash, quantity, trade, seasonal, and promotional.

DISCUSSION QUESTIONS

1. What is the purchasing process?
2. How would you explain the purchasing procedure to a small business owner?
3. What factors should the small business owner evaluate when choosing suppliers of materials and services?
4. Is it better for the small business manufacturer to make or buy components for a product? Explain.
5. Explain the importance of time in the purchase decision.
6. What is the significance of F.O.B. seller and F.O.B. buyer?
7. What is a consignment purchase?
8. Distinguish between a trade discount and a quantity discount.
9. What is meant by the term "1/10, net 30"? What is its equivalent annual interest rate?

THE BUSINESS PLAN: EVALUATING THE EFFICIENCY OF THE PURCHASING PLAN

The goal of the purchasing plan in the small business is to make the company more efficient. The following questions serve as guides for evaluating the efficiency of the purchasing activity in the small business.

1. Do you or your designated representative have final authority and responsibility for purchasing?
2. Do you have established policies governing the purchasing activity to ensure efficiency in all phases of the purchasing operation?
3. Do you have clearly established purchasing procedures?
4. Do you have reputable vendors from whom you make your purchases?
5. Is competition among vendors encouraged, and are purchases competitive whenever possible?
6. Do you strive to maintain good relations with vendors?
7. Do you attempt to develop new and better sources of supply?
8. Are materials and supplies being purchased at lowest prices consistent with quality requirements?
9. Do purchase records clearly show previous prices and suppliers so that you do not have to estimate prices when reordering?
10. Do you have a reliable but simplified method of pricing small orders to keep the cost of such orders lower than the value of the materials?

11. Are purchases made against written requisitions to guard against over-buying or unnecessary buying?

12. Are alternative sources of supply for critical materials maintained as a safeguard in emergency situations?

13. Do you have a follow-up system on orders with vendors to ensure timely delivery?

14. Have specifications of items you purchase been standardized where possible to obtain the advantages and economy of volume buying?

15. Are delivery receipts processed promptly so that you do not lose cash discounts because of delays?

ENTREPRENEURIAL PROJECTS

1. Contact a supplier and find out what discount would be available to you if you were an entrepreneur.

2. Interview a small business owner and identify the factors they consider most important in selecting a vendor.

3. Interview a small business owner and determine their perception of handling goods on consignment.

4. Interview a small business owner and determine if they take advantage of purchase discounts.

5. Interview a small business owner and ascertain the kinds of services that sales representatives provide for them.

CASE A

The Ranch House

The Ranch House, a chain of four small, locally owned convenience stores, has established the following procedure for receiving merchandise from suppliers.

Receiving Merchandise from Suppliers

Salespersons should be treated courteously and in a businesslike manner. While customers always come first, do not make salespersons wait any longer than is necessary.

To assure that the Ranch House is getting all of the merchandise that it is charged for, and to eliminate any possible confusion, the following procedure shall be followed at all times.

1. Credits and charges are written as separate invoices.
2. Credits and charges are handled in a neutral area, away from the sales/display area of the item being bought.
3. If any credits are due (stale items, empty bottles, etc.), the salesperson shall bring such credit items to the specified neutral area and write the credit ticket. Then, the employee shall check the credits, sign the invoice, obtain the salesperson's signature, and retain the original invoice without relinquishing control of it after signing. All credit items are then removed from the store.
4. All items being purchased will be brought into the store to the specified neutral area and the charge invoice prepared. After all the merchandise has been brought to the specified area, the employee shall check it in, sign the invoice, obtain the salesperson's signature, and retain the original invoice without relinquishing control of it after signing. After this, salespersons shall not be permitted to remove anything from the store, including trash. Trash shall be removed by the employee.
5. Checking merchandise involves more than signing an invoice. Go down the invoice item by item and be absolutely certain you received everything for which you are charged.
6. Do not let the salespersons rush you. Set your own speed at checking the salesperson in. If you are confused, tell the salesperson to explain until you are satisfied. Make sure prices on the invoices match the merchandise you are receiving.
7. Do not accept improperly prepared or charged invoices.

Questions

1. Evaluate this merchandise-receiving procedure in terms of strengths and weaknesses. Would you recommend any changes?
2. Why should the trash be removed only by the employees?

CASE B
Scientific Laboratories, Inc.

Scientific Laboratories is an independent testing laboratory of new products to determine their reliability and performance capabilities. A variety of materials and equipment are used in the testing process, and many of the testing materials are consumed in the testing process. The acquisition of these materials and equipment is a continuous process and requires specialized knowledge of testing materials. For these reasons, Scientific Laboratories has a full-time purchasing agent.

Donald Sands, purchasing agent for the laboratory, received a purchase requisition for 500 test tubes. A month earlier, he had purchased 1000 identical test tubes from Federal Glass Company for 49 cents per tube, F.O.B. buyer's destination. Donald telephoned Federal and asked for a price quotation on the 500 tubes. The quote was 51 cents per unit (F.O.B. buyer's destination). Donald looked up the previous quotes he had received on the last order of 1000 test tubes and found the following price quotations (all prices were F.O.B. buyer's destination).

Test Tubes, Inc.	57 cents per unit
United Glass	55 cents per unit
A-1 Glass Products	51 cents per unit
Federal Glass	49 cents per unit

Later that same day, Donald received a purchase requisition for a multipurpose analyzer, estimated to cost $2150. A request for a bids was sent to five companies that make the multipurpose analyzer and four bids were received: $2125, $2155, $2175, and $2225. The equipment on all bids was comparable and prices were F.O.B. buyer's destination. The $2125 bid from Johnson Equipment Company was accepted. When the invoice for the equipment was received, Johnson Equipment billed Scientific Laboratories $2150.

On another order, Sterling Electronics had delivered a portable computer to Scientific Laboratories on October 4. The cost was $985, terms 3/10, net/30. Sterling's invoice was dated October 10. On October 19, payment was made in the amount of $955.45. Sterling Electronics claims that the full price, $985.00, should be the proper amount, since the computer was delivered on October 4.

Sterling Electronics has offered a trade discount of 30 percent, 15 percent, and 5 percent to Scientific Laboratories for three orders of $1000, $625, and $5750, respectively.

Donald must also purchase consumable items, such as paper towels, used in the washrooms and as cleaning materials in the lab. These towels have been purchased from a local supplier in quantities of 5 cases, which is equivalent to one month's supply. The supplier has always delivered the goods on time. Last week, a salesperson from a large paper manufacturer called and offered Donald paper towels of comparable quality but at a price that is 10 percent lower than is currently paid to the local supplier, based on a quantity purchase of 50 cases. The manufacturer is located 600 miles away, but terms would be F.O.B. buyer's destination.

On a bottled chemical used in the lab, the annual demand is 2400 units. The procurement cost is $20 per order and the carrying cost per unit is $0.60.

Questions

1. Is the 51 cents per tube price quotation from Federal Glass considered a reasonable price for the 500 test tubes?

2. Should Donald solicit more price quotations from other suppliers or should he issue a purchase order for the 500 units from Federal?

3. What should Donald do about the overcharge on the bill from Johnson Equipment Company?

4. Does Scientific Laboratories owe Sterling Electronics more money on the portable computer?

5. How much should Scientific Laboratories remit to Sterling Electronics for the three orders on which the trade discount is offered? How much is the actual discount on the three purchases?

6. What factors should Donald consider in evaluating the salesperson's offer of the lower price on the quantity purchase?

7. What would be the correct number of units of the bottled chemical for Donald to order?

Notes

1 "Purchasing for Manufacturing Firms," *Business Basics,* No. 1015 (Washington, D.C.: Small Business Administration, 1980), p. 6.

2 Clifton Smith, "Policy and Procedure Manuals," in *Aljian's Purchasing Handbook,* 4th ed., ed. Paul V. Farrell (New York: McGraw-Hill, 1982), p. 3–31.

3 *Purchasing and Cost Control* (Washington, D.C.: Small Business Administration, 1984), p. 27.

4 J. H. Westing, I. V. Fine, and Gary J. Zenz, *Purchasing Management,* 4th ed. (New York: John Wiley, 1976), p. 53.

5 "Purchasing for Manufacturing Firms," p. 23.

6 Westing, Fine, and Zenz, *Purchasing Management,* p. 307.

7 Ibid., p. 308.

8 Caleb Johnson, "Inventory Management," in *Aljian's Purchasing Handbook,* 4th ed., ed. Paul V. Farrell (New York: McGraw-Hill, 1982), pp. 12–35, 12–36.

9 Myron Frye, "Price Considerations," In *Aljian's Purchasing Handbook,* 4th ed., ed. Paul V. Farrell (New York: McGraw-Hill, 1982), p. 10–9.

KEY WORDS

CHAPTER 15

INVENTORY CONTROL

After reading this chapter, you will understand:

1 That inventory control is important to small business because it reduces costs while aiding customer relations.

2 How keeping a record of customer requests for items not in stock aids in inventory control.

3 How the basic perpetual inventory system works and how some firms use specialized forms of perpetual inventory control.

4 How visual, periodic, and partial inventory control systems operate.

5 The importance of the two basic methods of physical inventory counts.

6 How to identify and clear slow-moving items in inventory.

7 The value of shelf space analysis and how it is performed.

ENTREPRENEURIAL PROFILE

Ed Shorma

WAHPETON CANVAS

He invented a beltless tarp that rolls automatically over a truck full of grain. His hardwood veneers adorn many a renovated home across the land. But what makes Ed Shorma most happy is that there are at least 15 nationalities among his 220 employees at Wahpeton Canvas in North Dakota.

You wouldn't expect Malaysians and Indonesians to work in 30 below zero weather, or what Northerners call "white-out" storms. But Shorma has sponsored dozens of refugees from many lands, and gone one step further: he has given them jobs.

Perhaps it has something to do with growing up in Wyndmere, North Dakota, among Czechoslovakian immigrants, and not speaking English until he entered grade school. Today, Shorma not only has command of English, but many of the exotic languages his employees speak.

In 1954, Shorma borrowed $1500 from a local bank in Wahpeton, located 47 miles south of Fargo on the Minnesota border, and purchased an old shoe repair shop. His first year of soles and shines brought in $5600.

Two years later, still operating out of a basement, he began to make canvas covers for farm trucks, grain drill boxes, and fertilizer attachments. Shorma saw a need for this kind of potection for machines in bad weather. And he began to fill the void.

Up-from-the-bootstraps stories don't involve SBA—that's the conventional misconception. In 1970, after an unsuccessful stint at farming and a term in the state legislature, Shorma wanted to go full tilt with canvasmaking. To effect a move from the basement

to downtown space, SBA loaned Shorma $75,000. The extra space was put to immediate use manufacturing original equipment seats for Canadian farm equipment makers—helping the trade balance in the days when it wasn't so unbalanced.

At the time of SBA's first loan, Wahpeton Canvas had gross annual sales of $147,000, and 17 employees. Today the company sells $12 million worth of goods a year, and has 220 employees. Not a bad return on investment!

Source: Network (Washington, D.C.: Small Business Administration, November–December 1987).

Retail and wholesale firms carry merchandise for resale, manufacturing firms carry raw materials and finished goods inventories, and service firms carry parts and supplies. All of these firms incur expenses that are a result of their **inventory.** How much inventory they carry and how well they control it is very important to their business.

COST OF INVENTORY

The major costs of inventory are from (1) storage facilities, (2) spoilage and obsolescence, (3) insurance, (4) handling, and (5) interest.

Storage Facilities

The larger the size of the inventory, the larger storage facilities must be to accommodate the merchandise. Land, building, or rental costs or all three are major expenditures for the small business. The requirements of storage also may vary in cost. For example, construction and maintenance of a sheet metal shed is much less expensive than construction and maintenance of cold storage facilities.

Spoilage and Obsolescence

Some inventories are perishable, and larger inventories of these items usually result in some losses from spoilage. Other goods are subject to obsolescence owing to fashion changes, for instance, clothing. Inventory items may also suffer from obsolescence because better products are introduced on the market, and the greater the amount of the item in stock, the greater the loss.

Insurance

Various types of insurance should be carried to provide coverage on the inventory, primarily fire and theft. Larger amounts of inventory mean higher insurance costs because premiums are based, in part, on the dollar value of the inventory.

Handling

Generally, the more inventory a small business carries, the more often it must be handled. This handling is an expense to the business in terms of costs of manpower, equipment, and damaged goods.

FIGURE 15-1
GOOD INVENTORY CONTROL REDUCES COSTS AND AIDS CUSTOMER RELATIONS.

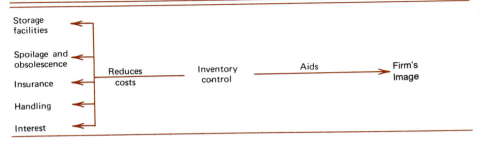

Interest

Inventory also requires an investment of funds. If the firm borrows money to maintain an inventory, it must pay interest on the borrowed funds. Even if the business does not borrow funds, it is still considered an expense because it would be able to use the funds it has invested in inventory for other uses. Even putting the funds into a savings account would earn the firm money that it will not receive if it is tied up in inventory.

Inadequate Inventory Control

All these are costs that the business firm must sustain in order to maintain an adequate inventory. However, if the firm carries too much inventory, it will significantly increase these costs. In additton, if the firm does not perform good inventory control, it can sustain additional losses in these costs. (See Fig. 15-1). For instance, one small retail appliance store discovered that it had several thousand dollars' worth of appliances that had been covered with other merchandise in a crowded storeroom for several years. The appliances were out of style and had to be sold at a large loss.

Poor inventory control encourages employee theft and prevents the business from recognizing shoplifting problems or even knowing how much is being lost to theft. Inadequate records of inventory cause problems in insurance claims in losses resulting from burglary. The small business that does not practice good inventory control may lose money it does not even know it is losing.

One example of how much a firm can lose without knowing about it is the case of a large store handling hardware and do-it-yourself items. The firm did not have an adequate inventory control system in its three stores in one city. It was notified by the police that three of its employees were caught in a police fencing operation run to trap thieves. The employees, it was later discovered, had stolen more than $100,000 of merchandise during the past year.

The store had no idea it had lost any merchandise until the police uncovered the loss.

INVENTORY AND CUSTOMER RELATIONS

A small business must carry sufficient amounts of inventory in order to maintain good customer relations. Customers who go into a retail store several times and are told the store is out of a product soon develop a feeling that they won't be able to find what they want if they return. They will soon trade elsewhere. The service firm that makes customers wait for service while the business obtains parts or supplies will suffer the same fate from its customers. The wholesaler who is often out of products retailers order will find that these merchants will soon patronize other wholesalers. Customers of manufacturers who experience too many delayed delivery dates will also shift purchases to other manufacturers.

The idea, then, is to balance inventory costs and customer relations. The firm must maintain as small an inventory as possible to reduce costs, yet maintain an inventory that is adequate to satisfy customer needs. Good inventory control is the key.

REQUESTS FOR ITEMS NOT IN STOCK

As a part of their inventory control system, small business firms should keep a record of all requests for merchandise that they do not have in stock. Inadequate reorder points can be easily spotted through this type of record. If a specific item that is regularly carried in inventory appears more than once over a reasonable period of time on the report, the firm should consider setting the reorder point higher. If an item that the firm does not stock appears more than once over a reasonable period of time, the business should consider adding the item to inventory.

INVENTORY CONTROL SYSTEMS

A business firm may utilize three basic types of inventory control systems: (1) perpetual inventory systems, (2) visual systems, and (3) periodic and partial control systems.

Perpetual Inventory Systems

A basic **perpetual inventory system** is used by many types of small business firms, including manufacturers, wholesalers, retailers, and service establish-

FIGURE 15-2
PERCEPTUAL INVENTORY CARD (GROCERY WHOLESALER).

Item Green Giant English Peas–303 Can

| Reorder Point | 100 cs | Order Amount | 400 cs | Stock Control # | CV-1604 |

In		Out		Balance
Date	Amount	Date	Amount	
				80
3/21	400			480
		4/1	60	420
		4/4	40	380

ments. In addition, specialized perpetual inventory systems are used by different types of businesses, particularly retail operations.

Basic Perpetual Inventory System

A basic perpetual inventory card is shown in Figure 15-2. Variations of this basic card are used by many small businesses. Some manufacturers, wholesalers, and service firms use **bin tags** that carry the same information as this card but are in the form of a tag. These tags are attached to the storage bin or shelf, and receipts and withdrawals of the item are noted on the tags when they are made. Retailers use several variations of the basic perpetual inventory system, which will be discussed later in this chapter.

The perpetual inventory card carries such general information as the name of the item, stock number, and reorder point. Every time additions to the inventory of this item are received from vendors, the number is recorded and added to the balance. Every time some of the items are used or sold, the withdrawal is recorded and subtracted from the balance.

If the perpetual inventory method is used, a look at the balance at any time will reveal the amount of inventory on hand for this item. According to need, other information may be recorded on the card, such as price, amount ordered but not received, specifications, location in stockroom, and what department uses the inventory item.

Firms that have a relatively small number of items and a small number of transactions per day are ideal for perpetual inventory systems using these in-out-balance cards. It does not take a person too long to record about 50 purchases a day. However, in small stores that have a large variety of items or a large number of purchases each day or both, it takes a considerable amount of time to post the daily purchases to perpetual inventory cards. For example, the small drive-in grocery would find it very time consuming to make a record of each item purchased and post them all to perpetual inventory cards.

Computerized Perpetual Inventory Control

Many firms with a wide range of inventory items and many additions and withdrawals each day have gone to **computer-based inventory control.** The same basic system is used in computer systems as is used in a manual operation. Instead of using perpetual inventory cards, the firm's personnel feed data on receipts and withdrawals of specific items into the computer, and a balance is retained in the computer's memory banks. Many of these firms tie their cash registers into their computer systems. As each sale is recorded on the cash register, it is also fed into the computer inventory control records.

Manufacturers universal codes are a particularly efficient method of recording sales from inventory in retail stores. Cash registers that are equipped with bar code readers scan the **manufacturers universal code** printed on the item and send it to a computer that keeps a complete up-to-the-minute perpetual inventory. The firm does not have to do anything to items placed on the shelf (such as adding tags with inventory coding). In addition, the customer is charged the correct current price, including sale prices.

The price of microcomputers and other associated electronic equipment has dropped during the past few years to such an extent that it is now feasible for almost all small businesses to perform their complete inventory control function on a computerized basis. In addition, computer software has become so "user friendly" that it takes very little training to use.

Specialized Perpetual Inventory Systems in Retail Stores

Retail stores often use specialized systems for collecting and transferring information into their perpetual inventory systems. Some of the more common methods are (1) sales ticket control, (2) stub control, (3) floor sample control, and (4) punched card control.

Sales Ticket Control
Sales tickets are one method of collecting perpetual inventory sales information. Sales tickets are completed each time merchandise is sold, listing such information as department, number of items sold, type of item sold, unit price, tax, and total price. This ticket is then used for posting to the card or computer perpetual inventory system. The sales ticket is also useful in accounting control, such as cash control and sales taxes payable. (See Fig. 15-3.)

MICROCOMPUTER INVENTORY CONTROL

The importance of inventory control to maintaining good customer relations and decreasing costs (which increases profit) has been discussed at length in this chapter. One of the more important functions of good inventory control is theft control. Without sufficient information about inventory, it is almost impossible to detect and pinpoint theft problems.

The number of items gone from inventory, sales amounts, and cash received must balance. If they do not balance, then there is an error or a theft problem. The business must investigate and determine which is the case. An inexpensive personal computer (PC) with a 10- to 40-megabyte hard drive can perform the inventory control function quickly and efficiently. It can also provide valuable information and reports that are usually too time consuming and expensive when the inventory control function is performed by hand.

The normal "canned" software package (program) for inventory control usually costs between $200 and $1000. Custom software packages for specific types of operations may cost considerably more. Some of the functions the "canned programs" will perform are these.

1. Posts sales transactions and prints reports for inventory sales performance by product, by class of product, by salesperson, and so on. It provides information about the contribution of profit by each item or group of items.
2. Creates and prints purchase orders. Lists open purchase orders and suggests items that should be ordered.
3. Lists the complete inventory with amount, price, code, and other related information.
4. Keeps a perpetual inventory record.
5. Keeps a record of and prints a report that contains a complete list of all vendors.
6. Prints work sheets that contain a complete list of all inventory with number of items and a space for the physical inventory count.

A good method for using sales tickets is to have a locked box with a slit in the top, and each time a sale is made, the clerk puts the ticket in the box. At the end of the day, the box is opened, and the total of the sales tickets is used as a check against the amount of cash in the register and the cash register tape. The sales tickets are then posted individually on perpetual inventory cards or entered into the computerized inventory control system. When the physical inventory count is checked against the perpetual inventory cards or computer records, any shortages are identified and managers immediately know if they have a theft problem.

Another method of using sales tickets for perpetual inventory control is common in some retail firms, such as automobile parts stores. A basic inven-

FIGURE 15-3
A VERY SIMPLE SALES TICKET SOLD BY MOST OFFICE SUPPLY FIRMS.

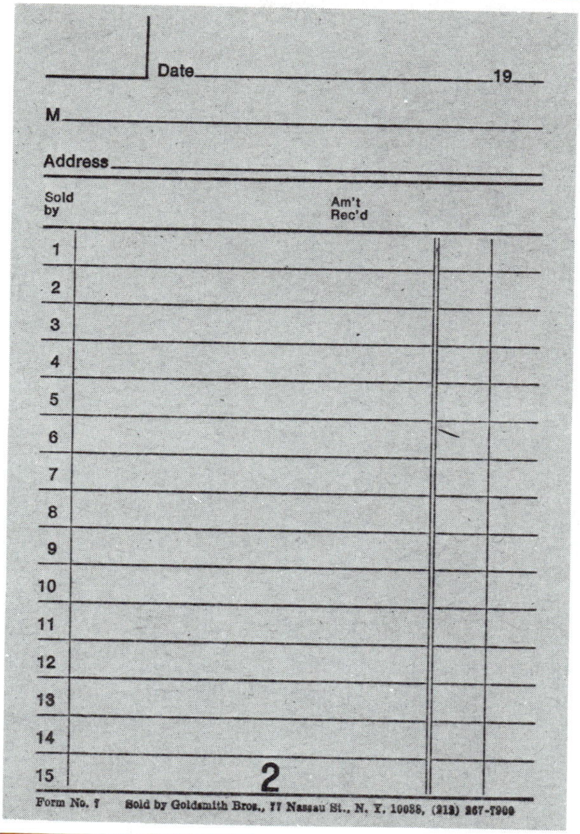
Date ____________ 19___
M ____________
Address ____________
Sold by
Am't Rec'd
1
2
3
4
5
6
7
8
9
10
11
12
13
14
15
2
Form No. 7 Sold by Goldsmith Bros., 77 Nassau St., N. Y. 10038, (212) 267-7900

tory is established on a yearly basis, and all items of the desired inventory are placed in stock. When a sale is made, a sales ticket is completed listing the part, its code number, and the number of units sold. Each day all items that appear on sales tickets are reordered to bring the inventory back to its original level. If the inventory on hand plus all items on order differ from the basic inventory, it is a warning signal to the manager that he or she has a theft or recording problem.

Stub Control **Stub control** of perpetual inventory consists of attaching a two part or more stub to each item that is offered for sale. (See Fig. 15-4). All the stub parts have such information as the department number, vendor code, types of merchandise, and any other coded information of value to the inventory and accounting systems of the store. When the merchandise is sold, one

FIGURE 15-4
SALES STUB INVENTORY CONTROL.

part of the stub is removed and placed in a collection container. The removed stub is then used to post to the perpetual inventory system and in accounting control procedures. If the customer returns the merchandise, the stub remaining on the merchandise is used to restock the merchandise and correct accounting records.

Floor Sample Control　**Floor sample control** is common to appliance- and furniture-type operations that place one of each item in stock (floor samples) in the show room area and then fill customer orders from inventory. One method is to have small pads with consecutive numbers printed on each page. The pads may be numbered from 1 to 100, and the total number of merchandise items that are received in stock is attached to the floor sample. For example, an appliance store may receive 25 units of a specific model of refrigerator. Numbers 26 through 100 are removed from a printed pad and the numbers 1 through 25 are attached to the floor sample. Each time a clerk completes a sale, he or she removes a number. Consequently, sales personnel are able to look at the remaining numbers on the pad and know immediately how many are left in stock.

Punched Card Control　A **punched card control** system uses two or more part tags or standard computer punched cards attached to the merchandise for sale. When an item of merchandise is sold, a part of the tag or punched card is removed from the item and placed in a collection container. The tags or standard computer cards are fed into a special ticket-converting machine or automatic card sorter for sorting into categories. The cards are then fed into specialized tabulating equipment or a computer to record inventory and accounting control information.

Visual Control Systems

Many small firms feel they are unable to maintain a perpetual inventory system for various reasons—high volume of small-volume items, large stock of small-value items, lack of funds to pay personnel to maintain a perpetual system, or an unfounded belief that computer systems are excessively complicated and expensive (or all of these).

The small business manager often is very familiar with inventory and knows approximately how much should be on hand at any given time. A daily visual examination allows the manager to estimate how much should be ordered.

Visual control is probably the most common method of stock control in small business firms and is the least effective. Visual control works better for firms that have stable sales, large numbers of each item in stock, merchandise that can be obtained quickly from vendors, and merchandise that is segregated on shelves or in bins. Inability to determine shortages of items is a major disadvantage of the visual control system.

For example, one small business located near a school was losing several thousand dollars each year owing to shoplifting and never realized the extent of the problem until one of the authors set up an inventory control system for the business. Shortages in inventory revealed by the inventory control system indicated the extent of the problem. By installing several shoplifting prevention techniques, the firm was able to increase its profit level significantly.

Periodic and Partial Control Systems

Small business firms that feel they are unable to maintain perpetual systems because of inventory volume, size, or cost of all three may elect a **periodic inventory system** or **partial control system** in conjunction with the visual system.

The periodic control system involves recording purchases and inventory levels at reorder times. For example, a sporting goods merchant would record the amount of baseballs on hand. When he or she feels it is time to reorder, the number purchased and the number remaining in stock are recorded. This record tells the merchant what normal turnover period is for each item and gives the merchant some approximation of how many items are on hand based on this normal turnover. It also has a major weakness of not identifying shortages.

A closely related system involves taking a complete inventory count of the business and then at the end of some period (such as three months) taking the entire physical inventory count again. The difference between the first and the second inventory count is computed, and all purchases for the period are added to the balance. All items that have the same percentage markup are then put in a category (such as 20 percent markup items into one group and 30 percent markup items into another group). By taking the cost of all the items and applying the markup for each group, the firm can come somewhat close to what its sales should have been for the period. If the sales total for the period differs significantly from the projected sales figure, the firm then knows it probably has a theft problem.

To help identify shortages, but still not use a perpetual inventory system for all merchandise, some small business managers use a partial perpetual inventory system. They may keep perpetual inventory records on more expensive items or items of merchandise more prone to theft. Other low-value merchandise is maintained by visual or periodic inventory control.

Some small business managers attempt to identify shortages by keeping a perpetual inventory on part of their merchandise on a rotating basis. For example, one drug retailer takes a physical inventory count on one part of total stock, such as gift items. He then keeps a record of all gift item sales and purchases for a month's period. At the end of the month, the drug retailer then takes another physical inventory count. By adding purchase to starting inventory and deducting the ending inventory, he knows how many gifts should have been sold during the month. By applying markup on gifts and comparing the total to sale of gifts, he is able to identify shortages from employee or shoplifting theft. The revolving perpetual inventory also allows the drug retailer to (1) identify reorder points more accurately, (2) establish optimum order size more accurately, (3) spot slow-moving items, (4) institute greater control over items more susceptible to theft, and (5) identify sections of the store that have greatest losses of merchandise.

Given the current low price of personal computers, inventory control software, and cash registers with bar code scanners, many visual, periodic, and partial control systems should be replaced with perpetual control systems.

PHYSICAL INVENTORY COUNT

Every small business should perform a periodic inventory count. Even if the firm has a perpetual inventory system that is designed to provide inventory information on a continuous basis, it should still perform a **physical inventory count** to identify mistakes and shortages. There are two basic methods of performing inventory counts.

One method is to perform it on all inventory at regular intervals, at least once a year. Retailers often run special sales to reduce their inventory just before inventory time. They then bring employees in on an overtime basis

An employee making a physical inventory count.

when the store is normally closed to perform the inventory count. This method provides the most accurate income statement if prepared at the same time as the inventory count. The count is also checked against the perpetual inventory at this time.

One very efficient method is to have the firm's computer (microcomputers will perform this function) print out a complete list of all items in stock with the number that should be in stock listed and a space for what is counted in stock. One person calls out the item and the number in stock, and another person marks the number actually in stock on the list. The number that should be in stock is next to the number that is actually in stock, and any deviation is instantly noted.

Another method is to perform a count of a few items each week on a continuous basis. These continuous inventory counts provide an ongoing check against the perpetual inventory system. This method sometimes allows the identification of mistakes and shortages sooner than the periodic count.

SLOW-MOVING ITEMS

Items in inventory tend to turn over at widely different rates whether they are raw materials or finished goods inventory of manufacturers, merchandise of wholesalers, parts and supplies of service establishments, or goods of the retailer. The slower the turnover of items in inventory, generally, the greater the chance of loss owing to spoilage or obsolescence. A good inventory system is necessary to keep this loss at a minimum by identifying slow-moving items. These slow movers may be specific products, colors, sizes, models, and so on. Once the slow-moving items are identified, there are various means that a small business manager may employ to deal with them.

One possibility is to eliminate the item from inventory. An analysis should be made to determine the amount that this item contributes to profit each year, relative to the cost of keeping it in stock. Many items that are slow movers cannot be eliminated from stock. The firm's customers may expect them to carry the item, and it may affect customer relations and patronage if eliminated. Also, some firms try to build an image of having almost anything you want so you don't have to go to several different stores. Many slow-moving items are necessary to this type store's image.

The most common method of dealing with slow-moving items is markdown. Markdown of merchandise is not only a method of clearing slow-moving merchandise but is also a good promotional technique. In fact, many retail stores offer markdowns on a wide range of merchandise at one time to maximize the promotional effect. Almost all retail stores engage in markdown sales, which are attempts to build customer patronage and store image as well as clear slow-moving items from inventory.

SHELF SPACE ANALYSIS

Up to now, we have talked in terms of slow-moving items and have generally ignored profitably of products. As a simple illustration, a firm may sell 10 watches in a month at a gross profit of $2 each and still make more money on them than by selling 100 toys at a 10 cent gross profit per unit. Another factor that has not been taken into consideration is the amount of store space required to sell a specific item. The store just mentioned might be able to sell watches and rings in the same space it would require just to sell the toy.

A technique called **shelf space analysis** is a means of measuring the

FIGURE 15-5
SHELF SPACE ANALYSIS.

Cost of item per unit	×	Percentage markup	=	Gross profit per unit
Gross profit per unit	×	Number of units sold during period	=	Total gross profit for period
Total gross profit	÷	Shelf space occupied in square inches	=	Gross profit per square inch for the period

profitability of each item in terms of turnover, profit per item, and amount of selling space required to sell the product. (See Fig. 15-5.)

To perform shelf space analysis, the firm must first measure each item it sells in terms of the amount of shelf space (in square inches) it occupies in the selling area. The average number of items it sells per month is then computed using beginning inventory plus all purchases for the year minus ending inventory and dividing by 12. Seasonal goods should be computed over the number of months they are actually carried in the selling area. Other seasonal goods may be carried in the same space during the other seasons. Examples are the following two items.

	Watches	Beach Balls
Beginning inventory	30	100
Purchases for year	50	1150
	80	1250
Less: Ending inventory	20	50
Total sold for year	60	1200
Divided by months in stock	5 (12 months)	300 (4 months)

The average cost of a unit plus markup is then computed to determine the average gross profit per unit sold. The average number of items sold per months times the per unit gross profit gives the gross profit per month.

	Watches	Beach Balls
Cost per unit	$20	$0.50
Times markup percentage	× 50%	× 40%
Equals gross profit per unit	10	$0.20
Times units sold per month	× 5	× 300
Equals gross profit per month	$50	$60

The amount of shelf space required for each item is then computed and divided into the average monthly gross profit to determine the amount of gross profit per square inch of shelf space each item produces. The linear inches of the front of the shelf space can be used in place of square inches when it produces just as good an analysis, such as when the depth of all shelves are the same.

	Watches	**Beach Balls**
Shelf space occupied	15 by 20 inches	40 by 60 inches
Total shelf space occupied	300 square inches	2400 square inches
Gross profit per square inch of shelf space per month	$50 ÷ 300 = $.167 *or* 16.7¢	$60 × 2400 = $.025 *or* 2.5¢

It is obvious in our example that watches are more profitable in terms of gross profit produced relative to selling area required.

This is a fairly simple process, but a more complex formula may be used that includes such items as storage cost, investment cost, spoilage and obsolescence costs, and frequency of stocking the items on the shelves. In addition, some shelf space may be more valuable than other shelf space, such as window space.

It would appear that shelf space analysis would be a large undertaking for a store with a large number of inventory items, such as a drug or grocery retailer. The best method of achieving shelf space analysis in this type of store is to use the computer or take a few items each week until the entire inventory analysis is completed. After the initial analysis is completed, it is necessary to perform the analysis on items that are added or on items that have undergone some drastic change in price, volume, or shelf space required.

From this chapter, it should be obvious that the small business manager must maintain good inventory control techniques to maximize profit.

SUMMARY OF KEY POINTS

1. The major costs of inventory are from (1) storage facilities, (b) spoilage and obsolescence, (c) insurance, (d) handling, and (e) interest.
2. A firm must maintain as small an inventory as possible to reduce costs, yet maintain an inventory that is adequate to satisfy customer needs.
3. A list should be kept that records all items requested by customers that are not in stock to evaluate reorder points and identify new items that should be carried in stock.
4. The basic perpetual inventory system records additions, withdrawals, and the balance on a continual basis.
5. Sales ticket control consists of the clerk's filling out a sales ticket for each sale, which is then posted to the perpetual inventory system at the end of each day.

6. Stub control consists of attaching a two or more part stub to the merchandise. One part of the stub is removed at the time of sale and used to post to the perpetual inventory control system.

7. Floor sample control is maintained by placing pads with numbers on them on the floor sample. One number is removed from the floor sample at the time of sale.

8. Punched card control is used when punched computer cards are attached to the merchandise and are removed at the time of sale for posting to inventory control records.

9. Visual control consists of viewing the inventory each day and reordering what looks low.

10. Periodic and partial control systems consist of taking inventory and adding purchases to see what should have been sold.

11. A physical inventory count should be taken on a periodic basis (at least once a year) to identify shortages.

12. The inventory control system should identify slow-moving items, which can be cleared from inventory in markdown sales.

13. Shelf space analysis measures the profitability of each inch of space of each product.

DISCUSSION QUESTIONS

1. Why is inventory control important from the standpoint of costs? From the standpoint of customer relations?

2. Why is the basic perpetual inventory control system called perpetual?

3. Which inventory control system is the most efficient? Why?

4. Briefly explain how the following work.
   a. Sales ticket control.
   b. Stub control.
   c. Floor sample control.
   d. Punched card control.

5. Which types of inventory control systems have failure to identify shortages as their major weaknesses?

6. What are the two basic methods of physical inventory counts?

7. What are some of the reasons for having markdowns of items in inventory?

8. Is there a good side to markdowns? Explain.

9. Why is shelf space analysis valuable?

THE BUSINESS PLAN: INVENTORY CONTROL

____ Will a Request for Items not in Stock form be of use to you?

____ Will you have less than 20 items in inventory? You could use a visual control system, but a perpetual system would be better.

____ Will you have more than 20 items in inventory and have more than 20 transactions a day? You can use a manual periodic or partial control system, but a perpetual system would be better.

____ Will you have inventory in your business? A perpetual inventory system is best because it gives you greater control in your business.

____ If you have less than 20 items and 20 transactions a day, a manual perpetual control system will meet your needs.

____ Could you use bin tags, perpetual inventory cards, sales tickets, stub control, floor sample control, or punched card control?

____ Will you have more than 20 items and 20 transactions a day? Your best system would be a computer-based inventory control system.

____ Have you selected a software package for your computer-based inventory control system? If not, go to a software store and select one that best meets your needs.

____ Do you have a large number of items with many transactions a day in a retail store? You should probably use a cash register with a bar code scanner tied in with your computer-based inventory control system.

____ How often do you plan to perform a periodic inventory count? Will you count it all at once or a few items each week? Be sure to identify slow-moving items and shortages.

____ Will there be a possibility of having slow-moving items in your inventory? How will you recognize them and how will you clear them out of inventory?

____ Will shelf space analysis be of any importance to you? If it will be, follow the simple steps presented in this chapter.

ENTREPRENEURIAL PROJECTS

Visit an area with a high concentration of retail stores such as a shopping center or mall. Select three small retail stores, and attempt to discover what types of inventory control system they use.

CASE A

Karen Kay Perfumes

Karen Kay last year leased space in a new shopping mall and opened a shop named Karen Kay perfumes. She stocked her store with several brands of perfume, one top line of cosmetics, and a limited line of higher-priced toiletries. The shop has a total of 60 different items offered for sale.

Sales have been good since she opened her shop, but she does not seem to be making as much profit as she feels she should, considering her volume of sales. In addition, she has had some complaints because a few customers were unable to purchase a particular item they wanted. Most of the time it was because Karen was out of the item in stock, and a few times because it was in stock, but she overlooked it and thought she was out.

Karen has exclusive distributorships for two brands of very expensive perfumes. She wants to get rid of one brand so that she will have room to add another perfume she feels has a very high profit potential. However, she is not sure which is the more profitable of the two brands she now carries. The following is some information she has gathered about the two brands:

	Brand X	Brand Y
Total yearly bottle sales	144	420
Cost per bottle	$15	$10
Markup percentage	100%	100%
Shelf space occupied	15 by 10 inches	20 by 10 inches

The difference in shelf space used for the two perfumes is the result of brand Y's requiring Karen to exhibit its perfume in a special display device on the shelf.

Questions

1. Does Karen need some type of inventory control? Explain.
2. What type of inventory control system would you suggest?
3. If she uses a perpetual inventory system, what kind would you suggest?
4. Would you suggest a physical inventory count and, if so, what type?
5. Perform a shelf space analysis on brands X and Y. Which should Karen eliminate?
6. How would you suggest she dispose of current stock of the brand you have chosen to eliminate?

CASE B
A to Z Hardware

A to Z Hardware is owned and operated by Alex Reese. The store sells a wide range of hardware items. The business has always been profitable and sales have grown over the past five years the business has been in operation.

Alex suspects that he has a theft problem. An expensive chain saw has recently disappeared, and no one remembers selling it. Alex does not know if this is a one-time incident or if it happens often. Alex has considered a manual perpetual inventory system for his inventory, but it seems out of the question since he carries more than 700 items in stock. About 300 of these items are less than $5 in value, and 300 are more than $5 but less than $20. The store averages about 80 customer purchases a day.

Alex has noticed that about three customers each day do not obtain what they came to purchase. He estimates that one-third of these requests are for items the store is out of and two-thirds are for items he does not carry. These customers concern Alex because he feels it is important for his store to project an image that he has what people want and they will not have to go to other stores.

Alex feels you have an extensive knowledge of small business operations and has come to you for help.

Questions

1. What kind of inventory control system will you recommend to Alex?
2. What might lead you to believe he has an inventory problem?
3. Would the "not-in-stock" incidents each day lead you to any other recommendations?
4. Do you think shelf space analysis would be beneficial to Alex? Explain.

MARKETING THE PRODUCT OR SERVICE

KEY WORDS

CHAPTER 16

MARKETING STRATEGY AND MARKETING RESEARCH

LEARNING GOALS

After reading this chapter, you will understand:

1 The meaning of the term "marketing."

2 The eight functions of marketing.

3 The marketing concept.

4 What marketing strategy is.

5 The significance of marketing research for a small business.

6 The sequence of activities in the marketing research process.

7 The types of marketing research data available to the small business manager.

8 The difference between observation, interview, and experimentation methods of data collection.

9 The use of sampling in marketing research.

10 A technique for conducting a sample survey suitable for use in the small business.

Betty Vhay

APPLEGATE FARM

Life with the 140-year old Applegate Farm in Montclair, New Jersey, was anything but bright for Betty Vhay. Since purchasing the dairy farm in 1981 with her husband, Vhay has endured more than the usual set of hard knocks. Money was chronically low; neighbors brought a lawsuit against the farm over "loud" machinery that was making ice cream (and making the place a "hangout" for area teenagers); she went through a bitter divorce. It seemed to her at times that the circumstances of the farm's purchase were an ill omen: after losing an unborn child in a car accident, she had taken $100,000 in settlement money to stake her future on Applegate Farm.

With two children to support by herself, Vhay pulled out all stops in the search for money to help the ice cream operation. Bank after bank turned her down as a credit risk.

Then in January 1987, the Money Store Investment Corporation took a chance on Vhay and provided her with an SBA-guaranteed loan of $170,000. For the first time since 1981, she had working capital, was sole owner, and recorded her first profit.

In 1981, Vhay employed 10; today she employs 52, most of whom are teenagers outfitted with their first job as ice cream barflies. Annual sales in 1987 were $700,000, a sizable increase over the $420,000 figure in 1981.

Until recently Vhay herself marketed her wholesale ice cream—one-quarter of the business—to area restaurants, nursing homes, and hospitals, though now she has hired a full-time marketer. In good weather Applegate Farm serves ice cream to over 25,000 people a week. Experiments include a green-tea flavored ice cream preferred by local Japanese restaurants.

Over 7000 daffodils and 300 azalea plants dot the picturesque spread. Walking around the five original buildings of the old farm, including the "new" barn (built in 1915) which serves as a freezer, is a comfort to Vhay today as is her success to SBA.

Source: Network (Washington, D.C.: Small Business Administration, May–June 1988).

THE ROLE OF MARKETING

Development of the marketing plan of the small business must rate as a high-priority activity. Unfortunately, many small business owners assume that the only requirement for success is to open for business and wait for customers. What they fail to comprehend is that marketing is a complex process. The perceptive small business owner understands that the firm is subject to influences found in both the internal and external environment that affect its level of operation. Internal variables include the firm's financial position, management capability, personnel resources, and products and services offered for sale. External variables include general economic conditions, characteristics of the population in the trade area, social and cultural forces, technology, competitors, and political and legal forces. Small business owners should realize, therefore, that the success of the firm depends largely on the ability to plan, organize, staff, lead, and control the marketing activities in relation to the firm's internal and external environment.

Today, the consumer is the center of attention in all marketing plans. **Marketing** is a process that has to do with "the performance of business activities that direct the flow of goods and services from the producer to the consumer or user." [1] If the marketing process is to be effective, the owner must ensure that the goods and services offered for sale will satisfy consumer needs. A crucial part of the marketing plan of the firm is the efficient performance of the marketing functions.

Marketing Functions

An understanding of marketing is not complete without an explanation of the functions that must be performed in the marketing process. The **marketing functions** include buying and selling; transportation and storage; risk taking, standardization and grading, and financing; and marketing research. Each function is described briefly in the following paragraphs and shown in Figure 16-1.

Buying and Selling

Buying and selling comprise the exchange process. The "buying" function involves the anticipation of customer demand and searching for and evaluating the materials and services that will satisfy these needs. Success in selling is directly related to buying. In addition to making sales, the "selling" function includes a determination of potential customers of the firm and using a combination of sales promotion techniques to stimulate demand for goods and services.

Transportation and Storage

Transportation and storage involve the movement and handling of goods. The "transportation" function makes efficient, long-distance movement of goods

FIGURE 16-1
THE FUNCTIONS OF MARKETING.

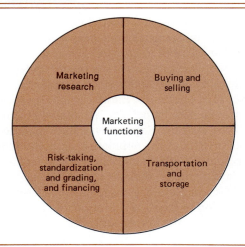

possible. The small manufacturer may locate a factory in an area in order to take advantage of any special attributes to that area (natural resources, labor supply) and then ship the manufactured goods to widely dispersed markets. Small retail, service, and wholesale firms depend on transportation systems to move the goods and services necessary for use in the operation of the business or for sale to the customers. Obviously, not all products are sold at the time they are manufactured. Thus, the "storage" function is provided by distributors in order to have goods available at the time and place they are needed.

Risk Taking, Standardization and Grading, and Financing

"Risk taking" is inherent in all business operations. Whenever goods are in storage, risk is involved because they may spoil, be stolen, or be destroyed as the result of a fire or storm. Consumer preferences may change, leaving the small business owner with large stocks of unsold goods. We emphasized earlier that some risk can be shifted through insurance coverage but the most effective means of dealing with risk is through sound management practices. The "standardization and grading" functions are important in that they facilitate buying and selling, such as enabling consumers to make comparisons of products. Standardization establishes the specifications for products that can be produced uniformly in color, such as size in clothing. Grading is used to classify products that cannot be produced uniformly in color, weight, or size, such as fruit or eggs. "Financing" is an integral part of the marketing plan.

Buying on credit from distributors allows the owner to stock merchandise for resale. The owner also "finances" sales by extending credit to customers.

Marketing Research

The purpose of "marketing research" is to provide current information about consumer preferences in order to plan for future needs. More coverage of marketing research is presented later in this chapter.

MARKETING CONCEPT

Over the years, the focus in marketing has shifted with the changing role of marketing in society. The first stage covered the period of the industrial revolution to the 1930s and concentrated on mass production of products at low per unit cost. The role of marketing was minimal. Companies set up sales departments, and the role of the sales personnel was relegated chiefly to selling the mass-produced goods. The other activities, such as advertising, were established as separate departments rather than being included as part of the total marketing effort.

The second stage, from the 1930s to 1950s, placed greater emphasis on selling. Producers became aware that it was not enough just to produce large quantities of goods but emphasis had to be given to the total system of selling goods. Thus, all marketing activities were grouped into a marketing department under the supervision of a sales manager.

Today's modern marketing programs embody the philosophy of the **marketing concept.** The marketing concept stresses that the objectives of the business are twofold. First, the needs of potential customers must be identified, and second, all the resources of the firm must be used to offer the goods and services that will satisfy customer needs while earning a profit for the firm. The owner must ensure that the firm stays on target and that all efforts are directed to achieving the goals of satisfying the customer and earning a profit. To accomplish these objectives, the business must develop marketing policies that provide the basis for the decisions required for maximization of customer satisfaction and profitability. Small business managers should incorporate the following basic guidelines into planning the marketing program for the firm.

1. Identify potential changes taking place in the firm's market that could materially affect the business.
2. Identify the firm's target customers.
3. Maintain an inventory of merchandise that appeals to the customers' needs in terms of price, quality, and selection or provide the services that satisfy customer needs.
4. Integrate all marketing functions and related activities to return a fair profit to the firm.

MARKETING STRATEGY

To develop an effective marketing plan, the owner must devise a marketing strategy for the firm. **Marketing strategy** is the course of action the firm will follow to achieve its established objectives stated in the business plan. Marketing strategy includes the two elements of market segmentation and marketing mix.

Market Segmentation

Market segmentation is the process of dividing a heterogeneous market of consumers into classes on the basis of similarity of characteristics, selecting any class or classes as the "target market," and striving to satisfy the needs of consumers in the target market with a distinct marketing mix. A small business has limited resources and cannot attempt to satisfy the needs of all consumers in the trade area. Instead, all efforts are geared toward the "target market." Through market segmentation, the entrepreneur develops a unique market niche for his or her firm that differentiates it from the competition. By concentrating on the target market, the entrepreneur's marketing effort is more efficient and effective. For example, the owner of a small hardware store ordinarily tries to attract customers from the local trade area, not the entire city. Occasionally, the need for a product or service is so general that the target market includes nearly everyone in the trade area, such as the need for the products and services of drugstores and grocery stores.

There are many bases for market segmentation. Small business owners should key their efforts to satisfying consumer needs in the specific target market. The following are some of the bases for market segmentation of ultimate consumers (those who buy products or services for their own personal or household use).

Demographics   Age groups, sex, family size, income level, occupation, educational level, religion, race, nationality.

Geographic   Urban, suburban, or rural; region of country (Northeast, Midwest); terrain of region (plains, mountains); size of city; size of state; climate.

Psychographic   Social class, life-style, personality type.

Product   Benefits of product (what consumers want from use of product), user or nonuser of the product, extent of use of product (heavy, moderate, light).

Another basis of segmentation is by industrial user. These are users who buy products or services to use in their own business or make other products.

Neil Balter, founder of California Closet Company, got the idea for his business while working as a carpenter. A friend asked him to build some shelves for a closet in the former's apartment. Balter turned the idea into a profitable business, identifying a specific market niche for his company. For an average cost of $400, Balter will analyze a customer's storage needs and design and build the closet.

Marketing Mix

The second component of the marketing strategy is to select the appropriate marketing mix to realize the dual goals of customer satisfaction and profitability of the firm. The **marketing mix** consists of four elements that owners integrate to service the needs of their target market. These four elements, referred to as the "4 Ps," are (1) products and services, (2) promotional strategy, (3) physical distribution, and (4) pricing.

Products and Services

To achieve the objectives of the marketing plan, the entrepreneur must select the correct combination of products and services that will satisfy the needs of the firm's target market. To accomplish this goal, the entrepreneur must define the product line and product mix. The **product line** is a group of products that are reasonably similar, such as furniture. The **product mix** refers to all products that the small business offers for sale and includes product depth and product breadth. **Product depth** refers to the models, sizes, styles, or colors offered within each product line while **product breadth** is the number of product lines carried. Because the firm can handle only a limited number of products or provide a limited number of services, the correct product line and mix are crucial to the firm's success because consumers buy to satisfy needs. The entrepreneur must stay abreast of consumer interests and add, modify, or drop product lines as demand changes.

Another decision facing the entrepreneur with regard to products and service centers around branded products. A **brand** is a "name, term, sign, symbol, or design or combination of them which is intended to identify the goods or services of one seller or group of sellers and to differentiate them from those of competitors." [2]

Selling brand-name products and services benefits both the entrepreneur and the consumer. Because consumers are familiar with brand-name products, such as product quality, they can more easily make their selection. The seller benefits because customers may prefer one brand that generates repeat purchases.

Owners must decide whether to sell national brands or distributor brands. A **manufacturer's brand** is owned by a manufacturer (producer) and is advertised and sold in all, or nearly all, sections of the country. **Private brands** or "distributor's brands" or "dealer's brands" are owned by an intermediary, such as a wholesaler or retailer, and are usually advertised and sold in a more limited geographical area, such as a region or a state, However, some private brands (Sears, Safeway, Penney's) are also sold nationwide. The advantage of selling private brands is that the seller's price is lower and profits usually higher than for the national brands.

The owner's decision as to whether to stock and sell national or private brands is important because the volume of brand name products sold by small

FIGURE 16-2
CHANNELS OF DISTRIBUTION FOR CONSUMER GOODS.

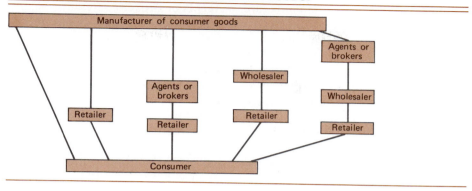

retailers is directly linked to the demand for the product. For the owner, the general guideline to follow should be to stock and sell the better known national brands promoted by national firms that have a good reputation for the quality of their products. The small business owner should find that the well-known national brands offer several advantages. They usually sell faster, and the owner is able to capitalize on the popular brand names when advertising.

Promotional Strategy

Promotional strategy informs customers about the firm's products and services by means of advertising, personal selling, and sales promotion. Promotional policies set the guidelines for the advertising program: what types of media to use, how often to advertise, how much to spend.

Promotional strategy policies also should set guidelines for special sales or promotional events. (See Chapter 19 for a more detailed discussion of promotional strategy.)

Physical Distribution

Manufacturers and intermediaries, such as wholesalers, must choose the proper channel of distribution for their products and services. The **channel of distribution** is the route that goods and services follow to the final user of the product. One criterion for selecting the channel of distribution is whether goods are consumer or industrial goods. *Consumer goods* are products that are bought by the ultimate consumer for personal or household use whereas *industrial goods* are goods used in making other products or in the operation of the business.

Figure 16-2 illustrates the alternative channels that the small manufacturer of consumer goods may use for the distribution of products. The channels available are these.

1. Manufacturer—Consumer.
2. Manufacturer—Retailer—Consumer.
3. Manufacturer—Agents or Brokers—Retailer—Consumer.
4. Manufacturer—Wholesaler—Retailer—Consumer.
5. Manufacturer—Agents or Brokers—Wholesaler—Retailer—Consumer.

Manufacturers of industrial goods have available four basic channels for distributing their products, as shown in Figure 16-3.

These four channels are

1. Manufacturer—Industrial Users.
2. Manufacturer—Agent or Broker—Industrial Users.
3. Manufacturer—Industrial Distribitor—Industrial Users.
4. Manufacturer—Agents or Brokers—Industrial Distribitor—Industrial Users.

Pricing Strategy

Customers must be charged a fair price for the products or services that will also produce a fair profit for the company. Pricing policies should give guidance in several areas. They must be set in accordance with the potential market to which the firm seeks to cater. Pricing should also reflect the pricing strategy of competitors. Other pricing decisions must include consideration of whether to adopt specific prices, for instance odd or even prices, and whether to use varying prices or a one-price policy as well as quantity discounts. (See Chapter 17.)

FIGURE 16-3
CHANNELS OF DISTRIBUTION FOR INDUSTRIAL GOODS.

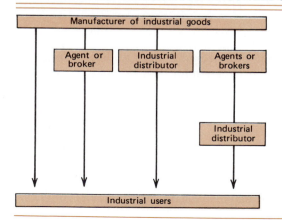

PRODUCT LIFE CYCLE

Whether manufacturer, distributor, or seller, the owner must constantly monitor products and services. Products follow a general pattern of development and decline called the product life cycle. Obviously, all products do not precisely follow this pattern, but it is a conceptual method for analyzing product demand that can aid managers in making decisions about when to push a product or drop a product. The **product life cycle** consists of four stages: introduction, growth, maturity, and decline. These four stages are illustrated in Figure 16-4.

Introduction

In the first stage, a product is brought into the market. When it is initially added to the product line, sales volume is generally low or weak as demand for the product develops. Special promotions may be offered to generate demand, such as a low introductory price or distribution of free product samples.

Growth

Sales volume and profit increase as consumer acceptance of the product grows. The market for the product expands and the number of competitors adding the product to their line is increasing.

Maturity

Sales volume rises to a certain level in this stage and then begins to decrease. At this stage, the owner may increase advertising of the product, find new

FIGURE 16-4
THE PRODUCT LIFE CYCLE.

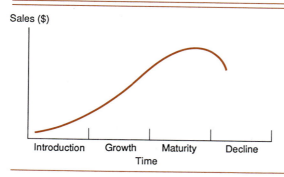

target markets, devise new uses of the product, or increase the frequency of use of the product.

Decline

In the fourth stage, sales drop as new products are introduced on the market. Consumer tastes change as well. At this stage, certain actions may be taken, such as lowering prices. If the decline cannot be reversed, the product will ordinarily be abandoned. Sometimes a product may be carried longer even if it is declining because it completes a product line offered by a producer.

MARKETING RESEARCH

Small business owners need accurate and current information on which to base their marketing decisions. For years, marketing research has been accepted by managers of large- and medium-sized firms as the basic tool for collecting the information needed for decision making. Small business owners, however, have almost completely ignored the practical application of marketing research for their firms.

Because of limited financial resources and expertise, some entrepreneurs rely on the **jury of executive opinion** rather than market research techniques to make forecasts concerning which products and services will satisfy consumer needs. The jury of executive opinion is the opinion or view of one person, usually the president or owner, or a few key personnel in the firm. These opinions, which are in reality intuition, form the basis for unscientific decision making. While this technique is simple, its major weakness is that it is based on opinion rather than a systematic collection of data. Managers offer products and services they "feel" will satisfy customers, seldom receiving feedback from customers as to the success of their efforts. As a result, many small business owners have instituted practices that are objectionable to customers. However, the small business owner may never realize that a problem exists.

Many small business owners feel they are doing an outstanding job. However, they are unaware of serious problems confronting them in the area of customer relations. To illustrate, an owner-manager of an automobile dealership in a relatively small community had a stated policy toward customers "to present a high-volume, low-price dealership that has a reputation for good service." However, a random survey of customers reported they felt his prices were too high. Two-thirds of the customers who had used his service department were dissatisfied with the service and indicated they would no longer do business with him.

It is also possible for the small firm to be located in an area where a large part of the population is unaware of its existence. For example, one small appliance store had been in business for six months in a town of 12,000 population. A random survey of people in the community indicated that 55 percent had never heard of the firm.

Cases such as these are common and stress the use and value that marketing research can have for the small firm. For example, in the second illustration just cited the appliance store manager was able to use the information to advantage. By changing its advertising policy and installing adequate store signs, the manager was able to inform the public of the firm's location, products, and services. As a result, sales were substantially increased.

Purposes of Marketing Research

Marketing research is the process of collecting, recording, and analyzing data pertaining to the target market to which the firm caters. These data include identifying (1) the market potential, such as size and income level of possible customers; (2) changes in consumer interests, tastes, and habits; (3) competitors' practices; and (4) economic trends in the market area.

Small business owners can benefit greatly by using marketing research techniques to survey customers' attitudes and opinions. Specifically, this marketing research survey can provide the small business owner with the means to accomplish the following.

1. To determine if the firm is obtaining a reasonable share of the market.
2. To decide if it is carrying a product brand and offering customer services best suited to the demands of its specific market segment.
3. To determine if the price range of the firm's merchandise is compatible with the demands of the market.
4. To uncover facets of the business that customers find objectionable.
5. To identify what customers like about the business so these features may be continued and reinforced.

The Marketing Research Process

If the survey is to produce the types of information desired, the marketing research process should be systematically planned. The marketing research process involves the sequences of activities shown in Figure 16-5.

FIGURE 16-5
THE MARKETING RESEARCH PROCESS.

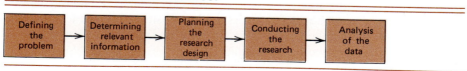

Define the Problem

The first step in the marketing research process, to define the problem, is the most important step. If a problem appears to exist, it is imperative that the owner distinguish between symptoms and causes. Declining sales are a symptom; the causes of the sales decline must be ascertained.

Correct identification of the problem places the owner in a position to specify what information needs to be collected and what marketing research technique to use for gathering the data. By concentrating more time, effort, and money on this most important step, the owner will likely realize substantial savings in time, effort, and money on the overall project.

Determine Relevant Information

Once the types of information that are needed have been identified, it is possible to assess what data are available from both internal company records and external sources. If the existing information is not adequate to provide answers, then the decision must be made as to what additional information must be collected.

Plan the Research Design

After identifying the additional information that is required, market researchers develop a research design that sets out in detail the plan that will enable them to gather the data. For example, if data are to be collected from customer interviews, a survey questionnaire must be designed and the number of people to be interviewed must be decided. In preparing the questionnaire, one must take care to see that it does not contain biased or prejudicial questions.

Conducting the Research

The first three steps in the marketing research process involve a considerable amount of planning. However, a thoroughly planned marketing research project expedites the data collection. A number of methods may be used to collect the data, such as interviews, observations, or experimentation. The methods used are determined by the research design and the information already available.

Analysis of the Data

When data are collected, they should be presented in a format that enables small business owners to analyze the results more easily. For example, data can be tabulated and presented in a table, chart, graph, or map format. After the marketing research process is completed and the data have been analyzed, small business owners are in a position to make a better decision because they are able to base their decisions on fact rather than relying solely on the ''jury of executive opinion.''

SOURCES OF ASSISTANCE FOR MARKETING RESEARCH

There are many sources of assistance readily available to small business managers to aid in the collection and analysis of market research data. One source for developing a market research effort can be drawn from the firm's own personnel resources. However, this alternative is not practical for most small businesses because they do not have employees who possess the specialized skills. A second source of assistance may be provided by various trade associations and business suppliers. A third alternative is the Small Business Institute (SBI). The SBI is a program sponsored jointly by the Small Business Administration (SBA) and participating colleges and universities. In this program, college students undertake and complete research projects in coordination with the needs of small business owners. (See chapter 22.) A fourth alternative consists of hiring a professional marketing research consultant, but the cost of this option may be prohibitive for most small firms.

In deciding which source to utilize, owners should weigh such factors as the following.

1. The availability in the firm of personnel with research expertise.
2. The availability of the required data.
3. The cost of the project and funds available in the firm.
4. The complexity and size of the problem to be studied.
5. The importance of the problem to the firm's survival and growth.

Sources of Marketing Research Data

When it has been established that data must be collected to complete the study, the source from which to gather the desired information must be determined. Sources of marketing information may be collected from internal company records and external sources.

Internal Company Records

The records of the firm should be the first area of investigation. Company records reveal a picture of the company's performance. Analysis of sales records discloses the number of units of each product sold, the products that were the best-sellers, whether the best-selling products were in the high-priced or lower-priced lines, the amount of the average purchase of consumers, the salesperson who had the best performance record in selling, the distribution of customers from various sections of the trading area, the amount of credit granted, and how much merchandise was returned.

External Sources of Data

An extensive array of data already in published form is available from external sources. A representative listing of sources of data is presented here.

A BRIGHT IDEA ISN'T ENOUGH

Marie-Jeanne Juilland

The capacity to become obsessed with an idea is a vital characteristic of an entrepreneur. It's what allows entrepreneurs to exert the herculean effort necessary to get a venture off the ground. Too bad it can't be turned off sometimes, like a light bulb. Your inspiration for a business needs to rest on the solid bedrock of information, the kind you can build only if you put your enthusiasm on hold for a while.

Being so obsessed with an idea that it's not possible to evaluate its viability in the marketplace is one of the most common mistakes of first-time entrepreneurs. ''A lot of them think, 'I experience a need and so does everyone else.' '' says Elaine Romanelli, director of the Center for Entrepreneurial Studies at the Fuqua School of Business at Duke University in Durham, N.C. The antidote to that problem is a few weeks to a year of solid library research.

Begin with a business school library, where you can learn your industry inside out. For starters you need to find out how big an industry it is, who your competitors are, and recent growth trends. Other questions to think about are: What are the logistics and costs of manufacturing this product or providing this service? Who will be my suppliers? What is my sales strategy? How much will consumers pay for my product?

Those are the kinds of questions Bruce Anderson is asking himself these days. He didn't the first time around and he suffered for it. Anderson's first venture, started in 1984 on little more than an impulse, a long-held desire to be his own boss, and $20,000 in savings, closed down after just 14 months.

Anderson had planned to import leather jackets from Korea at a wholesale cost of $32 apiece and sell them mail order for $79.95, roughly a third of the price charged by large U.S. department stores. The idea sounded great, but Anderson hadn't learned anything about the importing business before he started. He didn't know that experienced Korean sales agents, whom he needed to arrange the shipping of exports to the U.S., wouldn't find it profitable enough to work for his small company. Instead Anderson had to fly to Korea and do the job himself, which caused overhead to skyrocket.

He also discovered he had priced his jackets too low for U.S. consumers. Anderson is convinced they questioned the quality of a jacket priced so much below similar ones sold through retail chains.

Anderson, now 37 and a sales manager for a security fire systems company, is approaching his next venture in an altogether different manner. For starters he spent the last two years working with attorneys to get a patent on his idea for a way to easily keep men's dress socks paired. With that done, he started his market research. The local library provided articles and reports on the size of the current retail sock industry. A friend put him in touch with a venture capitalist uncle, who was able to give Anderson advice on funding alternatives. Most recently he has been visiting different sock manufacturing operations to learn about the business.

In Anderson's first venture he not only failed to research the industry, he also neglected the next step—testing the market, which can be standing on a corner asking potential customers how and if they would use your product, or sending out a professionally prepared questionnaire. He assumed that, given two products of equal quality, consumers would rush in droves to buy the less expensive one. He didn't consider consumer psychology, which made them suspicious of his jackets' much lower prices. Chances are, if he had done some field research, he would have found that out and either adjusted his price or decided not to proceed.

Source: Reprinted from the April 1988 issue of *Venture*, For Entrepreneurs & Business Leaders, by special permission. © 1988 Venture Magazine, Inc., 521 Fifth Ave., New York, N.Y. 10175-0028

Government Sources   Federal, state, and local government agencies published numerous resource materials that contain marketing information.

The federal government publications include those published by the U.S. Bureau of the Census. These census publications contain data on population, housing, agriculture, business manufacturers, and so forth.

Other government agencies, including the SBA, departments of Labor and Commerce, and the Federal Reserve Board, publish reports and pamphlets covering many subject areas, many specifically directed to the small business. Government agencies also publish special reports relating to specific industries, trades, geographic areas, and marketing operations. Retail trade and wholesale trade are examples of subjects of these publications.

State and local governments also publish vast quantities of data pertaining to specific geographic areas, such as industrial growth.

Trade Associations   A trade association is an organization that represents a particular type of business or industry, such as a restaurant association, builders' association, or hardware association. Association membership is voluntary, and the main purpose of an association is to further the best interests of the members. Trade associations offer many services and often develop statistical data and marketing research programs that assist membership in the following ways. A list of trade associations and their addresses is found in the Appendix.

1.   Accounting services (publishing comparative ratios).
2.   Advertising and marketing services (conducting studies or providing methods of merchandising).
3.   Aid to the disadvantaged (encouraging minority-group entrepreneur programs).
4.   Consumerism (publishing a code of ethics that includes requirements for consumer protection).

5. Ecology and environmental programs (conducting research to improve methods of waste disposal and to eliminate pollution).

6. Education (sponsoring short courses, clinics, seminars and workshops for industry).

7. Employer–employee relations (conducting surveys concerning members' employees—wages, work schedules, fringe benefits).

8. Government relations (informing members about federal, state, and local legislative actions).

9. Publishing (publishing magazines for the public, trade journals, newsletters, digests of laws, directories of suppliers and buyers).

10. Publicity and public relations (providing members with news stories that they can use in their own community).

11. Research, standardization, and statistics (regularly gathering and distributing data on orders, sales, production, construction, inventories, operating ratios, profits).[3]

Local Business Sources   The chamber of commerce is often able to provide information on local business conditions at no cost to the firm. Likewise, the telephone company, utility companies, banks, and local newspapers can provide market research information.

Bureaus of business research at colleges or universities provide data covering a wide range of topics, such as employment, market surveys, and economic conditions of the area.

Periodicals and Newspapers   Many business magazines and newspapers contain a wealth of information that may be beneficial to the data collector. Trade journals such as *Advertising Age,* business magazines such as *Business Week* and *Forbes,* and business newspapers such as *The Wall Street Journal* are invaluable sources of marketing information and current business trends.

METHODS OF COLLECTING MARKET RESEARCH DATA

There are three widely used methods of gathering information. These methods are observation, interview, and experimentation.

Observation Method

The observation technique involves collecting marketing data by means of direct observation. For example, observers may count the number of pedestrians or autos passing a site to evaluate if there is enough potential traffic to locate a store in the area. Or an observer, perhaps posing as a customer or a store employee, may record the comments of customers regarding the store, service, or layout. In this way, constructive steps may be taken to improve service, rearrange displays. Or add signs to make it easier for customers to complete their shopping. (A mechanical observation technique is accomplished by automatic counters that are used to make traffic studies.)

The major disadvantage of the observation method is that only a limited number of observations are possible because of time and cost factors. Thus, this method is not feasible for collecting much of the information needed for decision making by the owner–manager.

Interview Method

Interviewing is the most widely used method for gathering external data. This technique consists of interviewing a small number of people selected from a larger group. There are three basic interview techniques employed to ask respondents for their opinions in collecting external data: personal interviews, mail surveys, and telephone surveys. The best interview method is the one that yields the information needed with the highest degree of accuracy in the least amount of time at the lowest cost.

Personal Interviews

A major advantage of the personal interview is the likelihood of obtaining a higher percentage of responses when individuals are asked face-to-face for their opinions. A disadvantage of this technique is the high cost of collecting the data. Two types of personal interviews that may be conducted are the store interview and the home interview.

Store Interview
In the store interview technique, interviewers question a small number of customers at the point of sale or as they leave the store. Only a few, short questions should be asked to avoid irritating the respondent. Typical questions may include these: "How often do you patronize this store?" "Why do you shop at this store?" "Why did you purchase a specific product or brand of product?"

Home Interview
Although the home interview method can produce very useful information, it is also the most expensive interview technique. In-home interviews enable researchers to collect a broad range of data about consumer atttitudes, socioeconomic status, size of family, and other personal data. The personal nature of the interview is a positive feature. However, the success of the method depends largely on the effectiveness of the interviewers. If they lack motivation or are not properly trained, they may record incorrect data, ask the wrong questions, or offend the consumer. There is also the possibility that some individuals may refuse to participate in the survey.

For the results of home interviews to provide valid information, a representative number of homes must be included because it is impossible to survey every home in an area. Marketing research depends, then, on sampling. A sampling technique will be discussed later in this chapter that is practical for use by the small business owner.

Mail Survey

A second interview technique is the mail survey. Advantages of questionnaires are that they can be mailed to a large number of potential respondents and represent a less expensive method of data collection than personal interviews. However, care must be taken in the design of the questionnaire so that questions are clearly stated, easy to answer, and not biased.

Disadvantages of the mail survey are that the mailing list may not be accurate and respondents may be slow in returning the questionnaire. In addition, a low response rate has been a significant problem for users of mail questionnaires. Frequently, the response rate is below 25 percent, which makes users suspect that those who respond are different from the remainder of the population. However, most well-run general population surveys today get a 50 percent or greater return.[4]

Telephone Survey

Telephone surveys are an inexpensive means for collecting data as compared to personal interviews because one interviewer can interview many respondents. This technique is timely because interviewees are requested to answer questions immediately, thus providing instant feedback.

One disadvantage of the telephone survey technique is that interviewees can easily terminate the interview by merely hanging up. Furthermore, not all homes have telephones or listed numbers.

A Telephone Survey Technique   A practical method of conducting a telephone survey is outlined. This procedure has been used extensively by the authors, and results have been very satisfactory.

Step 1   The first stage is to determine the number of telephone exchanges in the trading area served by the firm.

Step 2   The second step is to determine the total number of telephones in each exchange of the trade area. Information for steps 1 and 2 can be obtained with the assistance of telephone company personnel.

Step 3   The third step involves selecting the telephone directory page numbers to be used to locate the actual telephone numbers to be dialed. If 100 telephone contacts are desired and if there are four telephone exchanges in the firm's trading area, then 25 pages must be selected. Random numbers selected must fall within the maximum number of pages in the directory. To illustrate, the Austin, Texas, telephone directory has 577 pages of listings of residential phones. Random numbers must be between 1 and 577. A table of random numbers was used to generate the following 25 random numbers. These numbers specify the page numbers to be used for the telephone survey.

1. 345	6. 199	11. 117	16. 354	21. 501
2. 423	7. 048	12. 435	17. 139	22. 163
3. 062	8. 164	13. 322	18. 341	23. 481
4. 356	9. 174	14. 046	19. 104	24. 167
5. 279	10. 136	15. 202	20. 004	25. 085

Step 4   On the pages selected, the first telephone number for each exchange prefix previously identified should be dialed. Thus, from each page, four numbers (one from each exchange) should be contacted. No business firms should be included in this survey. If a number is dialed and there is no answer, the next number with the same exchange prefix should be called until there is an answer for that prefix. If a selected page does not have any or all of the telephone exchanges, then either the next page can be used or the random numbers table can be used to select another page.

If there is more than one telephone exchange in the trade area, calls should be allocated according to the percentage of telephones in each exchange. This should account for the population density in the trade area. For example, suppose that 100 people are to be called, that there are two exchanges in the trade area, and that one exchange has 60 percent of the phones. Then, 60 percent of the calls should be made to that exchange, and the remaining 40 percent to the second exchange.

Based on actual usage of this sampling technique, we find that the number of calls necessary to provide satisfactory results will range from 60 to 100, with 100 calls preferred.

Experimentation Method

Some types of market research data can be gathered through experimentation. For example, the owner may use different ads to ascertain which is most effective in bringing in new customers. Or the store manager may experiment with staying open longer hours to conclude if sales sufficiently increase to justify the longer hours of operation. Another possibility for experimentation is test marketing different or new lines of merchandise to discover if they have customer appeal. A sporting goods store, for example, might consider the addition of a new line of camping equipment. Through test marketing, the store owner would be able to assess the probable success of the new merchandise line.

SAMPLING

The total of every person or every household in a city or trade area that is to be surveyed is called the **universe.** However, it is not feasible, both in terms of time and money, to make a complete survey. Instead, marketing researchers rely on sampling. A **sample** is the part of the total population (the universe) that is included in the survey. If the sample is to provide valid data, it is mandatory that the people who are included in the sample be representative of the universe because the results are obtained from the sample are used to make generalizations about the total population.

A representative sample can be obtained by use of random sampling. A random sample is designed so that every person in the universe has an equal and known chance of being selected. To illustrate, if there are 2000 people living in the market area and a random sample of 100 is to be taken, then the chances of being included in the survey are 100 in 2000. Because the sampling process is random, with each person having an equal chance of being selected, those surveyed should be representative of a cross section of the area's total population. The sample results can then be used to draw conclusions about the characteristics of the total population.

A Sampling Technique for the Small Business

The survey technique outlined in the following list presents a method of obtaining as random a sample as possible within practical limitations of time and money. This technique has been designed to meet the specific needs of the small business owner.

1. Draw equally spaced horizontal and vertical lines on a map of the market area. Spacing of the lines should usually range from ¼ to 1 inch depending on the size of the map. Usually more than 100 squares should result from the intersections of the lines. These resulting squares should then be numbered consecutively, eliminating all squares that are business districts and unoccupied land areas.

2. Determine the percentage of the market to be surveyed. Though statistical methods may be used, a more realistic approach for small business firms is to take into consideration cost, time, and size of the market to arrive at a sample size on a judgment basis. For this type of sample, 100 households is often an optimum size sample. It is usually a large enough sample to provide sufficiently accurate data without being too expensive and time consuming.

3. On small pieces of paper place numbers from one to the largest number appearing on the consecutively numbered map. From a table of random numbers or the slips of paper, select the numbered squares that are to be used in the sample, in a quantity equal to the size of the sample. Mark these areas on the numbered map.

4. The members of the research team should be "clean cut" and courteous. The team should inform customers interviewed that the survey is

being performed to measure customer opinion as part of the firm's continuing efforts to serve the community better.

5. A standardized pattern for selecting households to survey should be established—such as the first house in the selected area or the most northeastern house. If an interview cannot be conducted at this house—no one at home, refusal to answer the questions, and so on—the interviewer should then proceed to the next house until a survey has been performed in the randomly selected area.

Survey Questionnaire

The sample survey questionnaire shown in Figure 16-6 has been used successfully in making surveys of men's clothing stores. However, it can easily be modified to meet the survey requirements for a wide range of business firms.

FIGURE 16-6
CUSTOMER PROFILE.

1. Will you please give us some information about yourself?

   a. Age _____   d. Occupation _____

   b. Sex _____   e. Income _____

   c. Highest educational   f. Marital status Single _____

      level achieved _____   Married _____

                                     Other _____

   g. Number of females in household over age 16 _____

   h. Number of females in household under age 16 _____

   i. Number of males in household over age 16 _____

   j. Number of males in household under age 16 _____

   k. Area of residence _____

2. Answer the following for all purchases of apparel made by this household for males over 16 years of age in the average year. FILL IN THE NUMBER bought in each price range.

   a. Suits $95–125 _____ , $125–150 _____ , $150–200 _____ , $200–300 _____ ,

      Other _____ , None _____ .

      Where purchased? _____

      Why there? _____

      What brand? _____

**FIGURE 16-6
(CONTINUED)**

  b. Sports coats $50–65 _____ , $65–95 _____ , $95–150 _____ ,

  $150–225 _____ , Other _____ , None _____ .

  Where purchased? _____

  Why there? _____

  What brand? _____

  c. Slacks $20–30 _____ , $30–50 _____ , $50–70 _____ , $70–90 _____ ,

  $90–120 _____ , Other _____ , None _____ .

  Where purchased? _____

  Why there? _____

  What brand? _____

  d. Shirts $15–30 _____ , $30–50 _____ , $50–75 _____ , $75–100 _____ ,

  Other _____ , None _____ .

  Where purchased? _____

  Why there? _____

  What brand? _____

  e. Shoes $20–40 _____ , $40–60 _____ , $60–100 _____ , $100–150 _____ ,

  $150–200 _____ , Other _____ , None _____ ,

  Where purchased? _____

  Why there? _____

  What brand? _____

  f. Approximately how much is your total annual expenditure for undergarments,

  socks, ties, belts?

  $20–50 _____ , $50–75 _____ , $75–125 _____ , Other _____ ,

Check the three most important reasons in order of importance for your selection of
a clothing store.

Size of store: Large _____   Quality _____

                 Small _____   Merchandise

Convenience _____   selection _____

Adequate parking _____   Price _____

Other _____
                          (please fill in)

Analysis of the Survey Data

From the data collected, a "customer buying profile" can be developed that measures the firm's potential share of the market, suitability of brands to the market, and acceptability of product prices.

To determine the firm's potential share of the market, each response must be analyzed on a judgment basis to measure what part of the customer's total yearly expenditure for each item the firm should be receiving. The total of all item expenditure estimates is a measure of how much the customer would be expected to spend in the store after considering brand preference, price preference, and reason for purchasing at different stores. A total of all dollar estimates on all the surveys divided by the total number of surveys yields an average per household expenditure the firm should expect to receive. This average expenditure per household multiplied by the total number of households in the market area will produce the total amount of sales potential for the firm. This figure should then be compared to total yearly sales to determine if there is an excessive deviation. If the difference is large, the causes should be uncovered.

The profile also measures the distribution of consumer preference for different product brands as well as price ranges in the firm's market area. An´ analysis of the firm's competition and market helps determine which brands and price lines offer the greatest sales potential for the store.

SUMMARY OF KEY POINTS

1. Marketing is a process that includes the "performance of business activities that direct the flow of goods and services from the producer to the consumer or user."

2. The marketing functions are buying and selling; transportation and storage; risk taking, standardization and grading, and financing; and marketing research.

3. The marketing concept stresses that there are two objectives of the business: to satisfy the needs of customers and to earn a profit for the firm.

4. Marketing strategy is the course of action the firm will follow to achieve its objectives stated in the business plan and consists of two elements: market segmentation (the target market) and the marketing mix (the 4 Ps).

5. The marketing mix consists of the 4 Ps: products and services, promotional strategy, physical distribution, and pricing. The small business owner must select the proper combination of the 4 P's to achieve the dual goals of customer satisfaction and a fair profit for the firm.

6. Marketing research is designed to make sufficient, accurate, and current information available to the small business owners on which they can base their marketing decisions.

7. The marketing research process consists of defining the problem, determining relevant information, planning the research design, conducting the research, and analyzing the data.

8. Marketing research data are available from the internal records of the company and external sources.

9. Market research data may be collected by means of observation, interviews, and experimentation.

DISCUSSION QUESTIONS

1. How would you explain "marketing" to a small business owner?
2. What are the two goals of the small business as contained in the "marketing concept?"
3. What are the 4 Ps of marketing?
4. What is market segmentation?
5. Explain why marketing research is essential to the small business owner.
6. List the steps in the marketing research process.
7. Identify three sources of assistance to the small business owners when they wish to collect marketing research information.
8. What is the difference between the observation method and the experimentation method of collecting marketing research data?

THE BUSINESS PLAN: MARKETING GUIDELINES

Concerns to be addressed in developing a marketing plan include the following.

1. In developing a marketing strategy for your business, have you identified your specific market niche?
2. Have you defined the marketing objective in measurable terms, such as percentage of market share or percentage of increase in sales?
3. Has the target market for my business been correctly identified?
4. How large is the target market?
5. What is the growth potential of the target market?
6. How will you attract, maintain, and increase your market share?

7. Are you using the right combination of the 4 Ps to reach your target market?

8. Who are your competitors? Have you compared how your products and services meet consumer needs and how you compare with competition in terms of product–service mix, location, and so on?

9. Are there any environmental factors (legal, political, or social) that affect your market or product or service? (Environmental factors affect your business, but you have no control over them, such as rising tax rates).

10. Have you considered using marketing research techniques to aid you in identifying your target market, determining your product mix, and discovering consumer needs?

ENTREPRENEURIAL PROJECT

Use the customer survey instrument in Figure 16-6 and interview several people. Develop a "customer buying profile" for a retail store in your town or city.

CASE A
Children's World

Children's World is a specialty clothing store catering to children 12 years of age and under. The shop, owned by James and Susan Branson, is located in an enclosed regional shopping mall. The store offers a wider selection of children's clothing than any local competitor. Some merchandise is designed exclusively for Children's World.

Children's World faces strong competition from a number of different stores. Some of the competition comes from discount stores and other children's shops in the area of the city. Then there are the department stores and national chains such as Sears, J.C. Penney, and Wards within the mall. In addition, there are two other children's shops in the mall, although one will be closing at the end of this month.

The Branson's regularly advertise and use special promotional techniques, such as seasonal sales. They feel these techniques will enable them to remain competitive and to increase market share.

To gather information about how consumers perceive Children's World, the Branson's have requested assistance from the SBA to have a Small Business Institute (SBI) team design a market research questionnaire and conduct a market research study for Children's World. They feel this information will be useful in planning further sales strategy for the shop.

Questions

1. What is the target market of Children's World?
2. What market research techniques should be used to collect information about Children's World?
3. What types of questions should be included by the SBI team in designing the market research questionnaire?

CASE B

The Place for Books

The idea for The Place for Books originated with two brothers—Herb and Larry. They worked together on the idea for the business in the evenings after work. After two years of hard work and careful planning of all facets of the business, their idea was transformed into reality when they opened The Place for Books in a shopping center location in one of the most affluent areas of the city. Most people who were "experts" in the bookstore business gave The Place for Books little chance for survival. In fact, most predicted it would fail in a matter of months.

The experts were proven to be totally erroneous. Instead, the partners have been so successful with the first store that they have opened an additional store. They attribute their success to the marketing concept and marketing philosophy they developed for the business.

1. The Place for Books is first and foremost committed to maintaining an excellent stock and selection of books.
2. The Place for Books is a bookstore for readers of all ages and interests.
3. The Place for Books is committed to day-in, day-out value. "We do not run one-time sales; we do not mark up book prices and then discount them. We offer the lowest prices we economically can."

4. The Place for Books is planned with the customer as the center of the business. All phases of the store (policies, layout, hours of operation) are designed to cater to the customer.

The brothers realize, however, that they face stiff competition. Their chief competition comes from two national bookstore chain outlets. Recognizing the need to strengthen their customer-oriented philosophy, Herb and Larry have set out to conduct a market survey of their current customers in an attempt to serve their needs better. They expect that this market survey will enable them to increase their share of the book market by stressing the "customer-first" orientation of The Place for Books.

Questions

1. Design a customer survey questionnaire that could be used by the owners of The Place for Books to provide them with current information about their customers.
2. What techniques should be used to collect the desired type of information?
3. What is their target market?

Notes

[1] Committee on Definitions, *Marketing Definitions* (Chicago: American Marketing Association, 1960), p. 15.
[2] Ibid., pp. 9 and 10.
[3] James P. Low, "Association Services for Small Business," Management Aid No. 7.002 (Washington, D.C.: U.S. Government Printing Office, 1982), pp. 2–5.
[4] Harper Boyd, Ralph Westfall, and Stanley Stasch, *Marketing Research,* 6th ed. (Homewood, Ill.: Richard D. Irwin, 1985), p. 141.

KEY WORDS

PRICING

After reading this chapter, you will understand

1 How and why a small business promotes a price image to customers.

2 The relationship between price and volume of business.

3 That there are other factors that can offset price.

4 That retail establishments use one or more methods of setting price—markup on cost, markup as a percentage of selling price, suggested retail price, follow-the-market pricing, competitive pricing, and pricing for clearance.

5 How manufacturers set their price, using direct labor, raw materials, manufacturing overhead, and nonmanufacturing overhead costs, plus a margin for profit.

6 That wholesalers add all their costs to their cost of goods plus a profit to set their price.

7 That service firms usually set their price by charging an hourly fee plus list price for parts.

8 Why bidding is a difficult pricing activity for small business firms.

9 How a small business can use a bid, cost, variance system to measure profit on each job, set bidding prices, and see how far from the estimates its actual costs are.

ENTREPRENEURIAL PROFILE

David Kobos

KOBOS COMPANY

A young idealist of the 1960s—educated at Harvard and Reed College—journeyed with his wife to teach in the hard-bitten public school system of New York City. Within two years David Kobos was one of the last 7 (of 30) teachers in a special project remaining before the blackboard.

Discouragement—with both the huge metropolis and bureaucracy—found a respite in touring the specialty grocers of Little Italy and Greenwich Village. Kobos remembers his delight at "barrels of oregano"! Perhaps it was in that inhalation that he came up with an idea.

The young teachers returned to Portland, Oregon (where Reed College is located), and with only $6000 equity applied for and received an SBA loan for $17,000 to open a coffee and cookware retail store. From a strictly credit point of view, his was a weak application. One moment Kobos says he'll never forget is when SBA loan officer Bob Brown suggested adding $2000 to his loan request to ensure adequate working capital. "You could have knocked me over with a feather," he said. "I expected them to negotiate the loan downward."

Obviously, SBA recognized something special in Kobos; his business plan was neat and his academic training helped him research his ideas. He and his wife improvised; they painted a cabinetmaker's house in exchange for custom store fixtures. And as it happened they hit the gourmet food and kitchenware industries just as they were taking off.

Because the store was in an area of high unemployment, Kobos also took advantage of SBA's 7(j) counseling (which also helps minorities) when the new company had the classic problem of increased sales but shortage of cash. The inventory control system offered by the 7(j) consultant is still in use.

Today, Kobos Company has four retail stores in Portland and a year-old wholesale division featuring 27 varieties of coffee, 20 teas, and 100 different spices and herbs, along with its cookware. Kobos supplies 32 Portland restaurants.

The Kobos Company now has $2 million in sales and employs 45 people. When asked what he might have taken from his teaching experience to small business, Kobos said, "People skills. Training employees, educating customers—it's all people." And he hasn't given up concern for the education system. Kobos is now chairman of the local school board.

Source: Network (Washington, D.C.: Small Business Administration, January–February 1988).

Pricing of products and services is one of the more important decisions a small business owner-manager must make. **Prices** that are established set the firm's **price image** to the consuming public and to a large extent determine the volume of business the firm receives. Various types of small business firms have different pricing practices.

PRICE IMAGE

Any small business firm must determine the segment of the market in which the business is going to operate. It must then determine who its customers are (demographics, etc., that describe customers) and what they want. This establishes the image the firm must present to its customers. The firm should never do anything to damage this image. Its advertising, pricing, and so on, should always be pointed toward maintaining this image.

To a great extent, what the customer perceives as reality is more important to the small business than what reality is. Most customers are unable to judge accurately the quality of most products they purchase. Consequently, what they perceive as quality in products is what is important to the small business. For example, aspirin is a chemical compound that must be marketed in a certain state of purity to meet federal government standards. Consequently, all brands of aspirin tablets are, for all purposes, the same. If customers realized this, they would probably purchase the lowest-priced aspirin they could find. However, the largest-selling aspirin for many years is also one of the highest-priced aspirins. It would seem customers of this product perceive the brand to have a higher quality, which is not a reality. Advertising tends to continue this false perception of the product.

It is possible for a small business to build in its customers' minds a perception that may or may not be reality. For example, a small drive-in grocery must maintain higher prices than the supermarket. It is impossible for it to be price competitive. By offering items whose price the customer is familiar with (bread, milk, etc.) at competitive prices, it can somewhat build an image in many customers' minds that its prices are not as high as they really are. The customer still realizes there is some difference but thinks there is a narrower gap than there really is. An automobile parts house can do the same thing. It can offer items that the customers buy more often (spark plugs, oil filters, oil, etc.) at cost or slightly above cost. When customers see that prices on these items are competitive or below the discount house price, they tend to perceive the price image of the firm in the same light. The firm can have the same price markup or slightly higher on other products, and the customer will tend to see them as low prices. For instance, do you know, even within 50 cents, the price of a master cylinder repair kit for your car? This image building may not work for all customers, but it does for a large part of them.

Some of the images a small business actively tries to promote with prices are discount prices, high-quality products, or exclusiveness.

Discount Prices

It would be rare, if at all possible, to find a business that intentionally attempts to represent to the public that it handles low-quality goods. However, many firms attempt to convey to the public the idea that they offer quality products at **discount prices.** The discount house is an outstanding example. Discount houses attempt to maintain a pricing policy that holds prices at a low level in order to create an image of offering discount prices to the consumer. Most small businesses that stress discount prices are attempting to offer a low markup in order to build their volume of business.

Many manufacturers also attempt to build a price image on their products. Often they strive to convince the consumer that their product is of good quality and offered at "popular" prices. For instance, Black and Decker, a manufacturer of tools, has long maintained a reputation of quality for its line of tools. In recent years, it has used this image, along with low price, to achieve an image of good quality at low prices. By creating this image, the company is obviously attempting to use price as a means of increasing sales of its products.

High Quality

In direct contrast to the discount image is the firm that attempts to create an image of high quality and uses pricing decisions to reinforce this image. These small business retailers, manufacturers, and service firms are relying more on higher per unit profit than on volume. In fact, some firms use price to establish an image of high quality even when the quality is not high. In addition, some firms achieve high volume because of their higher price (this is the exception rather than the rule). To illustrate, the manufacturer of a perfumed shaving lotion had the option of offering its product at a low price because of the basic cost of producing the product. The final decision involved a choice between $.50 a bottle and over $3.00 a bottle. The firm selected the higher price in an attempt to establish a high-quality image. A large part of the per-unit cost of the after-shave was added on in the form of expensive packaging and advertising. This firm enjoyed a large volume of sales, probably many times higher than if it had decided on the lower selling price.

Exclusiveness

Exclusive stores often try to maintain a high price image to promote the idea of exclusiveness (high quality usually accompanies the exclusive image in the mind of the customer). These firms are attempting to stress per unit profit rather than volume of sales. To illustrate, high-fashion designers often price their creations in terms of hundreds and thousands of dollars. Their customers buy their creations because of the image of exclusiveness. Even though other firms copy their designs and reproduce them in the same, equal, or even better cloth, the customer of a high-fashion designer will still pay many times more for the original. Another example is Neiman-Marcus (a Dallas-based exclusive retail store), which uses its annual catalog offering expensive items such as his-and-her airplanes to build its image of exclusiveness.

PRICE VERSUS VOLUME

As a general principle, price does not move with **volume of business.** Most often, as price increases on a product, volume tends to decrease. Conversely, as price decreases, volume tends to increase. The shaving lotion example, mentioned earlier, is one of the exceptions.

As a result, most small business firms are faced with the decision to (1) offer low prices and strive to obtain volume, (2) offer high prices and make more per unit profit on fewer sales, or (3) set prices somewhere in between and obtain volume somewhere in between. It is often a difficult decision and usually a qualified guess as to which is the more profitable. To illustrate, suppose a manufacturer is considering three different prices for his or her product and each price will produce the following amount of sales.

Price		$ 15.00 each	$ 16.00 each	$ 17.00 each
Volume		40,000 units	35,000 units	25,000 units
Total sales		$600,000	$560,000	$425,000
Cost	$13 each	520,000	455,000	325,000
Profit		$ 80,000	$105,000	$100,000

It might appear that a small business would be able to experiment with price in order to determine its most profitable selling price. However, there are some problems with experimenting with prices. First, the firm may not have the financial ability to sustain fluctuations in business. Also, the firm presents one price image with one price and another price image with another price. This changing of price and price image will damage customer relations to some extent, possibly enough to ruin the firm. Consequently, the small business entrepreneur must perform an analysis of his or her market and make an estimate of the effect on profit for various pricing policies. Small business owners should then stay with such a pricing decision until they find evidence that another pricing policy is more profitable.

OTHER FACTORS THAT OFFSET PRICE

Price is important to most customers, but it is not the only thing that is important to them. As previously discussed, high quality and exclusiveness are able to offset and even negate price considerations. In addition, service, selection, and convenience are factors that offset price considerations to some extent.

Service

Many customers find different types of customer services important and are willing to pay higher prices, within reason, for these extra services. Some customers want credit and purchase from stores that offer credit even though the price they pay is usually higher. Customers of some small businesses, for example, drugstores, often pay higher prices to have merchandise delivered to them. In addition some customers are willing to pay a slightly higher price for products, such as appliances, to be sure of after-purchase repair and service.

Selection

Being sure of finding what they want at a store is important enough for some customers that they are willing to pay slightly higher prices. For example, some people may want specific merchandise and feel they could pay a little less for it at a discount house. However, they may go to another store because they are not certain the discount store sells it, and they are sure the higher-priced store will have the product. More than one store has built its patronage on his concept. One large do-it-yourself and building materials store has such a large selection of merchandise that a person is almost sure of finding what he or she needs at this store. The prices are a little higher on most products than at many other stores that do not have the same degree of selection. Many people patronize this store for the extensive selection of merchandise. They may be justified in their patronage because, if they have to go to several stores to find what they want, the cost of transportation can more than make up for the difference in price.

Convenience

Many people are willing to pay higher prices for goods and services because of convenience. For example, the small drive-in grocery almost always charges higher prices than the supermarket, but it is able to stay in business because of the convenience it offers customers on small purchases. Convenience is particularly important to consumers when small amounts of money are involved and becomes less important as the money amount of the purchase increases.

RETAIL PRICING

Retail firms use several methods in pricing their merchandise. Each firm may use one method or a combination of more than one method. The most com-

FIGURE 17-1
RETAIL PRICING PRACTICES.

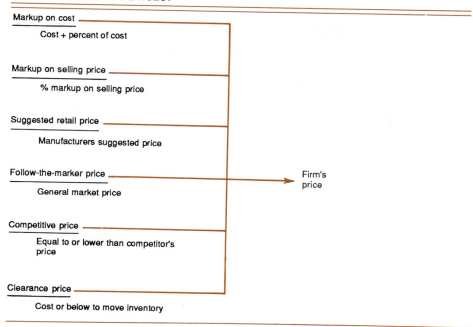

mon methods of pricing in retail establishments are (1) markup on cost, (2) markup as a percentage of selling price, (3) suggested retail price, (4) follow-the-market pricing, (5) competitive pricing, and (6) pricing for clearance. (See Fig. 17-1.)

Markup on Cost

Markup on cost by retailers is achieved by taking the cost of the merchandise (which includes incoming freight) from the vendor and adding a percentage of the cost to the amount.

Cost	$4.00	Cost	$4.00
Markup percentage	40%	Markup amount	1.60
Markup amount	$1.60	Selling price	$5.60

In our example, the 40 percent **markup on cost** of $1.60 is designed to cover all selling costs (sales personnel salaries, advertising, etc.) and overhead costs (rent, utilities, etc.) and provide a profit. For instance, the retail store may figure 20 percent for selling costs, 14 percent for overhead costs, and 6 percent for profit.

A retail store should calculate all its selling and overhead costs on at least a yearly basis and compare them to total cost of goods sold (see the income statement in Chapter 13) to arrive at what percentage these costs are. In our preceding example, if total selling costs were $79,200, overhead costs were $50,400, cost of goods sold was $360,000, and sales were $504,000, then the percentages would be these.

Amounts from Income Statement

Cost of goods sold	$360,000		Sales	$504,000
Selling costs	79,200		Cost	− 489,600
Overhead costs	50,400		Profit	$ 14,400
Total cost	$489,600			

Calculations of Percentages

Selling cost percentage: Overhead cost percentage: Profit percentage:

$$\frac{\$79,200}{\$360,000} = 22\% \qquad \frac{\$50,400}{\$360,000} = 14\% \qquad \frac{\$14,400}{\$360,000} = 4\%$$

It is obvious the firm is not realizing as much profit as had been planned because of an increase in selling costs. The firm must then raise the selling percentage or decrease its selling costs (which may result in lower sales) or accept a lower profit than planned or use some combination of the three. Competition and other market factors would probably dictate the decision.

The small business owner should be careful in determining what markup to add to the cost of goods. If the store has been in business for a time, then the firm's records will reveal how much selling and overhead costs have been, historically, in proportion to the cost of goods. If it is a new business, the small business owner should attempt to identify and estimate as accurately as possible every cost he or she expects to incur. Mistakes or overlooking a cost can be very costly to the firm because any increases will reduce profit. Good financial records are very valuable to the small business firm.

Markup on cost of goods can be used by the small business as a standard markup or as a flexible markup.

Standard Markup

A small business firm may elect to mark up all merchandise on one **standard markup** percentage. This policy usually is adopted by retail stores that have products that are alike or closely related. Many retail stores that are franchised operations, handle products in the same price range or have little competition often are able to use a standard markup.

The standard markup is easy to administer in daily operations; however, a retail store may find it difficult to maintain in the face of varying degrees of competition on different merchandise.

Flexible Markup

Flexible markup is used to adjust price when there is a change in competition or market demand. Increases in competition or decreases in market demand usually require a retail firm to lower its markup to maintain a satisfactory volume of sales.

Flexible markup is also used when there is wide variation in types and prices of products. For example, a department store may vary its markup from department to department to allow for the vast difference in products handled. If the department store were to attempt to adopt a standard markup for all products in the store, it would find that its volume of sales of some products would be very low.

Markup as a Percentage of Selling Price

Some firms **markup on selling price.** They multiply their suggested selling price by some percentage markup to determine what the price to their customers will be. For example, it is common practice in the textbook trade for the publisher to set the suggested retail price of their textbooks, then multiply by 80 percent to determine their price to bookstores. The resulting markup is 20 percent of the suggested retail selling price. For example,

Suggested retail price of textbook	$30.00
Less: 20% markup on price (20% × $30)	−6.00
Publisher's price to bookstore	$24.00

or

Suggested retail price of textbook	$30.00
Times 80%	80%
Publisher's price to bookstore	$24.00

Some small businesses like to tie their markup to their expenses by taking expenses as a percentage of their total sales. For example, a small business might calculate its total expenses (other than cost of the goods sold) based on last year's income statement and find it was $50,000. It could then derive its total sales for the same period and find it was $200,000. Its expenses as a percentage of sales then would be calculated as follows:

$$\frac{\text{Expenses (\$50,000)}}{\text{Sales (\$200,000)}} = 25\%$$

After analyzing its market and competition, the firm might regard 10 percent of sales as a reasonable profit. This would mean that 35 percent of each item's selling price would be markup. Knowing the cost of each item sold ($8 in this example), it would then be able to compute its selling price on each item as follows:

Selling price   100%
Markup   − 35% of selling price
Cost of item   65% of selling price

$$\frac{\text{Cost of item in dollars (8.00)}}{\text{Cost of item as a \% of selling price (65\%)}} = \$12.30$$

Using this method, the firm can easily derive expenses and total sales from its income statement each year and compute the ratio of expenses to total sales.

Suggested Retail Price

Many manufacturers print **suggested retail prices** on their products, supply catalogs with suggested retail prices, or give suggested retail prices on invoices. Some wholesalers also provide suggested retail prices to retail stores. For example, some wholesale grocers provide inventory lists to their customers that have both the wholesale price and a suggested retail price.

It is very common for small business firms to follow these suggested retail prices. It allows the small business owner to avoid the pricing decision. Many small business owners feel uncertain about the adequacy of their pricing decisions or do not want to go to the trouble of checking prices of other merchants.

The suggested retail price is easy to use. However, it may create a price image the small business owner does not want. In addition, it does not take into consideration competition, which varies to some degree by locale and type of business.

Some stores, such as retail automobile parts stores, use the manufacturer's suggested retail price as a base and then sell to the customer at a lower price, which is often the manufacturer's suggested wholesale price. Often the retailer lists both prices on the sales ticket to build an image in the customer's mind of getting a very good price on his or her purchase.

Follow-the-Market Pricing

Some small business firms do not attempt to lead in competitive pricing and simply follow the usual or average price of other firms. They achieve **follow-the-market pricing** by attempting to stay close in price to other firms. In fact, in small towns, it is not unusual for the owners of the same types of stores to agree to prices (this is actually a violation of antitrust legislation, which is not usually enforced in the case of small businesses because of the large number of them). For example, in the past, it had been standard practice in many small towns for the owners of gasoline service stations to meet and determine what prices will be in their stations. They often set categories of prices for major brands located on highways, major brands located in residential areas, and independents.

Competitive Pricing

Some firms strive to set prices on part of all of their products that are lower than those of most other firms. These stores often run competitive shopping lists on their competition. For example, a supermarket sends an employee to other supermarkets to record prices on various items of merchandise. From these lists, the supermarket then adjusts its prices to be highly competitive.

Competitive pricing can take the form of special prices for selected items for a specific period of time. For example, supermarkets run special price ads in newspapers each week trying to attract customers. It is fairly common for firms to get into price confrontations on specials for the same item. One store will offer a low price, and its competitor will then offer a lower price. Some firms make a practice of guaranteeing that they will meet or beat any advertised price of their competitors. The extreme of this occurred when one automobile dealer offered to beat any advertised price on an oil-and-filter change on a specific make of car. Its competitor then advertised it would change the oil and filter on the same make of car for 1 cent which meant that the original dealer would have to do it for free to beat the competitor's price.

Many retail stores adopt one of the previous pricing methods discussed, but, in addition, are often forced to adjust prices on some products to a more competitive price.

Pricing for Clearance

Pricing for clearance is common in retail firms. A large number of retail firms regularly reduce prices, sometimes below cost, to clear slow-moving items from their stock. In addition, many retail stores have loss leaders in which they sell merchandise at cost or below cost in order to attract customers for other products (this is a common practice of supermarkets). (A discussion of reduced pricing in order to clear slow-moving stock is contained in Chapter 15.)

Manufacturers sometimes find they have large stocks of a product on hand, and they offer the product at a reduced price to wholesalers and retailers so they can run specials on these products.

MANUFACTURERS' PRICING

Manufacturers usually base their product price on cost plus profit. The specific categories they use are direct labor, raw materials, manufacturing overhead, nonmanufacturing overhead (selling and administrative costs), and profit (See Fig. 17-2).

FIGURE 17-2
FORMULA FOR MANUFACTURERS' PRICING.

Some manufacturers take one additional step. They use the previously mentioned categories to determine their cost and then add on their profit plus the usual markup added on by the retailer. This then becomes their suggested retail price. They then sell the merchandise to retailers at a discount from suggested retail price. For example, a manufacturer might sell its product to a retailer for 70 percent of suggested retail price. This 70 percent covers the cost and profit markup. If the retailer uses the suggested retail price, 70 percent of sales price covers the cost of the product, and the 30 percent of sales price must cover all other expenses plus a profit for the store.

As in other types of businesses, manufacturers must take competition into consideration when pricing their products. They also must make a decision about volume relative to price. To obtain sufficient volume, they must balance price, advertising, and quality of their products in terms of market conditions, which include competition.

Manufacturers who have produced their products over a period of time are able to determine their labor costs by the number of products each work station is able to complete in a day's time. The number of products divided into the labor cost for each work station and totaled for the entire process provides per unit labor costs. The total of all raw materals used in the production of one unit of product plus waste allowances provides per unit raw material costs. Past records of expenditures for supervisor salaries, plant depreciation, machinery depreciation, supplies, plant utilities, and other factory-related costs provide a basis for arriving at manufacturing overhead. Office salaries, sales salaries, advertising, travel, office depreciation, office utilities, and administrive salaries are among the items that comprise nonmanufacturing overhead. All these costs plus a margin for profit, adjusted for market conditions and competition, provide the necessary information for the manufacturers to set their price.

Manufacturers who are producing a new product do not have historical records to provide this information. Consequently, they must estimate these costs and data to arrive at a price for their product. Manufacturers of a new type of product also face an important question about price. Should they price the product high until competition arises to recover as much development cost as fast as possible, or should they set the price low to discourage competition from entering the field as long as possible?

FIGURE 17-3
WHOLESALER PRICING PRACTICES.

Cost of goods from manufacturer + All costs + Profit = Price

WHOLESALER PRICING

Wholesalers generally base their price on cost of goods (which includes freight required to bring the product from the manufacturer to the wholesaler) plus a markup, which covers all other costs plus a profit. Wholesalers must take into consideration all costs when arriving at a markup, including such items as building rent or depreciation, warehouse salaries, office salaries, administrative salaries, selling salaries, delivery costs, utilities, and equipment depreciation. (See Fig. 17-3.)

Wholesalers must also pay close attention to competition and market conditions when setting price.

Many wholesalers print catalogs that contain both product listings and prices and provide them to retail customers. From time to time, they issue loose-leaf pages that notify the retailer of changes in price. However, the price they charge the retailer for products is, to some degree, inflexible for a period of time because its requires some time before they are able to notify customers of changes. This inflexibility means the price decisions must be sufficient to provide a profit while maintaining an effective competitive position.

SERVICE FIRMS' PRICING

Service firms often charge an hourly fee for the number of hours spent in providing service. Some even charge one amount for the main service person and another rate for a helper. This is common practice in the plumbing trade, where the hourly fee includes not only service salaries but also overhead, all other costs (except parts), and a margin for profit.

Some firms charge by the actual number of hours spent in repair. Others charge a standard number of hours the job should have required regardless of the time spent. For example, most automobile repair shops usually charge the customer so much per hour of labor. They may charge $60 per hour. However, they do not charge for the actual time spent in repair but, rather, consult a standard rate manual for how long it should take to complete the job. For example, the rate manual may list repairing a master cylinder at 1½ hours. In this case, the customer would be charged for 1½ hours times $60 or $90 in labor costs.

The amount the automobile repair shop charges for each hour of labor (ac-

FIGURE 17-4
PRICING PRACTICE OF SOME SERVICE FIRMS.

Actual time or standard time	×	Hourly rate	+	List price of parts	=	Price
Our example:						
1.5 hours	×	$60 = $90	+	$38.06	=	$128.06

tual or rate manual) is usually a matter of competition in the local community. If the automobile dealerships charge a labor rate of $60 per hour, most of the independent repair shops charge a lower rate to attract business, such as $50 per hour in our example.

A price for parts is also added to the labor cost charged to the customer. The automobile dealership will charge a list price that is roughly twice the cost of the part to the dealership. Independent auto repair shops usually follow a different procedure is pricing their parts. They often buy their parts from auto parts retailers. The auto parts retailer has catalogs from a wide range of manufacturers' with their parts and suggested prices. For example, the independent auto repair shop might buy a master cylinder (brakes) repair kit for a 1985 Ford LTD. The auto parts retail store's manufacturer's catalog would show the following:

Cost	$17.85	Cost to the auto parts store
Jobber	$19.85	Price to the auto repair shop
Dealer	$26.64	Price to individuals
Trade	$29.75	Price to individuals from higher markup store
List	$38.06	Suggested retail price

The independent auto repair shop would pay $19.85 for the part and charge the customer $38.06. (See Fig. 17-4.)

The automobile repair shop usually pays the mechanic a fee that is a part of the total labor cost. In our example, the automobile repair shop might pay the mechanic 50 percent of all labor costs, or $45 of the labor costs on the master cylinder repair job. The owner of the shop then keeps $45 for the labor costs plus the markup (list of $38.06 less jobber cost of $19.85 = $18.21) on the parts to cover the shop's overhead (equipment, building, utilities, office expense, supplies, etc.) plus a profit.

When price is based on a standard rate manual, the efficient mechanic who can complete the work in less time receives more per hour than does the mechanic who is not as efficient and takes as much as, or more time than, the manual allows. In this way, the customer is neither rewarded nor penalized for the speed of the mechanic.

Service firms that use actual hours or standard rate manuals usually adapt their price to meet competition by adjusting the dollar amount charged per actual or standard hour.

BIDDING

Bidding is probably one of the most difficult pricing activities in which a business can engage. Many times the firm has not produced a specific product or service exactly like the one on which it is bidding. For example, a construction firm may bid on construction of an apartment complex. Even though it has constructed other apartment complexes, there are usually problems unique to each job, such as site preparations, foundations, or new construction designed by the architect. It is often very difficult to figure the exact cost of each problem and technique before it is performed.

On the other hand, the firm that is bidding a job must be fairly accurate in its bidding. If the job costs more than expected, the firm sustains the loss. Conversely, if the firm bids too high, it probably will not get the job.

Another aspect of bidding is the costs to bid on a contract, which may range from a few hours of one person's time to the million or more dollars it sometimes costs aircraft manufacturers to design and build a mockup for a bid to the government. Consequently, a firm must be efficient enough in bidding to be assured that it has a reasonable chance to obtain contracts.

Another problem a firm faces in bidding on contracts that extend over long periods of time, sometimes in terms of several years, is continuing inflation of costs. Bidding usually requires a specific price. The firm that bids may find that costs have increased because of inflation to the point that fulfilling the contract costs more than the price it is receiving. However, it is becoming increasingly common to find contracts that contain some form of escalator clause as a hedge against inflation.

There are even cases when a small business might bid at cost of even below cost. If business activity is slow, the firm might consider a very low bid to keep its personnel and resources active. A bid to cover fixed costs and part of the variable costs might be the most profitable short-run action to take until business increases again.

Some service firms, such as accountants, hair care salons, business service firms, health care firms, and child care centers, use other methods of pricing their services. Some methods may be to charge what is customary in their area, what they think their services are worth, what their competition charges, the maximum amount they think their market will bear, or some other method of pricing.

BID, COST, VARIANCE SYSTEM

Any job order shop (one that does not produce to stock but only to fill customer orders) or most construction companies that bid or price based on estimated costs should maintain a simple **bid, cost, variance system** as shown in

Figure 17-5. It allows the firm to learn just exactly how much it is making on each job. In addition, it allows the firm to see how accurate its bids are and over a period of time makes the **bidding** of the firm much more accurate by showing how much variance there is from bid price to actual cost for direct labor, raw materials, manufacturing overhead, selling and administrative overhead, and profit.

Direct Labor

The amount of time each operation should take to complete the work is estimated and multiplied by the hourly rate paid the workers at each work station. For example, Figure 17-5 shows it is estimated that it will take the welder 2.4 hours to complete the task. Because the welder is paid $6.00 per hour, it is estimated that it will cost $14.40 to weld the job. However, it only took the welder 2 hours to complete the job, and the actual cost was only $12.00. Thus, the business saved $2.40 on this job.

Raw Materials

All raw materials that are needed to finish this job are estimated. Some firms call suppliers to check current prices at this point. Some items that are used in the job are difficult to assign to any one job, such as nuts and bolts. The welding rods used in Figure 17-5 are considered a supply rather than a raw material. These items are taken into account in manufacturing overhead.

In Figure 17-5 the cost of strip steel is estimated to be $210, but the firm was only charged $205, giving a savings of $5. On the other hand, angle steel had gone up, and it cost the firm $20 more than the estimate.

Manufacturing Overhead

A common shortfall of small business is to fail to apply overhead on a realistic basis in pricing. To illustrate, one small business bid $6800 on a city government job. Later it found city engineers had estimated the job at $8200, and the second lowest bid was $10,200. The owner of the business had been estimating his cost of direct labor and raw materals and then applying a 60 percent markup to cover overhead and profit. An analysis of past income statements showed that overhead costs were running 120 percent of each dollar spent in direct labor. The entire markup of 60 percent did not even cover overhead, much less profit. Needless to say, he lost money on the job.

Manufacturing overhead is computed by taking the total direct labor cost and multiplying it times the manufacturing overhead ratio. The manufacturing overhead ratio is determined by taking the manufacturing overhead cost from the income statement for the last year and dividing it by the total direct labor costs for the same period. Manufacturing overhead is comprised of such items as supervisors' salaries, machinery depreciation, supplies, utilities assigned to

FIGURE 17-5
BID, COST, VARIANCE SHEET.

JOB # 106	BID			ACTUAL COST			VARIANCE
Direct labor	Hours	Rate	Amount	Hours	Rate	Amount	Amount
Cleaning	0.5	$4.50	$2.25	0.5	$4.50	$2.25	$ 0
Cutting	0.8	5.00	4.00	0.6	5.00	3.00	−1.00
Welding	2.4	6.00	14.40	2.0	6.00	12.00	−2.40
Painting	1.1	4.50	4.95	1.0	4.50	4.50	− −0.45
Total direct labor			$25.60			$21.75	−$3.85
Raw materials							
Steel ¼ × 2 × 8 ft. strip			$210.00			$205.00	$−5.00
¼ × 4 × 8 ft. angle			300.00			320.00	+20.00
Paint 4 gal.			30.00			30.00	0
Total raw materials			$540.00			$555.00	+$15.00
Manufacturing overhead Direct labor × overhead ratio ____ × ___.55___			$14.08			$11.96	$2.12
Total manufacturing cost			$579.68			$588.71	+$9.03
Selling and administrative overhead Total mfg. × Total S&A cost overhead ratio ____ × ___.20___			$115.94			$117.74	+$1.80
Total cost of goods manufactured			$695.62			$706.45	$10.83
Profit markup 10%			$69.56			Price $765.18	
						Cost $706.45	
Bid price			$765.18			Profit $ 58.73	−$10.83

the factory, cost of the factory space in rent or depreciation, and insurance for the factory space and equipment.

In our example, the total of last year's manufacturing overhead was $264,000 whereas the total direct labor expense for the same period was $480,000. The calculation of the manufacturing overhead ratio would be:

$$\frac{\text{Manufacturing overhead cost (\$264,000)}}{\text{Total direct labor cost (\$480,000)}} = 0.55$$

Multiplying the job labor cost in Figure 17-5 of $25.60 by the overhead ratio gives $14.08 for estimated manufacturing overhead. Notice that the actual direct labor hours are also multiplied by the manufacturing overhead ratio. The labor cost savings are also reflected in a manufacturing overhead savings of $2.12.

Selling and Administrative Overhead

The selling and administrative (S&A) overhead cost is calculated by multiplying total manufacturing cost by the S&A overhead ratio. The S&A overhead ratio is calculated by taking all selling expenses and administrative expenses from the income statement and dividing them by the total cost of goods manufactured for the same period. Selling and administrative overhead is comprised of all expenses other than direct labor, raw materials, and manufacturing overhead. In Figure 17-5, the total selling and administrative expenses for the year were $280,000. The S&A overhead ratio should be

$$\frac{\text{Selling and administrative costs (\$280,000)}}{\text{Total costs of goods manufactured (\$1,400,000)}} = 0.2$$

In Figure 17-5, multiplying the estimated total manufacturing cost of $579.68 by the selling and administrative overhead ratio of 0.2 gives an estimated S&A overhead of $115.94. The actual manufacturing cost is also multiplied by this ratio to give the actual S&A overhead cost.

Profit Markup

The profit markup is a somewhat arbitrary percentage assigned by the small business. Of course, competition must often be a prime factor in setting the profit markup percentage. Our example in Figure 17-5 shows the firm wants to have a profit equal to 10 percent of total costs. Unfortunately, the small business missed its projected profit by $10.83 primarily as a result of estimating the angle steel price too low.

As with other forms of pricing, effective bidding is dependent on good records and careful analysis of costs. The small business firm that approaches pricing on a hunch or halfway basis usually doesn't stay in business very long.

SUMMARY OF KEY POINTS

1. A small business must determine its segment in the market and then maintain a pricing policy that is consistent with the image that is required.
2. Pricing helps promote an image of discounting, high quality, or exclusiveness.
3. Usually, the level of prices goes converse to the volume of business.
4. Service, selection, and convenience are factors that may offset price.
5. Retail pricing may consist of markup on cost, markup as a percentage of selling price, suggested retail price, follow-the-market pricing, competitive pricing, and pricing for clearance.
6. Markup on cost may be performed as a standard markup or as a flexible markup.
7. Manufacturers usually base their prices on direct labor, raw materials, manufacturing overhead, nonmanufacturing overhead, and profit.
8. Wholesalers usually base their price on the cost of goods plus a markup that covers all other costs plus a profit.
9. Many service firms compute their price by taking actual time spent or a standard time times the hourly rate plus list price of parts used.
10. Bidding is probably one of the most difficult pricing activities, and it must be fairly accurate if the firm is to make a profit.
11. A bid, cost, variance system should be used to calculate the bid price, record the actual cost, and measure the difference between the two.

DISCUSSION QUESTIONS

1. Name one type of small business that would use price to promote the following images—discount prices, high quality, and exclusiveness.
2. Explain the relationship between price and volume of business.
3. Is price the only factor that causes patronage of small business firms?
4. If you were to establish a neighborhood drugstore with delivery service, what type of pricing policy would you use? Explain your reasons.
5. What are some of the factors involved in the method manufacturers use to price their products?
6. What method of pricing is used by most wholesalers to set their prices?
7. If you set up an automobile repair shop, how would you set your prices?
8. Why is bidding one of the most difficult pricing activities in which a small business can engage?

9. If you owned a job shop manufacturing operation, would you use the bid, cost, variance system for bidding and recording actual costs? Explain how you would use it.

THE BUSINESS PLAN: PRICING

____ What is your niche in the market?

____ What image do you want to portray to the public?

____ What price image do you want to portray to the public?

____ Will your price image be for discount prices, high quality, or exclusiveness?

____ Will volume of business move opposite to price?

____ Can you charge a higher price because of services, selection, or convenience?

____ Will your business be a retail establishment? If so, will you use one or more of the following:

    ____ Markup on cost

        ____ Standard markup

        ____ Flexible markup

    ____ Markup as a percentage of selling price

    ____ Suggested retail price

    ____ Follow-the-market pricing

    ____ Competitive pricing

    ____ Pricing for clearance

____ Will your business be manufacturing? If so,

    ____ Will your cost of goods manufactured plus selling and administrative expenses plus desired profit margin determine your selling price?

    ____ Will you provide retailers with a suggested retail price?

    ____ Will your markup be a percentage of the selling price to determine your price to customers?

    ____ How will competition effect your price?

____ Will your business be a service establishment?

    ____ Will you use actual labor time, or will you use a standard flat rate manual (is one available)?

—— What will your standard labor rate per hour be?

—— How will you price parts to your customers? Will you use suggested list prices?

—— What is the customary price for your service in your market area?

—— How will competition effect your price?

—— Will you use bidding in your business?

—— Will inflation be a problem in your bidding? How will you allow for it if it is a problem?

—— Will a bid, cost, and variance system be of benefit to your operations? Remember it helps you become more efficient in your bidding and tells you how much you make of each job. If it will help you, use the form example in this chapter as a guide in creating your own form and system.

ENTREPRENEURIAL PROJECTS

1. Attempt to identify retail stores (one each) that use price to create
   a. A discount image.
   b. A high-quality image.
   c. An exclusive image.
2. Identify a retail store that attempts to offset price considerations by using service, selection, or convenience.
3. Attempt to identify a retail store (one each) that you feel uses the following pricing methods.
   a. Markup on cost.
   b. Suggested retail prices on some items.
   c. Follow-the-market pricing.
   d. Competitive pricing.
   e. Pricing for clearance.
4. Identify a service firm that uses a standard rate manual.
5. Identify a business that bids for jobs.

C A S E   A
Warren Auto Repair

Henry Warren has just graduated from the local community college where his training included business and auto repair courses. Henry has always been interested in automobiles and enjoys working on them. He would like to open his own auto repair shop, and his parents have said they would finance a small repair shop for him. Henry knows what type of equipment and tools he needs, but he is not sure how to price his services.

Henry has obtained an automotive flat rate manual and has been looking at standard times for various jobs. For example, replacing the water pump on a 1987 Chevrolet Nova is two hours. The local automotive dealer charges $55 per hour for labor and almost all the independent repair shops charge $50. Henry plans to use a nearby auto supply store that delivers as his source of auto parts. To check his costs, Henry called the supply store for the price of a water pump for the 1987 Chevrolet Nova. He was told that the jobber price was $23.60 and list was $45.10.

Henry has also been thinking about how he would promote the opening of his business. To save money on the amount of rent he will have to pay, he has selected a location that is one block off a major road on a small side street. He knows he must advertise if he is going to let people know where he is. He has decided to use handbills delivered in his market area. He knows he must give something that will be sufficient to attract customers to his location. He has thought he should include a coupon.

Questions

1. How much should Henry charge for his labor?
2. Compute how much Henry could charge for the water pump job and tell him how much he will make on the job.
3. Make a recommendation on what Henry should offer on the coupon.

CASE B

Jan's Sandwich and Ice Cream Shop

One month ago, Jan Sokol quit her job with a large corporation and bought out a sandwich and ice cream shop that had been in operation for two years in a neighborhood shopping center. The shop had been just breaking even during the two years it was open before she bought it. The previous owner had not advertised, and Jan felt the shop could be profitable with good promotion techniques. She was able to buy the business at a very good price because it had not been profitable.

The shop offers a good selection of various types of sandwiches, including hamburgers. It also carries a local ice cream that is considered by many to be the best ice cream sold in the city. Jan has improved the appearance of the shop and extended the hours that it is open. She has also distributed handbills in her market area with special price coupons on several items.

In Jan's market area there are three nationally franchised fast-food places, one chicken-oriented and two that are primarily hamburger-oriented. There is only one ice cream store in the area, and it also is a nationally franchised store. Jan made a survey of her competitors' prices and found that her ice cream prices were slightly lower than those of the ice cream store and found, too, that she was 20¢ to 30¢ lower on items the other three franchised food places sold that she also sold.

Jan is now wondering about her prices. She has asked your help in setting a pricing policy for her store.

Questions

1. Consider the retail pricing practices, and determine what should be Jan's overall pricing policy.
2. What should be her pricing policy for sandwiches? for ice cream?

KEY WORDS

CONSUMER BEHAVIOR AND PERSONAL SELLING

L E A R N I N G   G O A L S

After reading this chapter, you will understand:

1. That consumers purchase products and services to satisfy a variety of needs.
2. The phases of the purchasing process.
3. The buying motives that influence consumer purchases.
4. The significance of the business image of a firm.
5. Why good community relations are crucial for a small business.
6. Some techniques for creating positive customer relations.
7. The role of personal selling in the small business.
8. The difference between a service salesperson and a creative salesperson.
9. The value of training for salespersons.
10. The steps in the personal selling process.

ENTREPRENEURIAL PROFILE

H. Allen Ryan

NORTHCENTER FOODSERVICE CORPORATION

In the September–October 1987 issue of *D&B Reports,* there's a three-page spread on NorthCenter Foodservice Corp. of Augusta, Maine. Unmentioned in the article is that former company employee H. Allen Ryan's leveraged buyout in 1982 was made possible by an SBA loan of $200,000.

"The local bank insisted on an SBA guarantee as part of their commitment, meaning that without SBA's help the whole deal was likely to die," said Ryan.

"I found SBA to be detailed, professional, and very helpful during the negotiations for the guaranty. They asked tough questions as they sought to balance the interests of the taxpayer and their responsibility to assist small companies. In the end, they saved our deal.

"Without SBA's help I might not own our growing business today."

Since the first SBA loan, NorthCenter Foodservice Corp. has more than tripled its employees (from 20 to 75) as well as its annual sales, from $6 million to $21 million.

Give a lion's share of the credit to Ryan himself. The innovative president transformed a modest hot dog and lunchmeat producer into a dynamo offering 4000 different food and nonfood items to 1400 restaurants, schools, and hospitals. NorthCenter Foodservice is now competing in Maine with four huge national companies. Ryan feels NorthCenter has already surpassed another 36 food-service companies. "They haven't computerized, or modernized, so we're way ahead of them," he says.

What's in a name? For Ryan, changing the company name from Kirschner to North-Center was everything. (The logo has red sunrays shooting out from the "o" in North.) The name established the company in the heart of Maine, implying service to all points in the state.

The company has completely automated its fruit and produce department, helping provide "fresh is best" delivery. Food servicing is extremely difficult to computerize due to rapid turnover, price fluctuations, and spoilage. But NorthCenter's out-of-stock and spoilage rates are less than 1 percent each.

Another fresh marketing idea of Ryan's was the five-minute videotape all his salespeople carry, along with a five-inch player. The tapes tell the NorthCenter story: everything for your kitchen from blueberries to bluefish.

Ryan, Maine's Small Business Person of the Year in 1987, sees the crowding of Cape Cod as helping Maine's resort trade and boosting busines. Vacationers, after all, have to eat.

Source: Network (Washington, D.C.: Small Business Administration, November–December 1987).

"Why do consumers buy one product instead of another?"

"Why do consumers prefer one brand or product or service instead of another?"

"Why do consumers patronize one store instead of another?"

Of utmost concern to the small business owner is to find answers to these kinds of questions. By being sensitive to consumer needs, small business owners will have a superior understanding of consumer buying behavior. This information provides them with the knowledge of consumer needs and wants and to stock the products and offer the services so that they are available at the time consumers desire them. In this chapter, the discussion of consumer behavior is followed by another crucial activity in the small business, that of personal selling.

CONSUMER MOTIVATION

The business environment today is very competitive. Small business owners who anticipate consumer needs more accurately than competitors have a definite advantage. However, they cannot afford to become complacent, because consumer buying habits can change quickly. Since buying behavior is such a dynamic process, owners should recognize that it demands their full attention to be alert to sudden shifts.

The U.S. population is experiencing dramatic changes in life-style. For example, there is an upsurge in dual-career couples, a growing concern for wellness, and an emphasis on using leisure time constructively. These changes in life-style have a strong influence on consumer buying patterns.

The purchase of many goods and services is closely linked to satisfying needs of consumers at various stages in their family life cycle. Stages in the family life cycle are classified in several ways. One classification includes the following:

Single

Married

    Young married with no children
    Young married with oldest child under age 6
    Young married with youngest child over age 6 but under age 13
    Older married with older dependent children
    Older married with adult offspring living out of the home

Separated

Divorced

Widowed

Owner–managers need to be alert to the stages in the life cycle of their customers and key their selling efforts accordingly.

Clearly, the answer to the question of why people buy is that they are motivated to purchase products or services because they satisfy a need. An understanding of the motivational forces is critical for the small business owner, and the following discussion identifies some of the motivational forces behind consumer buying behavior at various stages in their life cycle.

Satisfaction of Primary Needs

In Chapter 8, we stated that motivation is the force that arises within an individual, stimulating the person to take action to satisfy an aroused need or reach a goal. Thus, only when the need is aroused or awakened will it serve as an energizer for action.

One set of needs that people are motivated to satisfy is physiological, safety, and security—the **primary or basic needs.** Purchases of food, clothing, and shelter are motivated by the physiological desire for survival. Other purchases are made to satisfy safety and security needs. For example, safety features may be added to the home, such as covering a slippery patio floor with outdoor carpeting. The concern for security may result in the home-owner's having a burglar alarm, burglar bars, and a smoke alarm installed. Though these purchases may satisfy the basic needs, they do not answer the question of why one product or service is selected in lieu of another.

Satisfaction of Secondary Needs

Other needs also play a major role in buyer behavior. These are the **secondary or higher-order needs.** Consumers make purchases that will satisfy their primary needs and also their secondary needs, such as recognition, peer approval, and status. When a person buys an automobile, the basic need for transportation is satisfied. However, the brand, model, color, style and price of the automobile satisfy higher-order needs as well. For example, a particular auto purchase can serve as a status symbol or a means of self-expression.

Thus, no single motive influences purchasing behavior. Instead, consumer buying behavior is stimulated by the desire to satisfy a combination of primary and secondary needs. Consequently, no simple answer exists to the question of why people make the purchases they do.

Figure 18-1 shows how small business owners can direct their appeals to consumers, offering possible means of satisfying their unique needs.

THE CONSUMER PURCHASING PROCESS

The actual purchasing process focuses on all the forces that influence the consumer in making choices. In the preceding section, we centered our atten-

FIGURE 18-1
THE LINK BETWEEN INDIVIDUAL NEEDS AND THE KINDS OF APPEALS USED BY RETAILERS THAT LEAD TO CONSUMERS' BRAND CHOICES AND STORE PATRONAGE.[1]

Individual Needs	Definition	Retailer Appeals
Self-fulfillment	To accomplish something difficult	Retailers of "do-it-yourself" home improvements and hobby products
Ego	To gain recognition	Fashion-oriented retailing
Social	Desire to be accepted	Retailers of flowers, greeting cards, sporting goods
Security	To take precautionary measures	Retailers of home security products

(Adapted from William R. Davidson, Daniel Sweeney, and Ronald Stampf, *Retailing Management*, 6th ed., John Wiley, New York, 1988, pp. 74–75.)

[1]Need classification based on Maslow's hierarchy of needs.

tion on the "why" of buying. Next we turn our attention to the purchasing process that influences "how, when, and where" the purchase will be completed. The purchase decision process includes the phases of recognition of a need, evaluation of alternatives, purchase decision, and postpurchase behavior.

Recognition of a Need

Whatever the product or service, consumer behavior is first awakened by the recognition of an unsatisfied need. Awareness of the need may be the result of a change in life-style, dissatisfaction with a current product, or a desire to upgrade a product. Recognition of a need that in turn influences the customer to purchase a certain kind or general class of product or service is classified as a **primary buying motive.** For example, the motor in a ceiling fan stops functioning, and it is no longer covered by warranty. The homeowner recognizes a need: repair the old ceiling fan, purchase a new model, or choose not to replace it. Because the ceiling fan is energy efficient and reduces cooling costs, the homeowner knows the fan is practical. The homeowner also determines that it will cost nearly as much to have the old fan repaired as to purchase a new one. Thus, the homeowner decides that a new ceiling fan is the best option.

Evaluation of Purchase Alternatives

When the consumer recognizes the need for the new ceiling fan (primary buying motive), his or her next step is to evaluate the possible alternatives for satisfying the need. The evaluation and comparison of ceiling fans to determine which specific fan to purchase is known as the **selective buying motive.** Before the actual purchase is made, the consumer will evaluate many alternatives of the product, such as special features, brands, styles, prices, and guarantees as well as the reliability and services of the sellers.

Rational Buying Motives

The consumer is influenced by other motives before making the final choice. One set of motives is the **rational buying motives.** A rational decision to buy involves a considerable amount of conscious thought and deliberation before the purchase is made. The consumer tries to evaluate all positive and negative features of the product or service. The consumer researches the products by gathering information from many sources, such as the *Consumer Reports* magazine. Some of the factors that would influence a rational purchase decision are economy, dependability, and convenience in use of the product or service.

Emotional Buying Motives

Another set of motives that influences the purchase is the **emotional buying motives.** Unlike rational purchases, emotional purchases involve little or no deliberation prior to the purchase. These are purchases characterized by impulse, by spur-of-the-moment action. Some motives that influence this type of purchase are a desire for social acceptance, emulation, and esteem.

Patronage Motives

Customers usually identify features about particular places of business that have strong appeal for them. These features are **patronage motives,** the factors that influence customers to return repeatedly to the same store to make their purchases. These motives influence *where* consumers will shop. The small business owners should seek to capitalize on these assets to build stronger patronage for the firm. Some representative patronage motives are discussed in the following sections.

Sales Personnel One factor that influences consumer opinion, especially about retail or service establishments, is the quality of the salespersons. Salespersons who are courteous and friendly and who volunteer assistance to customers do much to help create a positive store image. Customers frequently remark that they patronize a particular store because they enjoy the kind of service accorded them by the salespersons. Conversely, indifferent or discourteous salespersons are often the reasons many customers begin patronizing the firm's competitors. The importance of building and maintaining positive customer relationships should be constantly emphasized in the sales training program.

Customer Service   Customers may be attracted to a store because of the product-related services it provides. Service after the sale is especially important as products become more complex. Often shoppers are willing to pay more for an item because of the quality service that the store provides. Consumer-oriented services are frequently cited as significant patronage motives also. They may include layaway, delivery, product return policies, check cashing, receiving of payment for utility bills, selling of car license plates, or serving as a postal substation.

Convenience of Location   A convenient location is a prime reason for the growth of shopping centers and the drive-in type of store. Customers want to avoid traffic congestion and shop where parking is available.

Merchandise Selection   The variety and the breadth of assortment of merchandise are important patronage motives. When a store stocks a wide selection of merchandise, consumers can find much of the merchandise they want at one place.

Price and Quality   Customers expect to receive a dollar's worth of value for each dollar expended. A policy that encourages repeat purchases is to charge a fair price for the quality of merchandise offered for sale.

The Purchase Decision

After the consumer has searched for information and evaluated the alternatives, the culmination of the evaluation process is the actual purchase decision. In reality, it is difficult to separate the search and evaluation processes from the actual purchase because they are both closely related. Because there are always the elements of uncertainty and risk in any purchase, consumers often seek to take steps to strengthen their purchases, by buying brand-name products.

Postpurchase Behavior

After making a purchase, most consumers reevaluate their decision and wonder if they made the correct choice. They remember the positive characteristics of the product they did not select, especially if the purchase represented a substantial expenditure, such as an auto or major appliance. Each purchasing experience provides feedback that results in learning. Thus, each purchase experience has considerable influence in shaping the next purchase decision. Many consumers seek reinforcement for their choice by reading additional literature or talking with others about their purchase. The small business owner can use this knowledge of consumer behavior advantageously to build repeat business for the firm. One method of accomplishing this is follow up contact with customers after the sale to inquire about their satisfaction with the product or service and to provide postpurchase information.

THE IMAGE OF THE FIRM

Small business owners strive to create a unique image (or personality) for their firm. By electing to sell fashion merchandise, the retailer seeks to create an atmosphere of exclusiveness. Another retailer builds an image of value by advertising the lowest prices anywhere in the area. The service firm strives to build an image of reliability by stressing prompt and dependable service. Almost everything the manager does reflects on the firm's image because a firm and its owner are considered one and the same by most of the general public.

A firm's image is created by multiple factors. Two measures that go a long way toward creating a positive image in the community are the small business's public relations activities and customer relations.

Public Relations

Small business owners who actively participate in community activities acknowledge that public relations is an extremely beneficial means of establishing a firm as a part of the community. Quite often, the little things that the owner does in the community are the most important. Owner–managers should help formulate community policies and make sure their business activities conform to them.

One means of strengthening community relations is to keep informed about what the public thinks of the firm. By obtaining feedback from a cross section of the community, owners can develop a profile of public opinion. With this information, owners are then in a position to capitalize on their strengths and work to overcome any weaknesses.

Owners that view public relations as something to turn to only in time of trouble are actually doing themselves a disservice. Good public relations cannot be created in sporadic fashion. Rather, they must be conscientiously and actively developed on a continuous basis. Public relations are like the deposits made in a bank account. The resources are built up so that they are there when needed. The more owners deposit, the more there is to be drawn upon.

The astute owners consider what is best for the public at large as well as the firm when major decisions are made. In the long run, the interest of the community and the interest of the firm are inseparable. This interdependency is emphasized in the statement taken from a sales ticket of a small grocery store:

We are your friends and neighbors. The money you spend in our store stays in our town and helps support our schools, roads, churches, and other local enterprises. This is our way of saying THANK YOU—CALL AGAIN.

Owners should realize that by joining a service club or community service organization, they are communicating to the people in the community that they care about the community. If an entrepreneur does not participate in community activities, it may prove harmful to the entrepreneur and the small business.

The time invested in community activities will be more productive if owners participate actively in a few activities rather than trying to take on too many activities with half-hearted participation. Owners may also encourage employees to become involved in community activities. Some avenues for the owner to become involved in community service activities include the following.

1. Public service organizations (Lions Club, Rotarians, Kiwanis).
2. Professional associations (chamber of commerce).
3. Public schools (hiring students, working with student organizations).
4. Community projects (supporting local activities and special events by contributing time and money; contributing use of equipment during annual cleanup day; supporting programs that promote civic progress, such as bond elections for new schools).

Customer Relations in the Firm

An important consideration in creating positive customer relations is to make the customer really feel that he or she is number one in importance for the small business. An advertisement for Federal Express emphasizes this point: "If you don't take care of your customers, somebody else will. When you keep your customers satisfied, you keep your customers." Owners and employees alike must demonstrate through their actions and attitudes that they truly believe that they need the customer more than the customer needs the small business. Simply stated, without customers, there is no small business.

In front of Stew Leonard's grocery store in Norwalk, Connecticut, these words are chiseled on a 6000 pound piece of granite:

Rule #1   The customer is always right.

Rule #2   If the customer is ever wrong, reread Rule # 1.

The owner demonstrates his belief in this motto through such actions as cheerfully giving refunds to customers, even on goods purchased in other stores. The business is apparently doing something right because it is growing at an annual rate of 20 to 25 percent.[2]

Stew Leonard's motto, which is carved in stone at the entrance to his grocery, makes clear his dedication to service.

To emphasize that the customer is number one, the management of a chain of small convenience stores portrays its organization chart as an inverted pyramid with customers at the top followed in descending order by store personnel at level 2, stores managers at level 3, support staff at level 4, vice presidents at level 5, and the president at the bottom. The policy of the firm regarding customers is stated in the following manner.

First, we must have customers. Each customer must be welcomed warmly into the store and his or her business needs satisfied. He or she must leave the store wanting to return the next time he or she desires our kind of merchandise.

At a given time the customer is the most important person in the store. It is his or her money that backs your paycheck and pays the company's bills. The customer is truly the one indispensable person in our organization.

Only you, the employee on duty, can make the customers feel welcome and appreciated. Customer service must be your first and primary duty every day. You have a fine opportunity to meet interesting people, make people happy, and benefit both your employer and yourself.

Some of the actions that will promote healthy customer relations are presented in the following discussion.

1. Store owners and employees should empathize with customers. They should evaluate their firm objectively as the customers view it and ask themselves, "Do I like what I see?" and "Would I feel comfortable if I were a customer in this store?" Such an attitude is valuable in maintaining customers, especially since it costs five times as much to attract a new customer as it does to keep a current customer.

2. Positive customer relations are fostered by the fairness and honesty of the small business owner. These actions will result in strengthening the owner's reputation as a person of high integrity. However, illegal and unethical practices can do irreparable damage to the firm. For example, a garage owner advertised that he could rebuild American automatic transmissions for $159.00. When owners returned to pick up their cars, they were charged more than $300.00 because unexpected damage was discovered. In some cases, the transmission housing had only been spray painted to make customers think work had been done.

3. Customers should be treated courteously and attention given their special needs. Salespersons must provide fast, courteous assistance. The following statement of a small business recognizes this concern: "Personnel must be presentable, busy, friendly and helpful at all times. Welcome customers into the store—offer assistance—invite them back—SMILE—call your customers by name. Think of the *store* as being your *home,* and your *customers* as your *guests.*"

4. The advertising in the store should be truthful. False, misleading, or exaggerated claims must be avoided.

5. A firm that is attractive and maintained physically can aid in creating goodwill. The condition of the physical facility and the merchandise layout is an expression of the owner's pride in the firm. This statement of merchandising of a small firm stresses this point: "Merchandising is an art. Keep merchandise neat, straight, in its proper space, clearly priced, fronted, faced and dusted at all times. Displays should be creative eye-catchers rather than just stacks of merchandise that look like they were left there by mistake."

6. Customer complaints settled in ways that satisfy customers is another means of enhancing customer relations. Small businesses, in particular, often depend heavily on **word of mouth.** This type of product or service promotion can be beneficial or harmful to the firm. A satisfied customer frequently recommends the business to friends and relatives. A dissatisfied customer can start an epidemic of ill will by telling others about unpleasant experiences with the firm that can severely injure the firm's reputation if the matter is not resolved. For example, the Direct Selling Foundation reports that customers with complaints will tell an

Steve Bernard, founder and president of Cape Cod Potato Chips, launched his company in 1980 as a small storefront operation in Hyannis, Massachusetts. Today, Cape Cod Potato Chips have become the fastest growing chips in New England and the company has recently expanded to the West Coast.

average of 9 to 10 people about their gripes. And a business can retain as many as 95 percent of its unhappy customers by resolving the problems quickly. The strength of word of mouth is realized by Cape Cod Potato Chip Company,[3] a $5-million-a-year potato chip manufacturer based in Hyannis, Massachusetts. The firm's advertising budget is zero, and it relies solely on word of mouth to promote its product. The company relies on some of the thousands of tourists who visit annually its retail shop located at its manufacturing facility to return home and spread the word about Cape Cod Potato Chips to their local grocers. To ensure a steady flow of visitors the company relocated to a larger facility at Hyannis. This facility has a glass partition and walkways that enable tourists to view the entire potato chip manufacturing process. The goal of the founder of the company is to rely on word of mouth as long as possible in order to maintain the unique image of the firm.

Finally, we must reemphasize that customer relations encompass the total system of the firm's operations. This suggests that a program must be consciously developed to strengthen both community and customer relations to promote its products or services. It does not happen accidentally.

Customer Store Evaluation

The small business owner needs to be aware of the customer opinions of the firm. These data can be collected by using the "Customer Store Evaluation" questionnaire shown in Figure 18-2.

This questionnaire is designed to identify customers' perceptions of the many facets of the firm—store management, employees, and policies. The small business owner can measure the total reponses to each question to arrive at an overall picture of the perceptions of the firm. Visual observation of each completed questionnaire serves to highlight favorable and unfavorable attitudes toward the firm. The owner can then use this information to take any necessary actions to increase customer goodwill and enhance the image of the firm.

PERSONAL SELLING

Sufficient mention has been made to underscore the importance of the salesperson's role in developing patronage motives as well as in creating positive customer relations. **Personal selling** is the process of personally informing customers about a product or service through personal communication for the purpose of making a sale. Personal selling may be carried out on a face-to-face basis or by means of the telephone. Personal selling is especially vital for the small firm. In fact, customers of small firms usually expect personal service. Because many large retailers have gone to more self-service, the small business owner has an opportunity to fill this vacuum by providing personal services and may even gain a competitive edge in the process.

The goal of personal selling is to meet the consumers' needs by offering the proper mix of goods and services at the time, place, and price requested. When this goal is realized, the result is a satisfied customer, and there is the distinct likelihood that a long-term relationship between the firm and the customer will be established. In the remainder of this chapter, we will explore many facets of personal selling.

TYPES OF SALESPERSONS

In developing salespersons, the small business owners must identify the type of salespersons they need to sell their products or services. Most salespersons in small firms are classified as either service (order takers) or creative (order getters).

Service Salespersons (Order Takers)

Service salespersons, or **order takers,** assist the customer in completing a sale. In this sales situation, a customer has already made a decision to buy and has a good idea of what product or service to buy. The service function of the order taker is to provide the customer with the information needed to make the buying decision. For example, if a customer wants to buy new clothing, the salesperson's service selling activities center around showing the cus-

FIGURE 18-2
CUSTOMER STORE EVALUATION.

CUSTOMER STORE EVALUATION

Name of firm: _____ Town: _____

1. Have you ever traded with this firm? _____ Yes _____ No. If your answer is
   no, please state why _____

2. if your answer is yes, do you still trade with this firm? _____ Yes _____ No. If
   your answer is no, please state your reason for no longer trading with this
   firm _____

   _____

3. If you have ever traded with this firm, please rank the firm in comparison to
   other men's clothing firms by placing an X in the appropriate column.

	Very high	Above average	Average	Below average	Very low
Convenience of location					
Quality of goods or services					
Variety of choice of goods or services					
Quantity of goods or services					
Appearance of establishment					
Neatness					
Cleanliness					
Spaciousness					
Uniformity of appearance					
Number of hours a day the business is open					
Management's knowledge of product or service					
Availability of latest fashion or style					
Speed of service					
Prestige of business					

**FIGURE 18-2
(CONTINUED)**

	Very high	Above average	Average	Below average	Very low
Adequacy of merchandise displays					
Customer services					
Liberal credit policy					
Layaway					
Delivery					
Product guaranty					
After guaranty repairs					
Product return policies					
Purchase bonuses (trading stamps, etc.)					
Satisfies customer complaints					
Parking facilities available					
Quality of advertising					
Dependability of business					
Employees					
Knowledge of product or service					
Attitude: (1) Friendly					
(2) Helpful					
Appearance					
Adequacy of price of goods or service					
Acceptability of sales pressure					
Adequacy of traffic movement					
Street					
Sidewalk in front of store					
Inside store					

tomer various styles, fabrics, colors; providing assistance in measuring for size; making arrangements for alterations if necessary; writing up the sales ticket; and informing the customer when the purchase can be picked up or delivered.

Creative Salespersons (Order Getters)

The selling function of the **creative salesperson,** or **order getter,** is significantly more challenging. In creative selling, the potential customer does not have a purchase in mind. The order getter's selling activity is to recognize potential customers and to arouse their need for merchandise or services by providing them with necessary information. The creative salesperson tries to convert the customer's neutral attitude to a positive desire for a product or service.

Suggestion selling offers possibilities for the creative salesperson. In this sales situation, the salesperson tries to build upon the customer's initial need by suggesting additional or better quality products or services. For example, the salesperson could suggest a blouse to go with the purchase of a skirt. Or the salesperson may suggest that the consumer purchase a higher-priced, better quality item rather than the one initially considered.

Inside and Outside Sales Representatives

The sales activity may be classified on the basis of being performed inside or outside the business. The **inside sales representative** is sought out by the consumers who come to the place of business to make a purchase. This is characteristic of sales made to customers in retail stores and personal service firms. The inside sales representative performs both service and creative selling functions. By contrast, **outside sales representatives** call on the customer, such as in direct sales of a manufacturer's product to consumers. This type of selling is extremely challenging and requires individuals who can work on their own in the field without close supervision, keeping irregular hours, and spending substantial amounts of time traveling.

SELECTION OF SALES PERSONNEL

The owner–manager or some designated person has the authority and responsibility for selecting the sales personnel. As a means of making the selection process more efficient, the position requirements must be clearly defined. Position descriptions are a necessary aid for selecting the person who has the qualities required for the service or creative sales position.

The *Dictionary of Occupational Titles* (4th ed., Department of Labor, 1977) suggests some of the duties of a general sales position. This information is an entremely useful guide for small business managers as they develop the specific job requirements to match people with jobs. The job description for a retail and wholesale salesperson taken from this source follows.

> *Salesperson (ret. tr.; whole. tr.)*
> Sells merchandise to individuals in store or showroom, utilizing knowledge of products sold. Greets customers on sales floor and ascertains make, type, and quality of merchandise desired. Displays merchandise, suggests selections that meet customer's needs, and emphasizes selling points of article, such as quality and utility. Prepares sales slip or sales contract. Receives payment or obtains credit authorization. Places new merchandise on display. May wrap merchandise for customer. May take inventory of stock. May requisition merchandise from stockroom. May visit customer's home by appointment to sell merchandise on shop-at-home basis. Classifications are made according to products sold as SALESPERSON, AUTOMOBILE ACCESSORIES (ret. tr.; whole. tr.); SALESPERSON, BOOKS (ret. tr.); SALESPERSON, SURGICAL APPLIANCES (ret. tr.).

The employment of salespersons follows the selection process discussed in Chapter 9.

TRAINING THE SALES PERSONNEL

An effective training program for sales personnel follows and reinforces the employment selection process outlined in Chapter 9. Even though the small firm normally has only a few salespeople, the owner should understand the contribution that sales training offers to the success of the firm.

In providing the training and development that the sales staff requires, the small business owner is aware that they need at least three basic skills to make personal selling effective:

1. Salespeople must be skilled at learning the needs of the customer.
2. Salespeople must have a thorough knowledge of the merchandise and service offered by the retailer.
3. Salespeople must have the ability to convince customers that the merchandise and services offered by their store can satisfy their needs better than that of their competitors.[4]

The training and development process should begin immediately when the employee is hired. Starting training immediately has the advantages of reaching a reasonable level of employee productivity in the shortest possible time, avoids unnecessary expenses and lost sales, and takes advantage of the new employee's natural interest in the job and willingness to learn about it.[5]

Training is a continuous process during the employee's tenure with the firm. Experienced salespersons may need training to learn how to sell a new product line or service or to improve their selling techniques. Whatever the reason, there are a variety of training methods that can be used as we discussed in Chapter 9. Regardless of the method used, employees will derive the greatest benefit from training if the training cycle, outlined here, is followed step by step.

1. Analyze learning needs—what knowledge and skills do your people need for their work that they do not already possess?
2. Develop a training plan (in conjunction with the learner)—lay out what has to be done so that the learner will acquire the knowledge and skills that have been decided upon in the needs analysis.
3. Evaluate results—determine what has been learned and what remains to be learned and whether the results of that learning are indeed the ability to do the work better.
4. Follow up to see that additional learning takes place where needed and that the learning actually brings better work performance.[6]

Focus of Training

The ultimate goal of personal selling is the satisfaction of consumer needs because this is the key to the firm's survival and growth. The salesperson can work more effectively to attain this goal when given training that concentrates on the critical areas of product and service information, company information, customer information, and self-awareness. (See Fig. 18-3.)

FIGURE 18-3
FOCUS OF TRAINING FOR SALESPERSONS.

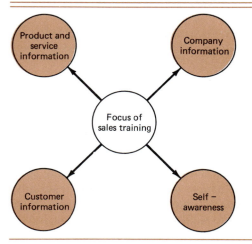

Product and Service Information

Knowledge of the attributes of the products and services one is selling is essential. However, the sales representative must also be able to emphasize how the product or service will benefit the customer. Product information includes a broad range of knowledge, including types, sizes, varieties, special features, and physical operating characteristics; quality; uses; and warranties. Product information requires some knowledge of the competitors' products in order to emphasize the product line that the salesperson is selling. Benefits stress what the product or service will do for the consumer, such as the suggestion by a professional carpet cleaning service: "Our professional carpet expert will save you money as well as headaches by cleaning your carpet thoroughly and safely. Many homeowners have replaced perfectly good carpeting when all they needed was good professional cleaning." Customers often are frustrated when a salesperson cannot adequately explain the features of the product or service. Training for developing product and service knowledge may be general or specific. General knowledge may suffice if the salesperson engages in selling a wide range of merchandise or services. Specific knowledge is required when salespersons sell technical equipment, such as computer equipment.

Company Information

A portion of the training program should be devoted to informing the employee about the company. Employees who are familiar with the firm's operations can represent it more effectively to the public and have a better understanding of their role in the firm. Company information focuses on such topics as history of the company; objectives; organizational structure; departmental structure; policies on customer services, sales, advertising, and personnel; rules and regulations on work schedules, uniforms, use of equipment, and credit and collections; delivery; and pricing. Much of this information is found in the employee manual. (See Chapter 9.)

Customer Information

The discussion of consumer buying behavior is intended to help the salespeople do a more effective selling job by providing them with information about consumer needs, interests, characteristics, and purchasing behavior. One of the most important qualities that is stressed for the salesperson is the need for empathy. The empathetic salesperson closely identifies with the consumer. Consequently, he or she gives more personal attention to understanding the customer's problems and feelings and tailors the sales approach to products or services that will satisfy customers' needs. In turn, this sales approach helps build customer loyalty. One of the surest ways of developing empathy is by learning to be a good listener.

Self-awareness

Evaluating one's skills and personal qualities (physical appearance, personality, tact) allows each person to assess himself or herself. Through greater self-awareness, the salesperson is able to realize the type of image he or she projects and to identify areas that demand improvement. The old cliché "Good salespersons are born, not made" fails to account for the significant benefits derived from sales training. For example, a shy person can become a successful salesperson by becoming aware of the situation and making a concerted effort to work to overcome the shyness. The person with an outgoing personality can improve his or her skills in customer relations through training. The point of the matter is that greater self-awareness will not of itself make one a better salesperson. What makes a successful salesperson is the desire to change and to improve.

THE PERSONAL SELLING PROCESS

Personal selling is the most widely used technique for marketing goods and services. Therefore, salespersons must be well grounded in all phases of the selling process. Likewise the owner of the small firm must be familiar with the personal selling process and ensure that this information is made a part of the sales training program.

In the preceding section, we discussed the types of information that should be included in the presale preparation of salespersons. The personal selling process includes the activities involved in the completion of the sales transaction. Not all sales situations require equal emphasis on each of the phases in the selling process. For example, the service salesperson would ordinarily concentrate on the last five phases of the selling process whereas the creative salesperson would emphasize all phases.

We will examine each of the seven phases of the personal selling process in turn: prospecting, preapproach, sales approach, sales presentation, dealing with objections, closing the sale, and sales follow-up. (See Fig. 18-4.)

Prospecting

Prospecting is the process of developing a list of new customers. Leads of potential customers may be obtained from many sources. An excellent start-

FIGURE 18-4
SEVEN PHASES OF THE PERSONAL SELLING PROCESS.

ing place is with the firm's own sales records and current customers who may be considering the purchase of a new model of a product, such as an energy-efficient refrigerator. Present customers may also offer referrals of prospective customers who they believe are considering a purchase. Personal acquaintances of the salesperson, leads from the firm's advertising, and newspaper announcements of births, marriages, graduations, or relocations offer other sources. **"Cold canvassing"** or the cold-call prospecting technique is used when salespersons contact most of the persons or companies in a territory about products or services that have a high level of demand. For example, telephone contact may be used to generate sales of such products or services as auto insurance or home improvement (carpet cleaning, pest control). Door-to-door salespersons use the cold canvassing technique in their efforts to sell such items as home care products (vacuum cleaners) or magazines.

From the leads of potential customers developed through the prospecting technique, the salesperson evaluates the list to try to determine who are the best prospects. For example, if the firm has used a direct-mail advertisement, the salesperson contacts those prospects who responded to the ad.

Telemarketing

With a list of prospective customers, **telemarketing** can be a very effective sales technique. From a prepared telescript, the caller is given instructions of what they are to say to the client. Information is recorded on each contact. Marketing by telephone has both advantages and disadvantages, but it is essential that the telemarketing campaign be well planned.

One advantage of selling by telephone is that it is economical: many customers can be reached at one sitting, and geographically dispersed customers can be reached easily. Disadvantages include the impersonal nature of the contact, merchandise can only be described (not displayed), there is no face-to-face contact, and the customer may be interrupted at a busy time, such as dinner.

Preapproach

In the preapproach or preparation phase, the salesperson attempts to gain as much knowledge of potential customers as possible to plan how and when to approach them. The salesperson must be aware of the customers' needs and the products and services the firm offers that will satisfy those needs. The more prepared the salesperson is in terms of awareness of the needs of customers, the more effective will be the sales presentation.

Sales Approach

The proper sales approach is critical because this is the initial opportunity for the salesperson to make a positive impression on the potential customer of himself or herself and of the product or service being sold and also to create sufficient interest so that the customer will listen to the sales presentation. Selling in the small business is often conducive to the creation of a favorable initial impression because of the opportunity to develop a warm, personal, and sincere relationship. Salespersons who can learn to know their customers and greet them by name and demonstrate that they consider the needs of the customers of utmost importance will greatly improve their chances of success.

Sales Presentation

The salesperson must make an effective sales presentation to attract and hold the prospect's attention. The sales presentation is reinforced by demonstrating the product or explaining the service or allowing the customer to participate in a trial of the product to appreciate it fully, for example, test driving a new automobile or trying on new clothing. The salesperson should not dominate the sales presentation but should listen and allow the customer to ask questions. Some specific procedures that may be included in the sales presentation of goods and services are listed here.

1. Make strong, persuasive points about merchandise or service early in the presentation—there may be no second chance.
2. Work on "selling benefits"—the value should be established before discussing price.
3. Give the customer complete attention.
4. Never confuse the customer with too wide an assortment.
5. Whenever possible, try to show the item in use.
6. Whenever possible, involve the customer.
7. As a sales presentation progresses, be more specific and more emphatic.
8. Listen to make the customer feel important.
9. Look for polite ways to make the customer feel at ease.
10. Demonstrate enthusiasm and a sense of satisfaction about your job.[7]

Dealing with Objections

Dealing with objections in a satisfactory manner is probably the most difficult step in the personal selling process. Whereas salespersons should anticipate some objections, they should not raise them. Instead, objections should be handled as they arise. Customer objection may include these: "The price is too high; the merchandise is the wrong color; it is not the kind of material I want; or, I have an older model at home with which I am satisfied." Some common methods of handling objections are shown now.

1. Use the "yes-but" technique. (Turn the customer's attention to other factors. The key here is not to contradict.)

2. Ask questions of the customer.
3. Use the turn-it-around principle. (Give the customer confidence in his or her own thinking and a feeling the observation is his or her own.)
4. Select another feature for emphasis. (Turn customer attention from the objection point to another point with more appeal.)
5. Direct denial. (Handle very carefully so no offense is taken by the customer.)[8]
6. Probe for the real objection underneath the stated objection. (David Sandler[9] reports that professional sales people operate on the "Rule of Three." That is, it may take three questions to get to the prospect's "real intent." The first two answers supplied by the prospect are generally intellectual in nature; the third is often an emotional response which reflects the prospects *true* intent.) Here is an example not using the "Rule of Three":

Prospect:	"Do you have more than one of these?"
Salesperson:	"Why, yes!"
Prospect:	"I wonder just how many they make?"
Salesperson:	"Lots of people buy this model."
Prospect:	"I'm sorry to hear that, I was hoping it was one of a kind. I like exclusives."

Here is an example using the "Rule of Three":

Prospect:	"Do you have more than one of these?" (intellectual)
Salesperson:	"That's an interesting question. Why do you ask?"
Prospect:	"I was wondering just how many they make?" (intellectual)
Salesperson:	"That makes sense, Can I ask you why that's important to you?"
Prospect:	"I like buying exclusives." (emotional)

Closing the Sale

Salespersons should be prepared to close a sale at any time during the presentation or while handling objections. In closing the sale, the salesperson tries to find the appropriate time to get the customer to act—to buy the product or service. Among the reasons a salesperson fails to close a sale is that he or she pushes the customer to make a decision before the latter is ready or that the salesperson demonstrates a feeling of superiority over the customer. A number of closing techniques are offered now.

1. Use the principle of positive suggestion, and assume that the sale is made. If the customer does not stop the salesperson, the sale has been completed. This technique assumes the sale is made: "Will you take it with you or would you like it delivered?"
2. Offering an added incentive or emphasizing a bargain may help in

SMALL BUSINESS BRIEF

POWERFUL SALES PERSUADERS

One formula for the sales presentation is suggested by the "**AICDC principle** of selling."

The "A" is to remind you that you have the prospect's *attention*. Obviously, it's the first order of business. No attention, no sale because the selling message doesn't get through. The prospect's senses must be *actively* involved.

The "I" is for *interest*. Attention must be maintained. The stimulus must be prolonged and pleasurable. The interest must be long enough to engage the prospect in the actual presentation.

The "C" is for *conviction*. The customer must sense that what the salesperson claims is true. He must be convinced of the rightness of your proposition.

The "D" is for *desire*. Desire is a natural result of the senses being pleasantly stimulated and the feeling that something good is in the offing.

The last "C" is for *close*. This is the payoff. It's the point where the salesperson's skill in appealing to the prospect's senses is measured and rewarded. The prospect is moved because he is stimulated to move!

Source: Douglas J. Christopher, "Powerful Sales Persuaders," *Salesman's Opportunity,* Vol. 120, no. 6 (November 1982), p. 28. Copyright 1982, Salesmakers Syndicate Services, 22 Bittersweet Trail, Wilton, Conn. 06897-3934. Reprinted from *Salesman's Opportunity,* 6 N. Michigan Avenue, Chicago, IL 60602.

---

prompting customer action. If the customer appears hesitant about the purchase, the salesperson may offer an extra incentive. "If you purchase the VCR now, we will deliver and set it up at no extra charge." Or the salesperson may remind the customer that the product or service goes back to regular price next week. "The special price for cleaning the drapes in your home ends Saturday."

3. Summarize the major benefits of the product or service. Emphasize those benefits that match the customer's buying motives.
4. Close by stressing customer approval. "We guarantee complete satisfaction or your money back.
5. Asking for the order is an obvious but often overlooked closing technique. Many customers respond favorably to this sales technique.

Sales Follow-up

Follow-up after the sale is a supportive procedure by the salesperson that aids in developing goodwill and repeat patronage. This may be accomplished by a telephone call or by writing a short, courteous note thanking the customer for

FIGURE 18-5
GUIDE FOR IMPROVING A SALESPERSON'S PERFORMANCE.

One goal of measuring a salesperson's performance is to help him or her improve. The three steps in bringing about improvement, when, and if, it is needed are planning, measuring, and correcting.

Planning

- Get the salesperson's agreement about what he or she is to attain to exceed for the next year.
  1. Total profit contribution in dollars.
  2. Profit contribution in dollars for
     Each major product line.
     Each major market (by industry or geographical area).
     Each of 10–20 target accounts (for significant new and additional business).
- Get the salesperson's agreement about expenses within which he or she is to stay for the next year:
  1. Total sales expense budget in dollars.
  2. Budget in dollars for travel, customer entertainment, telephone, and other expenses.
- Have the salesperson plan the number of calls he or she will make to accounts and prospects during the next year.

Measuring

- Review at least monthly the salesperson's record for
  1. Year-to-date progress toward 12-month profit contribution goals.
  2. Year-to-date budget compliance.

Correcting

Meet with salesperson if his or her record shows that he or she is 10 percent or more off target. Review with him or her the number of calls he or she has made on each significant account plus what he or she feels are his or her accomplishments and problems. In addition, you may need to do some of the following to help him or her improve performance:

- Give salesperson more day-to-day help and direction.
- Accompany salesperson on calls to provide coaching.
- Conduct regular sales meetings on subjects that salespersons want covered.
- Increase sales promotion activities.
- Transfer accounts to other salespersons if there is insufficient effort or progress.
- Establish tighter control over price variances allowed.
- Increase or reduce selling prices.
- Add new products or services.
- Increase salesperson's financial incentive.
- Transfer, replace, or discharge salesperson.

(Raymond Loen, *Measuring Salesforce Performance,* Management Aid no. 4.003, Small Business Administration, Washington, D.C., n.d., p. 4.)

the purchase and offering to be of assistance to the customer any time in the future. Other follow-up techniques include handling complaints quickly and courteously and providing reliable service after the sale. Follow-ups are usually provided on larger purchases, such as major household appliances.

EVALUATING SALES PERSONNEL

The performance evaluation of the salesperson should be designed not only to gauge past performance but also to reinforce future job performance and provide opportunities for self-development. Performance evaluation should be applied in a systematic manner to benefit both employer and employee. Performance may be evaluated by using a rating scale similar to the one presented in Chapter 9. The reader is referred to Chapter 9, where performance evaluation was discussed in some detail. The Guide for Improving a Salesperson's Performance shown in Figure 18-5 can be extremely useful for counseling the salesperson in the areas of planning, measuring, and correcting performance.

SUMMARY OF KEY POINTS

1. Consumer buying behavior is a dynamic process.
2. Consumers are motivated to make purchases to satisfy both primary and secondary needs.
3. The purchasing process consists of the following phases: recognize a need, evaluate purchase alternatives, the purchase decision, and post-purchase behavior.
4. The buying motives that influence the consumer are primary, selective, rational, emotional, and patronage.
5. Patronage motives are the features that cause a person to continue to buy from a specific firm.
6. Small business managers attempt to create a unique image for their firm.
7. The small business manager can strengthen customer relations with the firm by involvement in community activities and through in-store actions.
8. The Customer Store Evaluation (see Fig. 18-2) offers insight into the consumers' perception of the business.
9. Personal selling is of critical importance for the small business.
10. There are basically two types of salespersons: service (order takers) and creative (order getters).

11. Selection and training of salespersons are areas that must be emphasized even in the small business that has only a few employees.
12. There are seven phases in the personal selling process.

DISCUSSION QUESTIONS

1. Why should small business managers be knowledgeable about consumer behavior?
2. What causes people to buy certain products or services?
3. Explain the difference between a primary and a selective buying motive.
4. Identify several rational buying motives and emotional buying motives.
5. What are patronage motives?
6. Why is personal selling so important, especially to the small retailer?
7. What areas of knowledge should be stressed in a sales training program?
8. Identify the steps that should be followed in making a sale.
9. Explain the difference between a service and a creative salesperson.

THE BUSINESS PLAN: GUIDELINES FOR CUSTOMER RELATIONS AND PERSONAL SELLING

Guidelines for Customer Relations

1. Do you make a constant effort to attract new customers?
2. Do you maintain a continuous check on customer turnover, and do you know why they stop doing business with you?
3. Are you aware of the reasons why customers shop at your store?
4. Do you know what products or services your customers most prefer?
5. Have you considered using a consumer questionnaire to aid you in determining customer needs?
6. Are customer complaints handled promptly and satisfactorily?
7. Are your prices in line with your competitors'?
8. Is the store's appearance neat and clean and is the layout attractive?
9. Do you stress a special appeal, such as lower prices, better quality, wider selection, convenient hours, better service, or convenient location to cater to a specific market segment?
10. Are you familiar with your customers' life-styles?

Guidelines for Personal Selling

1. Are sales representatives thoroughly familiar with the products they sell?

2. Do sales representatives have a strong desire to sell?

3. Are sales representatives well groomed and neat in appearance?

4. Are sales representatives familiar with the customer and the needs of the customer?

5. Are they enthusiastic, energetic, imaginative, and do they work on their own initiative?

6. Do they handle all nonselling tasks adequately?

7. Do they understand the selling process?

8. Do they demonstrate a sincere interest in the consumer?

9. Do they work cooperatively with other personnel in the firm?

10. Do they listen to customers?

ENTREPRENEURIAL PROJECTS

1. Select two stores that sell comparable merchandise. Use the Customer Store Evaluation found in Figure 18-2 for evaluating one store where you regularly shop and a store where you shop infrequently. How do the two stores compare based on the evaluation?

2. Recall a recent purchase you have made. Reconstruct the process you followed in making that purchase.

3. Concerning your own shopping habits, what factors do you consider most influential in your choice of a store to patronize?

CASE A
The Portable Audio Unit

Marvin and Karen purchased a portable audio unit with dual cassette tape player-recorder for their daughter as a Christmas gift. They also bought an extended protection contract covering a three-year period.

After the unit had been in operation about two a and a half years, the fast-forward button on the second tape control popped out. Karen contacted the retailer from whom the unit was purchased to find out the name and location of the company that performed warranty repairs. The company, Double E Electronics, performs warranty service for many audio-video manufacturers.

When Karen took the audio unit to Double E, the clerk at the front desk immediately questioned the validity of the extended protection plan. In fact, her initial comment was that the policy was not valid and even discussed the validity of the warranty contract with another employee. Finally, a third employee came to the front desk, examined the insurance contract, and determined that it was valid. When this point was settled, Karen was informed that it would be six to eight weeks before the unit could be repaired. Karen left the unit for repair.

In about six weeks, the clerk from Double E called Karen and informed her that the unit could not be repaired under the terms of the contract since the serviceperson claimed that the fast-forward button had been broken as a result of abuse by the user. The cost of repairing the unit was estimated to be $60.00. The clerk further informed Karen that if she did not choose to have the unit repaired, there would be a $35.00 charge for inspecting the unit.

Karen became very upset, because she knew that her daughter had not misused the unit. When Karen began questioning the clerk as to the reason why they would not repair the unit under the terms of the extended warranty agreement, the clerk became very defensive and angry, even hanging up on Karen while she was trying to get a clarification on the matter. Karen became even more upset when the clerk hung up on her.

After the clerk hung up on Karen, she called the retailer where the unit was purchased to discuss the matter with a manager. When Karen called, she discovered that the retailer was closing its doors for business that very day. Fortunately, Karen was able to talk to a manager who was available for the specific purpose of handling customer questions about purchases and warranty agreements. When Karen informed the manager, he noted that the retailer had always had good working relationships with the insurer and suggested that Karen call the insurer.

When Karen called the insurer, she received very courteous responses from the service agent. When Karen explained to the insurance representative that the Double E clerk had hung up on her and had a generally anticustomer orientation, the representative grew concerned because the repair firm handled extensive amounts of repair work for the insurer. The representative of the insurance company informed Karen that she would authorize the Double E firm to complete the repair at no cost to her. This eased Karen's mind somewhat, but she was still aggravated about the matter.

After another week passed, the clerk at Double E called Karen and informed her that the unit was repaired. Marvin made a special trip in late Friday afternoon traffic across town to pick up the unit.

When he arrived at Double E, Marvin tested the fast-forward button and found that it had been repositioned but now it was impossible to depress it. Obviously, the serviceperson had not tested the repair work after completing it. A serviceperson then came to the front desk and took the unit to the back. After a wait of about 25 minutes, the serviceperson returned with the unit. Marvin tested the fast-forward button and found that it worked properly now. Marvin signed the insurance authorization form and took the unit home. When his daughter attempted to play a tape, the tape would not turn. Furthermore, the AM-FM radio would not play either (this had not been a problem before the unit was taken in for repair).

Karen telephoned Double E late that Friday afternoon about the problem. Again the clerk was very discourteous and defensive, claiming that the unit had been working properly when it was released to Marvin. A short time later in the telephone conversation, the clerk admitted that the only part of the unit that had been tested was the fast-foward button.

On Monday, Marvin took the unit cross town to Double E and demonstrated what the unit would not do. The clerk and the serviceperson could not understand why the unit did not work properly. Both tried to play a tape and the radio but without success.

Finally, the serviceperson who repaired the unit came to the front. He observed that the unit did not work properly and took the unit to the back. When the unit had been disassembled on Marvin's original visit after it was discovered that the fast-forward button could not be depressed, the unit had not been properly reassembled. The serviceperson admitted to this fact. Finally, the complete unit now worked satisfactorily.

However, the series of events surrounding the whole matter left Marvin and Karen with a very bad impression of repair work performed by Double E.

Several weeks passed. One day, Karen and Marvin received a letter from the insurance company. In the letter was an evaluation form that they were asked to fill out. They were asked to evaluate how the firm (Double E) handled the repair work and whether the work was completed satisfactorily. Some of the questions asked were:

- Did the store where you purchased your product handle the claim properly and courteously?
- If you referred to an outside servicer, did the servicer handle your claim promptly and courteously?

- Has the repair been completed? If not, why not?
- If yes, are you satisfied with the way the work was done? The way the claim was handled?

Questions

1. What does the repair firm, Double E, have to sell? Is it fulfilling this objective?
2. Based on this experience, how would you describe the image of Double E?
3. What impact would "word-of-mouth" comments of customers (such as Marvin and Karen) have on this type of business (a service firm)?
4. How would you perceive that Marvin and Karen would answer the questionnaire?

CASE B
Byrd Enterprises

Byrd Enterprises is a retailer of frozen foods (meats, vegetables, ice cream, seafood, pizza, ethnic foods), frozen and nonfrozen juice drink concentrates, and specialty foods items, such as popcorn and cheeses. These products are sold exclusively through home delivery by outside route salespersons using a fleet of refrigerated delivery trucks. Salespersons have specific routes for each day, and a route is served every two weeks. Salespersons make calls five days a week. If a holiday falls on a weekday, such as July fourth, sales calls are made on the following Saturday. A typical workday is 14 to 16 hours. Salespersons leave the warehouse at about 7 A.M. and return when the route is completed, usually between 9 and 11 P.M. The distribution center (warehouse) is located in a town of about 10,000 population. Territories in which customers are served extend into surrounding small towns, rural areas, and a nearby large metropolitan city. Before leaving for the day's sales run, salespersons must be sure that their delivery truck is loaded with the right selection of frozen food items because product demand on each route is slightly different. Thus, if the proper selection of products is not on the truck, sales are lost. Since route salespersons are paid on a commission basis, it is essential that they have the proper selection of products to meet customer demand. Salespersons are permitted to draw against their commissions to meet unexpected financial needs.

For this type of door-to-door selling, it is imperative that salespersons make a positive impression on the customer. A major problem that the company has encountered is attracting and keeping top-quality salespersons. The primary issue seems to be the long hours that the job requires makes it difficult to keep the salespersons who fit the image that the company tries to present. The company has lost many good salespersons because of working conditions. The vacancies have been filled by what the firm has later described as ''undesirables,'' that is, salespersons who do not project the image that the company demands. Some of the ''undesirable'' salespersons have been discourteous to customers, while others have not covered their sales routes completely. Customers have telephoned the firm's owner complaining about the rude treatment they have experienced from several salespersons— speaking down to customers, uttering sarcastic remarks, using a hard-sell approach to get them to buy products they do not want, or trying to intimidate customers by aggressive actions.

Mr. Byrd is aware that he must develop a plan of action to correct the situation quickly so as to not lose established clientele. However, he is uncertain which alternatives will provide the results he must have.

Questions

1. What alternatives would you suggest to the owner that would enable him to attract and keep the high-quality salespersons necessary for door-to-door home delivery?

2. What should be the emphasis in the firm's training program?

Notes

[1] ''Profitable Community Relations,'' Small Business Management Series no. 27 (Washington, D.C.: Small Business Administration, n.d.), p. 32.

[2] Harry Bacas, ''Making It Right for the Customer,'' *Nation's Business,* November 1987, p. 49.

[3] John Persinos, ''An Advertising Strategy Worth Its Salt,'' *INC.,* vol, 7, no. 3 (March 1985), p. 132.

[4] Bert Rosenbloom, ''Improving Personal Selling,'' Management Aid no. 4.014 (Washington, D.C.: Small Business Administration, 1980), p. 4.

[5] ''Managing Retail Salespeople,'' Business Basics no. 1019 (Washington, D.C.: Small Business Administration, 1980), p. 19.

[6] ''Training and Developing Employees,'' Business Basics no. 1022 (Washington, D.C.: Small Business Administration, 1980), p. 2.

[7] C. Winston Bergen, *Learning Experiences in Retailing* (Pacific Palisades, Calif.: Goodyear, 1976), pp. 296–298.

[8] Ibid., p. 299.

[9] David Sandler, ''Techniques for Handling Objections,'' *Increasing Your Selling Power* (Washington, D.C.: U.S. Government Printing Office, 1984), p. 34.

KEY WORDS

CHAPTER 19

PROMOTIONAL STRATEGY

LEARNING GOALS

After reading this chapter, you will understand:

1 The issues involved in choosing the advertising strategy of the small business.

2 The purposes of advertising.

3 The difference between promotional advertising and institutional advertising.

4 Some of the limitations of advertising.

5 The advertising media that may be appropriate for use by a small business owner.

6 Various methods of preparing an advertising budget.

7 The importance of the timing of an advertisement.

8 The characteristics of a good advertisement.

9 The difference between advertising and sales promotion.

10 Some of the sales promotions commonly used by small business owners.

Dave Larsen

BROOKFIELD NURSERY AND TREE PLANTATION

How did Brookfield Nursery and Tree Plantation decrease yearly space advertising costs from $6500 to $50, yet increase sales by 140 percent? Easy. With help from an SBA-funded Small Business Institute.

In 1982, the Christiansburg, Virginia, nursery's owner, Dave Larsen, approached Virginia Polytechnic Institute for help in marketing and accounting. He couldn't figure out why a dollar's worth of sales cost 65 cents in advertising—a tight squeeze for his company. He also needed help with his books.

The SBI team at the Blacksburg campus mapped out a media saturation plan for Larsen's innovative idea that would ship Christmas trees directly from the plantation to the buyer's door. Press releases went out to over 1100 newspapers, radio and TV stations, and consumer journals. The unique way of helping consumers celebrate Christmas caught on: stories on the nursery appeared in *The Wall Street Journal, The New York Times,* and *Chicago Tribune,* as well as Larsen's local *Roanoke Times.* Larsen called the results "overwhelming."

In one year, mail-order Christmas tree sales jumped from $10,000 to $24,370. By 1986, Brookfield Nursery was selling about $100,000 worth of Christmas trees. Today the company's gross sales are $500,000.

Previously, Larsen was receiving only year-end statements from his accounting firm, useless in planning. The SBI team researched a good computer system and put the company's first three months of 1982 on a computer that generated monthly profit-and-loss balance sheets. Another computer helped him with direct-mailing processing, a system he said, that "paid for itself" in one season.

In 1983, Larsen wrote Senator John Warner of Virginia: "Small businesses are having a tough time now, and need all the support they can get. I am sure the work of the SBI team saved me two years or more in obtaining my goals in financial management and promoting our Plantation-Fresh-Direct Christmas tree. I am very, very pleased, and recommend as much support to the Small Business Institutes as can be provided."

Larsen declares today, "I still use that SBI counselor's report with new employees."

Source: Network (Washington, D.C.: Small Business Administration, September–October 1987).

Ralph Waldo Emerson said, "If a man write a better book, preach a better sermon, or make a better mousetrap than his neighbor, though he builds his house in the woods, the world will make a beaten path to his door." This statement embodies the assumption that a new or improved product or service is all that is necessary to generate sales for the firm. However, small business owners who sit back and wait for customers to beat a path to their business to purchase their products or services will likely fall victim to their competitors. Though the products or services form one of the major variables of the marketing mix, consumers will not buy them unless they know of their existence and believe that they will satisfy their wants and needs. Promotional strategy is the means of accomplishing this goal.

Promotional strategy is the means that small business owners use to communicate information about the firm and its products and services to potential customers with the objective of influencing customers to purchase the products or services that will satisfy their wants and needs. The promotional methods utilized by small business owners to communicate this information are advertising and sales promotion (both are discussed in this chapter) and personal selling (discussed in the preceding chapter).

THE ADVERTISING STRATEGY OF THE SMALL FIRM

Developing an advertising strategy for a small business requires systematic planning. A wide range of questions must be answered when designing an advertising strategy, as depicted in Figure 19-1. Because each firm is unique, the advertising strategy necessarily must be developed to meet specific requirements. The ensuing discussion offers guidance in developing the advertising strategy of a small business.

ANALYSIS OF THE FIRM AND CUSTOMERS

An initial interest of small business owners should be to analyze their own strengths and weaknesses as well as identify their target market. In this way, a coordinated advertising strategy can be developed and implemented.

The evaluation of the firm should reveal how well it compares to competitors—what unique services or products are offered that are not provided by the competition. Other facets to be evaluated include the quality of merchandise carried in the store, customer services offered, store location, and selling techniques used.

Furthermore, an effective advertising strategy necessitates the identification of the target market. Questions related to the target market include who are my customers, who needs my products or uses my services, and who will buy my products or services? Another variable relating to the composition of the customer market is to forecast changes that are anticipated. Espe-

FIGURE 19-1
SOME ADVERTISING DECISIONS OF THE SMALL BUSINESS OWNER.

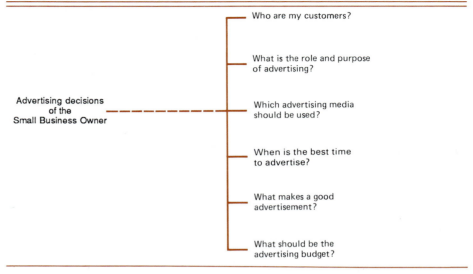

Advertising decisions of the Small Business Owner
- Who are my customers?
- What is the role and purpose of advertising?
- Which advertising media should be used?
- When is the best time to advertise?
- What makes a good advertisement?
- What should be the advertising budget?

cially pertinent is the determination of whether the market size is expected to increase or decrease, whether incomes will continue upward, and so forth.

THE ROLE AND PURPOSES OF ADVERTISING

Through small business owners may not feel that they can afford the expense of advertising their goods and services because of limited financial resources, such an attitude will significantly lessen the firm's likelihood for success. In fact, advertising should be considered an investment rather than an expense. Owners should realize the value of advertising and that advertising on a regular basis will materially increase the possibility for growth of the firm. Sales are the lifeblood of the small business. In the highly competitive business environment, a well-planned advertising strategy is one of the most effective means of increasing sales.

Personal selling was described as the personal communication between the customer and the salesperson. On the other hand, **advertising** is any type of sales presentation that is nonpersonal and is paid for by an identified sponsor. The advertising message, called the **advertising copy,** contains the written or spoken words of the ad or both. Owners may choose to place advertising messages in a single source (**advertising medium**) or in more than one source (**advertising media**).

Advertising has many purposes, depending on the type of the business and the kind of products and services promoted. For example, a manufacturer's

Robert McKnight and Jeffrey Hakman shared a dream of owning a business that would enable them to enjoy their endless summers of surfing. When they acquired the licensing rights for Quiksilver of Australia, a maker of boardshorts (tight-fitting swimsuits), they realized their dream. Subsequently, Quiksilver has grown to become a full-line activewear manufacturer. Quiksilver's promotional strategy includes providing free surfwear to 1000 kids who appear in their ads (for free) and giving clothing and $1000 annually to a select group of surfers. Quiksilver's A-Team consists of 10 professional surfers who wear the company's clothes and receive a monthly stipend.

advertising is designed to stimulate interest and increase sales in the line of merchandise. A service firm's ad is intended both to inform consumers of the various services the firm provides and to encourage consumers to use them.

In this section, we examine the promotional and institutional objectives of advertising as well as some of the limitations of advertising. While our attention is focused on retail and service firms, all other types of small businesses can modify these objectives to meet their specific requirements.

Promotional Advertising

The objective of **promotional advertising** is to inform and remind the target market of the firm about its goods and services. The greater amount of advertising dollars is spent for promotional advertising. Some of the specific goals of promotional advertising are discussed in the following sections.

Increasing Sales

A major purpose of promotional advertising is to create an action response on the part of the consumer that will result in sales of a product or use of a service. This advertising appeal is planned to increase sales or usage in the short term. Small business owners may emphasize specific appeals in their advertising message, such as offering a product at a special price for a specific time or a reduced charge for a service if used by a specific date. For example, a lawn maintenance service offers a reduction of 50 percent off the cost of the first mowing job if used before April 30.

Promotional advertising must also be focused on long-term growth. To illustrate, an owner may set a goal of increasing sales by 6 percent a year over the next five years. The advertising must be planned and coordinated to aid in reaching this objective. Likewise, all sales goals must be realistic. If an objective is to attract 10 percent more customers but the population is decreasing in the trade area and the market potential is not there, no amount of advertising will make the goal attainable.

Sales objectives for the year should be planned on a month-by-month basis. As each month passes, the owner is able to gauge sales performance and compare the sales forecast with actual results. In this way, the manager will be able to evaluate the effectiveness of the advertising program.

Creating Awareness of Product or Service

Advertising can provide customers with greater awareness of the firm's products or services. The message may center on the type of products or services sold, how the product or service can be used, where the product or service may be obtained, the benefits to be realized from using the product or service, and the price.

Attracting New Customers

Small business managers should not be complacent with their current volume of business and patronage. They may feel they have all the customers they can adequately serve and consequently see no purpose in advertising to attract new customers. However, the National Retail Merchants Association estimates that the small business would have to close its doors at the end of three or four years if it stopped advertising. This association reports that a store annually loses between 20 and 25 percent of its customers. Each year the market composition changes as people move in and out of the trading area. For example, the Bureau of the Census estimates that about 18 percent of the nation's population changes its place of residence annually. And customer tastes and shopping habits change. The younger generation has different demands from the older generation it replaces. To maintain the status quo, small business owners advertise to keep the firm's name before the public in order to attract new customers.

To increase patronage, we have emphasized the need for small firm owners to identify their market segment and develop their advertising strategy for this market. Markets may be segmented in many ways, as by age or by ethnic or geographical grouping. Thus, if the target market is teenagers, small business owners should discover such characteristics as where they live, their radio and television listening and viewing habits, and their income to direct advertising efforts at this specific market.

Promotion of a Special Offer or Special Sale

Advertising may promote a special event or a special sale. To illustrate, a pizza parlor advertises a special price on its pizza to help celebrate the pizza parlor's birthday. By purchasing one size of pizza at the regular price, the customer will receive the next smaller size of the same kind of pizza free. The ad also specifies how long the special price is good. Ads can be used to promote special sales, such as the 1 cent sale. Buy one item at the regular price and get a second for only 1 cent more. A men's store ad promotes a "one-day-only" sale of its famous-name brand suits at a specially reduced price.

Small business owners may find it useful to develop a promotion calendar to note opportunities for special events.

Special Dates	*Special Promotions*
Valentine's Day	Sidewalk sales
St. Patrick's Day	Seasonal fashion shows
Easter	Anniversary sale
Mother's Day	Grand reopening (after store has been remodeled)
Father's Day	Autograph parties
Labor Day	Free clinics
Thanksgiving	
Christmas	

Promoting Greater Uses of Product

Advertising may be used to inform customers of additional uses for a product or service. One of the premier examples is baking soda. Today this product is widely advertised as having many uses in addition to its original one as a baking ingredient, such as a deodorizer for the refrigerator, a cleansing agent, or a toothpaste. Some advertising is designed to increase the length of the buying season for a product. Antifreeze is advertised for its use as an engine coolant for summer driving as well as a protection against radiator freeze-up in the winter. This type of advertising may also suggest increasing the number of items purchased at one time or replacing the products more frequently.

Introducing New Products or Services

The product life cycle demonstrated the fact that products are introduced, grow, mature, and decline. As old products are phased out, new ones take their place. Advertising informs customers of these new products as well as any new services that the small business owner adds.

Institutional Advertising and Publicity

Institutional advertising is aimed at providing the general public with information about the company. Institutional advertising's purposes are to create goodwill toward the company, to build consumer confidence in the company, and to create or strengthen the image of the firm in the community. Through institutional advertising, the small business manager seeks to improve the firm's public relations stature by demonstrating that the owner is a concerned, active, socially responsible member of the community. For example, with the energy shortage, one firm advertised in a local newspaper a message reminding consumers and business firms alike of the critical need to employ energy conservation measures. The ad also contained suggestions on how energy might be conserved.

The small firm may also direct some of its advertising emphasis toward public service announcements. For example, announcements may be made informing the public of activities that are going to take place in the community. Announcements about special events, such as an arts and crafts show or activities of local civic organizations, may be sponsored by a particular firm. This type of advertising aids in fostering good public relations and strengthening the ties of the business to the community.

The company may also benefit from the publicity it receives. Publicity is not the same as advertising, however. **Publicity** is a news item about a company reported by the media because the information has some apparent news value. A firm may donate time, money, or merchandise to a civic project that is reported by the various media. Unlike advertising, publicity is not paid for by the firm. One way of getting publicity is for the owner of the small business to contact the media and inform them about themselves and what they are doing. This may be material for an article about the way the business was started. Or owners may get involved in public service activities, such as sponsoring a program to collect food for the homeless.

Limitations of Advertising

Although advertising is a powerful tool to aid the small business owner, its limitations must also be recognized. For example, advertising cannot force people to buy things they do not want. Another limitation of advertising is that, if a firm advertises extensively but offers poor service or inferior products, the advertising will not overcome these deficiencies. Many customers visit a store in response to an ad. However, if they are ignored or treated discourteously by sales personnel during their visit, the outcome will be dissatisfied customers who are unlikely to return to the store. If the small business manager charges higher prices than competitors for similar merchandise, advertising will not aid in selling the overpriced merchandise indefinitely. A further limitation of advertising is that it usually does not produce dramatic results immediately. Rather, the manager should follow an advertising strategy of advertising in several media and consistently in at least one medium. Furthermore, advertising effectiveness will be severely reduced if it contains false or misleading statements. Not only is this illegal but it also seriously damages the owner's reputation in the community. Additionally, advertising's value will be diminished if it is poorly timed or improperly prepared. In summary, the owner–manager should recognize these advertising limitations.

1. Advertising will not overcome discourteous treatment of customers by salespersons.
2. Advertising will not sell inferior products or services more than once.
3. Misleading or untruthful advertising will result in a loss of customer confidence in the firm.
4. A single advertisement will not bring about a sustained increase in sales and store traffic.

ADVERTISING MEDIA

Selecting the appropriate advertising medium or media that will satisfy the needs of a particular business is one of the significant decisions the owner must make. No formula provides the answer, but the following factors should be considered when choosing the media for advertising the company's products or services.

- *Trading Area* Do you serve or sell to an industrial market, a national market, a neighborhood market, a specialized market?
- *Customer Type* What does your potential customer read or listen to? Where? How often? What image does the medium you are considering suggest? Does it fit your customer?
- *Budget Restrictions* How will the amount of money you have to spend limit the media you can use? How does the cost per thousand compare with the media you are considering? How can you spread your money out over the year to give a repetitive, continual message?
- *Continuity of Message* How will the type of product or service, seasonal buying patterns, and customer profile affect your choice of media and the frequency with which you advertise?

- *Media Combinations* Would using more than one medium help you achieve your goals or not.
- *Assistance* Does the medium you are considering offer assistance to the small business person in preparing the ad or will you have to hire a professional or do it yourself?
- *Past Performance* What is the track record for use of the medium you are considering for your type of business?[1]

Newspapers

Newspapers are the single most important advertising medium for the small business manager. Nationwide, about 26 percent of all advertising dollars is spent for newspaper ads. An advantage of newspapers is that circulation covers a selected geographical territory (a section of a city, a single town, a number of adjoining towns, or a number of adjacent counties). In addition, newspaper advertising provides broad coverage in the trade area. Ads reach people in all economic classes. Newspaper ads are flexible and timely because they can be changed frequently. Newspapers have short closing times. "Closing times" refers to the deadlines prior to publication by which advertising copy must be submitted. For daily newspapers, this period seldom exceeds 24 hours, thus giving the advertiser the opportunity to make last-minute changes. Closing dates for Sunday supplements, however, are generally much longer, usually ranging from four to six weeks.[2] When compared with other media, advertising costs in newspapers are relatively low. This is significant for the small business manager who has a limited budget for advertising. Newspapers serve as a guide for shoppers who are looking for information about products or services. The ads inform them what is available, where it is being sold, when, and at what price. Managers should study the feasibility of using the newspaper coverage that matches their goals. If they are concentrating on a trading area of a specific section of town, they may advertise in a newspaper that has a circulation limited to one section of town, such as the *Southside News*.

A disadvantage of newspaper advertising is that its coverage is not selective. If the firm caters to a specific market segment, much of the newspaper ad coverage will be wasted. Another disadvantage to consider is that many ads are presented together in one newspaper, and a single ad may be missed. Most newspapers are read or scanned hurriedly and kept for a short time, which means the life of the ad is of short duration. Small business managers should analyze their firm's target market to determine whether newspaper advertising should extend to the larger audience or be limited to a more select audience.

Newspaper ads must meet certain criteria if they are to be effective. One set of guidelines for newspaper ads is the **AIDCA principle.** This principle outlines the basic requirements of a good newspaper ad.

1. *Attention*   Causes the customer to stop and read the copy.
2. *Interest*   Brings about a sense of curiosity.
3. *Desire*   Increases the urge to acquire.
4. *Conviction*   Substantiates that a decision to buy would be a good judgment.
5. *Action*   Actually moves the consumer to going out to buy.[3]

Radio

Across America, 99 percent of all households have radios, and the average number of sets per household is 5.4. Consequently, the medium of radio affords the owner the potential of delivering his or her advertising message into nearly every home in the trade area or selected homes as often as desired. A benefit of radio is that advertisers can direct their message to their specific market segment at the times they desire. For example, radio ads can be aired to selected groups—teenagers, listeners to certain types of music, or sports enthusiasts. Radio advertising is also flexible and timely. A commercial can be written and broadcast the same day. Likewise, the small business manager can direct the advertising to the target market at the time most likely to reach the largest number of listeners. For example, a larger share of the market can be reached before, during, and after sporting events.

Radio ads are sold in 10-, 30-, and 60-second spot announcements. Ad costs vary according to the time of day and size of the listening audience. Most expensive rates are usually for the prime time periods from 6 A.M. to 10 A.M. and 3 P.M. to 8 P.M. on weekdays.

Other factors influencing costs are (1) how often the business advertises in a given week; (2) how many consecutive weeks the ads run; (3) whether spots are scheduled on a run-of-the-station basis, that is, aired at times the stations elects, or in more costly fixed time slots; and (4) any combination packages of time amounts, slots, and frequencies.

Rates for a station are available from the station itself and are also quoted in the *Standard Rate and Data Service,* an industry survey of the costs of various media. For example, a spot announcement rate taken from this publication for a small radio station is shown with tables that follow along with its time rates.

There are some disadvantages associated with radio advertising. Obviously, radio advertising will not reach a person whose set is not turned on. Frequently, radios are turned on while people are engaged in other activities, and they may not be paying attention to the ad message. In addition, radio permits only a spoken message to describe a product or service, radio ads must be brief because of the time limit, and ads must be broadcast regularly to reach the target market.

RADIO TIME RATES

AAA	Monday through Friday	6 to 10 A.M. and 3 to 8 P.M.
	Saturday	10 A.M. to 8 P.M.
AA	Monday through Friday	10 A.M. to 3 P.M.
	Saturday	6 to 10 A.M.
	Sunday	9 A.M. to 8 P.M.
A	Monday through Saturday	8 P.M. to 6 A.M.

COST FOR EACH SPOT ANNOUNCEMENT, 1 MINUTE

	1 Time per Week	6 Times per Week	18 Times per Week	30 Times per Week
AAA	$33	$30	$28	$26
AA	28	26	24	22
A	14	13	12	11

10-second rate = 70% of 1-minute rate
30-second rate = 60% of 1-minute rate

Source: Spot Radio Rates and Data, Vol. 70, no. 8. (Wilmette, Ill.: Standard Rate and Data Services, August 1, 1988).

Television

Television is being used with increased frequency by small business managers. One reason for the growth is that advertising rates have been reduced, enabling more small business managers to fit this medium into their advertising budget. Like radio, television has the potential for reaching a mass audience. Census data indicate that 98 percent of American homes have television sets, there is an average of 1.83 sets per household, and in the average home a television set is turned on over six hours a day. Consequently, the likelihood of a firm's ad being seen and heard is quite high in the local market area. Television ads offer three advantages: (1) products or services can be advertised, (2) products or services can be demonstrated, and (3) the advertising message can be presented simultaneously with the demonstration.

Television time is sold in 10-, 20-, 30-, and 60-second spots. The 30-second spot is most popular with the small business owners. Spot announcements enable the advertiser to select the time, audience, and program for the commercial ad. The ad message can vary because it can be presented over different stations. As with radio advertising, the time and makeup of the viewing audience should be considered for the television ad. For example, a toy store can effectively present its ad during the Saturday morning time period when children's shows are being televised.

There are some disadvantages to television ads. They are projected onto the screen for a short time and may be missed by the prospective customer. Also, many trade areas have more than one television station, meaning only a part of the total viewing audience has the potential of seeing the ad. And the viewing audience usually does something else during commercial breaks.

A facet of television that is growing and should be considered by the small business manager is cable television and satellite television. About 47 percent of all U.S. households have cable. As these services expand and the number of users increases, this medium will become increasingly important for reaching specific markets.

In evaluating broadcast advertising, the small business manager should consider using smaller stations or stations in small towns. Rates on these stations are lower and frequently are more effective in reaching the desired target market.

Handbills

Handbills are one of the most inexpensive methods of advertising if properly managed. The cost of producing handbills is low because they are usually reproduced by either mimeograph or multilith methods. The small business manager is able to control the distribution of the handbills because they are distributed by store employees or others (school children) in a selected area. Handbills may be distributed door to door in specific neighborhoods, placed under the windshield wiper blade of cars parked in a shopping center lot, handed out to customers in the store, inserted in their shopping bag by cashiers as they check out, or laid out on a store counter where they can be picked up by the customers. (See Fig. 19-2.)

A disadvantage is that many customers consider handbills a nuisance and react negatively when they find handbills on their car or at their front door, and many are thrown away without ever being read.

Direct-Mail Advertising

Leaflets stuffed into monthly bills, flyers, catalogs, circulars, and postcards are types of direct-mail advertising. This is the most selective form of advertising, and the tone of the message should be personal. An advantage of direct-mail advertising is that small business owners can select the specific audience to whom they wish to send their message. However, a disadvantage of direct-mail advertising is that many people consider it "junk mail" and discard it, often without reading the message.

To be effective and efficient, mailing lists must be current and accurate. Usually the small business manager can compile his or her own mailing list from charge account records or sales slips. Lists can also be assembled from directories, such as that of the R. L. Polk and Company, publishers of over 1400 city directories. The Polk directories have four sections. Section 1 is a buyer's guide listing alphabetically all business and professional concerns in the community. Section 2 is an alphabetical list of residents and business and professional concerns. Section 3 is a directory of householders, including street and avenue guide. Section 4 is a numerical telephone directory.

Free lists are available from government licensing agencies, such as the

FIGURE 19-2
THE HANDBILL IS AN INEXPENSIVE ADVERTISING MEDIUM.

Grand Opening

BRODIE LANE LOCATION
8106 BRODIE LN. – IN BRODIE PLAZA

5th ANNIVERSARY

OAK HILL LOCATION
HWY 290 W

50% OFF
ENTIRE MENU!

MONDAY, MARCH 21st thru WEDNESDAY, MARCH 23RD

WE DELIVER TOO!

Register ALL WEEK
for a
FREE PORTABLE TV!

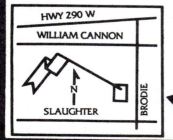

Grand Opening!
BRODIE PLAZA
8106 BRODIE LANE
280-1825

5th Year Anniversary
OAK HILL PLAZA
7101 Hwy. 71 West at the "Y"
288-3830

(As advertised in the *Austin Shopping Guide-11*, p. 33.)

FIGURE 19-3
PURPOSES OF DIRECT-MAIL ADVERTISING.

Solicit mail-order or telephone-order business.

Announce new products or changes in products and services.

Notify customers of price changes.

Precede or follow up on a salesperson's call.

Welcome new customers.

Regain lost customers.

Thank customers for their business at least once a year.

Remind customers or prospects of seasonal or periodic needs.

Announce special events such as special sales.

Create an image of the business.

(*Advertising Your Small Business,* Small Business Administration, Washington, D.C., 1984, p. 28.)

department of motor vehicles, chamber of commerce directory, the Yellow Pages, and club membership lists. Mailing lists may be purchased from firms that specialize in preparing them. Fees are charged on the basis of per thousand names for a general list or a cost per name for a specialized list.

Mailings may be made on a one-time announcement, such as a change in store name, location, personnel, or ownership. A series of mailings may be sent to promote the sale of a single offer. Often, a small business owner uses a regular mailing, such as the weekly mailing of a grocery store circular. Some mailings request the recipient to respond by filling out a coupon for additional information or entering a contest. Sales representatives then follow up by contacting them, usually by telephone. Some of the many uses of direct mailings are shown in Figure 19-3.

Store Signs

Store signs and other outdoor signs, such as billboards and portable trailers, are direct forms of visual advertising available to the small business owner.

Store signs are street advertising. Effective signs are clearly visible and readable. They are important because they provide easily recognizable information about the business and its products and services, give directions to the business, and help create the image of the business. Specific advantages of store signs are these:

1. Signs are oriented to your trade area.
2. Signs are always on the job repeating your message to potential customers.
3. Nearly everyone reads signs.
4. Signs are inexpensive.

5. Signs are available to every shop owner.
6. Signs are easy to use.[4]

Transportation Advertising

The company name may be painted and displayed on the sides of the firm's delivery vehicle. Another form of transportation advertising is to display an advertising message on a mode of public transportation—taxicabs, buses, commuter trains. Posters may be displayed on the sides of buses or on the backs of taxicabs, or rotating signs may be displayed on top of taxis. This type of advertising is relatively inexpensive, and the advertising area to be covered can be controlled.

Magazines

Magazine advertising can be used by the small business owner if it is used selectively. National magazines, which have high circulation and charge advertising rates that far exceed the advertising budget of the small firm, are impractical. However, magazines published in the local area, which have smaller circulation and lower advertsing rates, permit the small business owner to consider them as a medium for ads. There are a variety of types of local magazines that can adequately serve the needs of the small business manager.

City and Community Magazines

City and community magazines do not differ greatly from national magazines. The content of these magazines relates to the local area. Some of them are privately owned; others are sponsored and published by local groups, such as the chamber of commerce.

Visitor Magazines

These magazines emphasize places to go and things to do in the local area. Ordinarily, these magazines are placed in hotels and motels and are directed toward the tourist or convention visitor.

Publications of Special Interest Groups

Each locality has specific groups, such as women's clubs and fraternal orders. Frequently, these associations publish a magazine, either on a regular basis throughout the year or annually. If magazines are sent to a specific segment of the market to which the firm caters, the small business owner may wisely use this source as an effective vehicle for conveying advertising messages.

The advantage of advertising in a magazine is that the ads have a longer life expectancy than newspaper ads because magazines are kept longer and read in a more leisurely fashion. Disadvantages of magazine advertising are the fact that ads must be placed well in advance of the time of actual publication of the magazine and the higher cost for ad space compared to the newspaper.

Specialty Advertising

Advertisers are increasingly turning to specialty advertising as a means of placing their advertising in the hands of their customers. **Specialty advertising** refers to useful items that have the company name, logo, address, and telephone number embossed on them; are given free to customers with no direct commitment for making a purchase; and should make recipients feel good because it is free or something they can use. Whenever the person uses the specialty advertising item, such as the tote bag, pencil, coffee mug, or note pad, or whenever he or she needs to place an order, the customer is supposed to think of the company. Reasons given by business owners for using specialty advertising include the following:

1. Effective specialty advertising carries the imprint of the company that sent it.
2. Effective specialty advertising must have a long life, such as the 12-month life of the calendar.
3. Effective specialty advertising must be useful, novel, or attractive.
4. Effective specialty advertising is generally inexpensive.[5]

Directories

Small business owners commonly use the Yellow Pages of the local telephone directory for their ads. These ads have long life, usually a year, as well as wide circulation. Another benefit is that the telephone company extensively advertises the Yellow Pages, making potential customers aware of the value of looking in the Yellow Pages for specific firms. In addition to the Yellow Pages, other industry and trade groups frequently publish directories identifying their membership and their business products or services.

Other Advertising Media

Other media are used by the small business owners. Business cards are an effective advertisement for many owners. Other owners develop an advertisement on film or slides and show it regularly in movie theaters.

The advantages and disadvantages of various advertising media are shown in Figure 19-4.

TIMING THE ADVERTISING

Timing the advertising to reach the target audience is one of the most important considerations in attempting to maximize the advertising expenditure. Timing involves adjusting advertising plans to seasonal patterns, to the store's special days, and to special events in the community.

For a small retailer, advertising can be planned to coincide with the

FIGURE 19-4
ADVANTAGES AND DISADVANTAGES OF SELECTED ADVERTISING MEDIA.

	Advantages	Disadvantages
Newspaper	Selected territory Broad coverage of trade area Flexible Timely Costs relatively low for number of people reached	Coverage not selective to target market May not be seen Short life span
Radio	Mass audience potential Target market selectivity (usually local) Flexible Timely	Low attention by listeners Verbal presentation only Brief message
Televison	Products and services advertisement, demonstration, and message presented simultaneously Appeals to many senses Mass audience potential	Longer ad preparation time Higher cost than other media
Handbills	Least expensive Target market selectivity	Low readership Distribution problems
Direct mail	Most selective form Personal message Inexpensive for number reached	Low readership Reader perception of ad may be low ("junk mail")
Magazines	High circulation Longer life expectancy than newspaper Target market selectivity Reproduction quality high	Long lead time for ad preparation Higher cost of ad rates than for newspaper
Directory	Relatively long life Products, services, names of businesses listed alphabetically Reaches individuals who are searching for a particular item	Little variety in ad format

heaviest shopping days. Consequently, many grocery store owners plan their food ads to appear in Wednesday or Thursday newspapers. Other advertising should be scheduled to coincide with payroll days in the trading area. The small business owner must also consider what is to be advertised when deciding on the schedule of advertising, such as the introduction of new merchandise or end-of-the season closeout items. If the business is located in a college town, the owner can plan a special promotion to coincide with the school's homecoming activities or other special activities of the college, with advertising placed in the college newspaper.

The service firm may time special promotions with seasonal changes also. For example, a special promotion may stress the need to have the home furnace thoroughly checked before the winter season begins.

THE ADVERTISEMENT

There are a number of desirable qualities in an ad that assist in making it more effective in achieving the intended results. For example, consider the following.

1. Make your ads easy to recognize. Give your copy and layout a consistent personality and style.
2. Use a simple layout. Your layout should lead the reader's eye easily through the message, from the art and headline to the copy and price to the signature.
3. Use dominant illustrations. Show the featured merchandise in dominant illustrations. Whenever possible, show the product in use.
4. Show the benefit to the reader. Prospective customers want to know "what's in it for me." But, do not try to pack the ad with reasons to buy—give the customers one primary reason, then back it up with one or two secondary reasons.
5. Feature the "right" item. Select an item that is wanted, timely, stocked in depth, and typical of your store. Specify branded merchandise and take advantage of advertising allowances and cooperative advertising whenever you can.
6. State a price or range of prices. Don't be afraid to quote high prices. If the price is low, support it with statements which create belief, such as clearance or special purchase.
7. Include store name and address. Double-check every ad to make sure it contains store name, address, telephone number, and store hours.[6]

IMMEDIATE RESPONSE ADVERTISING

Immediate response advertising is designed to cause potential customers to buy a particular product from the small business within a short time—today, tomorrow, the weekend, or next week. An example of such decision-triggering ads is one that promotes regular price merchandise with immediate appeal. Other examples are ads that use price appeals in combination with clearance sales, special purchases, and seasonal items.

Such advertising should be checked for results daily or at the end of one week from its appearance. Because all advertising has some carry over effect, it is a good idea to check also at the end of two weeks, three weeks, and so on to ensure that no opportunity for using profit-making messages is lost.

In weighing the results of your immediate response advertisements, the following devices should be helpful.

1. **Coupons brought in**   Usually these coupons represent sales of the product. When the coupons represent requests of additional information or contact with a salesperson, were enough leads obtained to pay for the ad? If the coupon is dated, you can determine the number of returns for the first, second, and third weeks.

2. **Requests by phone or letter referring to the ad**   A "hidden offer" can cause people to call or write. Include—for example, in the middle of an ad—a statement that on request the product or additional information will be supplied. Results should be checked over a one-week through six-month period because this type of ad may have considerable carry-over effect.

3. **Testing ads**   Prepare two ads (different in some way you would like to test or set for different stations or broadcast times) and run them on the same day. Identify the ads—in the message or with a coded coupon—so you can tell them apart. Ask customers to bring in the coupon or to use a special phrase. Run two broadcast ads at different times or on different stations on the same day with different "discount phrases." Ask a newspaper to give you a "split run"—that is, to print "ad A" in part of its press run and "ad B" in the rest of the run. Count the responses to each ad.

4. **Sales made of particular items**   If the ad is on a bargain or limited-time offer, consider that sales at the end of one week, two weeks, three weeks, and four weeks came from the ad. You may need to make a judgment as to how many sales came from in-store display and personal selling.

5. **Check store traffic**   An important function of advertising is to build store traffic which results in purchases of items that are not advertised. Pilot studies have shown, for example, that many customers who are brought to the store by an ad for a blouse also bought a handbag. Some bought the bag in addition to the blouse, others instead of the blouse.

Source: Elizabeth Sorbet, *Do You Know the Results of Your Advertising?"* Management Aid no. 4.020 (Washington, D.C.: U.S. Government Printing Office, 1982), pp. 2–4.

THE ADVERTISING BUDGET OF THE SMALL BUSINESS

One goal of small owner-managers is to realize a maximum return of sales from each dollar expended for advertising. As stated in Chapter 16, one means for getting more results for each advertising dollar is to feature nationally advertised products in the ads. Millions of dollars are spent each year by manufacturers to promote their products and services nationwide. Incorporating brand names and symbols into advertising enables small owner–managers to capitalize on the pulling power that well-known products and services have.

In the preparation of the ad budget, the amount that should be budgeted depends on a number of factors.

1. Stores in less favorable locations or managers opening a new store or expanding a present store may require more advertising.
2. The intensity of competition increases advertising requirements.
3. The greater the number of special sale dates, the greater the need for an increased advertising budget.
4. The larger the competing firm or the more it spends for advertising, the more you may need to spend for advertising.

Methods of Preparing the Advertising Budget

There are a number of alternatives for preparing the advertising budget, some of which are recommended and others that are questionable.

Two questionable methods are the "spend what you can afford" approach and the "keep up with the competition" approach. The first method provides flexibility for increasing spending during a good month but is inflexible during an off month. The second method is a reaction to competitors. Instead of following the competition, the small business owner should stay ahead of it.[7]

Three alternatives that afford a realistic approach to preparing the advertising budget are the "percentage of sales" method, the "unit of sales" method, and the "objective and task" method.

Percentage of Sales Method

Owners most often use the **percentage of sales method** for establishing an ad budget. This method bases the ad budget on a percentage of sales and maintains the ad budget in a consistent relationship to sales volume. Guidelines are available from a variety of sources for setting percentages for specific types of businesses. Sources include trade magazines and associations, the Internal Revenue Service, census data, and financial reporting services, such as Dun and Bradstreet and the Robert Morris Association.

The sales period used to serve as the base for preparing the ad budget may be past sales, projected sales, or a combination of past and projected sales.

Unit of Sales Method

The **unit of sales method** requires that owner–managers set aside a definite amount of funds for each unit of the product that is sold. The advertising budget is based on the number of anticipated units to be sold rather than sales dollars. Thus, if the firm plans to sell 1000 units and it takes $2 worth of advertising to move the product, $2000 will have to be spent for advertising this product. This method is suited for specialty goods, such as automobiles. It is not very useful for style merchandise.[8]

Objective and Task Method

The most difficult and least used method for determining an advertising budget is the **objective and task method.** This is also the most accurate method and best accomplishes what advertising budgets should do.

1. It relates the advertising appropriation to the marketing task to be accomplished.
2. It relates the advertising appropriation under usual conditions and in the long run to the volume of sales so that profits and reserves will not be drained.[9]

To establish an advertising budget using this method, the small business owner needs to coordinate the marketing plan with specific objectives based on a survey of the markets and their potential. The objective and task method establishes what the owner must do to meet objectives and calculates the cost of advertising.

For example, specific objectives must be set, such as "Sell 20 percent more of product X or service Y by attracting the business of teenagers." Then determine the media that reach that target market and estimate how much it will cost to run the number and types of advertisements it will take to reach the sales increase. The process is repeated for each objective, and the total cost for all ads is the advertising budget.[10]

COOPERATIVE ADVERTISING

One plan for making each advertising dollar of the retailer go farther is through cooperative advertising. **Cooperative advertising** is the plan by which the cost of advertising is shared by manufacturers of nationally known brand-name products and the retailer who advertises and sells the products in the local trade area. An advantage of this type of advertising is that the retailers' share of the advertising expenditure is reduced by the percentage that the manufacturer contributes.

The most common cost-sharing ratio is 50:50, but percentages vary. Under special circumstances, the manufacturer may pay 100 percent of the cost of the ad if the ad features the manufacturer's products exclusively. National manufacturers may also supply the retailer with materials that are used in the advertisements. Small firms with limited funds for advertising can clearly benefit from cooperative advertising.

Most cooperative plans are drawn up for one year to coincide with the annual model and style changes. The manufacturers set aside funds for dealers based on an amount for each unit purchased or a stated percentage of total dollar purchases. To be reimbursed from the manufacturer's cooperative advertising fund, dealers must present proof of advertising and a copy of the receipted invoice. While the plan enables the dealer to get more advertising for each dollar spent because of the sharing of the cost with the manufacturer, it does increase the amount of recordkeeping, and enforcment of the plan sometimes puts a strain on the relationship with the dealer.

SALES PROMOTION

Another technique of promotional strategy is **sales promotion.** Sales promotion includes ''those marketing activities other than personal selling and advertising, and publicity, that stimulate consumer purchasing and dealer effectiveness, such as displays, shows and expositions, demonstrations, and various nonrecurrent selling efforts not in the ordinary routine.'' [11]

Sales promotion techniques are designed to give added sales push for products. The promotional events take place within the store as well as outside. A number of sales promotion techniques suitable to the needs of the small business owner are discussed in the following sections.

Point-of-Purchase Displays

Small business owners are constantly putting displays in their stores. **Point-of-purchase displays** are strategically located throughout the store and represent an effective means of generating **impulse purchases.** These displays are ways of drawing customer attention to a particular product or group of products. They are a means of merchandising a special or a promotion. Usually these displays are prepared by manufacturers or distributors of products and made available to the owner. Typical forms of display are wall or shelf displays, interior or overhead signs, freestanding displays, and counter displays.

Good displays that are attractively set up to catch the customer's eye are placed in a high customer traffic area and have point-of-sale material attached. They are a means of increasing sales on a particular product. Displays may remind customers of a product they need but had forgotten to include on their shopping lists. Another purpose of these displays is to suggest additional uses of a product. This technique is often successful in influencing a customer to purchase a product.

Many point-of-purchase displays are strategically located at the store's checkout counter to stimulate impulse purchases. For example, razor blades, chewing gum, and certain types of magazines and newspapers are placed where customers can purchase them on impulse.

Show Windows

As we discussed in Chapter 7, merchandise displays or signs in the show window should be appealing to the customer as well as attention getters. Show window displays should be designed for the purpose of presenting merchandise in such a way that the passerby stops, looks, enters the store to find out more about the merchandise, and is encouraged to make a purchase. Show windows can be effectively used to stimulate impulse buying. Show window displays should be changed regularly to make them most effective. If the same people pass your store daily, window displays should be changed more frequently.

Samples

One sales promotion technique is to distribute free samples of a product to customers. In this way, the small business puts the product in the hands of the customers for the purpose of getting them to try it. The expectation is that they will like it and become regular users. A sample tube of a new toothpaste, a sample box of a new detergent, or a sample jar of a new brand of freeze-dried coffee is given to customers to try. When a new food item is to be introduced, such as a new breakfast sausage, samples may be prepared in a grocery store. Customers are offered a sample, and its unique characteristics are explained. Customers who like the item then are encouraged to buy the product. An advantage of this sales promotion technique is that customer acceptance or nonacceptance of the product is known as soon as it is tried.

Contests

Some contests are intended to attract new customers to use a product already in existence or to introduce a new product. Other contests attempt to get customers into the store to register for a cash prize or merchandise to be presented at a drawing held in the store. For example, a small grocery store may have a contest or a drawing for a free turkey to be given away at Thanksgiving.

Premiums

Premiums are products that are offered free or at minimal cost to the customer. Consumers may receive a dish, glass, or other merchandise free if they purchase another product or make a purchase in excess of a stated dollar amount, such as over $10. A retailer may offer one pair of shoes at the regular price and the second pair of equal or less value for 1 cent more.

Coupons

A frequently used sales promotion technique is coupons. Coupons are intended to stimulate sales by offering the consumer a discount on purchases. For example, a retailer may offer a series of coupons that are redeemable during a specified week. Or a service firm may offer a coupon that provides a discount on a service, such as a $5 discount on the tune-up service for lawnmowers.

Fashion Shows, Trade Shows, and Demonstrations

These sales promotion techniques are designed to be informative, create goodwill, and increase customer traffic. A wide range of merchandise may be promoted by these events. A group of small retailers may jointly sponsor a fashion show presenting the newest clothing styles for the upcoming season. Likewise, a trade show, such as a home show, may be held in a large meeting hall to accommodate large numbers of people. In this trade show, individual business owners can display their merchandise for home improvement, such as solar energy heating and cooling equipment. At a trade show, demonstrations can be given to acquaint customers with how equipment functions, such as an exhibition of how to use a new model of woodworking equipment.

SUMMARY OF KEY POINTS

1. Promotional strategy is the means that small business owners utilize to communicate information about their firm and its products and services to potential customers.

2. An effective advertising strategy requires extensive planning.

3. Advertising is any type of sales presentation that is nonpersonal and is paid for by an identified sponsor.

4. Two general objectives of advertising are promotional and institutional.

5. Promotional advertising has many purposes, such as increasing sales, creating an awareness of products or services, attracting new customers, or promoting a special sale or special offer.

6. Institutional advertising is intended to create good will toward the company and to create a positive image of the firm in the community.

7. Small business owners should recognize that advertising has a number of limitations.

8. Small business owners must select the proper advertising media for the firm from newspaper, radio, television, handbills, direct mail, transporta-

tion, magazines, and specialty items. The store sign is an important source for identifying the small company.

9. The advertising budget may be prepared using a percentage of sales method, a unit of sales method, or an objective and task method as the guideline for the advertising budget.

10. Sales promotion includes the marketing activities other than personal selling and advertising and publicity that stimulate consumer purchasing and dealer effectiveness, such as point-of-purchase displays, shows, and demonstrations.

DISCUSSION QUESTIONS

1. What questions should a small business owner ask when developing a profile of the firm's customers?
2. Explain the difference between advertising and sales promotion.
3. What are some of the purposes of promotional advertising?
4. Discuss the difference between publicity and institutional advertising.
5. Specify some of the limitations of advertising.
6. What is cooperative advertising? How can it benefit the small business owner?
7. What is the objective and task method of determining the advertising budget?
8. Explain the role of point-of-purchase displays in sales promotion.
9. Is a trade show considered a sales promotion technique or advertising?

THE BUSINESS PLAN: GUIDELINES FOR PROMOTIONAL STRATEGY

The small business owner has a variety of advertising from which to choose to implement the promotional strategy of the firm. The following guidelines will aid in developing a promotional plan that allows the owner to make the best use of each advertising dollar by directing the advertising to the firm's target market.

Guidelines for Promotional Strategy

1. Have you identified the goals of your advertising program?
2. Have you developed a comprehensive profile of the customers in your target market?
3. Are the unique appeals of your business reflected in the store's image (high quality, special services, etc.)?

4. Do you know what you are trying to sell (product, idea, service, a company image)?
5. When you advertise, do you focus on your target market rather than advertise indiscriminately?
6. Have you considered how various media and promotional methods might be used for your firm?
7. Do you know which of your items can be successfully advertised?
8. Do you know when it is profitable to use institutional advertising?
9. Do you know when product advertising is better?
10. Do you record sales of merchandise advertised on each ad?
11. Do you check store traffic?
12. Do you know which of the media can most effectively reach your target market?
13. Can you make use of direct mail?
14. Do you have a mailing list and, if so, is it up to date?
15. Do you use coupons in your ads?
16. Do you concentrate promotional efforts on certain seasons?
17. Are certain days of the week better than others?
18. Do you use specialty advertising?
19. Do you use trade journals and out-of-town newspapers for promotional ideas?
20. Do you participate in activities of the chamber of commerce, better business bureau, other civic organizations?

ENTREPRENEURIAL PROJECTS

1. View local television programming, listen to local radio stations, observe transportation ads and outside signs, read newspaper and magazine ads, and, if possible, collect direct-mail ads and handbills of local small business firms. Make notes of the advertising messages and types of stores using the various advertising media. Also note how many different advertising media are used by the same stores.
2. Consult the *Standard Rate and Data Service* (available in most libraries), and determine the cost of advertising by means of radio on a station in your geographical area.

CASE A

Oakmont TV Sales and Service

Bill Griffith purchased Oakmont TV Sales and Service four months ago from Bob Andrews. When Bill bought the business, the products sold were two major brands of televisions, radios and stereos, videocasette recorders, and videodiscs. Since the business was purchased, Bill had decided to add a product line of household appliances (washers, dryers, refrigerators, freezers, and microwave ovens). The firm continues to offer full service for television re-

Demographics for Radio Stations A and B		
	Station A	Station B
Age		
Under 18	40%	6%
18–25	27	7
26–35	16	23
36–50	8	42
Over 50	9	22
Income		
Under $5000	16	5
$5000–10,000	64	8
$10,000–20,000	9	27
Over $20,000	11	60
Education		
High school graduate	55	12
College graduate	42	65
Graduate school	3	23
Occupation		
Student	35	5
Unemployed (nonstudent)	10	1
Clerical	12	8
Skilled	10	7
Unskilled	12	7
Technical	8	27
Managerial	6	26
Professional	7	19
Sex		
Male	46	73
Female	54	27

pair. Bill is aware of the value of advertising and advertises regularly in the local newspaper. However, he plans to intensify his advertising effort now that he is adding another line of products.

Sales representatives from two local radio stations have visited the shop this week. Each has attempted to sell Bill on the idea of purchasing advertising time on their station. Both stations broadcast into the same geographic area. The demographic data for each station has been shown to Bill by the respective sales representatives.

Questions

1. What are the demographic characteristics of each station's audience?
2. Which station would you recommend to Bill? Why?
3. Would television advertising be recommended for Bill's shop?
4. How does cooperative advertising aid a small business owner such as Bill?
5. What other advertising media would you recommend to Bill?
6. What sales promotion techniques, if any, should be recommended to Bill to further increase the public's awareness of Oakmont TV Sales and Service?

CASE B
A-1 Rent-All

Howard and Janice Carlisle, owners of A-1 Rent-All, opened for business in the spring of 1975. The business proved to be a success. In 1981, Mr. Carlisle died leaving Janice in charge of the business. Janice was unable to continue operating the business and put the business up for sale. In October 1981, Bob and Carol Whitney purchased the business.

They immediately began to expand the business, adding to the inventory of items available for rent. The business continued to grow, with sales and profits showing gains each year. By 1984, it became apparent that the business had outgrown its present location. Consequently, Bob and Carol began to search for a new site. After considering the sites available, they decided that none serviced their needs. Thus, they chose to construct a modern physical facility that would meet the demands of their rental business—adequate storage space, a parking lot with ample space for their customers, and outside land space of sufficient size that would be fenced for security purposes and used for storing the outside equipment.

The building and the move to the new facility have been completed. Now Bob and Carol realize the need to stress their advertising even more to expand the business.

A-1 Rent-All has three main target markets: business contractors, homeowners, and college students (the business is located in a college town). Contractors comprise about 48 percent of the business, students about 26 percent, and homeowners about 24 percent. The general public accounts for the remaining percentage.

Types of items and equipment rented include the following:.

Party equipment and supplies—chairs, tents, tables, linens, china, audio-visual, public address systems, silver.

Homeowner's tools—carpet tools and cleaners, pressure washers, ladders, sanders, grinders, typewriters, roll-away beds, post hole diggers, heaters, tents, exercise equipment.

Auto tools—pullers, torque wrenches, jacks, tow bars, car dollies, paint rigs, engine hoists.

Lawn and garden equipment—mowers, tillers, sprayers, weedeaters, fertilizers, trenching machines.

Contractor's equipment—air compressors and tools, pumps, generators, welders, scaffolds, scissor lift backhoes, dozers, forklifts, loaders, trenching machines, paint equipment, sandblasting equipment.

Bob and Carol feel that they can improve on their present advertising plan, which has been a blanket type of advertising to the general public, by continuing to advertise to the general public but also to develop an advertising plan to reach each target market.

Questions

1. What type of advertising plan could be effective in reaching the contractors?
2. What type of advertising plan could be effective in reaching homeowners?
3. What type of advertising plan could be effective in reaching the students?

Notes

[1] *Advertising Your Small Business* (Washington, D.C.: Small Business Administration, 1984), p. 24.

[2] James Engel, Martin Warshaw, and Thomas Kinnear, *Promotional Strategy,* 6th ed. (Homewood, Ill.: Richard D. Irwin, 1987), p. 332.

[3] C. Winston Bergen, *Learning Experiences in Retailing* (Pacific Palisades, Calif.: Goodyear, 1976), p. 259.

[4] Karen Klaus and R. J. Klaus, *Signs in Your Business,* Management Aid no. 4.016 (Washington, D.C.: Small Business Administration, 1982), p. 3.

[5] Judy Colbert, "The Gift for Doing Business," *Successful American Entrepreneurs* (Fall 1987), p. 15.

[6] Ovid Riso, *Advertising Guidelines for Small Retail Firms,* Management Aid no. 4.015 (Washington, D.C.: U.S. Government Printing Office, 1982), pp. 4 and 5.

[7] *Marketing Small Business* (San Francisco: Small Business Reporter, 1986), p. 15.

[8] Stuart Henderson Britt, *Plan Your Advertising Budget,* Management Aid no. 4.018 (Washington, D.C.: Small Business Administration, n.d.), p. 3

[9] Ibid.

[10] Ibid.

[11] Committee on Definitions. *Marketing Definitions: A Glossary of Marketing Terms* (Chicago: American Marketing Association, 1960), p. 20.

THE GOVERNMENT AND SMALL BUSINESS

KEY WORDS

CONSUMER CREDIT

LEARNING GOALS

After reading this chapter, you will understand:

1   How important consumer credit is to most small business firms.

2   How the traditional 30-day charge account operates.

3   How the revolving charge account functions and how small business firms use credit card companies to finance this credit.

4   How important bank credit cards are to small businesses and what functions they perform for them.

5   How installment credit functions.

6   How small business firms obtain credit information.

7   That the truth-in-lending law attempts to put credit on a more competitive basis and what information it requires business to disclose to customers.

8   The importance of the bad-debt ratio and the system for collection of overdue accounts.

ENTREPRENEURIAL PROFILE

Roberto Ruiz

MAYA CONSTRUCTION

Thank Roberto Ruiz for that drinking fountain to which you dip your head after a hike in the Grand Canyon National Park.

As a child in Nogales (Sonora), Mexico, Ruiz liked to build things. He came to Tucson in 1956 to study civil engineering at the University of Arizona. After stints with the Arizona Department of Transportation and a private engineering firm, he once again began to build things on his own. In 1977, on "gut instinct," he went into business for himself, with two employees. Ten years later, Maya Construction/Ruiz Engineering is the fastest-growing Hispanic-owned company in Arizona, and in *Hispanic Business* (November, 1986) was named the tenth fastest in the nation.

"I was very fortunate," Ruiz recalled. "I came out at a very good time when there was a boom and I was able to ride with the boom." The company now employs 250.

With SBA assistance, Maya was certified into the 8(a) program in 1978, and since then has received $62 million in government contracts. Annual sales at the time SBA entered the picture were $1748; today they are $23 million. For his first contract, Ruiz needed SBA surety bonding; today he has his own bonding ceiling of $25 million.

So extraordinary has been Maya's rise, the company will graduate a year early from 8(a) because its annual sales no longer qualify it as "small business"!

Ruiz has built everything from schools at Fort Huachuca, to a water distribution system (including drinking fountains) for the National Park Service in the Grand Canyon. Maya has had private and state building, roadway, and underground water and sewer projects, as well.

Seeing himself "as a coach, not a captain" of his company, Ruiz likes to act "as a cheering section for employees, to tell them when they're on target and guide them when they're not." Twice a year he retreats with his top managers for two days to plot Maya's business future.

Ruiz has garnered many accolades: Arizona Small Business Person of the Year (1983); National Minority Contractor of the Year, Department of Commerce (1984); and National Minority Contractor of the Year, Department of the Interior (1986). SBA likes to think of itself as a cheering section for this intrepid Mexican-American.

Source: Network (Washington, D.C.: U.S. Small Business Administration, November–December 1987).

Many small business firms extend either trade credit or consumer credit. Manufacturers and wholesalers often extend trade credit to their customers. This trade credit usually exists in the form of supplying products to their customers on 30-, 60-, or 90-day accounts. Various forms of trade credit were discussed in Chapter 5.

Consumer credit is credit extended by both retail and service firms to ultimate consumers. Consumer credit has been increasingly important in the United States since World War II. Today personal income has multiplied over 15 times what it was in 1950. Consumer credit multiplied by more than 28 times during the same period. For the same period, the population only increased by 1.6 times. Figure 20-1 shows the rapid growth of various types of consumer credit.

Consumer credit is extremely important to most business firms. Offering credit increases the number of sales and encourages repeat sales by customers. Many small firms would not be in business if they did not offer credit to their customers.

TYPES OF CONSUMER CREDIT

Although there are many deviations in consumer credit offered by firms to their customers, there are four basic types of consumer credit: 30-day charge accounts, revolving charge accounts, financial institution credit cards, and installment credit.

FIGURE 20-1
CONSUMER CREDIT, SELECTED YEARS 1950–1986.

Type of Credit	Amount (in billions of dollars)					
	1950	1960	1970	1980	1985	1986
Total Consumer Credit Outstanding	25.6	65.1	143.1	385.6	657.0	723.6
Installment	15.5	45.1	105.5	313.4	522.8	577.8
Automobiles	6.0	18.1	36.3	116.3	208.1	245.1
Revolving	NA	NA	5.1	59.9	122.0	135.0
Mobile homes	NA	NA	2.5	17.3	25.5	25.7
All other loans	9.5	27.0	61.6	119.9	167.2	172.1
Noninstallment	10.1	20.0	37.6	72.2	134.2	145.5
Single payment loans	3.6	9.1	19.3	39.9	70.1	76.6
Charge accounts	4.9	7.2	9.2	13.0	21.5	21.8
Service credit	1.6	3.7	9.1	19.3	42.6	47.1

(*Statistical Abstract of the United States*, 1988.)

NA–Not available.

Thirty-Day Accounts

The traditional **30-day charge account** extends credit to customers by allowing them to purchase merchandise on credit during the month and then pay the entire balance of the account at the end of the month. For example, a customer's record of charges and payments for three months might appear as follows.

	Credit Purchases During the Month	Payments at the End of the Month
September	$30	$30
October	44	44
November	68	68

Many firms with large numbers of credit accounts have gone to cycle billing. Cycle billing is used to reduce the pressure of billing at the end of the month and to utilize billing personnel better by spreading the billing process over the entire month. Every two or three days, a different part of the accounts is billed, usually in alphabetical order of the customers' last names. Instead of the account's being due at the end of the month, it is due in a specific number of days after the billing date shown on the statement (usually in 10 days).

Customers are usually not required to pay any interest on their credit if they pay it off by the due date. Some stores give their customers credit cards as a means of identifying them as credit customers. However, this is not the most common practice. Most stores offering traditional 30-day charge accounts use some form of credit slip, which lists purchases and dollar amounts and is signed by the customer.

Retail stores that use 30-day charge accounts usually carry the credit accounts themselves. These stores sometimes borrow money against their charge accounts from banks or factors as a means of financing them (a discussion of factoring is contained in Chapter 5).

Revolving Charge Accounts

The **revolving charge account** method is similar to the traditional 30-day charge account in that customers may purchase merchandise on credit and pay off all or part of it at the end of the monthly billing period. It differs from the traditional 30-day charge account in that customers are not required to pay off all credit purchases on a monthly basis. The revolving charge account method requires the customer to pay only a part of the total amount owed. The minimum amount customers are required to pay is based on the total amount they owe. Customers are charged **interest** based on the daily average balance of the account. A customer's revolving charge account for three months might appear as follows:

	Purchases During the Period	Interest Charged	Payment	Balance After Payment
January				$368.28
February	$54.60	$6.93	$50.00	379.81
March	0	6.65	50.00	336.46
April	35.38	6.20	30.00	348.04

Firms that issue **credit cards** place a maximum amount that may be purchased using the card. A common limit of credit cards is one that does not allow the cardholder to exceed a balance of $500. If requested, higher credit card limits may be established for individuals, depending primarily on their record and income.

Most retail firms charge interest based on the average daily balance. The average daily balance is calculated by totaling the balance outstanding for each day of the month and dividing by the number of days in the billing period. The most common rate of interest charged on revolving charge accounts is 1.75 to 2 percent per month, which amounts to an annual percentage of between 21 and 24 percent.

Almost all revolving charge accounts are set up to use credit cards. Firms sometimes carry their own accounts, but most small businesses accept credit cards issued by other companies. Some of the credit cards they accept may be from firms who produce a product and whose primary function is acting as something other than a financial institution. For example, many petroleum firms have their own credit cards and allow motels and other selected types of business to accept their credit cards for a fee.

Financial Institution Credit Cards

Financial institutions also issue credit cards that may be used to purchase a wide range of merchandise and services. Visa and MasterCard are the principal bank-issued credit cards. In addition, Diners Club and American Express are two firms that specialize in consumer credit for many products and services.

Bank-issued credit cards have been a real boon to small businesses. Several years ago it was common for the authors to hear a small business owner say the firm's biggest problem was credit and collections. Many small businesses have gone out of business in the past owing to improper control of credit and inability to collect customer credit accounts. The **bank credit cards** have largely eliminated this problem for most small businesses. The cards have become so common that most small businesses do not offer credit except on the credit cards.

The small business does have to pay a percentage of all charges to the bank. The percentage ranges from 2 to 6 percent of the amount charged. The percentage charged each small business is determined primarily by the average amount of sales charged on each ticket. For example, the small business that usually turns in charge tickets that only amount to a few dollars is charged a much higher percentage than the firm that turns in charge tickets amounting to several hundred dollars each.

Although small businesses do have to pay a fee for the service, they have usually found it well worth the cost. Every charge ticket they receive they enter on their bank deposit slip, and the amount is immediately added to their account. The bank then bills them for the cost of their tickets. The small business, in a sense, can count bank credit charges as cash to their business. In general, they run no risk of bad debts. The card also allows them to function on much less working capital, which is a cost to them. They do not have to process credit applications, and they maintain no credit or collection records.

One risk the firm runs is to fail to check the card against the invalid card list issued by the credit card company or to fail to telephone about all purchases over a specific amount. The small business must sustain the loss in these cases. Usually, credit card companies will pay a reward, usually about $25, to a clerk who calls the credit card company and takes up a card that appears on their invalid lists. This helps the small business by motivating clerks to be more diligent in checking the list in hopes of receiving a reward. Another risk is that the clerk does not properly imprint the charge ticket with the card machine. If the credit card company can not trace the customer, they will not accept the credit ticket.

Customers using bank credit cards are charged interest on the average daily balance. The rate charged varies with market interest rates and the amount owed. The rate has been between 1.5 and 2 percent per month. Some firms not only charge the customer interest and the business a percentage fee but they also charge the credit cardholder an additional yearly fee to use the card.

The U.S. government has passed several laws concerning credit cards. One requires that no one can be sent a credit card unless he or she has requested the card. Another limits the liability of the card holder to $50 if the card is lost or stolen provided the customer notifies the credit card company as soon as possible. A court decision also allows the small business to offer the customer a discount for cash without the danger of losing the bank credit card service. A law passed in 1975 prohibits discrimination in credit owing to sex or marital status, and another passed in 1977 prohibits discrimination in credit owing to race, national origin, religion, age, or receipt of public assistance. The Fair Credit Billing Law allows customers to withhold payment to the credit card company if the merchant refuses to help with defective products. Also, in this law the customer may refuse to pay the first $50 of a disputed bill if his or her written complaint is not responded to within 30 days or ruled on within 90 days or both, regardless of who wins the billing argument.

Credit cards are important to some customers not only because of the deferred payment but also because they provide information for their income tax returns. For example, some salespersons use credit cards as a record and means of proof of travel and customer entertainment expenses.

The small business can also use bank credit cards to allow employees away from the business to purchase needed items, such as gasoline, meals, and lodging for salespersons and truck drivers.

Installment Credit

Installment credit is primarily used when customers purchase items of merchandise that costs several hundred or thousands of dollars, such as appliances, automobiles, boats, and homes. Interest is calculated on the amount that is financed after the down payment if there is a down payment. The balance due plus the interest charge is then divided by the total number of months over which the purchase is to be financed to determine monthly payments.

The number of years allowed for the installment purchase to be repaid varies by item and financial firm. Some of the more common lengths of financing periods are large appliances, 1 to 3 years; automobiles, 3 to 4 years; boats, 1 to 4 years; and homes, 20 to 30 years.

Customers who obtain merchandise by installment purchases usually are required to sign an installment sales contract. This contract contains such information as total amount to be financed, interest rate, interest amount, repayment period, and an agreement in which the purchaser pledges the item purchased as security against repayment of the loan (installment credit is mortgage credit; legal aspects of different types of installment contracts are discussed in Chapter 21).

Some firms finance their own installment credit; however, most small businesses use financial institutions to carry their installment credit. They usually sign customers to installment sales contracts and then sell or discount the contracts to banks or sales finance companies. (Banks and sales finance company credit operations are discussed in Chapter 5.)

See Figure 20-2 for a comparison of the characteristics of the different types of consumer credit.

SOURCES OF CREDIT INFORMATION

Small business firms that carry their own customer credit have two basic sources of credit information about their customers: (1) credit application forms and (2) **retail credit bureau** reports.

FIGURE 20-2
CHARACTERISTICS OF CONSUMER CREDIT.

30-Day Accounts	Revolving Charge Accounts	Financial Institution Credit Cards	Installment Credit
Nonmortgage credit	Nonmortgage credit	Nonmortgage credit	Mortgage credit (chattel mortgage)
Store financed (may factor)	May be financed by store or other companies (such as oil company credit cards)	Financed by financial institution	May be financed by store, bank, sales finance company
No interest charged	Interest charged on balance	Interest charged to business and customer May have yearly fee Interest based on average balance	Interest added to amount financed
Paid off in full each month	Only a minimum amount must be paid each month and balance carried forward	Only a minimum amount must be paid each month and balance carried forward	Monthly payments for several months or years
May or may not use credit card	Usually involves credit card	Involves use of credit card	Sometimes requires down payment

The small business firm that does carry its own credit should require all credit customers to complete a credit application form. The small business may create its own application form or use a standardized application form.

Most cities have a local retail credit bureau to which the small business firm may belong to aid in credit decisions. These local credit bureaus are usually cooperatives owned by the local merchants. All local members supply the credit bureau with copies of all their credit applications. In addition, each month each member also supplies the local credit bureau with information on customer purchases, payments, and delinquencies. By collecting this information, the bureaus are able to obtain extensive credit files on large numbers of people in the community. Members of the local credit bureau are then able to telephone the bureau about new credit applicants and obtain credit ratings in a matter of two or three minutes. The bureau will also provide the small business with a more detailed report by mail if requested. In addition, if a small business has a delinquent account, the owner is able to obtain a "trade clearance" report, which summarizes the customer's more recent credit purchases and payments to other stores.

Most local credit bureaus also belong to Associated Credit Bureaus, which is a national organization. Thus the small business can obtain information on a nationwide basis.

Although local credit bureaus provide a valuable service to small businesses that grant credit, there have been some abuses. In some cases, information that was wrong or biased inadvertently found its way into the files of a few customers and created unwarranted problems for them. Federal law has been enacted that allows a customer to see his or her file on request and makes provisions for having the file corrected.

Although this chapter is devoted primarily to consumer credit, another source of credit information is used to such an extent by businesses that it seems practical to mention it at this time. Dun and Bradstreet sells to subscribers a publication that contains credit ratings of several million business firms in the United States and Canada. Dun and Bradstreet also prepares detailed reports on many of the companies listed in its reference publications.

THE TRUTH-IN-LENDING LAW

In 1969, the United States Congress passed the Consumer Credit Protection Act, which is popularly called the **truth-in-lending** law. This law was intended to put credit on a more competitive basis by helping consumers more easily know what credit costs them. Small businesses that offer credit must be familiar with the law to comply with its provisions.

The most important of the disclosure items are the finance charge and the annual percentage rate. The business firm must advise the customer of these two credit expenses in writing that is the equivalent of 10-point type, 0.075-inch computer type, or elite-size typewritten numerals. The finance charge is the total of all costs paid by the consumer for credit. It includes all interest, carrying charges, cost of insurance premiums if required for credit protection, and credit investigation costs. The annual percentage rate is the percentage interest rate charged on a yearly basis. This annual percentage rate must be reported to the nearest quarter of 1 percent.[1]

The truth-in-lending law requires specific information be disclosed for revolving charge accounts (called open-end transactions in the law) and installment contracts (called closed-end transactions).

Revolving Charge Accounts (Including Financial Institution Credit Cards)

The following information must be disclosed before the account is opened.

1. Conditions under which a finance charge may be made and the period within which, if payment is made, there is no finance charge (such as "30 days without interest").
2. The method of determining the balance upon which a finance charge may be imposed.
3. How the actual finance charge is calculated.

4. The periodic rates used and the range of balances to which each applies as well as the corresponding annual percentage rate—for instance, a monthly rate of 1.5 percent (APR, 18 percent) on the first $500, and 1 percent (APR, 12 percent) on amounts over $500.
5. Conditions under which additional charges may be made, along with details of how they are calculated. (This applies to new purchases when charges are added to the account.)
6. A description of any lien (secured interest) you may acquire on the customer's property—for instance, rights to repossession of a household appliance.
7. Minimum periodic payment required.[2]

The following information must be included on each and every monthly statement sent to the customer in the correct terminology, which is indicated in boldface type in the following quoted material.

1. The unpaid balance at the beginning of the billing period (**previous balance**).
2. The amount and date of each purchase or credit extention and a brief description of each item bought if not previously given to the customer.
3. Customer payments (**payments**) and other credits, including those for rebates, adjustments, and returns (**credits**).
4. The finance charge expressed in dollars and cents (**finance charge**).
5. The rates used in calculating the finance charge and the range of balances, if any, to which they apply (**periodic rate**).
6. The annual percentage rate, which must be expressed as a percentage after January 1, 1971 (**annual percentage**).
7. The unpaid balance on which the finance charge was calculated.
8. The closing date of the billing cycle and the unpaid balance as of that date (**new balance**).[3]

Installment Contracts

Installment credit must also provide certain information to the buyer under the truth-in-lending legislation. This information must be disclosed on a printed form (usually an installment sales contract) before the credit is extended. It must also be provided in the terminology, specified by the law, which is indicated as follows.

1. The cash price (cash price).
2. The down payment including trade-in (cash down payment, trade-in, or total down payment—as applicable).
3. The difference between the cash price and down payment (unpaid balance of cash price).

4. All other charges, itemized but not part of the finance charge.
5. The unpaid balance (unpaid balance).
6. Amounts deducted as prepaid finance charges or required deposit balances (prepaid finance charge) or (required deposit balance) or both.
7. The amount financed (amount financed).
8. The total cash price, finance, and all other charges (deferred payment price).
9. The total dollar amount of the finance charge (finance charge).
10. The date on which the finance charge begins to apply (if this is different from the date of the sale).
11. The annual percentage rate, which must be expressed as a percentage after January 1, 1971 (annual percentage rate).
12. The number, amounts, and due dates of payments.
13. The total payments (total of payments).
14. The amount you charge for any default, delinquency, and the like, or the method you use for calculating the amount.
15. A description of any security you will hold.
16. A description of any penalty charge for prepayment of principal.
17. How the unearned part of the finance charge is calculated in case of prepayment. (Charges deducted from any rebate must be stated.)[4]

BAD DEBTS AND COLLECTIONS

Small business owners would like to collect all their credit accounts, but this is not possible. The amount of bad debts they sustain on credit accounts will depend mostly on how effective they are in selecting people to whom they will grant credit and in the efficiency of their collection methods.

Small business owners should keep good records of credit accounts. By dividing **bad debts** by sales, they are able to compute the bad-debt ratio. They should calculate this ratio on a periodic basis to check the adequacy of their credit program. Once they have decided what is a realistic bad-debt ratio for the firm, any significant shift in the bad-debt ratio should be a signal that something is wrong. Small business owners should try to balance their credit policy so that they are not too restrictive and eliminate good customers or too lenient and have excessive bad debts.

Collection of overdue accounts requires considerable skill to balance effective collection without harming customer goodwill. If the small business firm initiates action too soon and with too firm a hand, it may lose many good customers. On the other hand, if it moves too slowly, while giving an impression of a lax attitude, it may never collect the account.

Collection timing and methods should vary to some degree with the credit record of the customer. However, a process of stages of collection methods should be employed in collection efforts. These stages should move from a soft approach to a final stern, legal approach.

FAIR DEBT COLLECTION PRACTICES ACT

Some debt collection firms used rather drastic methods of collecting debts in the past. Telephone calls in the middle of the night, banging on the door and yelling in a loud voice that the debtor would have to pay the debt, making repeated telephone calls to the debtor at his or her work, and threatening drastic actions they could not legally take were some of the common abuses. In 1978 the federal government passed the Fair Debt Collection Practices Act to eliminate these abuses.

The Federal Trade Commission summarized the act as follows.

How May a Debt Collector Contact You?

A debt collector may contact you in person, by mail, telephone, or telegram. However, it can't be at inconvenient or unusual times or places, such as before 8:00 A.M. or after 9:00 P.M. unless you agree.

A debt collector may **not** contact you at work if your employer disapproves.

Can You Stop a Debt Collector from Contacting You?

Yes, you may stop a debt collector from contacting you by saying so in writing. Once you tell a debt collector not to contact you, the debt collector can no longer do so, **except** to tell you that there will be no further contact. Also, the debt collector may notify you that some specific action may be taken, but only if the debt collector or the creditor usually takes such action.

May a Debt Collector Contact Any Other Person Concerning Your Debt?

A debt collector may contact any person to locate you. However, the debt collector must

Only tell people that the purpose is to try to contact you.

Only contact your attorney if you have an attorney.

The debt collector must not

Tell anybody else that you owe money.

In most cases, talk to any person more than *once*.

Use a post card.

Put anything on an envelope or in a letter that identifies the writer as a debt collector.

What Is the Debt Collector Required to Tell you About the Debt?

Within five days after you are first contacted, the debt collector must send you a *written notice* telling you

- The amount of money you owe.
- The name of the creditor to whom you owe money.
- What to do if you feel you do not owe the money.

If You Feel You Do Not Owe the Money, May a Debt Collector Continue to Contact You?

The debt collector must not contact you if you send a letter within 30 days after you are first contacted saying you do not owe the money. However, a debt collector can begin collection activities again if you are sent proof of the debt, such as a copy of the bill.

What Types of Debt Collection Practices Are Prohibited?

A debt collector may not *harass, oppress,* or *abuse* any person. For example, a debt collector cannot

Use threats of violence to harm anyone or anyone's property or reputation.

Publish a list of customers which says you refuse to pay your debts (except to a credit bureau).

Use obscene or profane language.

Repeatedly use the telephone to annoy anyone.

Telephone any person without identifying the caller.

Advertise your debt.

A debt collector may *not* use any *false* statements when collecting any debt. For example, the debt collector cannot

Falsely imply that the debt collector represents the U.S. government or any state government.

Falsely imply that the debt collector is an attorney.

Falsely imply that *you* committed any crime.

Falsely represent that the debt collector operates or works for a credit bureau.

Misrepresent the amount of the debt.

Represent that papers being sent are legal forms, such as a summons, when they are not.

Represent that papers are being sent are *not* legal forms when they *are*.

Also, a debt collector may not say

- That you will be arrested or imprisoned if you do not pay your debt.
- That he will *seize, garnish, attach,* or *sell your property* or *wages, unless* the debt collector or the creditor intends to do so and it is legal.
- That any *action* will be taken against you which *cannot legally* be taken.

A debt collector may not

- Give false *credit information* about you to anyone.

- Send you anything that looks like an *official* document which might be sent by any *court* or *agency* of the *United States* or any *state* or *local* government.
- Use any false name.

A debt collector must *not* be *unfair* in attempting to collect any debt. For example, the debt collector cannot

- Collect *any amount* greater than the amount of your debt, unless allowed by law.
- Deposit any postdated check before the date on that check.
- Make you accept collect calls or pay for telegrams.
- Take or threaten to take your property unless there is a present right to do so.
- Contact you by post card.
- Put anything on an envelope other than the debt collector's address and name. Even the name cannot be used if it shows that the communication is about the collection of a debt.

What Control Do You Have Over Specific Debts?

If you owe several debts, any payment you make must be applied as you choose. And, a debt collector cannot apply a payment to any debt you feel you do not owe.

What Can You Do If the Debt Collector Breaks the Law?

You have the right to sue a debt collector in a state or federal court within one year from the date the law was violated. You may recover money for the damage you suffered. Court costs and attorney's fees can also be recovered. A group of persons may sue a debt collector and recover money for damages up to $500,000.

Source: Fair Debt Collection Practices Act (Washington, D.C.: Federal Trade Commission, n.d.)

Collection Messages

The four steps in **collection** messages are (1) reminder, (2) stronger reminder, (3) inquiry and appeal, and (4) legal ultimatum.

Reminder

Most overdue accounts are collected with the first letter and are probably due to customers' oversight or procrastination. These people are valuable customers, so the reminder is intended to collect the money while retaining the goodwill of the customer. Consequently, the first message must start with the assumption that the customer fully intends to pay the bill but has overlooked it. The message must be very soft and must reassure the customer that the firm does not feel the individual is purposefully failing to pay the bill. The message should be a short note that includes something like "Have you overlooked us this month?"

Stronger Reminder

The second stage of the collection message should, **like the first, still assume** the failure to pay is the result of oversight or procrastination. The firm is still trying to collect the bill but also keep the person as a customer. However, the message should be a little firmer. The phrase "overlooked" is still used but a definite request for payment should be included in the message.

Inquiry and Appeal

The third stage of the collection messages assumes that the failure to pay is not an oversight, but there is something wrong. The firm is still trying to collect the debt and retain patronage of the individual. The firm does not, at this point, assume the customer is a customer it does not want on a credit basis. Consequently, the message should try to find out what is wrong and at the same time increase the pressure to pay. It should contain such phrases as "What is the difficulty?" and "Your credit rating is valuable."

Legal Ultimatum

The small business must at this stage assume that the customer is not going to pay the bill unless force is applied. The firm also reaches the stage at which it must assume the customer is no longer a valuable credit customer but a "cash-only" customer. The message must have urgency and outline the action the firm will take if the debt is not paid at once. Phrases such as "turned over to a collection agency" and "This action will destroy your credit rating" should be included. The small business should then follow with the action threatened if payment is not received.

Timing of Collection Messages

Credit customers differ, and so should the timing of the collection messages. The person who has a good credit record should be given a longer period in the four stages of the collection process. On the other hand, the person who has a record of slow payment should receive the messages over a much shorter interval. In general, the first reminder should be sent when the debt is 4 weeks overdue. The Inquiry and Appeal message should be sent when the debt is over 6 weeks overdue and the Legal Ultimatum when the debt is 10 weeks overdue. The debt should be turned over to a collection agency or attorney for legal action after 5 to 6 months.

SUMMARY OF KEY POINTS

1. Consumer credit has increased rapidly since World War II and is very important to small business firms.

2. Thirty-day charge accounts are paid in full at the end of each month and no interest is charged.

3. Revolving charge accounts are financed by the store, interest is charged on the average daily balance, and only a part of the bill must be paid each month.

4. Financial institution credit cards are financed by financial institutions, interest is charged to the business and the consumer, a yearly fee may also be charged, only a minimum amount must be paid each month.

5. Installment credit is a mortgage credit, may be financed by the business or financial institution, interest is added to the amount financed, monthly payments are required for months or years, and sometimes requires a down payment amount.

6. Credit application forms and retail credit bureaus are the two major sources of credit information.

7. The truth-in-lending law requires several things to be disclosed to the customer.

8. Small business owners who grant credit must make sure their credit policies are not so restrictive that they lose customers and not so lenient that they have excessive bad debts.

9. Collection messages should progress through four stages from reminder to legal ultimatum.

10. The Fair Debt Collection Practices Act specifies what rights the debtor has and what the collection firm may do to collect debt.

DISCUSSION QUESTIONS

1. Why is retail credit important to most small business firms?
2. How are traditional 30-day charge accounts different from revolving charge accounts?
3. How does installment credit differ from charge account credit?
4. What are some of the ways small business firms finance 30-day accounts, revolving charge accounts, and installment credit?
5. How does a small business obtain information about potential credit customers?
6. What was the reason why Congress passed the truth-in-lending law?
7. How does the truth-in-lending law attempt to achieve its goal?
8. What is a bad-debt ratio, and how is it used?
9. Should the collection system for overdue accounts be the same for all customers?

THE BUSINESS PLAN: CONSUMER CREDIT

_____ Will you need to offer credit to your customers?

_____ Will you offer 30-day accounts?

_____ Will you offer revolving charge accounts?

_____ Will you accept financial institution credit cards? This is usually preferable to offering your own 30-day or revolving charge credit.

_____ Which credit cards will you accept? You will have to pay a percentage of each charge. Check several financial institutions for the best percentage rate.

_____ Will you offer installment credit? Will you finance your own installment credit or will you use a financial institution? It is much less risky and easier to use financial institutions.

_____ Do you know how much interest and what period of time you will use in your customer credit? If not, ask your local banker for advice as to what is current practice in your community. If you are going to offer your own installment contracts be sure to refer to Chapter 21 for different types of installment contracts.

_____ What sources of credit information will you use? Credit applications and local credit bureaus are important sources of consumer credit information. Dun and Bradstreet can be a good source of business credit information.

—— Do you know federal disclosure requirements provided for in the truth-in-lending law? If you are going to provide credit to your customers, you should read the truth-in-lending requirements in this chapter for both revolving charge accounts and installment contracts.

—— Will you have to collect credit accounts? You should be aware of the correct stages of collection. You should also be aware of the provisions of the Fair Debt Collection Practices Act that are presented in this chapter.

ENTREPRENEURIAL PROJECTS

1. Identify a store that uses
   a. 30-day charge accounts.
   b. revolving charge accounts.
   c. installment credit.
2. Obtain a copy of a revolving charge account statement and an installment sales contract, and check them to see if they meet the requirements of the truth-in-lending law.
3. Obtain a copy of a credit application form, and analyze it to determine if you feel it does a good job of obtaining credit information.
4. Find out if your community has a retail credit bureau and, if so, who owns it.

CASE A

Sloan Music Store

Steve Sloan is in the process of opening a music store in a town of 30,000. His will be the only complete music store in the town. Steve will carry musical instruments, records, tapes, stereo sets and systems, and a broad range of music-related merchandise.

Steve is an accomplished musician and is knowledgeable about most of his products. He plans to carry a high-price and a low-price line in both instruments and stereo equipment. He has contacted the local high school band director and obtained permission to place instruments on display when the director meets with the parents of new band students each year.

The band director has told Steve that he must have some sort of financing available or most parents would not buy instruments from him. Steve agrees and feels that he must have credit available other than the few selected 30-day accounts he had planned on carrying. Steve has spent a big part of his funds for the store lease, remodeling, and initial inventory. He feels he has enough funds to provide working capital and support a few 30-day accounts.

He has agreed to pay you a fee if you will set up a credit system for him and advise him how he might obtain financing for customer credit.

Questions

1. What type of credit would you advise Steve to set up and for what types of merchandise would this credit be intended?
2. Will Steve have to pay any fees for any of the credit you have established?
3. If Steve carries the 30-day account credit as he plans, how can he find out about his credit customers?
4. What are the two main things Steve must tell his customers to comply with the truth-in-lending law? (Not all, just the two major items.)
5. Tell Steve about the bad-debt ratio and how he should use it.
6. Generally, how should Steve go about collecting overdue accounts?

CASE B

Lance Brian's Cozy Carpets

Lance Brian is the sole owner of Cozy Carpets, which has been selling carpet and other floor coverings to building contractors for two years. He extends credit to those contractors and has had some problems in the past; however, he now has separated customers into those who are reliable in paying their accounts and those whom he requires to pay in cash. He feels there is very little he can do to improve his credit and collection practices.

Lance recently moved his business to a new location in an attractive building. It is on a major thoroughfare and surrounded several miles in each direction by residential housing that is about 4 to 10 years old. Lance has had few retail sales to individual homeowners in the past, but now he feels the surrounding residential neighborhood could produce considerable retail sales. He realizes that he must have some kind of retail credit available because each sale represents from several hundred to a thousand dollars and more. Lance has the capital to offer retail credit if he desires.

Lance has asked you to help him set up a retail credit plan.

Questions

1. Would you advise him to offer 30-day charge or revolving charge credit?
2. Would you advise him to use bank credit cards? Explain your reasons.
3. Would you advise him to offer installment contracts? Should he finance them himself?

Notes

[1] Computations on installment sales can be complex for most people. To assist you, *Annual Percentage Rate Tables* is available from the Federal Reserve System in Washington, D.C., for $1.

[2] *Understanding Truth-in-Lending* (Washington, D.C.: Small Business Administration, November 1969).

[3] Ibid.

[4] Ibid.

KEY WORDS

CHAPTER 21

LEGAL CONSIDERATIONS

LEARNING GOALS

After reading this chapter, you will understand:

1 What the requirements are for a contract to be valid and enforceable in a court of law.

2 The various legal recourses available to a person when there is a breach of contract.

3 Why there is a Uniform Commercial Code, what it attempts to do, and what areas of commercial law it covers.

4 The different types of checks, how to minimize bad checks, and what to do when you receive a bad check.

5 That there are three different types of installment sales contracts, which of these are the best in terms of repossession, and how one should go about repossessing merchandise.

6 That patents, copyrights, and trademarks provide exclusive rights to the holder.

7 That small businesses must have various types of permits and licenses in order to operate.

ENTREPRENEURIAL PROFILE

Garrett W. Brown and Honie Ann Peacock

PYTHON DRILLING AND TESTING

A black man and a Jewish woman—not your usual business team in critical preconstruction testing! It happened in the Bronx.

In a highly specialized field hardly open to minorities and women, Garrett W. Brown, a Vietnam veteran, and Honie Ann Peacock, a consultant in employee relations, drill for "dirt" samples in the chasms of the Big Apple as Python Drilling and Testing

1980—their first year—was not a good one for construction. There were nights without dinner and weeks when payroll was met on a credit card. Peacock, a single parent, took, two outside jobs and worked full time without pay to help get the fledgling company off the ground. Brown, an ex-Marine sergeant who specialized in heavy construction equipment and diesel engines, brought 20 years of experience in the construction industry to the company. He designed and built their first drill rig in his living room.

Peacock wrote the loan proposal and marketing plan that enabled the company to receive a $50,000 direct loan from SBA, which bought them their first big drill rig and truck. Today their 16-person crew has been trained completely from within and represents a virtual "United Nations," including blacks, Filipinos, Hispanics, Irish, and Finns, both male and female.

Though it has been an uphill struggle to gain the confidence of their numerous clients, Brown and Peacock maintain a positive attitude. And why not? From the time of SBA's loan, annual revenues have grown from $30,000 to over $1 million.

Source: Network (Washington, D.C.: U.S. Small Business Administration, January–February 1988).

Small business firms exist in an environment governed by laws. In fact, business of any size could not exist without laws to set standards and requirements of conduct. Daily, the small business engages in activities that are governed by law. If small business owners are to succeed, they must know their rights and responsibilities under the law.

CONTRACTS

The small business owner deals almost daily with some form of **contract**—written or verbal. (See Fig. 21-1.) For example, if a customer orders a sandwich in a restaurant, he or she and the business are entering into a verbal contract. The restaurant is agreeing to provide a sandwich, and the customer is agreeing to pay the advertised price for the sandwich. Examples of contracts in written form would be leases, deeds, warranties, and installment sales contracts. Because small business owners are engaged in contracts on a continuing basis, they must know what is required for a contract to be valid and enforceable. They must also be aware of their rights in case the other party does not honor the terms of the contract.

Requirements of a Valid Contract

Each state establishes its own laws concerning contracts. As a result, there are some variations in legal requirements for valid contracts in various states. However, the states do have the same basic requirements.

For a contract to be valid and enforceable in any state, it must meet the requirements of (1) competent parties, (2) consideration, (3) legal purpose, (4) mutual assent, and (5) legal form.

Competent Parties

All parties to a contract must be competent parties under the law. The law defines parties that are not competent as drunkards, convicts, insane persons, and persons who are below the legal age. Laws in the 50 states vary between 18 and 21 in terms of minimum legal age. Generally, persons under the legal age specified by the state can enforce contracts against adults, but adults cannot enforce contracts against them. An exception exists in many states when the contract is for necessities, such as food, shelter, clothing, and ordinary education.

The small business owner should be aware that, although the law declares that drunkards and insane persons are not competent parties, it does not automatically mean that the person who appears intoxicated or acts abnormally cannot be a party to a valid and enforceable contract. In general, a person must be adjudged by the courts to be a confirmed drunkard or insane before he loses his status as a competent party. Intoxication and abnormal actions

FIGURE 21-1
SECTIONS OF A CONTRACT: A STANDARD LEASE FORM.

A 185—Blumberg's Improved Gilsey Form Lease

JULIUS BLUMBERG, INC., LAW BLANK PUBLISHERS
80 EXCHANGE PLACE, AT BROADWAY, NEW YORK

This Agreement BETWEEN

as Landlord

and

as Tenant

Witnesseth: The Landlord hereby leases to the Tenant the following premises:

for the term of

to commence from the   day of   19   and to end on the

day of   19   to be used and occupied only for

upon the conditions and covenants following:

1st. That the Tenant shall pay the annual rent of

said rent to be paid in equal monthly payments in advance on the   day of each and every month during the
term aforesaid, as follows:

2nd. That the Tenant shall take good care of the premises and shall, at the Tenant's own cost and expense make all repairs

and at the end or other expiration of the term, shall deliver up the demised premises in good order or condition, damages by
the elements excepted.

3rd. That the Tenant shall promptly execute and comply with all statutes, ordinances, rules, orders, regulations and requirements of the Federal, State and Local Governments and of any and all their Departments and Bureaus applicable to said
premises, for the correction, prevention, and abatement of nuisances or other grievances, in, upon, or connected with said
premises during said term; and shall also promptly comply with and execute all rules, orders and regulations of the New
York Board of Fire Underwriters, or any other similar body, at the Tenant's own cost and expense.

27th. Landlord shall not be liable for failure to give possession of the premises upon commencement date by reason of the
fact that premises are not ready for occupancy or because a prior Tenant or any other person is wrongfully holding over or
is in wrongful possession, or for any other reason. The rent shall not commence until possession is given or is available, but
the term herein shall not be extended.

And the said Landlord doth covenant that the said Tenant on paying the said yearly rent, and performing the covenants
aforesaid, shall and may peacefully and quietly have, hold and enjoy the said demised premises for the term aforesaid, provided however, that this covenant shall be conditioned upon the retention of title to the premises by the Landlord.

And it is mutually understood and agreed that the covenants and agreements contained in the within lease
shall be binding upon the parties hereto and upon their respective successors, heirs, executors and administrators.

In Witness Whereof, the parties have interchangeably set their hands and seals (or caused these presents to be
signed by their proper corporate officers and caused their proper corporate seal to be hereto affixed) this
day of   19

Signed, sealed and delivered

in the presence of

_____ L. S.

_____ L. S.

_____ L. S.

are usually not a defense against a valid contract unless the actions are so extreme as to prohibit intelligent action.

Consideration of Both Parties

Both parties to the contract must give some form of consideration for it to be a valid, enforceable contract. For example, a relative creates a contract in which he promises a young man that he will give him $5000 on his twenty-first birthday. This would not be an enforceable contract because the young man did not give any consideration in the contract. However, consideration does not have to be in the form of money or tangible goods. For example, if this relative promised to give the young man $5000 on his twenty-first birthday if he would refrain from drinking intoxicating beverages, it would be an enforceable contract because the young man would give consideration by not drinking intoxicating beverages.

A Legal Purpose

Contracts must be for a legal purpose to be valid and enforceable. In other words, the law will not enforce a contract requiring an act that the law itself declares illegal. For example, if a political candidate agreed to pay a person to break into his opponent's home for material to use in the campaign against her, the burglar could not force payment of the fee because it was for an illegal purpose and, therefore, not a valid contract.

Mutual Assent

For a contract to be valid and enforceable in a court of law, it must have mutual assent from both parties to the contract. The law recognizes four areas that violate the concept of mutual assent: (1) duress, (2) fraud, (3) mistake, and (4) undue influence.

Duress   **Duress** exists when a person is forced by threat to enter into a contract against his or her will. For example, if a person threatens bodily harm to another person unless he or she signs a contract, the resulting contract would not be valid and could not be enforced under the law.

Fraud   **Fraud** exists when there is intentional misrepresentation of fact. If fraud is present in a contract situation, then the contract is not valid and enforceable. For example, if a person intentionally turns back the speedometer of an automobile that he or she is selling and intentionally represents it to have a lower mileage, that person is intentionally misrepresenting the automobile. A contract signed under these conditions would not be valid and enforceable. However, it should be pointed out that, though the law declares fraud illegal, proving intentional misrepresentation in courts is not always an easy task.

Mistake   When one party to a contract makes an obvious mistake and the other party to the contract is aware of the mistake and takes advantage of it, the contract is not valid and enforceable. For example, if a contractor bid on a job and in listing costs added them together incorrectly, the other party could not take advantage of it and make him or her perform the job at the miscalculated price.

Undue Influence   If one party to the contract has undue influence on a person because of their relationship and causes the other party to contract to his or her harm because of this relationship, it cannot be a valid and enforceable contract. For example, an agent who has his or her client sign a contract to perform in a nightclub the agent owns at an unreasonably low fee could not enforce the contract because of the undue influence the agent had as a result of their relationship.

Legal Form

Contracts may be in either verbal or written form with certain limitations specified by the states. Some states specify that all contracts involving real property (real estate) must be in writing. Some other states specify that all contracts involving sums of more than a specified amount ($500 is a common amount) must be in writing. Some require both to be in writing. For example, if one person verbally tells another he will sell his golf clubs (personal property) for $200 and the other person accepts, it is a valid contract. On the other hand, if one person verbally offers to sell another person her home for $20,000 and the other person accepts, it is not a valid contract in states that require real property contracts to be in writing.

Most contracts are of the verbal variety, such as the earlier example of the person ordering food in a restaurant. Though verbal contracts are valid and enforceable (with the exceptions noted earlier), they are sometimes difficult to prove in courts of law because of their verbal nature. Consequently, the small business owner should always insist on contracts of a significant value to be in the form of writing regardless of state requirements for legal form. (See Fig. 21-2.)

Recourse for Breach of Contract

When one party to a contract does not fulfill his part of the contract (**breach of contract**), the other party to the contract has certain rights of recourse under law. In courts of law, he or she may (1) force performance of the contract, (2) cause the contract to be discharged, or (3) collect damages resulting from nonperformance of the contract. (See Fig. 21-3.)

Performance of the Contract

One party to a contract may go to court to force the other party to the contract to fulfill his or her part of the agreement. For example, Joe sold Don land and received payment for it. Then he changed his mind, tried to give the money back, and kept Don from entering the land. Don could go into court,

FIGURE 21-2
REQUIREMENTS FOR A VALID CONTRACT.

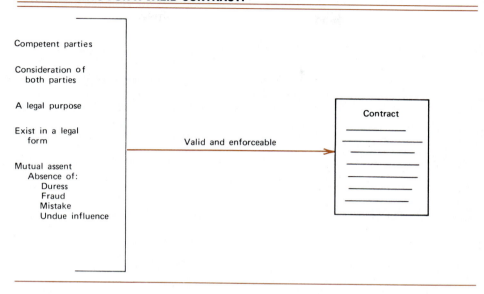

prove his claim, and the courts would direct Joe to turn the land over to Don. If Joe still refused, he would be declared in contempt of court and liable for criminal actions.

Discharge of the Contract

If one party to the contract fails to perform his or her part of the contract, the other party is not obligated to fulfill his or her part. For example, if one per-

FIGURE 21-3
RECOURSE FOR BREACH OF CONTRACT.

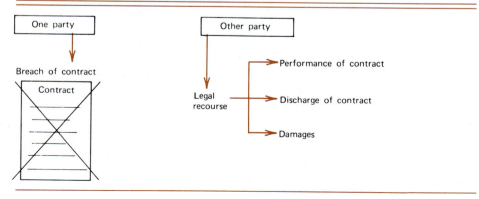

son agrees to sell another an automobile and then does not give this person the automobile, this other person is under no obligation to pay the purchase price.

Collect Damages

If one party to a contract suffers loss or damages as a result of the other party's not fulfilling his or her part of the contract, the injured party may recover damages in a court of law. For example, if a school hires a football coach and signs a contract for one year of employment and the coach is released from his or her duties after six months, the school must pay this coach wages for the remaining six months if he or she cannot find an equal position at another school.

UNIFORM COMMERCIAL CODE

Each individual state establishes its own laws (within the limits set by the U.S. Constitution and its state constitution) governing *intrastate* commerce (commerce within the state). The federal government establishes rules governing *interstate* commerce (commerce between the states).

Because each state establishes its own laws governing intrastate commerce, the early years of the United States witnessed a wide range of state statues and judicial rulings. Conflicts and confusion were common because of the difference in state laws. In 1890 a move was initiated to encourage the states to adopt uniform laws governing commerce. By 1945 over 60 uniform statutes were formulated and adopted by a large number of states. In 1945 work was begun to combine all these uniform acts into a code encompassing the field of commercial law. In 1952 the **Uniform Commercial Code** was first published and then revised in 1958 to its present form. With the exception of the state of Louisiana, all 50 states have adopted the Uniform Commercial Code.

The general areas of law and some of the major provisions of each area that are included in the Uniform Commercial Code are these.

1. *Sales*   Requirements of contracts—rights of seller and buyer.
2. *Commercial paper*   Requirements of negotiable instruments including time, liability, acceptance, alteration, and delivery.
3. *Bank deposits and collections*   Banking practices, such as cutoff time for posting.
4. *Letters of credit*   Rights and duties of bank, receiver, and customer.
5. *Bulk transfers*   Provisions preventing dishonest merchants from buying large quantities of goods without paying for them and selling them to third parties.
6. *Warehouse receipts, bills of lading, and other documents of title*   Reg-

ulates documents of title to personal property entrusted to others for various reasons.

7. *Investment securities*   Regulates registered and bearer bonds, stock certificates, and other investment paper.
8. *Secured transactions, sales of accounts, contract rights, and chattel paper*   Legal aspects of pledges, assignments, chattel mortgages, liens, conditional sales contracts, leases, and so on.

BANK CHECKS

Almost all small businesses receive and issue **checks** drawn on banks almost every day. Businesses that receive checks usually have a problem with bad checks. Retail and service firms usually suffer more than other businesses from bad checks, but manufacturers and wholesalers also find them a problem. Good check cashing procedures and collection practices help reduce losses from bad checks.

Types of Checks

The basic types of checks are (1) personal checks, (2) two-party checks, (3) payroll checks, (4) government checks, (5) counter checks, and (6) traveler's checks.

Personal checks   A personal check is a check made out by the individual signing the check and made directly to the small business. A small business should require positive identification on all personal checks. If the state issues driver's licenses with photographs, this is one of the best means of identification. If not, the store should require the driver's licence and note carefully the signature and description of the person. Additional identification should also be required in the form of credit cards, government passes, or identification cards. Signatures on these should also be compared to the driver's license and the check.

Two-party checks   A two-party check is a check made out by one individual to another individual who endorses it so it can be cashed by the small business. Generally, a small business should not accept two-party checks. The possibility of it being a stolen check or forgery is too great a risk.

Payroll checks   Payroll checks are issued by a business to an employee for his or her salary. They usually have the word *payroll* printed on them and often have the amount imprinted on the check by a machine. The small business should require identification as described earlier. In addition, it generally is not a good policy to cash out-of-town checks. Thieves sometimes steal blank payroll checks from firms and then pass them to small businesses in other towns.

Government checks   Government checks are checks issued by the local, state, or federal government. They may be for such purposes as wages, tax refunds, pensions, social security payments, welfare allotments, and veterans' benefits. It is not at all uncommon to find thieves who specialize in stealing government checks from mailboxes. In fact, in some metropolitan areas, stealing has become so common a practice that some banks will not accept government checks unless the person has an account in the bank. The small business firm should follow the same cautious identification procedure it uses with personal checks when accepting government checks.

Counter checks   Banks usually have checks with the bank's name on them placed on counters in the bank so depositors may use them to withdraw funds from their accounts without having to have their personalized checks with them. Unless the small business knows the customer well, he or she should not honor a counter check.

Traveler's checks   A traveler's check is a check sold by firms through banks to persons who do not wish to carry large sums of cash with them when they travel. The buyer signs each traveler's check in the presence of the bank teller and then must sign below the original signature when he or she cashes the check. A comparison of the two signatures identifies him or her as the owner. The small business employee or owner who accepts traveler's checks should *always* require the second signature in his or her presence and carefully check the two signatures.

Money orders may also be cashed as checks. Private firms, banks, and the United States Postal Service issue money orders for a fee. Small business firms should not cash money orders because they are usually purchased to send in the mail and not for direct transactions.

In addition to careful identification, the small business owner or employee who is cashing the check should look for

1.   A difference in the written and the numerical amount on the check.
2.   Proper endorsements.
3.   Old dates or postdated checks.
4.   An address of the customer and the bank.
5.   Erasures and written-over amounts.

Types of Bad Checks

Checks may be bad because of (1) insufficient funds, (2) no account, (3) a closed account, or (4) forgery.

Insufficient funds   Checks that are returned from the bank marked "insufficient funds" should be redeposited a second time after the customer is notified. Most of these checks are collected. State laws and bank practices vary, but, generally, if the check does not clear the second time, the bank will no longer accept it, and it is the small business owner's responsibility to collect it.

If the small business owner is unable to collect the check and resorts to prosecution in the courts, he or she should check state law to determine what actions must be taken to prosecute. Most states require the business owner to send the check writer a registered letter and wait from 5 to 10 days for payment before suit is filed.

No account   When a check is returned from the bank marked "no account," there is almost no chance of collection. This is usually evidence of intentional fraud by the check writer. However, before notifying the police, the small business owner should make an attempt to contact the check writer just in case he or she has changed banks and inadvertently written the check on the wrong bank.

Closed account   A returned check marked "closed account" is usually the result of a person's changing banks and forgetting he or she has a check outstanding. Also, the bank may have closed the account because of too many overdrafts. It may also be fraud on the part of the check writer. Collection should be attempted first and then prosecution begun if collection fails.

Forgery   The police should be notified immediately in cases of forgery. Forged checks are worthless, and it would be rare indeed for collection attempts to be of any value. If the forged check is a U.S. government check, the small business should notify the nearest local field office of the U.S. Secret Service.

Small business firms should automatically stamp on the back side of all checks received the notation "for deposit only" and the name of the business. This prevents the checks from being cashed if stolen. (See Fig. 21-4.)

FIGURE 21-4
TYPES OF CHECKS AND REASONS FOR BANK NOT ACCEPTING.

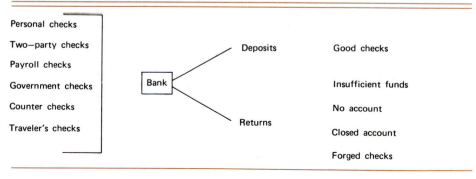

INSTALLMENT CONTRACTS AND REPOSSESSION

Installment sales contracts may exist in three basic types: (1) chattel mortgage, (2) conditional sales contract, and (3) lease–purchase.

Chattel Mortgage

Under the **chattel mortgage** contract, the title of the merchandise passes to the buyer at the time of the purchase. The contract is secured by the seller's having a lien against the merchandise.

Conditional Sales Contract

The **conditional sales contract** is the most common type used today. As the name implies, the sale of the merchandise is conditional on the buyer's making payments on time and meeting other conditions. These contracts usually require the purchaser to insure the merchandise and pay all maintenance costs until the merchandise is paid for. The title to the merchandise does not pass to the buyer until all provisions of the contract are completed.

Lease–Purchase Contract

Under the **lease–purchase contract,** merchandise is rented to purchasers until they have made a specific number of payments. After they have made the specific number of payments, they receive title to the goods. Some small business firms that specialize in lease–purchase types of sales try to appeal to persons who have poor credit ratings.

The conditional sales contract and the lease–purchase agreement are superior to the chattel mortgage in terms of repossession of merchandise. State laws governing repossession of merchandise under all three types of contracts vary widely. However, the chattel mortgage contract is more time-consuming and more expensive than the other two types of contracts in terms of repossession in most states. (See Fig. 21-5.)

The authors have known small business owners who repossess merchandise by going to the person's home, telling him or her they are there to repossess the merchandise, and then going into the house to take it back. *No small business owner should ever use this method of repossession.* Not only does it violate the rights of the customer, which can result in legal problems for the small business owner, but it can be very dangerous. Any small business owner who repossesses merchandise should first consult an attorney to learn the requirements of the state's laws and then carefully follow the requirements of the law.

FIGURE 21-5
TYPES OF INSTALLMENT SALES CONTRACTS.

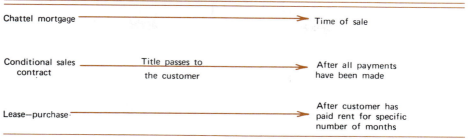

COPYRIGHTS, PATENTS, AND TRADEMARKS

The U.S. Constitution provides authors and inventors with exclusive rights to their works.

Copyrights

Copyrights are good for the life of the author plus 50 years. They are filed with the Library of Congress for a small fee. They may protect any of the following:

1. Books
2. Periodicals
3. Lectures
4. Dramatic and dramatic-musical compositions
5. Musical compositions
6. Maps
7. Works of art
8. Reproductions of works of art
9. Technical drawings or models
10. Photographs
11. Prints, pictorial illustrations, and labels.
12. Motion pictures other than photoplays
13. Motion picture photoplays
14. Sound recordings

Patents

Patent law gives inventors exclusive rights to make, use, and sell their inventions for a 17-year period. For an idea to be issued a patent it must be a

When Hallmark (left) introduced a line of greeting cards confusingly similar to Blue Mountain Arts's distinctive cards (right), Blue Mountain screamed trademark infringement. After an intense legal battle lasting over two years, Blue Mountain and Hallmark have struck a truce in the form of a consent decree—a formal written agreement. Under the terms of the consent decree, Hallmark will stop publishing its Personal Touch line of cards, discontinue the use of the Personal Touch name, and take steps to repurchase the cards from Hallmark stores.

unique new idea. If you wish to obtain a patent, you should probably retain an attorney that specializes in patents. The government Patent Office does not protect patents in court. The holder of the patent must prosecute patent infringement in the courts at the holder's expense. Of all patent infringements suits about 80 percent have been lost by the patent holder on a historical basis.

Trademarks

Registered **trademarks** give the owner exclusive rights without any time limit. The trademark must be distinctive and words in common usage are not eligible for protection.

LEGAL REQUIREMENTS CAUSE HEADACHES FOR SMALL BUSINESS

One or more common complaints for small business owners is about the time and paperwork that are spent meeting various laws of city, county, state, and the federal government. The experience of two people amply illustrates the problem.

One entrepreneur, whom we will call Joe, wanted to build an auto parts store on a major road in a city of a population over 300,000. Joe found what he considered the best location for his store. After considerable negotiations, Joe obtained an option contract with the owner and deposited $5000 earnest money with a title company.

Joe then spent half a day talking to various people at the city trying to verify the zoning. He finally discovered that the zoning had never been finalized and that the property was zoned for single family residence. Joe obtained all the information needed to try to get the zoning changed (it would take three months). Joe hired an architect to draw up a site plan taking into consideration all the various requirements of the city. Joe took his site plan to the city and was told he would have to see Planning to determine if it was a legal lot, Water Shed Management to determine the 100-year flood plain, Urban Transportation to determine parking requirements, Building Inspection to determine setbacks from the streets, and Landscaping to determine landscaping requirements. The second day while Joe was processing his application through these departments, he discovered that the city had an ordinance that required the property to have a 200-foot frontage on the main road to obtain direct access if there was another

road next to the property. The property only had 180 feet of frontage and did have access to another road, thereby denying access to the mainroad, which made the property unsuitable for his store.

Another entrepreneur, whom we will call Sam, set up a business (in the same city) in which he bought a large barbecue cooker on wheels from a firm that had obtained the right to sell barbecued food in a supermarket chain's stores on the weekend. The meat was cooked on the cooker in the parking lot and sold by an employee at a table in the supermarket. The table was equipped with a glass guard, heat lamps, and equipment to keep the meat and equipment clean. Sam had to obtain a health permit. The employee at the health department said Sam had a choice. He could permanently affix his table and cooking equipment to the barbecue cooker, or he had to build restrooms next to his cooker in the parking lot. The official agreed there was no health problem with the way it was done in other cities. It took an appeal to a city council member to get the official to change his mind.

Sam had to go to the state controller to obtain a sales tax permit. He had to fill in a rather lengthy form and place a specific amount of money on deposit, which he could not withdraw as long as he had his tax license. Sam collected sales tax, kept a record of it, filled out a form each month, and remitted the tax collected.

Sam obtained an employer identification number from the Internal Revenue Service (he had one employee). Sam withheld income tax and FICA tax from his employee's salary each week and filled out a form (he had considerable trouble understanding it) every quarter and remitted the money. He was required to pay an equal amount of the FICA tax. Sam also was required to pay a federal unemployment tax on his employee and fill out a form reporting this tax.

Sam also had to acquire a number from the state employment commission, fill out report forms, and pay a state unemployment tax.

Sam also was required to fill out several reports each year for various government bodies, such as the Economic Census Report for the Department of Commerce and the personal property tax forms for the city, county, and school district.

LICENSES AND PERMITS

Most states and many local governments require businesses to obtain various types of **licenses.** In addition, state and local governments often require employees of small businesses to obtain permits, for example, health permits. Some of the licenses are for control purposes, as is the case of a health permit. However, many are for taxation purposes, such as city business permits.

Individuals interested in starting a small business should first check and determine what licenses and permits are required for the business. In some cases, these may result in their not being able to operate a business. For example, if an individual built a tavern and then could not obtain a liquor license for some reason, he or she could not operate the business. Persons buying a business should also make sure the license and permits of the business will transfer to them or that they will be able to acquire them after they have bought the business.

From this chapter, it can be easily seen that legal aspects of small business can be complex and differ from state to state. The small business entrepreneur would be well advised to contact an attorney when he or she is starting a business.

SUMMARY OF KEY POINTS

1. The requirements of a valid contract are (a) competent parties, (b) consideration, (c) legal purpose, (d) mutual assent, and (e) legal form.
2. Recourse for breach of contract may be requiring performance of the contract, discharge of the contract, or collection of damages.

3. The Uniform Commercial Code was created because widely differing state laws were causing problems in interstate commerce.
4. Checks may exist in the form of personal checks, two-party checks, payroll checks, government checks, counter checks, and traveler's checks.
5. Checks may be bad because of insufficient funds, no account, a closed account, or forgery.
6. Installment contracts may exist in three basic forms: chattel mortgage, conditional sales contract, and lease–purchase contract.
7. City, county, state, and federal governments have numerous requirements that are placed on small business that require considerable time.
8. Exclusive rights may be obtained in patents, copyrights, and trademarks.
9. A new business must obtain various types of licenses.

DISCUSSION QUESTIONS

1. Who are competent parties in terms of a contract?
2. Does a contract have to be in writing, or may it be verbal?
3. What can a person do if another party does not honor a contract?
4. Do you consider the Uniform Commercial Code to be a good idea? Explain.
5. What types of checks would you advise a small business owner to accept?
6. How may a small business owner minimize bad check losses?
7. Which type of bad check returned by the bank is the most likely to be collected?
8. If you were a small business owner, which type of installment sales contract would you use? Explain.
9. How should a small business owner go about repossessing merchandise?
10. How long do patents, copyrights, and trademarks provide exclusive rights? Do they always provide protection?
11. Why should a prospective small business owner investigate licenses and permits before he or she starts or purchases a small business?

THE BUSINESS PLAN: LEGAL CONSIDERATIONS

____ Will you use contracts in your business?
　　____ Will they involve competent parties?
　　____ Do both parties give consideration?

_____ Will the contracts be for legal purpose?

_____ Is there mutual assent? Is duress, fraud, mistake, or undue influence present?

_____ Will they be in proper form (written if required)?

_____ Do you know what steps to take if there is breach of contract?

_____ What type of checks will you accept in your business? If you have employees that will accept checks, you should instruct them in proper identification and things that they should look for that could indicate a bad check.

_____ What will you do in case of a bad check—insufficient funds, no account, closed account, or forgery?

_____ Will you use installment contracts in your business? If so, will you use conditional sales, lease–purchase, or chattel mortgage contracts? Be sure to consider the ease of repossession.

_____ Will repossession be a part of your business? What does your state require for repossession?

_____ What licenses or permits does your city require for businesses of your type?

_____ What licenses or permits does your state require for your type of business?

_____ Will patents, copyrights, and/or trademarks be a part of your business? If they will be, check this chapter for details.

ENTREPRENEURIAL PROJECTS

Obtain a copy of an installment sales contract (blank or completed). If it is a blank contract, fill in the contract with fictitious information as if you were buying an appliance.

1. Determine if the installment sales contract meets the various requirements of a valid contract.
2. Determine if it is a chattel mortgage, a conditional sales contract, or a lease–purchase agreement.

C A S E A
Little Old Lady Cars

Kevin Johnson currently works as a salesman for a large manufacturer of electronic equipment. He likes selling but does not like the extensive traveling associated with job. He has always had a keen interest in automobiles and is skilled in making used cars look almost new by removing small dents, making the paint shine like new, and cleaning and improving the inside of the car. He is also able to perform tune-ups and minor repairs.

Kevin plans to open a used car lot on a piece of property with a small office on it on a major road in his community. Kevin has a considerable amount of capital and has decided to finance his own installment sales contracts for the interest he will earn on them.

Kevin has little knowledge about the legal aspects of operating a used car lot. Help him by answering some of his questions.

Questions

1. What can he do in terms of contracts to protect himself when he sells an automobile on the installment basis?
2. What should he do if someone does not pay the installments on the purchase?
3. What type of contract would you tell Kevin to use in his installment sales?
4. Kevin sells cars on Saturday and Sunday when the banks are closed and he takes checks for down payments. Tell him (a) what type of checks he should accept and what type he should not accept, (b) what kind of identification he should require and (c) what he should do if any are returned from the bank.
5. What should Kevin do about repossessions?
6. What should Kevin do about licenses and permits?
7. Kevin feels his name of the used car lot is unique and wants to protect it. He wants to know if he can patent, copyright, or trademark the name.

CASE B
Redell's Appliance Store

The Redell Appliance Store is owned and operated by Coy Redell. The store sells a well-known line of appliances—stoves, refrigerators, dishwashers, and others. It also has a complete service department for all the products it sells. Coy has been in business for 15 years and has been very successful.

Coy has been using a local bank to finance installment purchases for his customers. Because the business has been so profitable, Coy has quite a large sum of money accumulated in certificates of deposit in a local savings and loan association, and he has been looking for some place to invest it to earn more money. One day while filling in a loan application for a customer, Coy realized that the interest rate on the installment contract was considerably higher than the amount he was earning with his certificates of deposit. He decided that he would start financing his own installment contracts with his savings.

Coy has asked you to help him. He has several questions he needs answered.

Questions

Coy's questions are the following.

1. What should I do to make sure I have valid contracts with my customers?
2. What can I do if a customer does not make his or her payments on the installment contract?
3. What kind of installment contracts should I use?

KEY WORDS

CHAPTER 22

GOVERNMENT CONTROL, ASSISTANCE, AND INTERNATIONAL MARKETING OPPORTUNITIES

LEARNING GOALS

After reading this chapter, you will understand:

1 Which are the primary controls of business legislative acts, what they prohibit, and what agencies administer them.

2 What the Occupational Safety and Health Act is and how it affects small businesses.

3 What effect customer protection laws have on small business firms.

4 That the Small Business Administration is the main governmental agency providing assistance to small business.

5 That the Small Business Administration helps small business firms with loans, management assistance, training, set-aside contracts, and publications.

6 The opportunities for small business in international marketing.

ENTREPRENEURIAL PROFILE

William Gould

NATIONAL GRAPHICS

By 1974, William (Bob) Gould had had it. He resigned a cushy position as executive vice president of Western Litho Plate, a Bemis Company subsidiary, and started a small business in St. Louis making silver-based photosensitive film paper and chemistry for the graphic arts industry. Used to working with hundreds, he employed seven.

The firm, National Graphics, found itself in stiff competition with industry giants such as Eastman Kodak, 3 M, and Agfa Gevaert. Within a year, it realized it had to change its product line and marketing strategy drastically, or go under. Just as it began to do both, the recession hit.

In 1975, Chippewa Bank in St. Louis brought in SBA, which found National Graphics a good risk with its new ideas in spite of a bad business climate. Three SBA loans in three successive years worth $770,000 were made to the company. In particular, this helped boost the firm's attempt to get into the international market, where it soon boasted the widest variety of diffusion transfer products in the industry.

Today, National Graphics has not only paid the loans in full, but pays more in income taxes each year than the combined loan total! The firm now has 93 employees and has grown from annual sales of $524,000 the first year of SBA involvement to $15 million today.

Named National Small Business Exporter of the Year (1985) and Missouri Small Business Person of the Year (1979), Bob Gould says "SBA can be proud of its part in producing a strong taxpayer entity that will continue to put more and more people to work."

Source: Network (Washington, D.C.: U.S. Small Business Administration, March–April 1988).

Many states have social control of business legislation, but the more important pieces of legislation regulating business are federal laws that apply to interstate commerce. Major federal social control of business legislation exists in the form of the (1) Sherman Antitrust Act; (2) Clayton Act; (3) Federal Trade Commission Act; (4) Robinson–Patman Act; and (5) Food, Drug, and Cosmetic Act.

SHERMAN ANTITRUST ACT, 1980

The **Sherman Antitrust Act** prohibits restraint of trade and monopoly in business.

The two main sections of the act read as follows:[1]

Sec. 1 Every contract, combination in the form of trust or otherwise, or conspiracy, in restraint of trade or commerce among the several states, or with foreign nations is hereby declared to be illegal. . . .

Sec. 2 Every person who shall monopolize, or attempt to monopolize, or combine or conspire with any other person or persons, to monopolize any part of the trade or commerce among the several states, or with foreign nations, shall be deemed guilty of a misdemeanor. . . .

The restraint-of-trade section of the Sherman Antitrust Act has usually been applied to price-fixing arrangements between firms. One of the more famous cases of application of the Sherman Act was the conviction of several electrical manufacturers in the 1960s. For the first time in the history of the Sherman Act, several executives of the manufacturers were sent to prison under criminal prosecution of violations of the act.

The section of the Sherman Act prohibiting monopoly has been greatly eroded by the courts. In 1911, the Department of Justice (which is responsible for administering the act) brought suit against Standard Oil Company of New Jersey and the American Tobacco Company. The government asked for and received a judgment that dissolved both companies into several smaller companies. (It is interesting to note that both Standard Oil of New Jersey and American Tobacco are larger companies today than were their parent companies before the 1911 dissolution decree.) However, the courts, in reaching their decision, established what is known as the "rule of reason." The rule of reason held there was cause for dissolution of monopoly only when "alarming and ungentlemanly conduct" and an overwhelming percentage control of the industry existed. The rule of reason has, for all practical purposes, eliminated the use of the monopoly section of the Sherman Act.

As mentioned earlier, the Sherman Act is administered by the Department of Justice. The Department of Justice may use either criminal prosecution or civil injunction under the law. Under criminal prosecution, persons may be subject to fines not to exceed $100,000 (corporations $1 million) or imprisonment of no more than one year or both. Civil injunctions involve asking the courts to issue a decree correcting the violation of the Sherman Act. In addition, individuals or businesses may institute civil proceedings to recover three times the amount of damages proved plus attorneys' fees from persons or firms guilty of violation of the Sherman Act.

CLAYTON ACT, 1914

The **Clayton Act** was intended to strengthen antitrust action by the federal government. It was intended to provide more specific legislation than was contained in the Sherman Act. The Clayton Act prohibits four practices of business: (1) price discrimination, (2) exclusive and tying contracts, (3) intercorporate stockholding lessening competition, and (4) interlocking directors in competing corporations.

Price Discrimination

The Clayton Act prohibits price discrimination between different purchasers "where the effect of such discrimination may be to substantially lessen competition or to tend to create a monopoly in any line of commerce." This section was intended to prohibit a company from eliminating competition by selling at or below cost to selected customers. For example, one suit brought by the government charged that a manufacturer was selling spark plugs to automobile manufacturers at below cost to gain a large share of the replacement market (the government lost the suit because of the good faith provision discussed in the next paragraph).

The Clayton Act contained a provision that allowed price discrimination "when made in good faith to meet competition." The inability of the government to disprove good faith allowed almost a complete defense of this section of the Clayton Act. The inability of the Clayton Act to deal effectively with price discrimination led to the passage of the Robinson–Patman Act in 1936 (discussed later in this chapter).

Exclusive and Tying Contracts

The Clayton Act prohibits the following practices when their effect "may be to substantially lessen competition or tend to create a monopoly."

1. *Tie-in sales* For example, the case of a mortgage company compelling home buyers to sign a contract to insure their homes with a subsidiary of the mortgage company to obtain a home loan.
2. *Exclusive dealerships* These arrangements require the dealer to agree not to sell products of the seller's competitors.
3. *Requirement contracts* A contract that requires a customer to agree to buy all future needs from the seller.

4. *Full-line forcing*   The practice of selling a customer a product only if he or she agrees to purchase other lines of merchandise from the seller.

Intercorporate Stockholding Lessening Competition

This section of the Clayton Act prohibits a corporation from holding stock in another corporation when it would substantially lessen competition. For example, General Motors was forced by the courts to sell its stock in DuPont because DuPont supplied large amounts of paint to General Motors. The courts felt this intercorporate stockholding had the effect of lessening competition in the paint industry because General Motors used such vast amounts of paint.

Because the Clayton Act prohibited acquiring stock and not assets, many companies simply bought out the assets of competitors as a means of avoiding the act.

Interlocking Directorates in Competing Corporations

The Clayton Act prohibits a person from serving on the board of directors of two or more corporations that are or have been in competition if the effect could be to lessen competition. This section excludes banks, common carriers, and companies with capital of less than $1 million.

This section of the Clayton Act has not been as effective as intended by Congress because another person, such as a relative or employee, may serve on another board of directors and achieve the same results.

The Clayton Act is administered by the Federal Trade Commission with the following exceptions.

1. The Interstate Commerce Commission administers the Clayton Act when carriers are involved.
2. The Federal Reserve Board administers the act when banks are involved.

FEDERAL TRADE COMMISSION ACT, 1914

When the courts interpreted the Sherman Antitrust Act, they condemned unfair competition but declared the act did not make it illegal. Small business owners were concerned and demanded action from Congress. In response to public and small business pressure, Congress enacted the **Federal Trade Commission Act,** which contained the following provisions.

1. The Federal Trade Commission (FTC) was established to be comprised of five members appointed by the president for seven-year terms. No more than three members may be from the same political party.

2. Any unfair methods of competition were declared illegal.
3. The Federal Trade Commission was given power to issue cease-and-desist orders. These orders could be challenged in court by the defendant.
4. The Federal Trade Commission was empowered to collect information about a business and its conduct was to be made available to the president, Congress, and the public.

The most important sections of the Federal Trade Commission Act were the section declaring unfair methods of competition illegal and the section giving the FTC the power to issue cease-and-desist orders. The broad nature of the provision declaring unfair competition illegal provides legal authority for the Federal Trade Commission to deal with all types of business activity that injure competition.

Before the passage of the Federal Trade Commission Act, any individual or business suffering loss because of antitrust violations had to proceed directly through the courts under the Sherman or Clayton acts or both. This often proved to be a long and expensive process. Under the Federal Trade Commission Act, individuals can file a complaint with the FTC, and the commission has the power to issue a cease-and-desist order.

The Federal Trade Commission has become the primary agency enforcing antitrust legislation. Since it was formed, it has been empowered to administer the following acts.

1. The Clayton Act of 1914.
2. Parts of the Wheeler–Lea Act of 1938, which dealt with false advertising of food, drugs, cosmetics, and devices.
3. The Wool Products Labeling Act of 1939, which requires that all wool products except carpets, rugs, mats, and upholstering have a label attached that describes the kind and percentage of fiber contained in the product.
4. Parts of the Lanham Trade-Mark Act of 1946, which allows the Federal Trade Commission to apply to the commissioner of patents for cancellation of trademarks that are deceptive, immoral, obtained fradulently, or in violation of the Lanham Trade-Mark Act or a combination of these.
5. The McCarran Insurance Act of 1948, which regulates various activities in the insurance industry.
6. The Fur Products Labeling Act of 1951, which requires manufacturers to show on labels attached to garments the type of animal fur, country of origin, and specified processing information.
7. The Flammable Fabrics Act of 1953, which prohibits sale of highly flammable wearing apparel.
8. Part of the Food, Drug, and Cosmetic Act of 1938 (discussed later).

ROBINSON–PATMAN ACT, 1936

The **Robinson–Patman Act** was passed to close weaknesses of the price discrimination section of the Clayton Act. The Robinson–Patman Act prohibits (1) price discounts that cannot be fully justified by lower costs to the seller, (2) selling private brands of a product that are identical to regular brands at a lower price, and (3) giving buyers proportionally unequal advertising and promotional allowances. One of the major strengths of the act was that it placed the burden of proof for justifying price differences on the seller. In addition, the act not only makes the seller guilty under the act in cases of price discrimination, but it also makes the buyer guilty if he or she knowingly accepts a discriminating price.

The Federal Trade Commission may issue a cease-and-desist order when the seller is unable to show cost justification for price discrimination. The parties judged guilty may be subject to fines under civil proceedings and even subject to criminal action in certain instances. In addition, the act provides for any person injured by violation of the act to recover treble damages in civil actions.

FOOD, DRUG, AND COSMETIC ACT, 1938

In 1937 a drug manufacturer sold a drug contaminated with poison, which resulted in 93 deaths. The resulting publicity and public reaction caused Congress to pass the **Food, Drug, and Cosmetic Act,** in 1938. The Food, Drug, and Cosmetic Act of 1938 was considerably stronger than the 1906 act. The 1938 act prohibits (1) adulterated products, (2) misbranding, and (3) false advertising.

The Federal Trade Commission administers and enforces the false labeling and misbranding sections of the 1938 act. The Federal Trade Commission also has power to administer the prohibition of adulteration and false advertising; however, it has generally left these functions of the Food and Drug Administration of the Department of Health, Education, and Welfare, which also has enforcement power.

Figure 22-1 shows major business legislation.

OCCUPATIONAL SAFETY AND HEALTH ACT

There are about 10,700 deaths per year in the United States owing to occupational accidents. In addition, there are about 1.8 million workers who sustain disabling injuries on the job. In an attempt to reduce deaths and injuries related to work, Congress passed the **Occupational Safety and Health Act,** which is administered by the Occupational Safety and Health Administration

FIGURE 22-1
MAJOR GOVERNMENT CONTROL OF BUSINESS LEGISLATION.

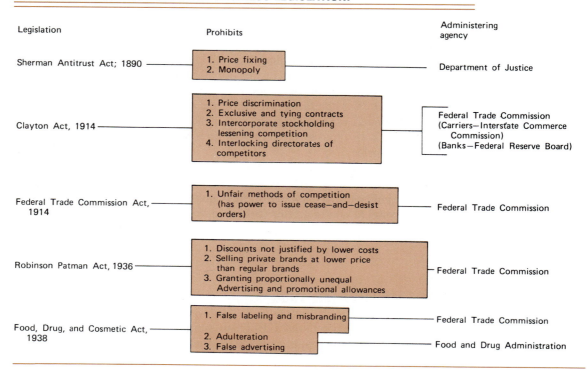

Legislation	Prohibits	Administering agency
Sherman Antitrust Act; 1890	1. Price fixing 2. Monopoly	Department of Justice
Clayton Act, 1914	1. Price discrimination 2. Exclusive and tying contracts 3. Intercorporate stockholding lessening competition 4. Interlocking directorates of competitors	Federal Trade Commission (Carriers—Interstate Commerce Commission) (Banks—Federal Reserve Board)
Federal Trade Commission Act, 1914	1. Unfair methods of competition (has power to issue cease—and—desist orders)	Federal Trade Commission
Robinson Patman Act, 1936	1. Discounts not justified by lower costs 2. Selling private brands at lower price than regular brands 3. Granting proportionally unequal Advertising and promotional allowances	Federal Trade Commission
Food, Drug, and Cosmetic Act, 1938	1. False labeling and misbranding 2. Adulteration 3. False advertising	Federal Trade Commission Food and Drug Administration

(OSHA). The act requires that all workers must be free from recognized hazards that could cause death or serious injury.

OSHA has considerable power to enforce compliance with the law. The law allows fines of up to $1000 for each violation and fines of up to $1000 per day unless the violation is corrected within a prescribed time. Also, if an OSHA inspector finds a violation he or she feels could cause death or serious injury, the inspector can obtain a court injunction and have the business shut down until the violation is corrected.

Employers of more than 10 people must keep a log and summary of occupational injuries and illnesses. All employers, regardless of size, are required to report within 48 hours accidents involving a fatality or hospitalization.

Prior to 1978, safety inspectors could enter a firm without advance notice to make safety inspections. However, in 1978, the Supreme Court ruled (*Marshall* v. *Barlow's, Inc.*) that OSHA inspectors must obtain a warrant to gain entry to a workplace when the owner demands it.

Some businesses have maintained that some inspectors are overly zealous to the point of absurdity or do not have the knowledge necessary to perform their jobs realistically or both. In fact, many people in business have accused many of the government agencies of the same weaknesses. For example, one OSHA inspector ordered a manufacturer of pet sanitary litter to give all its employees a two-week mine safety course, at company expense because it also owned a mine. Another agency was going to fine a person for flying a homemade helicopter 6 inches off the ground even though it was tied to the ground. The agency claimed he had failed to get FAA clearance. Publicity caused them to drop the case.

The small business owner should be aware of OSHA and the requirements for his or her type of business. The regulations cover, almost without exception, every type of business, even retail businesses. The requirements of OSHA can be very strict and most often are expensive. For example, the law requires any business that uses hydraulic jacks to have them inspected and serviced every six months by a certified dealer.

CONSUMER PROTECTION LAWS

The number of so-called consumer protection laws has been growing in recent years. The small businessperson must be aware of these laws and regulations in order not to violate their provisions. Some of the more important ones for small businesses are now discussed.

Cooling-off Periods

This Federal Trade Commission regulation requires a **cooling-off period** in door-to-door selling if the purchase exceeds $25. The buyer has three business days to cancel a purchase by written notification. The salesperson is then required to pick up the goods or make arrangements, at his or her expense, for the return of the goods within 20 days, or the customer can keep the goods. The salesperson must return in full any payment or trade-in received in the sale. The salesperson must also cancel any credit note or mortgage involved in the sale.

This regulation also makes provision for cooling-off periods in cases where the buyer's home is used as security in a credit transaction (not original purchase). Major repairs and remodeling often involve a second lien on the home. The three-day period is required in these transactions, and the creditor must give the buyer written notice of his or her right to cancel. Written notification is also required to cancel the purchase.

There are certain exceptions—purchases made entirely by phone or mail, purchases made in relation to earlier negotiations at a retail store, purchases of stocks and bonds from registered brokers, purchases of insurance, the rental of property, and parts and labor for maintenance and repair.

Fair Packaging and Labeling Act

The **Fair Packaging and Labeling Act** of 1969 requires that any manufacturer or distributor of a consumer product must display prominently on labels the true net weight or volume of the contents. The law also prohibits such terms as *giant quart* or *jumbo pound*. Under the law, a manufacturer can only advertise coupon offers or "cents-off" sales if the price is below the regular price. Any commodity labeled "economy size" or any other such term must be sold at a price that is at least 5 percent less than the per unit of weight or volume price of all other sizes of the same product sold at the same time. Introductory price offers can last no longer than six months and may be used only for new products, products that are substantially changed, or products being introduced for the first time in a particular marketing area. Manufacturers who elect to show the number of servings on their label must also show the amount of each serving.

This law also requires manufacturers to list on the label all of the ingredients of the product in decreasing order of weight for any nonstandard foods. The common name of the product and the name and address of the manufacturer must appear on the label of all goods except prescription drugs.

Federal Garnishment Law

The **Federal Garnishment Law** of 1968 deals with an individual's wages being withheld for the payment of a debt. The federal law prohibits garnishments of more than 25 percent of an employeee's disposable earnings (gross pay minus all deductions required by the law) in any one week or 30 times the federal minimum wage in effect at the time, whichever is less. The law also prohibits the employer from firing an employee because of one debt. The law does not prohibit firing if there are garnishments for two or more debts. If there is a state law covering garnishment of wages and it gives the debtor the better break, it is used instead of the federal law. Some states have laws prohibiting garnishment of wages and the federal law has no meaning in these states.

Magnuson–Moss Warranty Act

The **Magnuson–Moss Warranty Act** of 1974 provides that

1. No company can be forced to offer a written warranty.
2. Every term and condition of the warranty must be spelled out in writing.
3. All warranties must be written in ordinary language instead of in "legalese."
4. Any written warranty must be labeled either "full warranty" or "limited warranty."

THE INCREASING BURDEN OF FICA TAX ON SMALL BUSINESS

F.I.C.A. (Federal Insurance Contribution Act) tax is familiar to most people through their payroll checks and W-2 forms. Social security was instituted in 1934 as a mandatory insurance program. The program was extended in 1956 to provide benefits for disabled workers, and Medicare was added in 1965.

The benefits of the program have increased considerably since the start of the program, but the amount of contribution by worker and employer has also increased dramatically. The first tax rate was 1 percent for the employee, which was matched by the employer on wages up to $3000—a maximum of $30 each. The following chart shows the increase the employer has had to pay (the employee must pay the same amount) for selected years.

Moreover, small business owners must also pay an F.I.C.A. tax on their earnings.

Year	Percent Tax Rate	Maximum Income Taxed	Maximum Tax Amount
1976	5.85	$15,300	$ 895.05
1977	5.85	16,500	965.25
1978	6.05	17,700	1070.85
1979	6.13	22,900	1403.77
1980	6.13	25,900	1587.67
1981	6.65	29,700	1975.05
1982	6.70	32,400	2170.80
1983	6.70	35,700	2391.90
1984	7.00	37,800	2646.00
1985	7.05	39,600	2791.80
1986	7.15	42,000	3003.00
1987	7.15	43,800	3131.70
1988	7.51	45,000	3379.50
1989	7.51	48,000	3604.80

The rate has the same maximum income that is taxed; however, the rate is almost double the amount the employee pays. For example, the tax for self-employed persons in 1989 was 13.02 percent of all income up to $48,000 for a total of $6,249.60.

5. Full warranties require that
   a. Defective products will be fixed or replaced free including removal and installation if necessary.
   b. They will be fixed in a reasonable time.
   c. The customer does not have to do anything unreasonable.
   d. The warranty covers any owner, not just the purchaser.
   e. If the product cannot be fixed, the customer has the choice between a new one or his or her money back.
6. Warranties that do not meet all these requirements must be labeled "limited warranties."

Merchandise, Mail Order and Unordered

Mail-order firms must fill orders from customers within 30 days or offer the customers their money back. They must send customers a postcard allowing cancellation and the return of their money. If customers want their money back, it must be returned promptly. This regulation does not apply to magazines.

Free samples and merchandise mailed by charitable organizations soliciting contributions are the only **unordered merchandise** that can be sent through the mails. Other than these two categories, any merchandise that is unordered may be considered a free gift by the receiver. It is illegal for the business to bill or dun the person receiving unordered merchandise.

GOVERNMENT ASSISTANCE TO SMALL BUSINESS

Many agencies of the federal government offer various forms of assistance to small business. For example, the Commerce Department will provide information and assistance to small businesses to help them engage in international trade. The Department of Labor has sponsored programs that provide assistance to businesses in poverty areas for training workers. The Office of Minority Business Enterprise in the Department of Commerce has sponsored programs designed to increase the number of minority small business firms. However, the bulk of government assistance to small business has come from the Small Business Administration of the Department of Commerce.

The **Small Business Administration** (SBA) was established by Congress in 1953 to "help small businesses grow and prosper." The SBA strives to achieve this goal by offering various services to small business firms. Without a doubt, the most important function of the SBA has been in its loan programs discussed in Chapter 5. The SBA also performs other valuable services to small businesses in the form of (1) management assistance, (2) training, (3) set-aside contracts, (4) the Office of Advocacy, and (5) publications. (See Fig. 22-2.)

Management Assistance

The SBA provides management assistance to small business firms in the form of (1) their own field representatives, (2) grants to consultants, (3) the ACE program, (4) the SCORE program, and (5) University Small Business Institutes.

Field Representatives

The SBA has 98 field offices spread out over the United States, Guam, and Puerto Rico. These field offices have field representatives whose primary function is to administer assistance to small businesses, particularly those with SBA loans. Although usually understaffed, these field offices provide valuable guidance in all phases of operations to small firms.

FIGURE 22-2
HOW THE SMALL BUSINESS ADMINISTRATION HELPS SMALL BUSINESS (EXCLUDING LOANS).

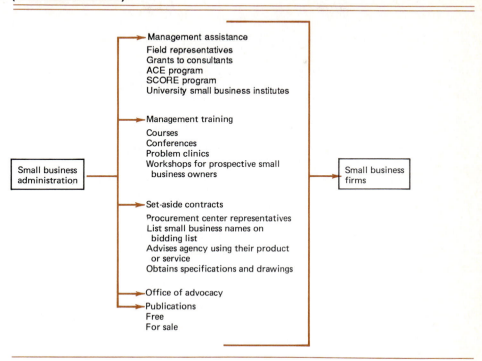

Grants to Consultants

The SBA provides funds, when they are available, to various types of consulting firms to assist loan recipients and other small businesses. The type of consulting sometimes varies from year to year, with such services as accounting and general business consulting being offered. The amount of funds made available for this type of service has been relatively small when compared to the amount of loans the SBA has outstanding. The SBA feels the program more than pays for itself in terms of improving the ability of loan recipients to repay their loans.

ACE Program

The **ACE** (Active Corps of Executives) program is one of the ways the Small Business Administration attempts to provide management consulting to small businesses. The SBA recruits persons actively engaged in small business, trade associations, major industry, professional fields related to small business, and educational institutions to join its ACE program. These volunteers provide free consulting (except for expenses that are paid for by the small business) to small business firms.

SCORE Program

The SBA forms **SCORE** (Service Corps of Retired Executives) chapters in cities and towns, consisting of persons who are retired from careers in business and business-related fields. These chapters include such persons as retired accountants, lawyers, engineers, economists, bankers, retailers, whosesalers, manufacturers, and educators. When a small business feels it needs help in solving problems or increasing efficiency of the business, it contacts the SBA field office, which in turn contacts the nearest SCORE chapter. The SCORE chapter then sends out one or more of its members who are best suited to help the small business. Today there are more than 4000 SCORE volunteers across the country helping small business firms. SCORE services are free to the small business except that the small business pays the out-of-pocket travel expenses of the volunteer.

University Small Business Institutes

The SBA contracts with colleges to provide business consulting to small firms through **University Small Business Institutes.** The SBA pays the school a small sum (currently, $400 each) for each business consulted. The methods of providing the service varies from school to school. Sometimes the instructor is directly involved in the consulting with his or her students. Sometimes the consulting is provided entirely by students. The school is required to provide periodic reports to the SBA and provide both the business and the SBA copies of the consulting recommendations. The service is entirely free to the small business. This program is designed to provide assistance to small business firms and give students exposure to real business firms and their problems. Both authors are involved in this program at their colleges and feel the program is very beneficial to both students and small businesses.

Management Training

The SBA provides management training through (1) courses, (2) conferences, (3) problem clinics, and (4) workshops for prospective small business owners.

Courses

The SBA cosponsors training courses for small business owners with educational institutions, SCORE chapters, and other civic organizations. Instructions are given by teaching staffs of colleges or other professionals. The small business owners who attend pay a small fee to cover expenses of the course, which usually consists of one day a week for several weeks.

The course may vary from general courses on policy and goals of small business to such specialized courses as bid preparation on government contracts or how to engage in export trade.

The SBA provides mailing envelopes and postage and helps with the publicity of the course. The institution provides the speaker and the room for the course.

Conferences

Conferences sponsored by the SBA are intended to help the small business owner with specific problems. They usually last only one day and cover such specialized topics as taxation. The SBA usually cosponsors these conferences with colleges, chambers of commerce, trade associations, and other civic groups. These conferences usually consist of a professional speaker, panel discussions, and question-and-answer sessions. The SBA provides mailing envelopes and postage for advertising the conference and helps with publicity.

Problem Clinics

The SBA also joins with cosponsoring institutions to offer problem clinics for small business owners. SBA contribution to the clinic is the same as for courses and conferences. The group of small business owners is led in a discussion of a common problem by a leader well versed in the specific problem. Problem clinics help small business owners exchange knowledge of a common problem and help them share in various methods of dealings with the problem.

Workshops for Prospective Small Business Owners

The SBA establishes workshops in cooperation with civic organizations in an attempt to help prospective small business owners understand the need for preparation before starting a new venture. SBA personnel or professionals hold a one-day session or several evening classes to instruct prospective small business owners in how to start a new business. Training materials are provided by the SBA to both the instructor and the prospective small business owners.

Set-Aside Contracts

The federal government contracts with private business for billions of dollars worth of goods and services each year. The various purchasing agencies of the federal government offer **set-aside contracts** on which only small businesses may bid in an effort to promote small business. The SBA has Procurement Center representatives in major government procurement agencies to review and recommend additional set-aside contracts for small business. The Procurement Center representatives also provide lists of small business sources to the procurement agencies and often recommend relaxation of restrictive specifications so that small firms may bid on them.

SBA field offices have personnel who help small firms in government contract bidding by performing such functions as advising which agency uses their products or services, helping them get their firms on bidding lists, and helping them obtain bidding specifications and drawings.

Office of Advocacy

"In recent years, high interest rates, inflation, and excessive government regulation have inhibited the performance of the small business sector."[2] Complaints from small business owners to the federal government are well summarized in this statement. In 1976, Congress created the **Office of Advocacy** within the Small Business Administration. The office was created to protect, strengthen, and represent small business within the federal government.

Its mandate from Congress is to

- Act as the primary spokesperson for small business and represent its views and interests before Congress and other Federal bodies.
- Serve as a conduit through which suggestions and policy criticisms are received.
- Inform the small business community of issues that affect it, and assist the entrepreneur with questions and problems regarding Federal laws, regulations, and assistance programs.
- Examine the role of small business in the American economy with regard to competition, innovation, productivity, and entrepreneurship.
- Measure the impact of Federal regulation and taxation on small entities and make policy recommendations that may enhance the performance of small businesses.
- Evaluate the credit needs of small business, particularly with regard to the free flow of capital to minority and women-owned enterprises.[3]

Publications

The SBA offers a wide range of for-sale publications designed to help the small businessperson in a wide range of problems. These publications are sold by the Government Printing Office at cost. A list of Small Business Administration publications and SBA field office addresses is presented in the Entrepreneur's Business Planning Guide at the end of the book. (A list of trade associations is also presented.)

INTERNATIONAL MARKETING AND SMALL BUSINESS

Foreign trade plays an increasingly vital role in the U.S. economy. With the growth of worldwide markets, international business opportunities have opened for small business owners.

Large firms have always been the principal American **exporters.** However,

Julie Just arranges for fishermen to ship salmon directly from Alaska to her wholesale customers in the States and abroad. Her finest compliment? She sent a Japanese client, known for his particularly high standards, a sample of the fish that was filling his 15,000-pound order. "He told me later that he didn't even look at it. He said, 'I didn't have to—I know I can count on you.' That's a sign that we're doing something right."

small businesses, which account for about 10 percent of total U.S. exports, offer unique possibilities for international trade, as seen in the following statement.

> They produce a wide variety of goods and services, often of exceptionally high quality, and can profitably penetrate small markets in ways that large companies find difficult. They are flexible in accommodating a foreign customer's special packaging and labeling requirements. Because they are entrepreneurially oriented, small firms can adapt quickly to fluctuating market conditions.[4]

The SBA estimated that about 15 percent of the over 17 million small businesses in the United States could participate in the field of international trade. As a result, the SBA made international trade one of its priorities. Approximately 700 international trade conferences a year present information to small business owners wanting to enter exporting and others wanting to expand their export markets. The SBA publication *Exporter's Guide to Federal Resources for Small Business* is a valuable aid for the firm interested in exporting. It can be obtained from the Government Printing Office.

Pros and Cons of International Marketing

The potential for exporting is increasing because many countries around the world are realizing substantial economic and social development. The rise in the standard of living among the people of these developing nations creates demands for new products and services. Exporting has distinct advantages. One, the firm can increase its profits by expanding its sales territory. Two, the diversity of markets served may help to reduce the impact of an economic downturn in one country if the economy is on the upswing in other markets. Three, there is a favorable tax advantage allowed exporters by the U.S. government. Four, because many products have a seasonal domestic market, it may be possible to sell merchandise to other countries in the off-season.

However, small business exporters face some potential barriers, and we examined some of these issues in the earlier chapter entitled Franchising. See Chapter 3. For example, entry into a foreign market requires that the small business owners understand and conform to the laws, social customs, business practices, and special regulations of the host country. Furthermore, the owners must decide how to organize their export strategy. If they lack the necessary management and technical skills, someone must be trained or hired to perform the duties of export manager. Small business owners also need experience and knowledge of financing as well as tariff and nontariff barriers to exporting.

A concern, especially for consumer products, is establishing an after-sale service network that can be time consuming and expensive. Creating an exporter-owned and operated service system in each country is beyond the financial and managerial means of most small businesses. Another barrier is the different measurement systems and varied product dimensions required by foreign-market users, such as the use of metric system of weights and measures. Because of such complications, small business owners have frequently been reluctant to enter world markets.

Selling in International Markets

We have stated that exporting is the most common means of access to world markets. A number of export distribution channels are available to assist the owner in selling in international markets. One method is for exporters of merchandise and manufactured goods to sell products to firms that buy for export. These "buyers for export" purchase merchandise from the firm for resale overseas. Most buyers for export specialize in specific merchandise categories, such as department store merchandise.

A second export opportunity is to sell directly through a foreign selling agent, distributor, retail store, or to customers. Shipping goods to the foreign markets remains the responsibility of the exporting firm.

An **export management company** (EMC) is the most likely export channel used by small businesses. An EMC is an independent firm that serves as the exclusive sales department for noncompeting producers. An EMC may operate either as an agent or distributor. As an agent, it uses the producing firm's name. Invoicing is made to the producing firm that bears the risk of nonpayment and may also have to extend credit. The agent is paid on a commission basis.

A distributor–EMC operates on a "buy–sell" arrangement. It purchases goods from the manufacturer for resale to the foreign customer while still marketing the product under the manufacturer's name. A distributor–EMC bears the risk of nonpayment and may extend credit; in some cases it determines the export price.

In 1982, the **Export Trading Company Act** was passed, creating another exporting channel for small and medium-sized firms. Prior to the act, U.S. businesses had been constrained in setting up joint exporting operations for fear of antitrust prosecution. Under this act, companies can form **export trading companies** (ETCs) and consequently pool a full range of export services. Thus, the act permits manufacturers to join with banks, transocean shipping companies, advertising agencies, distributors, and others to complete the distribution process necessary to handle a product bound from a U.S. factory to a foreign consumer. An ETC operates in a manner similar to the distributor–EMC, in that it buys from a U.S. producer for sale abroad and operates as an independent exporter.

EVALUATING THE FOREIGN MARKET

When evaluating a foreign market, small business owners should conduct a market research. This research will provide indicators of potential product demand and market share. In effect, this market research activity affords the same data as a domestic market research study. Specifically, the market research should be centered around discovering answers to the following questions.

1. How large is the market for my type of product?
2. What types of customers are in the market?
3. Where are the customers located (urban or rural)?
4. How much of my type of product is being sold in the foreign market?
5. What share of the market is each of my competitors getting?
6. What are the selling prices for my competitors' merchandise and what is the best way to price my products?
7. What kind of and how much advertising do my competitors offer?

8. How do my products compare with competitors in terms of style, price, advertising, and services?
9. Is the country an agricultural or an industrial nation?
10. What is the income level of the population?
11. What is the educational level of the population?
12. Are products made in the United States allowed in the country?

Sources of Assistance for the Small Exporter

A wide range of services is available from both public and private sources to assist the small exporter in evaluating foreign markets. For example, the Bureau of International Commerce of the U.S. Department of Commerce is specifically responsible for promoting overseas trade and helps small businesses in the following ways.

1. How to find overseas buyers and learn about specific, current opportunities for selling, exhibiting, and promoting their products abroad.
2. How to keep abreast of important marketing, economic, government, and other developments abroad.
3. How to exhibit their products overseas and meet foreign buyers through sponsorship of trade missions, trade exhibitions, trade fair exhibits, and other specialized events.

Other sources of assistance are the 43 field offices of the U.S. Department of Commerce, the Bureau of East–West Trade, international banks, and freight forwarders. Still other sources include industry trade organizations, local, U.S. and foreign chambers of commerce, export management companies, air freight carriers, and international consulting firms.

ALTERNATIVE FORMS OF INTERNATIONAL MARKETING

Although exporting is the predominant means of entry into international markets, small business owners may want to consider other forms. These other forms of entry are licensing and joint ventures. These two methods may be the only means available of gaining entry into some countries because of national interest.

Licensing

Under the licensing arrangement, a foreign manufacturer is authorized to produce the products of the domestic company. The production process and the patents remain under the control of the domestic firm. An advantage of this method is that entry can be gained into a foreign market with a minimum of investment while the company maintains control of the product. However, the licensing agreement must clearly stipulate the responsibilities of the licensee to manufacture the goods according to the quality standards. A disadvantage of the licensing agreement is that the domestic firm may be creating a competitor because the licensee may operate independently after the licensing agreement expires.

Joint Venture

Another form of entry into the international market by small business owners is the joint venture. This arrangement is similar to licensing except that the domestic firm acquires an equity interest in the foreign firm. Share of ownership may be any percentage basis. An advantage of the joint venture is that the equity ownership gives the domestic firm some control in the decision making and operation of the firm.

SUMMARY OF KEY POINTS

1. The Sherman Antitrust Act prohibits restraint of trade and monopoly.
2. The Clayton Act prohibits price discrimination, exclusive and tying contracts, intercorporate stockholding lessening competition, and interlocking directorates in competing corporations.
3. The Federal Trade Commission Act prohibits unfair methods of competition.
4. The Robinson–Patman Act prohibits price discounts that cannot be fully justified by lower costs to the seller, selling private brands of a product that are identical to regular brands at a lower price, and giving buyers proportionally unequal advertising and promotional allowances.
5. The Food, Drug, and Cosmetic Act prohibits adulterated products, misbranding, and false advertising.
6. The Occupational Safety and Health Act requires that all workers must be free from recognized hazards that could cause death or serious injury.
7. Cooling-off periods, fair packaging and labeling, the Federal Garnishment Law of 1968, the Magnuson–Moss Warranty Act, and regulations about unordered merchandise are some of the more important consumer protection laws.
8. The Small Business Administration aids small businesses with management assistance, training, set-aside contracts, the Office of Advocacy, and publications.
9. Opportunities for small business owners are growing in international markets.

10. Small business owners must select the method of distributing goods in the foreign markets.
11. Small business owners should conduct a market research study to establish the potential of the foreign market.
12. There are many sources of assistance to aid the small business owners as they evaluate the potential of foreign markets.

DISCUSSION QUESTIONS

1. What does the Sherman Antitrust Act prohibit, and how effective is it?
2. Who may sue for violations under the Sherman Act?
3. What does the Clayton Act prohibit, and is it effective?
4. What are the two most important parts of the Federal Trade Commission Act?
5. What are the major provisions of the Robinson–Patman Act?
6. Who administers the Food, Drug, and Cosmetic Act?
7. If you were a small manufacturer, would you be concerned with the Occupational Health and Safety Act? Explain.
8. Name at least one type of small business that could be affected by the following ''consumer protection laws,'' and tell how it could be affected.
   a. Cooling-off periods.
   b. Fair Packaging and Labeling Act.
   c. Federal Garnishment Act.
   d. Magnuson–Moss Warranty Act.
   e. Mail-order merchandise.
   f. Unordered merchandise.
9. What forms of management assistance does the Small Business Administration offer small firms?
10. How does the Small Business Administration assist small businesses in terms of government contracts?
11. What is an export trading company?

THE BUSINESS PLAN: GOVERNMENT CONTROL, ASSISTANCE, AND INTERNATIONAL MARKETING OPPORTUNITIES

—— Are you or any of your competition likely to be in violation of any of the following federal laws?

—— Sherman Antitrust Act—price fixing

_____ Clayton Act—price discrimination, exclusive and tying contracts, intercorporate stockholding, or interlocking directorates.

_____ Federal Trade Commission Act—unfair methods of competition.

_____ Robinson–Patman Act—price discounts not justified by costs, selling private brands at lower price, buyers given unequal advertising allowances.

_____ Food, Drug, and Cosmetic Act—prohibiting adulterated products, misbranding, false advertising.

If you are likely to violate any of the above you need to change your plans. If any of your competition is in violation, you should contact the Federal Trade Commission.

_____ Are you or any of your competition likely to be in violation of any of the following consumer protection laws?

_____ Cooling-off period—door-to-door selling exceeding $25 must allow three days for customer to change mind.

_____ Fair Packaging and Labeling Act—display true net weight or volume of contents.

_____ Federal Garnishment Law—garnishment not more than 25 percent of employee's weekly pay, not fire because of debt.

_____ Magnuson–Moss Warranty Act—full or limited warranty—if you plan to offer a warranty, you should read this chapter.

_____ Merchandise, mail order and unordered—if you plan to mail merchandise you should read this chapter.

_____ Would government assistance help you?

_____ Management assistance—SBA personnel, consultants, ACE program, SCORE program, or University Small Business Institutes.

_____ Would government-sponsored training programs help you?

_____ Are you providing a product or service that could be used by the federal government?

_____ Do you have problems with the government that the Office of Advocacy help with?

_____ Would any of the government publications help you?

If you answered yes to any of the above questions, you should contact the SBA at any of its field offices listed in this book.

_____ Will you produce a product that could be exported to other countries? Obtain a copy of *Exporter's Guide to Federal Resources for Small Business*.

_____ Could you use an export management company for exporting your product?

ENTREPRENEURIAL PROJECTS

Take the list of Small Business Administration publication to a small business, and find out which the owner–manager thinks would be of interest to most small businesses.

CASE A
The French Bakery

George and Linda McCoy opened their French Bakery one year ago in a small shopping center. They offer French bread and a wide assortment of French-style pastries. They have a small but loyal number of customers.

Their rent is rather high, and they have lost money from the very day they opened the business. They can't understand why they don't have more customers because everyone who tries their products seems to like them very much. They feel part of the problem might be the fact that their shop is not very visible from the street. Their only advertising has been in the restaurant section of the local newspaper.

They need immediate help and have asked you where they might get help. Their funds are so low that they cannot afford to pay someone for assistance.

Question

1. What type of help is available to George and Linda?

CASE B
Federal Trade Commission Expert

Recently, you graduated from college, and you have just accepted a job with the Federal Trade Commission. The first day on the job you had several letters on your desk. A description of each letter is presented as follows.

Letter A   A small businesswoman writes that she recently sent out bid requests and received three bids, each of which quoted exactly the same amount, $2416.52.

Letter B	A small businessman writes that he is having to pay almost twice the amount for a product paid by a large competitor who buys from the same firm.
Letter C	A small businessman writes that he was forced out of business by a competitor who sold his product at below what he could produce it for; then, after he went out of business, the competitor raised his price.
Letter D	An individual writes that she bought a product that, according to the label, was supposed to weigh 8 ounces, but it only weighed 7 ounces.
Letter E	An individual complains that he bought a vacuum cleaner from a door-to-door salesperson. He decided he didn't want it and asked for his money back. The company refused to refund his money.
Letter F	A worker writes that he was fired from his job because of a garnishment of his wages to pay a debt.
Letter G	A small businesswoman wants to know if her product warranty meets the full warranty or limited warranty requirements.
Letter H	A small businessman complains that he was sent equipment through the mail even though he had not ordered it. He does not want the equipment, and the company is sending him nasty letters threatening to ruin his credit.
Letter I	A small businessman writes that he has heard that the government provides assistance to small firms, and he wants to know whom to contact.
Letter J	A small manufacturer wants to sell his product overseas but does not know how.

Question

1. How would you answer each letter?

Notes

[1] United States Code, Title 15, Section 1-8.
[2] SBA Advocacy: *A Voice for Small Business* (Washington, D.C.: Small Business Administration, n.d.).
[3] Ibid.
[4] *The State of Small Business* (Washington, D.C.: U.S. Government Printing Office, March 1984), p. 292.

THE ENTREPRENEUR'S BUSINESS PLANNING GUIDE

The Entrepreneur's Business Planning Guide presents detailed information that the prospective or current small business owner will find beneficial to plan for the growth and prosperity of the firm. The Entrepreneur's Business Planning Guide includes the following parts.

1. The Business Plan
2. Small Business–Related Trade Associations
3. Private Sector Resources
4. Small Business Administration Field Offices
5. Small Business Administration Publications

THE BUSINESS PLAN

ENTREPRENEURIAL SELF-ASSESSMENT

The following list of personal characteristics is designed to help you determine if you have what it requires to be a successful entrepreneur. Analyze yourself carefully and honestly as you answer each question.

	Yes	No
Do I really have the desire to be my own boss rather than work for someone else?	___	___
Do I have the need to do things on my own?	___	___
Am I a self-starter?	___	___
Do I have sufficient management skills?	___	___
Do I have experience in the type of business I am interested in owning and operating?	___	___
Can I accept the responsibility of seeing things through to the end?	___	___
Am I a well-organized person?	___	___
Can I accept the risk of possible loss of investment if the venture fails?	___	___
Do I have the desire to lead and direct others?	___	___
Do I have the need to be in control of the business?	___	___
Can I make decisions quickly if I have to?	___	___
Do I have good health and the high energy level necessary to be an entrepreneur?	___	___
Do I have the financial resources, as well as future credit resources I need to begin?	___	___
Can I sustain my business through the early, formative years?	___	___
Can people (customers and employees) trust what I say?	___	___
Do I have the need to set and achieve difficult goals and move on to other challenges?	___	___
Do I have the desire to be innovative and creative?	___	___
Do I prefer having a plan of action (business plan) before I begin an activity?	___	___
Is my spouse supportive of my plan?	___	___
Do I manage my time efficiently?	___	___
Am I willing to work the long hours it takes to be an entrepreneur?	___	___

	Yes	No
Do I have the desire to stick with the business even in troubled times?	——	——
Am I willing to do all the tasks (glamorous and not so glamorous) that are necessary for the successful operation of the business?	——	——
Am I a hard worker?	——	——

There is no "passing" score. However, if most of your answers are "yes," you probably have what it takes to become an entrepreneur. If you answer "no" to about half the questions, you may need a partner to reinforce the areas where you are weak. If most of your answers are "no," then entrepreneurship is likely not for you.

THE BUSINESS PLAN FOR BUYING AN EXISTING BUSINESS

—— Why does the owner want to sell? If the business is really making an adequate profit, does the reason given sound reasonable?

Physical Facilities

—— Are the physical facilities adequate for the business you are planning?

—— Will you have to spend money to improve the building, equipment, machinery, inventory, and so on?

—— Do you have sufficient funds to achieve these improvements?

The Market

Composition

—— Have you studied maps, lists of customers, traffic patterns, and travel times to determine the actual market area of the firm?

—— Have you defined the natural and psychological barriers in defining the market area? Do you expect them to change?

—— What are the characteristics of the population in the market area—income, education, unemployment, ethnic composition, average family size, and size of age groups.

—— What has been the trend in population for the past 10 years and what trend do you expect in the future? Watch for factors that would indicate a decrease in population for your business.

—— Estimate the number of potential customers in the market area.

Competition

—— How many direct and indirect competitors are there in the area? Plot them on a map.

_____ How many competitors have gone out of business or entered the market area in the past 5 years? Try to find out the reasons for those that went out of business.

_____ Compare the volume of business of the competition with the business you are investigating. Try to find out reasons for any differences. Can you change them?

_____ What are the pricing policies and customer services of the competition? Do you plan to meet or exceed them?

_____ How much effort does the competition put into advertising, promotion, and sales effort? What do you plan to do in each of these areas relative to your competition?

_____ How attractive to customers are competitors?

_____ Is there any information about possible future competition in the market area?

Customer Attitudes

_____ Do the customers have a positive attitude toward the business? If not, can these attitudes be reversed with reasonable effort? A customer attitude survey will answer these questions.

Financial Condition

_____ What has been the trend of profit and cash flow over the past 10 years?

_____ Has profit and cash flow been consistent?

_____ What has been the trend in sales for the past 10 years?

_____ Are assets valued realistically in the balance sheet? Watch out for large amounts of intangible assets and/or unrealistic depreciation.

_____ Will you have sufficient funds to operate the business after the initial purchase? Consider purchases, current debt, salaries, living expenses, and so on.

_____ Are expenses listed in the income statement realistic? Can you reduce some?

_____ Can you obtain (at least 5 years) balance sheets, income statements, income tax returns, and cash flow statements? If the owner is not willing to provide any of these you should ask yourself why. You probably will need an accountant.

Legal Aspects

_____ Investigate the evidence of ownership.

_____ Is the business properly zoned?

_____ Are there any liens or debts that will be assumed by you?

_____ Does the business have the required licenses and permits and will they be available to you in the future?

_____ Are any patents, trademarks, copyrights, and trade names defensible in court? Make sure they are transferred to you.

_____ Are any exclusive dealerships or franchises transferrable to you? When do they expire and what are the terms of the agreement?

_____ Is there a union contract and what is in the agreement?

_____ Obtain copies of all leases.

_____ Is there any litigation pending?

____ Are there any existing commitments of any kind?

____ Is the seller willing to sign an agreement that prohibits future competition from the seller for a reasonable number of years?

Value

____ Compare the book, market, and replacement value of the assets of the business with the asking price. Use any favorable to you in the price negotiations.

____ Determine the degree of risk of the venture.

____ Multiply the expected yearly profit of the business times a factor that is representative of the risk involved to determine a fair price for you to pay. This factor is normally between four and eight times with a normal range of risk.

The material covered in this section is discussed in detail in Chapter 4 and in other chapters of the textbook.

THE BUSINESS PLAN FOR STARTING A NEW BUSINESS

The number in parentheses following the division headings denotes generally the chapter of the textbook where the information is discussed in detail. If a different number in parentheses follows any item under the heading, it is discussed in detail in the chapter that corresponds to that number.

Marketing Niche and Customers (Various chapters)

____ What will be your niche in the market? (16) Consider such factors as price, quality, exclusiveness, selection, convenience, and service.

____ Will your niche in the market be sufficient to support your business? (4)

____ Have you defined the marketing objective in measurable terms, such as percentage of market share or percentage of increases in sales? (16)

____ Has the target market for your business been correctly identified? (16)

____ How large is the target market? (16)

____ What is the growth potential of the target market? (16)

____ How will you attract, maintain, and increase your market share? (16)

____ Will you use the right combination of the "4 Ps" to reach your target market? (16)

____ Are there any environmental factors (legal, political, or social) that affect your market or product or service? (16)

____ Who are your competitors? Have you compared how your products and services meet consumer needs and how you compare with competition in terms of product–service mix, location, and so on? (16)

____ Who is your customer? (4, 16) Do any demographics correlate to your customer—age, income, education, sex, and so on?

____ What does your customer want in terms of your business? (16)

____ Do you need to perform a customer survey to determine who are your customers and what do they want (customer profile)? (16)

____ When you determine your customer profile, you must use this information to determine the image you want your business to always portray to your customers. (4)

Market Area and Location (Chapter 6)

____ Does any market area in your locale have more people that meet your customer profile? (4)

____ Have you considered the amount and quality of competition in the various marketing areas? (4)

____ Have you considered the demographics of the market and projections for changes in the market? (4)

____ Have you established the psychological and physical barriers of the market area? (4)

Potential of the Trading Area

How big is the trading area? _____ square miles.

What is the customer potential within 5 miles? _____ customers. Within 30 minutes travel time? _____ customers.

What is the density of population? _____ people per square mile.

Is there adequate transportation? _____ Yes. _____ No.

What is the income level of the trading area? $ _____ per capita.

Is the local employment pattern good? _____ percent people unemployed.

What is the general makeup of the community? _____ Residential. _____ Old. _____ Growing.

What are the trends in population and income? _____ Up. _____ Down.

Is new construction on the increase? _____ Yes. _____ No.

Are school enrollments up? _____ Yes. _____ No.

Are retail sales on the increase? _____ Yes. _____ No.

Have average business improvements been made recently? _____ Yes. _____ No.

Is there a high vacancy rate for business property? _____ Yes. _____ No.

Have shopping patterns changed drastically in recent years? _____ Yes. _____ No.

Are customers moving to or away from the potential location? _____ To. _____ From.

What are the present zoning restrictions? _____

Can Customers Get to the Location?

Is the area served by adequate public transportation? _____ Yes. _____ No.

How broad an area does the transportation service encompass? _____ square miles.

Is the area generally attractive to shoppers? _____ Yes. _____ No.

Can it be easily reached by automobile? _____ Yes. _____ No.

Is public parking adequate and relatively inexpensive? _____ Yes. _____ No.

How many spaces in the available, nearby parking space are taken up by all-day parkers? _____ Many. _____ Few.

If located on a highway, is the location easily accessible from the main traffic flow? _____ Yes. _____ No.

What are restrictions on signs and store identification _____

If on a limited-access road, how close is the nearest interchange? _____ miles.

Is the location accessible to delivery trucks? _____ Yes. _____ No.

Is the traffic speed too fast to encourage entrance by automobile? _____ Yes. _____ No.

Are the customers who drive past the location on their way to work or on shopping trips? _____ On way to work. _____ On shopping trip.

Will nearby stores help you? Are the other stores in the shopping center, neighborhood, or highway location of a nature that will attract customers who will also become patrons of your store? _____ Yes. _____ No.

What are the prospects for changes in traffic flow in the near future? _____ Slight. _____ Likely.

Will anticipated changes improve or damage the location? _____ Improve. _____ Damage.

Are zoning changes planned which would affect accessibility of the location? _____ Yes. _____ No.

Judging the Competition

Are there other businesses of the same kind, and, if so, how many, between the prospective location and the most highly populated area? _____ stores.

Is this spot the most convenient store location in the area? _____ Yes. _____ No.

How many other stores of the same kind are in this trading area? _____ stores.

How many of them will compete with you for customers? _____ stores.

Do they have better parking facilities? _____ Yes. _____ No.

Do they offer the same type of merchandise? _____ Yes. _____ No.

Do you consider them more aggressive or less aggressive than your own operation will be? _____ More. _____ Less.

What other competing stores are planned in the near future? _____
_____

Are other potential sites that are closer to the majority of customers likely to be developed in the near future? _____ Yes. _____ No.

Are your major competitors well-known, well-advertised stores? _____ Yes. _____ No.

Is there actually a need for another store of this kind in the area? _____ Yes. _____ No.

How well are the demands for this product being met? _____ Good. _____ Fair. _____ Poor.

If there are empty stores or vacant lots near the location, what is planned for them? A competitor store? _____ Yes. _____ No.

Can the Location Attract New Business?

Is the location in an attractive business district? _____ Yes. _____ No.

Are there numerous stores that will draw potential customers for you into the area? _____ Yes. _____ No.

Is the location near well-known and well-advertised stores? _____ Yes. _____ No.

Is this location the most attractive one in the area? _____ Yes. _____ No.

Is the location on the side of the street with the biggest customer traffic? _____ Yes. _____ No.

Is the potential location nearer to the general parking area than locations of competing firms? _____ Yes. _____ No.

Is the location in the center of or in the fringe of the shopping district? _____ Center. _____ Fringe.

Is it near common meeting places for people, such as public offices? _____ Yes. _____ No.

Are most of the people passing the store prospective customers? _____ Yes. _____ No.

Are the people who pass usually in a hurry or are they taking time to shop? _____ In a hurry. _____ Out shopping

Cost of the Location

What will your rent be? $ _____ per month.

Who will pay the utility costs? _____ You. _____ Others.

Who pays additional costs such as taxes, public services, and costs of improvements? _____ You. _____ Others.

What are the possibilities for eventual expansion? _____ Good. _____ Poor.

Are good employees available? _____ Yes. _____ No.

Will potential income justify your costs? _____ Yes. _____ No.

Promotional Strategy and Advertising (Chapter 19)

___ Have you identified the goals of your advertising program?

___ Have you developed a comprehensive profile of the customers in your target market?

___ Are the unique appeals of your business reflected in the store's image (high quality, special services, etc.)?

___ Do you know what you are trying to sell (product, idea, service, a company image)?

___ When you advertise, do you focus on your target market rather than advertise indiscriminately?

___ Have you considered how various media and promotional methods might be used for your firm?

___ Do you know which of your items can be successfuly advertised?

___ Do you know when it is profitable to use institutional advertising?

___ Do you know when product advertising is better?

___ Do you record sales of merchandise advertised on each ad?

___ Do you check store traffic?

___ Do you know which of the media can most effectively reach your target market?

___ Can you make use of direct mail?

___ Do you have a mailing list, and if so, is it up to date?

___ Do you use coupons in your ads?

_____ Do you concentrate promotional efforts on certain seasons?

_____ Are certain days of the week better than others?

_____ Do you use specialty advertising?

_____ Do you use trade journals and out-of-town newspapers for promotional ideas?

_____ Do you participate in activities of the chamber of commerce, better business bureau, other civic organizations?

Customer Behavior and Personal Selling (Chapter 18)

Guidelines for Customer Relations

_____ Do you make a constant effort to attract new customers?

_____ Do you maintain a continuous check on customer turnover, and do you know why they stop doing business with you?

_____ Are you aware of the reasons why customers shop at your store?

_____ Do you know what products or services your customers most prefer?

_____ Have you considered using a consumer questionnaire to aid you in determining customer needs?

_____ Are customer complaints handled promptly and satisfactorily?

_____ Are your prices in line with competitors'?

_____ Is the store's appearance neat and clean and is the layout attractive?

_____ Do you stress a special appeal, such as lower prices, better quality, wider selection, convenient hours, better service, or convenient location to cater to a specific market segment?

_____ Are you familiar with your customers' life-styles?

Personal Selling Guidelines

_____ Are sales representatives thoroughly familiar with the products they sell?

_____ Do sales representatives have a strong desire to sell?

_____ Are sales representatives well groomed and neat in appearance?

_____ Are sales representatives familiar with the customer and the needs of the customer?

_____ Are they enthusiastic, energetic, and imaginative, and work on their own initiative?

_____ Do they handle all nonselling tasks adequately?

_____ Do they understand the selling process?

_____ Do they demonstrate a sincere interest in the consumer?

_____ Do they work cooperatively with other personnel in the firm?

_____ Do they listen to customers?

Pricing
(Chapter 17)

_____ What is your niche in the market?

_____ What image do you want to portray to the public?

_____ What price image do you want to portray to the public?

_____ Will your price image be for discount prices, high quality, or exclusiveness?

_____ Can you charge a higher price because of services, selection, or convenience?

_____ Will your business be a retail establishment? If so will you use one or more of the following:

    _____ Markup on cost

        _____ Standard markup

        _____ Flexible markup

    _____ Markup as a percentage of selling price

    _____ Suggested retail price

    _____ Follow-the-market pricing

    _____ Competitive pricing

    _____ Pricing for clearance

_____ Will your business be manufacturing? If so,

    _____ Will your cost of goods manufactured plus selling and administrative expenses plus desired profit margin determine your selling price?

    _____ Will you provide retailers with a suggested retail price?

    _____ Will your markup be a percentage of selling price to determine your price to customers?

    _____ How will competition effect your price?

_____ Will your business be a service establishment?

    _____ Will you use actual labor time or will you use a standard flat rate manual (is one available)?

    _____ What will your standard labor rate per hour be?

    _____ How will you price parts to your customers? Will you use suggested list prices?

    _____ What is the customary price for your service in your market area?

    _____ How will competition effect your price?

_____ Will you use bidding in your business?

    _____ Will inflation be a problem in your bidding? How will you allow for it if it is a problem?

    _____ Will a bid, cost, variance system be of benefit to your operations? Remember it helps you become more efficient in your bidding and tells you how much you make on each job. If it will help you, use the form example in this chapter as a guide in creating your own form and system.

Source of Funds
(Chapter 5)

The funds to buy or start a business come from money you have, money for which you can sell part ownership of the business, or money you can borrow.

Fill in Figures 5-1 or 5-2 to help you determine how much money you need to start or buy the business. Try to think of other costs you will have that may not be on these two figures (such as purchase of land).

How much money do you have to contribute to the business? Do you plan on taking in a partner or selling stock in a corporation? How much money will this contribute to the business? Have you considered a Small Business Investment Corporation or venture capitalists?

Will you have to borrow additional funds? Take into consideration the amount, time, and interest rate to determine if you will have the ability to repay the borrowed funds.

Will you use a commercial bank for some of your funds? Talk to several banks about working capital loans and a line of credit. Try to obtain the best interest rate possible. Could you use a commercial bank to discount accounts receivable or installment contracts?

If you are buying an existing business do you have balance sheets, income statements, and cash flow statements to take with you when you talk about a loan? If you are starting a business, do you have a projected balance sheet, income statement, and cash flow statement?

Create a personal financial statement like the one presented in Figure 5-6. Take this with you when you talk to any financial institution.

Determine who your vendors will be and find out their credit terms.

Can you finance your accounts receivable by using factors? Will you use sales finance companies to purchase your installment sales contracts?

Have you considered insurance companies if you are financing shopping malls, apartments, or other large real estate ventures?

Are private investors a possible source of funds? Take into consideration that their interest rates may be higher than other sources of funds. Make sure you are not dealing with someone associated with crime or usury.

If you are turned down by commercial banks (one in small towns and two in large cities), you may be eligible for a Small Business Administration–guaranteed loan. Check the eligibility requirements and ineligible applications sections in this chapter to see if you are eligible for a loan.

If you plan on obtaining a SBA-guaranteed loan, read carefully the loan application information in this chapter.

From the amount of money you decided you need, subtract the amount of money you have and the amount of money you can obtain from selling part ownership in the business, to determine how much you will have to borrow. Can you obtain this amount from the financial sources listed in the chapter?

Form of Ownership (Chapter 2)

How many people will be needed to start and operate the business?
How much time will be required to run the business?
How much money will be required to establish the business?
Do I have all the knowledge necessary to establish and operate the business?

Do any of the owners need to be shielded from unlimited liability?

_____ I will be able to establish and operate the business by myself.

_____ There is no special reason to shield myself from unlimited liability.

_____ The business profit being taxed to me on my personal income tax is no special problem.

_____ Continuity of the business is no special problem to me or my family.

If you checked all the above, there is a strong possibility that the sole proprietorship form of ownership is suited to your needs.

_____ Two or more people (but not more than five) will be required to establish and operate the business.

_____ The partners are able to get along with each other and operate efficiently.

_____ Unlimited liability is no special problem for the general partners. If there is a problem with any other partners, they can meet the requirements to be limited partners.

_____ Each partner being taxed on partnership profits on their individual income tax does not create any special problems.

If you checked all of the above, there is a good possibility that the partnership form of ownership will fit your needs. If you decide on the partnership, you should consult an attorney to draw up the Articles of Copartnership. See page 47 for information that will be needed.

If the partnership is not for the continuous operation of a business, but is a joint ownership for a given limited purpose, a joint venture must be considered.

_____ A large number of people will be required to provide the capital to start and operate the business.

_____ There is a need for limited liability.

_____ There is a need for continuity of the business.

If you checked all of the above, the corporation form of ownership is a strong possibility for your needs. If you use the corporation form of ownership, you need to contact an attorney who will obtain a charter from your state. Page 52 lists information you will need to provide.

If you wish to retain all the profits in the corporation for growth, you may want to be taxed as a corporation. If you meet the requirements of a Subchapter S corporation, you may want to be taxed as a partnership. Consult a tax expert before you elect to become a Subchapter S corporation.

Franchising (Chapter 3)

_____ Is franchising a possibility for your business?

_____ If it is, is there a franchise operation that suits your type of business?

The Franchise

_____ Did your lawyer approve the franchise contract you are considering after he or she studied it paragraph by paragraph?

_____ Does the franchise call upon you to take any steps that are, according to your lawyer, unwise or illegal in your state, county, or city?

_____ Does the franchise give you an exclusive territory for the length of the franchise or can the franchisor sell a second or third franchise in your territory?

_____ Is the franchisor connected in any way with any other franchise company handling similar merchandise or services?

_____ If the answer to the last question is yes, what is your protection against this second franchisor organization?

_____ Under what circumstances can you terminate the franchise contract and at what cost to you, if you decide for any reason at all that you wish to cancel it?

_____ If you sell your franchise, will you be compensated for your goodwill, or will the goodwill you have built into the business be lost by you?

The Franchisor

_____ How many years has the firm offering you a franchise been in operation?

_____ Has it a reputation for honesty and fair dealing among the local firms holding its franchise?

_____ Has the franchisor shown you any certified figures indicating exact net profits of one or more going firms that you personally checked yourself with the franchisee?

_____ Will the firm assist you with

     _____ A management training program?

     _____ An employee training program?

     _____ A public relations program?

     _____ Capital?

     _____ Credit?

     _____ Merchandising ideas?

_____ Will the firm help you find a good location for your new business?

_____ Is the franchising firm adequately financed so that it can carry out its stated plan of financial assistance and expansion?

_____ Is the franchisor a one-person company or a corporation with an experienced management trained in depth (so that there would always be an experienced person at its head)?

_____ Exactly what can the franchisor do for you that you cannot do for yourself?

_____ Has the franchisor investigated you carefully enough to assure itself that you can successfully operate one of their franchises at a profit both to them and to you?

_____ Does your state have a law regulating the sale of franchises and has the franchisor complied with that law?

You—the Franchisee

_____ How much equity capital will you have to purchase the franchise and operate it until your income equals your expenses? Where are you going to get it?

_____ Are you prepared to give up some independence of action to secure the advantages offered by the franchise?

_____ Do *you* really believe you have the innate ability, training, and experience to work smoothly and profitably with the franchisor, your employees, and your customers?

_____ Are you ready to spend much or all of the remainder of your business life with this franchisor, offering his product or service to your public?

Your Market

_____ Have you made any study to determine whether the product or service that you propose to sell under franchise has a market in your territory at the prices you will have to charge?

_____ Will the population in the territory given you increase, remain static, or decrease over the next five years?

_____ Will the product or service you are considering be in greater demand, about the same, or less demand five years from now than today?

_____ What competition exists in your territory already for the product or service you contemplate selling?

    _____ Nonfranchise firms?

    _____ Franchise firms?

Physical Facilities (Chapter 7)

Facility Plans

_____ Shall a new facility be constructed or shall the firm be housed in an existing structure?

_____ Shall the facility be leased or purchased?

Store Exterior

____ Does the store's exterior design project the image the entrepreneur wishes?

____ Does the store's exterior blend with the other shops in the surrounding area?

____ Does the facility have an appropriate store sign (proper size, easy to read, clearly identifies the business, correct placement and positioning)?

____ Is there a display window that allows merchandise to be displayed effectively?

____ Are store entrances adequate (correct location, clearly marked, easy to open and close, nonthreatening—no obstacles or barriers to shoppers entering or leaving the store)?

Store Interior

____ Does the store's internal environment encourage shopping and project the desired image (flooring, walls and ceiling, lighting and fixtures, climate control, color scheme)?

____ Is maximum space allocated to selling activities, making sure that nonselling activities do not infringe on valuable selling space?

____ Does the layout plan demonstrate a true concern for the convenience of the customer?

____ Does the layout encourage self-selection of merchandise whenever possible so that customers have "hands-on" opportunities to examine the merchandise?

____ Is the layout plan appropriate for the type and size of store?

Management (Chapter 8)

Effective Communication

Small business managers must realize that effective communication does not occur in a vacuum. Instead, it is the result of conscious efforts by the manager to create an effective communication network. Some guides for creating an effective communication network are listed below.

As an owner–manager, do I

____ Encourage employees to express their ideas and opinions?

____ Listen with understanding to ideas, suggestions, and complaints?

____ Keep employees informed on all changes affecting work?

____ Keep informed on how employees are feeling and what they are thinking?

____ Encourage two-way communication?

____ Award recognition for good work and express appreciation for jobs well done?

____ Try to make communication messages accurate, complete, and clear?

____ Explain the "why" of decisions?

____ Strive to create a climate of trust and confidence by reporting facts honestly to employees?

Effective Leadership

Through their leadership role, owner–managers have a unique opportunity to create positive employee relationships. These guidelines offer some specific suggestions for becoming a more effective leader.

As a leader, do I

_____ Strive to improve my understanding of human behavior?

_____ Accept the fact that others do not always see things as I do?

_____ Respect differences of opinion and consider the possibility that I may not have the right answer when there are differences of opinion?

_____ Show employees that I am interested in them as individuals as well as employees?

_____ Treat employees as individuals; never deal with them impersonally?

_____ Give explanations insofar as possible for management actions?

_____ Provide information and guidance on matters affecting employees' security?

_____ Make reasonable efforts to keep jobs interesting?

_____ Encourage promotion from within?

_____ Express appreciation publicly for jobs well done?

_____ Offer criticism privately in the form of constructive suggestions for improvement?

_____ Keep my staff up to date on matters that affect them?

Management Organization Guidelines

_____ Do you have a written organization chart?

_____ Are all important activities adequately supervised?

_____ Does each person in the company know to whom he or she reports?

_____ Is authority and responsibility delegated to key members in the company?

_____ Does each person clearly understand his or her job?

_____ Are you giving thought to where the company will be five years from now?

Personnel (Chapter 9)

_____ Are job descriptions and job specifications based on job analysis?

_____ Are employees recruited from sources both within and outside the company?

_____ In the selection process, are the application blank, personal interview, and employment tests used to fullest advantage?

_____ Are new employees given a complete orientation to the job and the company?

_____ Are training opportunities made available to all employees according to their unique needs?

_____ Are a variety of training techniques used to provide for all needs of the company and employees?

_____ Are counseling services available both formally and informally?

_____ Are performance appraisals used to enhance employee performance and are they provided on a regular basis?

_____ Is the compensation plan perceived by all employees as being equitable?

_____ Are the laws that affect the small business understood and followed?

Computers (Chapter 10)

The following questions should be addressed to study all aspects of the microcomputer: applications system software, hardware, and the vendor. This step is necessary to determine the suitability of the microcomputer system to the unique needs of the small business owner.

Software Analysis

_____ Does the software package come with effective documentation?

_____ Is the operations manual written for the inexperienced computer operator?

_____ How easy is the software to use ("user friendly")?

_____ How easy is the software to change? (Can data that have already been processed be changed? Can the user change the program instructions, such as payroll withholdings rates, or does the vendor have to make the necessary changes?)

_____ Will the user be required to change any business practices? If so, will the changes provide the type of accounting and decision-making information the user needs?

_____ Does the software system have security features, such as passwords or user identification codes?

_____ Is it easy to increase the size of the files?

_____ Does the software have all the features that you must have for your particular business?

Hardware Analysis

_____ Does the microcomputer have sufficient storage capacity for the needs of the business now and in the future?

_____ Does the printer produce the desired quality of output?

_____ Is the speed of the printer satisfactory?

_____ Is the monitor adequate in terms of size, color, and so on?

_____ Is the processing speed of the microcomputer adequate?

_____ Can the microcomputer system be expanded when the need arises?

Vendor Analysis

_____ Is the vendor an authorized distributor for the microcomputer system under consideration by the small business owner?

_____ Do salespeople listen to customer needs and problems and genuinely try to offer a system that addresses those needs and problems?

_____ Does the vendor offer a financing plan?

_____ Does the vendor deliver the system, set it up, provide for on-site continuing education and training, and make a complete set of user manuals available to the small business owner?

_____ Is the vendor reliable and is the business stable?

_____ Does the vendor emphasize business needs first and price only after business needs have been analyzed?

_____ Does the vendor offer a complete demonstration of the system's capability?

_____ Does the vendor offer a service contract (for a fee) that extends beyond the basic warranty period?

_____ Will the vendor provide you with a list of names of customers who are using the system that the vendor installed to verify vendor claims of customer satisfaction?

_____ Will the vendor provide on-site service at your place of business?

Risk Management (Chapter 11)

Insurance

_____ Do you need fire insurance on the building, equipment, fixtures, or furniture?

_____ Is burglary, robbery, or embezzlement a possibility?

_____ Could you be liable for

    _____ Acts of you or your employees?

    _____ Conditions in the business?

    _____ Products you manufacture or sell?

_____ Would loss of earning power be serious to you?

_____ Will customers require surety insurance?

_____ Will the business own or lease any automobiles or trucks?

_____ Is there a need for life insurance to assure survival of the business if you or a key member dies? Be sure to consider term insurance.

If you answered yes to any of the above questions, you should contact at least one insurance agent. Consulting two would be better so you can compare prices. Be sure to weigh risk to cost.

Shoplifting

_____ Do you carry any merchandise that could be shoplifted?

If your answer is yes, then follow the practices to reduce shoplifting and ticket switching listed in this chapter.

Employee Theft

_____ Will you need to employ people in the business?

If the answer is yes, follow the steps listed in this chapter that reduce employee theft.

Burglary

_____ Will you keep money or anything of value in the business facilities?

If you answered yes, follow the list for burglary prevention in this chapter. Police in most towns will inspect your business and give advice for burglar protection.

Financial Recordkeeping and Cash Control (Chapter 12)

_____ Can you use the cash method of accounting?

Contact the IRS to see if you can use the cash method of accounting. If you are allowed to use it, it is probably the best method for you. If you must use the accrual method, you may need an accountant to help you.

_____ Can you use a manual bookkeeping system?

Unless you have a large number of accounting transactions each day, you should start out using a manual system so you have more intimate knowledge of your financial dealings and status. If you have a large number of transactions, you should obtain a computer of the size you need and inquire about software packages.

_____ What columns do you need in your sales journal?
_____ What columns do you need in your disbursement journal?

Construct your sales journal and disbursement journal using the examples in the chapter as guides.

_____ Will you need to offer types of credit that will require you to maintain accounts receivable cards? It is usually better to accept bank credit cards unless competition forces you to carry customer accounts.
_____ Who will keep your accounting books—you, employee, part-time employee, or public accountant? You will probably need an accountant to file your income tax return each year.
_____ Will you need a change fund?
_____ Can you avoid keeping currency overnight in the business? If not, how will you keep it safe?
_____ Will you need a sales and cash receipts form to be completed each business day?

Accounting Statements and Analysis (Chapter 13)

Set up a balance sheet that will represent the value of the business the first day of operations. Use the one presented in the chapter as a guide.

Estimate the budget for the first year's operations using the chapter example as a model.

Project the first year's cash flow statement, month by month.

Set up a combined monthly income and cash flow statement format. Be sure to key the columns in the sales and disbursement journals to the items in the statement. Duplicate this form and fill in the blanks from the totals in the journals each month.

Go to the library and find one or more financial ratio books. Decide which ratios would be important to you. At least once a year, calculate these ratios and compare them to the ratio standards for your type of business. Be sure you know what each ratio measures and how to use it.

Purchasing (Chapter 14)

_____ Do you or your designated representative have final authority and responsibility for purchasing?

_____ Do you have established policies governing the purchasing activity to ensure efficiency in all phases of the purchasing operation?

_____ Do you have clearly established purchasing procedures?

_____ Do you have reputable vendors from whom you make your purchases?

_____ Is competition among vendors encouraged, and are purchases competitive whenever possible?

_____ Do you strive to maintain good relations with vendors?

_____ Do you attempt to develop new and better sources of supply?

_____ Are materials and supplies being purchased at lowest prices consistent with quality requirements?

_____ Do purchase records clearly show previous prices and suppliers so that you do not have to estimate prices when reordering?

_____ Do you have a reliable but simplified method of pricing small orders to keep the cost of such orders lower than the value of the materials?

_____ Are purchases made against written requisitions to guard against overbuying or unnecessary buying?

_____ Are alternative sources of supply for critical materials maintained as a safeguard in emergency situations?

_____ Do you have a follow-up system on orders with vendors to ensure timely delivery?

_____ Have specifications of items you purchase been standardized where possible to obtain the advantages and economy of volume buying?

_____ Are delivery receipts processed promptly so that you do not lose cash discounts because of delays?

Inventory Control (Chapter 15)

_____ Will a Request for Items Not in Stock Form be of use to you?

_____ Will you have fewer than 20 items in inventory? You could use a visual control system, but a perpetual system would be better.

_____ Will you have more than 20 items in inventory and have more than 20 transactions a day? You can use a manual periodic or partial control system, but a perpetual system would be better.

_____ Will you have inventory in your business? A perpetual inventory system is best because it gives you greater control in your business.

_____ If you have fewer than 20 items and 20 transactions a day, a manual perpetual control system will meet your needs.

_____ Could you use bin tags, perpetual inventory cards, sales tickets, stub control, floor sample control, or punched card control?

_____ Will you have more than 20 items and 20 transactions a day? Your best system would be a computer-based inventory control system.

_____ Have you selected a software package for your computer-based inventory control system? If not, go to a software store and select one that best meets your needs.

_____ Do you have a large number of items with many transactions a day in a retail store? You should probably use a cash register with a bar code scanner tied in with your computer-based inventory control system.

_____ How often do you plan to perform a periodic inventory count? Will you count it all at once or a few items each week? Be sure to identify slow-moving items and shortages.

_____ Will there be a possibility of having slow-moving items in your inventory? How will you recognize them and how will you clear them out of inventory?

_____ Will shelf space analysis be of any importance to you? If it will be, follow the simple steps presented in this chapter.

Credit (Chapter 20)

_____ Will you need to offer credit to your customers?

_____ Will you offer 30-day accounts?

_____ Will you offer revolving charge accounts?

_____ Will you accept financial institution credit cards? This is usually preferable to offering your own 30-day or revolving charge credit.

_____ Which credit cards will you accept? You will have to pay a percentage of each charge. Check several financial institutions for the best percentage rate.

_____ Will you offer installment credit? Will you finance your own installment credit or will you use a financial institution? It is much less risky and easier to use financial institutions.

_____ Do you know how much interest and what period of time you will use in your customer credit? If not, ask your local banker for advice as to what is current practice in your community. If you are going to offer your own installment contracts be sure to refer to Chapter 21 for different types of installment contracts.

_____ What sources of credit information will you use? Credit applications and local credit bureaus are important sources of consumer credit information. Dun and Bradstreet can be a good source of business credit information.

_____ Do you know federal disclosure requirements provided for in the truth-in-lending law? If you are going to provide credit to your customers, you should read the truth-in-lending requirements in this chapter for both revolving charge accounts and installment contracts.

_____ Will you have to collect credit accounts? You should be aware of the correct stages of collection. You should also be aware of the provisions of the Fair Debt Collection Practices Act that is presented in this chapter.

Legal Considerations (Chapter 21)

_____ Will you use contracts in your business?

    _____ Will they involve competent parties?

    _____ Do both parties give consideration?

    _____ Will the contracts be for legal purpose?

    _____ Is there mutual assent? Is duress, fraud, mistake, or undue influence present?

    _____ Will they be in proper form (written if required)?

_____ Do you know what steps to take if there is breach of contract?

_____ What type of checks will you accept in your business? If you have employees that will accept checks, you should instruct them in proper identification and things which they should look for that could indicate a bad check.

_____ What will you do in case of a bad check—insufficient funds, no account, closed account, or forgery?

_____ Will you use installment contracts in your business? If so, will you use conditional sales, lease–purchase, or chattel mortgage contracts? Be sure to consider the ease of repossession.

_____ Will repossession be a part of your business? What does your state require for repossession?

_____ What licenses or permits does your city require for businesses of your type?

_____ What licenses or permits does your state require for your type of business?

_____ Will patents, copyrights, and/or trademarks be a part of your business? If they will be, check this chapter for details.

Government Control and Assistance and International Marketing (Chapter 22)

_____ Are you or any of your competition likely to be in violation of any of the following federal laws?

    _____ Sherman Antitrust Act—price fixing

    _____ Clayton Act—price discrimination, exclusive and tying contracts, intercorporate stockholding, or interlocking directorates

    _____ Federal Trade Commission Act—unfair methods of competition

    _____ Robinson–Patman Act—price discounts not justified by costs, selling private brands at lower price, buyers given unequal advertising allowances

_____ Food, Drug, and Cosmetic Act—prohibiting adulterated products, misbranding, false advertising

If you are likely to violate any of the above, you need to change your plans. If any of your competition is in violation, you should contact the Federal Trade Commission.

_____ Are you or any of your competition likely to be in violation of any of the following consumer protection laws?

_____ Cooling-off period—door-to-door selling exceeding $25 must allow three days for customer to change mind

_____ Fair packaging and Labeling Act—display true net weight or volume of contents

_____ Federal Garnishment Law—garnishment not more than 25 percent of employee's weekly pay, not fire because of debt

_____ Magnuson–Moss Warranty Act—full or limited warranty—if you plan to offer a warranty you should read this chapter

_____ Merchandise, mail order and unordered—if you plan to mail merchandise you should read this chapter

_____ Would government assistance help you?

_____ Management assistance—SBA personnel, consultants, ACE program, SCORE program, or University Small Business Institutes?

_____ Would government-sponsored training programs help you?

_____ Are you providing a product or service that could be used by the federal government?

_____ Do you have problems with the government that the Office of Advocacy could help with?

_____ Would any of the government publications help you?

If you answered yes to any of the above questions, you should contact the SBA at any of its field offices listed in this book.

_____ Will you produce a product that could be exported to other countries? Obtain a copy of *Exporter's Guide to Federal Resources for Small Business*.

_____ Could you use an export management company for exporting your product?

SMALL BUSINESS–RELATED TRADE ASSOCIATIONS

Selected Small Business-Related Trade Associations

American Bankers Association	Washington, D.C.	(202)663-5000
American Council of Life Insurance	Washington, D.C.	(202)624-2000
American Electronics Association	Santa Clara, Calif.	(408)987-4200
American Farm Bureau Federation	Park Ridge, Ill.	(312)399-5700
American Financial Services Association	Washington, D.C.	(202)289-0400
American Health Care Association	Washington, D.C.	(202)833-2050
American Hotel and Motel Association	New York, N.Y.	(212)265-4506
American Institute of Certified Public Accountants	New York, N.Y.	(212)575-6200
American Insurance Association	New York, N.Y.	(212)669-0400
American Retail Federation	Washington, D.C.	(202)783-7971
American Society of Association Executives	Washington, D.C.	(202)626-2723
American Society of Travel Agents	Washington, D.C.	(202)965-7520
American Trucking Association	Alexandria, Va.	(703)838-1800
Associated Builders and Contractors	Washington, D.C.	(202)637-8800
Associated General Contractors	Washington, D.C.	(202)393-2040
Association of American Publishers	New York, N.Y.	(212)689-8920
Association of Data Processing Service Organizations	Arlington, Va.	(703)522-5055
Automotive Service Industry Association	Chicago, Ill.	(312)836-1300
Computer & Business Equipment Manufacturers Association	Washington, D.C.	(202)737-8888
Electronics Industry Association	Washington, D.C.	(202)457-4900
Food Marketing Institute	Washington, D.C.	(202)452-8444
Grocery Manufacturers Association	Washington, D.C.	(202)337-9400
Health Industry Distributors Association	Washington, D.C.	(202)857-1166
Health Industry Manufacturers Association	Washington, D.C.	(202)452-8242
Independent Insurance Agents of America	New York, N.Y.	(212)285-4250

Independent Petroleum Association of America	Washington, D.C.	(202)857-4722
Information Industry Association	Washington, D.C.	(202)639-8260
International Communications Industries Association	Fairfax, Va.	(703)273-7200
National Association of Broadcasters	Washington, D.C.	(202)429-5300
National Association of Chain Drug Stores	Alexandria, Va.	(703)549-3001
National Association of Convenience Stores	Alexandria, Va.	(703)684-3600
National Association of Home Builders	Washington, D.C.	(202)822-0200
National Association of Realtors	Chicago, Ill.	(312)329-8200
National Association of Truck Stop Operators	Alexandria, Va.	(703)549-2100
National Association of Wholesaler Distributors	Washington, D.C.	(202)872-0885
National Automobile Dealers Association	McLean, Va.	(703)821-7000
National Business Incubation Association	Carlisle, Pa.	(717)249-4508
National Forest Products Association	Washington, D.C.	(202)463-2700
National Home Furnishings Association	Chicago, Ill.	(312)595-0200
National Industrial Transportation League	Washington, D.C.	(202)842-3870
National Lumber and Building Materials Dealers Association	Washington, D.C.	(202)547-2230
National Restaurant Association	Washington, D.C.	(202)638-6100
Printing Industries of America	Arlington, Va.	(703)841-8100
Travel Industry Association of America	Washington, D.C.	(202)293-1433

If the industry, organization, or association you are looking for is not listed, the American Society of Association Executives, located in Washington, D.C., may be able to help you. The telephone number of ASAE is (202)626-2723.

PRIVATE SECTOR RESOURCES

Small Business Organizations	(213)478-0437
American Entrepreneurs Association	
2311 Pontius Ave., Los Angeles, Calif. 90064	
Chamber of Commerce of the U.S.	(202)659-6000
1615 H St., N. W., Washington, D.C. 20062	
National Association of Development Companies (NADC)	(202)785-8484
1730 Rhode Island Ave., N.W., Suite 209, Washington, D.C. 20036	
National Association of Entrepreneurs	(303)440-3322
8735 Sheridan Blvd., Westminister, Colo. 80003	
National Association of Manufacturers (NAM)	(202)637-3046
1331 Pennsylvania Ave., N.W., Suite 1500, Washington, D.C. 20004	
National Association of Small Business Investment Companies (NASBIC)	(202)833-8230
1156 15th St., N.W., Suite 1101, Washington, D.C. 20005	
National Association of Women Business Owners (NAWBO)	(312)346-2330
600 South Federal St., Chicago, Ill. 60605	
National Federation of Independent Business	
150 West 20th Ave., San Mateo, Calif. 94403	(415)341-7441
600 Maryland Ave., S.W., Suite 700, Washington, D.C. 20024	(202)554-9000
National Small Business United (NSBU)	
69 Hickory Dr., Waltham, Mass. 02154	(617)890-9070
1155 15th St., N.W. Suite 710, Washington, D.C. 20005	(202)293-8830
• The Small Business Association of New England (SBANE)	(800)368-6803
	(617)890-9070
• The Smaller Manufacturers Council (SMC)	(412)391-1622
• Independent Business Association of Wisconsin (IBA)	(608)251-5546
• Council of Smaller Enterprise (COSE)	(216)621-3300
• Small Business Association of Michigan (SBAM)	(616)342-2400
• Texas Small Business United	(512)366-0099
• Independent Business Association of Illinois (IBAIL)	(312)692-7306
• Ohio Small Business Council (OSBC)	(614)228-4201
Selected Minority Small Business Organization	
National Association of Investment Companies (NAIC)	(202)347-8600
915 15th St., N.W., Suite 700, Washington, D.C. 20005	
National Association of Black and Minority Chambers of Commerce	(415)451-9231
654 13 St., Oakland, Calif. 94612-1241	

National Association of Black Women Entrepreneurs (313)341-7400
   Box 1375, Detroit, Mich. 48231
National Association of Minority Contractors (202)347-8259
   806 15th St., N.W., Suite 340, Washington, D.C. 20005
National Business League (NBL) (202)829-5900
   4324 Georgia Ave., N.W., Washington, D.C. 20011
U.S. Hispanic Chamber of Commerce (816)531-6363
   4900 Main St., Suite 700, Kansas City, Mo. 64112

SMALL BUSINESS ADMINISTRATION FIELD OFFICES

SBA FIELD OFFICES

Field offices are the first stop for getting assistance from the SBA. The first office listed under each region is a regional office, the others are district offices. Contact the office nearest you for more information about programs such as SCORE. If an office is unable to provide what you require it will be able to refer you to the nearest office that can.

Region I

Boston	60 Batterymarch Street, 10th Floor, Boston, Mass. 02110	(617)223-3204
Boston	10 Causeway St., 2nd Floor, Boston, Mass. 02222	(617)565-5590
Springfield	1550 Main Street, Room 212, Springfield, Mass. 01103	(413)785-0268
Augusta	40 Western Ave., Room 512, Augusta, Me. 04330	(207)622-8378
Concord	55 Pleasant St., Room 210, Concord, N.H. 03301	(603)225-1400
Hartford	330 Main St., 2nd Floor, Hartford, Conn. 06106	(203)240-4700
Montpelier	87 State St., Room 204, Montpelier, Vt. 05602	(802)828-4422
Providence	380 Westminster Mall, Providence, R.I. 02903	(401)528-4561

Region II

New York	26 Federal Plaza, Room 29-118, New York, N.Y. 10278	(212)264-7772
New York	26 Federal Plaza, Room 3100, New York, N.Y. 10278	(212)264-4355
Melville	35 Pinelawn Road, Room 102E, Melville, N.Y. 11747	(516)454-0750
Hato Rey	Federal Building, Chardon Ave., Hato Rey, P.R. 00919	(809)753-4002
St. Croix	P.O. Box 4010, Cristiensted, St. Croix, V.I. 00820	(809)778-5380
St. Thomas	Veterans Drive, Room 210, St. Thomas, V.I. 00801	(809)774-8530

Newark	60 Park Place, 4th Floor, Newark, N.J. 07102	(201)645-2434
Camden	2600 Mount Ephraim Ave., Camden, N.J. 08104	(609)757-5183
Syracuse	100 S. Clinton St., Room 1071, Syracuse, N.Y. 13260	(315)423-5383
Buffalo	111 W. Huron St., Room 1311, Buffalo, N.Y. 14202	(716)846-4301
Elmira	333 E. Water St., Elmira, N.Y. 14901	(607)734-8130
Albany	445 Broadway, Room 242, Albany, N.Y. 12207	(518)472-6300
Rochester	100 State St., Rochester, N.Y. 14614	(716)263-6700

Region III

Philadelphia	1 Bala Plaza, Suite 640, Bala-Cynwyd, Pa. 19004	(215)596-5889
Philadelphia	1 Bala Plaza, Suite 400, Bala-Cynwyd, Pa. 19004	(215)596-5822
Harrisburg	100 Chestnut St., Suite 309, Harrisburg, Pa. 17101	(717)782-3840
Wilkes-Barre	20 N. Pennsylvania Ave., Wilkes-Barre, Pa. 18701	(717)826-6497
Wilmington	844 King St., Room 5207, Wilmington, Dela. 19801	(302)573-6294
Clarksburg	168 W. Main St., Room 302, Clarksburg, W.V. 26301	(304)623-5631
Charleston	550 Eagan St., Charleston, W.V. 25301	(304)347-5220
Pittsburgh	960 Penn Ave., 5th Floor, Pittsburgh, Pa. 15222	(412)644-2780
Richmond	400 North 8th St., Room 3015, Richmond, Va. 23240	(804)771-2617
Baltimore	10 N. Calvert St., Baltimore, Md. 21202	(301)962-4392
Washington	1111 18th St., NW, 6th Floor, Washington, D.C. 20036	(202)634-4950

Region IV

Atlanta	1375 Peachtree St., N.E., Atlanta, Ga. 30367	(404)347-4999
Atlanta	1720 Peachtree Rd., N.W. Atlanta, Ga. 30309	(404)347-2441
Statesboro	52 N. Main St., Room 225, Statesboro, Ga. 30458	(912)489-8719
Birmingham	2121 8th Ave. North, Birmingham, Ala. 35203-2398	(205)731-1344
Charlotte	222 S. Church St., Suite 300, Charlotte, N.C. 28202	(704)371-6563

Columbia	1835 Assembly St., 3rd Floor, Columbia, S.C. 29201	(803)765-5376
Jackson	100 W. Capitol St., Suite 322, Jackson, Miss. 39269	(601)965-5338
Gulfport	One Hancock Plaza, Suite 1001, Gulfport, Miss. 39501	(601)836-4449
Jacksonville	400 W. Bay St., Room 261, Jacksonville, Fla. 32202	(904)791-3782
Louisville	600 Federal Place, Room 188, Louisville, Ky. 40201	(502)582-5971
Coral Gables	1320 S. Dixie Hwy., Suite 501, Coral Gables, Fla. 33134	(305)536-5521
Tampa	700 Twiggs St., Room 607, Tampa, Fla. 33602	(813)228-2594
W. Palm Beach	3500 45th St., Suite 6, West Palm Beach, Fla. 33407	(305)689-2223
Nashville	404 James Robertson Parkway, Nashville, Tenn. 37219	(615)736-5881

Region V

Chicago	230 S. Dearborn St., Chicago, Ill. 60604	(312)353-0359
Chicago	219 S. Dearborn St., Chicago, Ill. 60604-1593	(312)353-4528
Cleveland	1240 East 9th St., Room 317, Cleveland, Ohio 44199	(216)522-4180
Columbus	85 Marcoi Blvd., Columbus, Ohio 43215	(614)469-6860
Cincinnati	550 Main St., Room 5028, Cincinnati, Ohio 45202	(513)684-2814
Detroit	477 Michigan Ave., Room 515, Detroit, Mich. 48266	(313)226-6075
Marquette	300 S. Front St., Room 310, Marquette, Mich. 49855	(906)225-1108
Indianapolis	575 N. Pennsylvania St., Indianapolis, Ind. 46204	(317)269-7272
Madison	212 E. Washington Ave., Room 213, Madison, Wisc. 53703	(608)264-5261
Eau Claire	500 S. Barstow Commons, Room 37, Eau Claire, Wisc. 54701	(715)834-9012
Milwaukee	310 W. Wisconsin Ave., Room 400, Milwaukee, Wisc. 53203	(414)291-3941
Minneapolis	100 North 6th St., Suite 610, Minneapolis, Minn. 55403	(612)349-3550
Springfield	4-N, Old State Capital Plaza, Springfield, Ill. 62701	(217)492-4416

Region VI

Dallas	8625 King George Dr., Dallas, Tex. 75235-3391	(214)767-7643

Dallas	1100 Commerce St., Room 3C36, Dallas, Tex. 75242	(214)767-0605
El Paso	10737 Gateway West, Suite 320, El Paso, Tex 79935	(915)541-7586
Albuquerque	5000 Marble St., N.E., Albuquerque, N.M. 87100	(505)262-6171
Harlingen	222 E. Van Buren St., Room 500, Harlingen, Tex. 78401	(512)427-8533
Corpus Christi	400 Mann St., Suite 403, Corpus Christi, Tex. 78401	(512)888-3331
Houston	2525 Murworth, Room 112, Houston, Tex. 77054	(713)660-4401
Little Rock	320 W. Capitol Ave., Room 601, Little Rock, Ark. 72201	(501)378-5871
Lubbock	1611 Tenth St., Suite 200, Lubbock, Tex. 79401	(806)743-7462
New Orleans	1661 Canal St., Suite 2000, New Orleans, La. 70112	(504)589-6685
Oklahoma City	200 N.W. 5th St., Oklahoma City, Okla. 73102	(405)231-4301
San Antonio	727 E. Durango Blvd., San Antonio, Tex. 78206	(512)229-6250

Region VII

Kansas City	911 Walnut St., Kansas City, Mo. 64106	(816)374-5288
Kansas City	1103 Grand Ave., Kansas City, Mo. 64106	(816)374-3419
Springfield	309 N. Jefferson, Springfield, Mo. 65805	(417)864-7670
Cedar Rapids	373 Collins Rd. N.E., Cedar Rapids, Iowa 52402	(417)864-7670
Des Moines	210 Walnut St., Des Moines, Iowa 50309	(515)284-4422
Omaha	11145 Mill Valley Rd., Omaha, Nebr. 68154	(402)221-4691
St. Louis	815 Olive St., St. Louis, Mo. 63101	(314)425-6600
Wichita	110 E. Waterman St., Wichita, Kans. 67202	(316)269-6571

Region VII

Denver	999 18th St., Suite 701, Denver, Colo. 80202	(303)294-7002
Denver	721 19th St., Room 407, Denver, Colo. 80202	(303)844-2607
Casper	100 East B Street, Casper, Wyo. 82601	(307)261-5761
Fargo	657 2nd Ave. North, Fargo, N.D. 58102	(701)237-5771

Helena	301 S. Park, Room 528, Helena, Mont. 59626	(406)449-5381
Billings	2601 First Ave. North, Billings, Mont. 59101	(406)657-6047
Salt Lake City	125 S. State St., Salt Lake City, Utah 84138	(801)524-5800
Sioux Falls	101 S. Main Ave., Sioux Falls, S.D. 57102	(605)336-2980

Region IX

San Francisco	450 Golden Gate Ave., San Francisco, Calif. 94102	(415)556-7487
San Francisco	211 Main St., San Francisco, Calif. 94105	(415)974-0642
Fresno	2202 Monterey St., Room 108, Fresno, Calif. 93721	(209)487-5189
Sacramento	1011 10th St., Sacramento, Calif. 95814	(916)551-1445
Las Vegas	301 E. Stewart St., Las Vegas, Nev. 89125	(702)388-6611
Reno	50 S. Virginia St., Room 238, Reno, Nev. 89505	(702)784-5268
Honolulu	300 Ala Moana, Room 2213, Honolulu, Hawaii 96850	(808)541-2990
Agana	238 O'Hara St., Room 508, Agana, Guam 96910	(671)472-7277
Los Angeles	350 S. Figueroa St., Los Angeles, Calif. 90071	(213)894-2956
Santa Ana	2700 N. Main St., Room 400, Santa Ana, Calif. 92701	(714)836-2494
Phoenix	2005 N. Central Ave., 5th Floor, Phoenix, Ariz. 85004	(602)261-3732
Tucson	300 W. Congress St., Room 3V, Tucson, Ariz. 85701	(602)629-6715
San Diego	880 Front St., Room 4-S-29, San Diego, Calif. 92101	(619)293-5440

Region X

Seattle	2615 4th Ave., Room 440, Seattle, Wash. 98212	(206)442-5676
Seattle	915 Second Ave., Room 1792, Seattle, Wash. 98174	(206)442-5534
Anchorage	701 C St., Room 1968, Anchorage, Alas. 99513	(907)271-4022
Boise	1020 Main St., Suite 290, Boise, Idaho 83702	(208)334-1696
Portland	1220 S.W. Third Ave., Room 676, Portland, Ore. 97204	(503)221-2682
Spokane	W920 Riverside Ave., Room 651, Spokane, Wash. 99210	(509)456-3786

SMALL BUSINESS ADMINISTRATION PUBLICATIONS

SMALL BUSINESS ADMINISTRATION PUBLICATIONS

The Small Business Administration offers an extensive number of publications. these publications are available for a nominal sum, usually $1.00 or less, subject to price changes. The asterisk (∗) denotes the best-sellers of the SBA list.

Financial Management and Analysis

MA 1.001	*ABC's of Borrowing**
MA 1.002	*Profit Costing and Pricing for Manufacturers*
MA 1.004	*Basic Budgets for Profit Planning**
MA 1.006	*Understanding Cash Flow*
MA 1.009	*A Venture Capital Primer for Small Business*
MA 1.010	*Accounting Services for Small Service Firms*
MA 1.011	*Analyze Your Records to Reduce Costs*
MA 1.015	*Budgeting in a Small Business Firm*
MA 1.016	*Sound Cash Management and Borrowing*
MA 1.017	*Recordkeeping in a Small Business**
MA 1.019	*Breakeven Analysis: A Decision-Making Tool*
MA 4.013	*A Pricing Checklist for Small Retailers*
MA 4.014	*Pricing Your Products and Services Profitably*

General Management and Planning

MA 2.001	*Effective Business Communications*
MA 2.002	*Locating or Relocating Your Business*
MA 2.004	*Problems in Managing a Family-Owned Business*
MA 2.007	*Business Plan for Small Manufacturers*
MA 2.010	*Planning and Goal Setting for Small Business**
MA 2.011	*Fixing Production Mistakes*
MA 2.014	*Should You Lease or Buy Equipment*
MA 2.020	*Business Plan for Retailers*
MA 2.021	*Choosing a Retail Location*
MA 2.022	*Business Plan for Small Service Firms*
MA 2.025	*Going into Business**
MA 2.026	*Feasibility Checklist for Starting Your Own Business*
MA 2.027	*How to Get Started with a Small Business Computer*
MA 2.028	*The Business Plan for Home-Based Business*
MA 2.029	*How to Buy or Sell A Business*
MA 2.030	*Purchasing for Owners of Small Plants*
MA 2.031	*Buying for Retail Stores*

MA 2.032	*Small Business Decision Making*
MA 2.033	*Business Communication*
MA 2.035	*Developing a Strategic Business Plan*
MA 3.005	*Inventory Management*
MA 3.010	*Techniques for Problem Solving*
MA 5.009	*Techniques for Productivity Improvement*
MA 6.004	*Selecting the Legal Structure for Your Business*
MA 7.007	*Evaluating Franchise Opportunities*

Crime Prevention

MA 3.006	*Reducing Shoplifting Losses*
MA 5.005	*Curtailing Crime—Inside and Out*

Marketing

MA 4.002	*Creative Selling: The Competitive Edge**
MA 4.004	*Marketing for Small Business: An Overview**
MA 4.005	*Is the Independent Sales Agent for You?*
MA 4.012	*Marketing Checklist for Small Retailers*
MA 4.015	*Advertising Guidelines for Small Retail Firms*
MA 4.016	*Advertising Media Decisions*
MA 4.018	*Plan Your Advertising Budget*
MA 4.019	*Research Your Market**
MA 4.023	*Selling by Mail Order*
MA 7.003	*Market Overseas with U.S. Government*

Personnel Management

MA 5.001	*Checklist for Developing a Training Program*
MA 5.002	*Employees: How to Find and Pay Them*
MA 5.007	*Staffing Your Store*
MA 5.008	*Managing Employee Benefits*

New Products—Ideas—Inventions

MA 2.013	*Can You Make Money with Your Idea or Invention?*
MA 6.005	*Introduction to Patents*
SBIR-TI	*Proposal Preparation for Small Business Innovation Research*

GLOSSARY
OF KEY WORDS

Accounting equation The equation that assets equal liabilities plus capital, on which accounting is based.

Accounts receivable Funds that are owed the business by customers.

Accrual accounting The accounting method by which transactions are recorded when they happen regardless of when money is received or spent.

ACE (Active Corps of Executives) Individuals who are actively involved in work related to small business who provide consulting services to small businesses.

Acid test ratio Cash plus accounts receivable plus marketable securities divided by current liabilities.

Advertising Any type of sales presentation that is nonpersonal and is paid for by an identified sponsor.

Advertising copy The written and/or spoken words in an advertisement.

Advertising media The sources used to advertise the entrepreneur's products and services, such as radio, television, and newspaper.

Advertising medium A single source, such as radio, used by an entrepreneur to advertise the products or services of the firm.

AICDC principle The sales formula stressing attention, interest, conviction, desire, and close.

AIDCA principle The advertising principle that outlines the basic requirements of a good newspaper ad: attention, interest, desire, conviction, and action.

Analytical thinking The ability to analyze various problems and situations to deal with them effectively.

Application blank Written record of a job applicant's qualifications.

Application system software The computer software that instructs the computer to perform specific tasks, such as processing data.

Apprenticeship training Formal type of training that

combines formal classroom learning and on-the-job experience.

Assets Anything of value. Assets can be tangible or intangible.

Autocratic leader A leader who strives for maximum control with little delegation of authority and emphasis on one-way communication.

Automobile insurance Insurance that protects against loss related to an automobile.

B

Bad debts Debts of customers that are not collected.

Balance sheet An accounting statement in which all assets, liabilities, and capital are recorded.

Bank credit cards Credit cards issued by banks that allow customers to charge at a large number of businesses.

Bankruptcy Selling the assets of the business and dividing them among creditors and owners of the business when there are more liabilities than assets.

Bid, cost, variance system A system of calculating various costs and profit to arrive at a bid price. If the bid is successful, the actual costs are recorded and compared to the bid.

Bidding Quotation of a price by a business firm to another firm for goods or services.

Bill of lading A certificate issued to shippers by transportation companies to show that certain merchandise is in their possession.

Bin tags A system of inventory control in which tags are attached to bins and withdrawals, receipts, and balance of the items are recorded.

Bona fide occupational qualification A legitimate job requirement that permits employers to discriminate in hiring employees on the basis of religion, sex, or national origin.

Bond A certificate of debt by a corporation. Bonds are not ownership and have an interest rate, maturity date, and amount.

Brand A name, term, sign, symbol, or design or combination of them that is intended to identify the goods or services of one seller or group of sellers and to differentiate them from those of competitors.

Breach of contract The act of not honoring all terms of a contract.

Budget A projected income statement for a future period of time. It shows estimated sales and expenses.

Burglar alarm systems Devices that warn if a burglar is breaking into a business.

Burglary The breaking into a business and stealing of merchandise or money by a person or persons.

Business format franchising A fully integrated relationship with the franchisee and the newer type of franchising.

Business plan The plan of action for the firm that is a comprehensive, well-thought-out, written document that establishes the necessary guidelines for entrepreneurs.

C

Capital The part of the business that represents ownership. Assets minus liabilities equal capital.

Capitalization Multiplying the yearly profit of the business by some number to estimate the value of a business.

Cash accounting The accounting method in which transactions are recorded only when money is received or expended.

Cash discount Incentive offered the business owner for prompt payment of merchandise.

Cash flow statement An accounting statement that shows receipts and expenditures of cash.

Change fund The money that is retained from the previous day to make change for money transactions.

Channel of distribution The route that goods and services follow from the manufacturer of the goods or provider of the services to the ultimate consumer of the product or service.

Charge account credit Goods or services are bought on credit and are paid for at a later time. This does not include installment sales contracts.

Chattel mortgage A mortgage obtained when something is sold on credit and a lien against the item is retained against whatever was sold. Title passes at the time of sale.

Check A negotiable instrument that instructs a third party (usually a financial institution) to pay a second party a specific sum of money that the first person has on deposit.

Civil Rights Act of 1964 The law that prohibits discrimination in employment on the basis of race, color, religion, sex, or national origin. Religion, sex, or national origin may be a basis for discrimination if any can be shown to be a legitimate job requirement. The Act of 1964 pertained to firms with 25 or more employees, but this number was reduced to 15 in 1972.

Clayton Act   A law providing for social control of business that prohibits price discrimination, tying contracts, intercorporate stockholding lessening competition, and interlocking directorates in competing corporations.

Cold canvassing   The cold-call technique that is used in telephone sales or door-to-door sales. The salesperson attempts to create interest in a product or service while also developing a list of prospects.

Collection   Collecting money that is owed by customers.

Combination franchising   A franchising plan whereby two franchises share the same location. In some instances, they are managed by the same manager. The purpose of this plan is to reduce operating costs.

Commercial bank   A bank that offers checking accounts and savings accounts, loans money, and provides other business services. Savings and loan institutions are not included.

Committee on Economic Development   A body of people that has defined a business as small if management is independent, capital is supplied, and ownership is held by an individual or small group; if the area of operation is mainly local; and if the business is small when compared to the largest units in its field.

Common stock   A certificate of ownership in a corporation, which usually does not have a fixed rate of dividend, is paid after preferred stock, and entitles the owner to a vote at shareholders' meetings.

Communications ability   The skill to convey written and oral information effectively so that understanding is created between sender and receiver.

Community shopping center   Consists of many shops in a community location. The shops offer shopping goods and serve a population of from 40,000 to 150,000.

Competitive pricing   A pricing strategy by which a business tries to maintain lower prices than other business in the market.

Composition of population   The distribution of various factors in the population of people in a given market, such as age, income, race, education, and so forth.

Computer hardware   The computer and peripheral equipment.

Computer program   The detailed set of instructions that outlines the specific sequence of operations the computer is to perform.

Computer service center   A business that processes business data for other firms for a fee.

Computer software   The languages, programs, and instructions used to communicate with the computer and direct its operation.

Conceptual ability   The skill to understand the overall organization of the small business and how each unit fits together as a unified whole and contributes to the success of the firm.

Conditional sales contract   An installment sales contract in which title to the merchandise does not pass until the item is paid for.

Consignment purchasing   A stockless purchasing system whereby the vendor's merchandise is displayed in the small business and the vendor is responsible for the merchandise display and ownership stays with the vendor until the goods are used or sold.

Consumer credit   Money owed by ultimate consumers

Contract   A legal agreement between two or more parties.

Control   A management function. Control is the process of determining if current operations conform to established plans.

Convenience goods   Goods that the customer needs immediately and that are usually purchased from the most convenient source.

Conversion franchising   A method that allows an already-established small business owner to become associated with a franchisor to gain the advantage of name recognition and services of the franchisor.

Cooling-off period   A cooling-off period required by law in door-to-door selling when the purchase exceeds $25.

Cooperative advertising   An advertising plan by which the manufacturer shares in the cost of the advertising with the retailer, such as on a 50:50 basis.

Copyright   The exclusive right to publish a book, composition, picture, and so on granted by the government for the life of the author plus 50 years.

Corporation A form of business ownership that must be chartered by 1 of the 50 states. It has three or more owners and issues stock certificates as evidence of ownership.

Corporation tax A federal income tax levied on corporation profit.

Cost of goods manufactured A section of an income statement of manufacturers that shows direct labor, raw materials, and factory overhead.

Cost of goods sold A section of an income statement of retailers and wholesalers that shows how much the merchandise they sold during the period cost them.

Counseling Direct, interpersonal communication between owner and employees, which may be either formal counseling or informal counseling.

Creative salesperson A type of salesperson who attempts to create a need for a service or merchandise in the mind of a customer.

Creative thinking The ability of the entrepreneur to adapt his or her actions to the needs of the business in various situations.

Credit Money owed; also, when liabilities, capital, or income is increased or when assets or expenses are decreased.

Credit card Plastic card that allows the customer to charge goods or services.

Cumulative quantity discount Quantity discounts that are granted if purchase exceed a specified quantity or dollar amount over a predetermined time period, such as a year.

Current ratio Current assets divided by current liabilities.

Customer attitude survey A questionnaire survey of customers to determine what they think about the business relative to various factors.

Customer attitudes What the customers of a business think about the business concerning factors such as service, quality, price, and so on.

D

Database The computer program that permits the user to collect and store business information in a central file (floppy disk or hard disk).

Debit Condition when assets are increased or expenses are incurred or when liabilities, capital, or income is decreased.

Debt capital Money that is put into a business that comes from borrowing.

Debt to net worth ratio Total liabilities divided by net worth less intangible assets.

Decision-making ability The skill to select a satisfactory course of action from among alternatives to guide the company in attaining objectives.

Disbursement journal A basic accounting book in which all expenditures are recorded.

Discount prices A smaller than usual markup resulting in low prices.

Discretionary buying power The part of the income that is not required for the purchase of the basic necessities of life.

Disposable personal income The amount of money consumers have available to spend.

Dissolution Selling the assets of a business and dividing them among creditors and owners of the business. There are more assets than liabilities.

Dividend A payment of profits paid to stockholders in a corporation.

Domestic international sales corporation A corporation that can be set up that allows manufacturers to pay no tax on an export income up to $100,000 and defers taxes on 50 percent of the income above that amount.

Drive A person's motivation toward a task.

Duress Forcing a person to act against his or her will.

E

Economic order quantity Often referred to as EOQ, it is a technique for determining the right quantity to order that minimizes the total variable costs in buying and maintaining merchandise in inventory.

Emotional buying motive A purchase decision that involves little thought or deliberation.

Empathy The ability to put yourself in someone else's position and know how that person feels and perceives the situation.

Employee theft Theft of merchandise or money by employees.

Entrepreneur One who organizes a business undertaking, assuming risks, for the sake of profit.

Equal Employment Opportunity Act of 1972 An amendment to the Civil Rights Act of 1964 that was designed to prohibit discrimination in employment on the basis of race, color, religion, sex, or national origin in firms with 15 or more employees.

Equipment manufacturers and distributors Firms that sell equipment to businesses. They may make equipment or buy it for resale.

Equity capital Money invested in a business by the owners.

Exclusive agency contract An agreement that gives the distributor exclusive rights to sell goods or services within a designated territory.

Exclusive distributorship Agreement whereby a manufacturer gives the distributor exclusive rights to sell goods or services within a designated area.

Expenses Money that is spent.

Exporter A person or company that sells products in other nations than the one in which it is produced.

Export management company An independent firm that serves as the exclusive sales department for noncompeting producers.

Export Trading Company Act Law that permits companies to join with banks, ocean shipping companies, advertising agencies, distributors, and others to complete the distribution process necessary to handle a product from a U.S. factory to a foreign consumer while being exempt from antitrust prosecution.

F

Factors Firms that buy or discount accounts receivable.

Fair Labor Standards Act of 1938 Law that regulates the number of hours worked and provides for overtime pay in excess of 40 hours.

Fair Packing and Labeling Act Law that requires manufacturers to display the net weight or volume of the contents.

Fashion centers More suited for high-income areas, these centers consist of apparel shops, boutiques, and handcraft shops that sell high-price and high-quality merchandise.

Feasibility study A survey of the current information requirements of a firm, the areas of the company that would benefit the most from a computerized system, an evaluation of the computer systems that would meet the firm's requirements, the anticipated cost savings of the system, and a recommendation of the preferred system; also, a systematic study of the profit potential for a new business that has not been established.

Federal Garnishment Law A consumer protection law that prohibits more than 25 percent of an employee's disposable earnings from being garnishee and prohibits an employee's being fired for only one garnishment.

Federal Trade Commission Act A federal law that established the Federal Trade Commission and prohibited unfair competition.

Financial condition The financial health of a business; the total monetary strength of the business.

Financial control Using financial records to record and analyze money transactions.

Fire insurance Insurance that insures loss due to fire and other damage.

Flexible markup Occurs when various percentages of markup are added to different types of merchandise.

Floor sample control An inventory control system used when large items are in stock in a warehouse area. Pads of numbers are pasted on the item, and each time one is sold, a number is removed, thereby showing how many are left in stock.

F.O.B. buyer Title to goods passes when the merchandise is delivered to the buyer's place of business.

F.O.B. seller Title to goods passes as soon as the seller delivers the merchandise to the shipper.

Follow-the-market pricing A pricing strategy in which the business sets a price that is comparable to the going price charged by other firms.

Food, Drug, and Cosmetic Act A federal law that prohibits adulterated products, misbranding, and false advertising.

Franchise disclosure statement Detailed information about the franchise that the franchisor makes available to the franchisees, such as profit and franchise renewal.

Franchisee A licensed, affiliated dealer of the franchisor.

Franchising A continuing relationship in which the franchisor provides a licensed privilege to do business plus assistance in organizing, training, merchandising, and management in return for a consideration from the franchisee.

Franchisor The owner of a product, service, or method.

Fraud Intentional misrepresentation of fact.

Free-flow layout   A store layout, which may be circular, octagonal, or U-shaped and has no uniform pattern of arrangement.

Free-rein leader   A leader who emphasizes minimal contact with employees.

Fringe benefits   Indirect payments to employees.

G

General partner   A partner in a partnership form of ownership who has unlimited liability. There must be at least one in a partnership.

Grid layout   Rectangular store arrangement that features a main aisle and secondary aisles that are located at right angles to the main aisle.

H

Hedging   Shifting risk to others by buying and selling in the futures market.

Human relations ability   The ability to work effectively with others.

I

Immigration Reform and Control Act of 1986   The law that granted amnesty to many illegal aliens living in the United States. This law requires all employees who are hired after November 6, 1986, to show proof of identity and eligibility to work.

Impulse goods   ''Spur-of-the moment'' purchases.

Impulse purchases   Purchases made without pre-planning.

Income   Money that is received by the business.

Income statement   An accounting statement that records income less expenses for a specific period of time.

Input data   The data fed into the computer.

Inside sales representative   The sales function performed in the firm where consumers come to the place of business to make a purchase.

Installment credit   Goods and services are bought and paid for on a regular installment basis. This does not include charge account credit.

Installment sales contract   A contract in which a customer promises to pay for merchandise by making installment payments over a period of time.

Institutional advertising   Advertising aimed at providing the general public with information about the company.

Insurance company   A business that insures all sorts of risks in exchange for payment of premiums.

Interest   The amount of money that is charged for debt.

Internal organization environment   The climate of the firm, including the social, physical, and economic factors.

International Franchise Association   A nonprofit trade association that represents franchising companies in the United States and around the world.

Inventory   Goods carried on hand by a firm.

Inventory turnover   Cost of goods sold divided by beginning inventory plus ending inventory divided by two.

J

Job analysis   Systematic investigation to collect all pertinent information about each task.

Job description   Written record that defines the major and minor duties of each task.

Job evaluation   The systematic and orderly process for determining the correct rate of pay for each job in relation to other jobs.

Job specification   The qualities, knowledges, skills, and abilities an individual needs to perform a task satisfactorily.

Joint venture   A form of a partnership that is created for a specific purpose and not for a regular day-to-day business; a foreign manufacturer is authorized to produce the products of the domestic company, but the domestic company also has an equity interest in the foreign company.

Jury of executive opinion   The opinions held by one person or several persons. These opinions are based on the intuition of the small business owner. The jury of executive opinion forms the basis for unscientific decision making.

L

Layout   The arrangement of selling and nonselling departments, aisles, fixtures, displays, and equipment in the proper relationship to each other and to the fixed elements of the building structure.

Leading   A management function. Leading is the process of influencing employees toward the accomplishment of company goals.

Lead time   The time needed for delivery of materials so that they will be available when needed in the business.

Leasing employees   A situation in which employees are leased to and work for a small business but the employees officially work for the leasing company that pays their salary and fringe benefits and handles all employee-related paperwork for the lessee firm.

Lease–purchase contract   An installment sales contract in which the buyer or renter pays rent until an amount that equals the sale price is received. Title passes when the entire purchase price is paid.

Legal aspects   Matters of a business that relate to the laws of various governments.

Letter of credit   Letter issued by a financial institution requesting that money or credit be given a business or person and promising to pay up to a specific amount if defaulted.

Liabilities   All debt.

Liability insurance   Insurance that protects against being liable owing to acts of employees, conditions in the business, or products they sell or manufacture.

License   A certificate issued by a government agency allowing a business to do certain things.

Licensing   An arrangement whereby a foreign manufacturer is authorized to produce the products of a domestic company.

Life insurance   Insurance that pays for loss of life.

Limited partner   A partner in the partnership form of business ownership. This partner has liability only to the extent of the person's investment.

Line of credit   A commercial bank establishes a line of credit by agreeing to make loans automatically up to a certain established limit.

Long-term loan   A loan that has duration in excess of one year.

Loss of earning power   Insurance that protects against some event that causes the loss of ability to earn money.

M

Magnuson–Moss Warranty Act   A federal law that regulates warranties.

Manager   One who supervises the work activities of employees to see to it that they accomplish their specific tasks.

Manufacturer's brand   A national brand advertised and sold in all or nearly all sections of the nation.

Market barriers   Psychological or physical barriers that define a market area. They limit customer access to the business.

Market segmentation   The process of dividing a heterogeneous market of consumers into classes on the basis of similarity of characteristics, such as age or income.

Marketing   The performance of business activities that direct the flow of goods and services from the producer to the consumer or user to satisfy their specific needs.

Marketing concept   The objectives of the business are to identify the needs of customers and then use all resources of the firm to offer the goods and services that will satisfy consumer needs while earning a profit for the firm.

Marketing functions   The activities involved in the marketing process—buying and selling; transportation and storage; risk taking, standardization and grading, and financing; and market information.

Marketing mix   The strategy of the firm, which involves choosing the right mix of the four variables of products and services, promotional strategy, physical distribution, and pricing.

Marketing research   The process of collecting, recording, and analyzing data pertaining to the target market to which the firm caters.

Marketing strategy   Consists of the two elements of the market segment (target market) and marketing mix.

Markup   The percentage added to the cost or other basis to arrive at a selling price.

Markup on cost   A percentage of cost added to cost to produce a selling price.

Markup on selling price   A percentage of a suggested selling price that determines the price that is charged the retailer.

Master franchising   Sometimes referred to as subfranchising, it is the major method of entry into a foreign market. The franchisor divides a market into large areas (contiguous countries or regions) and each area is assigned to a master franchisee who in turn subfranchises in the local area and provides support to local franchisees.

Mental ability   The overall intelligence (IQ), creative thinking ability, and analytical thinking ability of the entrepreneur.

Merchandising service establishment   Firms such as barber shops, beauty shops, and motels whose focus is on customer convenience and attractive physical appearance of the facility.

Microcomputer The smallest computers. They are either IBM compatible or noncompatible. Well suited to the small business.

Microprocessor An integrated circuit called a "computer on a chip" that contains the central processing unit of the microprocessor.

Minimall A shopping center designed for customer convenience with major tenants being a junior department store; food, drug, or variety store; and a number of specialty and service outlets.

Modem (acroynm for MOdulator/DEModulator) A modem converts a computer digital signal to analog signals that are carried over telephone lines.

Morale The mental attitude of individuals and work groups toward their work environment.

Mortgage credit Credit on goods or real property that is secured by a lien against the goods or real property.

Motivation The inner drive that ignites behavioral actions to satisfy needs.

N

Neighborhood shopping center Ordinarily serves a population of 2500 to 40,000 within a driving time of 6 to 10 minutes. Firms in the center offer convenience goods and personal services; a supermarket or drugstore or both are the anchor stores.

Noncumulative quantity discount Quantity discounts that are granted if a large volume of merchandise is purchased in a single order.

O

Objective and task method A method of advertising budgeting that relates the advertising appropriation to the marketing task to be accomplished and to the volume of sales so that profits and reserves will not be drained.

Occupational Safety and Health Act A federal law passed to reduce deaths and injuries related to work.

Office of Advocacy A division of the SBA that helps small businesses that have problems with the federal government.

100 percent location The optimum location for a retail store.

On-the-job training Training given on the job. It is the most often used technique for training in the small business.

Operating system software The computer software that controls the overall operations of the computer components and is called "OS."

Order getter A salesperson who attempts to recognize potential customers and to arouse their need for merchandise or services by providing them with necessary information.

Order taker The type of personal seller whose main activity is taking the orders of customers who have made up their mind with regard to a specific purchase.

Organization chart Graphical representation of the authority and responsibility relationships among personnel as well as the formal channels of communication in the company.

Organizing A management function. Organizing is the process of coordinating the human, financial, and physical resources of the firm so that they follow the course needed to reach stated objectives outlined in the planning process.

Outside sales representative The sales function performed outside the firm where the sales representative call on customers, as in direct sales.

P

Partial control system A system of inventory control in which the business maintains perpetual records on part of its inventory on a rotating basis.

Participative leader The leader who shares decision making with employees.

Partnership A form of business ownership in which there are two or more partners (owners) of the business. It is not a corporation that issues stock.

Par value The stated value of stock on the face of the stock certificate. It usually has no relationship to market value.

Patent The exclusive right to produce a product for 17 years.

Patronage motives The factors that influence customers to return repeatedly to the same store to make their purchases.

Percentage of sales method The method used in preparing an advertising budget that maintains an ad budget in a consistent relationship to sales volume.

Performance appraisal The evaluation of each employee's job performance at periodic intervals.

Periodic inventory system A system of inventory control in which purchases and inventory levels are compared at reorder time.

Perpetual inventory system A system of recording inventory additions and reductions so that the balance of inventory on hand is known at all times.

Personal selling The process of personally informing customers about a product or service through personal communication for the purpose of making a sale.

Physical facilities The plant or building of the business.

Physical facility design The type of image that the business seeks to project to consumers by means of both exterior and interior features of the physical facility.

Physical facility planning The exterior and interior design of the physical facility, including the layout of the store's interior.

Physical inventory count Inventory in stock is counted and compared to inventory records.

Planning A management function. Planning is the process of setting objectives and choosing the course of action that will enable the entrepreneur to attain the objectives of the small business.

Point-of-purchase displays Displays located throughout the store, usually prepared by the manufacturers or distributors of products, and made available to small firm owners.

Preferred stock A certificate of ownership in a corporation that usually has a fixed rate of dividend, must be paid before common stock, and does not give its owner a vote.

Price image How the customer perceives the business relative to the degree of price, such as a discount price image.

Prices The amount of money charged for merchandise or service.

Pricing for clearance Marking down the price of merchandise to get it out of stock.

Primary buying motive Awareness of the existence of the need to purchase a certain kind or general class of product or service.

Primary needs Basic needs such as physiological, safety, and security needs.

Private brand A distributor's brand or dealer's brand owned by an intermediary and advertised and sold in a more limited geographical area, such as a region or a state.

Private investor An individual who loans money or one who invests in business ventures.

Process layout The type of layout in plants where many different kinds of products are produced or are produced for customer specifications.

Processing-type service establishment Businesses that have processing operations separate from where customer orders are taken, such as print shops.

Product and trade name franchise The traditional type of franchising common among auto and truck dealers, gasoline service stations, and earth-moving equipment dealers as well as the soft drink industry.

Product breadth The number of product lines handled by a firm.

Product depth The models, sizes, styles, or colors offered within each product line.

Product layout The type of plant layout used for mass production of goods.

Product liability Insurance can be purchased to protect retailers who sell or manufacturers who make products that are defective and cause damages.

Product life cycle The four stages of a product: introduction, growth, maturity, and decline.

Product line The group of products that are reasonably similar, such as furniture or hardware.

Product mix All the products that the small business owner offers for sale.

Progressive discipline A disciplinary approach that applies a minimum of discipline to a first offense but that increases the degree of discipline for subsequent violations of rules or policies.

Promotional advertising Advertising to inform and remind the target market of the firm about its goods and services.

Promotional discount A discount offered by means of a supplier paying for part of the advertising done by the buyer that features the supplier's products.

Promotional strategy The means that small business owners use to communicate information about the firm and its products and services to potential customers with the objective of influencing customers to purchase products or services that will satisfy their wants and needs.

Publicity A news item about a company reported by the media because the information has some apparent news value.

Punched card control An inventory control system in which punched cards are attached to merchandise and removed at the time of sale. They are then processed by equipment and recorded in perpetual inventory records.

Purchase order The legal order that requests the vendor to supply the materials or services to the firm.

Purchasing The process of buying the right quality of materials, products, and supplies in the appropriate quantity at the best price and at the proper time from the right vendor.

Purchasing agent The person who has authority for purchasing in the small business. The purchasing agent may be the owner or some employee designated by the owner. May be referred to as the purchasing manager.

Purchasing manager The person who has authority for purchasing in the small business. The purchasing manager may be the owner or someone designated by the owner. May be referred to as the purchasing agent.

Q

Quantity discount Discount made available on larger purchases.

R

Rate of return The amount of profit generated by a business relative to the amount of money invested.

Rate of return on assets Profit divided by total assets less intangible assets.

Ratio A calculation that compares one or more categories of income or expenses to other categories of income or expenses.

Rational buying motives A buying decision that involves a considerable amount of conscious thought and deliberation before a purchase is made.

Regional shopping center Caters to a trading area that has 150,000 people or more and that may extend 10 to 15 miles or more in all directions. One or more full-line department stores serve as the anchor stores, and the variety of stores offers a wide range of shopping goods, apparel, furniture, general merchandise, and home furnishings. May have as many as 200 small specialty shops.

Regulatory Flexibility Act of 1980 The purpose of this act is to require federal agencies to revise or drop excessive rules and regulations that are a burden to the small business.

Retail affinity Stores located near each other because they sell similar or complementary merchandise.

Retail credit bureaus An agency that is owned by participating merchants that keep and report credit records on customers.

Revolving charge accounts Goods or services are bought and paid for based on 30-day periods. Not all the money owed must be paid for at the end of the period, but some minimum amount is due.

Risk Exposure to injury or loss.

Robinson–Patman Act A law providing for social control of business that closed the weaknesses of the price discrimination section of the Clayton Act.

S

Safety factor The volume decided upon to be kept in inventory to meet the contingencies in the company.

Sales and cash receipts record A record that is kept each day to compare money received and what is on hand in the cash register.

Sales finance company Financial firms that purchase installment sales contracts from other businesses.

Sales journal A basic accounting book in which all sales are recorded.

Sales promotion The marketing activities other than personal selling or advertising and publicity that stimulate consumer purchasing and dealer effectiveness, such as displays, shows and expositions, and demonstrations.

Sales ticket control Part of an inventory control system in which all sales are recorded on sales tickets and posted to perpetual inventory control records.

Sample A part of the universe or total population.

SBA Small Business Administration.

SCORE (Service Corps of Retired Executives) Managers who have retired from active business management who volunteer their time and talents to counsel prospective entrepreneurs.

Seasonal discounts Discounts offered by suppliers during the off-season to encourage sales.

Secondary needs Higher-order needs such as recognition and peer approval and status.

Section 8(a)   A program of the Small Business Act designed to provide assistance to small businesses owned and operated by economically and socially disadvantaged persons.

Selective buying motive   The evaluation of possible alternative products or services that will satisfy a need.

Service salesperson   A salesperson who primarily functions in the capacity of assisting the consumer in making a sale.

Set-aside contracts   Government contracts that are offered only to small business.

Shelf space analysis   An analysis that provides the amount of profit each item makes in terms of the number of inches required to stock it on shelves.

Sherman Antitrust Act   A federal law that prohibits monopoly and price fixing.

Shoplifting   Theft of merchandise by customers.

Shopping center   A group of architecturally unified, commercial establishments built on a site that is planned, developed, owned, and managed as an operating unit related in its location, size, and type of shops to the trade area that the unit serves.

Shopping goods   Goods sold through a select number of outlets; the cost is usually substantial so that consumers shop.

Short-term loan   A loan that has a duration of less than one year.

Small business   A business defined by the SBA as one that is independently owned and operated, is not dominated in its field of operation, and is operated for a profit.

Small Business Administration   An agency in the Department of Commerce that helps small businesses obtain loans and also offers management assistance.

Small Business Investment Corporation   A financial firm that borrows part of its capital from the SBA and lends or invests the funds in small business ventures.

Small business owner–manager   The person in charge of the business where the owner is also the manager or where the manager is a paid employee.

Sole proprietorship   A form of business ownership in which there is only one owner.

Specialty advertising   Advertising that has the name and advertising message of the advertiser printed on useful items, such as pens or key rings.

Specialty centers   A center that caters to unusual, special market segments and consists of many small specialty shops and restaurants.

Specialty goods   Items that have a special quality or characteristic.

Spreadsheet   A computer program modeled after an accounting spreadsheet that is used to record routine business transactions and as an aid in planning and budgeting.

Staffing   A management function. Staffing is the process of selecting and placing people in positions for which they are qualified so that a proper balance is achieved between people and tasks.

Standard markup   Markup that occurs when the same percentage of markup is added to all goods sold.

Stockholders   Persons who own either preferred or common stock of a corporation.

Stress   How people respond to events in the environment that pose a threat.

String street location   Retail outlets located in an unplanned fashion along a heavily traveled street or highway.

Stub control   Part of an inventory control system in which two or more part stubs are attached to merchandise and part of the stub is removed at time of sale for posting to perpetual inventory control records.

Subchapter S corporations   Corporations meeting certain requirements that may elect to be taxed as a partnership, according to an Internal Revenue Service code.

Subcontracting   Taking part of a job and paying someone or some other firm to complete the task.

Suggested retail prices   Prices suggested by manufacturers that can be charged for the merchandise at the retail level.

Suggestion selling   The sales technique of suggesting additional items after a customer has made an initial decision to buy or suggesting a better quality of merchandise.

Surety insurance   Bonding to assure customers of the firm's ability to complete contracts.

T

Technical knowledge   The ability to work with "things."

Telecommunications   The process of sending information from one computer to another.

Telemarketing   A telephone marketing technique in

which the caller telephones a list of prospective clients and attempts to sell a product or service by using a prepared telescript.

Theft insurance   Insurance to insure loss due to theft.

Theory X   An assumption of human nature that supports the belief that people basically dislike work and will avoid it if possible. It also assumes that people must be coerced, directed, and threatened with punishment to get them to work. Further, it assumes that employees desire security above all.

Theory Y   The assumption about human nature that holds that people put forth mental and physical effort naturally and seek responsibility. It also sets forth the belief that people will exercise self-direction and self-control to accomplish objectives to which they are committed.

Theory Z   A contingency theory of leadership that holds that there is no one best form of leadership but that leadership style will vary according to the situation.

Thirty-day charge accounts   Charge accounts in which goods or services are bought and paid for at the end of a 30-day period.

Time management   The systematic analysis of how the owner and employees are using time in performing job tasks.

Title   Legal ownership to merchandise or property.

Trade area   The geographic area that provides a major portion of the continuing patronage necessary to support the individual business or a larger shopping district.

Trade discount   The discount available to purchasers on the basis of their trade classification wholesaler or industrial buyer or retailer).

Trademark   The legal right to sole use of a brand name.

Traditional bank loan   A commercial bank loan in which the money is loaned for an entire period instead of being repaid in installments.

Traffic count   A measure of the amount of pedestrian and vehicle traffic passing a site that represents potential customers.

Travel time   The amount of time it takes to reach a business location from various points in the market area.

Truth-in-lending law   A federal law that requires the disclosure of specific credit information to the customer.

Turnover   Total cost of goods sold divided by the average inventory.

U

Uniform Commercial Code   A common legal code that covers areas of business law that was established and adopted by 49 states.

Unit of sales method   The method used in preparing an advertising budget whereby a definite amount of funds is set aside for each unit of the product that is sold.

Universe   The total population under study.

University Small Business Institutes   A joint effort between the SBA and universities to provide management consulting to small business.

Unordered merchandise   According to law, unordered merchandise sent through the mail can be considered a free gift.

V

Value analysis   The systematic study of a component or a product to determine whether any changes in parts or function can be made that will provide the same value to users at less cost or greater value at the same cost.

Variable interest rates   The amount of interest charged on a loan in which the interest percentage is based on the prime interest rate for specific periods.

Vendors   Firms that sell any type of goods or supplies to a business.

Venture capital   Capital supplied to new firms by individuals or firms in exchange for part ownership of the firm.

Visual inventory system   A system of ordering inventory by looking at how much is on hand at regular intervals.

Volume of business   The amount of sales over a specific period of time.

W

Word of mouth   Impressions of a business that are passed from one person to another through conversation.

Word processing   The computer program that permits the user to compose, edit, format, store, and print text electronically.

Worker's compensation   Insurance for employees who suffer a job-related injury.

PHOTO CREDITS

INDEX